CW00670265

COSTUMING FOR FILM

COSTUMING FOR FILM

The Art and The Craft

Holly Cole and Kristin Burke

SILMAN-JAMES PRESS   **LOS ANGELES**

Copyright © 2005 by Holly Cole and Kristin Burke

All rights reserved. No part of this book may be used or
reproduced in any manner whatsoever without written
permission from the publisher, except in the case of brief
quotations embodied in critical articles and reviews.

First Edition
10 9 8 7 6 5 4 3 2 1

Library of Congress Cataloging-in-Publication Data

Cole, Holly, 1951-
Costuming for film : the art and the craft / by Holly Cole and Kristin Burke.
p. cm.
Includes bibliographical references and index.
ISBN 1-879505-80-0
1. Costume design 2. Costume. 3. Costume designers.
I. Burke, Kristin, 1970-II. Title.

TT507.C648 2005
791.4302'6--dc22

2005046422

Cover design by
Wade Lageose

Printed and bound in the United States of America

Silman-James Press
1181 Angelo Drive
Beverly Hills, CA 90210

Contents

5. Breakdowns   149

6. Costume Budgets   181

7. Prep   **243**

Acknowledgements and Special Thanks

James Acheson, Catherine Adair, Jennifer Barrett, Angee Beckett, Yvonne Blake, Tom Bronson, David Brookwell, Bruce and Rose Mary Burke, Kevin Burke, Lloyd and Florence Burke, Pat Burke, Molly Campbell, Eduardo Castro, Judy Corbett, Le Dawson, Jean-Pierre Dorléac, Diana Eden, Larry Estes, April Ferry, Marcy Froehlich, Chris Gilman, Julie Glick, Marcy Gossett, Cynthia Hamilton, Hope Hanafin, Bill Hargate, Tina Heinz, Oliver Hess, Donn Hook, Richard Hornung, Stacy Hughes, Barbara Inglehart, Susan Jakel, Virgil C. Johnson, Sandra Berke Jordan, Robert Joyce, Paula Kaatz, Madeline Kozlowski, Jeffrey Kurland, Carolyn Lancet, Alfred Lehman, Dan Lester, Josh Logan, Brad Loman, Betty Pecha Madden, Sean McNamara, Mina Mittelman, Sue Moore, Joe and Marie Mullin, Deborah Nadoolman, Daniel Orlandi, Kara Owens, Edwina Pellikka, Arianne Phillips, Porchlight Entertainment, Wendy Reynolds, John David Ridge, Rita Riggs, Julie Robar, Donna Roberts, Susan Roberts, Jaci Rohr, Jean Rosone, Ann Roth, May Routh, Susanna Sandke, Paul T. Sessum, Pamela Shaw, Buffy Snyder, Evelyn Thompson, Ret Turner, Robert Turturice, Pat Welch, Durinda Wood, Marcus Zakrzewski.

List of Figures

PART ONE

Orientation to the Field

A Day on the Set

It is 7:30 A.M. on an already hot summer day. I've just pulled into the parking lot of a red brick church, in the San Fernando Valley. As I slam the car door, the smell of bacon seizes me by the nostrils: The catering truck is here, and breakfast is on. Today is *the* big day on the set of *The Mating Habits of the Earthbound Human*. The costume designer is Kristin Burke. That's me. This is the day we shoot the Wedding Scene—the culmination, the alpha and omega, the essence of our film. Production could only secure one day at this location, so everything needs to run smoothly.

Our call sheet looks like the menu at Jerry's Famous Deli: Cast notes spill across two pages. Every principal actor and day player to hit celluloid on this shoot is going to be in this wedding scene, and everyone needs to look great. The greatest-looking of all, though, needs to be Carmen Electra, our leading lady. In the wedding scene, Carmen's character, Jenny Smith, is supposed to be nine months pregnant. Reading the script, I remember thinking, How charming, until the reality of the words "Maternity Wedding Gown" sunk in. Who makes maternity wedding gowns? I knew that, in the interest of time, money, and aesthetics, we would be *building* this gown.

As it is, we don't have anything in the way of a budget on this show. The line producer has given me well under ten thousand dollars to do all the costumes. Our leads, alone, have fifty changes each, the film takes place over two years, and then, there's this wedding scene! I have done all I can to secure product-placement deals for the film, and, thanks to Carmen's magnetic pull, I've done well. People love her—and they should: She's a charming, beautiful woman who could make a sack of flour look sexy. Still, we are cruising past the boundaries of our budget, propelled primarily by this wedding scene. The dress is a major expense, and we don't have the money to make two of them. If she spills coffee on it, or if someone steps on the train and rips it, we are shit out of luck.

I design the gown (fig. 1.1) and have it built by the wardrobe crew at The Costume Collection, in Los Angeles, where I set up an office during prep. The people at The Costume Collection are down-to-earth, friendly, and extremely hardworking; I appreciate that. We look over the design, I bring them fabric, and we are on our way. They make a "muslin" of the gown, in time for a quick fitting before principal photography begins. Carmen's schedule is tight, but we need to get going. We fit her with a pregnancy pad, and the basic silhouette takes shape. We have another fitting, about a week later, in the real garment. All of the seams look good; the hem is about right; the sleeves are comfortable. The dress is delivered less than a week later, wrapped in a big white cotton sheet.

And here we are: the big day. We have two extra costumers working with us, setting actors' dressing rooms, and ironing as though their lives depended on it. You have never seen five more industrious people. Within forty-five minutes, all of the actors' rooms are set, with the exception of Carmen's. We have close to twenty additional background players coming in this morning. I send the costume supervisor to do the preliminary wardrobe checks. I will come in when she is finished, to give final approvals. I still haven't had breakfast, so I run to the catering truck and pound a breakfast burrito. Bad idea: gut bomb.

FIG. 1.1 3

**Kristin Burke's design for Carmen Electra
in *Mating Habits of the Earthbound Human***

Carmen is ready to get into to the makeup chair. I have told the AD staff that I will not put her in the wedding gown until the last possible minute, I am not going to risk getting the gown soiled. In this one instance, production may have to wait on wardrobe. I hate saying this, but waiting five minutes for Carmen to get dressed is worth it if the gown stays fresh. I load an Adidas track suit and some shell toes in Carmen's trailer. We just got them in this morning, through product placement, and she squeals with delight when she sees them.

A "specialty extra" has been added to the cast, a young Hula Hoop artist, who needs to look vaguely "fifties cheesecake." Yesterday afternoon, I received her sizes, and pulled a costume for her. As I get the costume out to inspect it, the AD delivers the bad news: said "specialty extra" has cancelled, to be replaced by one of the wedding-guest extras, chosen, more or less, at random. Did I mention that the breakfast burrito was a bad idea? Stomach churning, I imagine the AD on a bull horn, in the extras' holding area: "Anyone here know how to Hula Hoop?" *Oy vey.*

They bring me a woman who looks like my aunt. "Wow," I think, "how are we going to do this?" Her measurements may have matched the cancelled extra's—once—but gravity has reorganized their proportions. She is pleasant enough, but it is all I can do to keep from clutching my stomach and grimacing. I take her into a changing room, and get her into the costume. It looks so-so: It doesn't sing, it doesn't look "cheesecake." I run back to the trailer. Along the way, the ADs are screaming for actors to get to the set. I see my costume supervisor, chatting happily with her cohorts, pulling her trademark little red wagon full of supplies. I think, It will be all right, she has her bases covered. I run back to the Hula Hoop woman, armed with pads. I pad her breasts—a little here, a little there—and soon she is looking better. Which is good, since we have no choice: They're ready on the set, and they're calling Carmen for rehearsal.

I lug the wedding gown and pregnancy pad to a piano room adjacent to the chapel where we are shooting. This will be Carmen's temporary changing room. I sit down at the keyboard and play a few measures of Chopin's *Funeral March*, just for effect. Rehearsal is over, and Carmen needs to put on the veil. I walk her back to makeup, where she is coifed and sprayed. We set the headband in her hair, and with a mischievous glint in her eye, the makeup artist plucks five perfect rosebuds from a vase and sticks them in around the headband. We all look at each other: funny and pretty. We decide to keep the look.

Carmen is quite a sight in her Adidas track suit and wedding veil. We get back to the piano room and it is show time. It takes about five minutes to adjust things, get all the bulges in the right places. I am sweating like a pig—the Valley sun has treated us to a heatwave of grand magnitude—but, beyond even this, the "heat" is on: This is the debut of the wedding gown costume—the visual epitome of the film—and I am hoping and praying that everybody is happy. I will be trailing Carmen today, like a water-skier on the back of a boat, carrying her train and lifting the gown, following her everywhere she goes so that it never touches the ground. I could get a costumer to do it, but this is my baby. No one will be as anal as I am, and it just makes me feel better to do it myself. Carmen and I look at each other, and share a moment of insane laughter. This has been a stressful shoot, for myriad reasons, but the sheer comedy of this costume gives us a break from the stress—for now. I grab the train of the dress, and we head to set.

Waiting for us is the director, the producer, and the line producer, a dopey grin on every face. Carmen is radiant. The director approaches, stunned and, it looks like, a little teary-eyed. "This is the most beautiful, *funniest* thing I have ever seen—I mean, so beautiful; so funny; so beautiful!" He shakes his head, "So funny! It is exactly, totally right!"

These are the moments we live for. Everyone is smiling, even the grips and electrics. Especially the grips and electrics. The final camera rehearsal begins. Carmen enters the chapel. My costume supervisor sees me from across the room, smiles and nods and gives the thumbs up. All is well in the world of wardrobe. I feel like I want…a cigar. But given the fact that I have to attend to Carmen all day, I decide to wait on the cigar until after work. I take a seat in a pew and watch the rehearsal. The director calls, "Cut," and looks over at me, beaming.

This is a good day, indeed.

So, You Want to Work in Film?

Visions of Merchant-Ivory films dance in your head? Humphrey Bogart in a trench coat? Indiana Jones in a fedora? The dazzle of Oscar night? If you're an aspiring costume designer, this is the stuff that dreams are made of. The big stars, the exotic locations, the lavish budgets and cushy salaries that you find in film are certainly seductive. And film may be seen by generations. Pretty heady stuff to those seeking fame, fortune, and artistic work.

Many of us harbor delusions about the glamour of filmmaking. The reality is that glorious work does get up there on screen—courtesy of a lot of unglamorous, back-breaking work. Film budgets can seem lavish. Top star salaries are legendary. Costume budgets of $250,000 for a $20-million-dollar film; $3,000 to $5,000 per episode for a weekly television series; even the $35,000 costume budget for a low-budget feature can make designing for film very attractive. Union costume design salary minimums of $1,404 to $2,500 a week; union costume supervisor minimums of $1,288 to $1,800 a week; even the lowly costume department production assistant rate, starting at $13.56 an hour, may seem enticing. But it can be startling how far those budgets have to stretch, and how underpaid you can feel, when you're working in this high risk business.

> Don't kid yourself. It's not about glamour. *(Bill Hargate, costume designer, and owner of costume workroom Hargate Costumes)*

Star power is a palpable force in the industry. A star with major box-office appeal can green-light a project. Millions of dollars will come in based on this "pull." A star's image can be money in the bank, literally. As a result, pressure on the star is extreme. Keeping the star happy and looking good are production, and costume department, priorities.

Even with top talent, a film is not guaranteed blockbuster status. Producers walk a razor's edge as they try to get their investments to pay off. The out-of-control production costs you hear so much about usually have more to do with escalating high-end actor's salaries than with design department abuses. However, to pay stars' salaries, producers often try to scale back other costs, including costume design budgets and costume department personnel. Costume budgets that seem high often need to be stretched over hundreds, sometimes thousands, of costumes. On a high-end studio feature, the costume budget is, on average, only two percent of the total production budget. Lower-budget films, with or without stars, follow this model. In fact, since the nineteen-fifties, with the downsizing of the studio system and the extreme escalation of the cost of filmmaking, general interest by the film industry in costume artistry has declined significantly. The few producers and directors who truly value beautiful costumes, and understand the artistry that it takes to produce them, are a rarity in today's industry. With few exceptions, money, not art, moves the industry now. Compare the production values in a daytime television series to those in a Merchant-Ivory film, then think about how much money, and how many jobs, that difference represents.

> Clothing takes up one third of the screen. Break it down. There is that body out there, dressed in clothing. You can tell a story through clothing. You don't need, in many, many cases, a lot of set behind it. If you've got the costuming, you can tell a story. One third of the screen image, and yet, we do not get one third of the budget. We are lucky if we get one percent. Right there, from the get-go, they're heading down the wrong road when they want to take all the money away from costumes. We've got a lot of money if we get one percent of the budget. Our dream? Five percent. If you can give me ten percent, the sky's the limit, honey—you can have anything you want. *(Betty Pecha Madden, costume designer for features, including* Baby Geniuses *and Michael Jackson's* Moonwalker, *and television movies, including* The Water Engine *and* The Heidi Chronicles*)*

Ever seen a movie being shot on location? All those trucks? All that equipment? It's like a small army. And it's just the tip of the iceberg. Film productions are, by nature, highly complex units (fig. 1.2). Newcomers to the industry can be stunned by the lexicon of job titles

FIG. 1.2

for industry personnel. (To get a small sense of all the personnel involved, take a look at fig. 1.3, "The Power Structure of a Production," which reflects only the actual production end of a film; it doesn't include development, marketing, or postproduction staffing in any detail. For job descriptions, see fig. 1.4, "Selected Production Job Descriptions.") If you take a look at any average feature film and start tallying the number of actors and extras on screen, you will see quickly how many hundreds of costumes go into the making of a film. Hence, the need for costume budgets in the tens of thousands of dollars, and a hearty crew of costume department personnel.

Who Does What? Basic Film Costume Personnel

The size of a production's costume crew is determined by two principal factors: the funds available for staffing, and the complexity of the project. Many costume departments are small, comprised of a designer, who doubles as costume supervisor, and a set costumer. Some departments are very large, staffed with a host of costume professionals, supplemented by a costume department accountant. A designer and costume supervisor may decide that it is most cost effective to develop their own costume workroom, staffed with custom made personnel, or they may opt to job out work to professional costume workrooms.

Learning the titles, categories, and basic job descriptions of those who work in the profession is a necessary step in orienting yourself in any field. In the field of film costumes, the *costume designer* carries the primary responsibility for creating look of the costumes, and ensuring their quality. The *costume supervisor* oversees the physical setup of the costume department and its general day-to-day operations. Design support staff, including *assistant designers* and *sketch artists,* assist designers by doing research, costume

FIG. 1.3: A PRODUCTION DEPARTMENT POWER STRUCTURE*

*Detailed non-costume-area job jurisdictions are discussed in *Job Descriptions, Responsibilities, and Duties for the Film and Video Craft Categories and Classifications* by William E. Hines, *How to Make It in Hollywood* by Linda Buzzell, and particularly good notes on production-office job definitions are given in *The Hollywood Job-Hunter's Survival Guide* by Hugh Taylor.

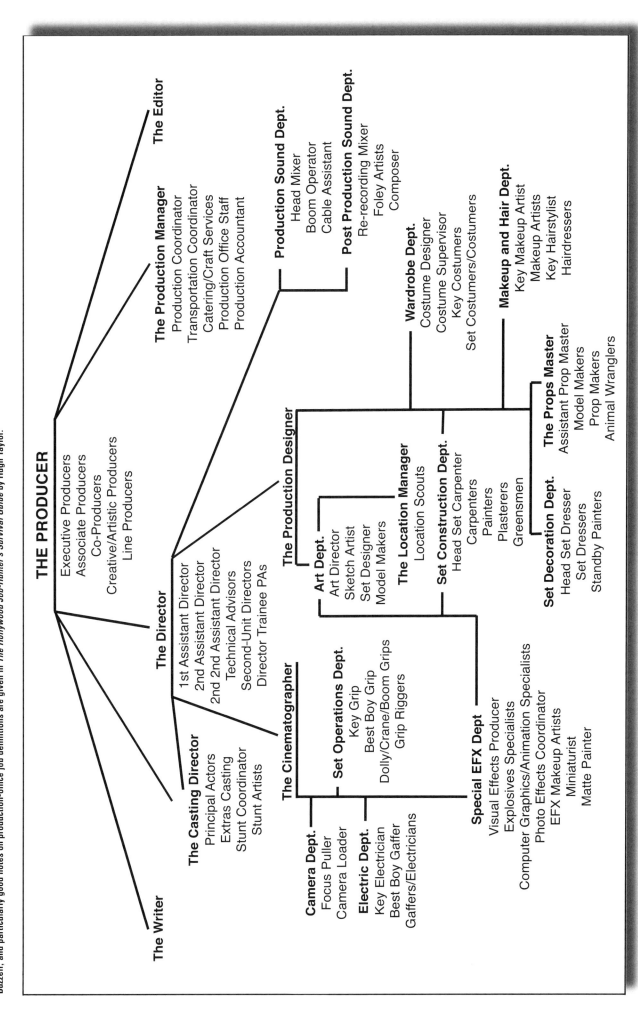

THE PRODUCER
Executive Producers
Associate Producers
Co-Producers
Creative/Artistic Producers
Line Producers

The Writer

The Director
1st Assistant Director
2nd Assistant Director
2nd 2nd Assistant Director
Technical Advisors
Second-Unit Directors
Director Trainee PAs

The Casting Director
Principal Actors
Extras Casting
Stunt Coordinator
Stunt Artists

The Production Manager
Production Coordinator
Transportation Coordinator
Catering/Craft Services
Production Office Staff
Production Accountant

The Editor

Production Sound Dept.
Head Mixer
Boom Operator
Cable Assistant

Post Production Sound Dept.
Re-recording Mixer
Foley Artists
Composer

Wardrobe Dept.
Costume Designer
Costume Supervisor
Key Costumers
Set Costumers/Costumers

Makeup and Hair Dept.
Key Makeup Artist
Makeup Artists
Key Hairstylist
Hairdressers

The Production Designer

Art Dept.
Art Director
Sketch Artist
Set Designer
Model Makers

The Location Manager
Location Scouts

Set Construction Dept.
Head Set Carpenter
Carpenters
Painters
Plasterers
Greensmen

Set Decoration Dept.
Head Set Dresser
Set Dressers
Standby Painters

The Props Master
Assistant Prop Master
Model Makers
Prop Makers
Animal Wranglers

The Cinematographer

Camera Dept.
Focus Puller
Camera Loader

Electric Dept.
Key Electrician
Best Boy Gaffer
Gaffers/Electricians

Set Operations Dept.
Key Grip
Best Boy Grip
Dolly/Crane/Boom Grips
Grip Riggers

Special EFX Dept
Visual Effects Producer
Explosives Specialists
Computer Graphics/Animation Specialists
Photo Effects Coordinator
EFX Makeup Artists
Miniaturist
Matte Painter

FIG. 1.4: SELECTED PRODUCTION JOB DESCRIPTIONS

PRODUCTION DEPARTMENT

Producer. Although many "producer" credits may be given on a finished film or television project, these primary supervisors are generally of three types: the *executive producer*, the *producer*, and the *line producer*. The *executive producer* is often a studio "suit," responsible for the project in the "big-picture" sense. S/He is the prime developer and shepherd of the production, and often holds primary responsibility for arranging a project's financing. He or she oversees development, production, and promotion of the project; supervises budgeting and scheduling; selects the director and takes a significant part in script development, key casting, and the selection of key artistic department heads. In television, the executive producer or creative producer plays a significant part in supervising the design of the project, among other aspects of the production. The producer is the person who assembles the team for the film, working in tandem with the executive and line producers. Often, the producer is the person who brings the project to a studio and the executive producer, and has a sense of "ownership" of the project – it's his/her baby. S/he is the closest and most integral person to the director in relation to filmmaking, and s/he controls the purse strings. The *line producer*, on the other hand, is a logistics specialist, who directly oversees the actual physical production, supervising budgeting, scheduling, and shooting on a day-to-day basis.

Production Manager (PM)/Unit Production Manager (UPM). The production manager (PM), also known as the unit production manager (UPM), is responsible for assembling a production's overall budget, and for controlling it during the shoot, day to day. He or she is also responsible for doing the breakdowns for each day's shooting, revising daily schedules and budgets under the direction of the producer, hiring crew, and arranging for required equipment, transportation, and cast and crew accommodations. In addition, the PM/UPM supervises day-to-day budget disbursements, including payroll, the payment of bills, the disbursement of petty cash, and other financial transactions.

First Assistant Director (1st AD). The first assistant director is responsible for assisting the director in planning and running the production; developing preproduction breakdowns and shooting schedules with the UPM; aiding with day-to-day production scheduling; following, and carrying out the director's orders, including the making of announcements for cameras and sound to roll; maintaining order on the set; acting as liaison between director and production manager, and other members of the crew; supervising the on-set use of extras; and keeping the production on schedule.

On some low-budget productions, the first AD will double as production manager. In episodic television work, there are two key first assistant directors: one for current episode on-set shooting, one for next-episode planning.

Second Assistant Director (2nd AD). The second assistant director is responsible for assisting the first assistant director and production manager; acting as key intermediary between the production office and the set; acting as a liaison between the set and the actors off set; tracking all call times; keeping crew informed and "in line"; "running talent" (making sure that actors arrive on location, make it from trailer or dressing room to set, and are properly "wrapped out"); assisting the 1st AD in the placement of extras on the set; supervising crowd control; and putting together all production reports and daily call sheets.

Second Second Assistant Director (the "second second"). The "second second" assists the 2nd AD with both on-set and off-set cast control. This is the person who physically walks the actors to the set. He or she also informs off-set departments of on-set events and what's up next.

Production Coordinator. The production coordinator is in charge of the production office. He or she heads off-set communications, correspondence, travel arrangements, deal memos, cast and crew lists, time cards, office supplies, and the set up of all charge accounts. In addition, the production coordinator is responsible for production office space rental, office equipment rental, and vendor relations.

Location Manager. The location manager scouts locations; arranges for permits and directs access to locations; coordinates production vehicle parking with police department and transportation department; provides for information on local resources, including local emergency services like hospitals.

Casting Director. The casting director, in collaboration with the producers and the director, is responsible for casting principals and day players.

Extras Casting Coordinator. The extras casting coordinator, who may be an individual or a representative of an extras casting agency, is responsible for casting extras (atmosphere) and featured extras for a production, for delivering costume and prop notes to extras, and for "wrangling" extras on set (handing out and collecting vouchers, supervising extras' conduct for set, and so forth).

Stunt Coordinator. The stunt coordinator heads the stunt team. He or she is the key source of information on stunt casting, the nature of stunt action, and stunt-related requirements for costumes and protective gear.

Script Supervisor. The script supervisor is responsible, before shooting begins, for an initial breakdown of "story time" (the counting of story days and nights in a script). Once shooting begins, the script supervisor is responsible for recording each take's continuity details, including take number and duration, script action and dialogue covered, lenses used, placement of camera; basic movement of actors, and the use of props and wardrobe in scenes, when their use is related to action.

CREATIVE PRODUCTION PERSONNEL

Director. The director is in charge of realizing the script on film. He or she chooses the designers in consultation with producer; directs the casting of the principal talent of the production in collaboration with the casting director and producer. He or she is also responsible for the look of the film—the physical staging, the photographic style, the direction of the actors, and the production and costume designers. The director usually oversees the film's assembly and, occasionally, the film's final cut, in collaboration with the chief editor and the producer(s).

Director of Photography (DP)/Cinematographer. As head of the camera, lighting, and grip departments; the DP is responsible for arriving at a visual style for the production, in collaboration, primarily, with the director. He or she is responsible for photographing the film, directing all lighting and camera work; and supervising all camera, light, and film usage.

Sound Recordist/Production Mixer. The sound recordist/production mixer is the head of on-set sound. His or her most basic task is to provide a clean dialogue track.

Postproduction sound work is the responsibility of several groups of people: re-recording mixers, music mixers, sound designers, and Foley artists (the latter being responsible for all non-music and non-dialogue sounds created in post production).

Production Designer. The production designer is responsible for the overall physical appearance of the production; for the design and dressing of all exterior and interior spaces; for the choice and preparation of all location shooting sites, in coordination with the location scout, the director, and the cinematographer. The production designer also directs the set construction, set decoration, and property departments, works closely with (supervises) the special effects creator, and has artistic influence in costume, hair, and makeup departments (in consultation with the director and the director of photography).

Costume Designer. See below, fig. 1.5, "Costume Department Job Jurisdictions and Duties."

Set Decorator. Head of the set dressing department, the set decorator, under the direction of the production designer, is responsible for providing a set's furnishings, ornamentation, and art work, regardless of whether on location or in the studio. Set dressers and swing gang work under the set decorator, and are responsible for dressing and striking all set furnishings.

Property (Prop) Master. The prop master is responsible for maintaining and placing necessary props (non-costume handheld items used by actors, including food, handbags, briefcases, umbrellas, walking sticks, cigarettes, newspapers, glasses, key jewelry, etc.).

OTHER KEY PRODUCTION WORKERS

Catering. "Catering" provides the major meals served during the production day. (Caterers can be very helpful for emergency bottled water, club soda, etc.)

Craft Services. Craft services provides the just-off-set munchies and beverages available between catered meals.

Transportation. The transportation department is responsible for providing, placing, moving, and maintaining production vehicles and providing selected transportation services for crew and talent. (The transportation department can be of great service to the costume department, providing, on occasion, convenient trailer placement, emergency dressing space, and emergency manpower in moving your illegally parked car—none of which is within a drivers' job jurisdiction.)

design sketches, breakdown work (a formal charting of costume-related information, based upon a detailed analysis of the script), fabric swatching (sampling), shopping, and character styling (outfitting).

Finished costumers work with "finished" costumes (rental and ready-made clothing). They shop, rent, and organize the costumes or dress the actors on the set, according to their individual job definitions. The finished costume staff includes *key costumers*, who are the principal assistants to the costume supervisor (they may specialize in either men's or women's costumes).

Custom-made costumers alter clothing and make made-to-order (MO) costumes. Custom-made personnel include patternmakers, tailors, cutters, fitter/drapers, and seamstresses, whose job it is to build, fit, and alter clothes, and craft artisans, like milliners (hat-makers), cobblers (shoemakers), dyers, costume agers, spacesuit makers, and others, who do special craft work.

Set costumers dress the actors, prepare and maintain the daily wardrobe for the shoot, and document the look of the characters. Costume department *production assistants* (wardrobe PAs) and interns are "go-fer" personnel, who do anything and everything that the boss asks.

For job titles and detailed job descriptions, see fig. 1.5, "Costume Department Job Jurisdictions and Duties."

The industry thrives on production teams that work together over and over again. Most costume designers develop a loyal group of costume personnel with whom they work on a regular basis, to help them survive production mania. Design assistants and costume supervisors are hand-picked, to support the costume designer in areas where she or he is either weak or overwhelmed. On-set personnel will be the designer's eyes and ears, reporting unauthorized costume changes, revisions in the shooting schedule, and the on-set politics that can affect the design integrity of a production. Loyal made-to-order personnel and rental-house staff regularly bale out their favorite designers when they get hit with radical schedule changes or impossible budget problems. A costume designer is only as good as the team he or she assembles, and its loyalty must be earned.

> For me, filmmaking is all about flexibility, challenge, and change. The keystone is finding a supervisor and crew I trust, and who will back me. After that, it is all about communication. Through experience and time, you put together groups of people who work very well together, and who understand each other. *(Catherine Adair, costume designer,* Win a Date with Tad Hamilton, BASEketball, Beverly Hills Cop III, *and* I Know What You Did Last Summer*)*

The Film Costume Process

Like the filmmaking process itself, the film costume process has three basic phases: *prep, shoot,* and *wrap.* Prep is short for *preparation* or *preproduction*—that is, before "production" (shooting) starts. During prep, a design concept is developed for the film, and preliminary and final designs are approved and produced; most of the *costume stock* (a collection of costume items for general use on performers during the production) is gathered, organized, and prepared for filming.

To prepare a film's costume stock, the head of the costume department does a *script breakdown*, a script analysis that targets the costumes that will be needed. This requires a detailed analysis of the action of the script, its atmospheres, and the passage of "story time." After the script breakdown is completed, *character breakdowns* are done for each principal and day player. These breakdowns fix where in the script a character changes costume, and, ultimately, what that costume change is. Once character breakdowns are finished, a *budget breakdown* is done—an estimate of the costs of all the clothing, accessories, services, supplies, and equipment the costume department will need for all three phases of the production. Prep personnel then go about compiling, organizing, fitting, and otherwise preparing the costumes and costume stock for filming.

During phase two, the *shoot* (the filming process itself), some costume personnel dress the actors at the shooting site and keep a watchful eye on the costumes and costume continuity on set, while other costumers prepare for future scenes.

Wrap, the third phase, which happens in bits and pieces throughout the production process, happens with finality when the shoot is over. In the most basis terms, wrap entails inventorying, packing, and storing production-owned wardrobe, and returning rented and borrowed costume stock to the appropriate sources in as close to original condition as possible, at the end of its use.

These processes and production phases are detailed in Part 5, *Breakdowns;* Part 6, *Costume Budgets;* Part 7, *Prep;* Part 8, *Shoot;* and Part 9, *Final Wrap.*

Filmmaking Rules of the Road

Filmmaking is an inherently expensive, complex process—an art, a craft, and a business that demands flexibility from its personnel, and an ability to accept, and cope with, the following four axioms of the filmmaking process: (1) perpetually evolving productions are the rule; (2) the shooting schedule determines work priorities; (3) work conditions are expected to vary; (4) the industry is geared to cope with rapid changes. These axioms are the only things in production that never change.

PERPETUALLY EVOLVING PRODUCTIONS ARE THE RULE

Scripts evolve. The industry trades on new scripts, and a constant flow of script changes is common. As a script changes, it is standard practice for new script pages to be delivered in a new color. The first wave of changes is on blue paper, the next on pink, then yellow, then green. Many costumers talk about scripts that have been through the full rainbow and back again before shooting was completed.

Staffing evolves. Film prep and shoot periods run, on average, from six to fifteen weeks. Costume department personnel ebb and flow over the course of a production. On

FIG. 1.5: COSTUME DEPARTMENT JOB JURISDICTIONS AND DUTIES

According to Costume Designers Guild Union Local 829 guidelines:

Costume Designer

- Directly communicates with producers and director
- Breaks down the script, to assess costume requirements
- Develops the costume budget and controls the disbursement of funds
- Plans the development of costume stock
- Supervises the hiring and distribution of costume personnel
- Oversees the acquisition of costume area supplies, equipment, and coordinates wardrobe-related transportation
- Carries primary responsibility for the quality of the "look," and for delivering the costumes on time and on budget

Assistant Costume Designer

- Aids and assists the costume designer in the implementation of the designer's creative activities
- Does research, swatching, shopping, script and budget breakdowns, and styling

Note: This position is very similar to the theatrical costume design assistant with the important proviso that on a union shoot, the design assistant must respect all costumer union job jurisdictions.

According to Motion Picture Costumer Union Local 705 guidelines for Finished Costumers:

Costume Supervisor

- Manages, supervises, and handles the general day-to-day operations of the costume department on a production
- Holds primary responsibility for setting up the physical department, i.e., setting up a place to house and contact the costume department
- Establishes a workroom and arranges for all necessary construction, alteration, and craftwork
- Obtains necessary wardrobe trailers and equipment in coordination with transportation and other departments
- Supervises the purchase of wardrobe supplies
- Supervises and hires all union costume personnel (Local 705, in Los Angeles, Local 764, in New York City)
- Is responsible for communications among all costume personnel, and for keeping track of everything related to costumes on the production
- Is in contact with the set every day
- Sees that the department functions properly and provides all necessary costumes
- Is directly responsible to the producers for any production delays due to costume problems
- Determines the script's costume requirements
- Breaks down the script to define period, establish change numbers, determine the need for doubles, triples, etc., and determine the passage of time, in consultation with the script supervisor
- Establishes the number of extras per scene who need to be costumed
- Researches the design and design sources for the costumes
- Stands in for the costume designer when the designer is unable to attend concept meetings with the producer and director
- Addresses both men's and women's wardrobes, ensuring a level of visual continuity
- Assesses the costume budget requirements, including all costs related to principal, day player, and extras wardrobes
- Plans for all other costume cost factors, including supplies, cleaning, foul-weather gear, loss and damage, etc.
- Submits the costume budget to the production manager
- Administers and maintains the costume department budget, accounting for and disbursing funds for all purchases, rentals, and made-to-order work
- Works with the production office to establish all accounts with costume department vendors, suppliers, and service providers
- Assembles the costume stock and supervises the preparation of wardrobe for shooting
- Supervises and participates in wardrobe purchases and costume rentals
- Supervises the manufacture of duplicates of existing garments, costume copies from photos, and all alterations
- Handles men's and women's wardrobe, helping the designer materialize the characters in the script

- Sets up all fittings and arranges for all fitting spaces, making sure all appropriate actors, actresses, stunt persons, and custom-made personnel are available for the fittings
- Fits or directs the fitting of all costumes when the designer cannot be present

Costume Department Foreman
- Manages, supervises, and handles the general operation of either the men's or women's costume departments under the supervision of the wardrobe supervisor
- Sees that the costume department functions properly and assists in avoiding production delays

Note: The costume department foreman is not allowed to function as a costume supervisor, key costumer, set costumer, or journeyman costumer, except in cases of emergency.

Key Costumer
- Works under the supervision of the wardrobe supervisor
- Breaks down the script and acquires research materials
- Assists in the assembly of the costume stock
- Fits and handles wardrobe.

Note: A key costumer may work on the set and help to fit principals, bit players, and extras.

Set Costumer
- Works on set and is responsible for on-set continuity tracking and wardrobe maintenance (general duties duplicate those of a key costumer, but are more detailed)
- Is present on set at all times while shooting (cannot leave the set without providing a replacement or notifying either a Local 705 co-worker, or the first or second AD or script supervisor)
- Is responsible for maintaining the look of all of the characters on the set; including the principal players, bit players, stunt persons, and extras
- Is responsible for any on-set aging of the costumes
- Records and tracks costume continuity
- Checks the actor before each shot, to make sure that he or she maintains costume continuity
- Takes costume continuity Polaroids and organizes them in the set book
- Records costume continuity, taking proper and legible notes
- Updates notes in the set book each day
- Keeps script supervisor informed of costume continuity issues
- Keeps the costume supervisor fully advised of what is happening on the set, including all on-set changes to costumes
- Meets deadlines for dressing actors, arrival of actors on set, and other costume-related deadlines set by production
- Confirms, with the second AD, that the company is shooting "per call sheet," noting changes where necessary
- Studies the shooting schedule and the call sheets, in preparation for the day
- Makes sure that the next change of costumes for each actor is laid out in advance, so that no production time is lost
- Checks, with the second AD, at the end of the day, for any changes that may not be on the call sheet
- Prepares and maintains the daily wardrobe and dressing areas
- Checks in the cleaning at the start of the day
- Makes sure the day's wardrobe is ready
- Prepares the dressing rooms and the daily costume changes
- Removes the costumes from the dressing rooms when actors are wrapped, and reassembles the costume changes at the trailer, replacing any tags that were removed
- Sends out the cleaning
- Makes sure the required costumes are ready for the next day
- Respects set and trailer etiquette
- Makes sure the set book is always accessible to the entire costume crew
- Maintains an orderly, focused environment on set

(continued)

Journeyman Costumer

- Assists the costume supervisor and key costumers with their regular duties, but cannot fit principals, bit players, or extras

Note: This level of costumer is primarily assigned to the maintenance of the costume stock and equipment. A journeyman costumer may also deliver wardrobe to and from sets.

Costumer: Entry Level

- Duties, and constraints, mirror those of the journeyman costumer (see above).

Custom-Made Costumers

Most custom-made costumer jobs follow guidelines established in large Broadway costume houses that have separate divisions for men's and women's wear and specialty craft areas. The job titles date from the Hollywood boom period, when very large workrooms were maintained. Few workrooms currently have the full range of jobs listed in fig. 11.3, "Finished Costume Division Structures," in Part 11, *Working in New York or L.A.* Below is a list of work classifications, the job description of which are not obvious from their titles.

According to Motion Picture Costumers Union Local 705 guidelines for Custom Made Costumers:

Manufacturing Foreman. The manufacturing foreman supervises either the men's department or the women's department (or a section thereof), under the direction of the custom-made department head.

Womenswear Division

Pattern Maker and Fitter—Class 2. Pattern Maker and Fitter, Class 2, makes patterns, cuts and fits from sketches or specified designs, assists in selecting materials, and supervises construction.

Women's Garment Tailor—Class 3. Women's Garment Tailor, Class 3, cuts, fits, and makes tailored suits, robes, and coats from sketches or specified designs and supervises their construction; may also make patterns and assist in material selection.

Tailor's Helper—Class 5. A tailor's helper, Class 5, who assists a women's garment tailor, Class 3, may do finishing, trimming, binding, button holes, sew in linings, and other special work on tailored items.

Women's Alteration Fitter—Class 3. A women's alteration fitter, Class 3, fits and makes alterations on stock costumes.

Women's Figure Maker—Class 3. A women's figure maker, Class 3, develops commercial dress forms from measurements, and makes muslin patterns to fit the forms and the artists. This title was assigned in the days when studio workrooms produced massive amounts of custom-made work for actors who were under contract to the studios. Dressing the same actors over the years of a contract, and many movies, made it practical for the studio workroom to a create dress forms to match the actors.

Women's Table Person—Class 3. A women's table person, Class 3, supervises the work of a group of finishers or workers at their table. Like an East Coast "first hand" position, a table person may cut material from patterns, pin and prepare for finishers, and generally assign work to his or her table group. He or she may also supervise a group in a specialty department.

Women's Draper—Class 4. A women's draper, class 4 , drapes material on models and figures, trims and finishes certain specially assigned costumes, bastes and pins gowns and costumes in preparation for finishers.

Women's Finisher—Class 5. A women's finisher, Class 5, stitches by hand or machine, and also presses.

Women's Special Operator—Class 5. A women's special operator, Class 5, does general artwork under the supervision of a cutter and/or table person, and does special work, like making masks and other items of buckram, fur, plastic, wire, etc. They may also do special designing on materials, with the use of dyes.

Menswear Division

Men's Tailor Cutter and/or Gang Boss—Class 2. A men's tailor cutter and/or gang boss, Class 2, drafts patterns, cuts fabric, and fits tailored suits and other costumes from sketches or specified designs, assists in the selection of materials, and supervises the work of fitters, tailors, and tailor's helpers.

Men's Tailor Fitter—Class 3. A men's tailor fitter, Class 3, fits and alters new or stock items.

Men's Alteration Tailor—Class 4. A men's alteration tailor, Class 4, presses, alters, sews trims, etc., on men's stock suits and costumes under the direction of a tailor cutter or tailor fitter. A men's alteration tailor may also make miscellaneous men's items.

Men's Tailor's Helper—Class 5. A men's tailor's helper, Class 5, finishes, trims, binds, makes buttonholes, and does other special work under a tailor cutter, a tailor fitter, or a specialty tailor.

Men's Wardrobe Specialty Manufacturer—Class 3. A men's wardrobe specialty manufacturer, Class 3, repairs, alters, and revamps special wardrobe items and accessories, such as men's hats, military caps, badges, shoes, belts, leather pouches, and other leather items.

Specialty Costumes Division

Key Special Costumer—Class 2. A key special costumer, Class 2, supervises the construction of clothing using foam, wire, plastic, cloth, leather, etc., for creature-type costumes, and also supervises special costume manufacturers, Class 4.

Costumer Union Guidelines for Live Television Costumers

Supervising Costumer. A supervising costumer functions like the costume supervisors mentioned earlier, with the exception that the live television supervising costumer can remodel costumes.

Wardrobe Master. A wardrobe master assists the wardrobe department head; fits, makes, alters, remodels, and repairs costumes; handles, buys, and rents costumes; and supervises the men and women assigned to the costume department.

Wardrobe Men and Women. Wardrobe men and women assist supervisors and wardrobe masters; fit, handle, remodel, alter, and make costumes; check clothing in and out; and dress actors. They may also assist in styling.

Junior-Grade Wardrobe Men and Women. Junior-grade wardrobe men and women do dressing, stock-handling, and inventory work. They do not fit, sew, purchase, rent, or check costumes in or out.

Seamstress. A seamstress does alterations and repair work, but does not do major alterations, remodeling, the making of costumes, stock room, or dressing work.

films with substantial costume crews, only the key members of the costume team work the entire prep and shoot; most are brought in for limited periods of time. Costume designers may only be employed until their designs are "established" (recorded) on film, and then they may be dismissed. Set costumers come in shortly before shooting begins. Additional costumers may be brought in only on days with large numbers of extras.

Casting evolves. The casting process can continue throughout production. In the film and television industries, late casting is the norm—even for principal players. Production-office casting priorities are, in order of importance: (1) *stars,* who are critical to producers' ability to raise production funds and make distribution deals; (2) *principals* (leading men and women) who get extensive screen time; (3) featured players (also known as *day players*, because they are only involved in shooting for a few days); and (4) extras (also known as *atmosphere* or *background*), who are generally cast the day before they shoot. It is standard practice for a film's costume department to provide "walk-in styling" for extras from the wide range of sizes available in its costume stock.

Workloads evolve. Because a film's production is strung out over weeks, sometimes months, of shooting, all departmental workloads are spread over the prep and shoot periods, according to shooting schedule priorities. Costume stock evolves as pieces are added or retired (wrapped), according to shooting schedule.

The design and performances evolve during shooting. Few films devote much prep time to "rehearsal" periods. Featured actors may get lucky and be given a week or two of rehearsal, but this is rare. In most cases, all they get is a read-through and an on-set camera blocking rehearsal (in which the actors, director, and camera crew plan the action and camera moves for a scene). The result: The "organic," evolving part of filmmaking is not confined to prep; it extends throughout the shooting period. Unlike theater, where the design and blocking "freeze" during the performance run, in film the performance is "alive" throughout the shooting period; text, acting, and design all evolve in response to the immediate shooting circumstances. In effect, film directors use the process of filming shot after shot as a means to rehearse the script.

Each shooting day's costumes and sets must be opening-night perfect; but to get the most interesting shot, the film's entire crew is poised for change. All costume designs are considered in flux until they are recorded on film. On set, anything can change—and regularly does.

THE SHOOTING SCHEDULE DETERMINES WORK PRIORITIES

Every member of a production unit is focused on getting the cameras rolling. It takes so much to get a shot set up—the efforts of so many grips, electricians, camera crew, set dressers, actors, stunt players, sound techs, costumers, and others—that an army of folk stands around, waiting to get the shot. This affects the production in two key ways: It creates the need to take maximum advantage of each shooting location, and it creates the need to streamline the shooting process.

The expense and difficulty of getting everything together in the right place at the right time dictates that every scene using a particular set will be "shot out" before leaving it. This means that the shooting schedule is drawn up according to the logic of location: Scenes are shot in an order determined by the requirements of location, often ignoring the continuous action of the storyline, a process known as "shooting out of continuity." As a result, on-set, the costume department must track *costume continuity* (the exact details of what each actor wears in a scene, and how the actor wears it), to ensure that all actors are dressed correctly when scenes are spliced together in correct story order. (For sample principal player continuity pages, see figs. 1.6 and 1.7.)

On the set, time is money—*major* amounts of money. Everyone is under great pressure to move as quickly and efficiently as possible. The camera department sets the shooting pace. Each scene is shot many times, from many different positions, to aid final editing. Each setup demands adjustments in camera and lighting—a time-consuming process involving camera tracks, dollies, lights, and lots of other equipment. It is impractical, and politically unwise, for anyone to slow down production, so the most important rule for the costume department on set is this: *Production should not have to wait for wardrobe.*

When actors arrive on set, they must be dressed correctly. If changes are required on set, stock should be on hand, and changes made within fifteen minutes. Action and adventure flicks, a staple of the film industry, can chew up wardrobe and require stunt artists to "double," or fill in, for actors. If the action is dirty or destructive, or if there is stunt-doubling, the costume department is expected to provide costume *doubles* or *multiples* (copies of the garment pieces) for additional takes, to keep the cameras rolling.

> I had a terrible mishap on the very first movie I did. We had a young child who was wearing a knit stocking cap with a pom-pom on top. The cap said something on the front. It was a horribly rainy day and the set was about three blocks from the trailer. I was a set costumer and I had the whole set to take care of by myself—approximately five principals and twenty-five extras. The mom had the kid in tow, but this kid was picking things off his body and throwing this and that, and the mother did nothing to help the situation. I was following them back to the set, but when I got there, I discovered that the child did not have his red hat. And we didn't have a double, of course. The hat had already been on camera, so I was in a panic. I ran back to the designer, and I thought, for sure, I was going to get fired. I was so nervous, I was crying. I told her what happened. She handled it with great grace. She said, 'Okay, let's see what we've got here.' She opened up the sock drawer and found a red sock. So, we made a hat. It was instantaneous! I cut up another sock, and made a pom-pom, and sewed it on. For the time that the hat was on camera, you never noticed that the little name that was on the thing wasn't there. (*Jaci Rohr, costume supervisor, member of Motion Picture Costumers Union Local 705*)

WORK CONDITIONS ARE EXPECTED TO VARY

The movie business is a business that asks you to be prepared for anything.

Costume budgets are all over the map. There are thousands of different kinds of production companies, each with their own peculiar way of doing business. A television commercial may have a costume budget of $150,000, while a feature film may struggle to put hundreds of costumes together for $35,000. Staffing, budgets, shooting schedules,

FIG. 1.6: WARDROBE CONTINUITY PAGE FOR A PRINCIPAL PLAYER

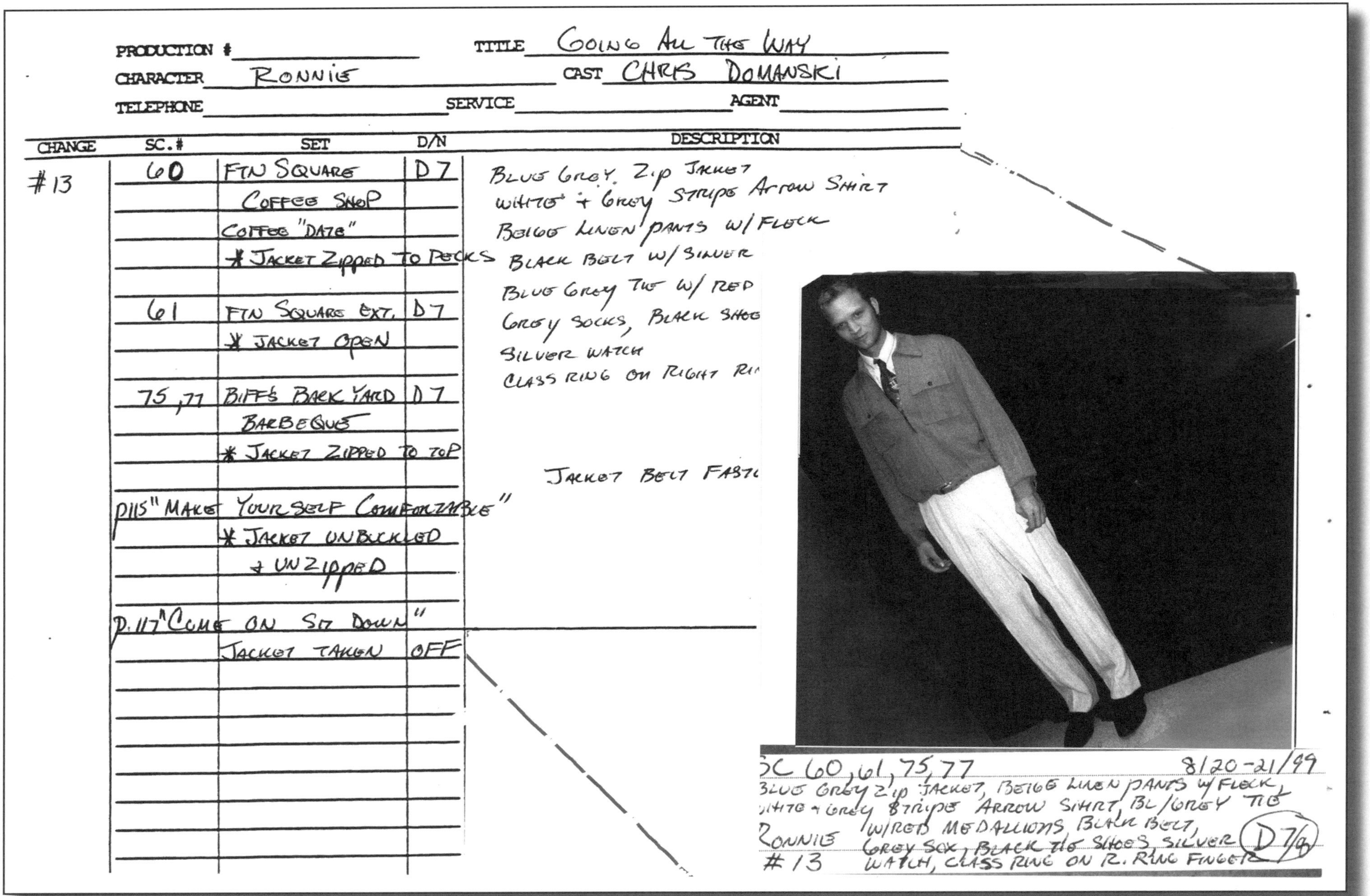

PRODUCTION #: _____ TITLE: GOING ALL THE WAY

CHARACTER: RONNIE CAST: CHRIS DOMANSKI

TELEPHONE: _____ SERVICE: _____ AGENT: _____

CHANGE	SC.#	SET	D/N	DESCRIPTION
#13	60	FTN SQUARE	D7	BLUE GREY ZIP JACKET
		COFFEE SHOP		WHITE + GREY STRIPE ARROW SHIRT
		COFFEE "DATE"		BEIGE LINEN PANTS W/ FLECK
		* JACKET ZIPPED TO PECKS		BLACK BELT W/ SILVER
	61	FTN SQUARE EXT.	D7	BLUE GREY TUT W/ RED
		* JACKET OPEN		GREY SOCKS, BLACK SHOES
				SILVER WATCH
				CLASS RING ON RIGHT RIN...
	75,77	BIFFS BACK YARD	D7	
		BARBEQUE		
		* JACKET ZIPPED TO TOP		JACKET BELT FAST...
	p115	"MAKE YOURSELF COMFORTABLE"		
		* JACKET UNBUCKLED		
		& UNZIPPED		
	p.117	"COME ON SIT DOWN"		
		JACKET TAKEN OFF		

DC 60 61 75 77   8/20-21/99

BLUE GREY ZIP JACKET, BEIGE LINEN PANTS W/FLECK

WHITE + GREY STRIPE ARROW SHIRT BL/GREY TIE

TWISTED MEDALLIONS BLACK BELT

RONNIE   GREY SOX BLACK TIE SHOES SILVER

WATCH, CLASS RING ON R. RING FINGER

#13   (D 7/8)

FIG. 1.7: WARDROBE CONTINUITY PAGE FOR A PRINCIPAL PLAYER

WARDROBE CONTINUITY SHEET

PRODUCTION # _____ TITLE __Going Are The Way__

CHARACTER __May__ CAST __Charlotte Wartzel__

TELEPHONE _____ SERVICE _____ AGENT _____

SC 60
Beige Huggar Hat, Pink/Green Floral
Chiffon Dress, Pink Crinolins, Pink Strapless
Bra + Pads, Pearl Floral Earrings, Pearl
May Necklace, w/ Nylon Gloves w/
#3 Roses, Beige Straw Wedgies D7
8/20

CHANGE	SC. #	SET	D/N	DESCRIPTION
#3	60	Fountain SQ	D 7	Beige Straw Huggar Hat
		Coffee Shop		Pink/Green Floral Dress-Chiffon
		Coffee "Date"		Pink Strapless Bra + Pads
				Pink Crinoline
				Seamed Natural Hose
				Beige Straw Wedgies Shoes
				Pearl Floral Earrings
				¼" Pearl Necklace - White
				Nylon Gloves w/ Rose Bud

FIG. 1.8

The Theory of Everything,
NBC Pilot

***Ocean Park* Studio location**

Photos courtesy of Rae Robison

Location shoot for *Closing the Deal* by MAC Films 2000

and work methodologies vary according to a script's complexity, and the standards of its producers. Career costume personnel adapt to every kind of budget by knowing the nitty-gritty of how to shop the stores, pull from rental collections, and collaborate with costume workrooms.

Costume prep periods vary. You may have two years, two days, or two minutes in advance of shooting to plan and produce a costume for a film. It is not unusual for modestly budgeted films to have only four weeks to prep. A single television episode may have only two or three days. Higher budgets tend to imply longer prep periods, but, in general, the business is increasingly cutting back. Costume personnel have to know how to hustle. Careers can be built on how quickly a designer and a supervisor can pull together a production.

Shooting schedules vary. Different production formats dictate different shooting schedules. The key production formats, with their typical shooting schedules, can be broken down this way:

- Feature films (low- to high-budget) shoot forty to sixty days
- Very low-budget features shoot as few as twenty days
- Movies-of-the-week (MOWs) shoot from twenty to thirty days

FIG. 1.9

21

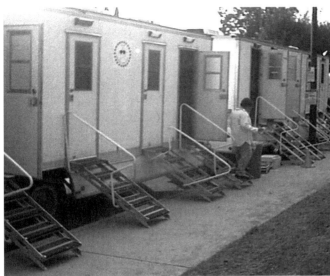

Ah, the glamour of the honeywagon . . .

Photos courtesy of Rae Robison

The number of pages per day a production shoots determines, in large part, the pace at which a crew is expected to work. Feature films generally shoot two to three pages of script per day, but very low-budget features can shoot as many as eight pages per day. Television movies generally shoot six pages per day.

Shooting conditions vary. Films are shot in many places—on *soundstages* (warehouses equipped for film production, with space to build sets, rig lights, and record sound); on *back lots* (the back acreage of a film studio, on which sets are built); and "on location" in the real world, where a set will be built, or existing scenic elements "dressed" (painted, adjusted, decorated) to match descriptions in the script. On location, film personnel must adapt, and often improvise, finding workspace and drawing on local resources for additional staff and services. Sometimes, the costume department office is conveniently located next to the costume storage area; sometimes, it's in your car. Costume department heads rent or create costume department offices, costume stock storage areas, fitting rooms, and costume workrooms, as the situation requires.

Location shooting demands portable work strategies for all production departments (fig. 1.8). The costume department can go mobile by using motor homes and dressing-room trailers called "honeywagons" for the principal actors (fig. 1.9) and special wardrobe trailers for costume storage. Costume construction work, fittings, and extras dressing rooms all get improvised on the shooting site. One designer told of a final fitting of a very expensive custom-made suit, with a very famous Rambo-like action hero, in which the star stood for final pants hemming on a toilet seat in a dimly lit hotel bathroom in Canada.

THE INDUSTRY IS GEARED TO COPE WITH RAPID CHANGES

Shooting schedules change, designs change, budgets change, with regularity. Industry personnel are expected to take rapid changes in stride. The industry labor unions trade on the flexibility and expertise of their members. The frenzy inherent in the business helps give personnel leverage to bargain for higher salaries. The result: Salaries can be high, but every penny will be earned as crews are put through the wringer. Production companies know that they ask the impossible on a regular basis; they expect to be told the cost, so they can make choices and establish priorities.

> I only had four weeks to prep *Maverick* [fig. 1.10]. It was nuts! I was starting in Lone Pine, California—the first location—in the morning; driving to Los Angeles for fittings in the afternoon; then back to Lone Pine, for wrap. Fortunately, I had fabulous actors to dress, who were as nice as they were talented. I had a marvelous cutter-fitter, John Hayles, who still makes things for me, contemporary and period. Also Tommy Velasco, a wonderful tailor. We would be lost without these skilled people! *(April Ferry, costume designer,* Terminator 3: Rise of the Machines, Donnie Darko, *and Academy Award-nominated* for Maverick)

In the two strongest film centers in the country, Los Angeles and New York, films are supported by a network of costume services that can speedily provide production companies with lavish costume offices, workrooms, rental collections, costume storage areas, cleaning services and delivery, fireproofing, dyeing, and shopping. Fashion design firms can shower your production with donated goods. Rental houses can deliver dozens of Chicago police uniforms, "camera ready"—correctly altered, with all the right patches and accessories—over night. Specialty companies can provide made-to-order buttons,

FIG. 1.10

Design by April Ferry
Sketch by Lois DeArmond
Dress by John Hayles
Photo by Ed Wassall

April Ferry's designs for Annabelle in *Maverick*

Maverick, **a film with beautiful period detailing produced by Warner Bros. garnered designer April Ferry an Oscar nomination in 1994. This film was prepared in four weeks. The meticulous detailing on this dress for Jodie Foster is characteristic of the kind of detailing necessary for principal player costumes.**

buttonholes, shoes, pleating, embroidery, knitting, beading, millinery, and trims. All of it is available, for a price. In every department, film personnel learn to improvise, tap local services and sources, and quote the costs.

Forget "It's not my department." Always say yes, if you can, but learn how to estimate the costs. Nobody wants to hear your problems. Find a way to solve them. Filmmaking—it's all about flexibility and change.

I did a movie with the Zucker Brothers. They had this wonderful half-time scene based on a spoof of hula girls. The scene was going to shoot on Tuesday. The Friday before, at about two in the afternoon, I saw the final dance rehearsal. Because it was a new piece of writing, it was all about clearances: The final music had been chosen based on what could be approved in time. This turned out to be rumba music, and the choreographer had come up with a brilliant number. I sort of blanched. I went up to the director and I said, "This is very funny and it's great, [but] remember those Hawaiian hula outfits that you approved two months ago? Are they still going to work with a rumba number?" And he said, "Oooo, good call. What can we have instead?" I said, "Carmen Miranda, perhaps, is more what you had in mind?"

So then we had a weekend to make two dozen [Carmen Miranda costumes]. That's when costume design takes on a different meaning: You are in a car, being driven to a fabric store, calling them at rush hour, on a Friday afternoon, at a quarter to six, asking them to stay open. Then, you are literally looking at bolts of fabric, saying, "Is there enough of this?" So, it's not, "Gosh, what would I like?" or "What could we custom-dye?"; it's, "Can I do twenty-four [of them]?" When you've got twenty-four dancing girls, yardage goes awfully quickly—especially if there are lots of ruffles. So then you're calling the person to cut the pattern over the weekend, and do the sample. You show them the fabrics on a Friday night; they cut the pattern on Saturday and make the sample for you to approve Sunday morning. Then they cut them in bulk on Sunday evening. They are mass-producing them in the workrooms on Monday, so that you can hand them to the girls and dress them as they walk on to the set on Tuesday morning. The blessing is that you had a three-day weekend!

At the same time, you are also having a budget dilemma. Before all [of the above] gets going, you have to call your line producer and say, "I've just had a meeting with the director, and this is what's happened. We have discovered that it is possible to do this [at the original cost] within the time frame, and this is how much it is going to cost. I need authorization to do it now because we need to put it into work now. Do I have authorization?" *(Catherine Adair, costume designer)*

So, Why Do It?

It's a gas and a half. As hairy as the production process sounds, it is not impossible. It's like moving to a big city: You just start to move faster, naturally. You cope with all the pressures of this field by getting into the Zen of the work. Most of all, you have to have passion. When faced with the fact that you have to style several hundred extras in short order, you embrace improvisational styling, creating characters in a matter of minutes, out of a stock of costume goodies. As you relax into the pace of the day, you find, after the initial flurry of dressing, that there is time between shots to tweak a collar here, a shirt tail there. If you are faced with ironing hundreds of formal shirts at the back of the truck on a hot summer day, you get into the Zen of ironing, the lack of stress in the moment. Every now and then, you drift on over to the craft service table, get a cool drink, chit-chat with the grips and the extras, and generally drink in the wacky atmosphere of the set.

Filmmaking is always a short-term, team effort. Film costuming—whether you are interested in designing, supervising, shopping, working on set, or building costumes—is essentially a freelance job, and as such, getting work is all about who you know. The ability to collaborate is key to building and maintaining a career in film costuming. A feel for the filmmaking process, a grasp of diplomacy, and a gift for "reading" a situation are vital skills. Understanding the entire costuming process—from design and construction to set work and final wrap—gives designers and costumers the flexibility they need to solve problems under the high-pressure deadlines on which this field thrives. Highly developed survival skills will hold you in good stead when dealing with "high maintenance" producers, difficult directors, and evolving productions.

Still interested? To get into the costume groove, first check your ego at the door. If you want to work in this field, you must be really hungry to do it. The unions are tough to break into, and job sources are often a jealously guarded secret. Getting to do the work you really want can be a long struggle, with lots of "dues-paying." If you come to the field with a long history of accomplishments in theater or fashion, you may be surprised by how unimpressed with it film people will be. To be brutally honest, unless you have film contacts who will vouch for you, the film professionals doing the hiring care more about your stamina than your fabulous portfolio. Even with an MFA or two years of Broadway or fashion-industry experience, on a film, you can still find yourself ironing shirts and sorting dirty socks.

There is very little formal training available in the nitty-gritty of costuming a film. Some costumers see the advantages of theater training, especially as a way of acquiring good construction, research, and collaborative skills. Others see merit in working with people who have strong retail and fashion backgrounds, believing that they may be more savvy when it comes to stock organization and modern dress resources—and that they may have less "attitude" than trained theatrical costumers when it comes to the kinds of work they feel is "beneath" them.

Film costumers have grown accustomed to training people on the job, so if you're smart, fun to work with, learn quickly, and have an ardent desire to work in film, dig in and get started. Talent isn't exactly held against you in film, but it takes a whole lot more than just talent to make it in this field. A great personality, a positive attitude, and a willingness work your butt off will help you succeed. You'll also need a thick skin, sensitive "antennae," and lots of hustle.

Conversation One:

On Working Your Way Up in the Industry, with Eduardo Castro

Eduardo Castro is the costume designer of the feature films *City of Industry*, *Kama Sutra: A Tale of Love*, and *The Perez Family*, among others (figs. 1.11 and 2.1). He has also designed for television, including the series *Miami Vice* and *Judging Amy*.

Eduardo, how did you come to design costumes for film? You're one of the few people I've met who came up the "traditional" Hollywood route.

Yes, that traditional route doesn't exist the way it did when I came back to Los Angeles in 1977. I'm from Los Angeles originally, and one of the first jobs I had while I was at Los Angeles City College was ushering, downtown, at the Music Center, which has three theaters: Dorothy Chandler Pavilion, Ahmanson Theatre, and Mark Taper Forum. All of a sudden, I was transported to this world I'd never known about—the world of theater—and I started to become intrigued.

I'd always liked to draw, and I'd always had this connection to clothing. I had always admired clothing in movies, but I'd never really thought I could be a part of it. I would look at the programs, and I would look up the designers and where they went to school. There was a resident designer at the Ahmanson Theatre, James Trettipo; I noticed that he went to Carnegie Mellon University. And then [costume designer] Ann Roth came to town and did some shows, and she came from Carnegie Mellon. And then, Suzy Tsu was doing *Godspell*, and she came from that school. So I said, "Why not give it a shot?" I applied, and I did a portfolio based on what I thought design for the theater was. I had no formal training, but I got accepted.

That was formal training, from the ground up. It's the place where you learn the hard way. When I came out to L.A., I realized that it doesn't have to be the hard way. I came out on Christmas break, in 1977, and I interviewed with the head of Disney. He said, "You must go to Western Costume [Company]; that's where you're going to learn and [where you're going to] see everybody." I interviewed at Western, and the head of the company, Bob Newmar, said, "Come on in."

No one can do this anymore?

No one can do that anymore, and it's sad, because back then, Western was the largest costume company in Los Angeles. It was almost like the only costume house, because they had everything under one roof: They had the shoemaker, the hat maker, and custom made-to-order. They had a dry-cleaning facility, a dyeing facility, milliners, everything. And, basically, you started doing stock—really menial labor—and then worked your way up.

You started in the rental collection at Western Costume?

I started below rental—worse than rental. They led me to the back area of Western, on the hottest day of the year. In this open cement area, they opened these corrugated gates, and there were three forty-foot trucks. On these trucks was a film I was to unload, and wash out, on the cement. The movie was *Apocalypse Now*. So I started my career *washing*. It took me two weeks just to hose down everything that had come in from the Philippines.

FIG. 1.11

Eduardo Castro's design for *Kama Sutra* (1996)

A little hard on your recent MFA ego, I would think.

No, I had no ego, at that point. I was tired of the academic world, and I was looking forward to a job for a while, to clear my head. I just thought, "Give me a job from nine to five, let me go home, and let me have a life!" The last year at school had been torturous. "Mindless" was fine for a while. I started there, and little by little…. You know, word gets around pretty fast about what one can do and what one can't, and you start to move up the ladder.

From hosing down the wardrobe from *Apocalypse Now*, I had to rearrange the armor section in the rental collection. That was just trying to find all the pieces of the lost armor in that vast place. Then, it was putting away belts and sizing shoes. And all the time, while this is happening, you're catching glimpses of the world you are eventually going to be a part of—the world of Edith Head, Dorothy Jeakins, Theadora Van Runkle. They were all doing big productions at the time, and coming through the shops. You'd go, "Oh, my God, look, they're preparing this movie called *Grease.*" And it looked like fun. Or *The Deer Hunter.* And some big musical going to Chicago. Or Ann Roth would come in. The variety was just so exciting. As people got to know who I was, and what I was like, I moved up to being a costumer "on the floor," either doing commercials or what they called "private rentals," with private clients.

Back then, those people who worked on the floor at Western were actually in-house costumers. Theadora Van Runkle or Edith Head could come in without anybody else (without a design assistant or her own costumer), and say, "Give me a man in the men's department; give me a lady in the ladies' department—this is what I'm going to do." You're functioning as a design assistant, a wardrobe assistant, an all-around assistant. After about a year there, I graduated to doing all the made-to-order films that came through Western. I was in charge of the big films that were made-to-order.

You were functioning as a design assistant, but also overseeing the workroom?

Yes, back then, that was the position: I was in charge of either swatching (sampling fabrics) or getting the fabrics and getting them washed and into the workroom. I learned the whole rhythm of doing made-to-order. People don't know what it really takes sometimes—all the elements. I learned right away not to leave the buttons until the last minute. I choose the buttons when I do the fabric. It's something I learned at Western, because we had to do so much, so fast, and so big.

I was working with some of the greatest. There was this wonderful couturier named Lilly Fonda; she was just fantastic. She'd worked on *The King and I* and *Hello, Dolly,* with Irene Sharaff, and all those people who'd done those big musicals of the fifties and sixties. I remember doing a film called *Hurricane,* which was big for me. The designer and her people came through town and gave me all of these instructions, and I was left alone while they were in Fiji or Tahiti. I had to fit Trevor Howard, Max von Sydow, and Mia Farrow, and I had to do the military costumes. Working with all these people, they started to request me.

I did a big musical, with Ann Roth. This was 1979, 1980. I think that was when things—the Hollywood tradition—started to fall apart. Little by little, Western was out-pricing itself. Little costume shops started to spread out. We were doing the musical *They're Playing Our Song;* Ann Roth came in, and we were to prepare it. I worked on it for about two weeks, but the bid at Western was too high and the producer said, "You've got to move the show." So, they moved to New York—it was cheaper than Western—and that's when Western was no longer the only game in town. This world wasn't going to handle it anymore.

After that, word got around that I could sketch. One of my first jobs was sketching for a film with Robert Redford, which didn't end up happening; then I got on a movie called *The Long Riders,* with designer Bobby Mannix. I sketched for that film, and that got me in to the designer's union. That was 1980.

How did you start to get a feel for on-set life?

I was offered a job on the set of a television show called *Paper Dolls,* which was this *Dynasty*-like series. I became the set person on it. It's amazing: a whole different social strata; a whole different way of being with actors. Basically, you're taking care of the actor. There is a lot of down time when they're lighting, it's not as creative, but I'm glad I did the set work, because, unless you do it yourself, you really aren't prepared, as a designer, to prepare your *own* set people.

From set work, I got picked up to do this and that, little jobs here and there: sketching, and assisting Julie Weiss on a project called *I'm Dancing as Fast as I Can.* It was her first movie as a designer, and my first movie as a costume supervisor. It was like the blind leading the blind, but we got through it.

One of my bigger breaks came when I was men's costumer on a television series that was huge called *Fame,* about the students and faculty of the New York City High School for the Performing Arts. It was exciting to work on this kind of show because we were doing production numbers. It taught me how to deal with fast-paced kids. I was on that for a year. Then, I got a call from designer Richard Shissler, who asked me if I would work with him and Milena Canonero on the third season of the television series *Miami Vice.* I turned it down twice, and they kept coming back until they made the offer quite nice. Basically, they promised me that if I supervised the wardrobe for that year, they would, in turn, recommend me to design the following year—which is what happened.

It took me about four or five shows to acclimate myself, because *Miami Vice* was a different kind of show than *Fame*. We were dealing with much higher-end clothes, and stunts. We were dealing with actors who had much more to say about their clothes than the *Fame* kids, so it was about keeping Don Johnson and Philip Michael Thomas and the two girls happy, and making [the design concept and the costuming process] cohesive and wonderful. It was all location work—very little soundstage work. Like a film. We shot seven days: every seven days, a new script. In many ways, I felt the supervisor's job—my job—was harder than the designer's, because I had to be responsible for all the technical ins and outs of the production. We would be shooting first-unit and second-unit; we would be shooting second and third stunt units; we'd be shooting inserts in New York City, where a jacket for Don Johnson would be. And, oh the budgeting! When I became the designer on *Miami Vice*, things became a lot easier.

I left *Miami Vice* after forty-four shows, then hooked up with costume designer Wayne Finkelman, on a movie called *Protocol*. I was on the very bottom rung: I was doing shoes. Wayne's assistant designer got fired or something, and I sort of stepped in and said I could do it. Wayne said, "Grab my hand and don't let go of it." I worked my butt off for him, and he paid me back ten thousand times, by giving me this movie, or offering me that film, or moving me up the ladder. I was his co-designer for a while and we did several films together. And then, he handed me my first film, which was *Bird on a Wire*, kind of a little gift on a silver platter. He was Goldie Hawn's costume designer, and he was also doing a film called *The Two Jakes*, starring Jack Nicholson. He couldn't commit to both, so he said, "I'm only going to do Goldie; you do the rest of the picture." Well, I ended up doing half of Goldie's costumes, plus the rest of the picture. That was my jumping-off point, because I was able to acquire an agent.

With all your experience, you weren't able to get an agent before that?

Agents don't want to touch you unless you have something solid they can go with to pitch you. Getting the agent was one thing, and that started a group of things. Since then, I've done every kind of venue: television, commercials. I still do everything.

Do you have any general advice for newcomers?

My main advice to people who want to get in to the business is not to be in a hurry to be in the hot seat. Spend your time learning, because if you fall on your face on a fifty-million-dollar movie, it's hard to get back up again. If you fall on your face as an assistant, on a little movie, it will be okay. You have to learn from the bad and the good. Try to work with people whom you're going to learn from. That's where you get ahead in the business. I learned so much from the good people I worked with: I learned how to talk from Julie Weiss. (She's the best talker in the whole world; that woman can talk her way into any situation.) I learned to draw from Theadora Van Runkle, who is the greatest, the greatest.

Who taught you how to handle a fitting with grace?

Ann Roth.

You've been blessed with many angels in the business. Of course, you've also more than earned your way. All those problems you've had to deal with!

Of course, there are going to be problems. But we'll solve them, and go on to the next thing. It's solvable. It's doable. You don't have to make it drudgery. If we can't have fun, why even bother doing it? Life's too short.

Fig. C.1: Hope Hanafin's designs for THE LONG ROAD HOME (1991) artfully combine strong character work with tightly controlled color and texture palettes coordinated to harmonize closely with the landscape) in order to produce subtle but powerful images.

FIG. C.2: Designs by Eduardo Castro for the film KAMA SUTRA (1996). Photos published with permission of RASA Film, Inc.

FIG. C.3: Hope Hanafin's photoboard from HBO's VENDETTA (1999) combines fabric swatches with photos to create a scene-at-a-glance palette board.

Fig. C.4: Research board by Hope Hanafin.

Fig. C.5: Hope Hanafin's color board uses swatches, paint chips and xeroxes to flesh out the world.

Fig. C.6: Hope Hanafin's designs for Cecily Tyson in A LESSON BEFORE DYING (1999). Photos by Bob Greene, reproduced courtesy of HBO Film and Home Box Office.

Fig. C.7: Hope Hanafin's designs for A LESSON BEFORE DYING (1999). Hope's designs show the kind of meticulous costume aging that is needed for camera. Photos courtesy of HBO Film and Home Box Office.

Fig. C.8: Eduardo Castro's design for Odell's gang in CITY OF INDUSTRY (1996) shows a photoboard approach to a color palette. Fitting photos were edited into the board to display the scene at a glance.

CITY OF INDUSTRY   ODELL'S GANG

Fig. C.9: J: Script pages from PLUTO NASH with Costume Notation.

===

Illustration: Costume script notation for Pluto Nash by Neil Cuthbert, courtesy of Castlerock Entertainment.

This story takes place in a fairly sophisticated colony on the Moon that is rife with shysters and mob guys. Pluto, our hero, is an Eddy Murphy/ Will Smith kind of smoothie whose bar has just been firebombed by gangsters, so he's out for revenge. Bruno is his antiquated side-kick robot.

Sc 19 EXT. A STREET OUTSIDE "THE PERFECT VACUUM" N2

It's a dimly lit backstreet in a very poor neighborhood. From the apartments above, babies and children can be heard screaming. The CAMERA PANS along a wall past a VIK RILLS poster. Somebody has scrawled, "VIK BLOWS!" on it. There's a doorway with a red light. A sign reads: "Girls, $350 and up. Real Girls, $3000 and up."

                              PLUTO
        Bruno....Bruno.
BRUNO is nowhere to be seen. PLUTO checks his pistol, takes a deep breath, and crosses the street.

[handwritten right margin: Pluto #2x ? Robot Whores? Beggars? Drunks? Kid? Hood? Drive Bys?]

Sc 20 INT. THE PERFECT VACUUM CLUB N2

It's a dive. Pictures of robot boxers on the wall; beat up chromium chairs and tables. Around the second floor is a railing, almost like an Old West saloon. The entire place is lit by one fluorescent light.

PLUTO enters and sees KELP and the mustachioed HOOD #1, the man who killed NILO, sitting at the bar along the side wall. PLUTO heads toward them.

                              PLUTO
        Hey, Kelp.

KELP and HOOD #1 swivel around in their barstools. The results of PLUTO's firefighting efforts are still evident.
                              KELP
        Well, if it isn't Pluto Nash. What happened, Pluto, the ilmenite mines let out early?

Two or three guys at the bar laugh.
[handwritten: Drunks or Hoods?]
                              PLUTO
        I got a message for Rex Crater.

[handwritten right margin: Pluto #2x, Kelp #2, Hood #1 — change #2, Bartender?, Whores?, Waitress?, Robot Boxer, Drunk #1, Drunk #2, Drunk #3]

===

Speaking women	Speaking men	Extras
General atmosphere & costume notes		
Dirt & distress _____	Damage/Stunt	Blood ●

                              BRUNO
        Oh, boy.
BRUNO draws his pistol and opens fire. His aim isn't so great, but his big old fashioned pistol makes a big noise and blows very big holes in tables and walls. BRUNO fires another blast, demolishing a support post causing a section of the upper tier to collapse. Three HOODS come crashing down.
[handwritten: #6,7 #3,4,5]

Two other HOODS open fire from the bathroom and side door. The bar and mirror get puckered with smoking burn holes. PLUTO pops up, fires once to his left, spins and fires once to his right, dropping both HOODS. His every appearance is followed by a barrage of laser blasts.

He scuttles along behind the bar, so they never know where he's going to pop up next.

DINA, still behind a table, sees PLUTO'S PEARL-HANDLED REVOLVER lying on the floor, a scant five feet away. She starts to crawl towards it. A series of laser blasts burn the floor in front of her. She makes an abrupt U-turn and crawls furiously back behind the table.

PLUTO jumps up and nails the HOOD shooting at DINA – A laser shot from KELP singes PLUTO's shoulder.
[handwritten: #8 Pluto #2xx stunt doubles 2nd phase distress]

We ANGLE ON PLUTO, dropped down behind the bar examining his shoulder. It's just a flesh wound.

Sc 20B ANGLE ON DINA INT VacuumClub N2

Still taking cover behind an overturned table, DINA sees PLUTO stand and start firing in the opposite direction. Suddenly, from the other side of her table, a HOOD crawls DIRECTLY IN FRONT OF HER and picks up PLUTO's PEARL HANDLED GUN. Although no more than three feet away, the HOOD is totally oblivious to DINA as he stands and takes dead aim at PLUTO. DINA jumps up, vaults off a chair, and lands on top of the HOOD, just as the HOOD fires. The laser shot narrowly misses PLUTO. Bottles are shattered. PLUTO is showered with glass and booze as he ducks down behind the bar.

[handwritten: Dina #2x stunt double, Hood #5, Pluto #2xx stunt doubles 3rd phase distress]

===

Speaking women	Speaking men	Extras
General atmosphere & costume notes		
Dirt & distress _____	Damage/Stunt	Blood ●

[handwritten top: How many Hoods at Hogostrada? ... N2]

...OD hiding behind the door to the back room, his gun drawn. Out of the corner of his eye, PLUTO detects movement up top – three other gunmen strategically placed, their lasers aimed at PLUTO.
[handwritten: "Fallen" Hood?, Gunman?, Hood #2?]

PLUTO takes it all in without batting an eye. Realizing his predicament, he makes his move. He drops to his knees and begins a wild, sobbing rant.
                              PLUTO
        Please don't kill me!!!! He can have the club. I don't even want the four million. I'll give him four million....

[handwritten right margin: Moonco Hood, "Fallen Hood", Gunman, Hood #2, Pluto Dirt Potential]

Sc 20A *A little later in the scene Pluto's soon-to-be girl, Dina, and his antiquated robot, Bruno, arrive:* **Int Vacuum Club N2**
Just then, DINA bursts through the door.
                              DINA
        Pluto, it's a trap!
PLUTO turns, momentarily distracted. KELP knocks PLUTO's gun out of his hand. It skitters across the floor. PLUTO pushes KELP into HOOD#1, who is now back on his feet and charging. From all angles, HOODS begin firing.
[handwritten: #2,3,4,5]

DINA scrambles behind a table.

PLUTO dives headfirst over the bar. He lands on another HOOD who is crouching there. The surprised HOOD jumps up. Another GUNMAN shoots him. PLUTO grabs the FALLEN HOOD's gun, pops up and fires a quick burst, taking out the GUNMAN. KELP and HOOD #1 fall back to the cover of a nearby video game.

DINA spots BRUNO in the doorway. He's just arrived.
                              DINA (continuing)
        Bruno....sic'em.

[handwritten right margin: Dina #2x Dirt Potential, Pluto #2xs stunt doubles, Kelp #2, Fallen Hood stunt doubles, Gunman stunt doubles, Hood #2, Hood #1 chang#2, Bruno #1]

===

Speaking women	Speaking men	Extras
General atmosphere & costume notes		
Dirt & distress _____	Damage/Stunt	Blood ●

Fig. C.10: Design by Dan Lester for the "Back from the Dead" coat for Spawn. This leather coat took roughly a week to age. The SPAWN production set up a special "aging" department to distress the clothes to cut down on per piece charges. Photo courtesy of New Line Cinema.

Fig. C.11: Design for the artist formerly known as Prince by Stacia Lang. Gene Mignola, the painter who created this print, made a montage of photos of the band to create one large silkscreen. He then screened the yardage with black paint. After that he hand painted the colors onto the yardage. Development of the silkscreen cost roughly $1,000 because of the amount of halftones. They printed 7 to 10 yards at $75 to $100 a yard.

Fig. C.12: Design for the clown in SPAWN by Dan Lester. The stunts in this production required 12 to 14 jackets. Material costs per jacket were roughly $200, but painting took three days and aging took an additional two days of labor. The result was an overall cost of $1,000 per jacket using an in-house aging team. Designs and photos courtesy of Dan Lester.

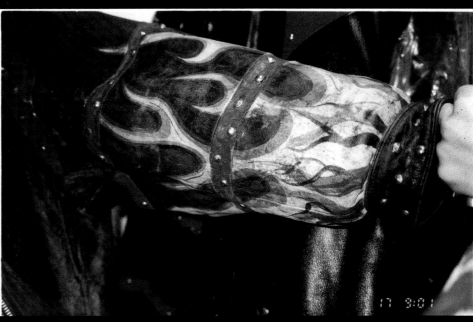

Fig. C.13: Jean-Pierre Dorleac's designs for HEART AND SOULS and THE LOT. These designs typify some of the design range of a Hollywood costume designer. Careful character detailing, whether you are doing naturalism or glamour, is the key to a successful career.

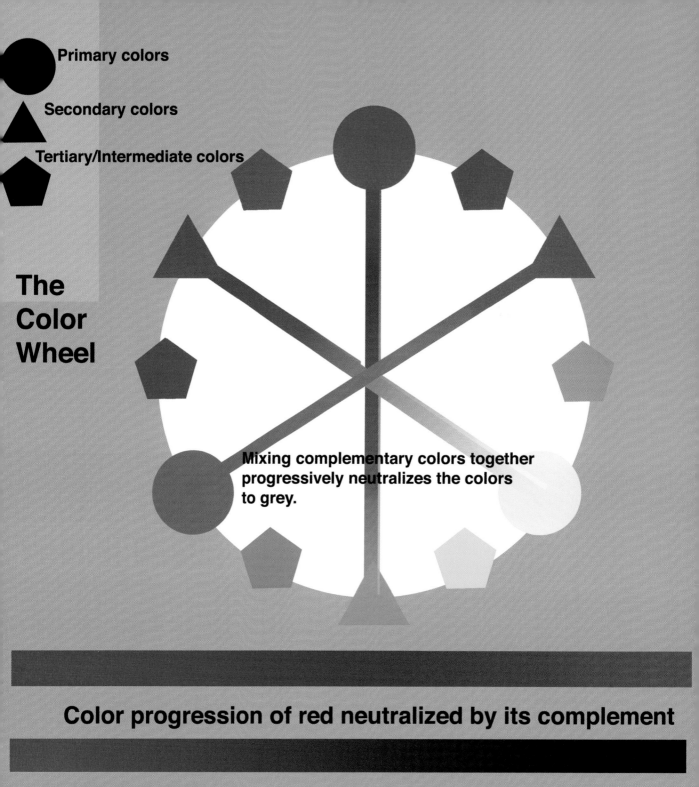

The Color Wheel

Primary colors

Secondary colors

Tertiary/Intermediate colors

Mixing complementary colors together progressively neutralizes the colors to grey.

Color progression of red neutralized by its complement

Color progression into shades

Color progression into tints

Value Chart

High light tone

Low dark tone

An analogous color scheme with a dominant blue-grey hue.

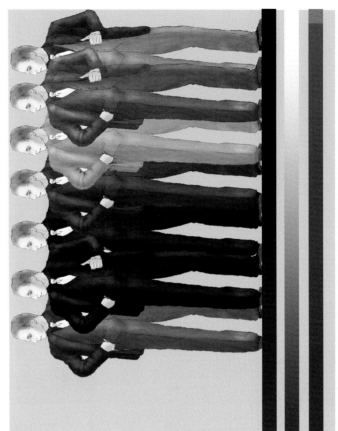

A monochromatic color scheme.

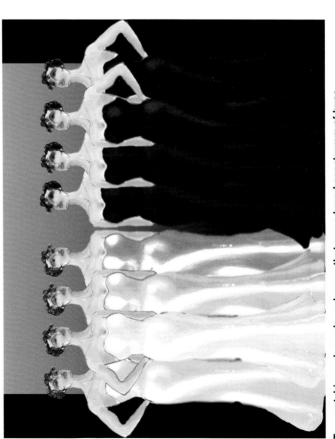

Two matching value color schemes that use a broad spectrumm of hues.

Contrasting values in a color scheme.

Contrasting intensities in a color scheme.

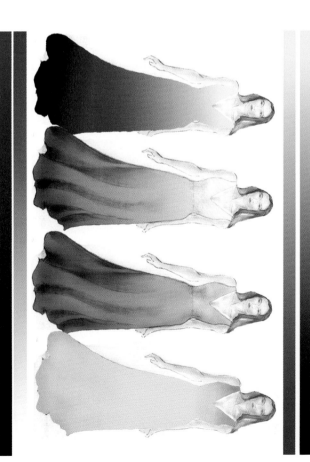

A complementary color scheme.

A limited warm and cool color scheme.

Fig. C.17

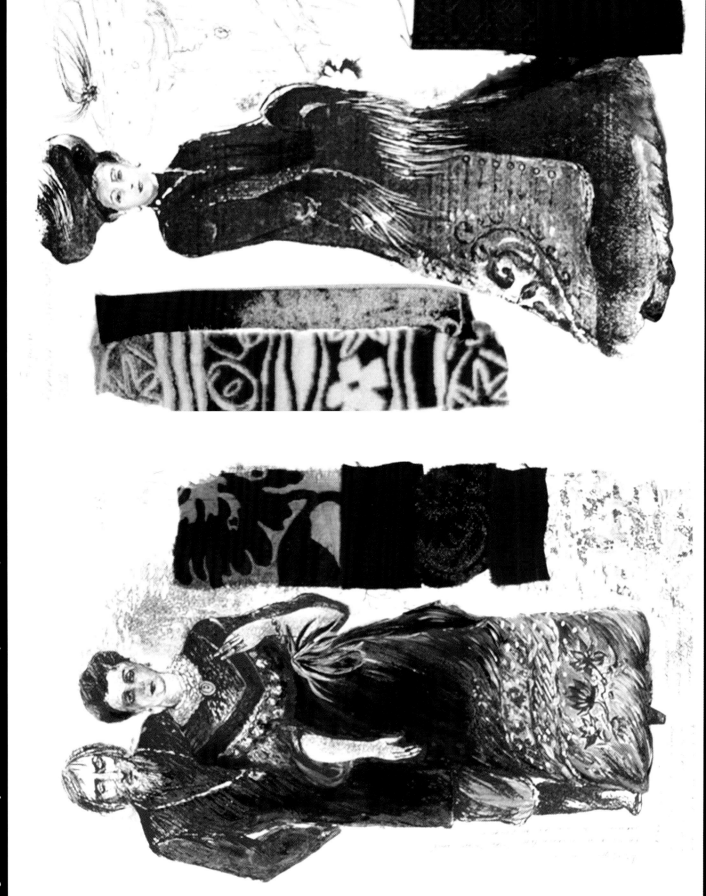

Design and sketches by Natasha Landau for the HBO production of *Rasputin.*

April Ferry's designs for Warner Bros. 1994 *Maverick*.

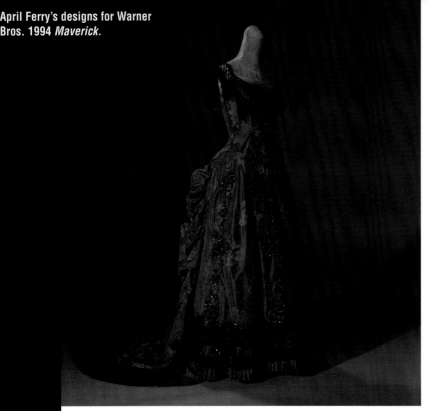

PART TWO

Fundamentals of Costume Design for Film

Costume Designers: The Forgotten Artists

Costume designers are generally a misunderstood group. For many outsiders, real Hollywood costume design died with Edith Head. In matters of prestige and respect, modern designers have been shortchanged, suffering in comparison with high-profile designers of the Hollywood glamour era—the nineteen-thirties and nineteen-forties—like Adrian, Travis Banton, Cecil Beaton, Howard Greer, Edith Head, Walter Plunkett, and Irene Sharaff. These designers were supported by a studio system that allowed them to design endlessly for female stars, while costumers put together the menswear and costumes for all the other characters in a film. Shops staffed with hundreds of fabulously talented tailors and dressmakers cranked out made-to-order work in great volume. Studios invested in costume stock that could be used again and again on the hundreds of films they produced each year. Costume designers' reputations were used to recruit stars. Art directors and cinematographers also flourished during this period and, in concert with costume designers, defined state-of-the-art glamour.

In the nineteen-fifties, postwar inflation hit the Hollywood dream factory hard. The weakening influence of the studios, the rise of independent production, and the social revolutions of the nineteen-sixties and seventies combined to create a demand for new kinds of films. The *cinema verité* movement (literally, *cinema truth*) brought location shooting and an interest in gritty realism to the forefront in the industry. As a result, costume designers were forced to work in new ways, putting whole films together "off the rack"—straight from readymade inventory available in any store.

The nineteen-eighties brought us the "corporatization" of Hollywood, and the idolization of the fashion designer, a trend epitomized in *American Gigolo's* 1979 homage to Giorgio Armani. The mass marketing of designer fashions, via the "boutiquing" of America, contributed as well. The movie industry's values changed, and so did the industry's understanding of the costume design process. Made-to-order and customized designs—the foundation of Hollywood's costume glamour—were traded by producers for off-the-rack wardrobe. The hours of fittings endured by stars were traded for plastic surgery, personal trainers, and couture goods. Why would a producer need a costume designer and a workroom when a shopper could buy an Armani?

The nineties brought the "stylist," a term that comes from the fashion advertising market. When the term first gained currency in film, a "stylist" was an expert in fashion who was employed by a star. The stylist created an "image" for the star, and built his or her personal wardrobe. Over the course of the decade, stylists built reputations based on close working relationships with fashion houses, which allowed them access to both exclusive goods and the latest styles. Now, stylists have thoroughly infiltrated film and television design, creating fierce competition among traditionally trained costume designers for the already limited number of jobs.

Since most productions—features and television shows alike—are designed from shopped goods (fig. 2.1), the difference between "designing" and "styling" seems fuzzy to outsiders; however, to traditionally trained costume designers, it is a difference with

FIG. 2.1

31

Eduardo Castro's design for Stephen Dorff in *City of Industry* (1996) is a good example of a "shopped" look that creates a compelling character.

deeply personal meaning. Costume design is about the creation of characters; styling combines readymade, off-the-rack clothing to create a "look." Indeed, some costume designers maintain that a stylist does nothing but make an actor look good. "All style, no substance." "Too much about display of the latest fashion—to the detriment of the character or the reality of the situation." "Characters created by stylists have the soul of a magazine layout." So say some costume designers. "Where's the poetry beneath the style?" they demand.

Today, Seventh Avenue and Milan supply the glamour to the Academy Awards. The Adrians, the Edith Heads—great designers, who designed not just film costumes for the stars, but elaborate personal wardrobes—seem all but gone.

> When I started working in the business, in 1978, there was more of a love of filmmaking by the production companies. It was an art form run by a family-oriented industry. Now, it's a global industry, where cost factors matter greatly. I've seen the pendulum swing away from the small boutique production companies, like MTM, where I started out, and which is now gone. Now, here I am, working for a major studio, a big corporation. We're a publicly owned company, and we're scrutinized by everybody, from New York to California, from Iowa to Nebraska. It's a totally different atmosphere. *(Pat Welch, costume designer,* L.A. Law, Snoops, *and Emmy-nominated for* Frank's Place*)*

> Designers just aren't as respected as much in this business as they are in theater. Very rarely do you get that respect. I've gotten it on several films, but I think it depends on the producer. The worst is modern television, because television producers assume their taste is better than anybody else's. *(Eduardo Castro, costume designer)*

The Costume Designer's Job

Costume designers, like fashion designers, are often given the job of making actors look good. But costume designers do much more than this. They create pictures that tell stories and illuminate the meanings of a script. Employing the tools of the costume design trade, they delineate character, clarify atmosphere, illuminate motivation, and augment mood. They also head the costume department.

To lay it out plainly, a costume designer fills three key roles on a film production:

1. *Storyteller.* Costume designers tell stories, through the costumes they design, about character, family, social conditions, ways of life. They also tell stories about the world or worlds from which the characters come and in which they end up. Costumes reflect the effects of history and of contemporaneous events, as well as the changes in a character's internal condition.

2. *Interpreter.* A costume designer interprets the script, orchestrating character harmonies and contrasts to fuel plot, crystallize motivation, and clarify any confusions in the script. A designer materializes a character's—and an actor's—strengths, weaknesses, idiosyncrasies, and emotional states; heightens drama, intensifies mood, and manipulates style, to illuminate the underlying meanings of a screenplay and express the director's point of view.

3. *Manager.* A costume designer manages the logistics of costume production, supervising the department's crew, supporting the actors, performing budget wizardry, and driving the timely delivery of costumes to the set.

To succeed, any costume designer must also develop an "eye" for design. Seeing in your mind's eye the combination of costume elements needed to support actor, character, story, and style of production is—without question—an art. Having an eye for design means that you have the ability to do the following:

- *Visualize the goods on the actor.* You can look at a body and see what shapes will flatter, or disguise, that form; you can look at fabric and imagine how it can be made into a garment; and you can look at clothing on a hanger and imagine how it will look on the body.

- *Identify the costume elements that most strongly reveal character and story.* Whether you are looking at people in the street, photographs in books and magazines, or clothing in stores and rental houses, you are able to determine the costume pieces key to telling the story, revealing its hidden meanings. You must be able to pick out the costume pieces that are emblematic of a character's idiosyncrasies, a character's emotional and circumstantial changes, the values of the world the character inhabits, and the nature of the events and atmosphere in the script.

- *Visualize a costume in the context of a scene, a set, an entire film.* You can imagine how a costume plays against the other characters in the scene, and against the set, as well as how it looks in different lights. You can visualize how a costume is revealed on film, including the moment-to-moment shifts in camera point of view, scene-to-scene changes of place and time, and character and event developments.

- *Visualize how style can be used to create the most compelling images for a character and a story.* You can see, in your mind's eye, how to manipulate color, texture, line, and shape for maximum dramatic effect. You can imagine how costume can be used to materialize a director's vision.

Telling a story with costumes

Anyone who enjoys people-watching understands that what you wear, and how you wear it, reveals a lot about your character and the way you live your life. As storytellers, costume designers must be able to recognize meaning in clothing elements, and distill those meanings into the essence of character, situation, and world. Using clothing as clues, we deduce social status and personal idiosyncrasies, physical condition and sexuality, season and occasion (fig. 2.2). Costume designers learn to identify—and make use of—costume elements to create characters, and the worlds in which they live.

A case in point: Eduardo Castro's work for actor Alfred Molina in *The Perez Family* (1994). Castro needed to design costumes for Molina, whose character is named Juan Raul Perez (fig. 2.3). Juan, a formerly wealthy man jailed in Cuba as a political prisoner, seizes the opportunity to escape to Miami, where he is caught, and held in a refugee detention camp. Castro's designs for Mr. Molina beautifully express the character's development over the course of events (the "character arc") through a series of different outfits (costume "changes") that show the change in Juan's status from political dissident tortured in a Cuban prison to prisoner in an American detention camp. In costume change number one, the drab institutional uniform, sadly deteriorated, reveals the char-

FIG. 2.2

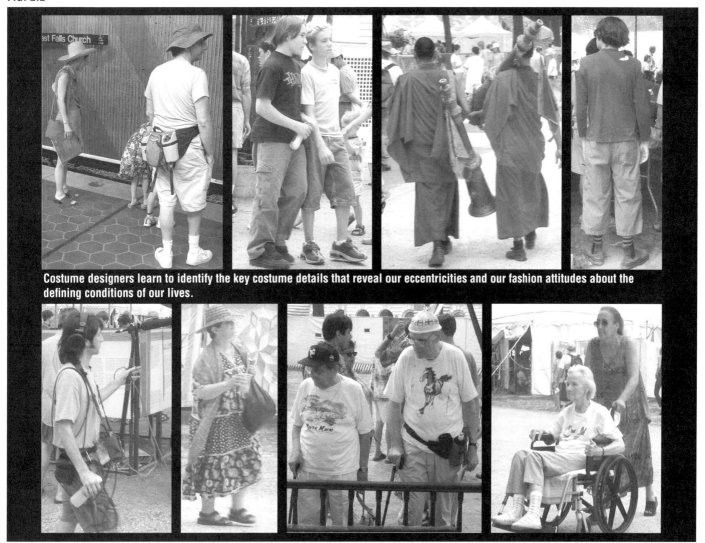

Costume designers learn to identify the key costume details that reveal our eccentricities and our fashion attitudes about the defining conditions of our lives.

FIG. 2.3

Eduardo Castro's designs for Alfred Molina in *The Perez Family* (1994) took him from a tortured political prisoner to a Cuban boat refugee living in Miami.

Photos by
Eduardo Castro

acter's misery and degree of degradation. Change number two is the character's Florida detention camp outfit. The poor fit of the tropical shirt suggests that this clothing has been donated by a local charity. Castro's costume choices show that while Juan's status has improved, his lot in life is still a sad one.

Costume designers take all the pertinent societal fashion rules and regulations of the world of the script and filter them through their design aesthetic to create clothing that crystallizes the elements of character and heightens the dramatic tension of the events. Using color and textural palette control, manipulating the garment shapes on the actors, and playing with the effects of visual harmonies and contrasts, designers can add tension and depth to the characters and reveal what is driving the action. (For more on this, see Part 4: Composing Costume Images: The Art and the Craft, "The formal language of design—compositional elements.")

If we want a demonstration of what costumes can do to materialize a character's attitude and backstory, look again at Eduardo Castro's designs for *The Perez Family*, especially his designs for the characters Armando and Felipe (figs. 2.3 and 2.4). Castro uses contrasting fashion vocabularies from the worlds of the story to make explicit the contrasts in background and attitude of these characters. The sharp, high-contrast graphic of Felipe's shirt, the way he lets his dark pants sink fashionably low on his hips, is in street-slick contrast to Armando's old farm hat and worn-down jeans. Even though Armando has some jazzy qualities, with those "shades" and that jewelry, he suffers in comparison to the hip Felipe. Contrasts in color and texture are deployed to reinforce the subtext: Armando is dressed in muted tones and worn, natural textures; Felipe is

FIG. 2.4

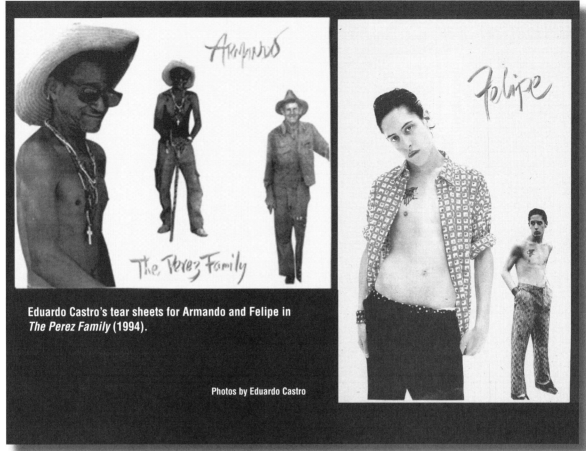

Eduardo Castro's tear sheets for Armando and Felipe in
The Perez Family **(1994).**

Photos by Eduardo Castro

dressed in sharp tones and slick textures. Look at the canny way Castro and his actors play with shape, and how similar shapes convey contrasting messages: while Armando's garments just seem baggy, the bagginess of Felipe's garments seems hip. Now, look at the messages these costumes send about where the characters come from. With his straw hat and old jeans, Armando feels rural; with his flashy shirt and his polka-dot boxers showing above the waistband of this pants, Felipe feels absolutely urban. Each of Castro's designs sends detailed messages about a character—his past, his attitude, his condition. All these messages add depth and resonance to a performance, a scene, and the film as a whole.

Of course, costume designers develop their knack for character costuming not only by studying psychology and design, but by studying the clothing rules-of-the-road for the societies represented in the script (fig. 2.5). Different regions, different times, different sects all develop their own sophisticated systems of clothing meaning. Fashionable business attire for a Hollywood mogul, for instance, is a far cry from what is cool for the Wall Street crowd. Even if you design for sci-fi, a designer must create a set of characters who communicate through clothing the rules and regulations of their society. Look at Durinda Wood's designs for *Star Trek: The Next Generation* (fig. 2.6). Even without of the context of the story, we know that these designs are for otherworldly folks: Their forms are humanoid, but one set of characters is very "techno-robot," the others' dress is an echo of Earth fashions, although not identified with any recognizable place or period. While it's obvious that these characters come from different groups, we can't get a "read" on their societal status until a few more of their own kind show up. And, we can't know if this is work or casual costume unless we can see them in the context of the group and the setting.

FIG. 2.5

Each sub-sect of society has its own fashion rules and regulations that its members abide by.

FIG. 2.6

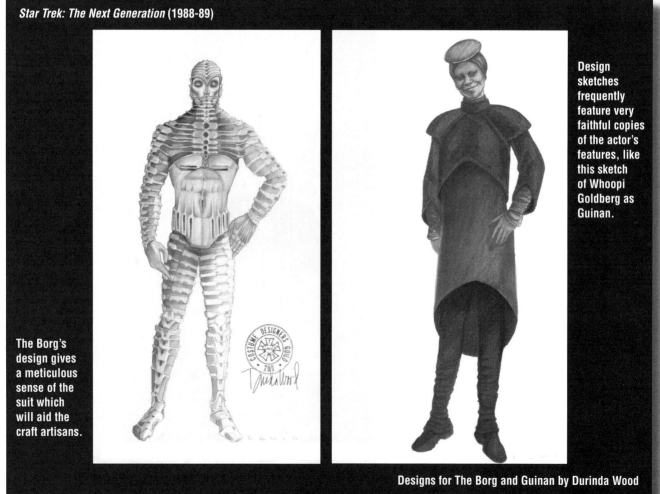

Star Trek: The Next Generation (1988-89)

The Borg's design gives a meticulous sense of the suit which will aid the craft artisans.

Design sketches frequently feature very faithful copies of the actor's features, like this sketch of Whoopi Goldberg as Guinan.

Designs for The Borg and Guinan by Durinda Wood

Here's the challenge in designing a character arc: You can only hope and pray that, when it's all edited together, your design actually holds up—that you haven't lost the missing link. Your design has to be flexible, so that if you take any one piece out of it, it will still work. What I often do is take the photographs from a fitting and organize them so that I can see them in sequence. Then I can look at the pattern made by one character's costumes next to the pattern made by the costumes of other characters, and get a sense of what's going on. You need to look and say, "Okay now, if this scene goes away, does the design still make sense? And, if it doesn't, can I—artistically, according to my own standards—come up with something that bridges the gap?" *(Catherine Adair, costume designer)*

Interpreting the script

Costume designers must be able to recognize the forces at work beneath the surface of the script. As a designer closes in on the look and tone of the characters, and the world they must illuminate, they are looking to clarify the emotional undercurrents of the story—and the emotional impact of their design. Costume designers want to reach people at a gut level; they want the audience not only to understand the story intellectually, but to *feel* it emotionally. Look at Eduardo Castro's designs for the 1996 film *Kama Sutra: A Tale of Love* (fig C.2). He creates a sexy, opulent world that seduces the audience with its lurid colors, lavish surfaces, and sexy shapes. Contrast this world with the world in the 1999 film *Vendetta*, as embodies in Hope Hanafin's design for the extras (fig. C.3). The dark, earthy palette, the shapeless layering of the garments, the rich, coarse textures create a world of tight harmonies that speak of endurance, not sensuality.

Managing the process

No matter how gifted you are as a designer—how skilled as a collaborator, how thoroughly planned your designs—you can still get screwed. Well-planned character arcs can be cut to bits in the editing room. Changes in shooting schedule and prep-crunch absurdities can force a designer into a mode I call "survival costuming": basic needs met, no art.

Sometimes I feel I should wear a T-shirt that says, "It's not my fault: I was fucked in the timing and screwed in the edit." *(Anonymous costume designer)*

Given the huge, expensive machine that a film production is, a costume designer needs to cultivate a talent for management. This means striving to keep the whole process in perspective, and developing some serious survival skills, among them, flexibility, the know-how to streamline the process, and a knack for creative problem-solving. It also means owning a solid, portable "wardrobe kit"—a personal stock of costume supplies and materials.

One reason you need a good costume designer is, you need one person who is overseeing everybody and coordinating things. Without one, sometimes things fall through the cracks. For example, when there's no designer on a TV show, you might see three actors in a scene together, all wearing blue shirts. The male and female costume supervisors might have been doing their own thing, or they could have been working on different floors, or in different buildings. One of the things a costume designer does is make sure we're all doing the same movie. *(Madeline Kozlowski, costume designer,* Oceans of Fire, Red River, The Tower, *and the series* Battle Dome *(1999-2000), among other feature and television projects)*

Flexibility. The filmmaking process comes at you from all directions. Late casting, actors who won't take fittings, late script additions, budget pressures, the limits of available goods: All this, and more, will make your job as a costume designer difficult. In fact, it can drive you crazy. Flexibility is the quality that will save you. You have to be able to take the chaos in stride. Every interview in this book contains hair-raising stories that illustrate the kind of flexibility a designer needs when the only source of comfort amidst the craziness is her paycheck.

Streamlining the process. Film demands of a designer a highly streamlined process. The pressure to be efficient on the job is extreme. Short prep and late casting mean you have to be quick with your key design decisions. Research quickly, sketch quickly, budget quickly, shop quickly, sew quickly. On feature films, principal actors are often cast in the last week of prep. In television work, you regularly get a script on Wednesday, fit the actors on Friday, and shoot on Sunday. To survive as a designer, you have to know how to assemble a film's wardrobe around late casting problems, how to tap instantly into local labor, service, and costume resources. You have to keep your car in good shape. Get a cell phone. And a laptop. Get email and a connection to the Internet.

Creative problem-solving. How do you survive insane script changes? The leading man got dumped and you start shooting the day after tomorrow. The director changed the mascot for the football team and you've got three hundred patches embroidered with the logo of the old mascot. What are you supposed to do, get lucky?

It's not about luck, it's about knowing your resources. *(Hope Hanafin, costume designer,* Normal; Winchell; After Dark, My Sweet, *among others)*

Knowing what's available quickly is only one aspect of being resourceful; a designer needs to have an eye for converting one garment into another—a sock into a cap—and adapting techniques from every quarter to produce what you need on the spur of the moment. I (HC) worked with a designer who was doing a film that was set in the eighteen-forties, which required one hundred children as extras, all in period clothing— already a challenge, since local sources were not chockablock with kids' clothing from that period, and the style of the production dictated a limited color palette and an overall folksy charm. But when production informed us that several hundred more children would be needed for the shoot, in two weeks' time, the designer didn't bat an eye. I asked her how she could remain so calm, and she said that this kind of thing happens all the time. She knew exactly what back-ups she had in our costume stock; how much more she could pull together from rental collections; and she knew we could go thrifting at a slew of local Salvation Army stores in the area. She also knew we could accessorize and recombine items from our costume stock to hide the kids' modern clothes.

Knowing how to improvise a period look, deliver three hundred new patches over night, fake the leading man's look on ten different stunt men, or invent a sci-fi look from welders' jumpsuits demands design creativity, an eye for unexpected resources, and a nose for unsuspected technical solutions. As a designer, you have to get off on the creativity of it all and trot out your best hunter-gatherer instincts.

Designer kits. As a survival tool, many designers (as well as costume supervisors and costumers) put together what is called a "wardrobe kit" to bring with them to a job. Designers accumulate their kits over time, tailoring them to the kind of costume work they get most often. Some designers have warehouses of goods from old projects; some have small, select collections. The rule of thumb is to build up a stock of general emergency clothing, accessories, and supplies, to collect unique or rare items that are particularly good for your design tastes. Standard kit items, aside from supplies, include underwear (male and female); ties, belts and suspenders; scarves and handkerchiefs; jewelry (male and female); sweaters and hats (male and female); standard and "character" clothing for the genres in which you work most; and robes, towels, and foul-weather gear. From our point of view, when it comes to assembling a kit, our motto is, "Too much is never enough."

A kit gives a designer quick access to goods she knows and likes. It allows a designer to respond handily to all kinds of costume emergencies. On productions with small budgets and prep crunches, a kit can help defray the cost of per-piece rentals. When, of necessity, a budget must be devoted to purchased or produced goods, a designer's kit can be the source of otherwise unaffordable special touches. A rental fee for this kit should be established during salary negotiations with production. (For information on contract negotiations, see Part 7, *Prep*. For more information on costumers' wardrobe kits, see figs. A.30-A.32.)

> In film, it's all about flexibility. In the theater, you have the stage—a beautiful black box. Once you know what that box is, you have the basic parameters within which to create your world. In film, you have to accept that however well-prepared you are and however determined you are to have control over your palette, your world, your environment, there will always be a part of the filmmaking process that is a bit like mercury: It's always going to be slightly in flux, it's always going to be moving.

> [In film], you need a sense of humor, an ability to laugh, and a realization that it's not necessarily personal. You have to realize that these people you're working with aren't necessarily doing whatever they're doing it to deliberately screw you over, or tie your hands behind your back. You are part of a collaborative, creative process that is always being reorganized and restructured, not just for your needs, but for everybody else's, too. And sometimes, if everybody else's needs are different from yours, you are going to get the short end of the stick. So, instead of spending energy and time on frustration, you say, "Okay, it is what it is; how do we solve the problem? How do we take advantage of this, and enjoy the creative challenge that has been put before us?"

> Realize that as a film designer your ability to solve problems creatively is a part of why you're being hired. Yes, you want to be hired because you are gifted and you have a

lovely sense of design, but you're also being hired because you can function under the pressure. Producers don't want to hear you complaining continuously; they want you to come up with solutions. They already know that they have made it difficult; they already know that it is complicated; they already know that it can be a nightmare. They don't need to be reminded of it. They want somebody who is going to come in and say, "Yes, it can be done. This is what it is going to take to do it." So there is a substantial part of the job that is problem-solving.

It's not my job to say, "No, you can't have something." If I don't feel it is visually appropriate, that's different. But in terms of technically achieving it, unless it is positively going to kill my crew, my philosophy is to say, "You need another five hundred extras by tomorrow morning and it's now five o'clock in the evening? Okay, it probably can be done, but this is how much it's going to cost you." Or you can say, "You know what? We cannot do it by tomorrow morning, and this is why. We could do it by such and such a date, but it is going to require this many more people and this many more man-hours and this much more time and money." If they choose not to spend the money, that's their business. Or if they choose to reorganize the schedule because they really feel that it is visually important to the piece, you make it happen. That's where team effort, having a crew around you who can help you fulfill that dream, takes on a completely different resonance. This team of people that you are working with is your life's blood.

…I honestly used to think that if I got to a certain level of the business, I'd have time to really think about the design, plan for it. It doesn't really happen often. You get job interviews because of your flexibility. A big hunk of what you're getting paid for is your ability to deal with chaos. *(Catherine Adair, costume designer)*

Designing the Character

Trying to find the perfect pieces to express the subtleties of character can be like trying to find the perfect outfit to wear to a job interview or on a blind date—you have one chance to express the complexities of your character.

The way a person dresses can suggest answers to certain fundamental questions about them, and suggest certain "defining conditions," among them, the following:

- *Current circumstances*. Is the character indoors or outdoors? In public or private? At home or at the office? In a city or in a suburb? In the United States, or elsewhere? What time of day is it? What time of year? Which year? Is the character at work or at play?
- *Inherent and acquired characteristics*. What age, sex, race, religion is the character? What is his or her state of physical health, mental health? To what degree is the character formally educated, sophisticated, worldly?
- *Social, political, economic, cultural conditions*. Does the character live in poverty or in wealth? Among dancers, musicians, or farm workers? What are the fashion rules of the social group to which he or she belongs? What are those rules at home, at the office, at social events? Is he or she involved in social or historical events (a party, a political campaign, a war)? Has the character been affected by events in the natural world (a rainstorm, a mudslide)?
- *Attitudes and eccentricities*. Is the character ambitious? In what ways? Is the character socially savvy or socially inept? What is his or her attitude toward social regulations? Is he or she self-aware or cut off from his inner life? Does the character have a sense of humor? An interest in fashion? What are the character's tastes in color, texture, shape?

Think about your own appearance. How have your circumstances changed over the years? How have your tastes your taste changed as you've matured? How has your sense of what's important changed? How has this been reflected in the way you dress?

Finding the perfect details to express the inner life and backstory of a character requires that a costume designer commit to the story he or she wants to tell with a design, and understand the part each character plays in the telling of that story. To design character images, a costume designer makes use of the following vehicles:

- The *actor*, his or her body (its shape and proportions; its age; its physical condition, including the articulation of muscle and fat; the skin quality and color; the hair texture and color; eye color; the nature and degree of physical attractiveness relative to the world in which the character lives); and less tangible qualities like character, personality, and public persona
- The *garments* available to the time and place of the story (within the limits of the style of the production), including underwear and outerwear
- The *accessories* available to the time and place of the story, again within the limits of the style of the production—the shoes, hats, gloves, scarves, handkerchiefs, watches, jewelry, purses, bags, glasses, belts, suspenders, insignia, etc.

Designing for the Performer

Your success in designing film characters is, in large part, a function of your ability to work with, and design for, the actor. To make a "character transformation" real for your audience, you have to design a character into whom your actor can believably transform. If you have to create design guidelines for principal characters before casting is locked, be prepared to make adjustments or re-design.

Three major factors must be taken into consideration in your designs for an actor: the actor's body shape, the actor's personality and public image, and the amount of "screen time" a performer will get.

- *Body shape.* Whether you are working with a star or an extra, you have to be able to work well using the raw materials of an actor's body shape. Costume designers create "body illusions" with their designs, carefully disguising and reconfiguring actors' shapes by manipulating the compositional elements of line, shape, color, texture, and the design principles of harmony, contrast, and balance to suggest that the body is thinner, bulkier, longer, shorter—in sum, less (or more) shapely than it is.

From the earliest days of the profession, costume designers developed tactics for making the best of a less-than-perfect figure. How do you make a short actress look taller? Use a line of contrasting buttons, or a striped fabric, or a long dark cardigan worn open to reveal a contrasting white shirt, which guides the eye to another point of focus. How do you distract from those expansive hips? Disguise those hips with a non-clinging fabric or additional layers.

Traditionally, in a medium-tight shot (the dominant frame in film), the point of focus is the face. A bright scarf or a large brimmed hat or bold jewelry, a contrasting collar or tie, can help the audience focus on the actor's face, and away from figure flaws. In a long shot, you want to focus the audience on the principal players. Try color contrast—bright against

FIG 2.7: DESIGN TACTICS FOR UNUSUAL BODY TYPES

FOR WOMEN

The "apple body" (thick on top, very skinny legs and arms):
- Use no patterned fabrics around the midriff.
- Get perfect alterations done so that the pieces fit the body well.
- Use longer, clingier separates to lengthen the line of the body.
- Use 3/4 length sleeves and cropped pants to expose slender wrists and ankles.
- Stay away from heavy sweaters and thick fabrics on top.
- Don't use drop-waist dresses or ensembles of any kind.
- For eveningwear: use strapless column dresses in clingy fabrics with long leg-slits.
- Asymmetrical hemlines are good for pulling focus to slender, shapely legs.
- Use color wisely: incorporate elements of the color of the skin tone, hair, and eyes into the ensemble.
- It is very important to have just the right hair, makeup, and jewelry.

The "pear body" (skinny on top, thick in the bum and thigh area):
- Don't use boldly patterned pants or skirts.
- Get perfect alterations done so that the pieces fit the body well.
- Use long coats, dusters, etc. to lengthen the body and smooth transitional areas.
- Use bold tops, if character-appropriate.
- Use beautiful fabrics, colors, and accessories close to the face, to draw attention upward, if character appropriate.
- Use deep v-necklines and/or plunging necklines, so that no one will be looking anywhere else.
- For evening wear: use 1950's-style ball gowns (with a floor-length big skirt), strapless or halter-top to emphasize the slender torso. Think Grace Kelly.
- Use color wisely: incorporate elements of the color of the skin tone, hair, and eyes into the ensemble.
- It is important to have just the right hairstyle, makeup, and jewelry.

Very large calves and thick ankles:
- Don't use short skirts or short pants.
- Use long skirts or pants, especially 1940's-style wide-leg, pleated trousers (think Kate Hepburn), or denim jeans that fit well on top and either flare slightly or cuff on the bottom.
- Use beautiful tops and top layers, to pull focus upward and away.
- Use stretch boots or rugged outdoor boots.

The "big all over" body:
If a gal is big but well-proportioned, she can wear almost anything. But keep in mind the following:
- Don't use print fabrics with a pattern larger than the palm of your hand.
- Get perfect alterations done, so that the pieces fit the body well.
- Stay away from garish colors and animal prints.
- For eveningwear: Use a dress with sleeves or a beautiful wrap. An elegant, sexy gown with sleeves will be most important.
- Accessorize, accessorize, accessorize—to find just the right distraction devices.
- It is important to have just the right hairstyle, makeup, and jewelry.

The "gravitationally challenged" body (we're all going to feel it one day):
- Get a Wonderbra, or other shelf-like miracle brassiere.
- Try using breast enhancers like "Curves," which are placed inside a brassiere. "Curves" have the weight and feel of a natural breast, and they are available at most lingerie stores.
- Use bum-lifting underwear. These can come with pads already in them or in nuclear-strength Lycra. Pity the person who tries to sneak a pinch on a bum in those Lycra pants; they really work. A "bodyshaper" or "bodyslimmer" can lift and/or shrink a gal significantly. Most department stores, and some retailers (like Victoria's Secret), carry bodyslimmers. Use them. Corsets are especially appropriate on a period show. A good corset would make Newton blush.

The "Olive Oyl" body (frail, shapeless, thin):
- Use a Wonderbra, "Curves," and/or bum-lifting underwear (see above) to pad out the body.
- Exploit and exaggerate the look, using one or more of the following suggestions:
- Cigarette pants and obvious graphic patterns (plaids, stripes).

- Boat-neck tops and slim-fitting tops.
- Body-hugging jersey, flimsy cottons, diaphanous fabrics, and pale colors, to push the "waif" look.
- Hair pulled back, to reveal a slender neck.

The little-boy body (athletic, no body fat, no boobs or hips):
- In a period piece, you just put this body into a corset. In a contemporary piece, you may need to give her a little more shape, with one or more of the following:
- Wonderbra, "Curves," and/or bum-lifting underwear (see above).
- Soft, rich colors like pumpkin, fawn, chocolate, cadet blue, melon, moss green, etc.
- Soft, touchable textures like mohair, suede, silk, fur, and chenille.
- Layers of wardrobe, to build out the silhouette.

Pregnancy:
Designing for an actress who is pregnant, and will be pregnant for the duration of the shoot (whether feature or TV series), try the following tactics:
- Use stretch fabrics.
- Use comfortable shoes.
- Use dark-colored bottoms (pants, skirts), so that the expansion is less noticeable.
- Make multiples of the costumes, to account for belly growth.
- Draw focus to the face, using beautiful fabric or scarves close to the face.
- Maintain alterations so that clothing always fits properly.
- Accessorize, accessorize, accessorize.

FOR MEN

"Beer muscle" (belly):
There are not many ways to hide this, particularly if the beer belly is a whopper. Often, an actor will get cast because of his particular physicality (a beer-belly, for example), and the look will be exploited. So, what do you do when he needs to look razor-sharp?
- For a suit, use vertical stripes, especially in a three-piece suit. This can be infinitely slimming.
- Use bold neckwear, a sharply contrasting necktie, for example, to pull focus to the face.
- Accessorize with hats, jewelry, watches, sunglasses. The more perfect the accessory, the more razor-sharp he will look. Include fabulous shoes and hosiery; they may say you never see them, but it's a lie.

Super tall:
- Find an excellent "big and tall shop" in your area. Make friends there.
- Stay away from garish colors, animal prints, and patterns larger than your palm.
- Make sure that the clothing is altered properly, and fits the body well.
- Get extra-long ties. Purchase neckwear at a big man's store, to ensure that the ties are proportioned for a taller man.
- Stay away from obvious vertical stripes.
- Avoid hats, especially big hats. It makes for a difficult frame line if the tall actor is in a scene with a shorter person. Don't use hats, unless it is a character trait (think John Wayne).

Super short:
- Find a "short man's store" in your area. Make friends there.
- Stay away from patterned clothing, unless it is a character trait.
- When choosing a suit, opt for vertical stripes to elongate the lines of the body.
- Stay away from light-colored sport coats, as this tends to chop the body in half and shorten it further.
- Make sure that clothing is altered properly and fits the body well.
- Choose colors carefully, and take into consideration the skin tone, hair and eye color when making costume color choices.
- Work with the actor's special physicality and "look."

Super tall or big all over ("grande"):
- Call your friends at the big-and-tall store; they should have big sizes in the tall section, too.
- Alterations, alterations, alterations. This is critical in a big-and-tall or thick-all-over man.
- Use comfortable shoes.
- Avoid garish colors, animal prints, and patterns larger than your palm, unless it is a character trait.
- Get his stuff custom-made, if you have the budget, particularly if the costume is a specialty piece like a wetsuit or a military uniform.
- Buy lots of undershirts and underwear, and multiples of things like dress shirts, so that the costume can be changed out if he gets too sweaty. (A big-and-tall or big-all-over actor often has problems with excessive perspiration.)

FIG. 2.8

Photo courtesy of
New Line Cinema

Spawn (1997) by New
Line Cinema

Dan Lester's ferocious
design for The Clown
played by John
Leguizamo brought
the dark world of the
comic to life.

Fitting photo and designs courtesy
of Dan Lester

FIG. 2.9

Photos courtesy of designer Dan Lester

Fitting photos of
John Leguizamo as
The Clown in *Spawn*
(1997)

dark, bold against dull, warm against cool. These are a few of the many techniques deployed by resourceful costume designers. (For more suggestions, see fig. 2.7, "Design Tactics for Unusual Body Types." In addition, see Part 3, *Composing Costume Images: The Art and the Craft*, which considers, in detail, ways to "pull focus" and solve figure problems by manipulating individual elements of design.)

In order to teach yourself to solve figure problems using the compositional elements of design, study books, catalogues, and magazines that feature real human beings with real figure problems (as opposed to glamorous fashion models). If your actor has already been cast, research the way that actor looks in other films, or the kinds of fashions the actor wears in life off-screen. Surprisingly few fashion design texts address designing for figure problems (although costume designer Bob Mackie has written an interesting book titled *Dressing for Glamour*, which does detail how to dress performers with figure problems). Designers really learn how to design for different body types in the fitting room, and at extras "call" (see Part 7, *Prep*, "Fittings").

Of course, even a beautiful body can profit from being artfully displayed. If ever you need evidence of this, watch the Academy Awards, and listen to Joan Rivers trash the Oscar crowd's clothes. As quickly becomes evident, "couture design" is no guarantee that the outfit is right for the actor.

• *Personality and image.* A designer must work *with* casting, not against it. A designer designs for a particular actor's personality, as well as for his or her shape. In the mind of the audience, each well-known performer is identified with certain qualities—sweetness, elegance, vulnerability, "edge." Your design must be built on these known qualities, or seek to illuminate qualities that have not yet been seen. Because the economic viability of a star depends on their public image, work *with* the actor on their screen image if "pushing the envelope" is what the project calls for.

A designer gauges the strength and boldness of the design not only in relation to the persona of the performer, but to the dramatic energy of the scene. Costumes are meant to serve the actor, but also the character, the story, the performance. A designer never wants to hear a director say, "The actor can't get in front of the dress; the dress was the performance." Look at Hope Hanafin's low-key, beautifully detailed design for Cecily Tyson, in HBO's 1999 film *A Lesson Before Dying* (fig. C.6). Her designs build on this actress's natural grace, and help create a very real, very dimensional character. Designer Dan Lester takes another approach to an actor's public image in his design for John Leguizamo's character "Clown" in the 1997 film *Spawn* (figs. 2.8 and 2.9). Lester's design is an audacious translation of the actor's dark, explosive comic persona, and a product of the actor's gutsy trust in his designer.

• *Screen time.* The choice of clothing and accessories for a character is, in part, dependent upon how much time that character spends on screen *(screen time)*. Leading actors *(principal players)* are on screen for the greatest amount of time. As a result, their costumes require the highest level of attention to overall design impact, depth and subtlety of detail, and quality of construction. *Day players* are actors who are featured on screen for short periods. A designer needs to provide them with a clear costume image that can be "read" relatively quickly.

FIG. 2.10

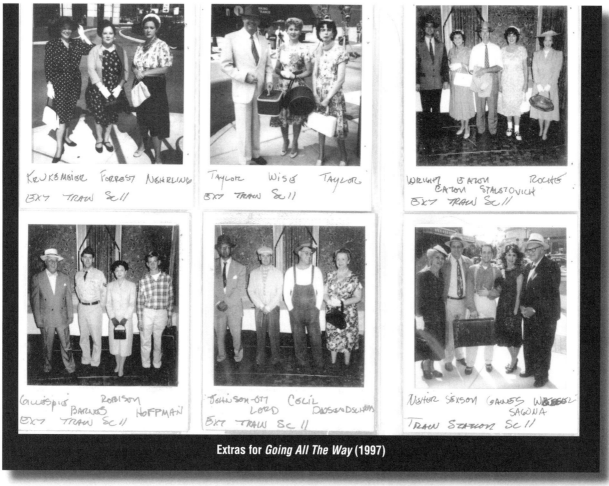

KRUKEMEIER FORREST NEHRLING
EXT TRAIN SC 11

TAYLOR WISE TAYLOR
EXT TRAIN SC 11

WRIGHT EATON ROCHE
EATON STALGTOVICH
EXT TRAIN SC 11

GILLESPIE ROBISON
BARNES HOFFMAN
EXT TRAIN SC 11

JOHNSON-OTT CECIL
LORD DAUSENDSCHON
EXT TRAIN SC 11

NISTLER SEXSON GAINES WHEELER
SAGONA
TRAIN STATION SC 11

Extras for *Going All The Way* (1997)

FIG. 2.11

Extras are frequently restyled into several different "looks" over the course of shooting.

In feature-length formats, a designer can create costumes that reflect the emotional and physical changes in a character over the course of the story (a progression called a "character arc"). In television, where commercials and the remote-control reign (especially in half-hour or one-hour episodic formats), first impressions are important, and character designs must be clear and committed. In episodic television, it is only after weeks of viewing that the subtleties of a character's costume and performance emerge.

Background players are called *extras,* or *atmosphere,* in the film industry. When it comes to extras, it is the charge of the designer to create a design scheme for extras that establishes "world" (or "worlds") of the story, and reinforces its more ephemeral mood or atmosphere (used here in the sense of the psychological environment, the feeling or tone conveyed by a place and a scene). The costume design scheme for extras can also help an audience focus on the principal players on screen. Since screen time for extras is commonly short and sweet, a designer's image for background players must do its job with tremendous visual efficiency (fig. 2.10).

If an extra has a specific function—a cab driver, for example, or a doorman—the costume should be designed as a quickly recognizable type, which then "goes away" visually for the audience. Because extras are often reshuffled during shooting, to create more than one set of character atmosphere, it is important that the design scheme for extras let the audience focus on principal players (fig. 2.11). Indeed, an audience's awareness of atmosphere should remain largely subliminal. One designer commented that if you can't make an extra really interesting, make them as indistinguishable as possible. (For more on this, and the "fitting time" factor in the designing of extras, see Part 7, *Prep,* "Fitting Extras.")

Designing for the World of the Script

Costume designers must be able to define a character in any context—past, present, future; known and unknown worlds. In order to do this, and to understand how clothing rules change, costume designers study contemporary fashion, historical fashion, cross-cultural fashion, and sub-cultural fashion. Current film standards demand authenticity—authentic silhouette, fabric, detailing. But authenticity alone is not enough. Designers must use costumes to amplify the "human resonance" of a foreign culture or time by creating images that help an audience connect emotionally with the characters. Back in the days of Bette Davis and Errol Flynn, costume designers often "updated" period shapes. By applying modern tailoring or shaping techniques to period designs, they made the characters who wore them more "present" to contemporary eyes.

Since the nineteen-seventies, period films have increasingly found a way to be true to period shapes and proportions, while creating strong, dramatic characters. The Academy Award-winning costumes designed by Sandy Powell and Humberto Cornejo for *Shakespeare in Love* (1998) are a particularly good example of this skill. Elizabethan clothing is about as dehumanizing as clothing can get: strangely shaped, and padded to distort the human form. Stiff and often excessively ornamented, it *challenges* the costume designer to humanize it. In Powell's design, William Shakespeare slouches about in a perfectly correct period doublet and pumpkin hose. The strong tone of the doublet's leather—a masculine forest green—makes the character a dashing young man. But it is the relaxed way in which the actor, Joseph Fiennes, wears the clothes that makes "Will" Shakespeare an artist with an attitude—and this, too, is part of Powell's design concept. Golden colors and cascades of blonde curls play up the romantic openness of Gwyneth Paltrow's character, Viola De Lesseps, in spite of the stiff, confining clothing in which she is bound. As Queen Elizabeth, Judi Dench is a ship of state in high dudgeon; Geoffrey Rush, as Philip Henslowe, is comically tricked out in all the weird proportions of the period. The commanding personalities of these actors easily "conquer" their period costumes. By finding ways for the characters to "relax" the clothes, by emphasizing the strengths of her actors' personalities, and by resisting the temptation to turn her characters into clothes horses, Ms. Powell designed costumes that support the story and the characters first, historical period second.

In science-fiction or fantasy films, a designer must create worlds that surprise an audience with new shapes, new rules, new ways of combining images—all while telling the human story. Futuristic designs demand that a costume designer look at clothing shapes in different ways—hunting for shapes that say "timeless" or "future" to the audience. Contemporary fashion designers often create designs that have a futuristic spin, and many film designers borrow from contemporary fashion to create future worlds (fig. 2.12). The brilliant fashion and film designer Jean-Paul Gaultier in *The City of Lost Children* (1996) and *The Fifth Element* (1997) is particularly imaginative in his reinvention of contemporary fashion. Some designers, like James Acheson, in Terry Gilliam's film *Brazil* (1985), or Jean Giraud, Michael Kaplan, and Charles Knode, in Ridley Scott's film *Blade Runner* (1982), draw from both the past and the present to create a vision of the future. The designs for *Brazil* and *Blade Runner* take off from clothing shapes of the nineteen-forties, as well as from contemporary (nineteen-eighties') dress. Some designers, like John Mollo, in his Academy Award-winning designs for *Star Wars* (1977), are inspired by the timeless shapes of Asian, African, and Middle Eastern fashions. Many designers use industrial clothing, military uniforms, and other clothing forms not identified solely with a single period or place to create future and fantasy looks, streamlining shapes, inventing new color palettes, and creating new insignia and decorations.

FIG. 2.12

Design by Dan Lester for the character Priest from the film
Spawn **(1997)**

Photo courtesy of New Line Cinema

To help an audience feel grounded in the new world of a science fiction film, a designer must create entire societies, with a way of life, a hierarchy, and a social structure comprehensible visually, at gut level—no program notes allowed. And, of course, even the designer of science fiction and fantasy costumes must keep in mind *context*—how characters will come together in a variety of scenes, and how they will look on location, or in a constructed set.

Designing for the Set

We "read" scenery the way we people-watch—looking for the visual details that clarify character or tell us a story. The architectural style and condition of the buildings in a neighborhood tell us about the people who live there. The *set dressing* of an interior—the furnishings, the drapes, the rugs, the art on the walls, the flower arrangements, the goods on counters and shelves—tells us a lot about its occupants. Seasons, events, and professions deposit costumes, props, and set dressing in the spaces of our lives. Most often, costumes and scenery reflect the taste and conditions of the world in the script.

The costumes must be designed in the context of the "set" (in its broadest sense, which includes real-world locations). Does the costume, and the action required of it, match the realities of the set (weather, "ground" conditions, and so forth)? Will the actor have to run in high heels across rotting planking or a muddy field? Is this practical, safe? What about the simple matter of whether an actor can be seen against a set. What about the stunning black evening gown on the deck of a yacht in pitch-black night? How does a designer make sure that the principal players stand out from the set, that they don't become "floating heads" on the screen? Costume designers have found a number of ways to solve this basic visual problem, among them, the following:

- The color palette can be developed that contrasts characters and sets—warm tones versus cool tones, light colors versus dark colors, grayed tones versus intense tones.
- The texture palette can be controlled to achieve contrast—shiny versus matte textures, complicated surfaces versus plain surfaces, sheer versus solid textures.
- The lines and shapes can be controlled to achieve contrast—complex versus simple forms, linear versus plain shapes.
- If push comes to shove, the director of photography can backlight and sidelight the actors, to help them stand out.

(For more on color and texture palettes, line and shape, see Part 3, *Composing Costume Images: The Art and the Craft*.)

A character's costume design must also respond to the intangible messages sent by the sets. Does the eccentricity of the house match the eccentricity of its occupants' clothing? Are the principal characters comfortable in their world or are they oppressed by it? Are they dehumanized or romanticized? Do the costumes and scenery work together in ways that reflect the mood of a scene, or the events that take place in it?

For characters in harmony with their world, the sets and the costumes might share a style and a palette. Take a look at Hope Hanafin's designs for John Korty's 1991 television movie *Long Road Home* (fig. C.1) for an example of harmony between characters and their world. The muted tones of the garments, the soft droopy shapes, the low-key textures of the costumes blend with the earthy feel of the sets and locations to create a world of visual harmonies that implies a close bond between the people and the land. For an example of how a designer might echo the conflicts in a script by contrasting costumes and their surroundings, look at Colleen Atwood's designs for Tim Burton's *Edward Scissorhands* (1990). Edward's spooky black-leather-and-metal outfit is violent contrast to the radically "happy" colors and near uniformity of the suburban women and their neighborhood.

With luck, the designer will get detailed information on the style of the sets, their color and texture palettes in conferences with the art director, the DP, and the location manager. When the style of the production is realism, making clothing style choices for characters can be relatively simple: photographs or period paintings can help a designer nail it down. But when the future, or any other imagined world, is what you are designing, the costume designer must work in concert with the art department. In Tim Burton's *Edward Scissorhands* (1990), the exaggerated pastel palette chosen for the sets and costumes of the townfolk created a surreal world. The crazy geometric prints and graphics on the women's costumes were part of a larger pattern of images that manifest in the film, in the form of giant topiaries and sculptural hairstyles. But this highly coherent, highly imagined world requires disciplined collaboration.

Designing for the Camera

A costume designer must develop a "camera eye"—an ability to look at the actor and at the outfit and imagine how that actor will look in that outfit on screen. In order to design camera-worthy costumes, a designer must (1) design for *motion pictures*—for a camera and actors in motion; (2) learn what the camera loves; and (3) design for the shooting process.

FIG. 2.13

"Wide shot"
"Waist up"

"Loose Cowboy"
"Close up"

Camera viewpoints. Photos by Kristin Burke. Actor: John Schuck.

• *Design for movement.* Look at your costume on a body, in motion and at rest, seated and standing, from the front and the back, in three-quarter and profile. Imagine the camera in motion (fig. 2.13). Will the "feel" of the costume be clear, will the costume fit and its visual focus "work" when the camera pushes in as well as when it pulls back? When it dollies and when it remains stationary? If you're mostly going to see an actress from the waist up, will she seem sexy enough in the scene when you can't see those gorgeous legs? Does the top half of her costume send the same message as the bottom half?

A designer must design for close-ups and long shots and every frame in between. Wide-screen images are particularly demanding: Everything is blown up to ten times life size. Detail is everything—collars must be perfect; insignia must be right. The pattern on a tie takes on new meaning in close-up on a forty-foot screen.

Because principal characters are on screen for the greatest amount of time, they usually get the greatest amount of detailing, but even extras' costumes can require detailed accessories and proper fit, since you never know quite how a scene is going to be shot (they may end up in the foreground). Understanding the effect of movement on a costume allows a designer to be practical about what needs detail and what can be done in broad strokes.

> You must see the world as a panorama, as well as under a microscope. *(Catherine Adair, costume designer)*

- *Learn what the camera loves.* Things that look good in the fitting room may not look right on camera. That beautiful, subtle tweed jacket can go flat on camera. That red dress that was so great in the dressing room and on the set just doesn't have the oomph you thought it would when you see it on film.

Study the impact of the complete screen image–the product of sets, lighting, camera framing, film stock and processing; analyze how the costumes take part in the total effect. Study how color and texture read on the screen. Study the way color is used to convey emotion. Have you ever noticed the subtlety of the color values on Hitchcock's famous blondes? Or how often the hue blue-gray crops up on screen? Present-day film stock is so exact in its reproduction of texture that designers must keep texture authentic, visually truthful. For this reason, many "period" pictures use actual period garments. In fact, historically, textural truthfulness in period work was always more important in Hollywood films than the accuracy of period shapes and colors.

Film requires finely detailed surfaces. Rather than using paints on the surface of clothes, film costume *agers* (also called *distressers*) prefer dye, colored waxes, bleach, and heavy washing effects to get surfaces to "read" as authentically as possible (fig. C.7 and *Conversation Eleven: On Dyeing and Distressing Costumes for Film, with Edwina Pellikka*).

There are also skillful ways to "cheat" costume details, but these, too, require a thorough understanding of what "reads" on screen. Costume designer James Acheson showed me a beautiful Chinese robe from his Academy Award-winning design for *The Last Emperor*. On screen, the robe looked encrusted with embroidery; in reality, its fabric is carefully silk-screened to simulate the colors and shadows of embroidery. (For more on designing for the camera, see Part 3, *Composing Costume Images: The Art and the Craft*, "Media restrictions.")

Designing for the Shooting Process

Long days of shooting can be hard on costumes. Actors sit around in their costumes for hours, eating, smoking, drinking, while they wait for camera setups. Designers are discouraged from using easily crushable fabrics like linen and rayon, or fabrics that wrinkle easily: They pave the way to maintenance hell.

Shooting "out of continuity"—not in the order scenes appear in the script—discourages the use of accessories that move easily on the body: large, loosely draped scarves and mufflers, for example, or strings of jewelry. Rolled-up sleeves and artfully flipped-up collars are problems waiting to happen. Of course, a great crew can meet all of these challenges with infinite grace; but in this age of shrinking departments, a designer can help his or her small staff by severely limiting the use of these kinds of pieces.

There are tricks of the trade to keep an actor looking perfectly groomed. To keep shirt tails from coming un-tucked, a designer might insist on a crotch strap, or that panties be sewn to the shirt. Get resourceful. But be careful that your solution doesn't create other problems, like the tacked-down scarf that stays in place, even in a stiff breeze.

Next!

Now that you have an overview of the role of the costume designer in film, and the fundamentals of costume design for film, you're ready for a primer on the basic tools of the costume design trade—basic costume design principles, the compositional elements of costume design, costume materials, and construction techniques. If you already know basic design, materials, and techniques, skip directly to Part 4, *Developing the Design.*

Conversation Two:

On the Status of Costume Design in Film, with Betty Pecha Madden

Betty Pecha Madden is a costume designer for feature films, including *Baby Geniuses* (starring Kathleen Turner and Christopher Lloyd) and Michael Jackson's *Moonwalker* (fig. 2.14). She has also designed many movies for television, including *The Water Engine*, *The Heidi Chronicles*, and *The American Clock*, and several television series. Betty is a member of the combined Costume Designer's Guild Local 892-Motion Picture Costumers Local 705 committee to represent labor concerns in the industry.

Has costume design in the film world been affected greatly by current "corporate" production attitudes?

It has, yes. Investors want to invest less and less because, with all the other production out there, their returns are getting smaller and smaller. They feel that the percentage of the market that they are impacting, and the window of time that they have to impact that market, is getting smaller. So they want to shrink the budget to match the target market they have out there.

Doesn't the "producing-by-committee" phenomenon also have an effect on the ability of a costume designer to do good work?

FIG. 2.14

**Design by Betty Pecha
Madden for "Moonwalker"**

Yes. In the present situation in Hollywood, there is a practice of giving many people producer titles. One season, my TV series had twelve producer titles. Twelve! Granted, these producers aren't making what producers with those same titles would have made twelve or fifteen years ago, but the salaries they are making are still large enough to affect the overall production budget. And they all have a say when everybody comes to the table.

Is this problem significantly worse in television than it is in feature film?

In the made-for-television movie arena, it hasn't had as big an effect. I don't think it's as bad in film. In the full-length features, I think you still have more of the old structure in existence. But you still have some problem with this because talent is being given more of a producer's voice in features. When you have stars being given a producer's voice, they make demands that often fragment the costume department. The lead actor's clothing is done by one costume designer, first-unit production is being done by another costume designer, and second-unit production may be done by a third costume designer. So you see the design vision being pulled in different directions.

Then, to complicate matters further, the director may come to the bargaining table with, "Well, I've got to have my DP, I've got to have my costume designer, my production designer." He has his list of people. Now, the writer-producer says, "Oh, but I've got to have *this* group of people." And the UPM (unit production manager) says, "I've worked with *this* crew of people; I've got to have this group of people." All of these producer-types are sitting at the table, and they're all vying for control of the project. There's a give-and-take thing going on. So the craft people out here, who have aligned themselves with a director, are being torn apart. Because if the director has to go to battle and he has a choice of keeping only one position (the costume designer, the DP, or the production designer), chances are, he's going to go for his DP first.

God knows, I don't have the kind of mind that can comprehend a solution. We all know that anytime you take an artistic story and dilute it with too many points of view, it's going to be watered down to the point of decimation. Instead of accomplishing what they set out to accomplish, producers have actually created their own time bomb, which just implodes because there were too many people with too much power providing artistic input. On the production end, we are given advice or instruction from so many sources that we struggle to stay afloat in that mire of creativity by committee.

The producers, the director, and the stars have input. And then many layers of other producers. Anybody I've missed?

No, you've got all of them lined up. Of course, you do have the "wife factor" or the "husband factor." All producers go home at night and their wives or husbands say, "I just hate the way she looked in that scene." And then the producer comes back to the costume designer the next morning and says, "Change her." And you are stuck. And the actress is now totally uncomfortable and insecure because now she has been told she doesn't look good. It becomes a downward spiral, everyone becoming more unsure about what they are doing.

How do you deal with that?

You have to try to be all things to all the people you're dealing with. You try to win their confidence and keep them comprehending the overall vision, while you are taking in all of this information—everything they're trying to say about the "look."

With a TV series or a miniseries, you have to be this incredible juggler of all these personalities! You try to project enough confidence to convince them to trust that you are making the right choices. This takes time. It can take a whole first season.

And you can still end up with the producers dictating the look.

And then when the final product comes out and it looks askew, they're saying, "Gee, those costume people really don't know what they're doing. I guess, they just didn't know how to do it." You end up taking the blame for decisions that are made without your input. How do I, as the costume designer, explain this to the big wide world out there, to those who are going to be viewing this? How do I explain that it wasn't my choice to have the producer's wife there, stealing the scene? That was the producer's call. How do I explain that to the moviegoer? Yet, I will have to take the burden, and the responsibility, of that in my career.

I've had directors and producers say, "Betty, why is it that all the atmosphere people and all the day players look just great, and yet, the lead actress, the most important person on the screen, just doesn't look right?" And when I've had the confidence, and I know I'm never going to get a job again with that person, I've said, "Because you dictated what that lead actress's costume should look like. Because you didn't pay attention to those background people and I did. Because the day player is somebody who you just hope is going to be dressed right when he comes on the set, but every time he comes on the set, you go, 'Wow, he looks great; but why does our lead actress look so….you know, she just doesn't look right?' Because you eliminated from the rack everything your wife doesn't like, you've eliminated from the rack everything that you don't like or understand. What's for you to understand, other than to trust that you have hired a *costume designer*, someone who has been educated, and trained, and has developed a skilled eye to see what is right for that character? You don't have to understand it. Just allow it to happen."

Aren't you also hearing them ask, sometimes on a weekly basis, "Why are you spending this amount of money on this?" Everyone I have talked to so far has mentioned how horrible the accounting is getting to be.

Absolutely. The amount of accounting work, for the designers, as well as for the supervisors! You have to constantly be adjusting the budget, because they are constantly rewriting that script. You have to adjust the budget and the design every time those new pages come out.

The reason why the tie-in with fashion has become so popular with production is because producers are seeing it as another way to cut costs—by getting "freebies." They really don't care what the clothing source is; the thing they hear is "free," and they think, "Good! Now I can take this money and I can spend it to paint the set; I don't have to spend it on the clothing. All I have to do now is give screen credit to this company. And, the clothes are by Armani!"

This is a total fallacy. The garment started out being an Armani suit, but had to be altered to death and restructured to fit the period and the character. So, yes, it's the Armani, but now you have completely reworked that suit to fit that character within that storyline, because that's what costume designers are all about. You are about that script! You're not about the Armani suit. You haven't put it with the tie and the shirt that the Armani look is about. You must "characterize" it. But you don't get any credit for that if it's an Armani suit, because the producers have to give the credit away, because they got the freebie suit. That reality isn't shared with anyone outside the film industry; that knowledge isn't out there for the public.

Does it make it easier for the costume department to deal with the fashion market instead of purchasing clothing? Sometimes, yes. Say, you get your talent list by 4:00 in the afternoon. You've got your tie-in with various fashion houses, so you get that garment picked up and it's brought in to you by 6:00 P.M. You do a fitting between 6:00 and 8:00 P.M., usually with a day player. Now, your cutter-fitter takes that garment and gets it pulled together for an 8:00 A.M. shoot. That all works, and it works beautifully, and it works in our favor, because we are not starting with a bolt of fabric. And that's where it works for us.

But what has happened over the years with costume designers is that the fashion industry has gone directly to production, and has become very bold and brazen about it, saying, "I will give you everything you will need for your production—$100,000 worth of clothing, or $500,000 worth of clothing. But for that, I want *credit*, a tie-in to your production. Let's form a package deal here." But what about the story? What about the characters in the script? "Oh, we have a costume department, they'll make sure the character is there." So, the producer hands the garments over to our costume department (which is then totally ignored, as far as credit for this transformation goes) and demands that we make everything presentable for camera, so it fits the character and the story! Most often, it is more of a burden to us than a help. A rounded character closet will usually need more than one label of clothing.

And it's demeaning. It's disrespectful.

And it's just not free. You do pay, in some form. For the fashion industry, it's cheap advertising—because if they have to pay for an ad, or do a TV commercial, it will cost them a lot more for that exposure.

As far as credit goes, television is especially bad. You've seen the split-screen credit that we're getting on television now—because the news is being flashed on half of the screen. All you see is this blur going by. That's your costume department's—and the rest of the film crew's—recognition. And the costume designer is listed right in there with the others. So what function do you perform on a production like this? I don't know that we can define the function that we perform. Certainly, we aren't acknowledged for what we do. Behind the scenes we are probably considered gods to make this happen, but in the public mind, and in the mind of some producers, the costume department's status is reduced to, "Oh, they shop stuff," or "They are our liaisons; they go out and get the stuff."

They don't understand that it takes an "eye" to buy, acquire, combine available goods to create a character. And characters need to be drawn from many sources— not just one designer label.

That's correct. It's a question of getting the *correct* necklace for that character, the *correct* earrings and hair accessories, the *correct* fit and styling. And now, what's showing up and making things look very bad on camera is the lack of fitting time. We're getting to the point where talent is refusing to put the clothing on ahead of time, in fittings! The assistant directors, who are supposed to schedule fittings, are saying, "Well, what do you have to fit it for? Just put it in the room; you know what size she is." Because we're supposed to know that actor's body. And somehow, magically, the wardrobe's supposed to fit. And it's supposed to look wonderful when that actor walks onto the set.

So often what goes on now on is that, in place of the fitting, the costume department has to hand the custom-fitter a mannequin that's supposed to represent the body of the actor. Now, we all know that when we put something in front of a camera, it has three-dimensional movement, right? It isn't a still photo. But on the dress form, the garment just hangs there—there is no movement, and no representation. The garment on the dress form is not a moving thing, which it must be on film. You need to see the garment in motion, on a live body, before it goes on camera.

So you have no dress rehearsal, as you do in theater, and no fittings, but the expectation is that your wardrobe still has to be able to walk onto set fitting perfectly and moving well?

Yes. We get, "Why isn't it picture-perfect quality? Why doesn't it look like old Hollywood? Why don't we have the glamour of old Hollywood?" Why? Because you're not investing time, money, and the artistic attention you need to invest to get the glamour of old Hollywood.

The careful planning and made-to-order design processes that are still basic to Broadway, you can't assume are understood in the film industry?

In the film business, the producers get up in the morning and put on their denim shirts, their denim jeans, and their sneaks, and they go out the door and think, "How much more difficult can it be for them in the costume department to do the exact same thing I just did? Just how difficult can it be?"

The thing that works against us is the fact that all of our work is done behind closed doors, and production doesn't see that process. I've had producers say to me, "Betty, I'd rather buy clothing from a good couture house than have clothing made for an actor, because it just never looks right." And my response to them is, "You are dealing with a sample garment. Every time you're making a garment, it's a first garment. If you do not have enough prep time for the process, the garment is not going to be finished when you put it on camera."

When someone is trying to give you a custom-made garment, you have to go through the basic process. When they are telling you that they need six weeks prep time to deliver the made-to-order (MO) garments and you agree to it in the beginning, you say, "Yes, well, okay, we'll make sure that you have your six weeks." Then, you get into your revised shooting schedule and your first assistant director says, "Well, things have changed. We need that garment the first week of shooting." Now, we have a problem. The process that was carefully planned has been interrupted.

Do you get that a lot from producers? A mistrust of made-to-order work?

Not a lot, but you do get it. They don't trust their own people in Hollywood. That's why they want to run off and find a designer who they *think* can do it right. So, they hire that person, and maybe they do that one film where everything is wonderful because they did have the time frame that they needed and they did give the designer the labor force that they needed to build it, and it's wonderful. Now, that designer wins an Academy Award or an Emmy and joins the Hollywood scene and becomes a victim like the rest of us. They've been given that one opportunity to represent that wonderful process, from beginning to end; but now, here they are, in the middle of Hollywood, where everything is "instant pudding," everything is, "I want it, give it to me now."

Between the months of January and July, I clothed 10,000 bodies in films. Ten thousand bodies! This was a feature film and two movies-of-the-week, with crowd scenes, very large groups of people: ballroom scenes, rallies, Grand Central Station—many big, big spaces, voluminous areas. These were period pieces: 1916, the 1929 crash, and 1947. Do you know how large my crews were? We had three to five people in my department and we clothed 10,000 people. Amazing. We were brilliant, but only we knew it.

In the industry, it sure looks like the camera department gets priority. They rely on the camera, the way they show the actor's face, to create character and emotion.

The industry is well-educated when it comes to how to light, how to photograph, how to direct, how to produce. That's wonderful technical stuff, and they put the money and the importance in those departments.

Hair and makeup make far more money than we in the costume department do. Often, the craft-service man on the set is making the same money, or more, than we are. That's a pretty good representation of just how bad it's become.

It seems like the producer's attitude is, "You're willing to take the salary, so you get the grief that comes with it."

From the moment that you sign your contract, your life is not your own. Not on any day or night of the week. Not for a minute. In reality, from the time your contract is signed until final wrap, you eat, sleep, and dream the production. As a matter of fact, I solve a lot of my problems in my few sleeping hours. It's a survival skill. If you're getting five to six hours of sleep a night and when you wake up you have a crew looking you in the face, waiting for solutions, then you're going to have to have those solutions ready for them.

If it's so horrible, if it's mercilessly unreasonable, why the heck do you guys do it?

Why do we do it? It's the only career that I haven't gotten bored with. Why? Problem-solving. I run on adrenaline. I am an adrenaline junkie. I get bored very easily once I have mastered something and figure out how it works. Don't ask me to be repetitive; I want to move on to another challenge. And this industry is the biggest challenge I have ever come up against. Every time the phone rings and I take on a new project, I am starting a new adventure—because no two scripts are alike, no two stories are told the same way. The working environment, the personalities you are dealing with, from the producer to the director to the talent, it's a whole new set of problems and people, a whole new set of circumstances.

It's miraculous that really beautiful work still happens in the middle of all of that torture.

It is. For me, to survive the process and actually have something that I can look at when I've finished and say, "I'm pleased with that," I have climbed a mountain. But often-times, I look at it and I cringe a bit and I say, "Well, okay, we gave it our best, and I can pay my bills and go on living. Maybe the next time, just maybe, I'll be able to have just a little bit more expression in the character development."

PART THREE

Composing Costume Images: The Art and the Craft

A Design Primer

Designing costumes for film is both an art and a craft. Learning how to interpret a script, manipulate visual compositions, develop design standards, work with other artisans, manage a department, and overcome limitations in the medium in which you are working are all a part of mastering the art and craft of designing costumes.

An ability to combine shape, color, and texture in perfect proportion to the actor's body, and to use these formal elements of composition to define character, is every costume designer's stock in trade. For costume designers, however, real artistry comes with the insightful use of these formal elements to illuminate character and crystallize narrative—that is, the elements of story. In order to perform this wizardry, a designer is required to be both artist and, if not master-crafter, at least apt student of costume materials and construction techniques.

Audiences "read" compositions with both their heads and their hearts. Costumes must communicate meaning both intellectually and emotionally. To do this, a costume designer must be fluent in two languages—the language of costume meaning and the formal language of design—and must speak them simultaneously.

The language of costume meaning—recap and refinement

Costume as narrative. The first charge of the costume designer is to identify the story that must be told, and then identify the costume elements that can tell it. We take for granted that costume details can communicate the "who," "where," "when," and "what's happening"—the narrative—of people's lives, that different seasons, different occasions, different professions, and different regions dictate specific clothing practices. Each culture and subculture has a "vocabulary" of garments, a "grammar" and "syntax" of clothing rules and practices that embodies its norms and values. What is worn reveals the relative wealth or poverty of the people, their trade practices, and the difficulty or ease of their lives, as dictated by terrain, weather conditions, and formative events.

What we wear and how we choose to wear it communicate not only our position in the world, but who we are (fig. 3.1). Our individuality is measured by how we conform to the rules of fashion. What a character deems appropriate to wear reveals both background and attitude. Wearing hip-hop clothes to a job interview tells a story about the wearer and the job. How people layer garments, or drape them on their bodies, can tell a story about background or psychological state. A blouse buttoned up to the neck says something different about its wearer than a blouse unbuttoned to flaunt cleavage. How a garment is made can reveal a character's social class, and the care he or she takes with matters of appearance. "Home sewing" can suggest a tight budget, as well as a mother's loving touch. A couture-tailored suit might speak to not only an ample bank account, but to a certain streak of vanity and aspiration. The physical condition of a garment also contains a narrative. Any mother who deals with hand-me-downs can read the history of a garment in its stains and battle scars. Indeed, aging and other techniques that "personalize" clothing to reveal character history are standard tools for costume designers and their crews.

FIG. 3.1

Costume designers manipulate what you wear and how you wear it to communicate character and story points. The evolution of this character's iconic character arc from "tough kid" to "hip business dude" uses costume pieces that crystallize the character's upward climb in status and sophistication. The trip from "anti-establishment" to "establishment with a twist" uses the hairstyle to provide a core eccentricity the character holds onto that becomes increasingly more daring through juxtaposition as he evolves into his business mode. Each look uses key elements that crystallize the character's increasing wealth (for example, the arc from camo cargo pants to sleek leather pants to expensive suit pants). The character's arc is expressed by the comparative messages sent by the different changes that reveal the changing fashion rules that the character lives by and the increasing cost and sophistication of the clothing.

THE TOUGH KID
The tough-kid image uses an arrangement of contrasting color values and textures, overlapping shapes, and loose, funky fit to emphasize the character's "anti-establishment" attitude.

THE ROCKER
The rocker image uses visual harmony in color and texture and slim body-molding shapes to lend power to the arrangement.

THE HIP BUSINESS DUDE
The hip business-dude image combines tight visual harmony in color and texture with the graceful tailored shapes and soft surfaces of hip designer suits. The laid-back quiet assurance of the suit is juxtaposed with the aggressively hip hair and sunglasses to achieve maximum contrast with the harmony of the arrangement.

In film work, as in life, garments take on—and help define—the shape and personality of the wearer. In so doing, they can crystallize the story of an entire life. Easily identifiable items like work clothing, uniforms, and clothing with logos can be useful as a means to clarifying characters who are on screen for a very short time. Parody and farce commonly employ the shorthand of costume stereotype: Lounge lizards wear shiny suits, Texans wear cowboy hats, car salesmen wear plaids. But complex characters can also be crystallized in a few essential costume pieces: Think of Indiana Jones's well-worn hat and leather jacket. Finding the essential piece is, for a costume designer, a little like finding the key piece in a jigsaw puzzle. Suddenly, it all makes sense. You can't picture the character without it.

Costume as symbol. Beyond telling a story about an individual and the world that individual lives in, clothing can serve as symbol, the embodiment of ideas and feelings larger than the garment and the person who wears it. A costume, or elements of its design, can stand for or suggest something beyond itself. It can be a visible sign of the invisible—and can stir reactions accordingly. In the right designer's hands, clothing can suggest an intangible trait, represent something in the unconscious mind, in the "collective unconscious" of a culture. It can suggest a relation to or associations with social conventions, belief systems, human archetypes, and institutions.

When the right character in the right clothing meets the perfect moment in time, a garment can become an icon, an image of mythic proportion, the epitome of an era and a sensibility. This can happen in life, or on celluloid, by chance or by design. In life, think Jackie Kennedy's Camelot-ending assassination suit. In film, think Humphrey Bogart, in his trench coat, playing the enigmatic character Rick in the 1942 film *Casablanca*. In wartime America, the trench coat was a symbol of mystery, secrecy, hinting at thrills and dangers very much alive in the spy-obsessed American imagination. Or think Marilyn Monroe in *The Seven Year Itch*, in her fan-pleated halter-dress. At once innocently white and incitingly sinful, the design, by Travilla, brilliantly materializes the conflict over what women were about—and about to become—in postwar urban America. By recognizing and working with garments and elements of design that carry the freight of symbolism, a designer can create costumes that underscore the mythic and metaphoric subtext of a script—and may become icons of an age.

Costume as expression. Costumes can be used not only as character statement, narrative, and symbol, but as vehicles to convey the vision of a script's writer and director. Directors like Fellini, Baz Luhrmann, Tim Burton, Peter Greenaway, the Coen brothers use strong visual images and powerful style statements to produce dazzling effects, to express the poetic subtext of a script, and to create a compelling world. The drunken frenzy of images in Baz Luhrmann's *Moulin Rouge* help the audience feel the drug-induced romance of *la vie bohème*. Fellini's fashion parade of popes in *Roma* reveal his wonderfully wicked sense of humor about the Catholic Church. Tim Burton's twist on suburban matrons in *Edward Scissorhands* made his "monster" refreshingly fragile.

In clumsy hands, stylized designs can lead to plot confusion, two-dimensional characters, stifled emotional content, and pretentiousness—or the simple all-style/no-substance effect of a bad science fiction film. But in sensitive hands, stylized designs can codify the vision of the director, and the meanings and feelings beneath the surface of a script.

The formal language of design

Working with the fundamental elements of composition (line, shape, color, texture), the design principles *harmony, contrast, balance,* and *emphasis,* and an almost infinite choice of materials and construction techniques, designers create costumes that produce visual effects, delineate character, support the story, underscore the mood and meanings of a script, and express the vision of its makers. Once the designer thinks through the "head" and "heart" messages the costumes should send, he or she can begin work on the "guts" of the costume—the visceral qualities of the design itself.

Basic design principles
Because the terms *visual harmony, contrast, balance,* and *emphasis* are used in every discussion of costume composition, especially in discussions of the compositional elements line, shape, color, and texture, it is important that you understand them up front.

VISUAL HARMONY AND CONTRAST. The principles of visual harmony and contrast are employed by a designer to give emphasis and clarity to a composition, strengthen the visceral effects of designs, and articulate the dramatic and emotional forces at work on the characters in the story (fig. 3.2).

FIG. 3.2

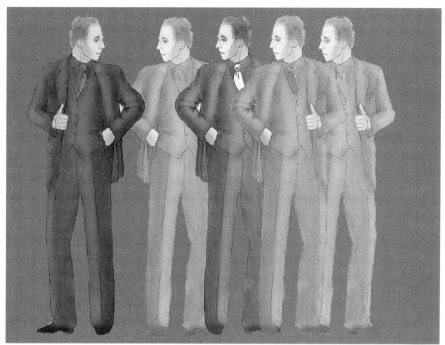

Visual harmony—pleasing arrangements of forms, colors, and lines—is achieved through the use of *repetition* (repeated elements), *gradation* (successive steps, or stages, in a series), and/or *progression* (advancement to a higher, or different, stage) (fig. 3.3). Visual harmonies can be used to support the emotional landscape of the script in several ways: by establishing a visual "norm" for a "world" or a group; by establishing visual alliances

FIG. 3.3

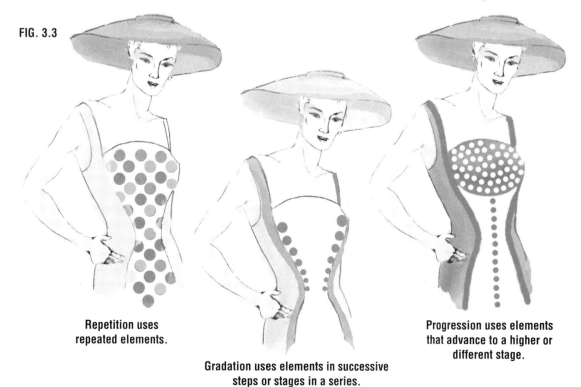

Repetition uses repeated elements.

Gradation uses elements in successive steps or stages in a series.

Progression uses elements that advance to a higher or different stage.

among characters; and by creating a comfortable atmosphere, a feeling of "safe harbor," for the characters. Tight color harmonies, orderly line patterns, motifs of related shapes can create a sense of "sympathetic vibration." In the world of Wall Street, for example, or the military, conformity in color range, line, and shape evokes a sense of unity and palpable strength. Images with repetitious arrangements of line or shape emphasize strength (the pinstriped suits and elongated forms of business wear, for example, or the repeated pleats of a judge's robe).

Designers use the principle of visual *contrast*—the juxtaposition of dissimilar elements—to strengthen the elements of conflict in a story; to establish the differences among characters and their surroundings; to add complexity and subtlety to a character; and to create visual excitation and direct the eye of the audience in the film frame, and in the film as a whole. To strengthen the elements of conflict in a story, a designer must heighten the contrasts in character that are emblematic of the conflicts of the drama. To get the leading man to seem ill at ease among his colleagues, a designer may play him against a block of coworkers who are costumed alike. By contrasting the costume of the leading man—its style, colors, textures and shapes—with his surroundings, the audience can *see* why the lead character doesn't fit in. The parts of a costume can also contrast: Costume compositions that are broken in to contrasting parts feel energized by the tension of visual conflict—a sensation that can range from playful to manic, depending on the nature and degree of the contrasts. The contrasting shapes and lengths of sportswear tops and bottoms, for example, may feel playful. Add contrasting colors and a mix of patterns and textures, and you've got costumes with explosive, even comic, potential.

To establish the differences among characters and their surroundings, costume designers often use the design principal of visual contrast. How rich, sexy, brash, vulnerable, odd, or powerful a character seems can be established by means of comparison (also called "co-positioning")—that is, how one character looks in relation to other characters in a scene, and how a character appears in relation to the set. A character's emotional arc can be expressed more powerfully by progressively heightening the visual contrasts from one costume change to the next, over the course of the story. Designers also heighten contrast among characters in a scene, and in a single character from scene to scene, in order to strengthen character motivation and reinforce the subtextual messages of the designs.

By way of example, watch *Star Wars* (1977) and compare the folks on the "Death Star" with the inhabitants of Luke's home planet, including members of his family. Inhabitants of the Death Star are encased in rigid, futuristic uniforms, with a limited palette, minimal decoration, and either high sheen or dull matte textures. Like a colony of ants, these costumes dehumanize the empire's legions, and reduce the world to black, white, and gray. In contrast, the inhabitants of Luke's home planet dress in soft, earth-toned wools made up into the simple, timeless shapes prevalent in desert lands. The city spaceport of this world is filled with eccentric characters and creatures who have a kind of funky, scruffy charm. Designed by John Mollo, the costumes for Luke's home planet support the emotional warmth and simplicity of his world, while, in sharp contrast, the militaristic "look" of the Death Star reinforces its cold, machine-like atmosphere.

FIG. 3.4

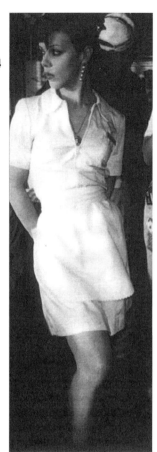

Debi Mazar's character options in the film *Red Ribbon Blues* (1996)

Designs by Kristin Burke.

Visual contrast can also be used to add complexity and subtlety to a character. Costume designers will mix "low impact" good (garments with low visual impact—for example, pants or tops in a neutral color) with "high character" goods (the eccentric old bomber jacket, covered with patches and insignia, or the jazzy Hawaiian shirt) to crystallize a character's attitude or eccentricity. Look at my (KB) photoboard for Debi Mazar's character in the 1995 comedy *Red Ribbon Blues* (fig. 3.4). The character's tough, cocksure attitude is crystallized in her leather jacket option, although many of her other options show the character's brazen confidence in more subtle ways (especially the sexy, eveningwear jewelry paired with her waitress uniform). The boldness of the details and the amount of screen time given a character dictate how many mixed messages an audience can absorb. In *Red Ribbon Blues*, Debi Mazar's character eccentricities are revealed over the course of a series of costume changes, not in one jarring shift. In the end, it is the contrast between the character's relatively "well behaved" waitress look and her "tough momma" leathers that really crystallizes the character's complexity.

Of course, visual contrast can also be used to pull the "eye" of the audience around and into the film frame, to direct the attention of the audience within the composition of a shot, a scene, a sequence. Costume designers use colors, shapes, lines, textures, and materials—in contrast and in harmony—to accomplish this. The rule of thumb says that the higher the degree of contrast between elements—one color and another, one line and another, one shape or texture and another, one mass and another—the more specifically focus is directed. How might a designer make an executive the center of attention, the wielder of power? He wears a suit in a strong dark tone, while the phalanx of "yes men" who surround him wear suits in a dull medium-gray. How could a designer get the leading lady to stand out in a ballroom scene? Her gown glitters with beading, the gowns of the extras don't; the star's gown is red, the gowns of the extras are pink.

Of course, the simple element of visual surprise—another version of visceral "excitement" through visual contrast—often has the strongest impact. Costume images that play against stereotype, or which otherwise surprise the audience, can pique its curiosity by challenging its expectations—the professor of archeology who turns into an adventurer in *Raiders of the Lost Ark* (1981); the angelic Uma Thurman turned into a gangster's moll in *Pulp Fiction* (1994). As audience members, we like to be intrigued. The principle of visual contrast, applied to expectations of character within a genre, or the juxtaposition of actor and role, can make an audience sit up and take notice.

The principles of harmony and contrast can also evoke subtle sensory and psychological responses. (For more on this, see below, "Basic compositional elements.") For an example of this, study Yvonne Blake's designs for the 1998 film *What Dreams May Come*, with Robin Williams (fig. 3.5). Max Von Sydow's Tracker seems particularly imposing and mysterious in his large, dark, all-covering costume when compared with Annabella Sciorra's Annie who looks soft, vulnerable, and exposed.

VISUAL BALANCE. Balance—the distribution of "visual weight" in a composition—is felt as visceral, often emotional, movement: Symmetrical arrangements feel balanced; static, asymmetrical arrangements feel dynamic. The arrangement of the parts and the

FIG. 3.5

Yvonne Blake's designs for *What Dreams May Come* (1998).

proportions of a composition can also produce visceral and emotional sensations in an audience. Large shapes, heavy lines, and long, unified images symmetrically arranged can create a sense of balance, weight, and strength. (It is these compositional elements that give evening gowns their drama.) Overlapping shapes, complicated line patterns, and other complex surfaces can feel tense and disorienting. An asymmetrical line or color contrast on a garment can feel more mysterious because it is off balance.

A costume designer can manipulate the distribution of visual weight in a composition to accomplish a wide variety of effects. A design can be "top heavy" (the upper half of the ensemble designed to be visually "weighty") in order to balance the silhouette of an actor with a disproportionately large lower half. A designer can create small points of interest, like areas of strong texture and color, to balance large areas of plain texture or muted tone. For the costume to feel balanced on an actor, the shapes that make up the garments need to progress harmoniously from toe to head. When a costume isn't working, most often the cause is discord in the shapes that make up the ensemble, or poorly balanced proportions—the size of the shapes in relation to one another, and to the actor's body.

VISUAL EMPHASIS. Closely related to contrast and balance, visual emphasis is a measure of the strength with which compositional elements are used by a designer to direct the audience's attention within a costume, among characters, in a set, in a frame, a shot, a sequence, and over the course of an entire film. Applying the principle of visual emphasis, a designer can visually answer questions like, "Which characters are allies and which are in conflict? How dangerous (or vulnerable, or fragile) is a character? Do the visual stakes of the costumes match the visual stakes of the story?

To determine where to place visual emphasis, designers follow four rules of thumb:
- Leading characters should be designed with a stronger visual focus than secondary characters and background players.
- Characters with important dialogue need designs that guide the audience's visual focus to the upper half of the body—preferably to the face.
- Costume designs should focus on the best elements of the actor's appearance, elements that translate to character. Whatever can't be featured must be fixed, via disguise or distraction.
- To strengthen the elements of conflict in a story, designs must visually heighten character contrasts and motivations. In this way, designs embody the forces at work on the characters.

Basic compositional elements

An ability to create costumes that convey meaning and feeling depends not only on the "head" and the "heart" of the designer, but on the designer's skill in using the principles of design, the basic elements of composition, and the materials and construction techniques in which they'll be embodied. The basic compositional elements of costume design are color, "line," shape, and texture.

COLOR

Costume designers use color to provoke emotion, clarify personality, control focus, and emphasize alliances and conflicts among characters and the worlds in which they move. Of all of the compositional elements of design, color has perhaps the greatest potential to express state of mind. Color harmonies and contrasts can underscore the dramatic elements of a story. Color can also illuminate a character's sense of self, and view of the world. To design well, you must anticipate how an audience will perceive—and emotionally respond to—color.

Designers manipulate color in three key ways:
- By color mixing, to adjust the purity and quality of a color
- By creating color harmonies and contrasts, to create focus and produce visual consonance or dissonance
- By manipulating the psychological "resonance" of color—the meanings and sensations commonly associated with certain colors—to evoke emotion and augment mood

Color theory—the analysis of the perception of color and color harmonies—is the subject of many books. Throughout the centuries, artists and designers have thoroughly explored the field by way of the intricacies of color mixing, and the development of color palettes. Color theory is, in fact, a very complex subject, one accompanied by an elaborate vocabulary and complicated scientific methods for analyzing light spectrums, electromagnetic waves, absorption and reflection effects, and a host of other phenomena that have to do with how color in *light* acts differently from color in *pigment*. For all designers, the detailed study of color theory and color mixing is highly valuable. (To this end, I recommend two excellent books, which explore the perception of color and how painters use it: *The Book of Color*, by Jose M. Parramon, and *Color Choices: Making Sense Out of Color Theory*, by Stephen Quiller.)

Although the primary subject of this section is how film costume designers use color to support a story and connect with an audience, I will be using the color terminology that visual artists and scientists have developed for talking about color in pigment. Why? Because costume designers work with color in pigment—from the watercolors they use for costume sketches to fabric dyes, and because the words used by the general public for color names and color qualities can be imprecise and confusing. After all, what color exactly is "fire engine red?" "Is a "bold" color the same as a "bright" color?

Color mixing. Artists and scientists who work with color have created a lexicon of terms in order to accurately describe color in pigment (fig. C.14). In this lexicon, the words for the three principle aspects of a color are (1) *hue*—the name of the color; (2) *tone*—its lightness or darkness (also called *value*); and (3) *saturation*—its vibrancy or intensity.

Every color can be analyzed for hue, tone (value), and saturation. The information produced by this analysis is necessary in order to mix and alter colors. How can you lighten, darken, warm, cool, or "gray down" a color? Whether you are mixing a dye bath to "take down" a white shirt or dyeing swatches (samples) of fabrics for a contrasting coat and dress, you need to know which colors make up a hue in order to understand how the addition, or juxtaposition, of other colors will affect it. If a costume designer does not understand how color works, she won't be able to mix the colors for her costume sketches, or develop a color palette for a project, or "tech" a white shirt, or subdue the blue of a skirt, or decide which green will go best with her actor's auburn hair.

An almost infinite range of colors can be mixed by using three highly saturated hues called *primary colors*. Primary colors are, by definition, hues that are pure—fully saturated, intense colors that have no trace of another color in them. As kids, we were taught that we could mix colors using the primary colors red, blue, and yellow. When mixed in pairs, these primary colors make the *secondary colors* violet (red + blue), green (blue + yellow), and orange (yellow + red). When secondary colors are mixed with either of their primary colors, they create the *tertiary colors* red orange, red violet, blue violet, blue green, yellow green, yellow orange (also called *intermediate colors*). All of these colors make up a "color wheel" (fig. C.14). Laid out in their proper positions on the color wheel, secondary colors fall directly opposite the primary color that is *not* part of their mix.

If secondary colors are mixed with the one primary color they do not include (violet + yellow, green + red, orange + blue), the result will be that both colors are neutralized (*de-saturated*), resulting in gray. This is true for any primary, secondary, or tertiary color mixed with its opposite hue on the color wheel. Colors that neutralize each other this way are referred to as *complementary colors*. When mixing colors, the purity (*intensity* or *saturation*) of a color has a huge impact on how predictable your results will be. Pure, full-saturation primary colors mixed with pure, full-saturation complementary secondary color will result in a perfect neutral gray. However, finding perfect, pure, full-intensity colors can be tricky. Dyes and paint pigments are derived from a variety of organic and chemical sources, and go through a series of different processes—all of which affect color purity.

For a costume designer, a hue has two key aspects that can be controlled: (1) its "tone," also called "value"—how light or dark the color is; and (2) its "saturation," also called or "intensity" or "vibrancy"—how raw or bold a color feels. Every color, whether primary, secondary, tertiary, or complementary, has a specific value (tone)—a relative lightness or darkness. When you mix a color with white, black, or its complementary hue, you affect both its *value* (lightness or darkness) and its *saturation* (intensity). To fully produce each color's *range of values*, a hue is mixed, in a stepped progression, with black (for a *shade* of the color) or white (for a *tint* of the color). This will give you a full range of tones for a color, called a *value chart*. When the hue is mixed with its complement, the grayed tones that are created may remain at the same value level, or they may get lighter or darker as they move toward gray.

By way of illustration: Let's say you have a fire-engine red shirt that you want to dye a brick red. First, you must determine if the fire engine red is a pure, primary red, a "yellow" red (shifted to the tertiary yellow/orange reds), or a "blue" red (shifted to the tertiary blue/violet reds). To achieve your perfect "brick red," you might, depending on what kind of red you start with, need to do one or more of the following: (1) "gray" the fire engine red—that is, neutralize some of the vibrancy or intensity of the color by mixing it with its complement; (2) "tint" the color (add white to the tone, to achieve a lighter terra cotta color) or "shade" the color (add black, to darken and deepen the hue); (3) add a "warm" tone (a color from the yellow through red-violet range of the spectrum) or a "cool" tone (a color from the violet through green range of the spectrum)—to add more vibrancy to the grayed tone. Note that when mixing colors, adding black can frequently muddy a color; but adding a dark chocolate, dark blue, dark purple, or dark green tone can both deepen a color and bring out its vibrancy.

In order to create harmonies and contrasts that will help illuminate character, heighten the drama, and intensify the emotional impact of the story on its audience, a costume designer must determine the collection of colors (called the *color palette*) to be used in each costume, and in the design scheme of the costumes as a whole. In doing this, the costume designer can control (1) the range of hues—the variety of colors used; (2) the range of tones or values—the variety of values used, from light to dark; (3) the range of intensities—how saturated or de-saturated (bold or muted) a color feels.

Setting color schemes (or palettes) for characters and background players is of primary concern not only to the costume designer, but to other members of a film's design team. By manipulating the range of hues, the range of values, and the range of intensities used in a color scheme, a costume designer can sharpen the dramatic shape of the story, create focal points in the narrative, and harmonize or contrast characters with one another, and with the production's sets.

Manipulating color to create focus. Each of the designers on a film—the director of photography, the lighting designer, the production designer, the costume designer—works to enhance the mood and drama of a scene with color. The costume designer uses hue, value, and intensity to create focal points in the narrative, to contrast (or harmonize) characters with the surrounding composition, to direct the attention of an audience to the important features of an actor and the important characters in a scene. In order for a design to succeed in these ways, the costume designer must agree with the production designer or art director, and the cinematographer, on a color palette for each scene, and for the entire picture.

When choosing colors for costumes, a designer must consider the range of hues, intensities, and values against which the costumes will play, and the way that the sets and costumes will be lit. Lighting may enhance, distort, or destroy our perception of a costume's colors, especially if colored gels are used to tint the light. A red dress can turn a muddy brown if lit with a blue-green light, but glow beautifully under a yellow-orange light. Extreme value contrasts between costume and set—bright white dresses in a black "world," for example—can also cause problems: when the camera lens and our eyes adjust for an extreme contrast like this, clothing detail can be lost. When costumes and set match too closely in hue or value, a "floating heads" effect is created, in which the clothing seems to disappear into the background.

Our perception of a costume's color also changes according to the colors that surround it—the colors of the set and the colors of other costumes. Artists have discovered that a color can appear to change according to the ground against which it is seen. This effect is called *simultaneous contrast*. Warm colors appear cooler in a cool environment. Dull colors appear brighter when surrounded by a muted complementary color. You think that's a "cool" lavender shirt? Watch it appear to change color when seen against a ground of yellow, red, or green.

For color contrast to succeed as a focusing device, color palette and color harmony must be firmly established, and controlled, in the entire composition. A film's designers will agree to use a restricted number of hues (a *dominant-color palette*) in each scene or sequence, or perhaps for the entire film. This means that each agrees to restrict the palette in his or her domain to the same set of hues, but to flesh it out with a specific set of tints, shades, and neutralized colors based on this palette. For example, let's say that the design team agrees to use a palette restricted to the colors blue, blue-violet, and violet (an *analogous* range of colors; see below). In order for the characters to harmonize with the "ground" of the sets, but also to be seen as separate from it—the costume designer and the art director will agree to a range of values within this color palette that each will use to distinguish the costumes from the sets. If the set designer chooses to use low-value blue-grays, the costume designer may then use high-value tints, and/or high-intensity blues and blue-violets.

To harmonize characters with one another, or with their setting, a designer can control the hues or the value range of their costumes' color palette in several ways:

- By using an *analogous* color scheme (fig. C.15). Analogous colors are derived from any three hues that are adjacent to each other on the color wheel. Analogous color schemes can include full-intensity colors, and/or their tints or shades, and/or the semi-neutralized grayed tones of each color. Because each base color in the trio has at least one color in common in its mix, these colors are, by nature, harmonious.
- By using a *monochromatic* color scheme. A monochromatic color scheme derives all of its colors from one hue, which is mixed with white, black, or its complement (mixed to the point where the color is fully neutralized to gray). This kind of color scheme is inherently harmonious because all the tones in the scheme share the same hue.
- By using a *cool* or a *warm* color scheme. The "cool" tones are the colors that range from violets through greens on the spectrum; the "warm" tones are the colors that range on the spectrum from yellow through red-violet. Limiting a color palette to either the cool or warm half of the color wheel extends the color harmonies of an analogous palette with three adjacent hues to six adjacent hues. A cool or warm palette can create tight color harmonies but allow more variety than an analogous palette. A cool or warm color scheme can also include the full intensity colors and their tints, shades, and semi-neutralized tones.
- By letting *one hue* or *one tone dominate* the color palette. A color scheme in which one hue or one tone dominates creates visual unity, even when accent colors (called *subordinate hues*) are present. For example, a formal party scene in which all of the men are in black tuxedos visually unifies the world, and allows the women to be in a variety of jewel tones or pastels.
- By *strongly limiting the value range* of the color palette. If you limit your value range, you can use a broader spectrum of colors and still achieve tight color harmony. For example, a muted palette or a pastel palette can harmoniously include a full spectrum of hues, as long as the all tones of the palette have matching values.

Once a dominant color range for a scene (or a costume) is established, a costume designer can use contrasting hues, color intensities, or color values to create special focal points within the composition, and to separate the characters from what surrounds them. A good designer can even create a sense of harmony from apparently discordant elements, as long as these contrasting elements (bold accents on a large muted ground, for example) are manipulated to achieve focus without causing imbalance.

To create color contrast, you can control the hue or the value range of your color palette in several ways:

- By using a *complementary color scheme* (fig. C.16). Artists have found that complementary colors—colors opposite one another on the color wheel—provide maximum color contrast when juxtaposed. Complementary colors have a unique effect: They bring out the intensity in one another. Juxtaposing a neutralized tone (like chocolate brown) with an intense version of its complement (like royal blue) makes the pure color "sing." Impressionist painters were famous for using complementary tones for shadows, to bring out full color clarity. Mixing complementary colors also tends to make far more beautiful grayed tones than mixing hues with white and black.

Strong complementary colors set side by side in equal amounts can compete violently for the eye. In their full intensity, they can clash uncomfortably. To give the eye relief, and to make complementary hues more visually compatible, costume designers can (1) combine complementary hues that have been mixed into tints, shades, or neutralized tones (a pale lavender blouse paired with a yellow-brown, "toast"-colored suit, for example, can work well together) or (2) allow one color to dominate the other (a deep forest-green velvet suit worn with a bright rust satin scarf, for example, can be stunning). Beautiful visual contrasts can be created, particularly if you use small areas of intense color in balance with large areas of a more muted version of its complementary tone.

Complementary colors also have a unique effect on our eyes: When we see a color, we simultaneously see its complement. Stare at a bright red object, then close your eyes and you will get an "after-image" of the object, in a complementary green. The eye actually seeks the visual balance provided by a color's complementary. This effect (noted above) is called *simultaneous contrast,* a term that refers to the fact that our perception of a color changes with the colors that surround it—a point worth a designer remembering, since costumes are designed to be worn by actors on sets.

• *By using contrasting hues (warm and cool), but limiting their range.* Artists and film designers regularly contrast warm and cool tones in their compositions, to create focus. But a "fruit salad" color palette (one that draws from the full spectrum), while it may create a lot of visual variety, dissolves dramatic focus. To create clear contrasts, you must allow the full screen to be dominated by only a part of the color wheel. The fewer the hues that dominate the image, the more hues allowed as color accents.

By contrasting warm accents with dominant cool tones (or vice versa), you can choose the visual focal point in an image. For example, you can use a red "power" tie against a blue suit to help an audience focus on the actor's face. You can help a leading lady stand out in a crowd scene by giving her a burgundy dress against the blue-gray background. If you are limited to a tight tonal color scheme (like in the 1997 film *Gattaca*), you can focus attention by using a contrasting hue. For example, for an Armani-inspired, matching-value suit-shirt-tie combination, you would do well to vary the hue of the tie if you want to direct attention to the face.

• By using *contrasting values* in the color scheme. Using the full range of a hue's low dark to high light values can provide visual variety to a composition, and make a monochromatic color scheme dramatic. If you are limited to a tight color palette (as in the 2001 film *Oh Brother, Where Art Thou?*), you can use contrasting tones to create focal points. For example, a designer using a tone-on-tone color scheme on her male lead may draw attention to his face by lightening or darkening the tone of the shirt and tie.

Establishing a palette with one dominant range of values allows contrasting values or intensities to be used to "pull focus." Beautiful visual contrasts can be created by using small areas of intense complementary color against large areas of more muted complementary tone.

Solving figure problems with color. By manipulating the hues and values of a character's costume, a designer can direct attention to the good points of an actor's figure, and disguise its flaws. Value and color contrasts can break the body into a series of shapes.

The shape you focus on first, and the way in which your eye travels from shape to shape, can be directed by the progress of colors around the body. The mass of a large body can be broken up by creating a series of visual focal points. A large woman in a dark pants suit, for example, is a massive dark shape. But try a long, dark coat, worn open, over a pale pants suit: The dark panels of the coat, worn open, frame a narrow vertical stripe of the light-toned pants suit, creating a slimming line, and softening the impact of a massive form. (For more examples of compositional tricks for solving figure problems, see fig. 2.9 and fig. 3.6.)

FIG. 3.6

The two garments on the left use contrasting values as a framing device to draw the eye to the thin, light, vertical shapes that run down the center of the form.

The two garments on the right draw the eye to contrasting shapes that also have contrasting colors or textures.

Using color to evoke emotion and mood. Color plays a major part in evoking both emotion and mood. Bold, intense colors can create a lively environment and suggest a forceful personality. Muted, neutralized colors can reinforce a subdued atmosphere and suggest more passive personality types. A dark palette can reinforce the dramatic or tragic; a light palette, the comic or romantic. Warm colors induce sensations of comfort; cool colors, emotional chilliness. Warm, low-value tones feel weighted, earth-bound, while pale tints feel airy.

The emotional changes in a character over the course of a story can be crystallized in changes or variations in the color palette. If a character grows insecure over time, for example, the designer may want the colors in the character's costumes to move from bold, intense tones to paler, or more muted, tones. As lovers come together in a story, colors may increasingly harmonize. For demonstrations of how color in costumes can contribute to the overall mood of a film, study the work of some of the designers represented in this book, particularly the hot, intense palette for *Kama Sutra: A Tale of Love*, chosen by designer Eduardo Castro to enhance the film's overall sensuality (fig. C.2). Then, study Hope Hanafin's muted, earthy palette for *A Lesson Before Dying*, which accentuates the film's loving realism (fig. C.7).

The degree of strength and subtlety of an actor's work will also help a designer determine the intensity of the colors to be used—provided this "call" comes from discussions with the actor before the palette for the costume is fixed. (The usually subtle actor may have decided to throw his style to the winds, if he or she believes that something "bigger" is called for.) Many designers use muted colors in a complex or strongly emotional scene to help the audience focus on an actor known for subtle, detailed performances. When it comes to a bold or "broad" actor playing a bold or broad character, however, bold color choices are not necessarily what's needed, even if that's what logic dictates. Sometimes, counterpoint works better, even in a comedy or a "swashbuckler": Compare the subtle colors Yvonne Blake and Ron Talsky chose for the 1973 version of *The Three Musketeers* (see figs. 10.10 and 10.11), starring Raquel Welch and Oliver Reed (actors known for their bigger-than-life personae), with the saturated palette Walter Plunkett worked with in the 1948 Technicolor version, featuring the immanently human, sweetly nuanced performance of Gene Kelly. In *Oh Brother, Where Art Thou?*, a light, monochromatic palette sets off an outrageously silly bunch of characters and performances.

It is also true that, given the right context, a character's dominant quality—indeed, the entire "flavor" of a picture—can crystallize around color used in ways that go against conventional color wisdom. *Men in Black* (1997) is a perfect example of this. Taking her cue from the script's title, costume designer Mary Vogt used muted colors and imposing shapes to monumentalize the formidable intelligence of Tommy Lee Jones and the chic severity of Will Smith, who then played, to brilliant ironic effect, against the comic phantasmagoria of the story.

Designers have also discovered that they can reinvent the emotional impact of color by manipulating its context. By working with the colors of a costume in harmony or contrast to the colors of its environment (including sets and surrounding characters), a designer can isolate a character, or place her in perfect harmony, with her environment. A character's vulnerability can manifest in pale tones worn in a dark world, or in rich colors worn in a dull world. By closely harmonizing costume and set palettes, a designer can add power to images. The brooding world of *Road to Perdition* (2002) was palpably frightening largely as a result of the dark palette shared by costumes and sets. Woody Allen's feelings about his childhood home are embodied in the warm palette shared by costumes and sets in his autobiographical film *Radio Days* (1987). The earthy, gritty feel of the world in *Oh Brother, Where Art Thou?* (2001) was amplified by downplaying sharp tonal contrasts between costumes and sets, and limiting the palette of both to earth tones. By controlling color harmonies and contrasts, designers artfully influence an audience's perception of power and romance, comfort and conflict.

Of all of the compositional elements of design, color suffers (and sometimes profits) from the greatest number of audience preconceptions. Color, by its nature, provokes a strong response in people. We have colors we love and colors we hate—especially in the clothing we wear. And, we weave meaning into our reactions. For some, muted colors are "safe," while bright colors seem clown-like, or vulgar. For others, muted colors seem dull, even lifeless. We harbor preconceptions about what colors symbolize: red means "whore"; white means "virgin"; pastel means "wimpy"; purple means "royalty." In reality, every "color rule" has been broken: Juliet can wear red and still be a virgin; comedy does not have to mean bright colors; couples do not have to have touches of the same color to be in tune with one another.

A designer must decide whether to tap into conventional attitudes about color, its moods and meanings—or defy them. Of course, a romantic scene can profit from the use of rose tones; a tragic scene can be enhanced with a moody black. A good designer takes advantage of the emotional associations we make with color when this choice is right for the design. But designers discover all the time that they can reinvent the emotional impact of a color: White can be used for a virgin or a whore—if the fabric and the cut are right. A villain can be villainous in gray if the value and tone of his suit are in sync with the steely world around him. What a designer does with color depends on the needs of the project. But it is true that intelligent use of color is more powerful than any preconception the audience may have. A designer with vision and insight can make an angel out of a sympathetic actor in a black suit and coat—just see Shay Cunliffe's design for Nicholas Cage in *City of Angels* (1998).

Developing an eye for color. You can study how color is used on the screen by renting some of your favorite films, turning off the sound, and watching the range of hues and values that are used. You'll be surprised by how many comedies and romances use gray, and how many tragedies use vivid color. Make a point of watching both high-budget and low-budget films. Look at how color is used in the Coen brothers' films *Raising Arizona* and *Oh Brother, Where Art Thou?*, and you'll discover that strong color control—the use of rich tones and vibrant hues in the first and a tightly controlled monochromatic palette in the second—can make relatively low-budget productions look stylish.

LINE

In addition to color, costume designers work with *line* to underscore the personality and mood of a character, to "nail" the period or culture, and to flatter or disguise the actor's body. By "line," I mean the two-dimensional effect produced by linear-print fabrics, seam lines, and rows of trim, as well as the three-dimensional effects produced by linear elements like pleats, gathers, lines of appliqué or buttons, layering of garments, the "cut line" of necklines, and the "body line" of garments that cling to the form—in other words, costume elements that create a conscious visual "line."

The compositional element called "line" has four key characteristics that a designer can manipulate: (1) direction—straight, vertical, horizontal, diagonal, or curved; (2) length—short, medium, long; (3) strength—weak, moderate, or strong; and (4) arrangement—opposition, transition, radiation, or serpentine. A designer uses the line of a design, in all its aspects, to create focus and express emotion (see figs. 3.7 and 3.8).

LINE – DIRECTION

FIG. 3.7

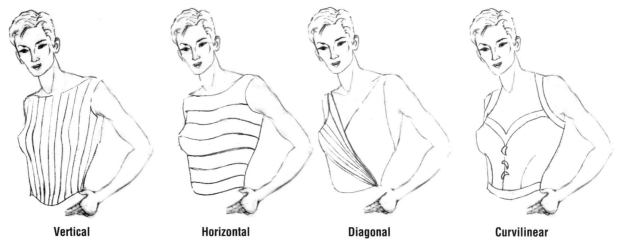

Vertical   Horizontal   Diagonal   Curvilinear

LINEAR ARRANGEMENT

FIG. 3.8

Transition   Opposition   Radiating   Serpentine

The images that illustrate "Transition" and "Radiating" use linear arrangements that are balanced and symmetrical. "Transition" uses a static arrangement to promote a sense of elegance. "Radiating" uses a dynamic arrangement to promote a sense of gaiety.

The images that illustrate "Opposition" and "Serpentine" use linear arrrangements that are balanced and asymmetrical. "Opposition" uses a dynamic arrangement to promote a feeling of clash or conflict. "Serpentine" uses a dynamic arrangement to promote a sensuous overtone to the garment.

Line and focus. The guiding of the eye along a line—called "line movement" by designers—is an important way to create focal points in any composition (fig. 3.9). The repetition, progression, and transition of linear arrangements collectively creates a palpable flow of movement that leads the eye to the focal points in a costume. Any woman with wide hips will tell you that a print with a horizontal line emphasizes breadth and mass as the eye is guided side to side, while a print with a long vertical line can guide the eye away from wide hips. A line of buttons or a long scarf can guide the eye up the body to the face. Strong vertical lines can even help short men look taller.

Using line to express emotion. Line can be manipulated to visceral effect. Long vertical lines can create feelings of sadness, strength, or elegance. Broken or conflicting

FIG. 3.9

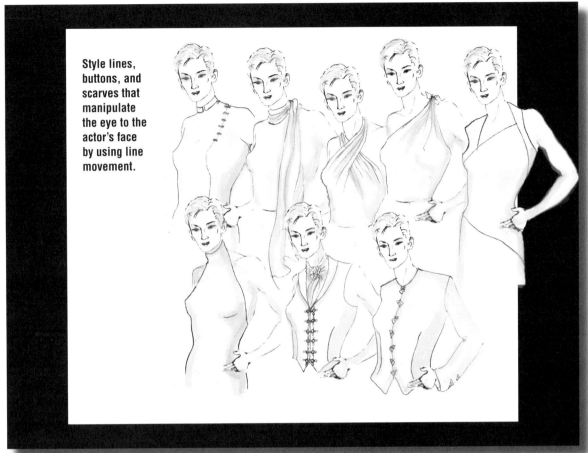

Style lines, buttons, and scarves that manipulate the eye to the actor's face by using line movement.

lines can create feelings of activity, tension, or chaos. Serpentine lines can feel sensuous, as they wrap around the body. Strong straight lines lend power to a composition. Curving lines can lend a feeling of gaiety. Parallel lines can feel static. Radiating lines, diagonal lines, and lines in opposition can feel dynamic. The pinstripes and long lines of a business suit can create a sense of power. Formalwear uses long, strong, elegant lines, and interesting line movement, to guide the eye up and around the body. The short shapes and active prints of sportswear can visually break the body into parts, and create a feeling of playfulness. A clinging dance leotard turns the body into one long dynamic line.

Developing an eye for line. To develop an eye for line, study how different couturiers use line in their sportswear, businesswear, and formalwear collections. Look at how costumes of different periods are identified with particular linear qualities—the soft vertical pleats of the ancient Greek toga, the drop of a skirt from an Empire-style bodice, the enveloping arabesques of the Art Nouveau garment and its nineteen-sixties revisions. Study the costumes of different cultures: the wrapped costumes of India, Malaysia, and Africa, for example. Also study how a designer manipulates line on large actresses, like Kathy Bates.

SHAPE

In addition to color and line, a costume designer works with the compositional element *shape*. When we talk about shape, we are talking about either the two-dimensional effect

QUALITIES OF TWO-DIMENSIONAL SHAPES

FIG. 3.10

| Free-form | Geometric | Organic |

QUALITIES OF THREE-DIMENSIONAL SILHOUETTE

FIG. 3.11

| Artificial silhouette | Fitted silhouette | Semi-fitted silhouette | Loose silhouette |

FIG. 3.12

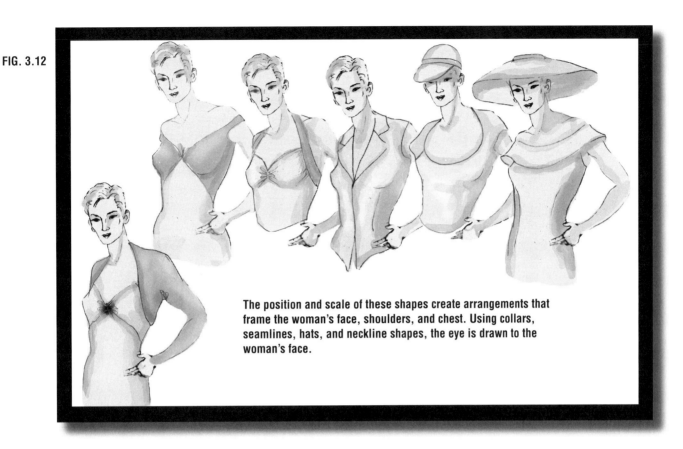

The position and scale of these shapes create arrangements that frame the woman's face, shoulders, and chest. Using collars, seamlines, hats, and neckline shapes, the eye is drawn to the woman's face.

of the shapes in a print fabric (floral prints, dots, and so on) or the three-dimensional effect of the shapes that make up a garment itself.

"Shape" has four key elements that a designer can employ: (1) the size of a shape—its area, scale, and mass; (2) the character of a shape (geometric, organic, free form, artificial) and its silhouette (fitted, semi-fitted, loose); (3) the position of a shape, and what body part it may frame; and (4) the arrangement of shapes, including their progression and their relative proportions (figs. 3.10, 3.11, 3.12).

Shape and character. A costume designer must first decide which serves the character and the production best: to have the body of the actor revealed or concealed by the shapes that make up a costume. Sometimes, to design a convincing character, you may need to glamorize an actor's shape by improving it using the shapes that make up the costume. At other times, you may need to enhance the comic potential of an actor's body. For example, you may need to help the very attractive Steve Martin create the illusion of a nerdy guy by visually narrowing his shoulders, raising his waistline, and shortening his pants. The art of manipulating *proportion* (the size and arrangement of shapes in relation to the actor's figure), creating focal points in a costume composition, and determining the degree to which the body is visible in, or disguised by, a garment all rely on a designer's eye for shape.

Revealing the body can add youth and vulnerability or sex appeal to a character—given the right body. To reveal the body, you can display *form*—that is, you can use form-fitting or clinging garments—or you can display *flesh*—that is, you can use sheer fabrics and abbreviated shapes. For example, if you want to reveal the body, but the film's period dictates long skirts, you still have many ways to go: You may need to use a short sleeve-length or a low neckline, transparent shapes, or form-revealing draping.

"Denying the body"—obscuring its lines—can add to a character's age, create a sense of defensiveness, or create the effect of asexuality. In order to "deny the body," to disguise exact body outlines, you can use layered shapes, long shapes, strongly geometric shapes, massive shapes, and artfully proportioned shapes. If the film's period dictates short skirts on an uptight gal, you can use a high-necked dress with a rectangular cut, or a long sleeved overcoat with straight lines, dark hose, and boots.

Altering the actor's form using shape. Every costume is shaped by its layers, from the skin out. For actors with figure problems (from flat to fat), you can use body-shaping devices like corsets, bras, girdles, fake butts. When the dictates of a character require an actor to change shape or age, you can use pregnancy pads, "fat suits," and "humps." A youthful actor playing an aging character demands artful padding, to simulate the thickening and sagging that comes with the territory. If you are working on a period film, be aware that different fashion periods favor different body types: The cone-like breasts and wasp waists of the nineteen-fifties, for example, demand appropriate period foundation garments.

Designers also manipulate focus and proportion to create visual illusions that disguise (or enhance) figure flaws. If you are working with actress Kathy Bates, and glamour is what the character, and the story, demand, you might look to create a slimming image by disguising her hips with a wide-shouldered, boxy jacket. The wide shoulders would make her hips look slimmer in comparison, while a square, or rectangular, jacket would disguise the lack of definition in the waist. You might also create an alternate focus, with a visually thinning shape—for example, the vertical rectangle of a blouse under a jacket worn open (fig. 3.13).

DISGUISING OR ENHANCING THE ACTOR'S FIGURE.

FIG. 3.13

You can manipulate seam lines or use flaring peplums to create the illusion of a narrower waist.

A chubby gal can use the shoulder pads and layering of a jacket to disguise the sides of her form...

...or she can use a voluminous wrap or large-headed sleeves to frame her torso and create the illusion of a narrow interior form.

If you are designing a comedy, you can manipulate the garment shapes to augment the elements of an actor's figure that have comic potential. For example, you can turn the tall guy into a taller drink of water by using long, thin shapes, or "high-water" effects (sleeve lengths and pant lengths too short). Make the little guy that much smaller by drowning him in big shapes—think Charlie Chaplin—or breaking up his form with contrasting shapes—a big jacket, a contrasting shirt, shorts, knee sox, a flat cap. Manipulating the extremes of how a person looks—how thin or fat, tall or short, distinguished or ditzy—always adds comedy to a character.

Working with period silhouettes. Clothing shapes, and the general arrangements and proportions of garments, are dictated by culture and historical period. *Period silhouette*—the head-to-toe overall proportions of a period's costumes—defines a "suit," an "evening dress," a "uniform" at any given period. It may dictate that women wear the tubular, geometric shapes of the nineteen-twenties or the triangulated torsos of the shoulder-padded nineteen-eighties. ("Phase 2: Preliminary research" in Part 4, *Developing the Design,* discusses how you can go about researching, and understanding, the shapes and aesthetics of a period.)

As noted, different periods dictate different body "ideals." The curvaceous Marilyn Monroe was never meant for the body-denying geometries of the nineteen-twenties fashions needed for *Some Like It Hot.* When faced with a body-versus-period-silhouette dilemma, designers may chose to abandon strict period restrictions, in favor of shapes that flatter the actor or actress—as Travis Banton did, to stunning effect, in his designs for this 1959 classic. Alternatively, a designer may dig further into the range of shapes available in a period, finding shape solutions available for the kind of body for which he or she is designing. Every period's fashion industry provides clothing for non-ideal body types. For example, in the nineteen-twenties, bias-cut dresses flattered the curvaceous figure, and women with big busts wore shapelier bras than did those with boyish figures—the period ideal.

The same visual geometry that works for problem bodies in modern fashion may also help with period-costume problems. Layered clothing that obscures the outlines of the body can help the chubby and waist-less in any number of periods. Color contrasts imposed on a period shape, with the use of trim or panels of a different color to break up the solid block of a gown, can create long, flattering verticals. Waists can be accentuated by broadening the shoulders, using effects like puffed sleeves, shoulder pads, broad collars, and contrasting shoulder yokes to triangulate the torso (fig. 3.14).

Using shape to distract is a tactic that can help problem bodies look well in both modern and period fashions. Creating shapes that draw the eye to a beautiful face, a gorgeous cleavage, an elegant neck, beautiful shoulders will help distract the audience from other problem body parts. In many decades of the nineteenth and twentieth centuries, hats with wide brims framed a face beautifully; short waists were disguised with dropped-waist belts, elongated vests, or long-line shell blouses; beautiful cleavage was featured in corseted or un-corseted fashions featuring low necklines, sweetheart-style necklines, open-necked blouses, or bustiers. Long, elegant necks can be gorgeous in high-necked or turtle-necked styles. Beautiful shoulders are delicious in drop-shouldered, boat-necked, and low-backed styles.

Twenties' period shape solutions for full-figured gals.

FIG. 3.14

The emotional effect of shape. Shapes can be manipulated to create or enhance the physical and emotional presence of a character. Tailored shapes that enhance the geometry of the body tend to evoke a feeling of power and authority. Shapes that hug and reveal the body can be sexy. Shapes that obscure the body's silhouette tend to neutralize the sexuality of a character. Garments that expose the neck and shoulders can create a feeling of vulnerability; garments that hide flesh or layer the form create a feeling of protection or withdrawal. Shapes that create an odd silhouette, or break up the body into odd proportions, can seem funny. Extreme silhouettes can feel eccentric, even "pushy" or egotistical.

The mass and scale of a shape can lend authority to a design, and direct focus. You want the leader to stand out in the crowd? Cape-like forms (the robes of office or overcoats draped cape-like across the shoulders) and long vertical shapes (suits, cassocks, gowns, and long overcoats) help create an air of authority. Broad-shouldered shapes can create an aura of strength or aggression (think of bomber jackets or football padding). Contrasting shapes that break up the body into chunks (short-sleeved shirts, shorts, layered shirts of different lengths) tend to promote a sense of the comic, unless the scale of the layers becomes aggressively more massive (like in the chunked-up look of hip-hop clothing).

For an example of the ability of shape (married to color and line) to evoke emotion, study Yvonne Blake's designs for the 1998 film *What Dreams May Come*, with Robin Williams (fig. 3.2). "The Tracker," Max Von Sydow's mysterious, powerful, but sympathetic, character is supported with a design that uses dark, voluminous shapes, humanized by the softness of fur and a clutter of smaller shapes, in the form of eyeglasses and other accessories. The vulnerability of "Annie," Robin Williams' "wife" (played by Annabella Sciorra), is supported by a costume that features pale colors, soft, "cradling" shapes, and a lot of exposed skin—neck and shoulders, belly and bare feet.

Developing an eye for shape solutions. Where you really learn to develop an eye for shape is in the fitting room. By fitting clothing on a wide variety of body types, you will discover fit and shape solutions to the problems of slim hips, barrel chests, beer guts, and big busts. Dressing extras on set is often a crash course in the use of shape to solve costume emergencies.

Your ability to solve problems using shape depends upon your ability to recognize and analyze your own instinctive responses to this element of design in clothing. One way to learn about the meaning of shape is to pick a mood or a "character quality" for which you want to find the visual equivalent (innocence, for example, or cruelty, or romance). Plaster a wall with images of clothing and characters that somehow embody these qualities for you. Look at the shapes, colors, and textures these images have in common, then target the shapes that resonate with you. Then learn to recognize those shapes in the course of formal costume research, and in the everyday act of people-watching.

TEXTURE

Fabric, and craft substances like fiberglass, plastics, and leather, are the all-important materials from which costumes are made. Texture (the way a material feels to the touch, its thickness, its firmness, its solidity) is determined by five key elements: (1) the physical composition of the material; (2) the construction of the material; (3) the material's surface effect; (4) the drape, or "hand," of the material; and (5) the durability of the material—all of which affect the work of the costume designer.

Physical composition of the material. The physical composition of the material includes the fibers that traditionally create cloth, including *natural fibers* made from plants or animals, and *manmade fibers* made from chemical solutions and petroleum byproducts. Fibers made from plants include cotton, linen, ramie, and the man-made natural fibers rayon, acetate, and nylon. Fibers made from animals include wool, cashmere, mohair, and silk (fig. 3.15). Man-made synthetic fibers include acrylic, modacrylic, polyester, metallic, and synthetic rubber (used to create the elastomer materials used in dancewear fabrics like Milliskin, Lycra, and Spandex). This category also includes other raw materials used in dressmaking and costume craftwork, among them feathers, furs, and leathers derived from animals or synthetic processes, and plastic resins, chemicals, and liquid rubbers used to create sheeting, or the fluids used in molding and casting. These include polystyrene, polyurethane, polyethylene, acrylic, latex, polyvinyl chloride, polyester, and chloroprene rubber.

The fibers or components that make up a material help determine its innate luster, drape, flexibility, warmth, colorfastness, strength, and absorbency. Silk and many synthetic fibers are lustrous; cotton and wool are dull. Polyesters attract static; natural fibers

FIG. 3.15

Refined silk cocoons

Raw and refined silk fibers spun into a range of different weight threads.

Raw silk cocoon

don't. Linen will never drape as softly as silk or wool. Neoprene rubber or Latex will by nature have more flexibility than fiberglass or polystyrene. Consider at the comparable merits of silk and wool in figs. 13.19 and 13.20.

How a material is made. Beginning costume designers often confuse the name of a *fiber* (the animal, plant, or manmade substance from which a textile is made) with the name of a *fabric* (the particular cloth into which the fiber is made). Silk, cotton, wool, and many synthetic fibers come in an enormous variety of fabrics, with an accompanying number of names used to distinguish weaves and knits, establish variations in weight, weave pattern, and thread count. For example, silk gauze, silk organza, china silk, and silk broadcloth are all plain-weave fabrics made from silk fiber; each type of silk fabric has a different thread count and a different thread thickness. The ability to distinguish among fibers, types of fabric, and weaves is a required job skill for any member of the profession.

Weaving methods include:
- *Plain weave*s (e.g., muslin), which can be manipulated to produce *basket weaves* (e.g., monk's cloth); or *rib weaves* e.g., taffeta or corded silk), which use yarns of contrasting thickness; (or *crepe weaves* (e.g., crepe, chiffon, or marquisette), which use high-twist yarns; or *iridescent weaves* (e.g., chambray or iridescent taffeta), which use two yarns of contrasting color
- *Twill weaves* (e.g., denim or military twill), which produce diagonal lines on the cloth and can be manipulated to produce herringbone patterns or hound's-tooth checks
- *Satin weaves* (e.g., satin or sateen), which float yarns over several cross yarns to produce a smooth, lustrous surface

FIG. 3.16

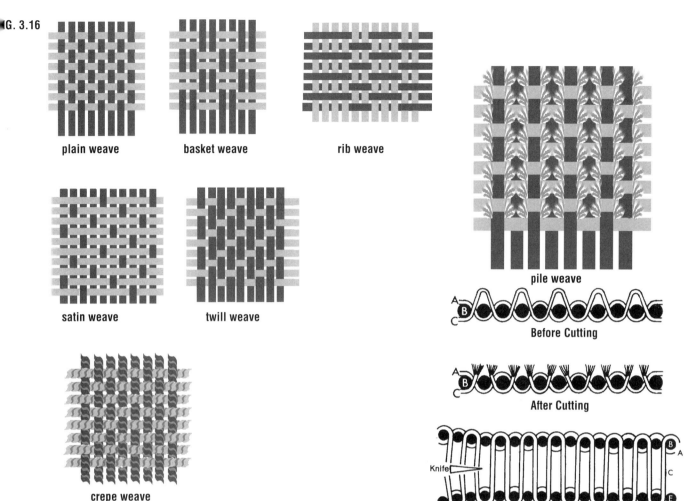

plain weave   basket weave   rib weave

satin weave   twill weave

crepe weave

pile weave

Before Cutting

After Cutting

- *Pile weaves* (e.g., velvet, velveteen, corduroy, or terry cloth), which create a fur-like surface
- *Figured weaves* (e.g., jacquard brocades, damask patterns, tapestry effects, dotted swiss, piqué), which use special loom setups to create woven patterns (see fig. 13.16)

Non-woven fabric or craft material construction methods include:

- *Knitting* (e.g., jersey knits, rib knits, double knits, tricot, velour, many imitation furs, and dancewear fabrics like Milliskin, Lycra, and Spandex)
- *Tanning* (the scraping and chemical curing of leathers)
- *Lace construction* (e.g., net, tulle, alencon lace, chantilly lace, galoon lace, etc.)
- *Bonded, laminated, or coated construction* (e.g., quilted fabrics, double-faced wools, rubber-backed upholstery fabrics, fiberglass)
- A variety of *molding* and *casting methods* used to create plastic and rubber sheeting, including foams and films in flexible and rigid forms

The combination of a fabric's fiber and construction technique will dictate its durability, draping quality, and surface effect. For example, silk fibers woven into a satin weave can be far more lustrous, malleable, and delicate than rayon fibers woven the same way.

For detailed information on fabric names there is *Profiling Fabrics: Properties, Performance, and Construction Techniques*, by Debbie Ann Gioello, a book with lavish photographs of hundreds of types of fabric, including shots of sample yardage draped on a dress form. The staggering variety of craft materials used in making armor, masks, spacesuits and creatures, theme park walk-around characters, jewelry, showgirl headdresses, fat suits, body padding, puppets, robots, and superheroes is gone into in exhaustive detail in the book *Costumes and Chemistry: A Comprehensive Guide to Materials and Applications,* by Sylvia Moss.

Surface effect. The surface effect of a material is the result of the following: (1) its transparence or opacity; (2) the way it reflects light (e.g., matte, gloss, or sheen effects); (3) the dimensionality of its surface (e.g., smooth, coarse, napped, ribbed, bumpy, or pierced); (4) its inherent or applied surface design (e.g., plain, printed, embossed, or woven into a pattern).

Weaving processes produce a wide variety of different fabric surfaces. Transparent weaves are a result of fine yarn size and low thread count. Both satin weaves and pile weaves produce a very lustrous surface, with the degree of sheen depending upon the fiber used. Dimensional surfaces can be the result of chunky yarns (like those used in raw silk fabrics or tweeds), high-twist yarns (crepe effects), unbalanced warp and weft threads (e.g., the very fine vertical threads and chunky horizontal threads used to produce a silk douppioni), or weaves that pull an extra set of threads through a plain woven base (pile weaves, boucles, terrycloth, corduroy). Knit processes can produce line effects (cable knits), dimensional patterns (like the "popcorn" pattern on an Irish fisherman sweater), lace-like patterns (leaf shapes, flowers, etc.), and looped effects (boucle knits, terrycloth knits, velour). Lace construction uses pierced effects, knotting techniques, and dimensional machine embroidery and beading. Twill weaves and basket weaves create patterns on the surface of a fabric by laying down the warp or woof yarns in a regularly repeated order and grouping (e.g., herringbone and houndstooth patterns). Figured weaves use looms that pick up groups of yarns during the weaving process in order to produce patterns (e.g., brocade and damask fabrics). There are a variety of specialty looms that do figured weaves, among them, traditional brocade patterns and embroidered, piqué, and dotted swiss effects. Any type of fabric can also be printed with fabric paints or dyes.

In addition to the surface effects produced through the weaving, knitting, or lace-construction processes, traditional fabrics are given *fabric finishes,* a multitude of processes and chemical treatments applied to fabrics to affect their durability, safety, and appearance. Fabric finishes are used to create etched velvet, cut velvet, moiré taffeta, seersucker, plissé, glazed goods, and other embossed and non-embossed effects. Garment construction techniques can also result in surface textural effects.

Dressmakers can manipulate fabrics to become more dimensional by using pleating, smocking, gathering, quilting, embroidery, appliqué, and beading. *The Art of Manipulating Fabric,* by Colette Wolff, displays a broad range of three-dimensional decorative dressmaking techniques. Fabric painters can etch, stencil, stamp, silkscreen, and print patterns onto fabrics. Craft artisans use molding techniques, appliqué, painting, electroplating, carving, embossing, shaving, sanding, and traditional dressmaker techniques to change the surface of their materials. For example, some craft materials are laminated or poured into (or onto) molds to take on the texture and form of the mold. Among the other means of producing this effect are *slush molding* (which entails brushing a slush-like coating of plastic or rubber into a negative mold), *injection molding* (which injects expanding plastic or rubber foam into a mold), and *coating* a mold with plastic resins or liquid rubbers. Plastic resins used in this way include polyurethane, acrylic, epoxy

FIG. 3.17

Polly Smith's designs for Miss Piggy in *Muppets from Space* (1999), a Jim Henson/Columbia Pictures Production, and Kermit from *Muppet Treasure Island* (1996), a Jim Henson/Walt Disney production.

(combined with fiberglass), polyester, and flexible or rigid polyurethane foam. Liquid rubbers used in this way include latex, foam latex, neoprene rubber, and silicone.

The casting resins and rubbers available produce a wide range of surface effects and flexibilities, running from the feel and surface of flesh (foam latex, silicone, or flexible polyurethane resins) to the high sheen and rigidity of jewels (epoxy, polyester, and acrylic resins). The thickness and density of the casting fluid, the size of air bubbles in the mixtures, and the depth of carving in the mold all affect the amount of surface detail revealed in the casting. Injection molding is used to produce the flocked foam Latex of the Muppet's Miss Piggy (fig. 3.17), slush latex molding to produce the oversize shoes worn by the Snuffleupagus and Big Bird.

Some craft materials are heated and shaped onto molds, to take on the texture and form of the mold. *Vacuum-forming* combines high heat with suction. *Heat-forming thermoplastic sheeting* becomes flexible when heated onto a mold via oven, heat gun, blow dryer, or hot water. Thermoplastic materials include the low-temperature-setting materials Friendly plastic, Hexcelite, Veriform, Fabric form, Wonder-flex, Solvoset, Protoplast, Polyform, Kydex, and Aquaplast, plus the high-heat-setting materials butyrate, acrylic (Plexiglas), ABS, polycarbonate, polyethylene, and polystryene.

The thickness of the material and the depth of the mold's carving determine the dimensionality of the final surface of the material. The surfaces of thermoplastic materials can range from dull to shiny, and set up into rigid forms, with limited flexibility. Thermoplastic materials are frequently painted, electroplated, or surfaced with fabrics, leathers, or trims. Many robots and much armor use vacuum-formed materials for their rigid suits.

Foam sheeting materials used by craft artisans have a variety of surface textures. Foam sheeting with an *open-celled structure* (e.g., Scott foam) has a surface that appears pierced with holes. Foam with a *closed-cell structure* (e.g., foam rubber) has a surface that appears smooth. Foam with a *flocked* surface has a velvety feel (e.g., the foam-cored Vellux Blanket). A shiny or matte material laminated on the surface of a material (e.g., Microcell) is called a *skinned* surface. Each type of foam sheeting tends to come in a range of densities (in open-celled foams, the density is determined by pore size). Foam materials can also be carved (and sometimes sanded) to produce textural effects, or they can be covered with other fabrics. Muppets Kermit and Grover are made of reticulated Scott foam covered with fabric, while Gonzo's nose is uncovered reticulated foam.

The drape of the material. The drape, or "hand," of a material refers to the way a fabric molds to a form and reacts to gravity. For traditional dress goods, how thick or thin a material is, what fiber is used, and how the material is constructed all affect its hand. In general, fabrics are classified as "crisp," "soft," or "bulky" (thick). Some fabrics, like cotton and silk, can easily range from soft to crisp depending on their weave and finish (fig. 3.18).

In dressmaking and tailoring, the hand of the fabric can be changed with the use of interfacing, interlining, flat-lining, lining, steaming, and even (on some occasions) washing. (Interlining and flat lining processes are the reason that you can take a drapey lamé and turn it into a tailored Elvis suit.) Appliqué, pleating, beading, quilting, embroidery, and the use of fabric paint will all change the hand of a fabric.

Craft materials are designated as "rigid" or "flexible," and a material's density and chemical makeup will determine its range of flexibility. There are flexible plastic foams and foam sheetings like polyethylene foam (Ethafoam) and polyurethane foam

Draping qualities of texture

FIG. 3.18

Soft   Crisp   Bulky

sheeting (Scott foam); flexible plastic sheeting like mylar, polyethylene sheeting, vinyl, and Naugahyde; flexible rubber sheeting and foam sheeting like neoprene sheeting, latex sheeting, and foam rubber; rigid plastic foams and foam sheetings like styrofoam, polystyrene, and polyurethane; and rigid plastics and plastic sheetings like acrylic (Plexiglas or Lucite), polyvinyl (Kydex and PVC), polystyrene, and ABS plastic. Some craft materials like latex, neoprene rubber, and polyurethane can range from rigid to highly flexible. Like fabric, flexible plastic or rubber materials can be made more rigid through paint, appliqué, and bonding processes.

Durability. The durability of a garment is a product of the following:
- The strength and flexibility of the fiber or components of which the base material is made
- The base material's construction (e.g., its thickness, the method of weave, and the fabric finishing processes)
- The construction methodology and support materials that have gone into making the garment

The garment industry rates fibers for relative merit, according to the following qualities:
- *Strength*—the ease with which it breaks when wet or dry
- *Elasticity*—the ability of a fiber to increase in length under tension and return to the original length when released
- *Flexibility*—the ability to bend easily
- *Resiliency*—the tendency to wrinkle
- *Pilling*—the unattractive way that fibers can break off and become "pills" on the surface of a fabric

Fibers vary radically in their relative durability and elasticity. Cotton knits, for example, will bag and sag over time more than any wool knit, but wool knits can't hold a candle to the enduring strength of elastic knits. Basic craft components also range in strength from brittle to highly flexible, and the durability of a craft material depends a lot on the thickness that is being used. For example, thin polystyrene vacuum-formed Halloween masks shatter easily, unless they are made in heavy-gauge polystyrene sheeting.

Construction, thickness, and density all play a part in a material's durability. Some weaves are more fragile than others—for example, pile weaves and satin weaves create surfaces that can be easily damaged, since they contain yarns that stick out from (or float over) the surface of the fabric. The result: Velvets "crush" easily; the threads on the surface of satins can get broken. Unbalanced weaves that weave thick, chunky threads through very fine threads (e.g., corded silk or douppioni silk) tend to fall apart with wear. The looped weaves of a bouclé or a terrycloth can snag easily. The density of some craft materials, like foam rubber, can be more important than the thickness of the material, for long-term durability. And fabrics with thick yarns (like many overcoat fabrics) are not necessarily stronger than closely woven fabrics with strong, thin fibers. What makes a weave strong? A high number of *interlacings* (one yarn passing over or under another yarn), and a high number of threads (or a *high thread-count*). Loosely woven or knitted goods with a low thread count or loose structure are more easily pulled out of shape (see figs. 13.19 and 13.20).

There are many ways to strengthen base materials, including chemical processes (e.g., fabric finishes or resin additives), painting or bonding processes (e.g., brush-on coatings or fusible linings), and dressmaking processes (e.g., flat-lining or quilting to a sturdier fabric). However, to keep construction and replacement costs down, it is best to

FIG. 3.19

CHOOSING FABRICS FOR A GINGER ROGERS-STYLE DANCE DRESS.
The preferred fiber: silk

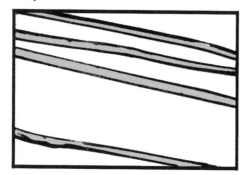

The naturally smooth quality of refined silk fiber helps create luster; its long, thin, triangular filament structure gives both strength and delicacy. As the thinnest and smoothest of all natural fibers, silk creates the most gorgeous, glowing satins; the thinnest and strongest nets and chiffons; and the most luxurious, drapable fabrics.

As a hydrophillic (naturally absorbent) fiber, silk dyes very well, discourages static cling, and "breathes" well, providing comfort for the wearer. Silk has fair resiliency, fair abrasion resistance, and good elasticity, giving it the kind of flexibility needed for this type of dress.

The preferred weave: crepe

Close-up view of crepe fabric

Plain weave of creped fibers

Dance dresses can vary widely in the weight and density of the fabrics used. Some have a weighted look, swinging heavily around the dancer's body. Some have a sheer gossamer look and appear to float around the figure. All dance fabrics must stretch and move with the dancer. The crepe weaves found in chiffons, marquisettes, crepes, and creped satins (like charmeuse and crepe-backed satin) use high-twist yarns that mold to the body and flex with its movement. Unlike stretch-knits, crepe fabrics can run the full gamut from the finest gossamer thin chiffon to heavy triple-ply crepe.

For strong dancewear, the strength of a fabric relies on three factors: the natural strength of the fiber used, the number of fibers twisted together to make the fabric's threads, and the number of threads used per square inch (the density of its thread-count). Silk's fine fibers can therefore be used to make very dense threads and weaves to create strong crepe fabrics that are still supple and fine in appearance.

MAKING THE DRESS. THE PREFERRED CONSTRUCTION TECHNIQUE: BIAS CUT

Dressmakers use two different approaches to achieve the fit and flow of fabric needed for dancewear: stretch or bias-cut construction. For the airy lightness of the overdress here, only bias-cut layers of chiffon-like fabrics will do. Bias cut uses the natural flexibility of the diagonal direction of a fabric to hug and flex with the body. The bias fabric molds to the torso, expanding and contracting as the torso moves and gracefully sliding down off the hips to hang in loose, graceful ripples at the hem. At rest, the bias cut creates a columnar beauty; in movement the skirts spiral out into huge circles as she twirls. Bias-cut clothes are based on the dynamics of movement—the garment and the body come together to form the dress.

weft yarns create crosswise grain

warp yarns create lengthwise grain

weft yarns

bias grain

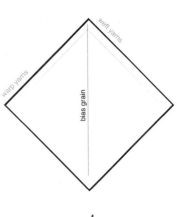

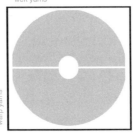

weft yarns

warp yarns

A circular cut of skirt allows the bias of the fabric to stretch the shape of the skirt into beautiful cascading waves of fabric. Creped fibers give more stretch and spring to bias cut.

FIG. 3.20

CHOOSING FABRIC FOR A BLUES BROTHERS-STYLE SUIT.
The preferred construction technique: traditional tailoring.

To achieve the broad shoulders, softly rolling lapel, and smooth, firm surface from the shoulders to mid-chest that these suits need, you will need to use tailoring techniques that mold the fabric of the suit to layers of interfacing and shoulder padding. A tailor will hand-tack, machine-stitch, and/or fuse a variety of shaping materials on the inside of a jacket to firmly stabilize the surface fabric and mold it into the correct shape. Non-traditional fusible tailoring techniques can save hours of hand-stitching; but for long-term usage, glue-bonded interfacings can break down, creating a pebbly "orange peel" look to the surface of the jacket that is disastrous on camera.

Traditional custom-tailoring patterning techniques also allow you to achieve the perfect fit you want on any type of body. Traditional bespoke tailoring develops patterns using the exact measurements of the body, customizing the proportions of the pieces to address any figure flaws and irregularities. So whether you are fitting the fit or the fat, the best or the worst posture, you will be able to use traditional custom tailoring to customize the suit to solve all figure problems.

The preferred fiber: wool.

Suits need a flexible fiber to help them retain their shape and appearance. A resilient fabric that does not retain wrinkles easily, fuzz, or pill is highly desirable, and a fiber with good elasticity and flexibility will help the suit not bag and sag from the normal wear and tear produced by the body bending, stretching, and sitting. Wool fiber has good resilience and flexibility. As a hydrophilic fiber, it absorbs water easily, making it comfortable to wear, easy to clean, and able to absorb a wide range of fabric-finishing chemicals that can help its durability and vary its surface appearance from soft and fuzzy to crisp and slick.

For traditional tailoring, wool has a unique advantage over all other fibers: It can shrink and mold to a shape by using steam. Wool fiber is more shapeable than other fibers because of its round, crimped, and scaly shape—with water and heat, the overlapping scales can stretch or shrink into each other (known as a "felting" effect). As a result, unlike working with any other type of fiber, tailors can artfully shrink and mold wool to suppress the waist or mold to the shoulders or hips. Using wool, they can make the hundreds of tiny hand stitches that go into the "rolling" of a collar or lapel disappear as the wool subtly steam-shrinks smoothly into place.

Wool fibers have a large diameter—relative to other fibers—and combined with the natural crimp, this makes wool look substantial, allowing the creation of a broad range of solid-looking fabrics of different thicknesses. Wool comes from about forty different breeds of sheep that produce different lengths of fiber, which are then twisted into wool yarns.

The preferred weave: plain or twill-weave woolen.

Suits need a malleable yet sturdy fabric. Loosely woven fabrics will pull out of shape too easily, so a high thread count is most desirable. Plain, balanced weaves with high thread counts could work well for the matte, dense look of the Blues Brothers-style suit; or a dense twill weave with a simple surface may be most desirable because twill weaves by nature are strong, plain weaves. Suitings should be a light to medium weight so that suits do not appear too thick or overcoat-like.

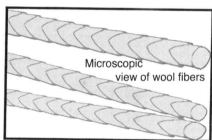

Microscopic view of wool fibers

Plain weave structure

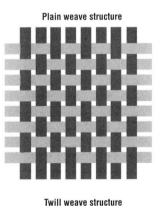

Woolen suitings are generally divided into "worsted wool fabrics" and "woolen fabrics." Worsted wool yarns go through processing that yields a finer, tighter, and more lustrous yarn than the processing used in woolen fabric yarns. Worsted fabrics tend to have a comparatively crisp hand and harsh, flat, firm appearance—a bit too slick and refined for the Blues Brothers style. Woolens often have a soft, napped surface and tend to appear duller, softer, fuzzier, and thicker—good for the matte, solid appearance of the Blues Brothers-style suit.

Worsteds are more durable than woolens, and the finer threads can be woven into finer, denser fabrics that help suits hold their shapes better. Woolen fabrics are woven much less tightly and are therefore less dense and less firm and do not hold their shape as well as a worsted over time. Since Blues Brothers-styling is not the look of a high-end business suit, the less firm, softer shape of a dense woolen fabric that molds itself into a more "comfortable" looking suit could be just the ticket.

If your Blues Brothers-style suit needs to endure very hard usage, you may opt for an "unfinished worsted" fabric with its dense weave and slightly napped surface for greater durability without the shine problem of a worsted wool.

Twill weave structure

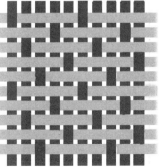

Worsted wool fabrics

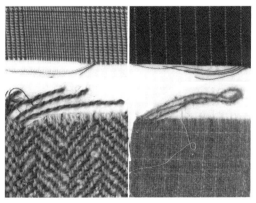

Woolen fabrics

start construction on a garment with the right type, weight, and weave (or composition) of material needed for the way the garment will be used.

Texture and focus. Contrasting surface textures can be used to create focal points in a costume composition, a tactic used to focus attention on the face of the actor, and, often, to draw attention away from figure problems. Common tricks that use texture to pull focus to a face involve using strongly contrasting textures on collars, ties, jewelry, scarves, shirts, lines of buttons, and appliqué or embroidery near the face. Busy textural patterns on large bodies lead to visual overload, so fashions for large men or women tend to use small patterns and/or contrasting surfaces of plain goods. To balance large areas of dull or matte goods and pull focus to the strong points on a less-than-perfect figure (the beautiful face or the fabulous cleavage, for example), you can use small areas of aggressive texture—strongly dimensional textures, textures with a high-contrast pattern, some transparency in the fabric, or a high sheen.

Texture and emotional resonance. Texture relays emotional content in two ways: through surface effect and as a result of the way the fabric moves on the body. "Crisp" goods seem almost to hold their shape without a body; they can lend a sense of strength and protection to the wearer. The outlines of the body can get hidden in them, and movement seems to stiffen or compress. Crisp goods can amplify a character's freshness and boldness, or formality and rigidity, or prickliness and brittle fragility. Soft, supple goods flow on, and with, the body. They lend sensuousness and ease to the wearer as they reveal his or her form. They can add comfort, grace, ethereal charm, and vulnerability. Bulky goods (whether they are soft or crisp) add visual weight by obscuring the form and turning it into a more massive shape. Bulk works against the sensuous movement of the body. Soft bulky goods—furs, thick sweaters, sweat clothes—can promote feelings of comfort or luxurious indulgence. They can bring out the Earth mother, or friendly bear, in a character. Crisp bulky goods, like motorcycle jackets or leather trench coats, can promote an aggressive, tough-guy quality in characters.

The tactility of the surface or print of a fabric can produce a visceral response in the viewer. It also affects how "busy" or calm the composition feels. Pile fabrics, cable-knit sweaters, furs, and velours make you want to sink your fingers into them. Low-pile suede surfaces and washed silks or rayons look soft and inviting. Sheer fabrics bring a mysterious vulnerability to an image. Plain fabrics can feel calming. Glittering fabrics are dazzling. The feel of a patterned fabric can range from lively to overloaded, as the scale of the pattern increases.

Texture can be used to play against the visceral effect of a shape or color, to add depth or subtlety to a design, and to work against, or in collaboration with, character stereotypes. A hooker can be dressed head to toe in white, but if the textures are supple and sensuous, the message won't get lost. On the other hand, a virgin might be dressed in a lively red, but if the textures are soft and delicate, an innocence and vulnerability will come through.

Choosing the right fabric. For a costume designer, the most difficult aspect of working with fabric is being able to determine the correct weight and drape of goods needed to make a garment. It is relatively easy to match a character in the script with the "character" of a color, a surface effect, or a print, but it is hard to learn the hand of the fabric you need to make a garment right. Unfortunately, there really are no good books that help young designers develop a palpable sense of the hand of different fabrics. If you are new to getting costumes made, and are responsible for supplying the materials, get advice from someone who really knows how to sew *before* you buy your yardage. If you can't get an expert's advice before you buy, take your sketch (or a photograph of what you want) with you, and ask the advice of a knowledgeable sales clerk. Alternatively, you can take a sample garment with you, one that has the weight and drape of the fabric you want, then compare the bolt goods to it.

Selecting a fabric for a particular garment is tricky stuff. Learning which fabric weights or fibers should be used for dancewear or eveningwear or tailored goods or uniforms can feel like negotiating a minefield. Different shapes, different seasons, different periods, and different uses all dictate different fabric weights and draping qualities. For example, supple fabrics with "give" and drape, like crepes, chiffons, jerseys, and knits, are best used for clinging or softly flowing shapes. Crisp, sculptural shapes need fabrics with body, and a measure of stiffness, like worsted wools, taffetas, bridal satin, douppioni silks, and most linens. Some period silhouettes need soft goods, others, crisp; some need natural fibers, others, synthetic. Until the nineteen-twenties, garments were made exclusively of natural fibers. The nineteen-sixties, nineteen-seventies, and early nineteen-eighties saw the blossoming of stretch fabrics, polyesters, synthetic knits, and metallic fabrics.

Action, adventure, even everyday usage can take a heavy toll on fine fabrics. Garments, like slacks, that get heavy wear need fabrics of sufficient weight and strength to endure the chronic use and abuse of sitting on a wide variety of surfaces; but to be attractive, a pair of slacks also needs fabric that has sufficient opacity, but not too much bulk. If you choose the wrong fabrics for a garment, you will drive up the time and cost it takes to make the garment, and you will discover that the garment just won't look right.

To give you a feel for the factors that go into the selection of a fabric, look at the fabric recommendations in figs. 3.19 and 3.20.

Other factors that come into play when you buy fabric, include:

- *The opacity of the goods.* In garments like dresses and suits, pockets, interfacings, zipper plackets, and facings may show through if made of translucent fabrics. Opaque linings or sheer interlinings can be used to partially solve this problem.
- *The wearability of the goods.* Test how wrinkle-resistant a fabric is by crushing it. Check the stretch and give of the fabric by testing the degree to which it springs back when stretched.
- *The scale of the pattern of the fabric.* The amount of fabric you need for a garment is determined by the nature of the print. Prints, plaids, and repeated patterns will need more yardage, to allow pattern-matching on seam lines.
- *The drape and weight of lining fabrics.* If a garment is to be lined, and the lining fabric and the fabric of the garment itself are to work well together, the lining fabric should match the hand of the garment's fabric, although in some instances, it can be lighter in weight, for comfort. Linings give garments a luxurious feel, and prolong the life of a garment, by covering construction details and protecting the outer fabric from abrasion during wear. Linings also help prevent the garment from stretching and wrinkling, and they can add body and help to preserve shape. Linings should always be smooth and slippery, to help the top fabric "glide" over it.

Developing a feel for fabric. Most costume designers learn how to use fabric by learning to sew, by closely studying what garments are made of, or by working with expert technicians who advise them. You need to study the drape of the goods and understand something about costume construction methodologies before you can intelligently choose fabrics. Learning to sew, you will handle fabrics and read patterns that give guidelines on the fabrics that should be used. Working in a costume workroom can expose you to a range of fabrics that you've never known, and give you access to fabric experts. Working in a costume rental house or crawling through designer boutiques and clothing stores will give you a tactile sense of the hand of different fabrics, and raise your awareness of luxury goods. If you really study, and feel, couture and period fashions (on a hanger and a dress form, not just in a magazine or book), you can get a real education in the drape and weight of fashion fabrics.

Magazines, and books with photos of fashion collections, do occasionally list the fabrics used in the garments they picture, information that can help you raise your awareness of draping quality and fabric names. There are also a variety of good books available that cover the nitty-gritty details of fabric, fiber, and craft material names and construction techniques. For the beginner, *The Vogue Sewing Book*, published by Vogue Patterns, is an all-around useful book. In addition to providing a primer on sewing techniques, it gives an introduction to fiber and fabric construction, includes a dictionary of fabric terminology, gives tips on fitting and shape solutions for problem bodies, and gives an overview of dressmaking, patterning, and fitting approaches used in men's and women's wear. For a crash course on the complexities of constructing tailored garments, study *Classic Tailoring Techniques: A Construction Guide for Men's Wear*, by Roberto Cabrera and Patricia Flaherty Meyers, which also has some great visual aids for fitting men's wear. Insight into the refined points and processes of couture design can be had by studying *Couture Sewing Techniques*, by Claire B. Shaeffer. For an advanced course in fibers and fabric construction, I recommend *Fabric Science*, by Joseph Pizzuto, a basic text of the fashion industry.

These texts all give a wealth of information, but be forewarned: For a beginner, they can seem fairly dry, and filled with technical details. Unfortunately, when working with fabrics, the devil is in the details, and the more you embrace an in-depth, hands-on approach to studying fabric and craft materials, the better designer you will be.

UNDERSTANDING CRAFTSMANSHIP

The craft of making clothing look good on screen is complex. Couture-style costume construction techniques are standard practice in the best shops in the industry. Dye artisans lovingly age garments to look as natural and authentic as possible. Craft specialists like Global Effects Inc. create spacesuits that match authentic NASA gear (fig. 3.21). To understand why expensive processes and goods can pay off, you need to study what the payoff is. A couture-quality finish (beautiful linings, hand-stitched detailing, etc.) improves the way the garment lays on the body, and can make the garment look better on camera. Well-designed foundation garments can transform a good-looking actress into a stunning vision, or create the illusion that a lumpy gal has a great shape. Designer-label suits can be cut to reveal, or disguise, an actor's shape. Some designer

FIG. 3.21

Christopher Gilman's Astronaut spacesuits   Photos courtesy of Global Effects

labels cater to a particular segment of the fashion market: A label may cater to athletic men, for example, or to an older clientele. In the hands of a brilliant artisan, custom-made goods can be fitted to any actor's body. And the goods just look right—they have a glamorous quality. This can be vital if your actor has difficult proportions or serious physical flaws. An authentic period look demands not modern tailoring, but the construction techniques and subtly different proportions of correct period tailoring.

As you look at couture fashion, you will notice that one of the most significant differences between designer-label goods and general off-the-rack fashion is the quality of the fabric. Beautiful fabric is one reason that designer goods work well on camera. The supple wools used in an Armani suit drape the body more subtly. A good silk has a richer luster, and more complex movement, than a silk-like lesser fabric. Many designers admit to never stinting on the ties they pull for a fashion-conscious lead: The luster and lay of a good silk tie is just too important to the on-screen look. In any event, great film designers develop a feel for goods that work beautifully on the body and look good on camera.

MEDIA LIMITATIONS

Every medium has its limitations. With film and video, some limitations are inherent in the nature of the physical medium; others come about as a result of production processes, still others as a result of personal taste.

Color palette distortion and production-stock issues. The stock on which a production is shot, the processing techniques used, methods of lighting and projection all have an impact on the truthfulness of color reproduction on screen. The accuracy of color reproduction is also affected by the nature of the materials used in a costume. Different fibers reflect light and color in different ways. Synthetics are particularly prone to color distortion when fluorescent or colored gels (especially red gels) are used in the lighting. Dyed-to-match garments of different fibers can occasionally appear to change color (*color shift*)—especially if synthetics are involved. Black polyester, for example, can read as green or red on screen.

Film stock, unlike videotape, has an acute sensitivity to color, and each brand and type of film has its own particular color sensitivity. Fuji stock tends to blue/green distortion, Aiwa film often has strong beige overtones, while Kodak is particularly good with reds. In spite of the overall sensitivity of film stock, and beyond the particular sensitivities of a given stock, a variety of color distortion problems crop up predictably, across the board, among them the following:

- Whites under very strong light can *over-burn* and glow, or *flare*. This distracting effect can draw attention from the actor's face.
- During film processing, colors are *color corrected*, most often to get natural flesh tones on the actors. Processing tricks are occasionally used to deliberately distort color, in order to produce the effect of night, or to create supersaturated effects or faded, over-bleached, de-saturated effects.

Videotape generally has poorer resolution and cruder color reproduction than film stock, although, with new digital devices that are coming into the industry, resolution and color problems are being solved every day. Nonetheless, the following problems are common to videotape:

- Primary colors can over-burn, especially primary red, which can also go nuclear orange.
- Purples, greens, and blues are particularly susceptible to going bluer. Navy and dark green can turn black.
- A dual-tone like teal or maroon will shift to one side of its hue or the other. Iridescent fabrics will do the same. Lavender will go gray or tan.

In video work, color correction is done in the studio, by a video engineer. Most video engineers correct for accurate flesh tones, but occasionally their artistic sense leads them to stronger palette distortions.

A number of different costume designers suggested the following to help control the potential color problems that crop up in film and on tape:

- Never let your whites be brighter than the actors' teeth or eyes.
- Avoid royal blue. In particular, don't use it on extras, since it's too easy to "track" in crowd scenes.

Reds and blues on video just zoom! They "bleed." You've only got to watch the soap operas to see this. To read a good red or scarlet on video, you would dye it almost a rust brown, or a wine color—a Bordeaux—and then it will read "red" on camera. And blue! Even on film, blue screams. When working on *Return of the Jedi* for George Lucas, we were told to avoid blues. We could use a muted teal, but never a true blue, because it always jumps out of the screen, and can give too much importance to only one character in a scene. (*Edwina Pellikka, owner of A Dyeing Art*)

Color palette control and lighting issues. Even with film stock, strong value contrasts—black figures on a white field, for example—will often result in a loss of detail, as the camera tries to compensate for the extreme range. In video, particularly, lighting can be so "hot" and white that pastels bleach out and dark/light contrast problems become acute. In this situation, white is likely to *over-burn* (or *glow*), black is likely to *black-hole* (all details eliminated, a black flare created). In video work, poor lighting can cause certain colors to go very dark, even black—certain reds are particularly susceptible to this problem.

To avoid or minimize these problems and others related to color palette control and lighting, a number of different costume designers suggest the following:

• Develop an acute sensitivity to value and contrast. Confer with the director of photography before shooting, to discuss color preferences and anticipate problems with palette extremes.

• Vary the hue, not the value. Low contrast tones may help the director of photography save time on lighting solutions.

• Use muted tones to emphasize the actor; they help an audience focus on both the actor's face and the drama.

• Give careful instructions on an acceptable range of color to the extras who supply their own costumes. This is key to palette control.

• When costuming extras in crowds, aim for the effect of "muted masses" or cool tone/warm tone separation, in order to let your leads stand out. You can get away with bright tonal "hits" on children in a crowd scene, if you want to get them to show up.

• Think twice about using a light, bright (high-value) tone for a shirt on a dark-skinned actor. In spite of efforts to achieve a light balance, you may lose detail in the face.

Color palette control and special effects (EFX) work. Costume color becomes critical in an effect called *chroma key*, the effect most commonly used to superimpose the TV weatherman in front of a satellite photograph. In chroma key work, an actor is placed in front of a screen filled with a single color, usually "chroma key blue," or "ultra matte green," since blues and greens are not found in skin tones. (Chroma key work can actually be "keyed" to any single color, so a costume designer can voice a preference for color to her director and cinematographer, during prep.) The chroma key color is the "key" to this special effect, since anything that uses this color, or tones close to it, will seem to "disappear" from screen. This allows the empty areas to be filled with images during the postproduction process. Because of the way chroma key works—"erasing" everything in the key color—costume designers must make sure that no costume item worn in a chroma key setup is in the chroma key color, or any tone close to it. If it is, the costume piece will magically "disappear," along with the screen behind it.

Color reflection problems. Problems with reflected color often cause designers to limit their palettes. Using extreme primaries and other strong colors on garments near the face can cause reflection problems in a close-up. For example, acid greens and yellows reflected on skin don't often work well.

With sensitive lighting and camera work, however, color rules can be broken, even though lighting setups for problem colors can take more time, which may not be available. To avoid problems with color reflection, a number of costume designers have suggested the following:

•   Avoid-high intensity colors—they overpower the actor and can cause color flare and color reflection problems in close-up.

•   Add smoky tones, or slightly faded tones, to your palette. They soften the value, and helps avoid reflection problems.

Texture distortion issues. While texture distortion is not really a problem with film stock, in this era, when most films are still transferred to videotape for rental release, it is important to anticipate video problems with texture, even when you are shooting on film.

Textures shot on videotape are acutely susceptible to distortion. The color and lighting problems mentioned in the previous section can cause a loss of textural details in over-burn situations. When high-contrast patterns of a particular scale (like a black and white one-eighth-inch stripe) are read by a video camera, a camera-scanning problem known as *strobing* (also known as *Rastar,* or *moiré,* effects) occurs. Strobing turns the lines of certain textured or patterned fabrics into a kind of undulating, pixillating wood-grain. Herringbone, houndstooth, one-half-inch to one-eighth-inch stripes, and checks or polka dots in high-contrast colors, are all susceptible to this problem (fig. 3.22).

Highlights on shiny, reflective fabrics and jewelry can flare and look over-burned on videotape. Compensate for this possibility by treating the pieces with an aerosol hairspray or a commercial "dulling spray," available at any art supply store.

Other media issues. The microphones used to record sound for film are extremely sensitive. This makes it difficult to use "noisy" fabrics, like taffeta or tissue lamé. Jingling jewelry is an obviously problem, but so are hard leather heels on shoes, in some situations. In a pinch, sound booties, shoe foam, and baby bottle nipples can provide a sound buffer for shoe sole and high heel problems, but rubberizing the soles of shoes and using composite soling are two methods that solve these sound problems over a long shooting period. You can get shoes resoled or rubberized at a good cobbler. Booties (soft slip-on shoe covers) and a roll of adhesive-backed shoe foam can be bought at a wardrobe supply stores like Motion Picture Supply (MPS) or the one situated at the Costume Rental Corporation (CRC), in Los Angeles.

> Logical "red flags" for me? Dark on dark and light on light are color problems for me. Picture-frame hats, which affect how the light hits an actor's face. Or things that might fog or steam up, for example, the Hazmat suits in films like *Outbreak*. Outfits where the actors look as though they're completely encased, and breath can fog the face mask. Reflective light, as with mirror or foil or any reflective surfaces. The problem here is the flare of the light; and the surface can turn into a mirror, and you lose the actor's face behind it. I learned that on a TV pilot called *The Burning Zone*. They wanted to place small lights inside the helmets, for TV purposes, because they didn't have the luxury of time to light for the reflections. Reflective colors that are hot or intense, like neon orange or neon yellow, can also create problems: They're going to bounce light onto faces, or onto other people or other clothes, especially in a close-up situation.

FIG. 3.22

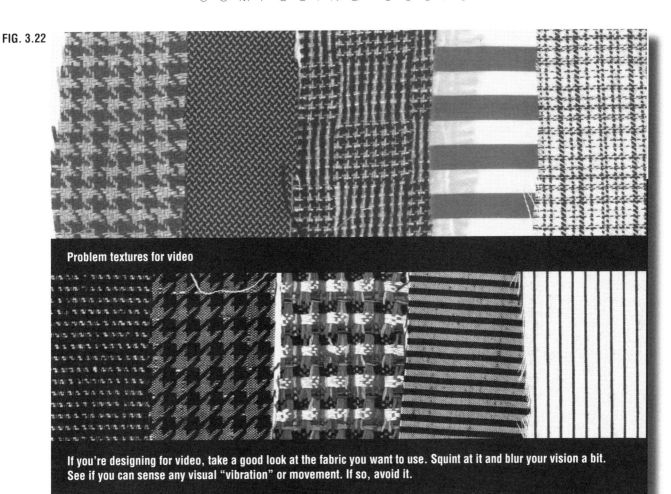

Problem textures for video

If you're designing for video, take a good look at the fabric you want to use. Squint at it and blur your vision a bit. See if you can sense any visual "vibration" or movement. If so, avoid it.

If you are doing TV, you also get things that fuzz or "ombre." For instance, a small houndstooth will shimmy once it goes onto TV; it will move because of the nature of video. Close stripes will do it, too. This can be either a color contrast problem, a problem with the scale of the pattern, or both. A quick trick is to squint at the fabric, shake it slightly, and see what it does (and hope you don't have a hangover at the time). On film, if you wanted a very thin stripe to make a statement, it might not be a problem—until it goes to the video shelf.

If the show is television to begin with, especially a three-camera show, where the lighting can have a kind of "flattening" effect, a good designer will find a way to compensate. On sitcoms, quite often, designers will use very specific, and very different, colors next to each other—just to give a little more punch. The sitcom *Designing Women*, I think, is one of the most remarkable examples of that, historically. The designer used very strong fields of color. But, again, if there is a rule, it will be broken. *(Catherine Adair, costume designer)*

YOUR DESIGN STANDARDS

The way in which you use the tools of design determine your design standards, and your design standards determine the kind of work you will get. Your design standards can get you typecast you in this industry. You'll only get the level of work that you can prove you understand. If you want to work on quality projects, you'll have to prove that you have high standards, and the skills to back them up.

A big budget does not equal great design. To advance in the industry, you must prove that you know the meaning of "high production values," and have the skills, determination, and resourcefulness to make them happen, regardless of the size of your budget. Even when money is tight, most productions want an "A-list" look—the best, or better, than their budgets can buy. The film market is flooded with high-fashion, designer-label goods that read beautifully on screen, but anyone who has ever listened to a fashion pundit trash the rich and famous knows that high-fashion goods are no ticket to looking good. It takes a costume designer with an eye for character, great taste, and an understanding of what works on the body and on camera to make a great designs for film.

Is there a recognizable A-list look? What rates an Academy Award or an Emmy? Take a look at Natasha Landau's Emmy and Cable Ace award-nominated designs for the 1996 HBO movie *Rasputin* (fig.s 3.23, C.17) and April Ferry's Academy Award-nominated designs for the 1994 feature *Maverick* (figs. 1.10, 3.24, and 3.25, fig. C.18). Meticulous detailing, beautiful fabrics, and strong character work are greatly prized in this business. Characters who have a flair for fashion are expected to wear garments that fit beautifully. Characters who have no fashion sense are expected to be perfectly unfashionable, accurate in every eccentric detail. Period productions are expected to feel authentic, worn-down garments to look authentically aged.

Designers can be merciless on the subject of other designers' work, but they also have a deep appreciation for good design. In a forum as public as the movies, where work is so easily studied, a costume designer's output is bound to be scrutinized, and judged. Costume designers appreciate a costume that doesn't overwhelm its wearer; they often criticize overly bright colors and tight fit, tagging them "too TV." Television design, all admit, can be very good indeed, but the compressed schedules of television production invite design shortcuts. Overtly trendy styles, in great number and often unrelated, end up on screen without even a laundering to make them feel real. This "catalog look," of chronic newness, not character, is often a consequence of too little prep time, and is seen too often (along with ultra-groomed hair and "beauty" makeup) in both television and film work. In both instances, the damage to dramatic effect and emotional authenticity is profound.

Good designers deplore design clichés. "Identikit" extras—instantly identifiable types—Texans in cowboy hats; Hawaiians in tropical shirts; respectable matrons in shapeless dresses, gangsters in dark shirts and pinstripes—crop up in both television and film. Network television comedies, especially sit-coms, are given to the use of homogenized casual wear, a sort of "California yuppie" style, but cleaner—very safe, very middle-American. Dirt and grunge mean poverty; vulgar glitz stands in for luxury, instead of the superb cut, texture, and accessories that represent real wealth. Acquiring a sensitivity to design cliché can help point you toward new solutions.

Some people look at the world, and some really *see* it. Flair and originality in design are measured by a designer's unique ability to heighten and reveal detail: A designer's understanding of fine craftsmanship and costume detailing are inseparable. A heightened use of the authentic and idiosyncratic in a costume can add depth and originality to a character. And you don't need made-to-order garments to display your originality; you can do it using shopped goods, from unusual sources—

FIG. 3.23

1996 Emmy and Cable Ace Awards nominee for best costume design for the HBO production of *Rasputin*, design and sketches by Natasha Landau. Rasputin - Alan Rickman,
Alexandra - Greta Scacci

FIG. 3.24

April Ferry's designs for Warner Bros. 1994 *Maverick* with Jodie Foster, Mel Gibson, and Graham Greene earned her an Oscar nomination.
Sketch by Lois De Armond
Dress by John Hales
Photo by Ed Wassall

FIG. 3.25

just look at costume designer Jeffrey Kurland's unabashedly brassy designs for Julia Roberts in *Erin Brockovich* (2000). The art of combining vintage and contemporary goods can be the foundation of a designer's career—just look at the current trend in dressing for the Academy Awards, in which both current and vintage designer fashions make an appearance.

Studying fashion, street clothing practices, and film design work can inspire creative design alternatives. Think about the work that knocks your socks off. Perhaps you love Colleen Atwood's whimsical designs for *Ed Wood* or *Edward Scissorhands*; the beautifully controlled palettes of the designs for *Room with a View* and *Howard's End*, by Jenny Beavan and John Bright; or Jeffrey Kurland's very humane sense of humor in his costumes for *Radio Days*, *Bullets over Broadway*, and *Erin Brockovich*. Are you a fan of Ann Roth's ability to capture character in *Working Girl* and *The English Patient?* Milena Canonero's eye for dramatic beauty in *Chariots of Fire* and *Out of Africa?* Ruth Carter's unfailing ability to nail atmospheric detail in *Malcolm X* and *Summer of Sam?* Study how designers achieve believability in the way characters dress, their approaches to texture, shape, and palette control, their eye for realistic detailing, their fitting standards. Notice how designers develop a color palette and spectrum of character eccentricities, even for a crowd of extras. Study the films that win awards: They are windows onto the standards of this industry.

It can be difficult to embrace the level of costume detail and subtlety of fit it takes to make a film with high production values. Too many costume personnel coming up through the ranks of low-budget production have a hard time adjusting to the design standards and budget practices required of A-list pictures. Designers who come up through the low-budget ranks look at the cost of designer goods, and made-to-order work, with its requirements of time and money, then dismiss them as unattainable, or worse, indulgent. Brought up on "make-do" processes, they forget how sloppy or clichéd their work can look. Working on a well-moneyed production in any capacity can help you gain an understanding, up-close and personal, of how money can be spent well. You will see what pays off and what doesn't. The higher the quality of the productions you want to work on, the higher the standards your current work must display.

Low- or high-budget, you can show a flair for the work, and an audacious eye. Great art is risky and rebellious, and it doesn't always require a big budget. How the hell could anyone bring in the costumes for *The Adventures of Priscilla, Queen of the Desert* for $15,000, even in 1994? Really creative designers, that's how. The Academy Award-winning costume designers of *Priscilla*, Lizzy Gardiner and Tim Chappel, have the kind of high standards and eye for design that are not limited by budget. Original vision can pay off in an industry that is always looking for "the next new thing." Quality work is not solely determined by budget, nor is it confined to any medium. Good work can triumph, in spite of circumstances.

And it will get noticed.

UNDERSTANDING THE COSTUME DESIGN PROCESS

Costume as narrative, symbol, and expression are almost always overlapping functions, much in the same way that formal elements of design are thoroughly interdependent. (As you have undoubtedly recognized, it is not always easy to distinguish among shape, line, and texture, for example.) And of course, it is the formal elements of design that are the vehicles for storytelling, symbolism, and expression. The design process itself does not easily or automatically divide into the intellectual activity of discovering a script's hidden meanings and materializing these meanings in concrete costume compositions—and certainly not in such strict order. The process is more organic than this, and often more mysterious: Meanings can reveal themselves when you are breaking down the script, making sketches, doing research, or fitting an actor. Sometimes, the most potent meanings do not become apparent until you see a costume on the set—or on screen. Meanwhile, it is left to the costume designer to master the elements of design that are controllable in what is, fundamentally, an alchemical process.

Practically speaking, of course, to make a career in Hollywood, a costume designer has to be able to make actors look great *and* create strong characters—most often while working from available modern fashion or costume rental stock. Defining a character with the right design choices and key costume details and combining line, shape, color, and texture in ways that are perfect for the actor are the largest part of the film designer's stock in trade. But a career in film costume design is also built on a foundation of strong script-analysis skills, dogged research skills, a talent for working with actors, an ability to "deliver the goods" on budget and on time, and production savvy—the art of navigating the politics of production collaborations. Armed with an understanding of these fundamentals, we can now get down to the nitty-gritty of the design process itself.

PART FOUR

Developing the Design

The Costume Design Process: An Introduction

In Part 4, *Developing the Design*, we will focus on the designer's artistic role in the production process by looking in detail at how a production's design guidelines are developed, and how principal players' costumes are designed.

Emmy award-winning costume designer Durinda Wood suggests that the costume design process can be broken down into seven basic phases.

Phase 1, *design analysis*, in which the designer develops a *design point of view*—a "design concept"—for the production. This is accomplished by means of detailed script analysis and preliminary conversations with the director.

Phase 2, *preliminary research*, in which the designer does the preliminary character and costume research needed to start design development

Phase 3, *preliminary design*, in which a designer does rough costume designs; does costume research; meets with key creative personnel on the production to clarify production details that may affect the costumes; and then, develops presentations of costume research and preliminary character designs

Phase 4, *design*, in which design guidelines for the film and specific designs for the principal characters are refined, in order to gain approval from the director and/or producer(s)

Phase 5, *prep*, in which most of the film's wardrobe is assembled and prepared for approval and shooting

Phase 6, the *shoot*, in which final refinements are made to the designs before being committed to film, and additional wardrobe is delivered according to shooting schedule deadlines

Phase 7, *final wrap*, in which the costumes are returned, if appropriate, and held or stored for additional footage and re-shoots that may be required after completion of *principal photography* (the footage shot during the original production shooting schedule)

[Note: Production restrictions, and complications like small budgets, short schedules, short prep times, unavailable design collaborators, and late casting, can cause phases three through six to overlap. For a more detailed step-by-step breakdown of the costume design process, see fig. 4.7.]

Phase 1: design analysis, in which the designer develops a design point of view by analyzing the script and talking with the director.

Analysis of the script. When you start to design costumes, you start with a careful analysis of the script, in order to develop your design "take" on the production—your design point of view. You have to commit to what you feel will connect best with the audience for this film. Eventually, you will refine your designs, and the costumes' details, to give power and depth to the characters, and to the story being told.

You have to have one essential vision for the design of a film. Make a conscious decision about the direction you want to go. *(Cynthia Hamilton, assistant costume designer,* Zoolander, Speed, Bugsy, *and others)*

As you analyze the screenplay, you are working on two levels: the *practical* and the *poetic.* The practical analysis of a screenplay is called a *script breakdown.* By "breaking down" the script, you get a handle on the script's logistics. In the process of breaking down a script, a designer figures out, among other things, the amount of costume stock needed to express the passage of time and fulfill the script's action demands. (The techniques for breaking down a script are detailed in Part 5, *Breakdowns.*)

Before doing your script breakdown, give the script a "close reading"—an analytical approach to reading meant to uncover the less literal, more "poetic" meanings hidden deep in a script. In order to take script analysis to this poetic level, actor Lawrence Fishburne says, "We have to apply our imaginations to the text." Every artist on a film—actor, director, cinematographer, art director, composer, costume designer—seeks the meaning *behind* the words in a script. Moving methodically from the details of each scene to "the big picture," each scene is read for its emotional impact. Step by step, the "feel" of a script will crystal-lize: glamorous or gritty; delicate or direct; comic or tragic; heroic or ordinary; polished or raw; stylized or "real." By discovering the nuances and hidden meanings in a text, a good designer will end up not just designing the events, but revealing—even determining—the meaning of the film. By skillfully controlling the ways in which a design resonates with these hidden meanings, a costume designer will have some say in how an audience responds.

Attacking the script on a poetic level has three primary objectives: (1) to address the characteristic quality or timbre of the story, the individual characters, and the scenes; (2) to illuminate the repercussions of the characters' interactions; and (3) to uncover the undercur-rents in each scene with which an audience will connect. Now, let's look at how to read a script to uncover its hidden meanings, step by step. (The questions in parentheses are meant to suggest additional lines of inquiry.)

Step 1: Identify the circumstances in each scene.
- Where is the scene set?
- Is it interior or exterior? Is it urban or rural? Rough or refined terrain?
- What is the occasion? (Is it a party? A hospital visit? The daily routine?)
- What is the weather? (Is it rainy? Snowy? Foggy? Steamy?)
- When does the scene take place? (What is the year? What is the season? What is the time of day?)
- What is the passage of time in the scene?
- Who is in the scene? (Look for the characters who are named, as well as those who are unnamed or implied, who would logically add to the atmosphere of the scene? A restaurant scene may need waiters and busboys, for example.)
- What is each character's social status?
- What is each character's profession?
- What is the sexual orientation of each character? How clearly should we "read" it?
- Do certain characters display eccentricities? What are they?
- Are there any specific references in the script to what the character is wearing? Consider the group of characters as a whole, and look at the kind of "society" they create.
- What is each character's attitude toward fashion?

- What happens in the scene? Who changes, externally and internally? How?
- What action is necessary? How does it affect the characters' dress?

Step 2: Look at the scene-to-scene flow of the script.

- Look at the *overall arc* of the script—the key incidents that create the rising and falling action of the script. Identify the point at which the climax occurs.
- What scenes are pivotal to the action of the script?
- Where are the most important emotional moments for the characters? Where and how does the character change significantly over the course of the script? (Look at each principal player's *character arc*–the flow of significant changes that "move" a character.)
- How does the mood of the story change from scene to scene, and over the entire course of the script.

Step 3: Look at what drives the action.

- How can contrasts among characters add to the power of the action of the script? (Example: If the leading man in a fight scene looks more vulnerable than his rival, will the fight be more interesting?)
- What purpose does a character, or a scene, have in the script? Think like a screenwriter and ask if the story works without this character or this scene? (Example: In *Star Wars*, Luke Skywalker's gentle aunt mollifies his abrasive uncle. If the character of the aunt were cut from the script, would we lose a sense of the forces that formed Luke's character? Would we *feel* less when we saw the charred bodies of his aunt and uncle?)
- How can you sharpen the undertone of the scene to add power to the action? (Example: Would the actions of the scruffy, eccentric law office in *Erin Brockovich* feel more heroic if the law office of its rival were filled with power brokers in head-to-toe Armani?)

Step 4: Look at ways to heighten the emotional impact of the action on an audience.

- What are the human repercussions of the story? Even if the world of the script is exotic or foreign to you, can you understand how the characters work?
- To what degree is realism or authenticity a design issue? Is the world of the script a "known" world—one that has existed in an actual time and place, or does the world of the script have a core humanity but exist in fictional time?
- Does the world seem to have an additional dimension? Is it an ordinary world in which things seem slightly surreal—*American Beauty*, for example?
- Can you find a visual metaphor for the world of the script? (The world in the script has the slickness of a magazine layout, for example.)
- Does the world of the film remind you of the work of an artist or the art of a particular period? (The world of the script has the quiet desperation of an Andrew Wyeth painting, for example, or the raw, dark abandon of the Ash Can school of painters.)
- How can you employ costume style to create the strongest response to the dramatic situation? Would naturalism help the audience relate to the story, or does it need more romance or more " edge" in order to draw in the audience?
- Can you heighten the drama with color choices? (Can you shift the color palette from bright to subdued as the hero gets trapped, for example?)
- Can you use texture to underscore the mood or feel of the scene? (Example: Would the romantic feel of the script be helped by bathing the romantic leads in visually "touchable" fabrics, like chenille or velvet or soft cashmere or thick cable knit?

A design analysis case in point: **Pulp Fiction**

Before meeting with a director, a costume designer should be well on the way to having a design point of view about the script. Frequently, film directors will interview several designers for a job. Crucial to getting hired is your ability to express your "take" on the script in the first interview. Imagine yourself going for a preliminary design meeting with the writer-director Quentin Tarantino, for his film *Pulp Fiction* (1994). Find a copy of the screenplay (available on the Internet) and read it through as if you've never watched the movie. Then, think about the pressure Betsy Heimann, the film's costume designer, must have felt. With its cast of well-known actors, *Pulp Fiction* was a stylish second feature for Tarantino, and a comeback for actor John Travolta. The script is edgy and violent, a wild ride filled with gunplay, drugs, and low-lives. It is also very funny—full of characters with foibles and quirks, who operate in a sexy, violent, iconoclastic—but very human—world. Cutting back and forth between the script's multiple storylines, the narrative is fragmented, and reassembled in circular form, a nice structural metaphor for the world the characters live in: In *Pulp Fiction*, what goes around comes around.

As a result, the costume design for *Pulp Fiction* must have grit and edge, a flair for character eccentricities. Sometimes the characters are slick and hip, sometimes wildly vulnerable. Playing up these contrasts in the design of the costumes gives the film visual variety, and helps the audience focus on the singularity of each character. In an ironical spin on the two-dimensional characters one might expect in a film with this title, the characters in *Pulp Fiction* have real depth. Unexpected, revealing moments arise for each of them, and the tables turn on most of them; every one of the principal characters surprises you in some way. And the costume design for *Pulp Fiction* must take this into account.

Let's take a look at two of the characters, Vincent Vega (John Travolta) and Jules Winnfield (Samuel L. Jackson), two eccentric hit men who enjoy each other's company. Jules is a philosopher, and one scary son of a bitch. Vince is a little thick, but sexy, and he sure can dance. Both are cold-blooded killers. The description of them in the script mentions their old, dirty car, their cheap suits and long coats. Lower on the food chain than their fearsome boss, Marcellus, but higher than the struggling boxer Butch Coolidge, Vincent and Jules present a unified front to the world: cheap, but jazzily eccentric.

During the course of the movie, we see these characters in several contexts: cruising in their car; committing an all-in-a-day's work murder of some dumb college kids; doing hideous clean-up detail (wiping brains out of the car); teaching a thing or two to would-be robbers Honey Bunny and Pumpkin while winding down at Denny's. Early in the script, Vincent is assigned the dream date from hell, with his boss's "squeeze," Mia (Uma Thurman). But dining and dancing at Jackrabbit Slim's is nothing but a prelude to an overdose—a reversal of mood typical of the whiplash narrative. From beginning to end, the character arcs in *Pulp Fiction* inscribe a roller-coaster ride through a landscape of hipness and twisted power.

If you were preparing to design *Pulp Fiction*, one of the first things you'd have to do is decide on how "cheap" and how "hip" these characters should look. In the comparison to the college kids who will be their victims, Vincent and Jules are cool killers, who literally call the shots. As the script suggests, they enter the college kids' apartment a unified front: dark figures in cheap suits and coats. The more alike they look, the stronger the effect—a force to be reckoned with. (Costume designer Betsy Heimann gave them a hip, chip-on-the-shoulder look. The head-to-toe black suits, with unfashionably small lapels, make them weirdly sinister, with a comic twist—the Blues Brothers as hit men.) The college-kid victims could be adolescent yuppies or dweebs. Which they are matters less than acknowledging, in costume terms, that they've been caught off-guard. They should look very casual, very ordinary, not at all unified visually; maybe one of them in a very just-rolled-out-of-bed kind of outfit, another in frat boy or surf dude gear. Keeping their fashion flavors generic serves two purposes: (1) it will make the coordinated suits and coats on Vincent and Jules, as cheap and out of fashion as they are, look intentionally intimidating by comparison, and (2) ironically, but importantly, it will keep the college boys "types" (and maybe makes their murders a little less personal to the audience), while keeping Vincent and Jules individual.

By the time Vincent and Jules arrive at the very average suburban home of Bonnie and Jimmie, the tables have turned. We see the hit men climb out of their car, covered in head-to-toe gore. The more ordinary and normal Jimmie and his house, the more surreal and bizarre the two bloody hit men. The subtext of the scene? Vincent and Jules are fish out of water. What was hip is now repulsive. And their suits couldn't be more inappropriate for the task at hand—mucking blood and brains out of the back seat of their vehicle. In their suits, in this garage, doing this job, Vincent and Jules become the embodiment of cool cats who've lost their cool.

In contrast, we have Winston "the Wolf" Wolfe—the mob "clean-up man," played by Harvey Keitel, who arrives at Jimmie's and proceeds to order Vincent and Jules around. Design-wise, "The Wolf" needs to be the new definition of hip: The cool guy on top, the one who keeps his wits about him in the middle of a mess. With "The Wolf" around, you get to show how cheesy Vincent and Jules really are. Keitel's costume needs to be smooth, controlled. He could even be in a tux, courtesy of the party he came from—almost a James Bond bad guy. But Mr. Wolfe is no Bond villain, oh so slick and black-hearted, as we'll see when he "lets his hair down" with the tow truck girl. He needs to be slick, but not cartoon slick. You could play a slick look against a not-so-controlled hairstyle, or just contrast the costume with the actor's courtly, quiet demeanor. Sometimes, the costume helps "act" the message, and sometimes the actor, unassisted, sends the subtle character messages.

Vincent and Jules hit rock bottom when they're stuck wearing Jimmie's cast-off clothes. Subtext? They've become whipped dogs. The more embarrassing and unfashionable their outfits, the lower they sink. But before you go all-out making them look stupid, remember that the designer can't let them sink too low, because the outfits they leave Jimmie's in are the same outfits we'll see them in at Denny's, where they push around Honey Bunny (Amanda Plummer) and Pumpkin (Tim Roth). The more foolish an actor looks, the more pressure he feels to "conquer" his costume. In the Denny's scene, Samuel L. Jackson could probably conquer anything, but "Kiss Me Stupid" paraded across his T-shirt is going to be pretty distracting when he reads Tim Roth the riot act.

And then there's the Jackrabbit Slim scene. Vincent's date with Mia is a dangerous dream. She's a babe and a half, but the wife of his boss, Marcellus. She and Marcellus have more money, and more power, than anyone else we will see on screen. Vince knows that if he steps out of line with Mia, Marcellus will kill him. You can help supply danger to the scene by developing how good Mia looks, and how good she and Vince look *together*. In fact, the better Vincent and Mia look together, the more dangerous the situation. (In Betsy Heimann's design, Mia is not only gorgeous, she's a hip "bad girl"—Vincent's dream date.)

Rather than settle for "sexy and dangerous," director Tarantino adds one more twist to the Jackrabbit Slim's scene: He makes it playful. The set is a dimly lit "retro" diner, filled with fifties and sixties icons of sex and violent death. The surrealistic chic of the diner's design is an invitation to trouble. For a costume designer, this scene and the overdose scene that follows are costume bonanzas—they set the tone for the entire movie.

At the end of the day, as you refine your design point of view about the character Vincent, you will understand who he has to harmonize with, when he needs to look powerful, when he does not. You will identify the emotional arc of his character and develop guidelines for his image. After you do this for each character in the script, you're ready to go on to the next step in Phase 1 of the design process: getting in sync with the director on design decisions.

Preliminary conferencing with the director. The costume designer's first conference with the director is a test, to see if your views of the script match. It is a time to compare your feelings with the feelings of the director—feelings about the characters and the subtext of scenes. Most importantly, it is a meeting in which broad tonal guidelines are established for story and characters, guidelines that point toward the final style of the production. At its best, this initial conference is a true collaboration: Both designer and director bring ideas to the table—fresh ideas that illuminate the script. For the costume designer, it is a crucial step. If you have never worked together, it can feel like a blind date, the elusive goal of which is instinctual rapport, instant understanding. How hard a director is willing to work to establish this level of understanding varies widely from director to director, and has a lot to do with how comfortable he or she feels talking costume design, and how buried by other work he or she is. (The section below called *Phase 3: preliminary design* will explore guidelines for collaborations with directors; for advice on establishing rapport with a director, see the section on interview technique in Part 10, *Entering the Market.*)

Furthermore, this meeting will determine the direction of your costume research. You need to understand the director's intent when it comes to matters of design and casting, his or her perspective on principal characters, and the atmosphere of the different scenes. You need to reach an agreement with the director on the arc of the events in the script and the arcs of the principal characters. Once you have clarified the general character arcs and scene atmospheres with the director, you can proceed with detailed script notation and character breakdown work, in which the script is analyzed for, among other things, the functional demands made on garments by the action in the script and the aspects of design that need researching before specific design choices are made (a technique explained in detail in Part 5, *Breakdowns)*.

Phase 2: preliminary research, in which the designer does the preliminary character and costume research needed to start design development

Once you've got a handle on the direction of the design, you need to sort out the clothing options available within the limits established by the worlds of your characters and their stories. Throughout time, each society and each period has created a limited number of styles; these styles become the standard by which is determined what is fashionable, what is commonplace, and what is eccentric in a given time and place. Unless the world of the script is wholly imagined (science fiction or fantasy, for example), a costume designer must choose, from historical or contemporary styles, costume elements that best support the mood and tone of a story and the characters who populate it.

Your research into costume styles can follow two paths: (1) the path to a detailed understanding of a society's clothing practices; and (2) the path to "tonal" research (seeking the strongest way to express visually the mood and character qualities you want to support).

The path to understanding clothing practices. Look at the clothing details of the period, and the society, in which the script is set, then search for answers to the following questions:

- What clothing styles are available in the period presented in the script? What are the exact lines and shapes of clothing and accessories available to men, women, and children that are appropriate to the world of the script, and its characters? (For nineteen-fifties' businessmen, for example, which suit lapel styles where current at the time? For eighteen-nineties' cowboys, what style of jeans did they prefer?)
- What fabrics, colors, and textile prints were available in the period; which were preferred by the group represented in the script?
- What clothing details define the look of the period or group? (On women, for example, the exaggerated shoulder pads of the nineteen-eighties or the skimpy-cut, worn with chunky heels, in the nineteen-nineties.)
- What clothing shapes and accessories in the period are more classic, less period-specific? (A man's conservative white dress shirt, with a plain spread collar, for example, was cut in about the same way during the nineteen-twenties as it is today.)
- What undergarments were available in the period, and how do they affect the look of the garments? (To look right, a nineteen-fifties' gal needs a bullet bra, not a nineteen-nineties' Wonder bra.)
- Where would the characters have shopped for their clothing?
- How are the societal rules of dress defined for the different seasons and occasions indicated in the script? How is status defined by the group's clothing?
- What are the rules of dress for the characters' professions?
- Do any clothing items mentioned in the script merit special attention (e.g., an anorak for a winter scene)? Do their details require researching?
- Do historical characters, whose clothing needs researching, appear in the story?

Period or societal clothing research can proceed in a variety of ways. If you are doing a contemporary film, you may want to look in the stores and at the magazines that would appeal to the characters whose costumes you are researching. You could hit the streets and photograph members of the group that you are studying in the context of the world in which they live. You could also investigate local costume rental sources to see what they stock that is contemporary, and immediately available.

As noted above, if you are doing a period piece, you will need to investigate *historical references* and *period costume collections*, in order to understand clothing rules and dress detail. (For example, if you were the designer on *Pulp Fiction*, your period research might include costume images of the fifties' and sixties' icons seen at Jackrabbit Slim's, and Vietnam-era military uniform and insignia for Captain Koons in the 1972 flashback sequence.) Costume designer Durinda Wood suggests using a variety of sources for this kind of research, including libraries, bookstores, movies, the Internet, and costume houses. If your research time is very limited, you may want to use a professional research service, which will, for a price, track down different historical costume resources for you. Also valuable are some of the websites devoted to researching historical costumes including: www.milieux.com, www.shootingstarhistory.com, www.killeenroos.com/link/victoria.htm, or even www.reconstructinghistory.com. (Research services will be discussed in greater detail in Part 6, *Costume Budgets.*)

At libraries, bookstores, and costume rental houses, you will find a host of specialized costume history reference books, most of which fall into a couple of different categories:

- *General surveys* that can go from the ancient Greeks to the nineteen-nineties, and will give the basics and key details of what men and women wore, along with the social context. The best of these surveys has both photos of real garments and period portraiture, so you can get a sense of the original colors, textures, and shapes of the period without having the clothing redrawn by a modern illustrator, who may add his own sensibility to the designs. *Survey of Historic Costume: A History of Western Dress*, by Phyllis Tortora and Keith Eubank, is one of the best in the field, and one of the few costume survey books to actually cover the nineteen-nineties.

- *Specialized surveys* that cover a variety of periods, and topics like the history of undergarments, the history of swimwear, and the fashions of a decade. The individual volumes in the series *Fashions of a Decade* (each volume covering one decade, beginning with the nineteen-twenties and ending with the nineteen-nineties) are useful for a quick overview of key fashion trends and subcultures. The series *Everyday Fashions as Pictured in Sears Catalogs* (one volume per decade, from the teens through the fifties) is especially useful for the range of garment details it covers, from shoe styles to suits. *A History of Men's Fashion*, by Farid Chenoune, will give you a good look at nineteenth- and twentieth-century tailoring styles, in addition to solid information on fashion trends and icons in each decade, up to the mid-nineteen-nineties. For a good wallow in the glories of the old Hollywood's glamour factory, look at *Those Glorious Glamour Years: Classic Hollywood Costume Design of the 1930's*, by Margaret J. Bailey. Particularly helpful in the "specialized surveys" category are the volumes on specialized military dress like *World Army Uniforms Since 1939*, by Andrew Mollo and Digby Smith.

- *Period costume construction and tailoring books*, which offer detailed studies of a range of period men's and women's garments. The best books in this category are drawn from detailed studies of period garments, among them, Norah Waugh's *The Cut of Women's Clothes, 1600-1930* and *The Cut of Men's Clothes, 1600-1900*, and Janet Arnold's *Patterns of*

Fashion: The Cut and Construction of Clothes for Men and Women c. 1560-1620. Other books in this category are written by expert theatrical drapers, for example, *Period Costume for Stage and Screen: Patterns for Women's Dress, 1500-1800,* and its companion volume, *Period Costume for Stage and Screen: Patterns for Women's Dress, 1800-1909,* both by Jean Hunnisett. These books are fabulous for historical recreations, and often give detailed explanations of foundation pieces and the layering used with these undergarments.

• *Books on different fashion designers and books that are developed from costume exhibits* are particularly good because they flood you with photographs of the real garments. There are wonderful books out on individual designers, among them, Armani, Balenciaga, Chanel, Dior, Galliano, Charles James, Thierry Mugler, Versace, and Vionnet, that really show the garments in detail.

• *Film books that have stills from many different films* (*The Films of the Thirties,* by Jerry Vermilye and Judith Crist, for example, or *Films of Bette Davis,* by Gene Ringgold). Books like this can give you a host of details on the costumes of different periods. Just remember that film costumes are always an interpretation by a designer, so use discretion when relying on them for historical accuracy.

While costume reference books are extremely helpful, a greater range of costume options can be found by going through *original period magazines, fashion journals,* and *portraiture* and *photography sources,* as we noted above. Many of the fashion-history reference books are good at giving bibliographic information on period magazines, and advice on where to continue researching a period.

Period costume collections (available at either costume rental houses or through museums and stores specializing in period garments) are the best places to visit if you want to understand the look of a period. Here you can get a very tactile sense of the fabric and trim details, as well as a full-scale understanding of the proportions of a garment and the scale of an accessory. Some of the most famous period collections in the country include the Costume Institute at the Metropolitan Museum, in New York; the Museum at the Fashion Institute of Technology, in New York; the Fashion Institute of Design and Merchandising Museum Foundation, in Los Angeles; and the Kent State University Museum costume collection, in Kent, Ohio. There are many other period and ethnic costume collections around the country, and many costume rental houses in New York and Los Angeles have authentic period garments in their stocks. To research the range and variety of these resources, you can use *Shopping LA: The Insiders' Sourcebook for Film & Fashion* or the *Entertainment Industry Directory.*

> CRC [Costume Rental Corporation] has a pretty extensive library, but even with a library, sometimes, you're really at the whim of who is on staff. At Eastern Costume and Warner Bros.' costume department, there are people on staff who know the resources. You can call on those people and pick their brains. It might take you ten hours to look up some sniggling detail, but the staff expert says, "Go to this book, look in this chapter, and you can find it."
>
> At CRC, you can only get access to the books when an employee is with you. The staff member will help you find something, or you can look for yourself. And, they'll make the photocopies for you. Eastern is more self-service, but they are also very helpful at finding something when you can't find it. (*Jaci Rohr, costume supervisor*)

If you've run through every available magazine and all the above sources, with disappointing results, or if you are designing for a contemporary subculture, researching on the Internet may be your best bet. A wide variety of "below-the-research-radar" groups, from bikers to psychobillies, have developed websites where you can get information on specialized costumes. The Internet also has a number of fashion history and costume reference sites, specializing in everything from sports gear to nineteen-fifties' collectibles.

Films, from 1912 to the present, are among the best costume research sources available. On film, you can see how a garment really "hangs"—assuming that the designer used contemporary fashions of the time. Videotapes and DVDs of period television shows, from the nineteen-fifties forward, are also rich sources for costume research. Movies and television shows made in the past, whether their subjects are historical or not, can be fabulous research sources. Just remember the proviso we mentioned above: that film costumes are always an interpretation by a designer, so use discretion when relying on them for historical accuracy.

Durinda Wood suggests two other sources for costume research: other costume designers and filmmakers, and the denizens of locations where shooting will take place. Other costume designers and filmmakers can, themselves, be experts on rules of dress, or may lead you to costume research sources that you might have missed. Talking to these experts can save you hours of research. Because films often shoot on locations where the script's real-life counterparts live, you can do costume research where the shooting will take place. By visiting a location during the preliminary design phase, and photographing its denizens, you will get a first-hand sense of what the people in this world really wear, and how they wear it (if, of course, your piece is contemporary). Even if you are working on a period piece, being in the landscape inhabited by your characters may lead you to discover colors and textures that may influence the palette of your designs.

The path to "tonal" research. In addition to researching correct clothing styles and detail, you also need to imagine ways of interpreting and presenting this research to the director and, ultimately, to the audience. The nature of the research that leads a designer to the kinds of interpretations that make costume design an art is more in the way of imaginative juxtaposition. Doing "tonal" research is really a matter of finding sources that can help a designer develop the "tone" of the piece— the pattern of images that will resonate with meaning, create a mood, and support the emotional underpinnings of the characters and their story.

This kind of "tonal" research can be done by finding images in documentary sources, as well as paintings and magazines that are not limited to a particular period but which convey a strong sense of a character in the script. You can also look at paintings, photographs, and other works of art that convey a strong sense of mood through color, texture, or imagery. By combine photographic images, color chips, and fabric swatches in your presentation to the director, you will be able to evoke your vision of the mood and feel of the design. For an example of this, look at designer Hope Hanafin's research board for a character called the Blue Fairy (fig. 4.1). It includes Xeroxes of paintings and photographs of the period (mid-nineteenth century), a Bette Davis film still, a photograph of a tutu from a costume collection, and Xeroxes of paintings from

FIG. 4.1

Research board
by Hope Hanafin

the Renaissance. All of these images inspired her preliminary rough sketch of the character. The combining of a sketch and research materials helps convey both the literal costume details and the more atmospheric tone—the feeling she wished her design to express. (For more on presentations, see below, *Phase 3: preliminary design,* "Preparing for conferences—preliminary design and research presentations.")

Phase 3: preliminary design, in which a designer does rough costume designs; collaborates with key members of the creative team; develops presentations of costume research and preliminary designs; and clarifies production details that may affect the costumes

Designing in sync with the filmmaking process. The next phase of the costume design process is conferencing with other members of the production's creative team. In doing so, you'll be proving to the director that you are on the right track for the look of the characters. You'll also be gathering information from the principal actors and the heads of the camera, lighting, and art departments, in order to make sure that you are in sync with their approaches to the script. At this point in the process, you are still gathering information that will shape your final design choices.

For the costume designer, getting a handle on a production's aesthetic guidelines is the tough part. Conferencing is often on the fly, sometimes nonexistent, and the amount of creative control a costume designer has can be very limited. Creative collaborations can be hellacious or divine or both, but the ability to collaborate constructively is key to building a career in film costume design. Remember, it's not just about you and your choices. As we discussed in Part 2, you must look at the costumes you design in the context of the whole filmmaking process: You must design the clothes to enhance the actor's performance; you must design for the way the camera reveals both the character and the story; you must design costumes for characters in the context of sets and lighting; you must design for the exigencies of the production process. An audience should be caught up in the story and its characters, not in your designs. Hence, design goal number one:

THE AUDIENCE MUST NOT NOTICE THE COSTUMES.

You must also design costumes that take into consideration the demands of the shooting schedule and other practical aspects of a production. If you can see your work in the context of the entire filmmaking process, you'll be able to deal more easily with the demands made on you every day of the shoot. If you don't, the work will drive you crazy. Unless you really love the process and understand the demands it makes, there is just too much shit that regularly hits the fan—and too little appreciation for what a costume designer does—to make sticking with it worthwhile. Thus, design goal number two:

DESIGN COSTUMES PERFECTLY IN TUNE WITH
THE SHOOTING PROCESS.

When you have achieved these goals, you are in sync with the production process.

Preparing for conferences—preliminary design and research presentations. To get the maximum value out of conferences with your collaborators, you must develop preliminary design and research presentations that create a crystal clear view of your design guidelines for characters and extras ("atmosphere"). To build good artistic rapport with your collaborators, these presentations must allow for interaction, and some changes in the design.

> You must be strong in your vision, and flexible in your details. *(Catherine Adair, costume designer)*

Costume designers create different kinds of preliminary design presentations. A costume presentation made to a director, or to other creative department heads, must strongly express the personality of the characters whose costumes you are presenting, and the mood or tone of the scene in which the costume appears. In preliminary design presentations, especially to a director, your presentations need to be uncluttered and as visually compelling as possible. Quaint fashion illustrations, or dull research details that do not create a "life" for the character, are detrimental to the presentation process. You should be able to remove or rearrange all sketches and research materials right before the director's eyes, to provide an instant picture of the changes he or she suggests.

The only danger in working with research presentations is that you and your collaborators may get wedded to a look that is either cost-prohibitive or not available through local costume resources. When you show research to your collaborators, you had better have a good sense that you can deliver the look on schedule, and on budget.

There are a number of different approaches to presenting character options and scene atmospheres, among them, *research books* and *research folders, rough sketches. research boards, tearsheets,* and *color boards.*

FIG. 4.2

Designs by Dan Lester for *Spawn*(1997)

Dan Lester's clown cheerleader options play with different levels of distress, different team logos, and different shoe options.

Design options for John Leguizamo

Illustrations courtesy of Dan Lester

• *Research books* and *research folders* are composed of research photographs and materials assembled in a ring binder or folder. The research book or research folder is easy to flip through and edit, but never has quite the same panoramic impact as carefully arranged research boards (see below).

• *Rough sketches* provide clear views of different options for a character. Rough sketches become particularly important when photographic research does not capture the flavor or style of a character. They can be vital for sci-fi production presentations, in which you need to create brand-new worlds. Look at the examples of designer Dan Lester's rough color sketches for levels of costume distressing and optional shoe choices for Clown, the demonic cheerleader in *Spawn*, played by John Leguizamo (fig. 4.2).

• *Research boards* and *tearsheets* are presentations composed of Xeroxes and photos carefully arranged on posterboard or presentation paper to reflect an individual character's costume options or the design scene for extras in a scene. For conferencing purposes, research boards and tearsheets have the advantage of showing the tone of a scene at a glance. And, research boards and tearsheets have a strong visual impact. They can, however, can be difficult to edit, unless the images are glue-tacked or pinned to the board.

In his research boards for *Spawn*, designer Dan Lester manipulates photographs and Xeroxes of costume research to materialize his vision of two contrasting crowd scenes that include a range of "character" extras (fig. 4.3). Eduardo Castro, in his research board for the character Roemello Skuggs in *Sugar Hill*, creates a spare, compelling vision for the character by displaying a very small number costume options in a dramatic, moody composition (fig. 4.4).

FIG. 4.3

Dan Lester's research is manipulated to create two contrasting crowd scenes in *Spawn*—"The Alley" (below) and "The Party" (left). He uses cut-and-paste techniques to create a range of characters that flesh in these atmospheres.

Tearsheets by Dan Lester for *Spawn* (1997)

FIG. 4.4

Eduardo Castro's tear sheets for Roemello in *Sugar Hill* (1994) create spare, striking compositions.

Rough sketches may be incorporated in research boards (as you saw in fig. 4.1, Hope Hanafin's research board for the "Blue Fairy"). So can *collages*. Using a computer, a scanner, a digitizing pad, and computer programs like Photoshop, you can easily manipulate pieces of Xeroxed research, changing scale and layering and artfully juxtaposing images (fig. 4.5).

• *Color boards* (also called "palette boards") are panoramic displays of images and samples intended to present the color palette for a scene or scenes, or for the world of the film. They are vital for presentations to the heads of camera, lighting, and art departments. In the color board in fig. C.5, Hope Hanafin draws on a wide variety of resources—costume history books, historical photography books, period paintings and photographs—for images of authentic period garments. She combines Xeroxes of these images with fabric swatches and paint chips, to clarify the color guidelines for the world of the script. In the color board in fig. C.3, for the HBO film *Vendetta* (1999), Hanafin combines photographs and fabric swatches to present palettes at a glance for a series of scenes.

Design collaboration guidelines

Once you have developed your preliminary design presentations on the characters and the atmosphere in a script, you are ready for conferences with your creative collaborators. Understanding the working agendas of your collaborators, and the pressures under which they are working, can be complicated. Personal neuroses, power trips, and secret agendas abound. In order to possess even a modicum of autonomy in the design process, you must learn to develop techniques for getting the information you need and gaining the trust of your colleagues.

FIG. 4.5

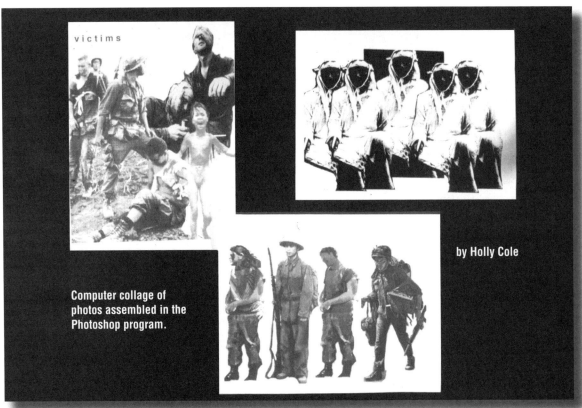

victims

Computer collage of photos assembled in the Photoshop program.

by Holly Cole

The better my communication, the more flexible I am, the more I make myself available, the more I end up with what I thought I was going to end up with on film. (Catherine Adair, costume designer)

Consider the following strategies for collaborating with producers, directors, production designers and art directors, directors of photography, the hair and makeup department, and actors.

• COLLABORATING WITH PRODUCERS. Producers must weigh the cost of artistry against a film's potential box office and acceptable profit margins. Producers can have great artistic vision, but they can also be stingy, self-serving bastards. Often, their priorities go to casting first, cinematography second, location and art direction third, makeup and hair fourth, and costumes last. Producers negotiate budget cuts that notoriously whittle away the costume budget before production even begins. Designers must be prepared, in a presentation, to focus on the practicality of the costume design, and not just its artistry. Many designers combine design concepts and budget projections in presentations to the producer, supporting arguments for design choices with arguments based on cost.

The producer's version of the costume budget is usually a good indication of what that producer knows about costuming. Does the producer's budget allow only for basic wardrobe costs—bargain-basement rentals and purchases, minimal services, supplies, equipment, and costume multiples? Is there any room for higher-quality goods or services like made-to-order work? Is there money budgeted to deal realistically with prep crunch, enough to pay crew to maintain the look during production? Can you get beyond survival mode and have some room for artistry?

Money in the bank is not the only way of upping the standards of a production. Many producers love (and depend upon) the use of *product placement.* In the world of costume design for film, this means designer-label or famous-brand clothing that is loaned, or given to, a production in exchange for screen credit. Thousands of dollars can be saved this way, and the designer goods can make cheap productions look much more expensive.

Costume designers tend to be of two minds about using these goods. While designer-label goods can create a quality look, they need to be used carefully. Armani, for example, doesn't work on everyone equally well. Some bodies look better in a particular designer's clothes than others. Actors can resent being forced to wear a particular brand or label, putting the designer in a difficult position. Sometimes a struggle ensues when a producer pressures a designer to use promo goods that are inappropriate to a character. No off-the-rack item gives a designer the design freedom that custom-made work can, and some designers resent the lack of freedom to design the costumes themselves.

The common use of shopped goods and product placement in the industry has created a legion of producers with an "off-the-rack" mentality. Unlike the producers of the nineteen-thirties, many of whom came from a garment industry background, most of today's producers don't understand the artistic value of a custom-made suit or dress, or why made-to-order work costs so much. Many producers really don't understand the basic garment development process; they don't understand the hours of craftsmanship it takes to make that Armani suit, nor do they understand that couture labor costs are spread out over the mass-market line the company puts out. Some producers—especially those with a background in television—need to be educated, not only on the subject of why fittings are necessary, but in the very basics of what a film costume designer does. Costume designer Madeline Kozlowski remembers working on a television series called *Battle Dome* (1999-2000):

> It was interesting working with producers who were TV-oriented—teaching them how to deal with a designer who does sketches. Often, producers supervise sitcoms, where they come in and say, "Okay, let's see the outfits you've got." For *Battle Dome*, I did tearsheets and designs, and they learned to deal with designs and appreciate them. They came up to me and said, "This is amazing; we've never done this before. Look at our characters, who look just like your drawings." I took a job teaching costume design at the University of California, Irvine, because I got tired of training producers.

When it comes to getting crucial production information, some producers don't know what a costume designer needs, so you need to seek them out and tell them. Kozlowski continues,

> I designed a made-for-television movie called *The Tower* (1993). Nobody told me there was going to be blue screen for a sequence in which an actor falls down the stairs. Now, I'm really good about reading everything in a script, and all production memos. Nowhere did anyone mention blue screen. Two days before shooting, I happened to overhear the producer and the DP discussing blue screen. I said, "Are you saying we're doing blue screen?" The producer said, "Yeah." I had a blue patterned shirt for my actor. I said, "You needed to tell me that. He can't wear the blue shirt." The producer said, "I'm sorry; I had no idea it had anything to do with costumes." How can you be a producer and not know that this is going to impact us? So three days before the shoot, I'm out running around for shirts.

A designer also needs to be savvy about elements of a production that can generate income.

> Two-thirds of the way through prep, on a large period show full of rustic peasants, the studio executive declared, "No brown allowed." I suspect his rule was more about the appeal of merchandise tie-ins than the actual show. *(Hope Hanafin, costume designer)*

Of course, many producers do understand the high cost of costume design and its onscreen pay-off, and they budget appropriately. If the budget is tight but they want quality, they may be willing to help you by scheduling a longer prep time or more fittings with the actors, or by limiting the number of extras (or their range of sizes) to what works for the costume department. Whatever their level of understanding, producers have the right to final approval of the designs.

> The big difference between television and film is that film is a director's medium and television is a producer's medium. Television is really where it's a little tougher, because you're dealing with two or three producers. And episodic television is different from sitcom television: Episodic is like doing a little film every week; a sitcom is more like theater, because you're rehearsing on stage, and it's like you're building up to one night. *(Eduardo Castro, costume designer)*

The degree to which producers want to be "hands on" in the creative process varies greatly from producer to producer, medium to medium, format to format, and production to production. Some producers review everything, at many points in the process. Others wait to voice their opinions when they get to the set. Because producers can be both a real pain and a source of future employment, costume designers cultivate relationships with them early in the process. Depending upon availability, and their interest in costuming, a designer may try to get producers to review and approve sketches, photoboards, and/or wardrobe racks, in an effort to get design approval *before* the shooting starts.

• COLLABORATING WITH DIRECTORS. Directors come from all kinds of backgrounds—from writing, from performing, from the camera department, from theater. In film, one of the primary responsibilities of the director is to pick the production's design team, and to direct the look of the production. Some have formal training in design, but there are many more who do not understand costume design, or the process of costume development.

Although theatrically trained directors may be comfortable collaborating with the costume designer, directors who come straight out of film can be acutely uncomfortable talking about clothes, or responding to costume sketches. Even though film is a visual medium, many directors are not able to look at a sketch or a rack of clothes and imagine the actor wearing the costume. They may even be uncomfortable when the clothing is shown to them arranged on a dress dummy. Many need to see the actor in the garment to know if they like it. They need the clothing to be "inhabited": Seeing it on a hanger or a dress dummy just doesn't hack it. And if the costume doesn't work for them on the actor, they want the costume designer to change it quickly.

> Most directors don't want to see the clothes, they want to see the characters. *(Cynthia Hamilton, assistant costume designer)*

Directors' schedules are so over-loaded, the demands on them so great, that their very last priority may be the costumes. Often, they'll want only minimal contact with the costume designer. The bottom line? Assume the director has little time to focus on wardrobe. You'll be lucky if you get two detailed design conversations with the director during prep. In Durinda Wood's step-by-step outline of costume design procedure, she lists three conversations with the director, including the job interview. (For a detailed version of Durinda's step-by-step outline, see fig. 4.6.) Another designer told me that on one major feature she worked on, she got *one* phone conversation with her famous director before shooting began on location.

In all events, you must be able to shape the design process to fit the needs of the director—what he or she needs to hear and see before shooting begins. Will he or she look at costume research or sketches or palette boards? Would he or she like to see the racks of clothes? Does the director want to be in on the fittings? If so, which ones? Many times you will have to work without much help from the director, going largely on instinct, and hoping it all flies when you get to set.

> I will always hire a costume designer who is happy doing the job, has a lot of talent, and makes you look good—someone who will put time and heart into the project. I am much more involved in other areas. The thing is to make sure that no characters are dressed like I am: I have no fashion sense. *(Miguel Arteta, director of* The Good Girl *and* Chuck & Buck*)*

FIG. 4.6

DURINDA WOOD'S COSTUME DESIGN PROCEDURE FOR A FILM

To prepare to design a film, you need an overall sense of the script-to-shoot process that costume designers go through. Emmy award-winning costume designer Durinda Wood suggests the following procedure for designing a film.

- **Phase 1, *design analysis***
    1. Read the script straight through the first time, making only a few notes.
    2. Hold preliminary discussion with the director. (Many times this is the job interview.)
    3. Break down the script
        a. Read the script again. The script is your blueprint.
            1) Mark it to separate principals, supporting, characters, and extras.
            2) Number days and nights.
            3) Underline character descriptions.
            4) Make notes about action
        b. Make a day/night schedule, to track the passage of time in the script; discuss this with the script supervisor and the director.
        c. Make a character breakdown chart [see Part 5, *Breakdowns*] for
            1) Principals
            2) Supporting characters
            3) Extras

- **Phase 2, *preliminary research***
    1. Make a research list.
    2. Make a prop list.
    3. Make a stunt breakdown.
    4. Make an extras breakdown.
    5. Make lists of questions for all departments, i.e., for the AD (assistant director), DP (director of photography), art director, etc.
    6. Research and Xerox, using
        a. Libraries and bookstores;
        b. Research agencies;
        c. Movies;
        d. Internet;
        e. Other costume designers and filmmakers;
        f. Locations where shooting will take place;
        g. Costume houses.

- **Phase 3, *preliminary design***
    1. Talk concept and exchange questions and ideas with visual departments, including
        a. Art department (look at drawings, locations, and storyboards);
        b. Set decoration;
        c. Director of photography;
        d. Prop department (go over prop list);
        e. Hair and makeup (if on-board).
    2. Develop preliminary designs and presentations (quick sketch and collage, etc.).

- **Phase 4, *design***
    1. Design costumes
        a. Do renderings
        b. Hire illustrators
        c. Swatch fabric
    2. Final design meeting with the director and/or producer(s)
        a. Show research
        b. Show designs
        c. Show samples
        d. Ask all questions that you have

- **Phase 5, *prep*, in which most of the film's wardrobe is assembled and prepared for approval and shooting**
    1. Make a budget, and meet with unit production manager and/or producers.
    2. Set up and hire the costume department.
    3. Meet with actors (many times by phone and fax).
        a. Discuss character.
        b. Show research.
        c. See them, if possible, and get measurements.
        d. Try on a few samples, to get ideas.
    4. Show designs to all visual departments (same procedure as in Phase 3)
    5. Talk logistics and exchange questions with production departments, including
        a. Assistant director (shooting schedule and day out of days)
        b. Stunt coordinator (go over stunt breakdown)
        c. Choreographer
        d. Special effects (blue screen, etc.)
    6. Gather costumes
        a. Made-to-order
        b. Rentals
        c. Purchases
        d. Product placements
    7. Fittings
    8. Alter, age, dye costumes
    9. Have meetings with logistical departments, same as above, plus the following:
        a. Extras casting (show them how you want extras to look)
        b. Locations (facilities, etc.)
        c. Wranglers and animal handlers
        d. Sound department
        e. Transportation department
    10. Outfit and load wardrobe trailer; set up on-location wardrobe department.

- **Phase 6, *the shoot*. Final refinements are made to the designs before being committed to film, and additional wardrobe is delivered according to shooting schedule deadlines.**

- **Phase 7, *final wrap*. The costumes are returned, if appropriate, and held or stored for additional footage and re-shoots that may be required after completion of principal photography (the footage shot during the original production shooting schedule). The designer may already be off payroll by the time final wrap is under way.**

Designers can do two things to help smooth the way to design approval: research the director's taste and get in sync with the rest of the creative staff on the production. With uncommunicative directors, you can look at their former films for a sense of their style and the subtlety of interpretation of which they are capable. Has the director used stylish costumes before or do sets and costumes tend to be neutral, while camera and lighting supply most of the visual mood and emotion? Does this director use a lot of atmospheric shots? What about a controlled palette? By conferencing with the actors, the art department, the director of photography, and the prop and set decoration departments, you can flesh out your understanding of the director's vision for the production, and build important production allies.

To take maximum advantage of your conference time with a director:

•   Prioritize the information you need from the director. What are the questions that only the director can answer? For example: What are the director's reasons for doing the film? What about the project compels the director? What is the director's "take" on the events and characters in the script? Does the director intend to use special effects? Where?

•   Talk with the principal actors to get information on the character guidelines the director has given them.

•   Work with the script supervisor to establish the passage of time in the script. Because the script supervisor must track day/night changes and continuity of action on the set, he or she and the director will be in close contact. Questions of when a character changes costume and why are critical for the costume designer, whose understanding of these matters must conform to those of the director and the script supervisor in order to avoid serious problems on set, and in the edit.

•   Make use of other members of the creative team to get information on the guidelines a director has established for the "look" of various scenes, and on the latest creative developments. Keep in touch, throughout the process, with the production designer, the art director, the set dressing department, the prop department, the director of photography, and the special effects department. The art director will be able to describe the shape of the spaces, the colors and textures of the seedy biker bar being designed for a scene, the set dressing department will tell you the character and tone of the posters and bar decorations, and the cinematographer will let you know if there will be lots of moody neon lights and smoke.

•   Pick the brains of other production team members for details on casting, shooting conditions, schedules, and other developments throughout prep and shoot. Keep in touch throughout the process with the first assistant director, the casting department, the stunt coordinator, and the locations department.

• COLLABORATING WITH PRODUCTION DESIGNERS AND ART DIRECTORS. The production designer and the art director are people you need in your camp. The art department is responsible for the creation of the sets and the transformation of locations on a production. The art department is headed by an *art director*, who directs the set designers (draftsmen), model builders, sketch artists, carpenters, plasterers, scenic artists, plumbers, and other department crew in the creation of sets for a production. The *set decoration department* is responsible for all the set dressing (the furniture, rugs, practical lighting fixtures, and all utilitarian and decorative objects, with the exception of objects principally handled by the actors). The *prop department* is responsible for all the hand props (objects handled by the actors, including cigarettes, watches, glasses, briefcases, food, etc.). While set decorators and prop masters consult with the art director, all three departments—art department, set decoration department, and prop department—fall under the direct supervision of the *production designer.*

The production designer is responsible for the overall look of the physical production and, as a result, has creative control not only over the work of the art department, set decoration, and props, but over the costume, hair, and makeup departments. The production designer's principal task is to conceive and direct the design and dressing of all exterior and interior sets. The production designer's interest in a production's costumes centers on matters of overall style and palette, rather than the inner workings of the department.

The production designer has the right to direct or approve your palettes for color and texture, and may take a strong interest in your interpretation of characters. The camera heightens the tactile quality of the details we see on screen—the creamy cheek of the leading lady, the drape of the Armani jacket, the satiny glow of the rosewood desk. As a result of the production designer's dominant vision and careful supervision, a costume designer and an art director can produce powerful images that are in sync.

Supervisory styles vary widely among production designers. Some are more "hands on" than others. If you are designing the costumes, cultivate a relationship with the production designer early, so that your design ideas can get heard before an overall look for the film is set in stone. Color boards, fabric swatches, sketches, and character paste-up boards are visual aids that can help you in this endeavor. Production designers and art directors are busy people, so they may not take the time or trouble to duplicate pictures of the sets for you. Their design processes, like yours, can be developmental—concepts can shift, locations can dictate colors and textures, set dressing can get improvised. One art director referred to the hectic pace of set building as "triage." As a costume designer, it is up to you to seek the information you need to stay in sync with the filmmaking process.

• **COLLABORATING WITH CINEMATOGRAPHERS.** Whether your wardrobe gets seen on screen, and how it is seen, is up to the *cinematographer* (also known as the *director of photography* or *DP)*—the head of the camera and lighting departments. The DP wields tremendous power during production. The choice of film stock, lenses, and framing all affect your work enormously. Some cinematographers are great craftsmen, with a talent for choosing the best lighting, lens, and framing for each shot. Some are true artists, who bring an emotional depth to their work that goes way beyond craft.

You should seek out and watch as much film as possible shot by each cinematographer with whom you will work. When you look at a cinematographer's work, look at the use of color and the use of light and shadow. Does this DP often backlight or sidelight? How well are the details of dark clothing revealed in a dark world, or in a world flooded with light? Are particular colors avoided?

Film stock, film processing, and the cinematographer's dictates on color palette have the greatest impact on you as a costume designer. A really good cinematographer can shoot any color, but some colors may create problems that take a good deal of setup time to solve, time that may not be available. Primary colors take more time to light. The *reflected glow* from a garment—the colored light that is the reflection produced by a highly saturated color hit by intense light—can cause problems on faces in close-ups and medium close-ups, especially if the color is unflattering or distracting (e.g., a reflected glow of neon green or canary yellow). Strong *color value contrasts* (e.g., black and white, forest green and bright yellow) in a scene are a problem for getting visual details balanced. Have you ever shot a photograph of someone in a dark garment, then discover when you looked at a print that the garment had lost its detail? Have you had colors shift in the processing? It can take some tricky lighting and camera setups to get the film stock to work equally well across a broad palette or color-value range.

Get color palette approval from the cinematographer. If you don't, you may find yourself redesigning on the set, or worse, getting screwed by color distortions that occur during film processing. If color accuracy is a major concern, try having a *palette test* done. In a palette test, the director of photography will shoot and process a small amount of film footage of the garments or fabrics that represent the costume color palette for the production. These days, there is rarely time to shoot real *wardrobe tests*—footage of the actors dressed in their wardrobe options.

A cinematographer will always shoot according to the dictates of the director, and with an eye to getting on film the maximum emotional impact of the moment. This means that occasionally you may have key wardrobe you love that never really gets seen on screen. This is part of the business of filmmaking: You have to take it in stride, for the good of the whole. Concentrate on the collaborative process. By establishing a strong rapport with the cinematographer, you may avoid the wholesale disregard for costumes that is an Achilles' heel for many designers. Show you care about the cinematographer's work and, with luck, he or she will care about yours. (For more on this subject, see *Conversation Three: On Working with the Cinematographer and Collaborating with Actors in Film, with Catherine Adair*, at the end of this part.)

• **COLLABORATING WITH HAIR AND MAKEUP.** The costume department is only one part of the departmental team that works to get the actors to look right. Hair and makeup will have its own point of view on character design. Hair and make up departments regularly work miracles. When a star's hair or makeup looks bad, the entertainment press has a field day, so productions often enroll in the just-make-sure-she-looks-good school of design. But "looking good" and "looking right" are not always synonymous, and costume designers and hair and makeup artists often do battle on the subject. Unless your director has established the costume designer's authority over the hair and makeup department before shooting begins, expect your control over the total look to be nil.

> For an actress, the three most important departments are hairdressing, makeup, and costumes, in that order. *(Irene Sharaff, costume designer,* The Best Years of Our Lives, The King and I, Who's Afraid of Virginia Woolf?, *and* Hello, Dolly, *among many others)*

There are many hair and makeup designers who do an exquisite job of developing appropriate looks for the characters that still flatter the actors. But there are too many examples in television and film of poor hair and makeup design: Characters in distress will have lips freshly rouged, no streaked mascara, and glamorized hairstyles that behave, under duress, less like real hair than like synthetic wigs. Then there's the period project, with historically accurate costumes but overtly modern, or patently odd, hairstyles. This is a problem for the costume designer who strives for period authenticity, extreme realism, or simply a visual unity in the look of the character.

So, whether you simply voice your opinions to your colleagues or do meticulous sketches of hairstyle and makeup ideas, as Jean-Pierre Dorléac did for the television movie *A Burning Passion: The Margaret Mitchell Story* and the independent feature *Walking to the Waterline* (fig. 4.7), remember this: The costume designer controls only the design of the character's clothing, not their total "look." Try to make friends with the hair and makeup department by sharing your research and soliciting their ideas about the characters. Try to see some of their previous design work, and comment on what you liked. Be sensitive to their needs. The color of a costume plays a major role in the selection of the hair and makeup color palette, so provide them with costume color boards that help their work. When transforming an actor into a character, hair color can be a particularly delicate issue. If tricky hair color problems arise, work with the hair designer. Provide copies of your sketches or fitting Polaroids so that he or she will know what they'll be working with. Work hard to agree on character interpretations. If push comes to shove, get the actor on your side and you might get the look you want.

• **COLLABORATING WITH ACTORS.** A costume designer's collaboration with an actor takes place in several phases: during preliminary conferences (frequently over the

FIG. 4.7

Jean-Pierre Dorléac's designs for an elaborate period hairstyle for *The Margaret Mitchell Story* (right) and a simple style for *Walking to the Waterline* (left) may only serve as guidelines for his discussion with the hair and makeup departments. Too often a costume designer has very little design control when it comes to a character's final hairstyle.

telephone); in fittings, and on the set during production. While Part 7 is devoted to costume prep (exploring in detail the collaboration between designer and actor that takes place during fittings), the present section will concentrate on the general shape of the costume designer's working relationship with actors.

As noted in Part 2 (*Fundamentals of Costume Design for Film*), costume designers base the amount of time and effort they can spend on an actor's costumes on two basic factors: (1) the actor's "star" status, and (2) the actor's *screen time*—that is, the amount of time an actor will appear on screen, based on the prominence of his or her character in the script. Stars, principal players, and day players (actors whose characters are important to the story, but whose screen time is short)—all must be courted by the costume designer, their design preferences and character ideas incorporated into the final design of their costumes. Extras are accommodated for comfort, when possible, but have no conceptual say in the design.

The costume designer must strive to win the trust of the principal players. Movie actors really know what they look like on the screen: They study it—and they have the power to do what they think they need to do in order to protect themselves. A featured actor must be comfortable in what you give him to wear or his discomfort will read ten times life-size on the screen. Speaking of her designer on *Charade, Breakfast at Tiffany's, Funny Face, Sabrina,* and half a dozen other films, actress Audrey Hepburn said, "[Hubert de] Givenchy's creations gave me the knowledge that I looked absolutely right. Givenchy's outfits gave me protection against strange situations and people because I felt good in them." Making the actor feel good is what it's all about.

With stars, you must contend with their public image. Stars are in a consummately vulnerable position on screen. Their hairlines, weight, muscle tone, sense of style, and other evidence of mortality are picked over by millions of fans and hundreds of critics. Stars have the right to opinions about what they look like on screen because they are going to have to live with any risks you take with their public image. And they've all known fashion disaster—and seen it replayed, *ad nauseum,* on forty-foot, and thirty-four-inch, screens.

> They've all been screwed along the line—or think they've been. *(Catherine Adair, costume designer)*

Beginning a collaboration with a principal player can be an uncomfortable business: Each actor you work with will need to be reassured quickly that the two of you are in sync. Often, your first conversation with an actor is your most important, and only, opportunity to gain that actor's confidence.

> I take the role of big sister, a caring partner who wants the best for them. I try to appeal to the actor in them, their character sense. *(Hope Hanafin, costume designer)*

The designer's understanding of a character evolves during the costume design process. To deepen that understanding, a designer should tap into the actor's ideas about the character. Talk about any "real world" counterparts to the character, and about the environment in which the character lives; ask the actor to imagine the places his or her character shops, the care he or she takes in appearance, and the eccentricities he or she might have. Discuss how the character evolves in the script, and how the costume changes can support the arc of the character. Impress the actor with how carefully you've thought about the character. Share your costume research with them. Embellish the character's costumes by "designing" elements that may not even show on camera—the character's undergarments, for example.

Other, more delicate, matters must be addressed with your actors, including an actor's insecurities about his or her appearance, an actor's clothing preferences, and the treatment he or she expects during production.

• *Exploring an actor's insecurities about appearance.* Some actors are very forthcoming about their clothing sizes, physical imperfections; and other clothing-related hang-ups; others are not. Let's face it, all of us have hang-ups about our appearance; sometimes we're right, and sometimes we're crazy. Many actors are embarrassed to share their size information; some will even refuse to be measured or fit (a situation I'll discuss further in Part 7, *Prep*). A film costume designer must cultivate extreme tact, and develop an eye for "sizing up" an actor—"guesstimating" clothing sizes and evaluating figure flaws without relying on the actor's assessment.

• *The actor's clothing preferences.* Common design strategies for working with stars include providing ample options, buying their favorite brands, using their favorite colors, and providing luxury details. (Some designers pamper stars with lavish goods that may or may not appear on camera, like beautiful undergarments, expensive set robes, and pricey accessories; for more on this, see below, *Star treatment.*) If permitted, a designer may visit an actor's home to get a feel for the shapes, colors, and labels in his or her closet. Film costume designers also study an actor's appearances in previous films, and contact other costume personnel who have worked with the actor in order to get detailed information on the actor's figure flaws, personal hang-ups, and costume preferences.

• *Star treatment.* One of the great film costume designers, Edith Head, developed personal relationships with the stars, encouraging them to confide in her about their wishes and vulnerabilities. She designed elaborate personal wardrobes for many of them, and furnished fitting rooms of lavish comfort. She accommodated their preferences, even allowing stars to choose the colors of their gowns. "If I had sketched a gown with a square neckline and the star wanted a round one instead, I let her have it. I never argued with her," wrote Edith Head in her autobiography, *The Dress Doctor.* Many designers and stylists have followed her lead.

More often than not, a designer will gain an actor's trust by stumbling upon the right set of words or the right rack of clothing options; only then will an actor let down his guard. Discussing clothing allergies, fashion preferences, image priorities, and personal wardrobe details with the actor will show you care. And if you do succeed in winning over an actor to your designs, you will have gained one of your staunchest allies.

Frankly, keeping the actors happy is a production priority. You can't afford to slow down the shooting schedule while an actor bickers over his wardrobe. As the designer, you are expected to design costumes that actors are willing to wear. A little pampering, a few design adjustments, some in-depth character discussion can all go a long way to getting actors to the set on time. But sometimes the character can get lost in the actor's personal preferences. As a designer, you must work to get the focus off the actor and onto the character.

When *Broadcast News* was being shot, angst about the look of the characters was rampant on the set. Many, many costume elements were picked over by many authority figures. The costume designer, Molly Maginnis, was put through hell. In a fitting, Molly and the actor William Hurt established a good rapport right at the beginning. She provided a number of outfits from which he could choose, but instead, he said to her, "What would you really like me to wear?" She selected an outfit and, blessedly, he walked right into it and looked great. When he appeared on the set, the angst routine started up again, but Hurt said quietly, "This is what I'll be wearing. Now, let's get on with it." That was all it took. *(Anonymous crew member,* Broadcast News*)*

Telephone your actors. Talk to them and listen. You can learn a lot. I will move mountains to get the actor on the phone; and I really try to listen to them. Most of them have been on the receiving end of some well-meaning person who is probably very gifted, but who was shooting in the dark and went in the wrong direction.

In the film I just finished, there is an actress who plays my leading man's girlfriend. She gets killed very quickly. She's only got two outfits in the entire film. Production didn't want to bring her in early—it was a money issue. She didn't want to come early, because she was working, and she was tired, and she was busy. I got on the phone with her answering machine and I said, "Hear me clearly. You only have two outfits in this entire movie. I know you are exhausted, but you are the reason that the whole rest of the story takes place. You are the reason that my leading actor goes through the storyline. You need to make a strong visual impression." I said, "I don't care if that means I get on a plane. I don't care if it means I have to buy you lunch and dinner. Even though you were cast four months ago and you have since done lots of other work, my responsibility is to make you everything that you need to be in terms of your clothing so that the whole audience will follow his journey afterwards. You have to be the light in his dark world." Once I explained that to her, she was great.

It's an attitude I've come to late in life—telling the truth, as I see it. You have to find a way to say, "Look, I know you've just had Christmas, I know you're usually a size two and you've gone up three dress sizes. What's the reality here? Because I need to make you look fabulous (or tragic, or vulnerable)." If it's a guy, and he has foot problems, "Let's talk about them. If that means we have to get an orthopedic for you, or I have to get something specially designed or adapted for you so that you are not miserable on your feet, on a concrete floor, fourteen hours a day—well, let's deal with it. Don't apologize for it. Don't pretend. Let's deal with it now, so that you can give the best performance you can."

With theater, you have that wonderful development period through the rehearsal process. In film, you don't. Two actors may be meeting each other for the first time doing an intimate love scene, on the first day of filming. Then, in four weeks, they may be doing their first encounter in the script. And two weeks after that, they may be doing the death scene. Somewhere in the middle, they may be doing the proposal scene. It is very unusual to shoot in sequence. A rehearsal period or a table reading before shooting is unusual nowadays. You have to realize that with this degree of vulnerability, you are going to be the actor's confidante, confessor, and psychologist, as well as costume designer. Actors are mostly very smart cookies, and they have, at some point, had a bad experience. We all have. And they don't want something that's ghastly on record for all eternity. *(Catherine Adair, costume designer)*

Production logistics and constraints—how they affect the design

Before the final designs are developed, a costume designer must seek out information on other aspects of the production process that may affect the designs. The limits in budget and prep schedules have the most fundamental impact on design, but other factors influence key design decisions, as well, among them, the pace and order of the shooting schedule, the nature and extent of the stunt work, choreographed movement, and special effects.

• **BUDGET.** If you were not given clear budget guidelines when you were hired, you must arrange for a preliminary conference with the unit production manager (UPM). As you prepare to design the characters, you must balance inspiration and practicality, and establish priorities in the expenditure of time and money. (The nitty-gritty of costume budgeting will be laid out in Part 6, *Costume Budgets;* the impact of budget constraints on costume design and costuming processes will be discussed in depth in Part 7, *Prep.*)

• **SPEED.** The filmmaking process thrives on speed, in prep and on the set. Because the shooting schedule sets all your work priorities, you should consult with the first assistant director at this point in the process, to get the latest version of the shooting schedule. From the information you get from the first AD, you can set priorities for additional research, sketches, meetings, and final presentations.

Keeping abreast of the shooting schedule will also help you decide on appropriate sources for your costumes—how quickly you must come up with the pregnancy pad, that wedding dress, those cheerleaders' uniforms. Even if you have the budget, do you have the time to build them, or must you rent or buy them? What can you find quickly? Can it be fit quickly? Can you return it for cash if it doesn't work? These are among the questions thrust on a costume designer by the speed of many productions—their short prep periods, limited fitting schedules, and on-set styling requirements.

As a designer, it pays to learn those tricks of the trade that will help you pull through in a pinch: for example, how over-layers, like coats and jackets, can hide a multitude of fitting sins, including the failed tailoring job done in no time on an odd body; and how knit garments can be fitted more quickly than structured goods because they adjust to the body so readily. (The part on prep that follows will explore in detail costume stock strategies, fitting methodologies, and tactical shortcuts used by costume designers to survive the speed of the filmmaking process.)

> How has all the pressure and speed of abbreviated prep times affected the costume workrooms? I think it has, profoundly. I think they've just had to get faster with everything, and the work is diminishing for them, too. I think it's a combination of both. I think that a lot less tailoring is going on now, especially in television. Have a look at what's on the air now. Do you really need to tailor those stretch Capris? I don't see a lot of television shows out there that demand a lot of high-fashion tailoring. Your lawyer shows, sure—and they look good. So there is work for them in the alterations department, but by and large, we are not terribly tailor-oriented at this point. Workrooms in the major studio costume departments have been kept

alive, as far as outside production goes, by refurbishment of existing stock. Because you can't shop period, that's been the saving grace. *(Pat Welch, costume designer)*

• **STUNTWORK.** At this point in the design process it is important for the costume designer to consult the stunt coordinator for guidelines on the stunts that will be featured in the film. Stunts and destructive action can demand the use of costume multiples. This need to produce multiples of the same costume, in addition to the nature of the stunt itself, will certainly affect the costume designer's final choice of color, material, shape, and style. Costume designers may opt to restrict designs for stunts to items available in quantity in chain stores, rather than overburdening the budget with made-to-order costs. Garments that can easily be duplicated—khaki pants, shirts in solid colors—are preferable to one-of-a-kind boutique items. Stunts demand garments that can withstand heavy wear and tear. Some stunt work, like fire and gunshot effects, can require the use of natural fibers. The use of special padding, flying rigs, and flexible shoes may be required for stunt choreography. (For more details on designing for stunts, see below, *Conversation Five: On Costuming for Stunts, with Madeline Kozlowski.)*

Designers must also develop an eye for garment styles, colors, and textures that will spotlight the dramatic effects of stunt and action damage. For example, a bloodstain may not show up on a dark garment enough to make its narrative and emotional point; a fabric in a lighter tone might be used to greater effect. In short, when a story calls for action, the costumes worn in these sequences must be designed in a way that maximizes the dramatic effect of the consequences of that action. For example, in the film *Romancing the Stone* (1984), costume designer Marilyn Vance cleverly designed a travel suit for Kathleen Turner made out of tussah silk, a fabric that she knew would rapidly, and realistically, self-destruct as this sheltered character crashed through the jungles of Colombia.

• **CHOREOGRAPHY/MOVEMENT WORK.** Some films require choreographed movement other than stunt work. Dance sequences, sword fights, extensive martial arts or boxing sequences, diving, magic, and sleight-of-hand work can require that special costumes be supplied. Certain kinds of choreographed movement require costumes cut or tailored in special ways, ways that can affect the design of the costumes and accessories themselves. At this point in the costume design process, designers must consult with the appropriate choreographers or movement specialists on the costume details that will be needed.

• **SPECIAL EFFECTS.** At this point in the process, the costume designer needs to know where special effects will be used in the production, and the limits imposed on the designs by these effects. The director of photography or the head of the special effects unit can give you this information. Special effects can restrict your color palette and texture selections, and it can dictate the need for costume multiples and miniatures.

Phase four: polishing the design, in which design guidelines for the film, and specific designs for the principal characters, are refined in order to gain approval from the director and/or the producer(s) and begin the steps necessary to producing principal players' costumes and gathering costume stock.

Whether you're at the drawing board, in front of a rack of clothing, or face to face with an actor, there comes a time when you have to pull the "look" together and commit to the final version of the characters' costumes. Your careful script analysis, costume research, sketches and collages all contribute to what you'll have on hand for that moment of truth—the final design presentation to the director. Even with all you know about the sets, lights, stunts, shooting conditions, shooting schedule, and the sum of money you have to work with, you should still ask yourself the following questions:

- Does the design say what I want it to say?
- Are the key character and story details reflected in the designs?
- Does the design nail the subtext and the tonal messages I want?
- Does the design look right on the actor?
- Does the design work well with the sets and locations?
- Will the design work well on camera?
- Does the design have flair?

Phase 4 is also the phase in which costume production strategies are set and budget priorities established, and, as such, is a critical test of the designer's eye and understanding of the medium. In Phase 4, a designer must focus on what needs to be gathered for the design—principal players' costumes, costume stock, services and supplies—and how to go about gathering it.

> The thing with wardrobe is, it's not important until it's wrong. *(Dan Lester, costume designer for* The Core, Spawn, *the television series* CSI: Crime Scene Investigation *and others)*

Final design presentations. Sometimes the kinds of presentations detailed in the section above called "Preparing for conferences" are all that are needed before budgets are developed and renting and purchasing can begin. At other times, the director and made-to-order personnel require final design presentations before final approvals are given and time and money fully committed. Short prep periods, directorial discomfort with sketches, and the costume designer's own level of comfort with sketching all play a part in determining the style of these final presentations, which may take any—or all—of the following forms: color sketches, collage boards, photo boards, and rack review.

- **COLOR SKETCHES.** Color sketches are important not only for presentations to the director but for made-to-order (MO) work. Sketches showing front views, back views, realistic proportions, costume details, and the character's attitude help the people building the clothes to do their work accurately. The more "photo-realist" the drawing style, the easier it will be for a director to imagine the actor in the costume. Lois De Armond's

FIG. 4.8

April Ferry's design for *The Babe* (1992). Sketches by Lois DeArmond.

FIG. 4.9

Designs by Dan Lester for *Spawn* (1997). Photo courtesy of New Line Cinema. Illustrations courtesy of Dan Lester.

sketches for the 1992 film *The Babe* (fig. 4.8), designed by April Ferry, are extremely realistic in their detailing, in comparison with Dan Lester's chic, loose sketches for *Spawn* (fig. 4.9).

> You must draw the character's attitude, as you perceive it to be. *(Ann Roth, Academy Award-winning costume designer for* The English Patient*)*

• **COLLAGE BOARDS.** If the director comes from a theatrical background, he or she may have no problem reading sketches, and may enjoy the dazzling artistry that stylish drawing techniques offer. But if the director is gun-shy with sketches, *collage boards* of Xerox- or computer-manipulated photos can help clarify the "camera-worthiness" of a design. If carefully scaled and artfully combined, Xerox-collage images or computer-collage images using Photoshop or similar programs can be particularly helpful, allowing the designer to combine photographs of the actor with research or magazine images (fig. 4.10).

FIG. 4.10

"Get the character's attitude on the page."

Collage sketch and tearsheet for a project design by Holly Cole

• **PHOTO BOARDS.** Photo boards are used for character-at-a-glance presentations, when a designer wants to show the progression of a single character from first appearance to last (fig. 3.1). One way to construct a photo board is to photograph your actors during fittings in all the costume options you have put together for them. To make your photo boards as visually compelling as possible, try eliminating distracting fitting room backgrounds and playing with the scale of the photographs (fig. 4.11). Photo boards can also be used for scene-at-a-glance presentations, in which the designs for multiple characters are clustered in a single presentation, to give an overall feel for the look of a given scene (fig. C.8).

Photo boards are great for presenting your ideas to producers, production designers, and cinematographers. They may be used by a designer when there is no time to sketch

FIG. 4.11

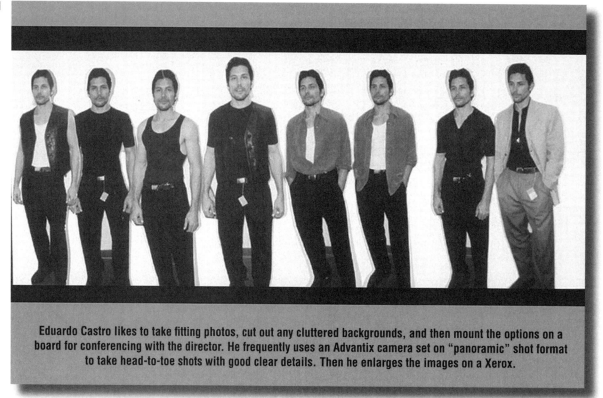

Eduardo Castro likes to take fitting photos, cut out any cluttered backgrounds, and then mount the options on a board for conferencing with the director. He frequently uses an Advantix camera set on "panoramic" shot format to take head-to-toe shots with good clear details. Then he enlarges the images on a Xerox.

or in a final presentation to a director who mistrusts sketches. In fact, using a photo board can be a good way for a designer to develop rapport with the director, prompting dialogue between the two of you. Often, when present in a fitting, the director spends his time developing a rapport with the actor, and, as a result, the designer's opinions get ignored. By presenting photo boards in a separate meeting, the dialogue between you and the director becomes the focus of the meeting.

• **RACK REVIEW.** When prep time is short and conferences are at a premium, a carefully designed wardrobe rack can become a fast track to design approval. A well-put-together wardrobe rack assembles key "character-defining" clothing articles (the perfect Hawaiian shirt; the jazzy two-tone shoes) and good wardrobe "basics" (the good pair of navy pleated gabardine dress pants; the well-fitted, lovingly aged pair of jeans) that can be combined in different configurations to "dress up" or "dress down" a character.

An inventively assembled rack of clothing options helps the costume process in several ways: (1) it provides design flexibility, allowing the designer options for recombination of items as actors, producers, directors, and others push for different "looks"; (2) it gives the production designer and cinematographer very tactile answers to critical questions of palette and texture; and (3) it allows the designer to improvise changes and substitutions from wardrobe already approved by the director, if problems arise during the shooting process. Trying the items on a dress form during a rack review makes your options even more vivid (for more on this, see Part 7, *Prep*, "Psychology of a fitting," and fig. 4.12.)

I start with photographic research, and color and texture research. I do color palette boards with fabric swatches and paint chips. I'll go through magazines or Xerox from

FIG. 4.12

Costumes can also be mocked up on dress forms to get approval from an actor who is unwilling to be fit. But for working with a director it is better to show them the clothing on the actor.

historical research sources, and tear and rip. I include details I like—bits of necklaces, collars, and cuffs. Bits and bobs. I take that into my director, in conjunction with fabric swatches and photographs from a first fitting with my actor.

The other thing I'll do now is use color Xeroxes of the 35mm fitting photos. You can sketch over them, which I find can be a big help, and it's quick! So, for instance, with Jennifer Love Hewitt, I let my director see different silhouettes of skirts on her. You can alter the photo and say, "Well, I liked the silhouette of this skirt and this top, but I think if we cut it down here, make it a little bit lower through the hip, open it up through here, do it in this fabric—" So you've got a shorthand sketch that's pretty close to the final effect, and they're looking at it on the actual body.

I remember a girlfriend of mine telling me that for the TV movie *Nine*, William Ivey Long took all the actresses, stuck them in leotards, and photographed them. Everything he designed was based on that. When I came out to L.A., I realized that I didn't have the time to sketch as I used to. I have, on a few projects, but not very often. So, I went, "Okay, what can I do? How can I use an old technique differently?" Color Xeroxes don't cost much, and it means then that the director, if he is visual, can sit there and noodle around, too. Then, when you take it to your cutter, they can see how the actor wears clothes. You can say, "This is the point I am worried about. We need to make sure that it is free-flowing from this point," or, "What if you lower the waist and it's curved a little more at the front and less at the back?" *(Catherine Adair, costume designer)*

Before We Move On

The final three phases of the costume design process—prep, shoot, and final wrap—will be covered in detail in Parts 7, 8, and 9 of this book. But before any of these phases can take place, two relatively simple, but essential, procedures must be completed: the breakdown of a script for costume demands and the development of working costume budgets. Both of these tasks are done as the designs are being developed. In fact, even preliminary designs cannot be produced (or research done, for that matter) until the script and basic character and scene breakdowns have been completed. In fact, the mastery of these tasks is essential to realizing your designs. The next two parts of this book are devoted to them.

Conversation Three:

On Working with the Cinematographer and Collaborating with Actors in Film, with Catherine Adair

Catherine Adair is a feature film costume designer whose credits include *Win a Date with Tad Hamilton, BASEketball, Beverly Hills Cop III,* and *I Know What You Did Last Summer.* She has also done television work, including a mini-series, movies-of-the-week, and a weekly series.

What kind of quality time do you get with a cinematographer on a feature?

Not a lot. You have to seek it out, given the speed with which everybody works and the limited prep periods that you're given. Increasingly, screen tests and wardrobe tests and color tests are a luxury. They do happen, but they are not the norm anymore. So it's a matter of being a little more aggressive as a designer—finding out who the DP is, calling, introducing yourself. It's a matter of trying to get a sense of how the colors are going to translate once they are on film, finding out what film stock they're using, what sort of stops they are going to be using, what kind of filters, what gels.

How did you develop your understanding of how film stock can affect your work?

I'm still learning. You find that most cinematographers do *some* testing. Often, they are making decisions up to the last minute—playing with lenses, film stock, et cetera. I have found on some projects that I have done that the colors are completely true to what I had imagined I would see in the finished product. On others, I have said, "Oh my!"

What kind of guidelines do you get from cinematographers?

It depends on the piece. Some of them love pure color, some of them don't. I've worked with cinematographers who've loved pure whites and pure blacks and punches of primary color. I've worked with other cinematographers who like a much softer palette. The best thing to do is ask. Find out early enough in the process. Don't hang yourself out to dry in a situation where suddenly you've got six dozen cavalier shirts that are white-white, in a scene on the battlements that takes place in bright hot sunshine. You could have dyed them all down and given the cinematographer a nice ivory cream, or a nice beige, instead. I've done films where we all agreed that we would avoid certain colors completely—that you would never see them. A color became an accent, a sort of subliminal color statement. I've had shows where I've worked a lot in very smooth surfaces—silks and satins and iridescent fabrics that caught the light, and others where I did lots of textural, nubbly things.

There are gobs of rules out there. There are actresses who say, "If I am in red, then nobody else in the scene is allowed to be in red"—that sort of thing. I've done pieces where they've said, "I want this to look 'normal.'" I've done things where I have deliberately put two people in very different plaids in the same frame, and I have had people call me on it and say, "You're not supposed to do that." Why not? What's the world we are creating? Whose rules are they? If they are my director's rules, that's one thing; otherwise, the rules are there to be broken.

With really gifted cinematographers, palette control is governed not by their abilities, but by the mood of the piece. Once you've found the parameters of the world that's being created by your director, your production designer, yourself, and your cinematographer, then you can ask about what they're going to use. "What is this gel going to do to the colors? What happens to the colors under limited light?" It's a matter of being aware *and* open to working as a team. You have to realize that, in a sense, you're only as good as the collective.

Please talk a bit about your experience with cinematographer Dean Semler on the Sylvester Stallone film *Eye See You* (2002). As I understand it, you had some interesting palette challenges. How did your designs develop?

It was my second time with the director, and my third time with the production designer. The three of us usually start from old masters' paintings, or photographs. That side of the process was lovely because we all started from the same color palette—mostly Vermeer. The production palette was extremely limited.

Once we worked out the palettes, I gave Dean Semler color boards for the different worlds we had created. He filmed those with the film stock he planned to use, and we looked at them under different light conditions—shade, exterior and interior light, with blue gels, with doubled areas of blue gels, under very low light, at different stops, et cetera—so I was able to see what the colors did, which ones stayed "true" and which ones distorted or went into a color area that wasn't part of the palette. Dean was wonderful. He used a lot of gel, and he gave me swatches of the principal colors that he was using. I was then in a position to go back to the workroom and, as they aged and distressed the clothes, look at them through those gels.

The set, when it was built, was a dark, deep gray, and because of the way the paint glazes had been applied, you got this extraordinary concrete monolith, with other colors and textures coming through, according to how it was lit—which Dean did beautifully. The palette and the lighting, combined, created a completely neutral world. It was such a limited world that any color just jumped out.

Since I was working in a very, very small range of colors against the gray concrete, texture took on a huge importance: That's what gave me the depth and definition between my actors and the walls. The walls had a life of their own in this concrete, modern-art sort of space, and, in order for my actors not to look flat against them, I went for nubbly, textural fabrics. For one of the older characters, I went for a woolly sweater that had a heathered quality; and then I got the dyer to "pill" it for me, so that it actually had the pilled shoulders and elbows. And the wrists were stretched out and uneven. That is what made this character's gray stand out against the gray of the wall. I asked the agers and distressors to sand and to lift the pile on fabrics, and then to dry brush them slightly with other colors, so that you got another dimension to the fabrics. Because of the nature of the palette, buttons with too high a contrast "popped" and looked like traffic lights, so I worked very hard to get all the buttons in colors very, very close to the palette of the clothing. Often, the buttons would get sanded down, or I would look for buttons that had a matte finish.

Did you shoot any color tests with the clothes?

I was lucky, we did. We pulled shirts in appropriate colors and textures, and we put the stand-ins in those and had them walk in front of pieces of the set. We also put them under different qualities of light. That was a luxury, and a big help. The challenge is that often these tests won't get done until just a couple of days before you actually have to start shooting, so if you are going to make changes, you have to do it very, very quickly.

Didn't you still have some real surprises crop up?

In spite of all the planning, the first day of shooting they added more blue gel, because everybody loved the look of it; so my blues popped more than they had in the original test, which meant that I had to dull them down further. You have to realize that a costume you shoot the first day of filming may not appear in anything you shoot for another two months, so if you don't like what you see on the first day, you may be stuck with that particular change, even though the next shot with that change may be two months away. I was fortunate on that first day of filming because we only filmed one scene with three actors.

Still, it must have been a continuity nightmare.

Well, you can get away with a few little changes in color because you are moving from one set to another, one light condition to another, and the color will look different as a result—so you can fudge color changes if absolutely necessary, and if the changes are subtle enough.

The cinematographer came to me halfway through the first day of filming and said to me, "I am using more blue than I anticipated." Later that same day, he did some additional tests for me. I was able to bring in other articles of clothing that other characters were going to wear down the line and check those. The good news is that you get an answer very quickly. You usually wait less than twenty-four hours to see processed film. The challenge, then, is making sure that you have a crew that can work tirelessly—sometimes through the night—to balance things. And you hope they don't change the shooting schedule!

In fact, my production designer came up to me after the first day of filming, and he'd seen the dailies. He was very upset because he felt that I had misunderstood him—that I hadn't understood that his color palette was very tight, very subdued, very restrained. There was a plaid shirt that I had used, which on film looked quite vibrant, and it really upset him. In no uncertain terms, he said, "I thought we were a team here. What the hell has happened?" Then, he came into the trailer and blinked and rubbed his eyes because he suddenly realized how limited and how muted the palette for the costumes really was. I said to him, "You find, on this truck, that shirt." This is one of the most gifted men I know, in his generation. And he couldn't find the shirt. When I pulled it out and showed it to him, he was hard-pressed to believe me—except that it was the only one of its kind on the truck. My point is, if you had done the same clothes outside in a park, in the middle of green trees and a blue pond, everybody would have said, "Why did you do such dull clothing?" But because it was against a completely neutral, gray background, the film stock absorbed the colors very differently.

How did you end up fixing the problem?

Where I still wanted the blue to pop, I left it. Where the blues started to be too hot, I balanced them by dipping the clothes in a brown dye bath. This just took the edge off of them, and made them not quite as vibrant on film.

Things can change even in postproduction. On the film *Seven*, after they had finished shooting completely, they developed a different way of treating the film in the printing. The sort of grainy, black and white, almost pewter quality that the film has was actually something that was done after they had finished filming. That happened to me on *Before Women Had Wings*. I worked with a very soft palette, based on the production design. They wanted the film to have the feel of tinted pictures—like very early color photography that had faded. Once they had finished filming it, the cinematographer played with another whole process in the final print, to which none of us was party. While the look of the film itself is quite beautiful, it is quite different than the palette that I had played with, and the palette that I saw in dailies while we were filming.

So you really had no sense of what the final version would look like?

No, I didn't. That's not always the case, but it can be. It's happened to me more than once.

You've worked in both television and film. The process of doing television work seems to be so much more rushed. How much room do you have for dialog with the director of photography in that kind of context?

A couple of the TV cinematographers that I've worked with have been super. On a series I was doing, after the fitting I would drive across the lot, Polaroids in hand, and get approval from my producers and directors. In TV, often it's your producers, rather than your director, who will have the first say. And then, from there, I'd go straight to the soundstage, wait until the cinematographer had three or four minutes, and say, "Here's what's planned for the next episode."

Once the show is up and running and they've got a sense of the characters and the personalities, then all you have to do is earmark something that you think might be a specific problem, or different, or peculiar. If you let them know, they can adjust. There is a lovely story of a film that shall remain nameless, where a leading lady was put in a black cocktail dress, on a yacht, in an exterior night shot, where the camera was looking out to sea. The costume designer didn't let the cinematographer know ahead of time. Now, the actress looked fantastic in the dress; in the fitting, it looked beautiful on her. But nobody really thought through the reality of being on a yacht, against the sky, which was black, against the sea, which was black, in a black dress, with a very white actress.

You really have to develop a "camera eye" as a designer, and think about framing, what reads on camera.

Yes. One of the things I often do to help my "camera eye" is to take photographs in a fitting. If I'm doing television, I'll do one photo at full length, then one that is very close to the frame that you will see on TV. If it's film, I'll do three shots—full-length, medium, and close-up. You have to decide, do you want the collar starched or do you want it rumpled? Things that are baggy in real life can look hip and cool on film, or they can just look "shlumpy." If you want the "shlumpy" look, you might have to go an extra degree one way or the other. Sometimes you have to exaggerate, but sometimes—remembering that the eye is only seeing a part of the image—you have to "pull back."

A director hired me, but I had to pass muster with the producers. They said to me, "What do you think is the ultimate simple, casual, sexy look for a woman today?" I thought about it for a while, and I said, "It depends on the woman—her shape, and her sensibility. You put a little Calvin Klein T-shirt on one young actress and she's going to look hotter than you could ever possibly imagine. Another actress may come off as very athletic, and rather tough and street-wise, whereas somebody else may come off as vulnerable, and somebody else may come off as if she's wearing her boyfriend's favorite piece from college. It depends on the size and the scale of it."

You have to see what the camera reveals. That takes quite an eye.

It takes a different eye. For example, shoulder pads can create a very different look on television than they do on film. Whereas shoulder pads can look fabulous in a full-length shot—the kind you see more of on film—if you're framing somebody very, very close, as often you do for TV, the actor can suddenly look as if she's got no space left between her ears and her shoulders. You start to look at details like this with a very different eye. You have to acknowledge that a good percentage of the time, you are going to be looking at somebody from mid-bust up—at some point, in any outfit, that's what you are going to see. I've done costumes where you never saw the full-length version of it, ever—especially on TV, but even in film. So you do need to think, "Not only do I have to love it walking into the room and making a statement, but also in that scene where she is going to be sitting at the dinner table and I'm only going to see her from the bosom up." So you make sure that, from the bosom up, the outfit is right. And if you've got a choice between two outfits, choose the one where the top half is doing what you want it to do.

I say the same thing with actors when they come to me about presenting awards at ceremonies. Yes, you have the walk in, but a lot of what you're dealing with, and a lot of what you are going to be seeing, is from the chest up—faces in the crowd or on the stage. So, with the guys, is the tuxedo lapel really doing everything it can for their shoulders? If it's a woman in a strapless gown, have you chosen the best piece of jewelry? You have to be careful, because you are not going to see much else.

How do you cope with getting the proportions right for the camera when you have not seen the actor in costume until that one-shot fitting, or until he or she walks on to the set?

You cover your bases. Choices, lot's of choices! Take whatever you can lay your hands on, even if it means you're packing six armloads of stuff, even if it involves fighting with production to give you fitting time.

Are you ever in a situation where the director is not happy with what pleases the actor?

Yes. And at a certain point, you either find a hybrid that works for both of them, or you put the three of you in a room together to work it out. Because sometimes, with the actor's choice, once the director sees him in it, and sees it in three dimensions—how it moves, how it "plays"—his opinion can be changed. Even if you spent the money on a good 35mm print (instead of a Polaroid) to show the costume to the director in a better light, a still photograph is still a flat canvas and film is moving pictures. If you possibly can, get the actor dressed, so that the director can see the costume in 3-D.

But you do shoot fittings with a 35mm still camera?

Yes. As I said before, often, I'll photograph the fitting with a regular 35mm camera, to see what the outfit looks like on camera. It's a comfort tool for the actor, too. The actor may fall in love with something in the fitting, you'll think *you* like it, then you'll look at it in the 35mm print, and you'll go, "Oh!" If the movie camera sees what that 35mm still camera sees, then, even though I'm not lighting it brilliantly, this outfit that you fell in love with *is* going to say something different on film than what we thought it said in the fitting. So, shooting stills in a fitting can help you develop your eye for what's camera-worthy.

If any of us go out to dinner, or to a special occasion, and we *thought* we had something fabulous on, but it's too tight, or the shoe is half a size too small, or the pantyhose are down around our knees, or the bra is pinching us, it's misery, and, on some level, it "reads." On some level, people can *see* what we're thinking: "I shouldn't have bought this shirt, it's uncomfortable." A film camera picks up everything. It picks up every nuance. And what a designer needs to remember is that you are going from a wide, broad canvas to a close-up that can show an actor's nose hairs. If the camera can read that much detail, why would it not read discomfort in clothing? Or mood? Or the sub-text of a strange doubt an actor has? It's very vulnerable, to stick yourself in front of a camera and then see yourself in forty-foot detail.

The thing for me is finding a balance of comfort for the actor, without overindulgence—acknowledging that if actors are comfortable, and if they feel safe in the clothes, and if the clothes help them with the character or the world that they are creating, then they will give a better performance. It's not just the outside layer, it's the inside layer, as well. So then, why not make sure that the underwear is believable and feels right? Why not explore whether a shoe half a size too big is going to change the actor's walk? If it helps, why not try it? I've had some unusual requests over the years, but I would have to say, nine times out of ten, they've paid off. So if it means one designer-label, special-care bra that you have to ask your set crew very sweetly to hand-wash and lock up every night, it might be worth it. Because if having on this hot piece of lingerie is going to make your actress feel phenomenally sexy, maybe it's worth it. Maybe it's worth looking at. If an actor gives a better performance, in a strange way, it's made me look better.

Conversation Four:

On the Art of Collaboration in Episodic Television, with Pat Welch

Costume designer Pat Welch has designed for seven different television series, including *L.A. Law*. In 1988, she garnered an Emmy nomination for her work on *Frank's Place*.

You started your career as a costume designer in TV?

The term "TV" is deceptive. There are two different avenues in television. There are the productions that are "made for TV," single-camera shows like one-hour dramas and half-hour sitcoms. These are shot on five- or seven-day shooting schedules. And then, there's what we call "live TV." The "live TV" show is shot in front of a live audience, and generally uses multi-camera setups. It's the closest thing we have to theater that's *not* theater.

In single-camera shows, you are shooting every day of the week, so you're prepping an episode, and then you start shooting it. About two or three days into shooting that episode, you start prepping your next episode. Prep and shoot overlap, and the clothes change out every five to seven days. In a multi-camera show, you have a live audience one night a week. On *WKRP in Cincinnati*, the show I started on, we prepped for three and a half days, then we shot what they call "block and tape"—you block a scene, then you shoot it. We'd have a dress rehearsal on Friday, and then a final taping with an audience.

Is this the way the format is taped today?

More or less. There may be two audience shows. They may bring in a second audience the same evening. They may not do block and tape, or they may do stop-and-go shooting, where they keep the audience while they repeat the scene until it's done correctly. There are many different options in a multi-camera show.

In episodic television, you have the same producer but different directors for each episode. Who creates more problems for the costume designer, the new young guys, who still have a lot to prove, or the old guys, who've been directing episodic for a long time?

The young Turks—the up-and-coming directors. They've come out of the school of guerilla filmmaking, so they're incredibly grateful for whatever you can bring them. And the old-timers have seen everything, and worked with everybody, so they are very much at ease, and very skilled at communicating, most of the time. I have always been very lucky to have extremely accommodating directors.

I think it's not so much whether the director has a theater background or a film background that helps in a collaboration; I think it's whether the director has a love of making a character on paper come to life. That's what makes a collaboration between a director and a costume designer really work—if the two can have a meeting of the minds about how they are going to breathe life into this black print on white paper.

What's the most fun?

Talking a producer or director into something. Somebody being appreciative. I did *Frank's Place*, and Hugh Wilson was the executive producer. He called me up and I went in and I met with him. He said, "Well, it's about this restaurant in New Orleans."

It didn't sound very interesting. I said, "How about if we do it retro?" And he said, "What a great idea! What do you mean?" I said, "Why don't we make it so that it's contemporary, but when you come to Frank's Place, when you come into the neighborhood, it's period. 1953." And he said, "Oh, I like that," and that's what I did. The main characters, when they weren't in Frank's Place, were in contemporary clothing, but the background players were always in period costume—hats, gloves, jewelry, dresses, hose, petticoats, underwear, shoes—the whole nine yards. That's what I mean about being able to pitch something and get away with it. Hugh Wilson was very gracious to allow me that freedom. And that's what made *Frank's Place* such a wonderful place for me.

With as little prep time as you have in television, do you only have time to "talk" the clothes, or do you have visuals for the producers and directors to respond to?

In the case of *Frank's Place,* I had visuals. At that time, in the mid to late eighties, the market was saturated with garments from the nineteen-fifties, so it was out there for cheap. I could spend a couple hundred bucks and say, "This is what I want to do for you." Hugh would come in and say, "This is really great," and "Yeah, that works." I also photographed every fitting, and I would have each photograph mounted and sent up to the producers and the directors, so they could see what was going on.

With the tight time frame, do you ever get a chance to look at something on a camera before a final taping?

Yes, that's where dress rehearsals and/or "block and tape" come in, because they do use the cameras.

Designers talk about the flattening effect of the lighting in television work, especially for a three-camera shoot. How can the costume department work with other departments on the production to compensate for this?

Actually, I think that the multi-camera, three-wall-set show has gotten a bad rap. If you've got a good lighting director, or a gaffer and a good cinematographer, you can get the depth that you need. And the set decorator and art director help. A good art department can bring a lot to the table to help that dead, flat look not happen.

I always work very carefully and very closely with the art director, who has usually been on the project longer than I have. Pretty much the first thing out of my mouth when we meet is, "Where's the color palette?" And then I hop, skip, and jump over to the set decorator, and say, "Any tricks in your bag for the upholstery fabrics? What are you doing for window treatments? We've got a bed scene here, and you are using striped sheets: How thoughtful of you!"

PART FIVE

Breakdowns

Breakdown Basics

Very early in the costume design process, production will want costume budget estimates. Not long after that—early in prep, at the latest—production will want a realistic working budget for the costume department. In order to produce these budgets, a careful determination of the general costume demands of the production is essential. Making this determination begins with doing a script breakdown (a task required of every department on a production), then doing costume breakdowns of various types. Costume breakdowns are time-consuming to do, but absolutely essential. They help you get organized, delegate work, and respond rapidly to production changes and budget-justification demands. When you are tracking hundreds of costumes, the more scrupulous your breakdowns, the better you can respond to emergencies of the organizational sort.

In the costume department, the job of doing script and costume breakdowns is often split between the costume designer and the costume supervisor, according to the priorities, and availability, of each. However, all costume personnel are expected to read and analyze the script and other production documents for clues to how the costumes will be used during a production, and as a means of determining the total costume count of the production and what it will require to produce it. In fact, in Los Angeles, both film costume unions (the Costume Designers Guild Local 892 and The Motion Picture Costumers Union, Local 705) require their members to be able to do costume breakdowns for a script. The unions use action/adventure scripts filled with stunt work to train their members in the master craft of accurate costume breakdowns.

Types of breakdowns

Costume designers and costume supervisors do a number of different types of breakdown over the course of preparing for a film, generally in the following, logical order:

1. *Script notation*—notes, on the pages of the script itself, indicating key information about the situation, the characters, and the action in each scene, and what it means in relation to the costumes
2. *Costume crossplot*—a graph-like representation of the entire film, intended as a kind of "cheat sheet," from which you can tell, at a glance, who is in a scene, what change they are in, and whether or not any doubling is necessary
3. *Scene breakdowns*—lists of all characters and extras in each scene
4. *Character breakdowns*—breakdowns configured to detail all of an individual character's changes
5. *Specialized* or *summary breakdowns* (also known as *breakouts*)—these forms are meant to detail and/or summarize special costume needs (military uniforms, for example)

Why do a script breakdown?

A script breakdown is done to accomplish the following:
1. To clearly mark scene breaks
2. To highlight who is in the scene

3. To highlight where the scene is set
4. To highlight when the scene takes place
5. To note the day/night sequence in a script
6. To note all script references to clothing items
7. To note all key actions that affect costume condition and count, including stunts, progressive damage and distress, and the need for character and photo doubles
8. To note key questions for the director
9. To note where costumes change and to assign these costume *change numbers*

Note: The *change number* is the sequential number of each outfit worn by a character. These numbers track the quantity of costume changes, often suggesting the passage of time and delineating the character arc. Films often have hundreds of scenes; and principal characters often have dozens of costume changes. In *Wyatt Earp* (1994), there were some 245 scenes; Kevin Costner alone had some fifty-six changes.

As costume designer, the first time you read the script, you read for the "feel" of the script, and for story (and its hidden meanings). Doing a script breakdown, you make notes that allow you to engage the director in dialog and develop your own design point of view. The "official" reading is to do an actual script breakdown. While the designer's initial reading of the script focuses on questions of dramatic situation and how it may be reflected in the design of the costumes, an official script breakdown, usually done by the costume supervisor or costume designer early in preproduction, focuses on how situations and action will affect the production and acquisition of wardrobe. Note will be made of any script elements that fundamentally affect the costume budget, and that will need to be discussed with the director and other members of the production team.

We recommend that whether you're the designer or the supervisor, you read the script at least four times: first, to get the "feel" and the story; second, to break it down; third, to check your work; fourth, to know it like the back of your hand.

The script breakdown process

Basic questions. When doing your full script breakdown, ask the following questions, and note or highlight the following information:

• *Who* is in the scene (the be-all and end-all of costume work)? The characters in the scene, and the range, style, and undertones of their costumes help to determine the atmosphere of a scene. Determining how a character's status, profession, sexuality, and attitude toward fashion are displayed in his/her clothing helps reveal the character's eccentricities and social position.

• *What happens* in the scene? What are the occasions or events of the scene? *Style* and *color palette* are often determined by the "event" of the scene (a party, a wedding). Major changes in events or a character's development will affect the costumes used to express the arc of the character. Stunts and destructive action dictate the *style*, the *color*, and the *serviceability* of the garments, and determine the need for *costume duplicates* (see below, "Noting costume duplicates").

• *Where* and under what special conditions does each scene takes place? Is the setting urban or rural, the terrain rough or refined, the locations local or foreign, the atmosphere sophisticated or unsophisticated? The answers to these questions, and questions like it, will affect the designer's choice of *style* and *tone*. Whether the scenes are interior or exterior, wet or dry, hot or cold will affect not only the design (the costume layering, for example), but the more practical aspects of costumes—the need for duplicates, for example, and for a stock of "comfort garments" for the actors—long johns, gloves, socks, hand warmers, and so forth.

•   *When* does the scene or sequence take place, and over what period of time? Historical period defines the range of costume options. The season determines the layering and color palette. The time of day affects style choices. And the passage of time is fundamentally important to determining the number of costumes a character needs.

•   *Why* does the scene exist in the script? What purpose does it serve in the narrative, for the characters, in terms of the tone of the piece? Does it provide clues to the hidden meanings in the script? How might the "why" of a scene be reflected in the design of the costumes?

•   *How* will the scene be shot? Are there indications in the script of how a scene will be filmed (e.g., montage or special effects sequences, close-ups, long shots)? How will these affect both costume count and how the costume silhouette or detail will read on camera?

Noting costume multiples. Because action that may damage costumes requires additional copies of that costume (elements of it or its entirety), it is particularly important that action in the script be accurately and thoroughly noted. In fact, several aspects of filmmaking can demand costume duplicates (also called *doubles* and *multiples*), including: (1) to dress a stunt specialist who substitutes for an actor in the performance of physical activities that cannot be performed by the actor him- or herself (*stunt doubles*) or duplicate a costume to facilitate stunt padding or rigging; (2) to provide costume duplicates for multiple takes in which a costume may get dirty (*distress doubles*) or to preserve duplicates of costumes in different phases of distress for continuity coverage; (3) to provide costumes for actors who substitute for a featured character in a non-stunt scene (*character doubles* or *photo doubles*); and (4) to keep a costume looking fresh during the course of shooting (*usage doubles*). For more on this, see Part 6, *Costume Budgets*, "Costume multiples coverage and cost guidelines," and fig. A.39.

•   *Stunt doubles.* Stunt specialists can perform any physical activity that cannot be performed by the original actor. Actions that can appear quite harmless—riding a horse, climbing a tree, even driving a car—can end up needing stunt doubles if the star is not inclined to do the action required, or is prevented from doing it for any reason, including insurance restrictions. Different stunt players with different specialties may substitute for the same actor when more than one stunt is involved. *Raiders of the Lost Ark* employed an entire team of stunt men: one substituted for Harrison Ford under a truck, one for Harrison Ford on horseback, one for Ford near a gasoline fire, and so on. When you think of the costly shooting delays that result when a star is injured doing stunt work, you can understand why producers demand stunt players and costume duplicates.

Whether using a stunt person or not, some stunts require protective equipment— padding or rigging, for example. Duplicate costumes in sizes that can accommodate flying rigs, padding, wetsuits, or fire-protective clothing can be required.

In designing for simple stunts, three is my magic number. For each stunt phase, I have three copies of the costume: one for the actor, plus one a size up, plus one two sizes up—to cover for padding and to give me a double. *(Madeline Kozlowski, costume designer)*

- *Distress doubles.* In stunt sequences in which costumes are destroyed, multiples are needed for retakes. Any stunt sequence can require the action to be shot over and over again, from many angles. Destructive action, like that staple of the film industry, the bullet "hit," requires a new costume or costume piece for each take. A bullet "hit" entails rigging the actor's body with a "squib"—a device with a detonator that causes a small explosive charge to rip through the actor's costume and trigger the explosion of a blood pack. To a producer, it is far more cost-effective to purchase costume duplicates than to delay the shoot.

Non-stunt sequences in which a costume may get dirty can require costume duplicates (*distress doubles*) for filming multiple retakes from different angles. That juicy hamburger that Vince eats in *Pulp Fiction*, for example, suggests the need for a duplicate shirt.

If a character's costume is supposed to be progressively damaged or dirtied, *multiple distress doubles* will be required. Since scenes are shot out of sequence, each phase of damage or "distress" must be preserved. For *Gone With the Wind*, Vivian Leigh had seventeen copies of her burning-of-Atlanta dress, one for each stage of distress.

- *Photo doubles* and *character doubles.* Actors who substitute for a featured player in a non-stunt scene are called photo doubles. Photo doubles require costume duplicates, also called "photo doubles" or just "doubles." For example, while the star is shooting the principal action on the soundstage with the director, a photo double may be working with a *second unit* (a second camera crew and director) to shoot supporting material—stunts, long shots, etc.—at a different location. (For more on this, see Part 8, *Shoot*, "Second unit.") Doubles of the character's costumes will be needed for this second-unit shoot. When an action is created that cannot be performed by a live actor (most often, special effects or pyrotechnics), the actor is doubled by a dummy, who will also need wardrobe that matches the principal. This double wardrobe is called a *character double*.

- *Usage doubles.* At a shooting rate of two to four pages a day, filmmaking is a lengthy process that can be hard on clothes, even when the action is minimal. Worn-out garments often need to be replaced, and even a deceptively simple film in which the heroine has one outfit can require many duplicates (*usage doubles*), just to cope with the long days of shooting.

Script notation

Elaborate coding and marking systems have been developed for the efficient notation of a script; ask any costume supervisor. Abbreviations, color coding, straight lines, wavy lines, tabs, arrows, underlining, circling—you name it, it's been done. Each costumer has his or her own preferences when it comes to script notation. Some prefer circling information to underlining information, some keep colors to a minimum; others use a rainbow of highlighters to mark key script data, including characters, timeline, action, and references to tone and atmosphere. The goal is to use enough markings, colors, and notes to help you find key information quickly when you do your character breakdowns and costume budgets. So, customize a system that works for you, but it should be *a system that someone else can figure out,* just in case you decide to become a nun in the middle of a difficult production.

As you debate life-or-death issues like whether to use a blue or green highlighter to indicate stunts, consider using the following marking system, as a place to start. It highlights key information while keeping the script fairly uncluttered (see fig. C.9, "Script pages from *The Adventures of Pluto Nash*").

One more word of caution: Although your script is your bible in many ways, it is an ever-changing bible—new pages are regularly generated and distributed by the production office. Important script notations can be lost as old pages are replaced, unless you are scrupulous about duplicating and distributing your notes.

Underline

1.   Draw a clear black line across the page indicating the start of each new scene.

2.   Underline the "slug line" of each scene—the scene number, interior/exterior status, set/location, and day/night status. If any of this information is not in the text, make notes and confirm your conclusions with the script supervisor.

Dark underlining helps you visually separate one scene from another. In chase sequences, however, or in sequences built of short, intercut scenes, underlining between every scene can be overkill. You may want to treat scenes or sequences like these as "scene blocks," by grouping together very short scenes in which costumes do not change.

Highlight

1.   Highlight the named characters and extras for each scene the first time they are mentioned in the scene. Buffy Snyder, former president of Local 705, suggests blue for male principals and day players, pink for the female equivalent, yellow for extras. (Note: A capitalized extra in a script is considered a day player.)

2.   Highlight any costume or costume-related "business" (action) in the script. Buffy Snyder suggests using green for all costume and action notes in a script, but I like to distinguish stunt or action usage that affects costume multiples from the bulk of costume-related text, so I suggest using the following additional color coding:

- *Brown* for tracking staining and other actions that affect costume duplication
- *Green* for stunts that create the need for costume doubling and multiple sizing
- *Orange* for general atmospheric or costume reference notes, including all period, season, and time indications; place and tonal atmosphere (characteristic style); any mention of still photos or videos of characters in the script that will appear on camera and add to the costume load; any costume references or actor business that affects costumes. Additionally, you may want to circle them or note them in the margins of the script.

Margin notes

1.   Note the number of the story day or night, as it is lived by the characters, in the top right-hand corner of each page. Note in the margin when a time shift occurs. Montage and fantasy sequences can be given their own scene numbers and time indications (as in "Fantasy 1/Night").

2.   Note change number of each of the featured players the first time they wear a change. Some costumers prefer to note the character's change number in *each* scene, as a quick reference. Because a character might wear a layered outfit, adding or subtracting layers over the course of several scenes, the costume change numbers can get a bit tricky. I suggest that a change number always begin with the first version of the costume as it appears on screen—for example, (change number) "1," Mia in bustier, shirt, and skirt. If a layer is added to the basic change, use the basic change number and a plus (+) sign—e.g., Mia in bustier, shirt, skirt, and over-jacket would be change number "1+." If a layer is subtracted from the basic change, use the basic change number and a minus sign (-)—e.g., Mia in bustier and skirt would be change number "1-."

3.   Note need for costume multiples (stunt doubles, distress doubles, doubles needed to preserve different phases of distress). The need for costume multiples can also be indicated with the following special notations:

- *Doubling* for stunts or distressing action can be indicated by a letter to indicate the nature of the doubling problem ("S" for stunt action/double problems, "D" for dirt/destructive problems). Examples: Mia in costume change #1 that gets vomit stains in the scene would become change number "1D"; Mia's stunt-driver double or the actor playing Mia in a duplicate of change number 1 with a special stunt rig for the hypodermic stabbing would become change number "1S" (for stunt).

- *Each phase of costume that must be preserved* can be indicated with x's. Examples: Mia in phase one distress of change number 1 becomes "1x"; Mia in phase two distress of change number 1 and rigged for a stunt becomes "1xxS."

- *Staining action* can be indicated using colored shading or dots. Examples: red for blood, blue for water, brown for dirt, and so forth.

- *Stunt sequences, special effects sequences, and key business* that requires multiple costumes can be marked with an adhesive arrow-marker or an index tab. Quick reference tabs that do not easily peel off the page can be useful to note the need for addition discussion or breakdown attention.

- *Description and count of implied, but unnamed, extras in the scenes, and any questions you have for the director,* e.g., questions on montage sequences, possible second-unit work, special effects sequences, and so forth may be noted in pencil in the margin.

Costume breakdowns

Costume breakdowns come in the following basic types: the scene breakdown, character breakdowns, specialty breakdowns and breakouts, summary breakdowns, and the costume crossplot. [Note: For the balance of Part 5, and all of Part 6, *Costume Budgets*, chart samples of costume breakdown and budget forms are based on what we're calling "Holly Cole's Hypothetical Production of *Pulp Fiction*." To test your understanding of costume breakdowns, study the script for *Pulp Fiction*, then use the blank forms provided in A.1-A.9 and A.13-A.17 to create your own breakdowns. (Check your work against the character and budget breakdowns in figs. 5.1-5.12 and 6.1 and budget breakdowns in A.18-A.29.)

The scene breakdown. The scene breakdown gives an overview of the script, laid out scene by scene. (See fig. 5.1, "Scene Costume Breakdown Form for Holly Cole's Hypothetical Production of *Pulp Fiction*.") Also known as the "long form," the scene breakdown lays out all of the characters involved in each scene, giving the gist of the costumes they are wearing. It also has room for notes on costume doubling or special costume business. While this form is not a show-at-a-glance chart the way the crossplot is (see figs. 5.2, 5.3, and 5.4), the scene breakdown does give you more basic information on the costumes in each scene. To costumers who loathe crossplots, scene breakdowns are very important.

Scene breakdown notation guidelines are as follows:

1.   Vertical columns list, left to right:
   • Scene number in the script
   • Day/night numbers (fantasy or montage sequences get separate numbering systems)
   • Set/action (location notes are combined with a one-liner that gives the key action of the scene)
   • Interior/exterior designation
   • Character (lists individual named characters and groups, some extras)
   • Change number (using above notation system for doubles, distress, etc.)
   • Costume description (only a brief description—the "gist"—of the outfit is noted in addition to special costume or stunt business and distress sources using the "action" color highlighting system (blue for water, brown for dirt, red for blood, etc.)

2.   Horizontal rows are used to list every scene's characters (hence the term "long form" for this form of breakdown).

The *scene worksheet* lets you see a character at a glance. (See fig. 5.5, "Scene Worksheet for the Jack Rabbit Slim's scene in Holly Cole's Hypothetical Production of *Pulp Fiction*.") This form can be used to simply record preliminary design ideas or developed into a worksheet. (See fig. 6.1, "Scene Budget Worksheet for Holly Cole's Hypothetical Production of *Pulp Fiction*" to help with costume count computations and budget figures.)

Character breakdowns. Doing a character breakdown for each principal and featured player is the next step in the process. (See figs. 5.7, 5.8, "Character Breakdown Form for Vince in Holly Cole's Hypothetical Production of *Pulp Fiction*," and A.5.) The individual character breakdown is a form that lists the number of changes worn by a given character over the course of the entire film, in what scenes each change is worn, what garments and accessories make up each change, the general condition of the garments (related to story action), and (sometimes) how they should be worn by the actor (if this has been determined by the designer to be part of the design). Like all costume breakdown forms, the individual character breakdown allows you to put your hands on specific information quickly, and is especially useful in developing summary breakdowns like those in the section that follows.

Like the design of a film, character breakdowns evolve over the design, prep, and shooting phases of a production. Character breakdowns of varying detail are used for a variety of purposes, among them
   • to reflect the arc of a character in his or her basic costume changes as they develop during preliminary research and conferencing;
   • to detail principal and secondary-player costumes, and to generalize costume requirements for extras in the early phases of production for the development of a preliminary costume budget;
   • to defend necessary purchases and eliminate unnecessary expenses in budget-cutting sessions;

- to provide quick costume summary information when gathering costume stock for extras; and
- to provide a form for recording every item of a costume change and how it is worn on film, for use as an inventory list and as a means of checking costume continuity.

There is no universal design for an individual character breakdown form. In designing one for your own use, be guided by the answer to this basic question: How much room do you need to record a necessary level of costume detail? Indeed, how much detail is necessary—or even possible—to record at the time you will be using this form?

We like to do character breakdowns even before we even shop a character. Character breakdowns help you visualize a character's arc and put together a budget for each character. Some designers even like to present an actor, at the fitting, with his or her individual character breakdown, then walk them through it.

Specialty breakdowns and breakouts. There are several adaptations of the individual character-breakdown form that are handy for particular tasks, among them the "character worksheet," the "scene worksheet," the "character breakdown for shopping," and "character continuity pages."

The *character worksheet* lets you see a character at a glance. (See fig. 5.5, "Character Worksheet for the Jack Rabbit Slim's scene in Holly Cole's Hypothetical Production of *Pulp Fiction*.") This form can be used to record preliminary design ideas or developed into a budget after the manner of fig. 6.1 to help with budget development.

The *character breakdown for shopping* is an individual character-breakdown form designed to including lists of costume pieces for an individual character and the basic size information on the actor who will play it. The form also provides space for source notation. (See fig. 5.8, "Character Breakdown for Shopping for Vince in Holly Cole's Hypothetical Production of *Pulp Fiction*" and A.6.)

Character wardrobe continuity pages are completed as designs are more or less finalized and preparations made to pack the wardrobe truck for the shoot. Basically dressing lists for principals, character wardrobe continuity pages get very specific in preparation for recording costume continuity. A continuity page must detail what an actor was wearing when a scene was shot and precisely how he or she was wearing it. (Sample pages, including wardrobe continuity notes, appear in figs. 1.6, 1.7, and A.12.) For more on wardrobe continuity, see Part 8, *Shoot*.

In order to develop costume budgets and acquire costume stock for extras, extras breakdowns are done, listing scenes in which atmosphere are required and describing by type and number the kind of costume stock needed. An *extras/featured extras scene costume breakdown* pulls information off the master-scene costume breakdown and gives you a list specifically detailing the count and character of background players, character groupings, and featured extras within each scene (see fig. 5.9), charting the information necessary for preliminary budgeting in these categories.

Summary breakdowns. The following costume summary breakdowns are useful for conferences, budgeting, and shopping preparation. (Principal player and extras costume summaries can be particularly useful in budget-justification conferences.)

The individual *character summary breakdown* is a short list of all changes for a single character (see fig. 5.10). It includes information on doubling and stunt work, and is particularly useful when doing the character budget summary work described in Part 6, *Costume Budgets*.

The *extras/featured extras summary breakdown* (see figs. 5.11, 5.12) is particularly useful when preparing to rent and purchase costume stock for extras. Since most of these performers will be costumed on a walk-in basis, it is body count that matters: how many kids, cops, prostitutes, and so forth. An extras summary can help you plan for the quantities you need. On action films, a *"kill" count*, also called a *stunt count*, can be helpful, providing, as it does, the total number of doubled costumes needed for each stunt. *Uniform summaries* are also common. Since these costume summaries are, ultimately, most useful for budget justification conferences, changes are only minimally detailed, if at all. It is the numbers that matter on these forms, since, when a production looks to save a significant chunk of money, the number of extras gets cut first.

Additional breakdown forms are detailed in Parts 6 *(Costume Budgets)*, 7 *(Prep)*, and 8 *(Shoot)*.

The costume crossplot. The costume crossplot is a graph-like representation of the entire script (see figs. 5.2, 5.3, and 5.4 (detail), and A.1). Intended as a kind of "cheat sheet," a crossplot allows you to learn, at a glance, who is in each scene, in what change, and whether any doubling of the change is necessary. While some costumers find it useful, others dislike this form because it gives little specific costume change information.

> To do a good budget, you need a good crossplot. *(Buffy Snyder, costume designer and costume supervisor, former president of Local 705, Motion Picture Costumers Union)*

The following notation guidelines are used in the costume crossplots illustrated in figs. 5.2, 5.3, and 5.4, and A.1:

1. The *first four vertical columns* give scene number, set/action, day/night number, and interior/exterior. In noting day/night numbers, remember that fantasy and montage sequences are given their own set of numbers.

2. *Additional vertical columns* list the characters. Starting at the far left, immediately after the interior/exterior column, principal players are listed, in order of importance. Day players and extras are next to one another, clustered according to their scene groups. Extras may be grouped by type. In order to keep crossplots, like the one for Holly Cole's Hypothetical Production of *Pulp Fiction*, in figs. 5.2 and 5.3 (detail), to a workable width, each page lists only the day players and extras that are in the scenes on that page.

3. *Horizontal rows* under the character columns note, by change number, the characters in each scene. Change numbers follow the action notation guidelines indicated above: "D" for a distress double; "S" for a stunt double; "x" for each phase of distress; plus (+) for an added layer; minus (-) for a subtracted layer; color dots to indicate the nature of staining action, including blue for water, brown for dirt, red for blood, and so forth). Nudity is indicated with an "N."

Note: In films that employ many extras, the crossplot can become unwieldy, especially when all extras are noted on each crossplot page. Noting extras and day players *only* on the page that includes their scenes is one way of keeping the crossplot to a manageable length. While this makes doing the total character count more difficult, it does keep the crossplot pages to a reasonable width. The more unwieldy the crossplot, the less you want to carry it around as a cheat sheet.

Breakdown Formats

In actuality, there are no universal costume breakdown forms, as we said above. Every costume designer and costume supervisor has his or her own particular approach to the process. There is, however, one universal law in the "breakdown" business: Costume breakdowns, and all other costume department paperwork, must incorporate the most up-to-date script-related information issued by production. This includes, but is not restricted to, the following:

1. scene numbers
2. story day/night number (e.g., day number one, also written as D-1)
3. interior/exterior (written as INT./EXT.)
4. names of characters
5. types and number of extras

This means that all costume department paperwork, beginning with breakdowns, should conform to the following production-issued documents:

1. The latest *shooting script*, with scenes numbered according to key story points, locations, and key camera angles (see C.9).

2. The latest *shooting schedule* (called a "one-liner" schedule, see fig. 5.13), which list the date on which a scene will be shot, along with key actors in each scene and types and numbers of atmosphere (also known as *one-liners*, because they reduce the key action of each scene to a single-line description).

3. The *day-out-of-days* (fig. 5.14), a schedule that lists the dates on which each actor starts work (S/W), continues work (W), and finishes work (W/F).

Given the vagaries of film production, and thus, film production paperwork, it is worth remembering (and compensating for) the fact that shooting scripts change, sometimes on a daily basis—and often vary, from draft to draft, in the amount of information they give regarding scene numbers, sets, story detail, and camera angles. Scripts are often unclear in their day/night notation and vague on the exact passage of time. (The final determination of the script's passage of time is often settled in discussions with the director and the script supervisor, and then incorporated into the other production office paperwork. Often, the costume designer is the first to do a day/night breakdown, because the costume designer is hired before the script supervisor comes on board. Reconciling the designer's day/night breakdown with the script supervisor's day/night breakdown is a step that should not be missed.) In addition, scripts often lack detailed notation on the types of extras in a scene, and many "logical" atmospheric extras may not be indicated (e.g., the ambulance crew at the roadside accident). How many and what kind of extras are to appear in a given scene are questions often answered in discussions with the director, the AD, the art director, the cinematographer, and the head of extras casting.

Doing costume breakdowns can take on the aspect of a private ritual, thanks to the level of concentration it takes and its importance to the success of your job. Consequently, many costumers have decided preferences when it comes to styles of notation and the look of the breakdown forms. However, expressing too decided a preference for a particular breakdown style can be a handicap in a job interview, unless you also express a willingness to be flexible.

All of this becomes moot, of course, if you take advantage of the computer software, now available, that standardizes breakdown and budget forms. There are a number of software packages for features and episodic television that create forms and can link databases, for the quick configuration and reconfiguration of character breakdowns, crossplots, and budgets. (Brad Loman, former Vice President of the Costume Designers Guild, and a television designer noted for his ability to design three series at once, developed a very useful computer program called CostumePro, used by many in the industry. It is available through Power Production Software, www.powerproduction.com.)

> I think, as we become more technologically oriented, there are more and more demands
> made on the artistic or crafts department. As the paperwork has increased, so have the tools
> with which to produce and move that paperwork. New budget programs can be utilized;
> and the creators of those programs are willing to work with individual clients to custom-
> tailor programs for each person's needs. *(Pat Welch, costume designer)*

In fact, well-honed computer skills make the revising of costume breakdowns and budgets a great deal easier, especial in this business, where scripts and budgets change daily. When scenes and characters are added or cut, when actions are rewritten and schedules changed, the computer can save you time in the altering of breakdowns and the recalculation of budget figures. And the flashiness of a slick computer print-out will score you points in budget-justification meetings with the production office.

FIG. 5.1: THE SCENE COSTUME BREAKDOWN FORM

Hypothetical *Pulp Fiction* Project

Sc	d/n	Set/Action	i/e	Character	Chng	Costume	Notes
1	D1	Denny's hold up	I	Vince	1	Dork outfit	
1	D1		I	Jules	1	Dork outfit	
1	D1		I	Pumpkin	1	casual daywear	
1	D1		I	Honey Bunny	1	casual daywear	
1	D1		I	Denny's waitress	1	waitress uniform	
1	D1		I	Denny's manager	1	Suit	
1	D1		I	Denny's cook	1	cook uniform	
1	D1		I	Denny's busboy	1	busboy	
1	D1		I	Denny's patrons	1	casual daywear	
2	D1	'74 Chevy go to hit	I	Vince	2	black hit man suit	
2	D1		I	Jules	2	black hit man suit	
3	D1	Nova trunk load guns	E	Vince	2	black hit man suit	
3	D1		E	Jules	2	black hit man suit	
4	D1	College apt. ctyd load in	E	Vince	2	black hit man suit	
4	D1		E	Jules	2	black hit man suit	
4	D1		E	College apt. dwellers	2	morning college duds	
5	D1	College apt. lobby gossip	I	Vince	2	black hit man suit	
5	D1		I	Jules	2	black hit man suit	
6	D1	College apt. elevator Mia gossip	I	Vince	2	black hit man suit	
6	D1		I	Jules	2	black hit man suit	
7	D1	College apt. hall massage chat	I	Vince	2	black hit man suit	
7	D1		I	Jules	2	black hit man suit	
8	D1	College apt. hit	I	Vince	2	black hit man suit	
8	D1		I	Jules	2	black hit man suit	
8	D1		I	Brett	1s/1xs	breakfast preppy casual	2 phase shooting-shoulder&kill
8	D1		I	Marvin	1	breakfast casual	
8	D1	College apt. hit	I	Roger	1s	breakfast surfer casual	stunt man for kill?

s-indicates stunt/stunt double   d- indicates a destructive action that indicates costume multiples
a red dot indicates blood   a brown dot indicates dirt   a blue dot indicates water   - indicates a stripped piece
x's indicate phases of distress   + indicates an added piece or layer

Costume Crossplot for Hypothetical *Pulp Fiction* Project

Sc#	Set/Action	d/n	i/e	VINCE	JULES	MIA	MARSELLUS	PUMPKIN	HONEYBUNNY	BUTCH	FABIENNE	LANCE	JODY	CAPT. KOONS	THE WOLF
1	Denny's robbery	D1	i	1	1			1	1						
2	'74 Chevy go to hit	D1	i	2	2										
3	Chevy trunk	D1	e	2	2										
4	Apt. Ctyd Mia gossip	D1	e	2	2										
5	Apt. Reception Mia gossip	D1	i	2	2										
6	Apt. elevator	D1	i	2	2										
7	Apt. Hallway	D1	i	2	2										
8	Apt #49 hit	D1	i	2	2										
9	Title card: Vince Mia date														
10	Sally Le Roy's Butch c.u.	D1	i							1					
11	'64 Malibu cool drivin'	D1	e	1	1										
12	Sally Le Roy's greet	D1	e	1	1										
13	Sally Le Roy's bar tiff	D1	i	1	1		1			1					
14	Lance's kitchen stud chat	N2	i	3									1		
15	Lance's bedroom heroin hit	N2	i	3								1			
16	Marsellus' house note	N2	e	3+											
7-29	Marsellus liv rm/dressing rm	N2	i	3+		1									
30	Jackrabbit Slim's arrival	N2	e	3+		1+									
31	Slim's ordering	N2	i	3+ 3		1+ 1									
32	Slim's ladies room cocaine	N2	i			1									
33	Slim's dining	N2	i	3		1									
34	Slim's dance floor	N2	i	3d-		1d-									
35	Marsellus liv rm find heroin	N2	i	3+ 3		1+ 1									
36	Marsellus bath rm	N2	i	3											
7-41	M liv rm/bathrm overdosing	N2	i	3/3d		1d									
2-43	64 Chevy movin	N2	e	3xs		1xs									
44	Lance liv rm answer phone	N2	i									2			
45	Chevy/Lance int phone chat	N2	i/e	3x		1x						2			
46	Lance's crash	N2	e	3xs		1xs						2			
47	Lances' bedrm to livrm Jody	N2	i	3x		1x						2	2		
48	Lance's spare rm panic	N2	i									2	2		
49	Lance's livrm stabbing	N2	i	3x		1xs 1xx						2	2		
50	Chevy dazed drive	N2	e	3x		1xx+									
51	Marsellus hs goodbye	N2	e	3x		1xx+									
52	TV-Speed racer	Flbk	i												
53	Butch's Mom's watch story	Flbk	i											1	
54	Butch locker rm prefight	N3	i							2 2+					
55	Title Card: The Gold Watch														
56	Alley long shot wait	N3	e												
57	Taxi-watch Butch escape	N3	i							2+x s					
58	Taxi -Butch arrival	N3	i							2+x					

Sc#	DENNY'S WAITRESS	DENNY'S MANAGER	DENNY'S COOKS	DENNY'S BUSBOYS	DENNY'S PATRONS	MARVIN	ROGER	BRETT	4TH KID	COLLEGE APT. PATRONS	ENGLISH DAVE	TRUDI
1	1	1	1	1	1							
2												
3												
4										1		
5										1		
6												
7												
8						1	1s	1D 1XS	1s			
9												
10												
11												
12											1	
13												
14												1
15												
16												
7-29												
30												
31												
32												
33												
34												
35												
36												
7-41												
2-43												
44												1
45												1
46												
47												1
48												
49												1
50												
51												
52												
53												
54												
55												
56												
57												
58												

Sc#	SLIM'S PATRONS	SLIM'S UNIFORMED STAFF	BUDDY HOLLY	ED SULLIVAN	RICKY NELSON	MARILYN MONROE	ZORRO	JAMES DEAN	DONNA REED	DEAN MARTIN	JERRY LEWIS	PHILLIP MORRIS MIDGET	MAMIE VAN DOREN	SLIM'S ENTERTAINERS
1–16														
7-29														
30	1	1												
31	1	1	1	1	1	1	1	1	1	1	1	1	1	1
32	1													
33	1	1	1	1	1	1	1	1	1	1	1	1	1	1
34	1	1	1	1	1	1	1	1	1	1	1	1	1	1
35–58														

Sc#	BUTCH JR.	BUTCH'S MOM	KLONDIKE	ESMARELDA	DEAD WILSON	WILSON'S TRAINER	FIGHT PATRONS	ACCIDENT BYSTANDERS	LOOKY LOO WOMAN	GAWKER 1	GAWKER 2	MAYNARD	ZED
1–52													
53	1	1											
54			1										
55													
56				1									
57				1									
58				1									

FIG. 5.2: THE COSTUME CROSSPLOT FORM

Costume Crossplot for Hypothetical *Pulp Fiction* Project

FIG. 5.3: THE COSTUME CROSSPLOT FORM

Cell	Set/Action	d/n	i/e	VINCE	JULES	MIA	MARSELLUS	PUMPKIN	HONEY BUNNY	BUTCH	FABIENNE	LANCE	JODY	CAPT. KOONS	THE WOLF	DENNY'S WAITRESS	DENNY'S MANAGER	DENNY'S COOKS	DENNY'S BUSBOYS	DENNY'S PATRONS	MARVIN	ROGER	BRETT	4TH KID	COLLEGE APT. PATRONS	ENGLISH DAVE	TRUDI	BUTCH JR.	BUTCH'S MOM	KLONDIKE	ESMARELDA	DEAD WILSON	WILSON'S TRAINER	FIGHT PATRONS	ACCIDENT BYSTANDERS	LOOKY LOO WOMAN	GAWKER 1	GAWKER 2	MAYNARD	ZED	THE GIMP	JIMMY	GAMBLERS	CROUPIER	LUCKY LADIES	MONSTER JOE	BAQUEL
59	Taxi whipping	N3	e							2+xs																2					1s																
60	Wilson's locker rm mourning	N3	i	4		2				2x-xs																								1	1												
61	Taxi chng clothes	N3	i			2				3d																								1	1												
62	Phone booth call in rain	N3	e							3x	1/N																					1		1	1												
63	Motel drop off	N3	e							3x	N																					1	1	1													
64	Motel lovemaking	N3	i							N/4	2																					1															
65	Motel shower	N3	i							4/5	3																																				
66	Motel watch hunt	D4	i							5s																																					
7-70	Honda rant & rave	D4	i/e							5																																					
1-73	Apt approach	D4	e							5																																					
4-75	Apt Ctyd approach	D4	e							5																																					
76	Apt get watch, kill Vince	D4	i	4-ds						5																																					
7-79	Ctyd/car escape	D4	e							5																																					
80	Honda hits Marsellus & runs	D4	i/e				3ds 3ks 3xs			5ds 5ks 5xs																											1 1sd											
81	Mason-Dixon fight	D4	i				3xxx			5xs																											1	1									
2-83	Mason-Dixon torture&escape	D4	i							5xs																													1	1	1					
84	Mason-Dixon find sword	D4	i				3xxx			5xxx																													1	1	1					
85	Mason-Dixon sneak up	D4	i							5xxx																													1sd	1sd	1					
86	Russel's rm killing	D4	i			3	3xxx			5xxx																																				
87	Pawnshop chopper escape	D4	e							5xxx	4																																				
88	Hotel rm worrying	D4	i							5xxx																																				
89	Chopper movin	D4	e							5xxx																																				
90	Hotel escape	D4	e							5xxx	4+																																			
91	Title card: Bonnie Situation																																												
92	College Bathroom	D1	i																																											
93	Apt. close up shooting	D1	i	2	2																	1 1x	1x	1																						
94	Apt.Vince & Jules react	D1	i	2	2																	1 1x	1x	1																						
5-96	Nova in & killing	D1	e/i	2d+	2d+																1d 1x 1xs			1																						
97	Jimmy's Nova pull in	D1	e	2x	2x																																			1					
98	Jimmy's bathroom cleaning	D1	i	2x	2x																1xx																				1					
99	J's kitchen bitchin	D1	i	2x	2x																																				1					
100	Marcellus dine rm call	D1	i	2x			3 4																																							
101	J's bedrm help call	D1	i		2x																																									
102	Wolf's hotel suite gambling	D1	i												1s																												1	1	1		
103	Title Card: 9 min 37 sec																																												
104	Jimmy's porsche arrival	D1	e	2x											1																															
105	J's Wolf arrival	D1	i	2x	2x										1																															
106	J's garage check out car	D1	i	2x	2x										1						1xx																									
107	J's kitchen strategy	D1	i	2x	2x										1																										1	1				
108	J's bedroom oak's nice	D1	i	2x	2x																																				1	1				
109	J's garage cleaning	D1	i	2xx	2xx																																					1				

FIG. 5.4: CROSSPLOT DETAILS

Head these columns with the character names
List principals/stars first, and then list characters as they appear.

Sc#	Set/Action	d/n	i/e	VINCE	JULES	MIA	MARSELLUS	PUMPKIN	HONEYBUNNY	BUTCH	FABIENNE	LANCE	JODY	CAPT. KOONS	THE WOLF	DENNY'S WAITRESS	DENNY'S MANAGER	DENNY'S COOKS		
1	Denny's robbery	D1	i	1	1			1	1							1	1	1	1	1
2	'74 Chevy go to hit	D1	i	2	2								2 change numbers are listed by scene							
3	Chevy trunk	D1	e	2	2															
				day/night and interior/exterior notes are made for each scene in these columns																
	Describe the location as well																			
	as the key action of the scene																			
	in these spaces																			

FIG. 5.5: SCENE WORKSHEET

Hypothetical *Pulp Fiction* Project

SCENE#S 31-34 JACKRABBIT SLIM'S

CHAR	Buddy Holly	Ed Sullivan	Marilyn Monroe	James Dean	Zorro	Young Elvis
	dinner jkt	grey suit	7 year itch dress	red zip jacket	black mask	50's sport shirt
	tux pants	white shirt	tap pants	jeans	black hat	tight black trousers
	formal shirt	thin tie	bullet bra	tee	black period shirt	sox
	tux accessories	sox, shoes,belt	pumps,hose	boots,sox	black spanish pants	pointy toe shoes
	Holly glasses	name tag	jewelry	name tag	black cape	belt
	sox,shoes		name tag		black cumberbund	name tag
	name tag				black gloves	
					name tag	

CHAR	Martin & Lewis	Donna Reed	Phillip Morris Midg	Mamie Van Doren	Ricky Nelson	5 rock musicians
	50's tux	50's shirtwaist	bell boy uniform	50's sweater	white shirt	50's sport shirts
	tux shirt	bullet bra	bell boy hat	pedal pushers	50s vneck sweater	black trousers
	tux accessories	crinoline	shirt	wide belt	dress pants	sox
	sox, tux shoes	jewelry	white gloves	hose	2 tone shoes	pointy toe shoes
	name tag	hose,pumps	sox, shoes	pumps	sox	belts
		name tag	name tag	bullet bra	name tag	name tags
				jewelry		
				name tag		

CHAR	Brenda Lee	Jerry Lee Lewis	50's Staff	Casual patrons	Dressy patrons
	50's prom dress	wild dinner jacket	1 carhop uniform	30 upscale men	20 dressy men
	bullet bra	tux pants	2 busboys uniform	Melrose casual	20 dressy women
	crinoline	tux shirt	2 bartenders uniforms	30 upscale women	10 twist men
	hose	tux accessories		Melrose casual	10 twist women
	pumps	2 tone shoes			
	hair bow	sox			
	jewelry	name tag			
	name tag				

FIG. 5.6: CHARACTER BREAKDOWN FORM

Production: Hypothetical <u>PULP FICTION</u> Project   **Actor: <u>John Travolta</u>**
Character: <u>Vince</u>   **Telephone: _____**

Ch#	Sc#	D/N	I/E	Set/Action	Costume	Notes
1	1	D1	I	Denny's hold up	Dork outfit	
1	11	D1	E	'64 Malibu drivin' cool	Dork outfit	
1	12	D1	E	Sally Le Roy's arrival	Dork outfit	
1	13	D1	I	Sally Le Roy's bar tiff	dork outfit	
1	112	D1	E	Jimmy's backyard dork dressing	Dork outfit	
1	113	D1	I	Jimmy's garage – drive plan	Dork outfit	
1	114	D1	I	Jimmy's garage – still photo	Dork outfit	
1	116	D1	E	Monster Joe's– Wolf flirts	Dork outfit	
1	117	D1	I	Denny's hold up	Dork outfit	
1	118	D1	I	Denny's bathroom	Dork outfit	
1	119	D1	I	Denny's hold up	Dork outfit	
2	2	D1	I	'74 Chevy go to hit	black hit man suit	
2	3	D1	E	Nova trunk load guns	black hit man suit	
2	4	D1	E	College apt. ctyd load in	black hit man suit	
2	5	D1	I	College apt. lobby gossip	black hit man suit	
2	6	D1	I	College apt. elevator Mia gossip	black hit man suit	
2	7	D1	I	College apt. hall massage chat	black hit man suit	
2	8	D1	I	College apt. hit	black hit man suit	
2	93	D1	I	College apt. Die Die miracle	black hit man suit	
2	94	D1	I	College apt. miracle killing	black hit man suit	
2s	95	D1	E	'74 Nova peel out	black hit man suit	stunt driving
2d/2d	96	D1	E	'74 Nova Marvin accident	black hit man suit	gets super bloody
2x	97	D1	E	Arrival at Jimmie's	black hit man suit	phase 1 bloody
2x	98	D1	I	Jimmie's bathroom wash up	black hit man suit	phase 1 bloody
2x	99	D1	I	Jimmie's kitchen complaint	black hit man suit	phase 1 bloody
2x	105	D1	I	Jimmie's living rm Wolf intro	black hit man suit	phase 1 bloody
2x	106	D1	I	Jimmie's garage check out car	black hit man suit	phase 1 bloody
2x	107	D1	I	Jimmie's kitchen: the plan	black hit man suit	phase 1 bloody
2xx	109	D1	I	'74 Nova cleaning	black hit man suit	phase 2 bloody

FIG. 5.7: CHARACTER BREAKDOWN FORM

Production: Hypothetical <u>PULP FICTION</u> Project

Actor: John <u>Travolta</u>

Character: Vince

Telephone: _____

Ch#	Sc#	D/N	I/E	Set/Action	Costume	Notes
2xx	110	D1	I	Jimmie's garage: clean car	black hit man suit	phase 2 bloody
2xx	111	D1	E	Jimmie's backyard:hose down	black hit man suit/nude/dork	phase 2 bloody, wet
3	14	N2	I	Lance's Kitchen: stud chat	date suit	carry coat
3	15	N2	I	Lance's bedroom: heroin	date suit	roll up sleeves for heroin, carry overcoat
3+	16	N2	E	Marcellus house: Vince arrival	date suit	wear overcoat
3+	17	N2	I	Marcellus house: Vince entry	date suit	wear overcoat
3+	19	N2	I	Marcellus house: find intercom	date suit	wear overcoat
3+	20-27	N2	I	Marcellus house: intercom chat	date suit	full view/video insert
3+	29	N2	I	Marcellus house: Let's go	date suit	wear overcoat
3+	30	N2	E	Jackrabbit Slim's arrival	date suit	wear overcoat
3+/3	31	N2	I	Jackrabbit Slim's order	date suit	take overcoat off
3	33	N2	I	Jackrabbit Slim's dining	date suit	
3d	34	N2	I	Jackrabbit Slim's dance floor	date suit	twist, sweat potential
3	35	N2	I	Marcellus house: dance entry/disco	date suit	no coat
3	36	N2	I	Marcellus' bathroom chat	date suit	
3	38	N2	I	Marcellus' bathroom chat	date suit	
3	40	N2	I	Marcellus' bathroom chat	date suit	
3d	41	N2	I	Marcellus' liv rm: body found	date suit	stains from body
3xs	42	N2	I	'64 Chevy movin'	date suit	phase 1 distress,stunt driver double
3xs	43	N2	I	'64 Chevy movin'	date suit	phase 1 distress, stunt driver double
3x	45	N2	I	'64 Chevy/Lance's phone intercuts	date suit	phase 1 distress
3xs	46	N2	E	Lance's car crash	date suit	phase 1 distress, stunt driver double
3x	47	N2	I	Lance's bedrm to livrm panic	date suit	phase 1 distress
3x	49	N2	I	Lance's livrm adrenalin shot	date suit	phase 1 distress
3xs	50	N2	E	'64 Chevy movin'	date suit	phase 1 distress, frazzled,driver double
3xs	51	N2	E	Marcellus' house good bye	date suit	phase 1 distress, frazzled,driver double
4	60	N3	I	Willis's Locker room	hit man suit	
4-ds	76	N3	I	Butch's apt. bathroom	hit man suit	lose duster, gets shot down,stunt double

FIG. 5.8: CHARACTER BREAKDOWN FOR SHOPPING

Hypothetical

Production: PULP FICTION Project

Agent: _____

Character: VINCE _____ **Telephone:** _____

Ht. _____ **Wt.** _____ **Suit** _____ **Shirt** n _____ /slv _____ **Shoe** _____ **Hat** _____

Pants w _____ /i _____ **Sweater** _____ **Trunks** _____ **Ring** _____ **Actor: JOHN TRAVOLTA**

Allergies

CHG#	SCENE	D/NI/E	SET/ACTION	COSTUME PIECES	NOTES	SOURCE
1	1,11-13	d1 i/e	Denny's, Sally Le Roy's	USanta Cruz tee shirt		
	112-116		Jimmy's, Monster Joe	Red shorts		
	117-119		Denny's	thongs		
2	2-8	d1 i/e	Chevy,college apt hit	black suit w/ thin lapel		
	93-95			white shirt		
	2d 96		Chevy Marvin accident	thin black tie	distress doubles	
	2xs 97-107		Jimmy's escape&plan	black belt	phase 1 distress, drive double	
	2xx 109-111		Jimmy's clean up	black sox	phase 2 distress	
				black shoes		
				shoulder holster		
				duster		
3/3+	14-29	n2	Lance's, Mia date prep	jazzy black suit		
	3d 30-34		Slim's	jazzy tie	stain potential	
	3d 35-41		Marcellus'-Mia o.d.	white shirt	stains from body	
	3xs 42-46,50-51		chevy movin'	black belt	stunt driver,distress phase	
	3x 47-49		Lance's panic	black sox		
				slip on shoes		
4	60 n3		locker rm	white shirt		
	4-sd 76 d4		Butch's apt death	thin black tie	stunt double, bloody death	
				black suit	distress doubles	
				black dress shoes		
				sox		
				coat		

FIG. 5.9: EXTRAS/DAY PLAYERS SCENE COSTUME BREAKDOWN

Hypothetical PULP FICTION Project

Sc#	D/N	I/E	Action	Characters	#s	Costume	Notes
1	D1	I	Denny's holdup	Denny's waitress	2	waitress uniform	
117-119				Denny's manager	1	Suit	
				Denny's cook	3	cook uniform	
				Denny's busboy	2	busboy	
				Denny's patrons	35	casual daywear	
				1 Long Hair Yuppie			
				12 average casual men			
				5 business men			
				10 average casual women			
				5 kids			
				2 character men			
4	D1	E/I	College apt. ctyd & lobby	College apt. dwellers	5	morning college duds	
				2 sorority types			
				1 punk guy			
				2 yuppie dorks			
8	D1	I	College apt. hit	Brett	3+stunt double	breakfast preppy casual	2 phase shooting
92-94				Marvin	4d rpt for 95	breakfast casual	stunt rig
				Roger	3d	breakfast surfer casual	stunt rig
				Fourth College kid	3d	breakfast casual	stunt rig
12-13	D1	E/I	Sally Le Roy's arrival	English Dave	1	slick outfit	
14,44-49	N2	I	Lance's	Trudi	1	druggy casual	
30-34	N2	I/E	Jackrabbit Slim's	Buddy Holly	1	Buddy Holly look alike	
				Ed Sullivan	1	Ed Sullivan look alike	
				Ricky Nelson	1	Ricky Nelson look alike	
				Marilyn Monroe	1	7 Year Itch dress	
				Zorro	1	Zorro look alike	
				James Dean	1	Rebel w/o a cause	
				Donna Reed	1	Donna Reed look alike	
				Dean Martin	1	Dean Martin look alike	
				Jerry Lewis	1	Jerry Lewis look alike	

FIG. 5.10: CHARACTER SUMMARY BREAKDOWN FORM

Production: Hypothetical <u>PULP FICTION</u> Project
Character: Vince

Actor: <u>John Travolta</u>
Telephone: _____

Change#	Scene#	D/N	I/E	Set/Action	Costume	Notes
1	1,117-119	D1	I	Denny's hold up	Dork outfit	
	11-13	D1	E/I	Sally Le Roy delivery		
	112-114	D1	E	Jimmy's house dork dressing		
	116	D1	E	Monster Joe's- Wolf flirts		
2 multiples	2-8,93-94	D1	I/E	College kid hit	black hit man suit	
2ds	95-97	D1	E/I	'74 Nova Marvin accident	black hit man suit	stunt driving, gets super bloody
2x	97-107	D1	E/I	Jimmie's plan&clean phase1	black hit man suit	phase 1 bloody
2xx	109-111	D1	I	Jimmie's clean&wash phase 2	black hit man suit	phase 2 bloody,wet
3 multiples	14-15	N2	I	Lance's Kitchen: heroin prep	date suit	carry coat, roll sleeves for heroin hit
3+	16-29	N2	E	Marcellus house pick up	date suit	wear overcoat
3d	30-34	N2	E	Jackrabbit Slim's date	date suit	overcoat on&off, sweat doubles?
3d/3x	35-41,47-49	N2	I	Marcellus' Mia overdose/Lance's panic	date suit/distressed	stains from body, phase 1 distress
3xs	42-46,50-51	N2	I	'64 Chevy movin'	distressed date suit	phase 1 distress,stunt driver double
4multiples	60	N3	I	Willis's Locker room	hit man suit#2	
4-ds	76	D4	I	Butch's apt. bathroom	hit man suit#2	lose duster, gets shot down,stunt double

Hypothetical
Pulp Fiction Project

Sc#	D/N	I/E	Action	Costume types	#'s	Character Notes
				UNIFORMS		
1,117-119	D1	I	Denny's holdup	Denny's uniforms	7	3cooks,2busboys,2waitresses
30-34			Slim's	Slim's uniformed staff	8	2carhops, 2bartenders,4 busboys
81-86			Mason Dixon	Redneck cop	3s	Zed
102	D1	I	Wolf's Hotel Suite	spencer tux	1	Dealer
					TOTAL 20	
				50'S /SPECIALTY		
30-34	N2	I/E	Jackrabbit Slim's	Slim's entertainers/staff	17	50's icons
81-86	D4	I	Mason Dixon	Black leather bondage	1	The Gimp
54-60	N3	I		bloodied fighter outfit	1	Dead Wilson
					TOTAL 18	
				SEMI FORMAL		
102	D1	I	Wolf's hotel suite	tuxes, semi formals	9	5Dressy Male Gamblers, 4 Lucky ladies
					TOTAL 9	
				BUSINESS/DRESSY WEAR		
1,117-119			Denny's	suits	6	Denny's manager, 5 Denny's biz patrons
30-34			Slim's	"Melrose" dressy	20m 20w	Slim's patrons
					TOTAL 46	
				UPSCALE CASUAL		
12-13,60	D1	E/I	Sally Le Roy's/The fights	Casual & jazzy	62	2 English Dave, 50m+10w fight crowd
30-34			Slim's	"Melrose casual"	80	Slim's Patrons 40m, 40w
					TOTAL 142	
				AVERAGE CASUAL		
1,117-119			Denny's	casual daywear	30	15m 10w 5k Denny's patrons
4-8,	D1	E/I	College apt. ctyd & lobby	college types	8	2 sorority girls, 1 punk, 2 frat boys
8	D1	I	College apt. hit	breakfast casual	16	Brett 3,Brett stunt2, Marvin 4
92-97						Marvin dummy1, Roger3, 4th kid 3
14,44-49	N2	I	Lance's	druggy casual	1	Trudi
99-114	D1	I	Jimmie's clean up adventure	Jimmie	1	breakfast casual
115-116	D1	E/I	Monster Joe's	casual worker	2	Monster Joe, Raquel
81-86	D4	i	Mason-Dixon pawnshop	redneck casual	3	Maynard

FIG. 5.12: EXTRAS/DAY PLAYER SUMMARY FORM

Hypothetical
Pulp Fiction Project

Sc#	D/N	I/E	Action	Costume types	#s	Character Notes
12-13,60	D1	I	The fights	character casual	25	15 men, 10 hoods
				TOTAL	86	
			EXTRAS/DAYPLAYER			
				SUMMARY TOTALS:		
				UNIFORMS	20	
				50'S/SPECIALTY	18	
				SEMI-FORMAL	9	
				BUSINESS/DRESSY	46	
				UPSCALE CASUAL	142	
				AVERAGE CASUAL	86	

Shooting Schedule as of 8/5/96 - (PREPRODUCTION) **

Sc #	INT/EXT	Location / Description	Day	pgs.	char #s
30	INT	PHONE BOOTH — The fella's eat and check in with mothers	DAY 4	4/8 pgs.	1, 2
60	INT	FOUNTAIN SQUARE COFFEE SHOP — The threesome sip coffee and speak about college	DAY 8	1 7/8 pgs.	1, 2, 6
61	EXT	FOUNTAIN SQUARE COFFEE SHOP — Marty leaves Gunner in a cloud of dust	DAY 8	1 3/8 pgs.	1, 2, 6
		-- END OF DAY 1 -- Mon. Aug 19, 1996 -- 3 6/8 pgs.			
95	EXT	MERIDIAN HILLS COUNTRY CLUB — Fight starts over beards and Jews	DAY 15	4 3/8 pgs.	1, 2, 4, 6, 9, 10, 11, 14, 15
		-- END OF DAY 2 -- Tue, Aug 20. 1996 -- 4 3/8 pgs.			
75,77	EXT	BIFF'S BACKYARD — Biff tells Sonny to go for it now, while he can	DAY 10	1 4/8 pgs.	1, 23
76	EXT	BIFF'S BACKYARD — SONNY'S FANTASY: Sonny in Biff's shoes	FANTASY DAY	1/8 pgs.	1
31	EXT	SHIN'S HOUSE — The fellas pull up to Shin's house	DAY 4	1/8 pgs.	1, 2, 11
32	EXT	SHIN'S HOUSE — The fellas approach the house and are welcomed by Shins	DAY 4	1 1/8 pgs.	1, 2, 11
32A	EXT	SHIN'S HOUSE - PATIO — Shin shares his version of The American Dream	DAY 4	3 1/8 pgs.	1, 2, 11
33	EXT	SHIN'S HOUSE — Sonny and Gunner walk quickly back to car	DAY 4	2/8 pgs.	1, 2
113	INT	WEDDING CHAPEL — SONNY'S FANTASY: Gail objects to the wedding	FANTASY NIGHT	2/8 pgs.	1, 7
		-- END OF DAY 3 -- Wed, Aug 21, 1996 -- 6 4/8 pgs.			
107	INT	THE ATHENEUM — Sonny meets the Gail Thayer	NIGHT 17	1 pgs.	1, 2, 6, 7
108	EXT	ATHENEUM RESTAURANT — The foursome eat drink and are merry	NIGHT 17	1 pgs.	1, 2, 6, 7
109,111	EXT	ATHENEUM OUDOOR DANCE PAVILION — The foursome dance and nestle	NIGHT 17	4/8 pgs.	1, 2, 6, 7, 29
110	EXT	ATHENEUM OUDOOR DANCE PAVILION — SONNY'S FANTASY: Sonny & Gail are Fred & Ginger	FANTASY NIGHT	2/8 pgs.	1, 2, 6, 7, 29
		-- END OF DAY 4 -- Thu, Aug 22, 1996 -- 2 6/8 pgs.			

FIG. 5.14: DAY OUT OF DAYS SCHEDULE

"GOING ALL THE WAY"

SCHEDULE AS OF Tue, Jul 30, 1996

August													
Day of Month:	19	20	21	22	23	24	25	26	27	28	29	30	31
Day Of Week:	M	Tu	W	Th	F	Sa	Su	M	Tu	W	Th	F	Sa
Shooting Days:	1	2	3	4	5	6			7	8	9	10	11
1. SONNY	SW	W	W	W	W	W			W	W	W	W	W
2. GUNNER	SW	W	W	W	W	H			W	W	W	H	H
3. MOTHER		SW							SW	H	H	W	W
4. BUDDY		SW	H	H	W	H			H	W	H	W	W
5. FATHER	SW	W	W	W	WF							SW	W
6. MARTY			SW	W	H								
7. GAIL						WF							
8. NINA									SW	W	W	WF	
9. BLOW		SWWD											
10. WILKS		SWWD											
11. SHINS		SW	WF										
12. BEAUTIFUL YOUNG GIRL													
13. WAITER													
14. MITZI		SWF											
15. RICHIE		SWF											
16. LUKE													
17. BIG QUINN													
18. LURLENE													
19. TEENAGE BOY													
20. DEEDEE										SWF			
21. JOCKO													
22. FRENCHY													
23. BIFF			SWF										
24. BURLY GUY													
25. FARMER													
26. MINISTER													
27. CONDUCTOR													
28. DOCTOR				SWF									
29. CROONER													
OLDGUY													

DAY OUT OF DAYS SCHEDULE

Conversation Five:

On Costuming for Stunts, with Madeline Kozlowski

Costume designer Madeline Kozlowski has had a wide-ranging career designing for a variety of productions, including a number of action/adventure projects for film and television. Movies-of-the-week *Oceans of Fire* (1986), *Red River* (1988), *The Tower* (1993), *The Return of the Hunter* (1995), and the series *Battle Dome* (1999-2000) are just a few of her credits (fig. 5.15).

You've done a wide variety of stunt-laden scripts. Could you talk about designing for stunts?

I've blown up oil rigs in the Gulf of Mexico, killed wagon-train immigrants in Westerns, and melted an actor in *The Tower*, an interesting picture about a building run by a computer. We fried the CEO in a sauna, chopped the head of security in half with an elevator door, and continued in this manner until the body count just couldn't go any higher.

How did you ever figure out the costume coverage you needed? How did you second-guess all the things that could go wrong?

There's nothing to be afraid of. You must always proceed with safety and caution, but the professional stunt coordinators and special effects supervisors are experts. They know how to do their stuff, and, basically, you do what they tell you.

FIG. 5.15

Madeline Kozlowski's design for Ken Norton in *Oceans of Fire* (1986)

When a project is stunt-heavy and costume multiples must be purchased and prepared in advance, how do you cope with late casting?

It depends. Many stars have regular stunt doubles. I did a Western with the actor Bruce Boxleitner, whose regular stunt double, Cliff McLaughlin, lives in L.A. I was able to fit him at the studio instead of on location.

Often, a production company will hire a stable of stuntmen and women to do stunts for a number of the actors. The stuntmen and women are represented by an agency that specializes in stunt actors. These agencies have the measurements for their clients on hand. You simply call the agency and request the sizes you need. For simple stunt work, a costumer generally buys three sets of a particular outfit: the first set for the actor, the second, one size up, and the third, two sizes up. This allows for padding worn underneath the clothes.

But don't you still run into surprises, even when you have size information in advance?

Oh sure. I did a film that was stunt-heavy, for Stephen Cannell, in Acapulco, Mexico. We took three stuntmen and two stuntwomen from L.A, and then picked up three more stuntmen in Mexico. Just as we were going to shoot the helicopter jump sequences, the stunt coordinator took the female stuntperson out of the shot and replaced her with one of the men, because the woman was not trained in jumps from that height. But because I had my magic three sets, I was able to dress the smallest guy in the largest outfit. They just had to be careful how they shot him. Most of the time, however, stunt casting is going to get as close to the actors' sizes as they can.

Is it three copies of the outfit for every stage of the stunt?

Generally, yes. Often an actor will have twelve to twenty-four changes in an action/adventure film. If he has a stunt sequence in change numbers one, six, and seven, you would need three sets of each of those changes. If it's a very difficult stunt, you would definitely need more sets. You discuss this with the stunt coordinator. Buy more sets if the costume goes through stages of distress. Example: stage one—actor falls down in the gorse bushes: dirt on knees, jacket sleeve torn, face dirty; stage two—he gets shot in the arm: blood runs down sleeve; stage three—he gets dragged by the bus: shoes get scraped, pants ripped, sleeve of his jacket ripped out entirely.

Generally, in a picture, the lead actor gets dressed, he goes to work, something happens, he goes home, changes clothes, and goes back to work the next day—not like the nightmare of a *Die Hard*, where one outfit gets destroyed over the course of an entire picture!

Didn't you work on a *Die Hard*-like movie, in which one outfit, on the leading man, goes through hell and back?

The Tower, a made-for-TV movie, starring Paul Reiser. The director was very specific about how he wanted the main character to look. And we were going to shoot blue screen, as well as miniatures and a number of other effects processes. I chose a beautiful olive green $2,500 cashmere jacket for Paul that had no blue in it whatsoever. The pants were a dark navy, Dolce & Gabbana, at $1,200 a pair. I remember the shirt exactly because it was such a problem to find something that tied the jacket and the pants together; it was a black and tan large check, from Perry Ellis. His tie was a black silk knit, and on his feet were beautiful black Madison loafers. He looked great, but this outfit cost a fortune, and we needed three sets, for twelve stages of distress—on a TV-movie budget!

Hair, makeup, and I made charts to determine these twelve stages of distressing—so we could have some kind of plan from the beginning, and since films are not shot in story sequence. How we did it: In stage one, the actor gets sprayed with a fire extinguisher on his brand-new jacket. In spite of the fact that I live by the "three" rule, I said, "Perhaps only two sport coats, at $2,500 a piece." I bought a piece of similar cashmere, scotch-guarded it to death, and had effects test it with the fire extinguisher foam (which was really shaving foam). It wiped off beautifully, but we found that we could actually blow the foam off with a hair dryer. With two jackets, we could easily get four to five takes, or better.

Now, I'm looking at how to afford a minimum of twenty-six pairs of the Dolce & Gabbana pants. Solution: real pants for the actor, and duplication for stunts. I bought fabric so close in color and material, you couldn't tell the difference, and a tailor duplicated the Dolce & Gabbanas for $200 a pair.

You have to realize that stunt sequences are not fabulous close-ups. What I needed was the cut, the fullness, and the silhouette of the originals in the fabric I bought to match. Some designers might think, "Well, I can't afford Dolce & Gabbana pants, so I won't buy them. But these pants were perfect for Paul Reiser in cut and style. Studio services at Neiman Marcus located eight pairs for Paul, and my tailor made eighteen pairs at $200 each. You have to be willing to solve problems and do the extra work. It was difficult to find the fabric to match, do the tests, and make the pants, but it paid off.

Were you trying to save money so you could spend it somewhere else?

Yes, budget is always a consideration.

Could you talk a bit about actually working with the stunt players?

Too often, stunt performers are treated like extras. But these are really important members of the team, so I take extra time with them. When I was in Acapulco on the television series *Palace Guard*, I called all the stuntpeople in and fit their clothes. You know what they said to me? "Nobody ever fits us." And I thought, "Yeah, but I want this picture to look the best it can." To not have fittings is just stupid. I mean, why not? Why not make sure that the stuntman's pants are the right length? Why not make sure he's got enough room to move, instead of being faced with yet another crisis on set?

Do stuntpeople provide their own stunt pads?

Yes. A stuntperson comes to work equipped with basic padding for the elbows and knees, baseball sliding pads for the hips, tailbone protection, etc., and, generally, black Reeboks for shoes.

When you design for stunts, you need to consider clothing that can accommodate protective pads, that can be altered for harnesses, and that covers the arms, to the wrists, and the legs, to the ankle. Remember: (1) flesh-colored pads look like flesh-colored pads; it's better to cover the body parts, (2) elbows, knees, hips, and other joints need to be protected, (3) cuts will heal, bruises will fade, but ball-joint injury could be disastrous.

I think that getting some sense of the rigging and mechanics of stuntwork can demystify it a bit. Can you talk about squibs and bullet hits?

In a stunt that involves a bullet hit, the stuntman wears a T-shirt, over which the "squib rigging" is taped. (Tape is best, because the squib rig needs to be fixed as tightly to the body as possible.) A squib is the electrical firing device that creates that appearance of an explosion. The squib rig can be best described as an inverted "saucer" made of brass. The saucer is riveted to a piece of shoe-sole leather about two inches in diameter. This disc of leather is then stitched to a piece of industrial felt about one-eighth inch to one-quarter inch thick. A piece of heavy-density foam, for additional padding, is placed between this rig and the T-shirt. The squib, which is made up of two parts—the safety switch, which turns the device on, and a button, which actually sets off the charge placed into the depression of the "saucer"—is held in there with modeling clay. The blood bag is placed over the squib. The wires run from the squib to a battery. This charge can be fired either by the stuntman himself or by an effects man, off camera.

And the clothing itself needs to be one hundred percent natural fiber?

Correct, because the fabric needs to be fireproof. Synthetic fabrics melt. The fabric over the hit is sanded from the back until it's very thin, and breaks easily. If the stunt involves being hit by an arrow, the end of the arrow pops from under the fabric and rips the fabric, looking as if the arrow is coming out of the person's chest.

Isn't it dangerous to squib actors?

Generally, the stuntman wears the squib, not the actor. That's what stunt doubles do.

Have you ever seen blood from a stunt hit splatter, and hit other actors?

Other actors are seldom very close. It's all about how the director shoots the scene. A good example would be an explosion. In *Oceans of Fire* (fig. 5.15), we blew up an oil rig in the Gulf of Mexico. A trampoline was placed on the edge of the rig. The stuntman runs, jumps on the trampoline, and is catapulted into the water. You don't see the stunt man jump on the trampoline because the director shoots the face of the horrified rig owner as he watches the carnage, and then the editor cuts from the explosion to the owner's face, and only then to the stuntmen vaulting over the railing into the flaming water. Good editing pays off here. This is called "plenty of coverage."

Flaming actors must be scary.

To me, fire is always scary. But we use burn suits for a flaming stunt. We had quite a bit of fire in both *Oceans of Fire* and *The Tower.* How it works: The stunt man wears a Nomex suit under the burn suit. These Nomex suits look like long underwear, with socks, gloves, and hood. The burn suit is made of fire-resistant material, and includes a full head covering and mask. The special effects man arranges for the burn suit, and handles the whole procedure. It's like packing your own parachute. The burn suits are bulky, and often this effect does not involve any real clothing. In *Oceans of Fire*, the oil rig workers wore jumpsuits, which is what the burn suit looks like. We put a hard hat on the stuntman so the silhouette was right. All you will actually see is the shape of a man on fire. And it will probably be a night shot—burn suits look best at night. This will not be a close-up, and they always try to get it in one take. If you are working with a guy who's going to be fully in flames, he's going to be very specific about his blocking, so the effects crew knows exactly where and when to put out the flames.

What about partial burns—when a stuntperson will be near flame or partially on fire? What would they wear under these circumstances?

Nomex fire-retardant underwear. They will wear something protective on their body, topped by a full suit of Nomex, and then the costume. In *Celebrity Daredevils*, I provided Nomex suits for all the race car drivers. But the special effects supervisor will tell you exactly what you need to provide. You need to maintain communication with the effects and stunt people.

Technology is improving effects every day. On *Battle Dome*, the fireworks effects were all "cold": There was no fire or heat whatsoever—but it still makes me hold my breath.

Is the effects guy always the authority on the stunt protective equipment?

Explosions and fire stuff, yes. But padding can be up to the stuntman. You work with both of them.

PART SIX

Costume Budgets

Budget Basics

Putting together a film's costume budget is a tedious, difficult task, one that requires resourcefulness, patience, and savvy. Figuring out all the costume pieces required for principal characters, accounting for the multiples of those pieces needed for stuntwork, and getting a price on all of them is just the tip of the iceberg. And the costume budget must account for many factors beside the cost of principal characters' costumes, as you will see in the pages to come.

To master the art and science of costume budgeting, you must learn to
- anticipate all costs and potential crises;
- factor in special deals that can be struck;
- anticipate contingencies, and find funds for them;
- prioritize what must be done, so the money ends up "on screen."

The costume budget for a film comes in three basic versions: the *budget estimate*, the *preliminary budget*, and the *master budget*. The budget estimate is generated by the production office well before the costume designer is hired, and generally embodies a producer's or production manager's idea of how much the costumes on a film should cost to create and maintain. The preliminary budget, on the other hand, originates ideally with both the costume designer and the costume supervisor. It represents their educated, well-substantiated estimate of what it will cost to do their jobs. The master budget is the direct result of negotiations between production and the costume department. In the course of these negotiations, production's budget estimate for costumes and the preliminary budget figures presented by the designer and supervisor are compared; labor, services, materials, and funds argued for; and a "master" figure for the production and maintenance of costumes settled upon.

In all events, the phrase "*the* costume budget" is deceptive, implying one fixed, definitive sum. In reality, the costume budget is an organic entity. Not only does its form change, but the numbers grow and shrink, according to an infinitude of variables, among them, cost overruns in various departments, shooting schedule changes, added characters, changed stunts, and other vicissitudes of production that invariably take their toll on the department's bottom line.

The budget estimate

The budget estimate—production's ballpark figure for the cost of a project's costumes—is put together as a part of the initial budgeting of an entire production. Most often, it is calculated by the producer or unit production manager (UPM), although on some studio productions, it is done by the head of the studio's costume department. In most cases, however, the production budget for costumes is done by non-costume personnel. In all events, the budget estimate for costumes is made up of four line items:
1. Department staffing
2. Facilities (the wardrobe office, costume stock storage and fitting areas, the costume workroom)
3. Transport (wardrobe trucks or trailers) and special location setup equipment (tents, chairs, etc.)
4. Costume stock, including equipment, supplies, purchases, rentals, and wardrobe-related services

The production budget, of which the costume budget estimate is only one part, is vigilantly guarded by production. Traditionally, it is for their eyes only. Keeping these figures close to the vest, a production manager has more leverage in budget negotiations with department heads. A unit production manager who is deliberately evasive when it comes to hard numbers for the costume budget is hoping that the department's preliminary budget figures are lower than production's—a tactic that may save the production money right out of the gate. If you can find out who put together the production budget for your department, you may be able to dig up more specific numbers than the UPM is willing to divulge. However, the best hedge against getting shorted is to do your homework.

Before beginning work toward a preliminary budget, it is traditional for the costume designer to meet with the UPM. In this meeting, the designer must ask basic questions that only production can answer, among them:

• What are the conditions under which the costume department will be working? Are there department offices and costume storage facilities available via the production company? If you are working for a studio, are there built-in rental arrangements for office space, a costume storage cage? Is an automatic "general stock" charged to the production for open access to the studio's costume rental stock? Are there automatic, in-house charges for this arrangement? (For more on this, see Part 7, *Prep*, "Varieties of costume department setups.")

• What is production's "standard accounting procedure?" What are the procedures for making purchases? (For more on this, see Part 7, *Prep*, "Purchasing Power.")

• How many fittings per actor is the production willing to pay for? (For more on fittings, see below, "Fitting requirements and costs," and Part 7, *Prep*, "Fitting the Actor" and "Fitting Extras.")

• How will costumes be transported to and stored on location? (For more on this, see Part 7, *Prep*, "Truck styles.")

> On my "episodic" [television series] budget of $8,000 a week, the studio got a guaranteed $1,700 a week rental for open access to pulling costumes from their collection. *(Barbara Inglehart, costume designer on the television series* Sliders *and co-author of the book* Shopping LA: The Insiders' Sourcebook for Film & Fashion*)*

Prepare to be pressured by production for a budget estimate of your own. If it doesn't happen in this meeting with the UPM, it may have already happened—in your job interview. Designer Eduardo Castro recalls that on his first day on the job for *Kama Sutra*, a job that he took over (in a huge rush) from designer Eiko Ishioka, he was asked by production for a budget estimate before he could even get oriented. Even under ordinary circumstances, costume designers and costume supervisors testify to the tremendous pressure exerted by production to produce a preliminary budget.

Indeed, if a preliminary budget is required by production before a costume supervisor starts work, the costume designer may be on her own to develop one. As a result, a costume designer must have a solid understanding of what's required to support a costume department, including the costs and availability of staff, facilities, supplies, equipment, and services. The ability to do rough-and-ready script notes and costume breakdowns is vital. These quick-and-dirty calculations may not be arrived at by doing formal breakdowns (which may have to wait until your costume supervisor is on board), but the ability to do breakdowns and budget estimates in your head is critical to producing a rough budget estimate. A stopgap measure at best, the budget estimate will keep production happy until the department can do the real thing. As you can see, the more complex the project, the more vital it is to bring the costume supervisor on board quickly.

> The simple question of "What's the budget?" is often a you-show-me-yours-and-I'll-show-you-mine contest. *(Robert Turturice, Emmy-award winning costume designer and a former president of the Costume Designers Guild)*

The preliminary budget

When the designer has answers to as many production questions as possible, it is time to begin work on the official preliminary budget, which production will want "as soon as possible." The preliminary budget includes all four line items above—that is, staffing; facilities; transport; and costume stock, including wardrobe equipment, supplies, and costume services—but the counts and costs must now be defensible, not just rough estimates.

While line items one through three are certainly negotiable, line item four—the cost of actual costume stock development and its maintenance—will be the most hotly negotiated figure in the budget. In this figure, the designer has the most at stake. As a result, preparing a formal preliminary budget becomes a critical task. Accurate script and costume breakdowns and summaries must be done if costume counts for featured characters and background players are to be reliable. The design conferences discussed in Part 4, *Developing the Design,* will need to take place. Additional conferences with the cinematographer, art director, prop master and set decorator, first assistant director, stunt coordinator, and effects department will help you develop a preliminary budget based on all known location, production, casting, and design mandates.

What makes up a preliminary budget? A formal preliminary costume budget is made up of the following: (1) a budget summary cover sheet; (2) principal player pages; (3) supporting character pages; (4) specialty atmosphere and general extras pages; (5) an "additional costs" page that summarizes estimates for supplies and equipment, cleaning and laundry, alterations services, miscellaneous costs like dyeing and distressing services and the purchase or rental of foul-weather/specialty gear. It also includes line items for tax and loss and damage charges.

To establish your department's credibility with the production office, you must be able to produce a preliminary budget that factors in cost estimates for the following:

1. *Costume stock,* including
   - the development of the wardrobe stock through purchase, rental, made-to-order work, or "product placement" deals (deals with companies that donate or lend clothing to productions in exchange for advertising and/or screen credit);
   - costume multiples for stunt and distress doubles;
   - costume multiples for photo doubles and usage doubles;
   - special protective stunt clothing not provided by the stunt department;
   - loss and damage coverage for rental or loaned items marred in the prep or shooting process.

2. *The costs of costume services,* including
- costume research costs;
- sketch artist costs;
- service charges for Xerox duplication;
- costs for shipping services;
- phone and fax charges for out-of-the-office situations;
- service charges for alterations;
- cleaning, fireproofing, dyeing, aging/distressing;
- studio service department charges (charges levied by the department store services that help film and television designers with purchasing);
- facility services charges levied by costume rental companies and costume workrooms for aid in pulling or re-stocking garments, processing paperwork, on-site Xeroxing, cleaning, dying, alterations, etc.;
- over-hire staff charges, for personnel over and above contracted production wardrobe staff, hired in work overload situations. (Note: While over-hire costs generally come out of the payroll/labor budget handled by the unit production manager, on rare occasions, over-hire labor may be charged to the costume budget.)

3. *The costs of the wardrobe supplies,* including
- costume office supplies (Polaroid film for fittings, computer supplies, notebooks, etc.);
- wardrobe supplies (socks, hose, boxes, cleaning supplies, etc.);
- wardrobe equipment (steamers, irons, sewing machines, laptop computers, etc.);
- special shooting situation clothing (foul-weather gear for the crew, modesty robes, sound-buffer booties, etc.).

Detailing the preliminary budget. How much detail do you need to include in your preliminary budget? Costume designer Robert Turturice firmly believes in submitting a highly detailed preliminary budget as a means to developing a strong, positive relationship with the UPM. A detailed budget, based on good research, will help answer the production office's money questions and help target areas of concern. A detailed preliminary budget also prompts discussion among departments.

The larger the project, the more staggering the detailing can, and should, be. Your budget will be examined thoroughly, and you should be prepared to go through your budget line by line, justifying all expenses.

> Increasingly, producers want to know where every dime is spent, and how it was spent. As a designer coming to film, you have to be able to explain how you are spending the money—and in a lot of detail. I went through a four-hour meeting not long ago, and we literally went through every single page of the script and explained the budget. Two producers, my studio representative, my director, and my first assistant director all sat there. [My costume supervisor and I] had earmarked the script, and we literally said, "If you turn to page five, scene three, you'll notice three guys who are drinking beer fall off the roof into a hedge. We've budgeted six changes, based on shopping it cheaply, from Kmart." With each stuntman getting wet, getting beer stains and grass stains, you're getting six takes: two masters and four close-ups—which is not very many. So, the question came up, "Do you really need six takes? Can't you do it in four?" And we all waited to hear whether we were allowed to keep it at six changes.
>
> This was a broad comedy, and there were many script changes during shooting. To protect my own reputation with the studio, my supervisor and I did an addendum to my budget, which itemized each of the additional costume "gags" that came up during filming. With so much going on, it is easy for people to forget.

Traditionally, the art department has a position called "art department coordinator." Increasingly, there is talk of creating a similar position within the costume department. The costume supervisor on a large show is now so bogged down with paperwork that rather than assisting and being part of the creative process with the designer, she or he is often locked in a deluge of endless computer entries and clerical accounting, which can be frustrating. Officially allocating one person to paperwork would, I believe, be a very good thing. *(Catherine Adair, costume designer)*

Buffy Snyder, former president of Motion Picture Costumers Local 705, suggests that for every principal character, every supporting character, and every scene that features "specialty atmosphere" (non-speaking characters featured in the script), you should prepare a budget worksheet, as noted in Part 5, *Breakdowns*. This worksheet can be used to detail the gist of each costume, which makes it easier to ballpark figures for purchase, made-to-order, and rental costs. (For an example of a character/scene budget worksheet, see fig. 6.1.)

After you have worked out the individual costume change costs, you can begin to put together the formal preliminary budget you will present for negotiation to the production manager. Here are some preliminary budget rules of thumb:

• *Principal and supporting players.* Detail all costume changes for principal and supporting players. Additionally, itemize individual pieces that require multiples in each change. It is left to the discretion of the person doing the budget whether to list every costume item in each principal change or to price the change as a unit. A production manager can be buried in budgetary minutia if every costume item is listed separately; however, noting cost estimates for individual items, especially ones that "play" in more than one change, can make the cost of each change crystal clear— and this kind of clarity and forthrightness can help built a relationship of trust with the production manager. (See A.14 and A.15 for blank forms and A.19–A.23 and A.24-A.26 for examples.)

• *Detail as "costume units" all specialty atmosphere changes,* including those for unnamed atmosphere, e.g., taxi driver who we assume is driving the cab the characters hail in scene 3, but who is not named specifically in the script). *List crowd atmosphere and any other atmosphere in summary numbers, according to the nature of their status* (e.g., "upscale," "average," "poor") and/or the nature of their look (e.g., "character/eccentric," "business," "student," "uniform type," "passersby," "urban," "country.") For example, your list might include 12 upscale businessmen; 20 average urban passersby; 3 poor country kids; 2 uniform cops; 1 Army soldier in fatigues, 1 waiter, 1 maitre d'. (See A.16 for blank form and A.27 and A.28 for examples.)

• *Detail, in summary numbers, as many items as possible on the "additional costs" page.* Some costumers do a limited amount of detailing here, especially for high-cost equipment and treatments like Nomex fireproofing. (See A.17 for blank form and A.29 for an example.)

• *Preface the budget with a dated cover sheet that summarizes the totals for all categories and gives a grand total for all wardrobe-related expenses.* Also note the basis of the budget formulation— for example, "The budget was prepared on August 1, based on a telephone conversation with the director. It does not fully reflect atmosphere count, EFX (special effects)

SCENE#S 1,117-119 DENNY'S HOLD UP

CHAR	Pumpkin	Honey Bunny	Vince	Jules	Denny's Manager
	hawaiian shirt $85	dress $150	red shorts $40	white shorts$40	blazer $45
	tee $10	sox $10	Santa Cruz tee $100	I'm with Stupid tee $100	pants $20
	jeans $35	boots $109	thongs $15	thongs $15	tie$5
	sox $5	jewelry $75			shirt $7.50
	boots $100				belt $5
	belt $20				shoes $7.50
	jewelry $100				sox $2.50
					name tag $2.50
	Total: $355	Total: $344	Total: $155	Total: $155	Total: $95.50

CHAR	waitresses 2	cooks 3	busboys 2	Casual m Patrons12	Casual f patrons10
	uniform dress $25	white sslv shirt $15	tee shirt $15	shirt $7.50-$25	shirt $7.50-$25
	apron $10	white pants $35	white pants $20	pants $12-$20	pants/skirt $12-$20
	red cross shoes $10	apron $10	apron $10	sox $3	sox $3
	hose $4	sox $2	sox $2	shoes $7.50-$15	shoes $7.50-$15
	name tag $2.50	black shoes $10	sneakers $15	opt. jacket $20	opt. sweater $20
		belt $5	belt $5	belt $5	jewelry $10
		hair net $1		jewelry $10	
	Total $51.50	Total $78	Total $67	Total $45-65-98	Total $40-60-93

CHAR	M Biz patrons 5	M character patrons 3	Kid patrons 5
	suit $65	shirt $7.50-$25	shirt $10
	shirt $7.50	pants $12-20	pants/skirt $15
	tie $5	sox $3	sox $3
	sox $3	shoes $7.50-15	shoes $7.50-$15
	shoes $7.50	hat $7.50	
	belt $5	belt $5	
	jewelry $10	jewelry $10	
	Total $103	Total $52.50-85.50	Total $$35.50 - 43

requirements, and final principal casting. Should there be any changes resulting from the in-depth meeting next week, I will advise you." (See A.13 for blank form and A.18 for an example.)

Many budget discussions revolve around attempts to reduce the number of extras in scenes and target key scene expenses that might be minimized (expenses like uniforms or stunt multiples). To prepare for preproduction discussions like this, you can create *character budget summaries* for principals, day players, and/or key-scenes budget using character or scene worksheet forms (see fig. 6.11 and A.3 and A.4) or develop budget summary forms after the manner of the character summary forms in A.8 and A.9.

Jurisdictional issues. Who does the preliminary budget and additional budget breakouts? Ideally, the costume designer and the costume supervisor join forces to do costume breakdowns and the preliminary budget and breakouts. In the process of doing this work, priorities are set that guarantee that the department will run smoothly and the costumes look right and are delivered on time. In fact, according to union contract, both the designer and the supervisor are responsible for delivering the costumes on time and on budget.

However, even during the preliminary breakdown and budgeting phase, the costume designer and the costume supervisor have different concentrations. The costume designer's primary focus is on the look and quality of the characters' costumes. Costume sources (designers, manufacturers, stores, rental collections) and services (made-to-order artisans, dyers, distressers, dry cleaners, etc.) are also of concern to the designer, to the extent that they have a bearing on the quality of design itself and its maintenance over the course of production. A costume supervisor's principal concern, on the other hand, is to manage the day-to-day operation of the costume department, including the administering and maintaining of the budget. She or he will direct the hiring of additional costume department staff; set up department facilities (department offices, costume stock storage areas, workroom, fitting rooms, etc.); direct the gathering and organization of costume stock, the acquiring of supplies and equipment (hangers, sewing and cleaning supplies, racks, sewing machines, steamers, etc.), and the contracting of services (made-to-order, cleaning, shipping, etc.) that will guarantee the delivery of costumes to the set on time and on budget.

What designer and supervisor bring to the making of a preliminary budget naturally reflects their respective specialties; however, there are no formal guidelines for how to divide the work of producing costume budgets. Instead, the workload is distributed according to the strengths and weaknesses of each individual, and the time available to each. (L.A. union guidelines for costume designer and costume supervisor job jurisdictions are set out in fig. 1.5, "Costume Department Job Jurisdictions and Duties"; costume designer/costume supervisor collaboration strategies are discussed additionally in Part 7, *Prep.*)

The importance of setting priorities. The priorities set in the preliminary budget establish the "quality" of the look of the production and provide for maintaining that look throughout the shooting process. The task of setting priorities in your preliminary budget is not just a matter of making sure you're covered, it's a display of the standards of the costume designer and his or her costume supervisor. Their ability to get the biggest bang for the buck is a measure of their talents. Delivering high standards at bargain-basement prices is one way of moving up the ladder.

But what is most tricky in budgeting is getting a handle on the production office's idea of quality. When is the $2,200 suit justifiable or the $600 pair of period shoes? Do the producers really care about quality like this? Costume designers and costume supervisors perpetually negotiate with producers and production managers for money to keep the production running smoothly. When it comes to keeping the star happy, being true to period, and creating rich visual atmosphere, standards are relative, and so are their price tags.

> The studios are subsidiaries of large corporations, run by businessmen with a bottom line: to answer to their shareholders. They don't see why they have to pay more for quality, because they don't fully understand the intricacies of the crafts, sets, and costuming. And the sad thing is that they do not even see that they have lost the look of magic. When you compare an old film with a new film, too often some new films can look "dead." There is still some very beautiful work produced, but much of the stuff lacks magic. *(Edwina Pellikka, professional dyer, owner of* A Dyeing Art*)*

Shooting for the best look you can get with the funds available is a driving force for many costume designers, who often opt for smaller staffs, fewer supplies, and less-comfortable working conditions in order to meet their own artistic standards. Costume supervisors—whose key responsibilities are to maintain the look, hold the line on the budget, and not hold up shooting—may prize crisis coverage and careful costume maintenance over a flashy look. This can lead to strains in the designer/supervisor work relationship. The more uncomfortable and difficult the working conditions, the less efficient the costume crew becomes, and the more the "look" is compromised. The designer and the supervisor must both assess the aesthetic and practical requirements of the production, then agree on a clear set of priorities for the budget. This will enable the team to hold up under the stress of unforeseen crises and the myriad demands that inevitably arise over the course of a production.

> When you treat people right—with respect for their craft—then you can get magic. So many persons—designers, cutters, costumers, colorists, whomever—if treated respectfully, are with you one-hundred-ten percent. They believe in what you are trying to do, and in what their input will mean. Because these people have artists' souls, they will give you magic. They will do more than you ask. They will give that indefinable touch. However, if you treat people badly, and disrespect their talents, they will do only what you ask them to. If someone comes into your workshop and is crass and rude and behaves as if you're nothing and a nobody, you will give them only the minimal service. *(Edwina Pellikka)*

Budget assessment: know thyself and thy marketplace. When developing your preliminary budget, remember this homily: "To thine own self be true." You are working up the numbers that you will be asked to live by, so you need to be realistic in your estimates. Both the costume designer's and the costume supervisor's preferences and practices have an impact on the budget. Do you love pricey ties? Do you love vintage goods? Do you need to see a full mock-up? Do you tend to change your mind a lot on made-to-order work? What are your fitting obsessions? Do you need six hours of alterations per change, or eight, for your glamorous leading man? How few multiples can you get away with? Can you recycle the extras stock? How many design options do you really need? The answers to all of these questions will have an impact on the budget.

Budget research resources and fees

Before you can start to put together a detailed preliminary budget, you need to research the costs of the different vendors and services, workspace and storage space, materials, supplies, and equipment that you want to use. Because budgets often need to be put together very quickly, the following sections are intended to give you some basic guidelines for costume research fees, rental charges and conditions, made-to-order charges and conditions, craft costs and conditions, special stunt-coverage costs; wardrobe equipment and supply costs, and over-hire rates.

The number of weeks or months you are given by production to prepare the show will determine if costume staff can do the research or research assistants or research services will have to be employed. A *research service* provides costume research services at the rate of approximately $250 a day, with a one-day minimum. Film studio and costume rental-house research libraries are available to costumers in Los Angeles. Some charge access fees; some allow free usage only if you are a costume rental client; and some provide a librarian who will do research for you for a research fee of $40 to $60 an hour. All have Xerox charges that may run anywhere from twenty-five cents to a dollar a copy (and very few have access to color Xeroxing). The book *Shopping LA: The Insiders' Sourcebook for Film & Fashion* lists the standard costume research resources in Los Angeles, as well as research and costume collections specializing in military, ethnic, couture, and period dress. (These collections may charge access fees, may restrict photo work, and may require an appointment for access.)

Wardrobe rental sources

L.A. and New York have a broad spectrum of costume rental sources. Some of these are IATSE (union signatory) companies (such as Warner Bros. Studios), with overall higher rental rates than the independents (such as Palace Costume & Prop Company). Often, both signatory and non-signatory companies have minimums (check with the source for rental requirements).

Each rental company's costume stock has its own strengths, weaknesses, specialties. The range of accessories, patches, and insignia available for rental vary greatly from company to company. Some companies have "more Armani than Armani," to quote one costumer; some have costumes that are beaten to death. Very few general rental companies stock *specialty craft costumes* (robots, astronauts, or space critters) or theme-park *walk-around* characters (dancing vegetables, giant cartoon characters, etc.). These must be rented from specialty rental companies, or they must be made-to-order.

Many of the rental houses cooperate with each other and do sub-renting and subletting. You know: "I don't have these patches for this show, can I get them from you?" That kind of thing. That's always very helpful. *(Jaci Rohr, costume supervisor)*

When it comes to costume rental, there are three standard rental periods: weekly rental (one week at a time), biweekly rental (two weeks at a time), "production" rental (a twelve-week package rental rate). Companies that cater to commercials or single-show TV work specialize in weekly or biweekly rentals. Companies that cater to feature film productions and episodic television series emphasize production rentals. Some rental companies allow goods to go out *on approval*, meaning for a short time, before being charged full rental price. The on-approval rate is fifteen to thirty percent of an item's standard rental rate. For the record, there is surprisingly little difference between the cost of a short-term rental and a long-term rental.

Rental pricing practices and deals. Compared to made-to-order charges or purchase prices, rental rates can be very attractive. However, costume designers need to plan carefully when using rental goods. (Compare costume costs in fig. 6.2, "Relative Cost Guidelines For Rental and Made-To-Order" and figs. 6.3 and 6.4 for comparative pricing for suits and uniforms, respectively.)

Some rental companies do *per-piece pricing*; others rent by the *costume unit*—a full outfit like a suit, a uniform, or a period gown, for a single price. In some instances, accessories will be included for this single price. (For example, a men's suit, including jacket, shirt, tie, and trousers, will also rent with hat, cuff links, belt, and shoes.) Other companies that price "per costume unit" may exclude accessories, which may be priced per piece. (A man's suit, for example, would include shirt, tie, jacket, trousers, but not hat, tie pin, cuff links, belt, or shoes, which would be charged additionally, at a per-piece price.) Other rental companies do strictly per-piece pricing.

Per-piece pricing can be murder. *(Pat Welch, costume designer)*

Some companies also rate a costume item according to its status, based on rarity and condition, and adjust its rental rate accordingly. "A" stock is costume stock that is in top condition, and, as a result, is higher priced; "B" stock is in mediocre condition and is priced accordingly.

Most costume rental companies are open to making deals, especially if they know you, know your work, and know that you are responsible for maintaining and returning their costumes on time and in proper condition (see below, *Rental conditions*). The sooner you prove yourself to the staff of your favorite costume rental house, the more likely you can cut a deal. In our experience, there are only two kinds of deals: There is the going rate and there is the, "We like you and we know you have no money" rate. A good deal is one that allows you to get what you need and still come in under budget.

Among the most common deals a designer or supervisor can cut for costume rentals:

- The volume deal (special rate breaks and longer "on approval" arrangements for volume rentals)
- The short-term deal (rate breaks on rentals kept for a shorter than standard period)

FIG. 6.2: RELATIVE COST GUIDELINES FOR RENTAL AND MADE-TO-ORDER FROM PROFESSIONAL WORKROOMS

MENSWEAR	RENTAL	MO
Military/Police Uniforms	$150 - $525	$500 - $2500
Suits	$45 - $140	$750 - $3000
Formal Suits	$85 - $125	$2000 - $4000
Period Suits	$100 - $200	$1500 - $4000
Sport Coats	$35 - $65	$500 - $1800
Shirts	$15 - $35	$150 - $450
Pants	$15 - $40	$75 - $450
Sweaters	$20 - $35	$400 - $1000
Vests	$15 - $35	$150 - $450
Overcoats	$55 - $125	$750 - $2500
Outer Jackets	$55 - $125	$750 - $2500

WOMENSWEAR	RENTAL	MO
Suits	$45 - $185	$750 - $2500
Day Dresses - Simple	$35 - $60	$750 - $1000
Cocktail Dresses	$75 - $90	$1200 - $3000
Evening Gowns	$90 - $400	$2500 - $20,000
Period Gowns	$90 - $400	$1000 - $20,000
Blouses	$15 - $35	$125 - $450
Skirts	$15 - $35	$125 - $500
Slacks	$15 - $35	$150 - $500
Sweaters	$20 - $35	$400 - $1000
Outer Jackets	$35 - $85	$750 - $2500
Overcoats	$55 - $125	$750 - $2500

ACCESSORIES	RENTAL	MO
Ties	$7 - $15	$50 - $100
Belts	$7 - $15	$25 - $400
Hats	$7 - $35	$300 - $750
Gloves	$7 - $15	$100 - $350
Shoes	$7 - $45	$350 - $1000
Jewelry Sets	$15 - $35	highly variable
Purses	$15 - $35	highly variable

CHILDRENSWEAR	RENTAL	MO
Suit/Dress	$45 - $150	$750 - $2500
Shirt/Blouse	$15 - $35	$100 - $450
Pant/Skirt	$15 - $40	$100 - $450
Sweaters	$20 - $35	$400 - $1000
Over Jackets	$55 - $125	$500 - $2000

SPECIALTY GOODS	RENTAL	MO
Walk-Arounds	$100 - $450 short term	$3500 +
Creatures	$400 - $2000 short term	$10,000 +
Space Suits	$1000 - $2500 short term	$10,000 +
Wet Suits	$25 (partial) - $95 (full)	$200 +

OTHER	RENTAL	MO
Women's Panties		$35 *
Bras		$75 *
All-In-Ones		$75 - $250 *
Elaborate Foundations		$1000 - $3500

* If you have a style that can
be made up in custom fabric
by a mass manufacturer

FIG. 6.3

Purchase
  Suit $300-$1,900
  Shirt $25-$400
  Tie $7-$60
  Belt $10-20
  Shoes $60-$365
Total $402-$2,745

Made to Order:
  Suit $500 to $2,000 plus materials*
  Shirt $150 to $540
  Tie $50 to $90
  Belt $25
  Shoes $300 to $500
Total $1,025 to $3,155 plus materials

*Suit-quality silks, wools, and linens vary widely in their costs. Estimating in the ballpark of $60 to $80 a yard for a 3-½ yard suit would provide for medium-quality suit.

For oversize problems add $500 to labor costs because of fitting problems and unavailable pattern blocks.

Rental
  Suit $45-$140
  Shirt $15-$35
  Tie $7-$15
  Belt $7-$15
  Shoes $30-$45
Total $104-$250 as available (12 week production rental)

- The early return or extended-use deal (price breaks for the early return or especially long-term use of rental items)
- The package deal (at wrap, the production company "donates" wardrobe purchases and made-to-order garments to the rental company in exchange for a break on rental charges)
- The substitution deal (a backend deal that mitigates exorbitant replacement charges for lost or damaged rental goods by "changing out," or substituting, bought or made costume items)

Note: All costume rental companies price costume stock and make deals in their own peculiar ways; as a result, many are reluctant to quote you standard prices. However, while rental prices can vary widely from company to company, there are ballpark figures for basic items that a designer and supervisor can use for budget estimates and preliminary budgets.

Special services. Some costume rental houses offer special services for additional fees, among them:

- *Pulling*—costume-rental company staff collecting pieces from the costume stock for you, in your absence. Rates to pull costumes go from $20 to $42 an hour, and may be restricted to one outfit per hour. Not all rental companies offer this service, so you may have to pull your own costumes at the rental facility;
- *"On approval"* rentals—rental goods sent for fittings and designer/director viewing and approval without a commitment to rent. "On approvals" are charged on a per-item basis, at ten percent of the weekly or monthly rate, with a charge for re-filing set at ten percent of rental rate per

FIG. 6.4

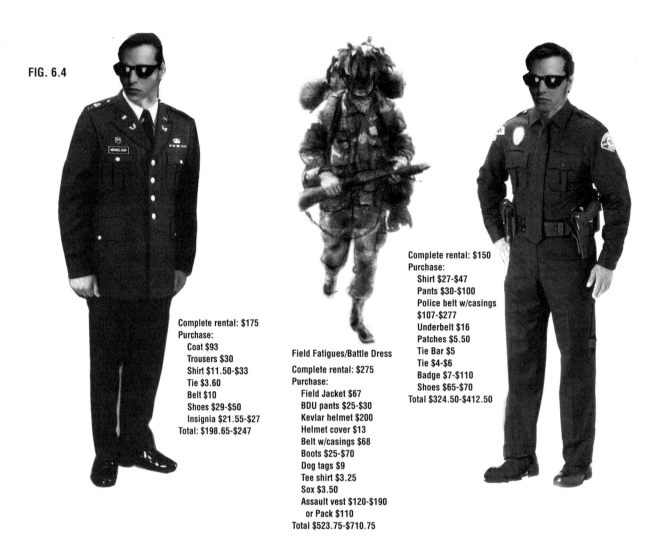

Complete rental: $175
Purchase:
  Coat $93
  Trousers $30
  Shirt $11.50-$33
  Tie $3.60
  Belt $10
  Shoes $29-$50
  Insignia $21.55-$27
Total: $198.65-$247

Field Fatigues/Battle Dress

Complete rental: $275
Purchase:
  Field Jacket $67
  BDU pants $25-$30
  Kevlar helmet $200
  Helmet cover $13
  Belt w/casings $68
  Boots $25-$70
  Dog tags $9
  Tee shirt $3.25
  Sox $3.50
  Assault vest $120-$190
   or Pack $110
Total $523.75-$710.75

Complete rental: $150
Purchase:
  Shirt $27-$47
  Pants $30-$100
  Police belt w/casings
   $107-$277
  Underbelt $16
  Patches $5.50
  Tie Bar $5
  Tie $4-$6
  Badge $7-$110
  Shoes $65-$70
Total $324.50-$412.50

item. "On approval" requires the goods to be returned within forty-eight hours of check-out, and may be unavailable on weekends;

- *Camera-ready* costumes—costumes altered for the actor and shipped ready to be photographed;
- *Dry cleaning*—charges for cleaning services may or may not be built into the rental rate;
- *Holds*—rental companies will hold "wrapped" costumes (character costume changes that have been used during a shoot and may be needed for re-shoots after principal photography has been completed) for some length of time—for a price;
- *Re-filing*—checking the returned garments against rental company paperwork and returning them to their place on the racks. Fees for rental company staff to re-file costumes vary from $1 to $1.50 an item, or a blanket fifteen to thirty percent of the rental fee. If garments are not returned in the order in which they appear on the rental paperwork, additional fees can be added for the required organization of the returned stock, and the extra time it takes to check in garments that have been returned helter-skelter;
- *"After hours" access* to the collection can incur security and costume staff charges as high as $265 an hour, with a four- to eight-hour minimum, plus electricity charges.

The following additional costume-related charges are standard at costume rental houses:

- Security deposits that can run three times the rental cost
- Loss and damage charges that can run ten times the cost of the rental

Costume rental companies may also bill for operational services, including:

- Charges for paperwork processing (charges vary from company to company, some bill this as an add-on charge)
- Phone, fax, and copy charges
- Shipping (always an add-on charge, but not always available)

Rental conditions. Each company sets its own *garment usage conditions*, but the global rule is that rental garments should be returned to the rental company in the "same condition or better" than they went out. In order to ensure that rental garments remain camera-worthy, alterations must be done to *industry standard* (nicely stitched, in a way that does not mar the fabric or create unsightly lumps; no major cutting, gluing, trimming, dyeing, or distressing done without negotiation; garments able to be restored to the original rental condition, if necessary).

Custom-made work

Cost guidelines and conditions. Custom costume construction can carry a steep pricetag: $2,000 for a suit (fig. 6.3), $15,000 for a beaded gown (fig. 6.5). Rates for the same item can vary greatly from workroom to workroom. Estimates for the same period shirt came in at $350 in one workroom, $450 to $600 in another, and $1,000 in a third. Each *workroom* (or costume shop) bases its charges on an hourly rate, between $25 and $45 an hour, with time-and-a-half or double-time fees for rush orders.

Pricing can reflect a shop's level of craftsmanship, but it is not the only element that comes into play. A shop head estimates costs based on the number of hours it takes

6.5

7-9 yds velvet
($23 a yard for
rayon, $45
for silk)

Built-in foundation

Labor costs:
$3,000 low end
$5,000 norm
$7,500 high end

9.5-11.5 yards of brocade
(@ $45-$70 a yard)
3-5 yards of velvet
(@ $22 a yard)
1.5 yards of coutil for
the corset @ $22 a yard
7-9 yards of cotton
for the petticoat @ $6 a yard
1.5 yards of drill
for the bustle pad @ $5
+ Trims & Fastenings

Labor costs:
Corset - $500-$1,000

"camera-ready interior"

Petticoat & pads
$1,100-$1,600

Dress $2,000-$5,000 low
$12,000 high

Photo by
Ed Wassall.

Dress designed by April Ferry for the film *Maverick*

3 layers of chiffon:
lame chiffon,
metallic chiffon,
beaded chiffon
@ $14-$28 a yard
10-15 yards

Underdress silk
@ $15 a yard
5 yards

Built-in
foundation

Labor:
low end $3,000
mid $8,000-$9,000
high $14,000

to build the piece, the number of workers who will be involved, and the cost of the required materials. Different materials dictate different pricetags, not only because of the cost of the goods but also because some fabrics can be more difficult to work with than others, and some can require special handling. Leather, silk chiffon, sequined fabrics, vinyl, rubber, and fabrics that are difficult to tailor (e.g., satin or velvet) can mean expensive handling fees. Tailoring techniques, bias cuts, corseting, and elaborate period understructures can drive up costs.

> Costume designers are generally focused on the color and texture of the fabrics, not the "hand" [the drape] of the goods (fashion designers are better at that). In fashion, you can't afford to "flat-line" with these things. It's just too expensive to use elaborate processes in place of getting goods that are the correct weight. *(John David Ridge, costume designer and owner of the John David Ridge costume workroom)*

A workroom can track the expenses of the construction process for you and give you an itemized tally of the costs of the different processes and materials used in the creation of a garment. In estimating the cost of custom-making a design, a shop head will build in overhead, including a percentage of what it costs the shop during the building of your project to run its facilities, do payroll, and make pension and welfare payments for its employees. Like costume rental companies, some workrooms also charge a production for after-hours security, telephone, fax, and Xerox charges, among other things. Subcontracting is another cost: A shop may need to job out *craftwork* (dye, beading, millinery, embroidery, costume painting, leather or plastics work) and will therefore add a subcontracting charge to its estimate. Additional service charges will be added for off-site fittings or shopping support (with charges based on the shop's hourly rate, including the amount of time spent shopping and traveling, plus transport costs). For example, a fitting might take one hour (at a $42 an-hour shop rate), plus four hours of travel in traffic for a total cost of $168 in service charges for an off-site fitting with one fitter.

Depending on how well you are known at a shop, a shop head may also build some "padding" into their budget, to compensate for possible design changes. Sometimes the padding is minor; sometimes it is grossly inflated. Shops can get badly burned by designers who are unclear, or who change their minds a lot. Major line or proportion adjustments can force shops to create numerous mock-ups; late changes in materials, dye, paint, or beading treatments can necessitate extra fittings, re-cutting, and even new purchasing. All of this drives up the labor costs of the garment. A shop head can only give a best-guess estimate based on the information provided by the designer about how the design may change as the piece is being built.

To get an accurate price on something you want built, you will need to present a detailed and understandable design to the shop head: a sketch with front and back views, photos with a view of the whole garment, or a sample garment that you want copied or adapted—something that helps the shop understand three-dimensionally the form and details of the garment. A workroom needs information on the materials, trims, treatments, and if the garment will be worn with other layers. If a designer has particular feelings about the line or movement of the garment being built, it is important to tell the *costume technician* (the draper or tailor or pattern-maker or specialty costume maker) early in the process, so that he or she can plan an approach to the construction. And, most important of all, the designer (or the designer's liaison to the shop) must clarify the time frame for building the garment, since this will dictate how many of the shop's personnel will be employed in the project and how much overtime can be anticipated.

Made-to-order costs can be negotiated based on time frame, optional materials, design simplification, and the number of costumes (or costume duplicates) needed. Competition for contracts is fierce among shops, and they will often bend over backwards to accommodate difficult designers and difficult production circumstances in order to get work. Price breaks become more feasible during a "dry season," when shops are particularly hungry for work. Much of the cost of a made-to-order garment goes into the development of the original pattern, so duplicating the garment (or grading the size of the pattern up or down, for costume multiples) can be considerably cheaper than the cost of the development of the original garment. Price breaks also become possible when a shop wants to impress a particular designer or production company that could bring more work to the shop in the future. A designer may also be able to negotiate a deal if the garment is returned to the workroom for the workroom's rental collection.

To keep costs as low as possible, you might find freelancers who have the skills you need for the project (e.g., dressmaking, tailoring, pattern-making, period construction). Many costume technicians in costume workrooms do freelance work, and some even advertise in industry guides like *Shopping LA: The Insiders' Sourcebook for Film & Fashion.* Some of the lowest-priced labor can be found in college costume shops. But, watch out for the level of training you'll get from freelancers at the college level: It may be less than you need for the garment at hand. Of course, the danger in working with low-priced technicians is the usual problem with bargains—uncertainty in the level of expertise and the quality of the workmanship. With any costume-construction work, the designer and the supervisor must understand the degree of technical difficulty involved in the production of a garment, since basic technical understanding is what will allow you to hire the right made-to-order personnel. (For freelance labor in Los Angeles, ask around at the fabric stores, contact FIDM (Fashion Institute for Design and Merchandise), look in the back of the fashion-industry trade publication *Apparel News,* and cruise the California Mart.)

On a low-budget film, where every dollar counts, costume designers and costume supervisors often opt to avoid high-cost workroom charges by using strictly low-priced workrooms, or by putting together their own crew to handle alterations and costume construction. On a film like 1981's *My Dinner with Andre,* which had a long prep period and a very small cast, an adept costume designer with sewing skills could do the work him- or herself. The film, however, would have to be an independent feature, since on a "union" film, the costume designer is prohibited from doing costume construction.

The shops that do lower-priced jobs are often thoroughly capable of doing beautifully detailed work, and they can save you a lot of money when budgets are slim. By learning the strengths of the lower-priced shops, you also add to your own creative problem-solving skills. In Los Angeles, check out the workroom at J&M Costumers, in particular. In New York, look at Michael-Jon Costumes, Jennifer Love Studios, Mr. Tony's Tailoring, Studio Rouge, and Carelli Costumes.

Estimating made-to-order. As you detail your budget, you'll need a sense of what pieces must come from made-to-order sources. To determine what a made-to-order design might cost, you can get estimates from costume workrooms. There is no charge for this service, and you can request that the workroom give you a written bid. These bids incorporate patterning and fitting costs, but may not include fabric costs. By going to a number of shops to get made-to-order cost estimates, you can compare the work methods and quality, determine a shop's level of expertise, then judge for yourself whether or not this is the level of expertise you need. You may also want to get information from other designers and supervisors about the reliability of these workrooms. Are their estimates accurate? Do they charge unfair overtime or unwarranted service charges?

A bid can take time to produce, so if you are pressed, you may opt to work out the rough cost of custom-made garments yourself (fig. 6.5). To determine the ballpark price of a custom-made garment, (1) price your fabric; (2) look up the kind of garment you have in fig. 6.6, "Yardage and Made-to-Order Labor Estimates"; (3) compute your yardage cost from this chart; (4) take your estimate of labor time from the chart and multiply it by a shop rate between $25-$45 an hour; (5) add an additional hour of fitting time, at the shop rate; (6) add all your figures together for the total cost estimate. It is also good to factor in some overtime charges on made-to-order estimates, in order to cover costs associated with late casting.

Generally, in doing custom-made estimates, we use the high figure ($45/hour) as a benchmark shop rate. Whether you end up paying overtime or not, it pays to figure overtime into your MO budget. (We add to the basic MO estimate another fifteen per cent of the total, based on rush rates.) If you need it, you're covered; if you don't, you'll come in under budget, and production will think you're a genius. For guidelines on estimating alteration costs, see "Estimating over-hire alterations personnel" and "Estimating alterations costs" later in this chapter.

Craftwork cost guidelines and conditions

Simply defined, *craftwork* is the comprehensive term applied to all costume-related specialty work, including, principally, fabric dyeing and distressing, hand painting, silkscreening, beading, millinery (the making of hats), embroidery, leather and plastics work.

Dyeing and distressing, hand-painting, silkscreening. Dye studios specialize in a broad range of pigment-related processes and services, principal among them:

- Dyeing, including deep color work, large-volume vat dyeing, and guaranteed color-matching
- *Teching* (pronounced "tekking")—taking the glare off white or bright fabrics via a dye bath

FIG. 6.6: MADE-TO-ORDER YARDAGE AND TIME ESTIMATES

WOMEN'S MANUFACTURING	Yardage	Construction time
Skirt - straight	1.5 yards	4 to 6 hours
Skirt - circle	8 yards	6 to 8 hours
Blouse	2 to 3 yards	8 to 10 hours
Jacket	3 to 3.5 yards	24 to 28 hours
Vest	1.25 yards	8 to 10 hours
Suit, two-piece	5 yards	36 to 40 hours
Suit, three-piece	6 yards	40 to 45 hours
Gown - Formal, straight	5 yards	16 to 20 hours
Gown - Formal, full	9 yards	20 to 28 hours
Overcoat	4 yards	35 to 40 hours

PERIOD MANUFACTURING	Yardage	Construction time
Woman's Corset	1.5 yards	40 hours
Woman's Bloomers	3 yards	8 to 10 hours
Woman's Chemise	1 yard	7 to 10 hours
Woman's Jacket	3 yards	8 to 10 hours
Woman's Blouse	2 to 3 yards	10 to 12 hours
Woman's Waistcoat	1 to 1.5 yards	4 to 6 hours
Woman's Skirt, long	6 to 7 yards	8 to 10 hours
Woman's Skirt, full	9 yards	8 to 10 hours
Man's Coat	5 yards	36 to 40 hours
Man's Tail or Frock Coat	5 yards	40 to 45 hours
Man's 18th-Century Court Coat	5.5 yards	40 to 45 hours
Cassock coat	11 yards	40 to 45 hours
Man's Waistcoat	1.5 yards	6 to 8 hours
Man's Breeches	2 yards	13 to 15 hours
Man's Pants	2 yards	11 to 15 hours

MEN'S MANUFACTURING	Yardage	Construction time
Pants, pleated	1.5 yards	10 to 12 hours
Pants, plain	1.5 yards	10 to 12 hours
Shirt	3.5 yards	10 to 12 hours
Sportcoat	2.5 yards	28 to 32 hours
Vest	1 yard	6 to 8 hours
Suit, two-piece	3.5 yards	35 to 40 hours
Suit, three-piece	4 yards	40 to 45 hours
Overcoat	4 yards	35 to 40 hours
Kilt	3.5 to 4.5 yards	16 to 20 hours
Robe	4.5 to 6 yards	16 to 20 hours

All of these estimates are strictly for manufacturing the garments. You need to double these time estimates to include full mock-up development and add fitting time. Plaids and large-scale patterns will need more yardage for seam-matching.

- Aging (also called "distressing")—the dyeing, bleaching, painting, and wearing down of garments to make them appear well worn, soiled, or damaged
- Hand-painting
- Silkscreen work (at some dye studios)

CUSTOM DYE WORK. There are a number of ways to go about having custom dye work done. Some dry cleaners do very straightforward vat dye work and stonewashing for the very reasonable rate of $8 to $10 per piece or per yard. But remember, cleaners are experts at getting out stains; dyers are experts in pigment. Vat dyeing at a dry cleaners is cheaper than at a dye studio simply because a dry cleaner does not, in most cases, have the color expertise that a professional dyer has. If you have a dry cleaner do your dye work, you are taking chances.

Many costumers do simple dyeing and distressing themselves. Big studio productions on location will buy or rent washing machines and dryers, then set up a workspace in the costume department for a full-time dyer-distresser. Some rental houses provide washing machines for dye work, and a few (but very few) costume workrooms do their own dyeing.

Elaborate dyeing, distressing, and costume-painting jobs that involve more hand labor generally need to be farmed out to a dye studio or a freelance dyer/painter. Silk-screening, used primarily for garment logos and names, occasionally for custom fabric printing, can be commissioned through a silkscreen studio or through one of the few of the film-oriented dye studios.

For purposes of rough estimates and preliminary budgeting, the following prices for custom-dye studio services can be used as guides when developing a preliminary budget:

Vat dying charges
- Sample setup charge (the cost of prepping the dye bath) ranges from $10 to $15 for color samples. (As a service, some companies provide color sample charts from which you can choose, in order to avoid sample charges.)
- Bath charges range from $75, for small dye baths, to $185, for extra-large dye baths; $165 for a stripping bath (to remove color from fabric).
- Per-piece charges of $6.50 to $16; per-yard charges of $13 to $25; per-pound charges ranging from two-pound minimum ($70) to 15 pounds ($278).
- Additional charges for special processes like acid washing, stone washing, or marbleizing; or the use of special dyes, like Procion (cold-water fiber-reactive dye) or Poly (dyes for polyester fabric).
- Additional charges for such specialty items as hats, "skins" (body suits), and shoes.

Hand processes charges
- On a per-piece basis, starting from a base rate of $13, and going up with the complexity of the work

The price structure of hand processes is less cut-and-dry than the price breakdown of vat dyeing processes. Hand-painting and distressing work may require many steps. Hand-painted goods can entail adapting artwork, setting up lines of dye-resist, and then hand-painting the design. Distressing may require that garments be washed and bleached in four-hour runs, dipped in multiple dye baths, and additionally airbrushed, sponged, and sanded, to name only a few of many possible techniques (figs. C.10, C.11, and C.12).

Silkscreen charges

- Artwork preparation can cost $200 to $400.
- Silkscreen preparation costs generally run $125 to $500; the larger the screen, the more expensive. Each color in the artwork requires a separate screen.
- The cost of the paints (prices, opacity, and permanence vary with different brands).
- Printing charges run $13 to $20 a yard for each color run.

In silkscreening, prices depend on (1) the state of the artwork (imperfect artwork, or artwork that is in other ways not silkscreen-ready, requires special handling); (2) the scale of the printing project, including the size and preparation of the printing table (high yardage counts mean large printing tables and higher costs); and (3) the number of colors required in the print.

Rush charges. While rush charges vary from one custom-dye studio to another, all studios base rush charges on a minimum number of hours required to complete a job. One-hundred percent to two-hundred percent markups can be expected for same-day service; fifty to one-hundred-fifty percent markups for next-day service.

Freelance dyers. Freelancers customarily work by the job or by the day. Day rates range from $175 to $240, plus kit rental.

Why is professional dyeing so expensive? Because dye type and fabric content and condition affect how well, and how permanently, goods will take the dye, custom dyeing can be a very tricky—and expensive—business. Some dyes called *fiber-reactive* dyes actually become a permanent part of natural fiber. Other dyes (*union dyes* like Rit or specialized dyes for nylon or silk) take to different fibers with different measures of success, and different levels of permanence. Fabrics with polyester content, acrylics, Ultrasuede, plastics, vinyls, and some fake furs can be extremely dye-resistant. Vintage goods, thrift-shop goods, and cheap yardage with grease or chemical stains that are not easily visible can create dye problems, since dyes react differently to stained and unstained fabric. Even goods that appear to be made out of the same fabric can react differently when dyed.

> I have had the experience, when dyeing a purchased shirt, of having the fabric used in construction not be the same for the entire piece, thus creating an unwanted parti-color effect upon dyeing. (*Marcy Froehlich, costume designer and author of* Shopping LA: The Insiders' Sourcebook for Film & Fashion)

Guaranteeing a permanent, beautiful dye job is a very tricky business. Even *teching* (taking the glare off a white or bright fabric via dye bath) is not as easy as it sounds. How evenly a new color takes on a fabric is affected by the size of the dye vat (the determining factor in how well the dye can flow and agitate around the goods) and how well the dry dye was liquefied in the vat. (It must be fully liquefied to avoid the problem of un-dissolved dye specks staining the fabric.) An almost-certain recipe for spotted, badly dyed goods? Dry dye dumped into a washing machine, agitated briefly, then followed by a pile of dry garments crammed into the washer and run through the wash cycle.

Even for skilled professionals, dyeing garments that have been constructed with interfacings and linings is a very, very difficult job. Each fabric used in a garment has its own potential for shrinkage. Tailored garments are very tough to work with, since each layer of interfacing, interlining, and lining may shrink in an entirely different way.

In dyeing and distressing, each garment presents its own challenges and can require multiple dye setups and processes. The multiple processes used to distress garments can require clever use of dye and paint techniques, as well as a solid understanding of what different fibers can withstand. For example, one costumer told a story of an inexperienced crew who had to distress satin "gang" jackets the night before a shoot. They were attacking the jackets with watered-down bleach and dyes. All was going well until they came to the two jackets that were synthetic duplicates of the other jackets. When the bleach hit the surface of the synthetic satin, the jackets literally melted before their eyes.

Conferring with the dyer. In the service of accurate estimates for custom dye work, be prepared to give accurate information to the dyer on the following matters:

- The specific color or effect you want (use a color chip or a swatch of at least two inches by three inches)
- The fiber and condition of the goods to be dyed
- Scripted action and unusual costume-maintenance challenges that will affect the dyed garments during production
- Lighting conditions that may cause color distortion, including fading
- The time frame for the job

For more advice on dyeing, distressing, and working with dyers, see *Conversation Eleven: On Dyeing and Distressing Costumes for Film, with Edwina Pellikka,* at the end of Part 7, *Prep.*

Custom knitwear, millinery, and shoes. When it comes to custom knitwear, millinery (hats), and shoes, the greatest difficulty is finding a vendor who is willing to do one-of-a-kind work, to your specifications (i.e., accurate-to-period research or in the custom colors or fibers you desire). Hat and sweater manufacturers can be approached to make up goods in special fabrics or colors, but, for the most part, these companies are interested in volume work. And since the knitting machines used by commercial knitwear companies can only handle certain fibers and gauges of yarn, up-front design restrictions are abundant. Multiple colors and multiple fibers escalate the price. As a result, custom work like this is done by freelancers or small specialty companies. We suggest seeking out manufacturers of a product that most closely resembles what you've designed.

Pricing is by the piece. Millinery can run from $200 to $600 an item. Shoes can run from $300 to $500. Sweaters can range from $400 to $900, on average. Sources for this kind of work are listed in *Shopping LA: The Insiders' Sourcebook for Film & Fashion* and *The Entertainment Sourcebook.*

Specialty costumes. Aliens, armor, spacesuits, theme-park walkarounds, fat suits, and muscle suits all require special techniques and materials to create. The price tags can be staggering, and the processes by which they are developed are very different from those used in common costume construction. This kind of work is most often done by special effects crews or by craft studios. Craft houses and effects studios deal with a broad range of materials and techniques: foams, fiberglass, metal, leather, vacuum-form plastic, and other plastics. Each material has its own methodology and its own pricetag.

A special effects studio frequently handles custom-made fat suits, fur goods, transgender foundations (e.g., the foundation garments that made Terence Stamp look like a woman in *The Adventures of Priscilla, Queen of the Jungle*), and anything science fiction (see figs. 6.7-6.9). Craft studios can specialize in leather work, light-up costumes, and costumes in unusual materials, like foam or plastic. Both craft houses and special effects studios handle walk-around costumes, and any studio may specialize in particular kinds of work, for example, spacesuits, or animal costumes, or armor (fig. 6.10).

Craft studio work can start at $35 to $42 an hour; a special effects studio may be as much as $100 an hour. Because costs are so tied to the look you need, the conditions in which the costume will be used, and the way it needs to move, price guidelines are almost impossible to give (see *Conversation Twelve: On Prep Collaborations with Craft Artisans, with Chris Gilman* at the end of Part 7, *Prep*). To get an accurate price on something you want built, you need to draw—or commission someone to develop—a very detailed rendering, one that gives front, side, and back views of the costume. Because shapes and proportions are unusual in these costumes, the craft house or effects studio has to understand very clearly how a human fits into, and moves in, the suit (figs. 6.11 and 6.12). Many shops develop their own work drawings (and bill for them), in order to accurately grasp proportion, joint placement, and human-eye placement, as well as details like the design and location of closures.

In general, craft-built costumes require a much longer time to construct than do regular costumes: The nature of individual crafts materials and the way they are combined in a single costume may involve many complicated and lengthy processes. A craft-built costume mock-up is not like a muslin: You can't take a tuck in vacuum-form plastic or preserve the correct proportions by carving away at a fiberglass form. In many cases, the process starts with a sculpture on which a mold will be based. That sculpture needs to perfect before anything else can be done. As a result, some shops prefer to do a full body cast of an actor, so that they can sculpt on an accurate armature. This approach—body-cast, then sculpt—can give you a fabulously subtle fit, but it is by no means cheap at $5,000 to $6,000 per casting.

Most of these special suits are extremely hot and uncomfortable to wear and have extremely tricky rigging. They can require padding, backpack frames (to support weighty materials), air systems, and "cool-suit liners"—the vest and pant combination that cools the actor via a "re-circulating liquid" system. They can even require a technician on set to handle all the tricky rigging. A suit like this can range in quality from bad theme-park outfit to museum-quality replica.

Negotiations with shops that make such costumes begin with discussions of time frame and budget limitations and proceed with review and discussion of the design, including the desired range of movement, the proportions of the shapes, and the costume's textural surfaces. The shop will suggest materials and design variants based on your budget and time limitations. Many finishing techniques are very time-intensive and can affect a shop's ability to deliver under "rush" conditions.

In price and schedule negotiations with a craft shop, you must understand what kind of mock-up process is possible, based on your designs. You must inform your shop contact of the number of fittings for which the actor(s) is available and the physical

FIG. 6.7

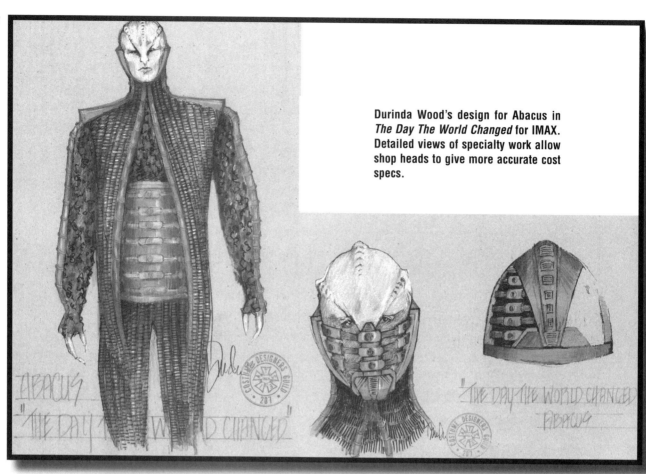

Durinda Wood's design for Abacus in *The Day The World Changed* for IMAX. Detailed views of specialty work allow shop heads to give more accurate cost specs.

FIG. 6.8

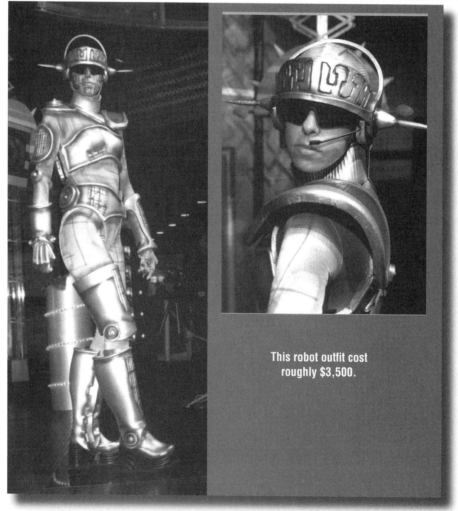

This robot outfit cost roughly $3,500.

FIG. 6.9

Dan Lester's design for Priest in *Spawn*. Photo courtesy of Mr. Lester.

This backpack was estimated between $6,000 - $15,000.

FIG. 6.10

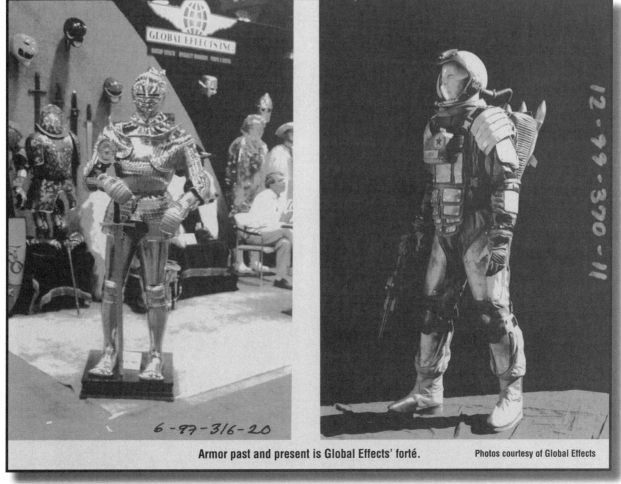

Armor past and present is Global Effects' forté.

Photos courtesy of Global Effects

FIG. 6.11

This kind of rigid suit needs to be fitted very precisely to the actor's body to allow for a full range of movement.

Body armor by Global Effects being fitted by Christopher Gilman.

Photo courtesy of Global Effects

FIG. 6.12

Photos courtesy of Global Effects

Variations in the proportions of rigid and soft parts in these suits can give them more flexible fit.

conditions under which the production will be shot. You must also inform your shop liaison of other costume work being subcontracted elsewhere, when that work needs to be coordinated with the craft costume work.

Deals can be cut with craft houses if you are building multiples, or if the shop can get the costume back for future rental. Although prices for craftwork vary widely, according to the nature of the design and the number of craft costumes required, you can get an idea of the enormous investment it takes to make even simple craft-work costumes: Chain mail armor can start at $1,000; spacesuits start at $10,000 to $40,000—for a prototype only; suits for theme-park walk-around characters start at $3500 to $10,000 (compare figs. 6.8 and 6.9). (See *Conversation Twelve: On Prep Collaborations with Craft Artisans, with Chris Gilman,* at the end of Part 7, *Prep.*)

Costume multiples coverage and cost guidelines

Action that deliberately damages the costumes—stuntwork or otherwise—has the greatest impact on the number of costume multiples for which you must budget. (A basic rundown on the types of multiples was given in Part 5, *Breakdowns,* "Noting costume multiples." A character worksheet used to help work out costume-duplicate computations for a few principal characters in the hypothetical production of *Pulp Fiction* can be found in fig. 6.13.)

Stunt coverage. While stunt personnel generally provide their own protective padding, flexible shoes, and a few other pieces of protective equipment and special effects (EFX) personnel supply the squibs, the flying rigs, and the other technical equipment needed in stunt and special effects work, the costume department is expected to budget for and provide stunt players with the following:

• The *character clothing and costume duplicates* that the stunt actor will need for the character he or she is playing. Some EFX rigging (especially if it involves squib and fire work) requires that the clothing use only natural fibers. Synthetic fabrics can melt with the heat involved in these stunts, and plastics can actually melt onto an actor's body. Stunt performers also need a flexible version of the shoe their character wears, if they don't supply their own.

• *Body padding* (fat suits, pregnancy pads, etc.) for stunt artists who double for principal players, and whose costumes include these elements. Padding is sometimes available at a costume rental house, but to perfectly match a principal player, the padding may need to be made by a craft studio or made-to-order costume workroom.

• *Protective wetsuits* for working in wet conditions (cold river work, long days shooting in wet tanks, etc.). Wetsuits can be custom-designed to be flesh-colored or custom-cut to be hidden beneath garments. Standard-cut wetsuits go for around $200 a piece; custom-cut work will be higher. Wetsuit manufacturers such as Body Glove are listed in *Shopping LA: The Insiders' Sourcebook for Film & Fashion.*

• *Garments made of Nomex (flame-proofed) fibers, or otherwise flame-proofed costumes.* When a performer plays in a fire sequence, the costume worn in the stunt should be made of natural fibers, professionally treated with a flame-retardant chemical. The performer

CHAR				
VINCE	**CHANGE #1** Scs# 1,11-13,111-119	**CHANGE#2,2d,2xs,2xx** Scs#2-8,94-111	**CHANGE#3,3d,3xs** Scs# 14-51	**CHANGE#4,4ds** Scs# 60,76
	red shorts	black jacket x6 +1 for stunt driver= 7	jazzy black jacketx3 +1 for stunt driver= 4	black suit x3 +3s =6
	US Santa Cruz tee	black pantsx6 6	jazzy black pantsx3 3	white shirtx3+3s=6
	thongs	white shirtx6 +1 for stunt driver= 7	jazzy shirtx3 +1 for stunt driver= 4	black tiex3+3s=6
		black tiex6 +1 for stunt driver= 7	jazzy tiex3 +1 for stunt driver = 4	sox,shoes,beltx2+1s=3
		sox,shoes,beltx2 2	sox,shoes,belt rpt rpt	duster rpt
		dusterx6 rpt for stunt driver 6	overcoatx3 rpt for stunt driver= 3	
		2D, 2xs -Marvin car killing, driving double	3d- dance/food stain potential, vomit retakes	Bloody killing w/ stunt double
	Diner/Jimmy's outfit	2x,2xx - Jimmy's arrival phase 1 distress	3xs distress phase 1 post vomit, driving double	no duster for stunt
		2xx car cleaning phase 2 distress		
	Total:1	Total: 6-7 +2 access.	Total: 3-4,rpt access.	Total: 6 outfit,3 access.

CHAR			
JULES	**CHANGE #1** Scs# 1,11-13,111-119	**CHANGE#2,2d,2xs,2xx** Scs#2-8,94-111	
	white shorts	black jacket x6 +1 for stunt driver= 7	
	I'm with Stupid tee	black pantsx6 6	
	thongs	white shirtx6 +1 for stunt driver= 7	
		black tiex6 +1 for stunt driver= 7	
		sox,shoes,beltx2 2	
		dusterx6 rpt for stunt driver 6	
		2D, 2xs -Marvin car killing, driving double	
	Diner/Jimmy's outfit	2x,2xx - Jimmy's arrival phase 1 distress	
		2xx car cleaning phase 2 distress	
	Total:1	Total: 6-7 +2 access.	

CHAR			
MIA	**CHANGE #1,1d,1xs 1xd,1xx,1xs** Scs# 14-51	**CHANGE#2** Sc#60	**CHANGE#3** Sc#100
	blouse x6+1drive doub+1dummy +1drive doub=9	dress	negligee
	bustierx3+1dummy +1 drive double= 5	jacket 5	slippers
	slacks x4+1dummy= 5	jewelry 5	
	jacket x1 not worn for vomit scene = 1	hose,pumps 1	
	shoes,jewelry x1 +1dummy= 2	2	
	1d sweat,food stain, vomit retakes	fights outfit	breakfast outfit
	1xs,1xd stain phase 1, driver and dummy double		
	1xx,1xs distress phase 2 ,driver double		

should also wear an under-layer beneath the flame-proofed garments, to protect the performer from an allergic reaction and to keep the flame-proofing chemical from being sweated away. A set of silk longjohns and gloves, costing about $70, is often used for this purpose.

Garments made of Nomex are permanently fireproofed, and can be dry cleaned and laundered without losing their fireproof properties, while fabrics and garments simply treated with flame-retardant chemicals will lose their fireproofing properties when dry cleaned or laundered. Flameproofing generally carries a minimum charge of $50, with final costs based on the size and number of items flameproofed. Pricing may be on a per-piece, per-square-foot, or per-yard basis, depending upon the vendor. Prices may start as low as $15 per piece, $75 per unit, or $1.25 per yard. Pure synthetics may not take the treatment at all or may show other problems when treated. (The process works best on pre-laundered goods.) The fireproofing process itself takes from half a day to one day to accomplish, including drying time.

You can flameproof costumes yourself using a flame-retardant solution called C-537, available at CRC (Costume Rental Corporation) in Los Angeles. You can pour C-537 into a spray bottle or Hudson sprayer and spray a thin coating on the garments. However, to best protect the actor from physical harm, and to protect the production company from liability, it is wise to have the garments treated by a professionally certified flameproofer, who will ensure that the production company gets get a "C.A. certificate." This certificate warrants that flameproofing was done by a licensed flameproofer and exempts the costume department and the production company from any future liability if problems arise during the use of these garments. Los Angeles-based flameproofers are listed in *Shopping LA: The Insiders' Sourcebook for Film & Fashion*. Regional sources can be tracked through local fire departments.

Estimating stunt multiples. As you draw up your budget, you may have little information available on how the stunt will be shot. To estimate the number of duplicates needed for stunts and other action, consult first with the director, the director of photography, and the stunt coordinator. The director and DP may be able to give you information on how they will shoot a scene and how many "takes" they need to get it. In the "master" of a scene (the version of the scene in which the camera sees all characters and all action in the scene in the same frame), every "take" will require a fresh set of multiples. Expect more "takes" than the director estimates; cover your ass by budgeting for more than the estimated number of multiples (fig. C.12). The stunt coordinator may know how he or she intends to staff the stunts and will know the number of stunt specialists needed. In fact, stuntmen and stuntwomen are often used as actors, cast as the sole performer in a role: that German officer on the passing motorcycle who got blown away? A stunt actor. For guidelines on estimating stunt multiples, see "Guidelines for Estimating Costume Multiples," page 568. A character worksheet used to help work out costume-duplicate computations for a few principal characters in the hypothetical production of *Pulp Fiction* can be found in fig. 6.13 and "A case study: estimating stunt multiples for Holly Cole's hypothetical production of *Pulp Fiction* can be found on page 212.

Because it is sometimes difficult to get time with the director, the DP, even the stunt coordinator, you may have to turn to the actors themselves for initial information. An actor can describe to you what action/stuntwork he or she can handle, but *always confirm this with an AD.* (Principal actors do occasionally perform their own stunts, when desire, agility and the production company's insurance policy permit them to do so; however, principal actors are only allowed to perform stunts, or be in perilous conditions, up to a limited, insurable point. Beyond this, a stunt double will be used, requiring a matching costume.)

Estimating distress multiples. Intentional staining or destruction of a costume dictates the need for a minimum of an original plus two copies of the garment for retakes. The most important items to duplicate are the big costume pieces: the jackets, shirts, pants, blouses, skirt, dresses. Duplicate shoes and jewelry can be "cheated" in medium and long shots.

Your script breakdown will reveal the "stages" of distress a garment must go through. If an action sequence is very fast and complicated, some costume staining may be obscured, but clear breaks in that action give the audience a look at the costume's dilapidated state or "stage" of distress. The discontinuity of the shooting process and the possibility of future re-shoots require you to save a copy of the costume in each stage of distress (see page 568, "Estimating Costume Multiples" and the *Pulp Fiction* case study on estimating stunt multiples, page 212).

Multiples for non-deliberate dirt and stain problems. Unintentional soil problems can come up during the action of a scene (an actor rolls on the ground, or eats a greasy hamburger, or downs a cocktail, for example). This can be prepared for with two copies of the outfit: one copy for use during shooting, a duplicate to use while copy one is off set, being cleaned. Many low-budget movies skimp on these numbers by choosing to depend on quick stain-removal hustle by the set costumers, or careful camera work, to disguise problems.

If a costume design is messy and worn down to start with, or if the clothing is dark and durable, you may be able to keep your costume-duplication costs down. Think about Indiana Jones and his great scruffy look: His leather jacket can go through a lot of wear and tear without looking much different at the end than it does in the beginning. But whether the look is scruffy or not, without sufficient costume duplicates, you always run the risk of delaying a shot (see page 568, "Estimating Costume Multiples").

Estimating usage multiples. Screen Actors Guild (SAG) regulations dictate that a costume must be cleaned every third day. Delayed deliveries from cleaners can wreak havoc on the set, so principal garments that get extended use are duplicated for costume coverage during cleaning. SAG regulations also dictate that intimate articles (including shirts and blouses) must be cleaned daily, so they get first priority for usage duplication. To estimate how many multiples you will need, check your shooting schedule to see how many consecutive days the principals must work in the same costume pieces.

Garments that wilt or get dirty easily can also demand duplication, depending upon the look required by the design. The filmmaking process is hard on garments—actors eat in their costumes, smoke in their costumes, sit around for long periods as lights and cameras get set up. Set costumers struggle to combat the effects on garments of dirt and grime, inclement weather, and simple perspiration. Costumes in pale colors, or in fabrics that crush

FIG. 6.14

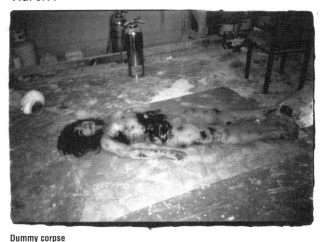

Dummy corpse

Kristin Burke cutting dress to set up stomach wound

Kristin Burke collaborating with Sota Effects, a special effects company.

Dummy corpse with dress

Dressing wound with stage blood

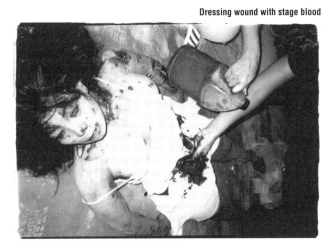

and wrinkle easily (like linen, silk shantung, rayon challis, or velvet), are difficult to maintain. Over the course of two days of shooting, even the most fastidious star can spill spaghetti on himself. Principals playing "suits"—lawyers, corporate executives, and the like—need two starched shirts a day just to combat the wilting effects of the heat from on-set lights. A rayon or silk suit shows wear faster than a wool suit, but if a wool suit isn't appropriate, you may need a duplicate to keep the lead at his or her most handsome.

The goal for costume coverage: *always have one clean copy available in case of disasters.* However, with garments that can cost thousands of dollars, or budgets that are excessively tight, this is not always possible. When deciding a number for usage multiples, costume designers and costume supervisors take into consideration the ability of their set costumers to solve stain problems quickly, the reliability of their dry cleaner, the number of costume department crew who can cover costume laundering and maintenance, and how many of the costumes are at high risk for heavy usage (see page 568, "Estimating Costume Multiples").

Estimating costume duplicates for photo and character doubles.

To help determine what costume duplicates may be needed for photo doubles, consult with the special effects department and the first assistant director. The special effects department dictates the scale and number of costume duplicates needed for dummy doubles and miniatures (fig. 6.14). The AD can apprise you of the number of actor-substitutes needed as a result of principals' schedule conflicts (second-unit work, for example, or conflicts with the star's personal schedule, which can require the use of photo doubles).

A case study: estimating stunt multiples for Holly Cole's hypothetical production of *Pulp Fiction*

Here's my (HC) take on estimating multiples for selected stunts in a hypothetical production of *Pulp Fiction*. (I have chosen a handful of stunts from the film and determined the number of costume multiples I would feel safe having if I were the designer or supervisor on this show; although the stunts are particular to *Pulp Fiction*, each is an example of a common stunt or "distress" scenario. As a result, you can use each of these examples as a rule of thumb.)

Stunt description

A minor featured player (e.g., Roger, the "surfer-type" college kid) gets "blown away," in one step.

Multiples required

- Three to four copies of the outfit, to accommodate out-of-sequence shooting. This gives you one outfit to get blown up on the first day of shooting and one or two backups, in case the special effects people have problems, or the director wants fifty angles on the action. If you purchase the garments new at a store with a return-for-full-refund policy, you can return the backups for cash, if they don't get used. This leaves you with one clean outfit for the scene with Roger *before* he gets killed, when his outfit is still clean, which they're going to shoot three days later.
- One pair of shoes—if the shoes are made of materials that can be wiped clean. If the shoes *can't* be wiped clean, then three to four pairs, as with the ensemble above.
- Save the "blown away" outfit for reshoots. Save the clean outfit for reshoots, as well.

Stunt description

A lead character or day player (e.g., Vince, in the bathroom shooting, or Maynard, one of the rednecks) gets "blown away" or his clothes get seriously damaged in one step.

Multiples required

- Three copies for the actor, assuming he has to appear clean before the stunt and scheduling prevents shooting in sequence. Save both a clean copy and the "blown away" copy for reshoots.
- Three copies for the stunt double. (You can always use the extra copy on the actor if someone messes up, and you can return it if it doesn't get used.) Save both a clean copy and the "blown away" copy for reshoots.

Stunt description

A featured actor gets seriously damaged in a two-stage stunt (e.g., Jules and Vincent, in their "hitman" suits, in the car shooting and subsequent cleanup; or Brett and Marvin, two college kids, get shot more than once).

Multiples required

The Jules and Vincent scene

Stage one of the damage:

- Three copies for the actor shooting the scene, to allow for multiple takes. No additional stunt multiples are needed, since no stunt players are required for this action, and Jules' and Vincent's costumes do not get damaged, only bloodied.
- Two outfits will be kept clean, for reshoots and out-of-sequence shooting.

Stage two of the damage:

- Three "prepared" outfits (outfits that already have the appropriate stage-one damage duplicated on them [bullet holes, blood stains, etc.]; some of the outfits that were backups for stage one can be reused here. The actor will wear the "prepared" suit in the scenes that take place between the stage-one and stage-two damage. Jules and Vincent only get intensely messy, so they need no stunt doubles.

- The stage-two outfit will be preserved for reshoots.

In sum, for the entire "stunt/action" (stage one and stage two combined), Vincent and Jules need six copies of each outfit (eight, for safety).

The Brett and Marvin scene

Stage one of the damage:

- Three copies for each actor, to allow for multiple takes. The character Marvin has very few lines of dialog, and could be played by a stunt actor, so stunt doubles of his wardrobe may not be required. Brett only gets a shoulder hit, and shoulder hits are easy. Squibs contain relatively little "blood," and since the squib hit is in Brett's shoulder, close to his face, it is more likely that the actor's hair and face, rather than the rest of his costume, will get bloody. If at all possible, this stunt will be shot in one take, using the actor himself. After all, who wants to re-dress the actor—one hour to shower, dry hair, and refresh makeup—and wait all of that time to shoot again? Even if things do go awry, you'll still have two more shirts for Brett, from his basic allotment of multiples.

Stage two of the damage:

- For each actor, three "prepared" outfits (outfits that already have the appropriate stage-one damage duplicated on them [e.g., bullet holes, blood stains, etc.]; some of the outfits that were backups for stage one can be reused here). The actors will wear the "prepared" suits in the scenes that take place between the stage-one damage and stage-two damage. If a stuntman is cast in the role of Marvin, no stunt double would be needed for his "stage-two damage" costume. Brett, on the other hand, goes through a hail of bullets in his stage-two costume. A stunt double will be required for this action. The "prepared suits" will be rigged with squibs for the stunt. Three of these "prepared" suits are needed, since many takes may be necessary.
- The damaged outfits will be kept bagged and bloody, for reshoots.

In sum, for this stunt (stages one and two, combined), Marvin needs six copies of his outfit (eight, for safety); for Brett, eight copies of his outfit.

Note: You will not be sad if you purchased eight suits for Marvin. Often, a squib will rip a hole that looks totally wrong—that is, totally unlike a hole ripped by a bullet. When special effects people set the squib, they make "hash marks" (they "score" the fabric in a crosshatch pattern, without actually cutting through the fabric). These hash marks are made to allow the fabric to explode more easily and in a predictable place. What they often do, in addition, is to leave a well-defined, implausibly clean-looking crosshatching of cuts in the fabric. When the stunt is done, ripping the squib backing and wires off can cause more damage to the garment than the squib itself causes, especially with delicate fabric.

Stunt description

A star has a three-stage stunt (e.g., Butch and Marcellus in the accident, plus the fight and rape at the pawn shop).

Multiples required

- Each actor requires twelve to thirteen copies of his outfit, assigned in the following ways:
- One or two clean copies for out-of-sequence shooting
- Three copies for reshoots (one copy of each of the three stages of destruction)
- Two damaged backups, for shooting the final stage; these two damaged backups will also double as multiples in filming the second stage of the action

- Two copies for the stage-one stuntman (before and after preserved for reshoots)
- Two copies for the stage-two/stage-three stunt man (before and after preserved for re-shoots). Note: The tumbling and stunt driving required for the stage-one accident may require a different stuntman from the "fighting" stuntman (driving doubles will wear only the upper half of the costume).
- Two copies for the actor and stuntman on stages two and three action, for retakes

A word of warning: You can never predict what will happen during a stunt, or even in which order the scenes will be shot, so, whenever possible, protect yourself with a reasonable number of multiples.

Workspace, equipment, and supply guidelines and costs

Workspace guidelines and costs. With very few exceptions, the production budget (not the costume department budget) covers the monies for the rental of costume department home-base office space, workspace, and costume storage space. Because of this, we have decided to cover the guidelines for choosing costume facilities, and their allied costs, to Part 7, *Prep* ("Choosing Costume Facilities and Services"). How these matters are decided are, of course, fundamental to the successful running of a costume department, and, as such, must be discussed early in the process—by the designer, in the job interview, if it seems appropriate, but certainly in the first conversation the designer has with the production manager. Thoroughly thinking through the material we cover in "Choosing Costume Facilities and Services" will help when you have to make a case for renting a warehouse space, a "cage" at a rental house, or a washer and dryer dedicated to teching and distressing.

EQUIPMENT AND SUPPLY GUIDELINES. Every costume department has to put together the equipment and supplies needed to assemble and organize the costume stock during prep and "run" and maintain the character costumes during shooting. As a result, you must budget for the following:

- Office supplies (computer supplies, ring binders, etc.)
- Stock-organization supplies (hangers, tags, garment bags, etc.)
- Dressing supplies (dress shields, shoelaces, insoles, etc.)
- Cleaning supplies (spot removers, Wet Ones, etc.)
- Craft supplies (dye, paint, etc.)
- Sewing supplies

To solve problems that crop up during shooting, the costume department is also expected to stock certain emergency supplies, including the following:

- Knee pads, sound booties (to baffle the sound made by shoes on hard surfaces), and mike packs (in which to tuck radio mikes under garments)
- For cold-weather shooting, you'll need longjohns, gloves, hand warmers, warming coats, boot dryers, space heaters, and umbrellas (although, as noted above, umbrellas are usually supplied by props). For hot weather, you'll need hand-held fans and underarm sweat guards. For inclement weather, regardless of temperature, you'll need foul-weather gear, stock towels, and stock T-shirts and socks, among other things. Wearable foul-weather gear (rain slickers, warm jackets, dry socks, sun hats, etc.; umbrellas are provided by props)
- Modesty clothing (pubic patches, penis covers, set robes)
- "Comfort" clothing (underwear, towels, etc.).

You will always need to budget for any equipment needed to prepare the costumes for shooting (irons, steamers, sewing machines, etc.). Every costume supervisor must also budget for key items needed to set up a costume department office, if these supplies and equipment are not provided cost-free, by production. Depending on your office setups on the set and at the home base, you may need to equip (1) a work area for the supervisor, complete with computer and a place to store production files, binders, and other production documents; (2) work areas for the designer and the costumers; (3) a workspace for costume construction and alterations personnel; (4) a costume storage area; (5) fitting rooms; (6) and possibly a dyeing and distressing workroom. Desks, chairs, work tables, cutting tables, rolling racks, a blackboard, bulletin board, dress forms, curtains and mirrors for fitting areas, folding chairs for extras fittings, and a small refrigerator and hot plate, among other things, may be required.

Regardless of the size of a production, there are certain key variables that have an impact on the quantity and range of supplies, equipment, and costume stock needed by a costume department, among them:

- *The costume requirements of the script*, which affect the kind of department workspace and stock storage you need
- *The ease of access to your costume storage site; the size of your wardrobe truck(s) and costume storage and workroom space; the accessibility of goods and services near shooting sites*, all of which determine the kind of facilities, equipment, and supplies needed
- *The number of advance fittings allowed with principals, stunt players, and "extras" (background players)*, which determines the need for and nature of costume options, fitting rooms, and on-set tailors, among other things
- *The amount of stuntwork, nudity, and special effects work in the script*, which dictates the number and nature of costume multiples, comfort clothing, additional set costumers, and so forth
- *The shooting conditions, which determine the need for a host of costume items.* Shooting in remote locations or at a studio that is near elaborate support facilities and costume services; shooting in relatively consistent weather conditions or in weather extremes; shooting with a full crew in your department or one that is barely adequate; shooting with workroom and storage facilities that match the task—all these conditions have an effect on your equipment and supply needs.

Is there a standard list of basic costume supplies and equipment needed on a production? Yes. It looks like a combination of the items on the supply list in figs. 6.15 and 6.16 ("Basic costume department supply specs for Holly Cole's Hypothetical Production of *Pulp Fiction*") and the wardrobe kit supply lists in A.30-A.33. Beyond the super-basic, however, different productions and different production circumstances dictate different kinds of equipment and supplies. A period production; a stunt-heavy production; an upscale, high-fashion production; a low-life, grubby production—each has its own varied requirements. Shooting conditions (soundstage versus location, for example) and format (episodic television versus feature film, for example) also have an effect on the range of wardrobe equipment and supplies required by the costume department. And, while some productions choose to job out all construction and alterations work to professional workrooms, a costume department may find it in their best interest to set up its own costume workroom, requiring additional equipment and sewing supplies.

Most of the supplies and some of the basic equipment a costume department needs will be part of the wardrobe kit owned by an experienced designer or costumer. It is customary for these kits to include collapsible rolling racks, sewing machines, steamers, irons, pressing boards and forms, and a host of other standard and exotic supplies. Kits are rented to the production company at a daily or weekly rate, in order to save the production the cost of major equipment purchases, and to provide back-up and emergency supplies.

Equipment and supply costs. The general rule of thumb in budget planning is to allocate three percent to seven percent of your costume budget for equipment and supplies. This figure should cover the cost of basic stock setup (racks, rack dividers, hangers, tags, pins, etc.); office and wardrobe expendables (computer paper, costume cleaning supplies, etc.); comfort and emergency wardrobe (set robes, foul-weather gear, etc.); and basic wardrobe maintenance equipment (irons, steamers, sewing machines, etc.).

The supply "specs" (for "specifications") in figs. 6.15-6.16 ("Basic costume department supply specs for Holly Cole's Hypothetical Production of *Pulp Fiction*") give you an idea of the equipment and supply budget for a medium-size project with a realistic production budget. Contrast this list with the list in fig. 6.21, "Guidelines for Streamlining Wardrobe Equipment and Supplies for a Starvation Budget," which gives guidelines for downsizing the wardrobe supply and equipment budget on a medium-size project with a super-small budget.

Estimating the cost of costume cleaning services

Costume cleaning costs vary with the scale of the production, the type of costumes, the period, and the kinds of fabrics being used. Dry-cleaning costs for elaborate gowns run $20 a piece and higher; leather goods can be $100 per piece and up. The intimate garments of the principal players (including shirts and blouses) require daily cleaning. Extras' costumes can need quick, high-volume cleaning to recycle the garments for other scenes. Wash-and-wear garments like T-shirts or underwear can be easy to handle, but high-volume ironing can be labor-intensive. Specialty costumes like suits of armor, or large foam or fiberglass suits, cannot be serviced by dry cleaners and must be hosed down by hand and sprayed with an anti-bacterial disinfectant.

When budgeting for costume-cleaning services, begin by determining the kind of cleaning services you need. Do you need laundry and dry cleaning? Do you need quantity service, as well as quality work? Do you need pickup and delivery services? Do you need overnight service? Remember, in many instances, garments can't leave the set until they are "wrapped" at the end of the shooting day and must be back on the wardrobe truck by call time—often, very early in the morning. In Los Angeles, overnight garment-cleaning services are available, but most of these "service" cleaners require a guarantee of $5,000 worth of cleaning to even set up an account. In small towns beyond Los Angeles and New York—not to speak of more remote locations—no dry-cleaning services may exist. If they do exist, they do not usually do overnight work with less than a twenty-four-hour turnaround (this is true even of large cities). Can you persuade a local dry cleaner to make special arrangements for the duration of your production? On a remote locations, can you hire a local family to launder and press overnight, for delivery at call time? Every tactic you can think of has been tried, with varying results.

Off-the-beaten path locations that lack a full range of cleaning services make it necessary to hire additional personnel to cover weekly cleaning and maintenance, but so do small crews, no matter where your location. Because your costume department staff will

Area/Item	Cost	Quantity	Total
OFFICE			
4" Ring Binders	$20.00	4	$80.00
2" Ring Binders	$6.00	3	$18.00
Notebook Dividers	$2 per 10 pack	33	$66.00
Cardstock Continuity forms	.20 per sheet	400	$80.00
Polaroid sheets	$30 for 100	400	$120.00
3 Hole Punch	$5.00	4	$20.00
Scotch Tape	$1.59	10 rolls	$15.90
Packing Tape	$3.00	10 rolls	$30.00
Gaffers Tape	$3.00	10 rolls	$30.00
Pencils	$1.29 a pack	3 packs	$3.87
Sharpies/highlighters	$16 a dozen	3 doz	$48.00
Rub-a-Dubs	$16 a dozen	3 doz	$48.00
Polaroid labels	$6 a box	4 boxes	$24.00
Computer paper	$3 per reim	3	$9.00
Computer ink cartridge	$27.00	3	$81.00
Legal pads	$12 per doz	1	$12.00
Post Its	$12 per doz	3	$36.00
White Out Tape	$4.25 per roll	10 rolls	$42.50
STOCK ORGANIZATION			
Manilla Tags	$30 a box of 1,000	2	$60.00
2" Safety pins	$26 a box	3	$78.00
Small Gold Safety pins	$15 a box	3	$45.00
Fabric silver pens	$3.50	12	$42.00
Ziplocks-quart	$34 a doz	1 doz	$34.00
Ziplocks-gallon	$41 a doz	1 doz	$41.00
Rack dividers	$50 per 100	4	$200.00
Tagging gun & supplies	$51.00	2	$102.00
Hangers-muslin	$8 ea	5	$40.00
Hangers-wire	$50 for 500	2	$100.00
Hangers-skirt	$44 for 100	50	$22.00
Garment bags	$33 for 100	2	$66.00
		subtotal	$1,594.27

Area/Item	Cost	Quantity	Total
Cleaning bag roll	$48 for 273	2	$96.00
Cardboard boxes	$1.50 ea	24	$36.00
Accessory Bags	$135 for 500	500	$135.00
DRESSING SUPPLIES			
Insole sets	$13 per doz	2	$26.00
Heel grips	$12 per doz	1 doz	$12.00
Barge Cement tube	$12 per qt.	1 qt.	$12.00
Shoelaces	$10 per doz	2 doz	$20.00
No skid pads	$1.50 ea	1 doz	$18.00
Shoe Stretch Qt	$6.50	1 qt.	$6.50
Moleskin roll	$15.00	1 roll	$15.00
Shoe Polishes	$2.25	3	$6.75
Military Shine	$5.00	3	$15.00
Saddle Soap	$2.30	3	$6.90
Static Guard	$44 per doz	1 doz	$44.00
Scotch Guard	$125 per doz	1 doz	$125.00
Dress Shields	$3.50 per 12	3 boxes	$10.50
Shoulder pads	$2.00	6 pair	$12.00
Bust pads	$2.00	1 doz	$24.00
Collar Extenders	$6.50 per 100	1	$6.50
Collar Stays	$1.35 a pack	1	$1.35
Lint rollers & refills	$6.25	3	$18.75
Topstick	$4 a box	2 doz	$96.00
Foot foam	$70 per roll	1	$70.00
CLEANING SUPPLIES			
Shout Wipes/ Wet Ones	$35 doz boxes	2	$70.00
Bleach	$1.29	2	$2.58
Laundry Detergent	$40 per 4	2	$80.00
Woolite	$2.40	2	$4.80
Clear Choice gal.	$32.00	1	$32.00
End Bac	$82 per doz	1 doz	$82.00
Trash Bags	$5.40	2	$10.80
		subtotal	$1,095.43

This supply budget assumes that the wardrobe setup has 1 trailer for the principal wardrobe and 1 trailer for the extras wardrobe + a cage storage area at a rental house. It also assumes that the wardrobe department consists of a designer, a design assisstant, a supervisor, and 2 set costumers. All told, there are 323 characters and 346 changes, not including the stunt multiples.

be eaten alive just running the show and preparing the costume stock, the smaller your crew, the more laundry services you will need. Hiring a union costumer to do laundry is a healthy expense, at a minimum of $18 per hour, with a guaranteed minimum call of eight hours. Using a laundry service on a distant location is usually more cost-effective, but there can be a downside: Uncommon fabrics can be mishandled; pickups and deliveries can be late (which, if you're low on costume duplicates, can be a disaster); local custom can dictate special, unasked-for touches, like extra starch and creases in denim jeans.

Non-union shoots can unload laundry chores on wardrobe interns and production assistants, but recognize that while these personnel may save you a bundle, you may be giving valuable wardrobe pieces to inexperienced personnel, and damage may ensue. Garment shrinkage, color bleeding, the elimination of sizing, and a host of other unwanted transformations can, and will, occur, if the person laundering your costumes doesn't know what to do. The only safe, practical solution when your crew cannot handle the work is to hire professionals.

Because cleaning loads and crew sizes vary enormously, it is not possible to give an exact formula for estimating cleaning costs. Using the model of a minimum $5,000 contract, you can average $200 per day (or $1,000 per week) for a five-week shoot, for dry-cleaning services. But, realistically, you may not have dry cleaning every day, or, if your show is a laundry show, you may choose to have your crew cover the laundry tasks. As a result of these variables, cleaning costs can run from $25 to $200 per day, depending on the style of the design, the number of stunts, the opportunities for dirt and distress. For a production like a sitcom, the cleaning would average $200 for each shooting day. Period shows or shows with a lot of leather or beaded goods will run much higher.

Estimating over-hire staffing requirements and costs

While basic costume-department staff salaries are covered under the "staffing" budget line, *over-hire staff*—that is, additional short-term costume staff for prep or shooting overloads or emergencies—can be charged to the "costume stock, supplies, and services" budget line. Understaffing happens on a production all the time, and if over-hire labor is not picked up in the production budget, you must include it in the department's budget, so you won't get caught short.

Estimating over-hire costumers. With your staff size and shooting schedule in mind, determine which days have the greatest number of extras. Even when the extras are expected to provide their own wardrobe or have been pre-fit, expect a substantial amount of setup time, including *onset styling*, "character designing" using costume pieces, and accessories pulled from your general stock (figs. 6.17, 6.18). Styling the extras can be as simple as looking over options they've brought, then telling them which items to wear, or as elaborate as pulling entire "looks" from the general stock.

Most shooting days need the extras dressed within the first hour of their call. Knowing how fast your crew can style is a vital factor in calculating how many additional costumers you will need, and when in the shooting schedule. The average rate is four to ten *period-dressed* extras per hour per costume team member.

FIG. 6.16: BASIC WARDROBE DEPARTMENT SUPPLY SPECS FOR THE HYPOTHETICAL *PULP FICTION* PROJECT

Area/Item	Cost	Quantity	Total
Laundry Baskets	$4.00	3	$12.00
Spray Starch	$1.50	3	$4.50
Distilled Water	$12 per 6	18	$36.00
Dish Soap	$1.30	2	$2.60
Zout 64 oz	$15.25	3	$45.75
Wet Ones	$3.50	2 doz	$84.00
Tailor's chalks	$2.15 per chalk	6	$12.90
BASIC CRAFT SUPPLIES			
Rit Dye	$2.10 ea	6	$12.60
Magix	$8 a can	4	$32.00
Deglazer	12.50 pr pt.	1	$12.50
Schmutz Sticks	$45 for 6	2	$90.00
Fuller's Earth 82 oz	$10-$13	2	$26.00
Cheesecloth	$2.25	1	$2.25
Mineral Oil	$4.00	1	$4.00
Glycerine	$6.00	1	$6.00
Stage Blood qt.	$20.00	6	$120.00
sand paper	$10 a pack	1	$10.00
Rubber gloves	$4.99	2 boxes	$9.98
Particle masks	$0.49	8	$3.92
Jewelry Repair kit	$6.00	1	$6.00
Barge	$2.75 per tube	1	$2.75
SEWING SUPPLIES			
Needle kit	$2.50	5	$12.50
Multi thread kit	$10.00	2	$20.00
Fasteners kit	$10.00	2	$20.00
Elastic	$1.25 per pack	3	$3.75
Seam rippers	$1.20	4	$4.80
Measuring tapes	$1.00	6	$6.00
Asstd. needles	$6.00	1	$6.00
Scissors	$5.25	3	$15.75
		subtotal	$624.50

Area/Item	Cost	Quantity	Total
WEATHER & PROTECTIVE CLOTHING			
Knee pads	$6.95	8	$55.60
Elbow pads	$8.50	8	$68.00
Shin pads	$6.95	8	$56.00
Forearm pads	$8.50	8	$68.00
Panties	$4 for 3	1 pack per 6 sizes	$24.00
Bras	$4-$10	6	$60.00
T shirts	$10 per 3	1 pack per 3 styles,4 sizes	$24.00
Briefs	$8 per 3	3	$24.00
Jocks	$18.00	3	$54.00
Sox	$5 for 4	36	$180.00
Hose	$5 for 4	12	$60.00
Courtesy Robes	$20 ea	4	$80.00
Rain Ponchos	$2.50	12	$30.00
Bath towels	$4 ea	12	$48.00
Handkerchiefs	$2.29per 4	2 packs	$5.00
Sound Booties	$1.75pr	3	$5.25
EMERGENCIES			
Tampax	$2.99	1	$2.99
First Aid kit	$11.95	1	$11.95
Spray Deodorant	$1.25	1	$1.25
EQUIPMENT			
Steamer	$165.00	2	$330.00
Iron w/ board	$46.00	3	$138.00
Sleeve board	$26.00	2	$52.00
Sewing Machine	$500.00	2	$1,000.00
Rolling Racks	$130or $5wk	4 racksx14wks	$280.00
Extension Cords	$30.00	3	$90.00
Computer	$1,200.00	1	$1,200.00
Printer	$200.00	1	$200.00
		subtotal	$4,124.04
		GRAND TOTAL	$7,438.24

This supply budget assumes that the wardrobe setup has 1 trailer for the principal wardrobe and 1 trailer for the extras wardrobe + a cage storage area at a rental house. It also assumes that the wardrobe department consists of a designer, a design assisstant, a supervisor, and 2 set costumers. All told, there are 323 characters and 346 changes, not including the stunt multiples.

FIG. 6.17

On-site styling
of extras is
common.

Kristin Burke styling extras

FIG. 6.18

Kristin Burke measuring and
fitting extras on set.

The crew's ability to dress extras quickly has a lot to do with

- the percentage of extras who provide their own wardrobe;
- the number of extras who were pre-fit and need only to have their wardrobe handed to them;
- the range of the costume stock, the costume crew's knowledge of it, and how well organized it is;
- the crew's familiarity with the costume designer's aesthetic and/or the period in which the film is set;
- the individual design talents and practical speed-styling abilities of the crew.

On "crunch" days, the costume crew's styling rate is a critical factor in getting the job done without holding up the shoot. This is one of the many reasons costume designers and costume supervisors prefer to work with a crew they know. When extras are expected on set and time is short, all available costume personnel are expected to pitch in and help—including the costume designer, the costume supervisor, the set costumers, and the design assistants. With a known crew, a designer and supervisor can estimate over-hire needs based on first-hand knowledge of styling speed, factoring in additional time for labor-intensive period shows.

To determine the number of set costumers you need on a shoot, begin by estimating the amount of time your staff needs to style individual extras. On a low-key modern production like *Pulp Fiction*, with a combination of seasoned costume crewmembers and over-hire labor less familiar with the stock and the "look," an average of twelve extras per hour can be dressed. Next, ask yourself how many members of your steady crew will realistically be available to dress extras. Keep in mind that, on all but the lowest of low-budget productions, it is not the job of the costume designer or the costume supervisor to dress extras. In any event, except in emergencies, neither will have the time. Also, remember that at least one of your full-time set costumers will be working exclusively with principals and day players. It is not uncommon, therefore, to look to the design assistant and the second set costumer, plus any prep costumers you can liberate, to be your only full-time crew available to dress extras on heavy days. In any event, you need to develop a pretty clear picture of how many hands you already have on deck to dress those twelve or so extras per hour.

Once you've done this, look at the extras breakdown and at the shooting schedule. Make a list of the scenes that have extras in excess of the number per hour that your full-time crew can handle. Next, look at the shooting schedule and make note of the number of days it will take to shoot each of the scenes on your list. Divide the number of extras in each scene by the number of extras dressed per hour (in the case of a contemporary show, approximately twelve per hour). This will give you the number of over-hire set costumers you'll need to dress extras in that scene. Once you've calculated the number of over-hire set costumers you need for each extras-heavy scene on the shooting schedule, add up the numbers, and you've got an estimate for total over-hire set costumers.

For example, if you have one shooting day with 84 extras, you have three available full-time crew to who can dress an average of 12 extras per hour (for a total per hour of 36), you'll have a balance of 48 extras who will need people to dress them. At 12 extras per hour, you'll need to budget four over-hire set costumers for one day. If you have scenes that will be shot over four days, with 130 extras per day, plus 30 pre-fit extras, you'll probably have to loosen up the formula and budget for six or seven over-hire set costumers to style extras on the first shooting day. For the next three days, cut back to two over-hire set costumers who can hand out, maintain, and collect the costume stock assigned to the extras the first day they "played." If the day with 84 extras and the day with 160 extras are the only days on the shooting schedule that can't be handled by full-time costume crew, then you'll be budgeting for 16 days of set-costumer over-hire (four for one day, six for one day, and two for three days).

Estimating over-hire set crew costs. Depending on your friends, connections, and the union status of the film, the set-costumer over-hire pay rate can run from $18 to $25 an hour, with time and a half paid after ten to fourteen hours worked in a single day (depending upon the overtime terms of your agreement with the production company). A normal shooting day runs twelve hours, and many production companies don't pay overtime until your work day exceeds those twelve hours.

Estimating over-hire alterations personnel. Depending upon the quantity and complexity of costume construction and alterations required for a production, alterations work will be done either "in house" or jobbed out to professional workrooms or freelance custom-made specialists. Union shoots have strict guidelines that forbid "finished set costumers" from functioning as "custom-made workers," and it is commonplace for a union shoot to bring in over-hire alterations personnel. Non-union shoots have no such protections: Costume personnel are not barred from doing costume alterations and construction work. However, non-union production often means low-budget production, and a costume department may have neither the luxury of adequate prep time nor adequate costume staff to do the work "in house." As a result, low-budget, non-union productions often job out their construction and alterations work.

In addition to standard alterations during prep, you must plan for on-site alterations personnel once shooting has started, in the event that a star's schedule or attitude prohibits fittings. Because alterations on the set demand the utmost speed and resourcefulness, most costume designers and supervisors will look for highly trained tailor/fitters or alteration fitters to cover star alterations. The high cost of on-site alterations personnel can cause hardship in a costume department budget, so the need to persuade your UPM that this should be a legitimate line item is very real (see page 569, "Estimating Staffing Requirements for Different Kinds of Films").

If you choose to assemble a freelance alterations team, this team will include some or all of the following custom-made specialists, listed below by Motion Picture Costumers Union Local 705 job titles for construction personnel on feature films.

- *Patternmaker/fitter*—someone who makes womenswear patterns, cuts and fits from specified designs (known on the East Coast as *draper*)
- *Tailor/cutter*—someone who drafts patterns, cuts and fits tailored suits from specified designs, and specializes in menswear or womenswear
- *Tailor/fitter*—someone who fits and alters men's tailored suits
- *Alteration fitter*—someone who fits and alters womenswear
- *Alteration tailor*—someone who alters menswear
- *Finisher/seamstress*—someone who does hand or machine stitching, minor alterations, and repair work on womenswear

Normally, weekly alterations loads are determined by the number of day players and pre-fit extras scheduled to work. To determine how many alterations personnel you may need per week, compute the weekly alterations load using the following equations:

- To calculate the number of alteration hours needed in a week, multiply the number of day players and fitted extras per week time three (the average number of alteration hours per performer)
- To calculate the number of alterations personnel required for that week, divide the number of alteration hours for the week into 40 (the number of hours in a standard work week)

Estimating alterations costs. To estimate the total number of hours needed for alterations, consider whether the following elements are necessary and budget accordingly:

- *Stars and "high-glamour" styling.* Costuming stars and creating "high glamour" styles require fastidious fitting adjustments for the best results (see Part 7, *Prep,* "Menswear Fitting Points for a Contemporary Businessman's Look" and "Glamour Fitting Points").
- *Costume multiples.* Costume multiples can require additional alterations, to compensate for oversize items purchased when correct sizes were no longer available. Even in territory crawling with malls, you can still dead-end on identical garments in the correct sizes.
- *Period costumes and craft-constructed costumes.* These require pre-fitting and will generally need longer alteration times. For period work, increase the estimated alteration times by two hours per costume.
- *Promotional wardrobe.* Even promotional items used for costumes can end up with a high alterations pricetag.

The general rules of thumb for estimating alteration costs are as follows: (1) assume six hours of alteration per change per principal; (2) assume three hours per change per specialty character. (Professional workroom time estimates for alterations can be found in fig. 6.19.)

If you go to a union costume workroom for alterations, expect fees to range from $35 to $45 per hour. Non-union workroom rates run between $25 and $45 per hour. Freelancers go from $18 per hour for a basic seamstress to $15 per hour for a tailor.

As you put together your alterations budget, factor in some overtime and rush charges, to cover late casting. The amount of overtime you'll need will vary with the length of your prep period

FIG. 6.19: TIME ESTIMATES FOR ALTERATIONS

Women's Alterations	
Dress down/up sizing & hem	6.4 hours
Down/up size a blouse	1.2 hours
Attach panty to blouse	1.2 hours
Men's Alterations	
Waist and seat down/up sizing	1.5 to 2 hours
Pants hem	1 hour
Shorten sleeves	1 hour
Lift shoulders	1 hour
Narrow sleeves	1.2 hours
Reset suit buttons	1 hour
"Military pinch" at jacket collar	1 hour

and the construction capabilities of your crew. You can build in rush charges by using higher workroom rates for all alterations work and slightly overestimating the time the alterations will take. With very short prep and/or very late casting, this is particularly important.

On a contemporary show, I figure about one week of alterations in a costume house is going to run us about $8,000—a little over $1,000 a day. If I use a costume rental house, I can drop between $8,000 and $10,000 a week in alterations and rentals if it's a reasonable movie. If it's a biblical epic, it's a different story. There are only so many hours in the day, right? You can only spend so much. *(Madeline Kozlowski, costume designer)*

Determining other over-hire needs and estimating over-hire costs. Very short prep periods and small crews can make the need for over-hire shoppers, researchers, launderers, and costume-pulling services at costume rental houses very real. Let the shooting schedule be your guide to prep and shooting crunches you must prepare for.

Preproduction over-hires can be spread across your budget under line item figures for research, purchases, and rentals. You'll need to foresee labor shortage problems and budget over-hire time to prevent them, factoring in pay rates for the required over-hire personnel. Below is a list of average rates for experienced free-lance personnel in Los Angeles.

Set costumers
Non-union $700 - $1200 per five- or six-day week
Union   starting at $21.13 per hour*

Shoppers/prep
Non-union $700 - $1200 per five- or six-day week
Union   starting at $18.81 per hour*

Researchers
Non-union $700 - $1100 per five- or six-day week
Union   starting at $18.81 per hour*

Seamstresses
Non-union $18 - $45 per hour
Union $35 - $45 per hour

Tailors
Non-union $15 - $45 per hour
Union $35 - $45 per hour

Crafts Artisans
Non-union $20 - $30 per hour
Union   starting at approx $35 per hour

*IATSE Single Production Signatory Low Budget Feature Length Motion Picture: "Low Budget Basic Agreement Wage Scales $1 – 3.6 Million Budget"

Freelance rates vary regionally, according to level of experience. Regional films use local seamstresses and college students as pick-up labor, and their rates vary enormously—from free "wardrobe interns" and just-above-minimum-wage workers to the rates listed above.

Actors' fittings: requirements and costs

Actors are paid to do fittings out of the acting salary budget in the master production budget. Screen Actors Guild (SAG) rules dictate that any performer earning less than $950 a day who is fit prior to a day of employment will be paid for a minimum one-hour call. If an actor spends more than one hour in a fitting, his or her payment will be prorated in fifteen-minute increments. Television arrangements are a little different: SAG television contracts grant producers two to four hours of fittings every three to seven days. There are no additional charges if fittings are done on a day when the actor is regularly called to perform. As a result, production sometimes pressures the costume department to arrange fittings for actors on the days they shoot. (For more detailed information on SAG fitting compensation guidelines and fitting regulations, see Part 7, *Prep*, "Fitting the Actor.")

The UPM can give you guidelines on the number of actor's fittings that the production company is willing to cover. On a period show, the production should be prepared to pay extras to be fit in advance. If you think you will need an unusual number of fittings with an actor (based on a difficult-to-fit body, for example, or a sophisticated or complicated custom-made design), make sure that you negotiate these extra fittings with the UPM, and make sure that the cost is picked up by production and not charged against the costume department budget.

Extras' fittings: rules and costs

Extras are often asked to bring three options for each scene they are in. In the past, extras were only compensated for garments that were used on the shoot; but recent television contracts have reflected a shift in this policy. Extras may now be compensated for all of the changes they are asked to bring, whether or not they are used. Fees for using an extra's personal clothing come out of production's master budget. However, if you need to pre-fit modern dress extras, you may need to make sure in negotiations with the UPM that the costs associated with these fittings are covered by production and will not be charged to the costume department budget.

> Seventy-five percent of the costume discussions on a film tend to be budget negotiations.
> *(Robert Turturice, costume designer)*

Budgeting for product placement

Although many production companies pressure costume designers to use promotional goods, designers are often reluctant to use them, since they can come with very specific conditions for use (only on the star, for example, or only for "wholesome" stories). Vendors who promise production-placement deals can also be unreliable, and the screen credit they are given by contract can also seem to devalue the costume designer's credit (see *Conversation Two: On the Status of Costume Design in Film, with Betty Pecha Madden*).

If the production company is counting on significant promotional costuming to keep costs down, you can "cover your ass" by submitting two budgets: one with and one without promotional wardrobe. If the availability of promotional goods is affected adversely by script or casting changes (if, for example, a company agreed to provide free clothes for Kevin Spacey, but very late in prep the casting changed to Danny De Vito, and, as a result, the promo company backed out), you'll be prepared, and the production company will be forewarned. In such a situation, the budget must be renegotiated, and if you have already submitted a budget without the promotional items factored in, you have sped the process toward a solution and established greater credibility with the producer by anticipating the problem.

Atmosphere coverage and costs

The single greatest budget problem confronted by designers is getting enough funding to cover costuming for extras. Many young producers don't budget money to costume modern-dress extras, assuming that the extras can provide their own costumes. They don't understand the problems this creates for a costume designer, including poor color choices, ugly goods, and inappropriate shoes and accessories.

The costume designer must prove the need for depth of extras' costume coverage to UPMs, who are generally unsympathetic to aesthetic demands, but do understand practical problems. Be prepared to justify your budget figures for atmosphere on the basis of logic, not art. Learn how to talk the talk. "Wardrobe things that hold up camera" (e.g., wrong colors, "poor" garments in a "rich" scene) is one reason that may justify extras' costume-coverage expenses. "Seasonal difficulties" (e.g., shooting a winter street scene in June, when the extras may show up to the call in summer duds) can trigger the approval of a higher costume-rental figure. "Location access difficulties" may help you justify renting more clothes before you get to the location (e.g., you're in Canada shooting a Florida scene, and need tropical duds; or, you're going to Cuba for a location, and quick access to your uniform source will not be possible). "The director wants" or "the DP wants" also gives you clout.

> Atmosphere coverage, other than period, can be a test of wills. *(Robert Turturice, costume designer)*

In any event, be prepared to estimate your extra's costume-coverage costs using the following formula:

1.5 outfits multiplied by the number of extras anticipated

Many costumers commented that a budget figure providing two-hundred-percent coverage for extras (two outfits per extra) will always get flagged by production. But reducing the number of changes on hand from two outfits per extra to one and one-half creates other problems, and the smaller the number of extras, the more the problems: To wit, four soldiers of unknown size are harder to pull from six stock outfits than one hundred soldiers of unknown size from one hundred and fifty stock outfits. You may be able to cut a deal for a volume costume rental that includes the right to pull stock for atmosphere, and this can prove enormously helpful, but such arrangements are generally only available at studio costume rental facilities, for studio productions.

Estimating loss and damage

The general rule of thumb is to allot ten percent of the total costume budget to loss and damage; although some costumers estimate as low as five percent. (Percentages vary, depending upon the percentage of costume stock devoted to expensive made-to-order and bought goods, uniform rentals, and other pricey items. Destructive action, a high percentage of fragile costume pieces, and rough shooting conditions (bad weather, high-crime location work, low security staffing, etc.), all suggest higher loss and damage estimates.

Estimating tax

It's amazing how fast taxes mount up. In New York or L.A., always figure in tax at eight percent across the board. In other parts of the country, different tax rates apply. In Canada, tax rates are much higher than in the U.S.

Contingency funds

The contingency line item in your budget is meant to cover overages. Ideally, the contingency figure is fifteen percent of your total costume budget. Shipping, rush charges, service charges, and any number of surprise costs are going to come out of these contingency funds.

Regrettably, this is a line item that producers like to cut, so you need to build contingency funds ("padding") into your budget in other ways, including the following:

- Rounding off costs on the high side
- Overestimating alteration costs
- Budgeting for costly made-to-order services
- Budgeting for purchases instead of rentals
- Budgeting high on supplies
- Budgeting for a costly dye studio instead of a freelance dyer

There is an art to padding a budget. You learn where to pad and where not to pad. On *Bulworth*, with Milena Canonero, we padded on alterations. We had a $30,000 alterations budget. We only spent $10,000, because we were very lucky with what we bought: Only a hem on Warren Beatty, and taking in the jacket waist a bit, because we found the perfect suit in New York. We bought great clothes for Christine Baranski, and they fit almost perfectly. For a movie of that caliber, a $10,000 alteration budget is unheard of. I know people whose dyeing samples are over $12,000. *(Eduardo Castro, costume designer)*

The amount of budget flexibility you have over the course of production—and with it, your ability to respond to costume crises with grace—depends upon the extent to which contingency funds remain in your master budget. Of course, the UPM is looking for padding, so you have to bury these extra funds carefully, and be prepared to tap-dance your way past any questions they prompt.

You just have to put money in spots where producers won't take it away. *(Dan Lester, costume designer)*

In fact, you have to have some budget flexibility to deal with unforeseen crises like script changes and late casting. And crises will happen. Whether designer or supervisor, you will be expected to handle these crises efficiently, with aplomb. Always, over the course of a production, changes take place—major ones and minor ones, many requiring additional costumes. At the same time, you may be asked by production to cut your budget. Your ability to graciously handle such "curve balls" can help you move up the career ladder, sometimes getting you hired on productions with bigger budgets, so when it comes to contingency funds, "CYA"—cover your ass.

Dated condition memos and budget cover sheets: coping with changes

Your budget estimates are tied to a particular version of the script and a set of work conditions known to you at the time you drew up the budget. When changes are made that affect the costume budget—when a gigantic ballroom scene is added, for example, or Faye Dunaway replaces an unknown in the cast, or the producers decide to change the shoot from New York to Poland—the budget will need to be renegotiated—and amended. The *condition memo* is a brief description of the assumptions under which you worked to produce this particular version of the costume budget (the stage of the script, the state of principal-player casting, and the level of information from other departments). A condition memo might read like this: "This budget was drawn up March 12, after the addition of scene 232 (beauty pageant), before seven of the principal players were cast, and before detailed conferencing with EFX."

Production delays often trigger additional costs for the costume department. Casting the leading lady one week before shooting means rush alteration charges. Moving the robot bar scene up in the shooting schedule means major overtime costs at the specialty crafts and dye studios you are using. Some costumers send cautionary memos to the UPM, reporting costs that will be generated if production decisions are not reached by a certain date.

As the script evolves and you are given new pages, adjust your budget to reflect the changes, attach a new condition memo, along with a dated *budget summary cover sheet* (blank form A.13), then send a copy of them all to the UPM. Keep all the original script pages, with the original budget, for future reference. If, at a later date, any of your expenditures are questioned by production on the basis that they are not required by the updated script, you can point to the original script pages and the original approved budget items that justify your initial purchases.

Advanced budget negotiations

After you've submitted your formal preliminary budget (see A.18-A.29 for a full sample budget for the hypothetical *Pulp Fiction* project), you'll begin negotiations with the production manager or UPM, consulting with the director to pare away the number of extras, the number of uniforms, and so on. Your ability to break out atmosphere costs and individual scene and character costs here is a distinct advantage. Once the director and the UPM have approved the costume department budget, you can really get under way.

Future budget negotiations are likely to be necessary as you encounter casting changes, rewrites, actor availability problems, star demands, special effects requirements, and so on. As before, use logic, not art, to justify your new expenses. In additional condition memos, you might say, for example:

- "Schedule changes caused rush charges";
- "Unexpected physical conditions demanded additional supplies";
- "Extras casting agreements were ignored";
- "Runaway action caused exceptional loss and damage";
- "Unforeseen star demands occurred";
- "Theft resulted from security problems";
- "Long distance fitting costs were required because of actor unavailability";
- "Late casting switches were made after made-to-order goods were finished."

Clarity, logic, and a positive, flexible attitude will help you greatly in your negotiations, but your budget figures must prove your case. Most importantly, your original budget should reflect advance planning for the normal crises of production.

> I just had [production] take $10,000 out of my $25,000 budget, to cover principal wardrobe over an entire season. So now, I have to go and fight about that. It's a constant battle. My wardrobe supervisor said, "Aren't you upset?" I said, "No." You know, there are ways of dealing with producers. They just have to see it in black and white. There's a way to ask for more money. You just don't go, "I need more money." If they've added a scene, or brought a scene up earlier or something, that's where the memo comes in.
>
> There's an art to writing a memo. You do not blame anyone for anything, you just state the facts. You say, "Due to the changes in the schedule, we have found ourselves in this situation, and in order to address it, or be on time, we will need additional funds. Blah, blah, blah. Please advise me. Can we meet to discuss this?" Or they've added a stunt where there's a $3,000 dress. You say, "This is what it's going to cost. Do we need the stunt?" You have to protect yourself in memo form—nicely, directly. People who get into trouble are those who do not advise the producers that there may be a possibility of going over budget. You keep the producers abreast of developments. *(Eduardo Castro, costume designer)*

Tight budget strategies

If, after negotiating the costume budget with the production manager, you find that you must make additional cost cuts, there are many ways to do so. Some are dangerous, some labor-intensive, some a godsend. They include the following.

Wheeling and dealing. Make a deal. Volume rental and volume made-to-order work can lead to special deals. You can negotiate a special price, and special arrangements, when you agree to rent costumes, costume storage space (a costume "cage"), office space, and workroom labor from a single source. Under such single-source arrangements, some rental companies have been known to let a designer pull freely from stock for mass fittings, charging only for what ends up being used—even though the designer may hold on to the goods for weeks.

Most often, the art of the costume deal requires good timing and a good reputation, although rental houses or made-to-order companies desperate for work during the slow season may cut a deal even with a newcomer. Low-budget costumers often try to obtain low rental fees or borrow goods with the promise that all of the production's bought and made items will be given to the rental company in trade when the production is over. Craft companies and made-to-order workrooms with rental stock may be willing to work at a reduced rate if, after the shoot is over, they get for rental the specially designed goods they've made.

There are many deals in the biz, and developing a good reputation is the most important bargaining chip you have. To establish a good reputation, you must return rental, borrowed, and promotional items on time, and in top-notch condition. You have to deliver on any promises you've made. You have to be clear and consistent when working with made-to-order sources, and you need to give them as much time as possible to do their work. When vendors help you in the hard times by cutting you a special deal, or saving you in a crisis, you need to bring them business when the good times roll. Be fair, be consistent, show them special consideration, and you'll earn a good reputation. (For more on this, see the section called "Product Placement" in Part 7, *Prep.*)

Using actors' personal wardrobe. Using personal wardrobe as costume is common practice with modern-dress extras. It is also a common tactic practiced with principal players on many low-budget productions. The extras are paid for the use of their personal clothing out of the production budget's extras' salary budget line, so this can save significant costume budget money. The extras have a wardrobe allowance box on their time card; they check it off, they get their money. The actors have no such option: Either they negotiate in their contract for compensation for the use of their wardrobe or the costume designer can compensate them with gifts of wardrobe from the production.

Using the personal wardrobes of actors and extras can get you some great clothes and help solve fitting crunch problems; but it carries the danger of not having multiples if they're unexpectedly needed, and not have clothing readily available for reshoots or inserts, or even, occasionally, for the next day of shooting—a continuity nightmare. Imagine, the actor had the nerve to wear his own clothes home! And instructing day players and extras in what to bring to a shoot is an art. Misinterpretation is rampant. Bad taste and inappropriate choices can leave you in the lurch, unless you've invested in back-up choices (see "The art of giving wardrobe instructions" in Part 7, *Prep.*)

> As far as getting extras to bring the right wardrobe, you're at the mercy of the extras'
> casting agency, which may not convey your requests to the extras they hire. You must
> fax the agency detailed descriptions or lists of what the extras need to bring with them,
> and even then, the extras get it wrong! *(Marcy Froehlich, costume designer and co-author of*
> Shopping LA: The Insiders' Sourcebook for Film & Fashion*)*

Using product placement. Promotional items or product placement goods can be a godsend, helping a designer stretch her budget. And large quantities of free shoes from Adidas, or clothing from Armani or Cerruti or Tommy Hilfiger, can significantly change the look of a film. However, promo deals often carry stiff conditions, and, as noted above, have been known on occasion to fall through. Companies don't want like-item competition in a film, so they can demand that no other logo-stamped clothes appear on screen.

Companies that provide promotional goods are concerned with their own image, and how their goods are featured in the film is a deal-breaker. Companies usually like attractive stars in cheerful films. They can be uninterested in helping with extras coverage. If there is a leading lady switch late in prep, if the script features drug trafficking or excessive foul language, the company may be uninterested in participating in the deal. One famous tennis shoe company allows no violence or drugs on screen in the productions to which they contribute. The time it takes for the contributing company's executives to okay the script and send the goods can be a problem: Most corporations do not work on "film time."

If you can make promos work under the conditions imposed by the companies and, in spite of them, develop a rapport with a corporate representative, you can save yourself thousands of dollars and get fabulous goods that take your low-budget movie to a higher level. Making a $30,000 budget look like a $70,000 budget can get you more work on projects with larger budgets, so the tight wire you walk in a promo deal may help your career. (For a guide to working with product-placement sources, see "Product Placement" in Part 7, *Prep*).

Designing day players and extras for maximum economy. In addition to making deals for volume rentals, using the actors' personal wardrobes, and using product placement when possible, there are several other budget-busting tactics, among them:

• *Whenever possible, design using stock that will fit instantaneously.* When you use stock that must be altered, don't get obsessive about subtle, labor-intensive fitting points that run up alteration costs—resetting sleeves, for example, or adding crotch straps to shirts, to keep shirt tails permanently tucked in. Luxuries like this are never advised for players who will not get extensive close-up work.

• *For the extras, design for "A," "B," and "C" status groups, using preferred stock to create stronger looks on the extras in the "A" group and passable looks on the "B" and "C" groups.* If you do this, your set costumers will have to work carefully to keep "C" extras in the deep background; but if your set crew is vigilant, this method can save a lot of money. Of course, to actually make this happen, you must have a team of most-understanding assistant directors.

• *Recycle the costume stock.* The recycling of costume stock items from one extra to another is a common practice during shooting, although not recommended: Recycling stock on principals, or any featured player, for that matter, is an accident waiting to happen. However, replaying costume stock on background performers is all too common a practice on low-budget productions. I (HC) worked on a shoot where we used a Panama hat on two dozen different men in the course of the shoot. We simply didn't have enough hats in reasonable sizes to go around. But recycling can make reshoots hell. Instead of costume units being wrapped after they've been used, then held for reshoots, the individual costume pieces get put back into stock, to use on other players. If you need to reshoot the scene later, you have to paw through stock to reconstruct the costume, based on sketchy notes, and often not-very-good Polaroids.

Using cost-recovery strategies. Buy clothing options that can be returned if unused. This practice is especially useful when designing for costume multiples. Save tags and billing for future returns. Sell stock back to the actors or staff when it is not needed for reshoots.

Streamlining made-to-order work and using multiple sources. Streamline patterning and prototype development. To keep costs down, costume construction can be compressed so that designers commonly see only half of a mock-up on a form before the garment is cut and fitted in real fabric. Farm out the work to different priced shops, according to the level of special work the goods need. For simple pieces, use low-price, quick turn-around costume shops or freelancers, whose staff won't "love" the garments too much with time-consuming couture techniques. Use higher-priced studios for difficult goods or goods that require fine detailing.

Using interns and production assistants. While union shoots thoroughly discourage using interns and non-union production assistants, there are plenty of productions that thrive on underpaid and overworked interns. Interns can be trained costume personnel who are new to film work, or complete beginners who had enough hustle to get attached to the production. There is plenty of low-skill work that needs to be done on a regular basis, so interns are often given work based on the following criteria: an exemplary attitude (a sunny manner and a willingness to do anything); an ability to drive and navigate around town; and an ability to consistently show up on time to work.

Productions with huge workloads and small crews also seek interns with costume training (sewing and fitting skills, styling and shopping skills, stock organization experience, etc.) and frequently dip into local theater departments, or advertise in local papers or trade magazines.

The often-extreme pressures of working in film frequently result in the gross exploitation of interns. The stakes can be so high on the job that trained personnel give minimal time or attention to teaching interns the ins and outs of the business. And sometimes bosses are just self-serving sons of bitches. To get the best from your intern staff, you must treat them humanely, and lay out clear ground rules and detailed techniques for organizing and handling the costume stock, making purchases and doing returns, doing laundry and costume maintenance. (Ways to become an intern will be discussed in Part 10, *Entering the Market.*)

Arranging for wardrobe kit rentals. As noted earlier, because work conditions vary so much in the industry, costume designers and costumers collect a wide variety of supplies and equipment from different sources to create a "kit" that they can take with them wherever they work. Kits are developed over time as personal funds allow, and it may take time to develop a kit strong enough to be worthy of a production rental. Personal kits that include computers, rolling racks, sewing machines, steamers, and sergers can save the costume department hundreds, even thousands, of dollars, and the range of supplies contained in these kits can help a costume department respond efficiently to a wide variety of crises.

Streamlining supply and equipment inventories. Cheating on the budgets for supplies and equipment makes it hard on a crew, but it can save you a lot of money. If you forfeit expensive plastic skirt hangers and opt for metal hangers, you will force your crew to pin each skirt or pair of trousers to the hanger. (This can take precious time—it's always a trade-off.) A short count on rolling racks means that the crew must shuffle garments on and off available racks on a daily basis. Buying dye and sewing supplies on an as-needed basis means a few dozen more trips to the store. (And, of course, that goes for bleach, soap, set robes, etc.) "Make-do" economizing can force the production to rely on a crew's kits to solve supply problems, or the crew's miraculous improvisational skills to fill in for supplies or equipment that aren't available. Of course, it can also leave you in the lurch, with only the hope that it won't hold up shooting or show on camera.

It is especially dangerous to pinch pennies on costume multiples. This can put the production at risk. Holding up production always results in frayed tempers, so it is worth the money to have at least minimum coverage. Too many costumers have stories of "squib happy" special effects folk or production glitches that caused more takes than anyone counted on. I (HC) worked on a shoot where the fantasy dance sequence in

FIG. 6.20: GUIDELINES FOR STREAMLINING THE WARDROBE SUPPLIES AND EQUIPMENT ON STARVATION BUDGETS

If you're working with a very low budget, streamline the supply list by reducing it to the most basic functional goods and buy goods with an eye to emergency coverage. The following list served the needs of a medium-sized feature film I worked on that had a cast of forty principal and featured players (and a total of 860 changes), a crew of four, and a starvation budget. Compare this list with the Wardrobe Department Basic Supply Kit in A.30.

Office Supplies: Forget Polaroid plastic sheets, computer supplies, Polaroid labels, and rubber stamps. Tell your crew they must supply their own hole punches, Polaroid rings, pencils, pens, staplers, and flashlights. Buy one box of Sharpies and six rolls of tape.

Equipment: Try to get all equipment through kit rental. If you can't, get one iron and ironing board setup for the principals and one setup for the extras. Rent one steamer, one sewing machine, and minimal rolling racks (the number will be dependent on your cage storage situation). Buy tools on an as-needed basis. Have the crew bring their own oversize golf-style umbrellas in case of rain or blazing sun.

Stock organization supplies: Forget skirt hangers, padded hangers, muslin hangers, wood hangers, dress labels, garment bags, and tagging gun supplies. Buy one storage box for each man's and woman's shoe size (grouping ultra small and ultra large together), one box for hats, one box for purses, three boxes of small Ziplocks for jewelry, two large boxes of tags and safety pins, a roll of dry cleaning bags, accessory bags for twice the number of cast, and four boxes of wire hangers by the box of 500.

Dressing supplies: Buy the following minimal emergency supplies and buy other supplies on an as-needed basis. Half a dozen sets of insoles, half a dozen shoe laces (black, brown, and white), a box of moleskin strips, one can of saddle soap or instant shoe shine, one can each of Static Guard and Scotch Guard, three collar extender, six boxes of Topstick, six pair each of black dress sox, brown dress sox, and white athletic sox.

Craft supplies: Buy the following minimal emergency supplies and buy other supplies on an as-needed basis.
One dark and one light Schmutz stick, a small bottle of mineral oil, three cloth diapers or hand towels.

Sewing supplies: Have the crew supply their own threaded-needle kits and scissors. You should supply one multi-colored thread kit.

Cleaning supplies: Get the following minimal emergencies supplies and buy other supplies on an as-needed basis:
one quart of Picrin and one bottle of Zout for spot cleaning, one large box of baby wipes, six white tailor's chalks, one dish soap, and one gallon of distilled water.

the open-air courtyard got increasingly wild. The action was great fun, but when the leading man, during a mambo, took off his white dinner jacket and started swinging it over his head, then whacking it against the floor—the *dirt* floor—we in the costume department wanted to die. We only had one jacket that fit this actor, so between each take, we blitzed the jacket with the stain remover Zout and white chalk. We survived the crisis—more or less—but it was a hair-raising experience.

A note on sleaze economies

Sad to say, there's a lot of unscrupulous behavior in the film costume world. Extras get stuck wearing someone else's dirty clothes after a minimal spray-down with disinfectant. Items get returned to stores "unused" after they've been worn by performers on set. Personal-kit expendables get used up and never replaced. Poor thrift goods are substituted for rental stock that gets trashed. Stock deals are made, then broken. Bills never quite get paid.

Unfortunately, everybody's been burned, which makes working in costumes tough all the way around. Take heed: While some of these tactics may save a production money, none will enhance your reputation with the vendors and individuals you depend on. Saving money via sleaze economics may make you look good to one or two producers, but when you really have to design a show on time and on budget, the vendors and individuals you screwed won't come through for you. A bad reputation is hard to shake in the very small world of moviemaking.

The master budget

Once the costume designer and costume supervisor have come to budget terms with production, a *master budget* can be produced, and money transactions can begin—purchasing, rentals, made-to-order work, the leasing of equipment, the buying of supplies—in short, all the preparations necessary for realizing the design. Of course, as noted above, the costume department must be prepared to renegotiate the budget with every change sent down "from above." As with the initial budget negotiations, the costume designer and the costume supervisor negotiate money issues with the unit production manager and/or producers, design guidelines that cause budget problems (e.g., the number of police extras needed for the big scene or the prohibitive cost of the "designer" look for the big stunt sequence) with the director. But once a master budget is agreed upon, costume "prep" can begin (see A.18-A.29).

Conversation Six:

On the Costume Craftwork Process and Budget Factors, with Chris Gilman

Chris Gilman is president of Global Effects Inc., a company that manufactures special costumes and props for film, including astronaut suits (fig. 3.21) for *From the Earth to the Moon* (1998), biohazard suits for *Outbreak* (1994), and Dracula's armor for *Bram Stoker's Dracula* (1992). This interview is the first part of a two-part conversation. (See Part 7, *Prep,* for the second half of the conversation, about the collaboration of the craft studio and the costume designer during prep.)

Designers and costumers are often intimidated by complex craftwork, and the costs can seem staggering to newcomers. Chris, how do you get costume designers to understand what you do and what you need from them?

Craftwork is very foreign to most costume designers. As a result, I see designers who are unsure of what they are doing. For a costume designer, making *traditional* costumes is not that scary, but if you are going to get into specialty wardrobe, you need a basic knowledge of what these special materials and processes can do—in the same way that a costume designer develops a basic knowledge of fabric. A common problem we run into is designers coming in and dictating the materials they want us to use. The problem with that is that most designers use the names of materials as catch-phrases: "I want it out of latex." Well, that's the only name for a rubber product they know. Or their friend Bob had something made out of latex, and they like the look of it. Well, part of our job is to *simulate* materials.

You need costume designers who are able to communicate the quality that they are looking for in a design, but who will allow you to dictate the materials, because the materials you use determine your work techniques, correct?

It affects techniques, and it affects how durable their product is. In collaborations, I try to guide a designer through the process because there are so many unknown factors. But in the end, I have to have faith that what they want is, in fact, what they want. And they have to have faith that what I'm telling them about how it can be done, can be done, and is, in fact, how it *should* be done. I've had designers argue with me. "No, we are going to do it this way. No, we're going to do it that way." For example, I was working with some people who wanted this prototype helmet. I said, "By the time I make this prototype helmet, I might as well make you the helmet." "Oh, no, no, just mock it up. Don't go through all that work." But it's not like I can do a "muslin" of a helmet; it's not like I can drape a helmet.

There are some techniques that require that I sculpt the design, mold it, and cast it. There are other techniques that allow me to just fabricate it out of aluminum, which I can do faster than I can sculpt it. Having the ability to form metal in almost any shape I want is a big advantage. It's something that other shops can't do. So in this case, for me to make this helmet was fairly simple. But it was, "Oh, no, no, no, no, just make a mock-up." I had a discussion about it with the person for at least an hour. My office manager overheard most of the conversation, and thought, "This person isn't listening to a word Chris said." This person has got it set in his mind that this is what he wants, and this is all he wants.

Many designers are accustomed to regular costume-house techniques, where you can see a mock-up on a stand or go to full mock-up fittings. They don't realize that your sculptural processes can be more time-consuming and the piece more difficult to alter afterward.

The important thing in the production of any sort of rigid costume is sculpting the correct form. When you are draping fabric, the design sketch does not have to be really detailed; its proportions don't have to be correct. There are a lot of "cheats," a lot of fine-finish detail that you don't have to put in the sketch. But if a crafts studio gets into a sculptural piece, whether it is armor or a spacesuit or a robot suit, lack of accuracy and detail in the design sketch is a problem. To fine-tune a form in fabric, it's as easy as moving a pin and saying, "This is how I'd like to end this." That process can be done in a clay sculpture as well, but it takes a lot longer, and a lot of money can be burned up in the sculptural process.

The training that most sketch artists get is exactly that—*training* in sketch art. There are two approaches to design sketching. One says, draw it as it's going to be. If the person who's going to wear the design is short and frumpy, design it short and frumpy—and do the best you can with those proportions. The other camp believes that you should make your sketch of the design as cool looking as you can and figure out how to make it work later.

If you cheat those dimensions when you are dealing with a robot suit or a suit of armor, you're going to be hindered in the sculpture stage. It is always going to be a battle of proportions. Say, you block out in the clay something of a particular length, then you step back from it and you say, "Wait a minute, I can't make that detail go to there because I have six other details that I have to get in, and I am already three quarters of the way down the leg—so I've got to re-proportion everything." And the problem with that can be that when you get the sculpture blocked in and you stand back from it, it loses the essence of the original sketch.

Take the case of Whitney Houston's Queen of the Night outfit from *The Bodyguard* (1992). The original sketch was done by Susan Nininger, a costume designer. In her sketch, the Queen of the Night outfit had a breastplate that looked like a solid piece of chrome, an abdomen plate with all these pleated fans coming off the waist, and a head-dress that looked like a helmet. The original sketch was a "costume-y" sketch: It gave us a general direction. The problem was that our sculptor couldn't sculpt from that. Not enough detail. Not enough information. Does this shape go in? Does it come out? What happens to it when it goes around the corner? Does it just abruptly end? Does it blend into another line? So we did what we usually do—have one of our illustrators, who's used to dealing with those things, "illustrate" the sketch, using realistic proportions and a little more realistic style of drawing.

Even if someone is a really good artist, he or she doesn't always have the ability to render really mechanical shapes. It can be easy to create an "Escherism," a term that

I coined. If you know who the artist M.C. Escher is, you'll "get" that an Escherism is an effect that happens when you draw a line that starts off as a "positive" (a bump), but becomes a "negative" (an indentation) by the time it gets around to one side, but when you are looking at the drawing, you don't notice it. Another Escherism is when people draw two versions of a costume, one from the front and one from the side, but you can't make both of them happen at the same time. If you go back and reference the front view, lines don't line up. People tend not to look at the mechanical details of the drawing, just the art of it—the general impression.

So, in effect, your illustrator does a technical drawing?

We look at it as a technical drawing only because we keep in mind the technical aspects of the design. But we try not to make it look like a technical drawing because you still have to pitch the idea; you still have to make it look glamorous, or whatever the emotion is that you are trying to get across. Sometimes designers don't want to spend the money on this step. They go, "We don't really need that. Let's not." The problem is this: Let's say it takes two days to work through sketches and really start to fine-tune the design. If you do it on the fly, in sculpture, it will take a week to make those same decisions and those same changes.

Your technical drawing is really a time-saving thing for you.

It is. To make the changes in the clay generally takes a lot longer than starting with a fresh piece of paper and just sketching out a different approach, so we try to fine-tune as much as we can in the two-dimensional stage. We try to do multiple views, or at least a three-quarter view, to give us an idea of how things change as you move around the form.

Sometimes it's easier for me to create the item in 3-D. No matter how much you fine-tune a two-dimensional image, as soon as it translates into three dimensions, it changes. And a lot of people really can't visualize the design until they see something they can move around. So we'll do an intermediate thing—a maquette, a miniature—somewhere between a sketch and a full-sized mock-up. And again, when it comes to this approach, there are two camps. In one camp, you make your maquette to sell the idea. In a maquette, you can give the actor forty-inch legs, or biceps thirty inches in diameter, to look impressive. In the other camp, you are true to the real proportions. The real advantage of a maquette is that a lot of details can be worked out very precisely, very quickly, since there is a lot less surface area on a maquette than there is on a full-scale sculpture. If your maquette is not directly proportional to the person you modeled it on, the design won't translate well.

So you use your sketches and models to confirm design proportions. In effect, in respect to basic proportions, these sketches and models are your "mock-ups"—a hedge against major, full-scale sculptural changes that take more time and cost more money. But for mold-making, you still need an accurate, full-scale sculpture.

If we are doing a sculptural piece, unless it's something simple like a helmet, we almost always require a body cast of the actor. That's five or six thousand dollars, right there. You have to cast the actor's hands separately, his head separately, his feet separately, and then you have to cast his body from his neck to his ankles to his wrists. Then, you have to clean it all up, fit it together, make a "positive," smooth it all out, and double-check the measurements, to make sure that, in fact, it is your actor—because it is easy to misalign pieces and have it a little off here and there.

Or we have the actor scanned and have a three-dimensional model of the actor machined.

Why not do elaborate measurements?

Well, with armor, if the sculpture has to fit the actor specifically, there is no way to use measurements. It is impossible to measure accurately where lumps and bumps appear on the person. You know, where is an actor's bicep, exactly? Where is the highest point of his bicep?

The fit of the parts at the joints is incredibly critical on a rigid costume. Otherwise, you can't do the things you need to do—like being able to bend, and kneel down. The biggest mistakes are making the backs of the knees too tight, not making the hip areas correctly, and not making the glove areas correctly. The fitting process—the process of figuring out where you are going to need the most room—can take the better part of a day.

You also have to keep in mind that you have actors who are whiners. I'm a card-carrying SAG actor. I have spent a lot of time in rigid suits. I try on every costume I make that I can fit into. I walk around in them, sometimes for long periods of time, in order to understand what the actors are going to have to go through. But, unless it's a pair of silk pajama pants, you can still have actors who are going to complain about how uncomfortable a costume is. So you have to deal with that.

A piece that is exactly molded to an actor's body is bound to be more comfortable. And it would save on fitting and alteration costs.

With fabric, you are pretty limited in the amount of "sculpting" you can do, whereas in clay, you can sculpt absolutely perfect shapes and forms. The sculptural form is more "tune-able." Also, with a rigid suit, if you put it on the actor and it's not right, you have some options for fixing it, depending on the material it's made of. With a fabric suit, if you make a small mistake, you can fix it. If the body bulges in a certain place, and you can see a little pucker, you just go, "Okay, we have to fix that." In a rigid suit, by the time you get to the prototype, you have invested a tremendous amount of time and money in your sculpture—figuring out the design, and then creating a mold of that sculpture so you can reproduce it. If you have a fitting problem, sometimes the only option is to completely re-sculpt and remold.

For a principal actor, you can generally get approval to spend enough money to do that kind of careful custom work, so certainly that process makes sense. But if you are dealing with army guys, a bunch of extras?

In that case, a design requirement is to make the item generic enough to fit many types of bodies.

We have done a lot of shows—for instance, *Beverly Hills Cop III*—that wanted robot suits built. We couldn't do body casts of every single guy who was going to play a robot, so we designed things with the intent of being able to grind them out, sand out different areas, open things up, and shorten a little bit here and there. Shortening is the hardest thing to do, generally. And we just said to the casting people, "Everybody you put in this suit has to be between 6'1" and 6'3", and between 180 pounds and 200 pounds."

You gave them very specific constraints?

Very specific. But if we know we have to fit a wide range of people, then we try to be a little loosey-goosey with the shape. Of course if I sculpt it with a half-inch of "slop," the lower legs look a little thick—almost thicker than the upper leg. "Can't you make the lower legs a little thinner, for a more dynamic look?" Those are the things that you balance against. So if you don't have a body cast and you are trying to balance the dynamic look of the part, you have to be careful of where you start to skimp on size. We also have options in what we use to make the product and the mechanical techniques used to make it, to assure the critical sense of the fit. Obviously, the more rigid the parts, the more critical the fit; the softer the parts, the little less critical the fit, so we try to mix and match those elements (fig. 3.5).

To get back to our process, if we get a final sketch or maquette approved, and we have a body cast of an actor, we'll start sculpting the full-size element on the body cast. If we don't have a body cast of an actor, we have a variety of casts in stock for different-size people. Sometimes, actors are claustrophobic. Sometimes, actors don't want to be body-cast. Sometimes, we'll even body-cast a "body double"—someone who is similar in size and shape. Also, quite often, actors have already been body-cast somewhere else, and you can get hold of the body cast. The downside to this is that body-casting methods can vary. Everybody takes measurements differently. Mold-makers don't want to trust the measurements of other mold-makers, just like costume people don't want to trust other costumers' measurements.

If the body cast is made, it is critical that it get seamed together correctly. Problems come up if the mold gets a dent in it; or if a plaster-bandage cast is left lying down, and the butt flattens out—that kind of thing. The actor may have gained weight or lost weight since the casting. These are all things that can make an old mold inaccurate. Then, when you make the costume and it doesn't fit, you'll have a problem. It becomes your responsibility, because, even though somebody else made a mistake with the body cast, you were the one who built the costume. And it costs you a lot of money to redo the costume.

Things that help speed the construction process include sketches that are proportionally correct and mechanically minded, accurate design maquettes and body casts, and flexibility when it comes to the kind of mock-up that the costume designer needs to see. What else can help keep costs down?

When I'm bidding the job and you say, "It really needs to look like this," I ask, "How *much* does it really need to look like that?" And I mean, *how much.* How much with dollars and how much with accuracy. If you have $10,000 to spend, or $50,000 to spend, then you have the money to make it look *exactly* like that. But if you have $6,000 to spend, you can't afford to have it look like that. If you draw something like a robot suit or a creature and say, "I want this little square thing with this little point sticking off it because I like the way it looks like an old TV," we have to *make* that. I have to sit down and machine a pattern, and machine these out of aluminum, and turn this, and do that.

But if you let me go down to the surplus store, I can probably find some things, and I can mock something up that looks close enough.

"No, it's got to be this."

Well, now, the part that I could go to the surplus store and buy for $5.00 is going to cost $5,000 if I have to make it to look specifically like your drawing. The reason the part at the surplus store costs $5.00 is that the government probably made a couple of hundred thousand of them.

Can you give me some up-front cost guidelines for craftwork?

Without seeing your drawing, without a discussion of the particulars of the item you want us to make, without knowing the time frame or the details of how it needs to work, there is no way for us to give you enough cost information for you to be able to make an intelligent decision. Basically, we use the same processes that you go through for any costume: You have to understand what the character is and what the character has to do. Sometimes when we have people come in to talk to us about prices, they are very wary about giving us budget figures. "We don't know the budget yet, can you give us a ballpark?" That's like going in to a car dealership and saying, "I don't know how much money we have to spend. What do cars cost?"

In the process of designing, we have to take into account the look of an item, the actions the actor has to perform in it, what conditions it has to go through, and how we are going to translate the design sketch into a very specific three-dimensional sculpture. How is the actor going to function in it? How are the pieces going to stay where you want them to stay? How long is it going to take the actor to get into the costume? What parts does he have to put on first, and what parts does he have to put on last? What does the "finish" have to be? What does the color have to look like? What kind of paint, what kind of dye, what kind of coating? Is it going to be on the surface or in the suit? There are some materials that paints and dyes don't stick to at all, so then it is important to put that color in the material.

How do you choose materials?

We select the material based on what the shape is, how much time we have, what the budget is, how much movement is required, and how much action is going to be involved. Are we making one? Are we making a dozen? Are we making one stunt suit? One real suit? All of these factors. We try to guide clients along budgetary lines. The biggest mistake is trying to buy a full-blown Mercedes for ten thousand bucks. You are not going to get it. You can get a nice used Toyota for ten thousand dollars, and if you invest a little bit of money in the outside of it, you can spiff it up—the analogy being that if you try to get too many details and too many exotic finishes, or too many exotic shapes and too many processes, you're burning up a lot of money.

Ninety percent of the time, designers are under budget in their estimates for craftwork by a factor of two; sometimes by as much as fifteen or twenty. I've had clients come in and try to get a $50,000 or $60,000 item for $2,000. They'll say, "Oh, we want this and we want this and we want that. We want to do this. We want this shape. And we have $5,000." Now, they think $5,000 is a lot of money. But when you add up all the man-hours, I would have $5,000 in the design, the sculpture, and the materials before we even get to the labor to put it together, or make the actual parts out of the molds, or make the molds. So all of a sudden, the budget isn't anywhere near what you think it is.

In other words, you help guide designers through the options they have?

We try to find out what they really want the most. It's just like buying a car. You go into a dealership; you don't want to spend any more than thirty grand. But you really want that air conditioner. And you really want that nine-speaker stereo system. And you really want those cool wheels. And you really want the sun roof. And you really…Well, it gets to the point where you've got to either cough up more money or live without some of these options. But those are tangible options; you can see them—whereas some of the processes in craftwork are an integral part of the item itself; you can't necessarily see them.

The thing that is really important is the detail. Really look at the detail. You can go to Armani or you can go to Sears to buy a sport coat. If you don't know anything about sport coats, $3,000 versus $125! If you don't understand the reason for the difference in price—if you don't see it—you will when you put it on. And then, you look at it and go, "Oh. I get it." We here at the shop have a tendency to be very particular about the details. We try to make sure that they're right, with the thought that the actor has got to be able to work.

So, very important rule of thumb when thinking about the budget: If your budget is limited, don't blow your money on too many details. Better to do the details that you *can* do right. Because if you make an involved costume and it's cheesy—if it's slapped together, lumpy and bumpy and not finished nicely—people are going to see that, and they are going to go, "That looks kind of crappy." But if it's simpler, and really finished and professional, they won't notice all those details that aren't there. They'll notice the fact that it's really finished and professional-looking.

To cut to the chase, the thing to ask is, "How much did you have in mind to spend?" I approach it by trying to give you the most bang for your buck. My reputation is based on everything that goes out of here.

How can a designer negotiate with you on costs?

We've done spacesuits on a "manufacture for rental" basis, for $6,000 a piece, and we've done spacesuits on a "manufacture for rental" basis, for $50,000 a piece.

Meaning that you custom-make them for the film, but they come back to you afterwards, to add to your rental collection?

Right. That will account for a savings of twenty percent to as much as fifty percent on an item, depending on what's involved. Now on the two suits mentioned, I would say that if I put the $6,000 one up against a $30,000, one you'd be hard-pressed to see that there was a $24,000 difference. But one is made of completely custom-built pieces while the other is built using off-the-shelf items. For the $6,000 suit, we used parts molds that already existed. The $6,000 spacesuit used off-the-shelf fittings that were originally designed as hose couplings. We cut them a little bit, polished them so they didn't look so cheap, and used them as spacesuit neck rings and boot rings. We happened to have wrist rings already made up, so we used those. The wrist rings alone, if we had to make them, probably would have cost $1,200 a pair. But because these items had been mass-produced, or were surplus, we saved a lot of money over the cost of a completely custom-built costume.

What else can help a designer cut costs?

Our shop rate for certain things, depending on the detail level, is between $65 and $75 an hour. Say we put in two hundred hours on a part. That's $1,500 dollars for that one part. The second part only takes me an hour to make out of the same mold, so now you have two parts, but it only costs $785. And now, I make twenty parts. And because I'm making twenty, I can condense my process and I don't have to make them one at a time. I also have techniques that I've come up with—ways of "cheating," of shortcutting—that allow me to do in a day what might otherwise take three days.

Everyone I've spoken with has talked about budget constraints, and how difficult things are getting as a result.

There is always somebody out there who's working out of their garage, who is trying to get a foothold, who will work for nothing. It's a crapshoot. That person might be the most enthusiastic person in the world, but Albert Einstein on a lazy day is going to be a far more effective thinker than a kid just out of high school, even if he is the most enthusiastic guy in the world.

If you make things cheesy, if you make them cheap, they're not reliable. They'll jam. They'll pop open when you don't want them to pop open. It's holding up production because it broke while you were putting it on. Now how much money did you save when the director and the producer are screaming at you because this thing broke, and you've got twenty or thirty people standing around with their arms crossed waiting for the costume to be ready? How much money did you save then? Not very much.

If a guy is willing to work for nothing, that means he doesn't have much overhead. He isn't paying for a bunch of machinery; he isn't paying for a bunch of guys; he's not paying for a big shop; he's not paying workman's comp—all those things that are required to do business. So you save a little money, but it's liable to catch up with you.

PART SEVEN

Prep

Introduction to Preproduction

"Prep"—short for "preproduction"—is, officially, the period before principal photography begins—the weeks, sometimes months, in which preparations for shooting are made. Unofficially, prep continues even after shooting begins. This is true for every department on a film, not just the costume department: No one has the luxury of finishing all preparatory work on a project before shooting starts. Keeping this in mind, there are many things that must be done, often simultaneously, as soon as the official prep period commences. Some of these tasks are completed before principal photography begins, while others begin in the formal prep period and are not finished until moments before a costume walks onto the set, somewhere deep into the shooting schedule.

The following is a more or less comprehensive list of basic things to do during prep:

- Establish the terms of the collaboration between the costume designer and the costume supervisor
- Establish prep priorities and develop work strategies
- Do a script breakdown
- Establish costume breakdown and budget research priorities
- Do costume breakdowns
- Establish priorities for acquiring costume stock
- Determine costume coverage and sources for principal players and extras
- Establish requirements and sources for facilities and services, equipment and supplies
- Research preliminary budget, including identifying costs that are unavoidable and deals that might be cut
- Finalize preliminary budget
- Negotiate costume budget with production, including costume stock rentals and purchases, salaried staff, over-hire and freelance costume labor, facilities and transportation support
- Tender offers to prospective staff and support personnel
- Negotiate final contracts with production
- Establish accounts with vendors
- Set up costume department office, on-site workrooms, costume storage, fitting rooms, on-site laundry, dyeing and distressing facilities, as needed
- Attend production meetings
- Collaborate with other departments (conferences and presentations)
- Gather costume stock for principal players and extras via purchase, rental, and product placement
- Work with made-to-order sources, including costume workrooms, craft studios, and other costume artisans, as necessary
- Organize the costume stock
- Prepare for fittings
- Schedule fittings
- Fit the actors
- Fit the extras, if necessary
- Work with set costumer to prepare the set book
- Discuss the practical look of all available changes, including the look of atmosphere
- Load and prep the wardrobe truck(s)

Some of these tasks have been discussed in detail earlier in the book. Others will be described in detail in the sections below.

The Costume Designer-Costume Supervisor Collaboration

The work style and emotional tone set by the costume designer and the costume supervisor set the style and tone for the entire costume department team. The designer and supervisor have to work in tight harmony. Issues of territory, responsibility, and control need to be resolved early on. According to industry standards (and union contracts), both designer and supervisor have their necks on the line when it comes to the budget, the quality of the look of the production, and the timely delivery of the goods. As a result, both parties need to fully understand the demands of the script, the priorities of the designer, the logistics of budget and schedule, and the assets and limitations of their crew. Both designer and supervisor break down the script (sometimes separately, sometimes together), establish budget and schedule priorities, put the staff together, and gather the wardrobe. Both designer and costume supervisor must understand how to run a department before they can stretch its resources and adapt it to the demands inherent in costume work.

Few hard-and-fast rules exist when it comes to how a costume designer and a supervisor divide the work of preproduction planning. The mandate to accomplish the tasks before them overrides strict job definitions. In an ideal designer-supervisor duo, the weaknesses of one party are compensated for by the strengths of the other. Work is taken on by the person who can best accomplish it. Rapport and respect between the designer and her supervisor are amplified by a mutuality of design purpose and organizational goals. Once these goals are defined, the designer and the supervisor will go about doing their respective tasks. Although each has his or her own way of going about the work, the individual duties of designer and supervisor are always conceived as a single shared plan of operation.

Mutual regard and common courtesy help to accomplish this plan of action, of course, but to really achieve harmony, the designer-supervisor team needs to find some balance in the way the workload is distributed and the production's details are handled. Traditionally, it is the costume designer who focuses on setting the project's visual goals with respect to the costumes and confers with other departments about the design. Costume supervisors, on the other hand, focus on making sure that the costuming process run smoothly. Logistics and conditions that affect the flow of the work are the supervisor's obsession. If an assistant designer is not hired, the assistant designer's tasks are distributed among members of the costume department staff, according to availability, aptitude, and—if the crew is union—according to guild and union job descriptions. These tasks may include character research, character breakdowns, shopping and rental research, "swatching" (sampling fabrics), developing made-to-order specifications, and supervising fittings, among other things. Often on productions with modest budgets the costume supervisor functions as the design assistant, and may act as the designer's eyes and ears in meetings, in the workroom, on the truck, and, sometimes, on the set.

FIG. 7.1

The diva designer at work....

"Oh, and after you're through with the budget, resarching the insignia, doing the crossplot, figuring out the stunt multiples, and setting up the accounts...could you pick up my dry cleaning?"

Great supervisors, like great cutters, have a strong design sense and a deep appreciation of good design. Great designers have an acute appreciation of good organization and a practical understanding of the demands made on their designs by the filmmaking process. Unfortunately, a fabulous design eye does not necessarily come packaged with great organizational skills. Many designers lack these qualities and need a great deal of support in this territory from their staff. Of course, control freaks and callous attitudes can crop up in both positions. Designers who share information only on a "need-to-know" basis are a particularly thankless lot to work for. Supervisors who are insensitive to a production's design standards make achieving those standards an uphill battle (fig. 7.1).

Traditionally, each member of the design team—the costume designer and the assistant designer(s)—has a set of duties during prep. Many of these duties overlap, which is why it is critical for designer and supervisor to agree on a division of responsibilities before prep begins.

Duties during prep: the design team and the supervisor

Before we delve into the prep process in detail, it might be worth laying out an overview of the respective, and sometimes overlapping, duties of the design team and the costume supervisor.

COSTUME DESIGN TEAM'S DUTIES DURING PREP
- Shop, pull, and coordinate character designs
- Coordinate design choices, conditions for use, and delivery dates with product placement sources

- Coordinate design choices and delivery dates with studio services departments
- Develop character boards
- Obtain design approval from the director and the producer
- Coordinate design choices with hair and makeup departments
- Research, select, and contract with made-to-order and craft shops
- Shop and supply decorative fabrics and trims
- Track made-to-order and craftwork progress
- Respond to samples and patterns
- Supply purchased or rented garments that affect fit and layering of made-to-order goods
- Coordinate delivery of goods on projects using multiple made-to-order sources
- Supply accessories and shoes to fittings
- Direct fittings, via critiques of the "spirit," fit, and proportions of garments on actors
- Supervise made-to-order revisions
- Track casting developments
- Draft wardrobe instructions for the extras, to be delivered to casting and extras casting departments
- Coordinate special costume needs and stunt casting with the stunt coordinator and stunt team
- Track shooting schedule and script changes
- Coordinate costumes with camera department, and special effects, when necessary
- Coordinate budget adjustments with unit production manager
- Develop detailed character breakdowns for character continuity pages

COSTUME SUPERVISOR'S DUTIES DURING PREP

- Arrange for and set up costume department office, if this has not already been done by design team
- Supervise the purchasing of all costume department equipment and supplies
- Set up accounts with vendors; coordinate and supervise all department-related accounting activities (letters of credit, deposits, rentals, direct purchases, purchase orders, credit charges, petty cash, etc.) with production accounting and vendors
- Supervise, in collaboration with the designer, the purchasing and rental of all character wardrobe goods
- Coordinate product placement deliveries
- Coordinate delivery of goods, services, and billing with made-to-order, craft, cleaning, and alteration sources
- Coordinate and schedule fittings with actors, designer, and, if necessary, made-to-order and craft sources
- Coordinate wardrobe transport, including scheduling and location logistics, with transportation department
- Coordinate fittings and wardrobe requirements for stunt personnel, in collaboration with the designer
- Coordinate costume design and construction requirements, including requirements for padding and rigging, with the special effects department
- Supervise ongoing acquisition and organization of stock, equipment, and supplies at department home base
- Order and organize stock, equipment, and supplies for on-location costume department
- Track billing and crediting for all costume returns
- Track wardrobe damage and loss
- Supervise the development of the set book
- Supervise loading and preparation of wardrobe truck(s)

A sidebar: design assistants

Many producers dislike hiring design assistants, especially when the production budget dictates that the design assistant will end up doubling as set costumer. What producers fear is a lack of trained—and available—costume help on set. After all, no producer wants camera held up because the set costumer is out shopping the next day's changes, or, conversely, that the design assistant working set has no idea what to do about the coffee spilled on the star's white tux. Sadly, producers often view design assistants as employees whose tenure must end with the beginning of the shoot. Many producers fail to realize that shopping and fitting continues throughout the shooting period.

A seasoned producer will object when a designer hires a design assistant who will double as set costumer—even if it's done to save money. On most films these days, the designer, plus one other person (the design assistant), will be needed to shop and do fittings throughout the shooting period. Even if the design assistant is trained to work the set, she or he won't be free to do so. As a result, the department would be underrepresented, camera would be held up—and, again, no producer wants camera held up.

The costume designer should be prepared to negotiate very skillfully for an assistant designer, reminding the producer of the particular prep and shoot conditions that justify this hire. Indeed, a design assistant can often direct fittings and make purchases, acting as surrogate in matters of design when the costume designer is unavailable, or overloaded with work. (For more on design assistants, see below, *Conversation Seven: On the Role of the Design Assistant, with Marcy Froehlich.*)

> "Design assistant" is not a very friendly term in Hollywood. Producers don't question costumers—'Oh, they're wardrobe people, they're fine'—but they do question assistant designers. To them, the need for assistant designers is a sign of a high-maintenance designer. The worst thing is a diva costume designer, and certain designers are high-maintenance. That gets around. And that starts to affect the status of all designers.
> *(Eduardo Castro, costume designer)*

Setting Prep Priorities

Costume prep is the art of prioritizing limited time. Costume prep periods vary from production to production, but many productions—especially television and non-union features—allow no more than four to six weeks to prep (sometimes less) before principal photography begins.

Many fundamental elements of a production—casting, script, the availability of locations, the weather, the details of action sequences, special effects and stunt information, among them—are in a state of continuous flux during prep. As a result, costume prep priorities, once established, will change. In order to set priorities and keep them real, the costume department must hustle as much information on these matters as it can from the first AD, the second AD, the camera department—any and all sources. But first, the costume department must get from production the most up-to-date edition of the *"one liner" shooting schedule* (fig. 5.13).

The shooting schedule—the list of scenes to be shot day by day in the order in which they'll be shot—determines the costume team's work strategies during prep. What works first? What works next? The answers to these questions help the costume designer and costume supervisor decide in what order costumes and stock must be readied.

> Prep time in feature films has really come to where television used to be: a three-week or four-week prep. In TV now, you get two to three weeks' prep. I have to say, I feel that people who have a history in features have been spoiled by the long prep periods and the huge crews. When you think of episodic TV, a lot of times it's a mini-feature produced in seven or eight days. You have to be tough. You have to be highly organized. You have to able to think ahead. *(Pat Welch, costume designer)*

There are certain rules of thumb for scheduling prep that are useful to know. Ideally, shooting-schedule logic has the production crew going to a location in the sequence in which the sets at that location are introduced in the script, but this seldom happens. The order in which locations appear in a script may not make sense when you are moving a crew and equipment from place to place; there may be difficulties in gaining access to a location; costly actors may not be available in the ideal timeframe. In general, productions do try to schedule exterior locations first. Once at a location, an attempt is made to shoot all the scenes that use that location in the order in which they appear in the script. Once again, however, reality isn't always so ideal. Shooting schedules can be seriously affected a number of factors, but most commonly by unexpected foul weather. If an exterior location is rained out, the scenes scheduled to be shot are replaced by interior locations called *cover sets*, and the originally scheduled scenes are rescheduled. This rescheduling is necessary in order to avoid idling the crew—a crew that may cost $50,000 per day.

Although studio features have a more leisurely prep schedule than independent features, a neophyte in the business will undoubtedly end up working on productions with prep schedules that more closely resemble the one outlined below ("Four-Week Week Prep Schedule for a Typical Independent Production"). On this preproduction schedule, the costume team has one week to develop design guidelines, set stock priorities, set up the office, research costume resources, and develop a preliminary budget. As a result, design and budget guidelines must be worked on simultaneously.

In all events, the shorter the prep period and the scantier the set-in-stone information the production office provides, the more efficient and creative the costume department needs to be. To get an idea of the creative ingenuity and energy, and the managerial strategies and bare-bones efficiencies it takes to prep a production in four weeks, look at the prep schedule below. Not an hour is wasted as both the costume designer and the costume supervisor improvise, based on available information.

FOUR-WEEK PREP SCHEDULE FOR A TYPICAL INDEPENDENT PRODUCTION

WEEK ONE: GETTING YOUR DUCKS IN A ROW

Week One goals: Set up the office; get preliminary costume design approval

Designer concentration: Design development and organization

- Produce research boards, tear sheets, and sketches
- Preliminary conference with art director on palette and design themes

- Preliminary contact with principal casting (after contracts are signed), for discussions on character, actor's clothing preferences, body issues, measurements, allergies, color, and shoe preferences

Supervisor concentration: Department setup and budget development

- Set up the office and "cage" arrangements
- Arrange for equipment (racks, steamers, irons, sewing machines, box storage, etc.)
- Purchase supplies
- Set up accounts with vendors (rental companies, made-to-order and craft sources, studio services, fabric stores, etc.)
- Start prep costumer(s)
- Preliminary discussions with transportation department about trailers, loading dates, and location logistics
- Arrange for wardrobe services (cleaning, research, shipping, etc.)

Designer and supervisor: shared tasks

- Break down the script (script notation, character and extras breakdowns, etc.); costume supervisor and script supervisor conform script day/night breakdown
- Design and budget research—character, period, and uniform research
- Rental, made-to-order, and purchase sourcing
- Product placement contacts
- Casting department reconnaissance (Who are they thinking of casting? What "look" are they going for?)
- Schedule fittings, in coordination with the casting department and actors
- If casting is *not* set, shopping/rental research and reconnaissance
- Pulling and tagging uniforms and other special-dress extras stock, at rental houses

End Week One: Designer presentation to the director (discuss script and design thoughts; discussion generally lasts three to four hours)

WEEK TWO: GETTING READY FOR THE INVASION

Week Two goals: Fit principals and day players, if available

Designer concentration

- Pull rental wardrobe
- Coordinate made-to-order (MO)
- Shop, using petty cash
- Style/design the day players and principals, if available

Supervisor concentration

- Preliminary budget approval
- Stock gathering
- Fittings
- Coordinate returns of wardrobe not approved

Note: Accounts are not necessarily fully set up by week two. In general, rental houses approve and set up accounts faster than studio service departments. This is because rental houses have more manpower in the accounting department and are set up to handle industry-related business more efficiently. To compensate for delays in studio services, most designers have personal studio-service accounts, which can be "rolled over" to production once a production account is approved.

EARLY PART OF WEEK TWO

Designer task

- Coordinate MO work

Supervisor tasks
- Budget submission, and budget corrections, for approval
- Trickle-in casting coordination, including calls for measurements

Designer and supervisor: shared tasks
- Pull wardrobe at costume houses, based on actor measurements and most recent meetings with director
- Pull special pieces (hats, shoes, accessories, and accent pieces for extras), in assorted sizes
- Coordinate with stunt coordinator

LATE IN WEEK TWO
THURSDAY (DAY)

Designer tasks
- Shop
- Memo out, on 24-hour approval, from rental houses (an arrangement that allows you to pull costumes for Thursday night fittings and, if they don't work, return them the next day, for a ten-percent restock fee)
- Style, and pull together, options

Supervisor task
- Organize the stock

THURSDAY NIGHT

Designer task
- Handle blitz of day player fittings

Supervisor tasks
- Polaroid fittings
- Record alterations on tags
- Coordinate alterations
- Tag and bag character changes
- Track rental memos and returns

FRIDAY

Designer task
- Confer with the director about changes, using photos from the fittings

Designer and supervisor: shared tasks
- Post-conference change-out and retagging, based on director's requests
- Return rental wardrobe not approved
- Coordinate additional alterations
- Copy producers on director-approved Polaroids of character changes

WEEK THREE: SHOP TILL YOU DROP

Week Three goal: Fit the principals

Designer concentration
- Gather wardrobe
- Coordinate made-to-order
- Fittings
- Conferences with other departments

Supervisor concentration
- Bring set costumer on board (ideally)
- Stock gathering

- Fittings
- Returns

Note: Accounts should be in place by week three, so studio services can memo out goods on five-day approvals and bill bought goods to the production account.

MONDAY THROUGH FRIDAY

Designer task
- On-location conferences with director of photography (DP), stunt and special effects coordinators

Designer and supervisor: shared tasks
- Shop
- Coordinate additional MO work
- Memo out goods through studio services
- Pull rentals
- Stockpile inventory and set up costume department offices for after-hours and weekend fittings.
- Production meeting (takes up four hours of one weekday)

Set costumer tasks
- Purchase supplies for truck and set
- Rent equipment for truck
- Learn costume stock and script details (backwards and forwards!)
- Go over the script, memorize which costumes go where
- Prepare "set book" (see below, "Production Tracking")
- Meet with costume designer to go over details of how costumes should be worn
- "Runs" (errands)

WEEK NIGHTS AND/OR WEEKENDS

Designer tasks
- Final casting conferences and fitting requests

Supervisor tasks
- Record, tag, and bag character changes and options
- Coordinate alterations
- "Honcho" (oversee) check requests

Designer and Supervisor: shared tasks
- Fit as many actors as possible

FRIDAY

Designer tasks
- Present director with principal fitting photos; director "signs off." After approval, note rejects and remove option tags. Change out goods as necessary.
- Get a copy of approved designs to director and producers

Supervisor task
- Organize returns and alterations (send out only after designer approves)

Designer and supervisor: shared tasks
- Organize next week's shopping
- Make list of costumes requiring multiples
- Strategize
- Make lists for final week of prep

WEEK FOUR: GOT HAIR? GONNA LOSE IT

Week Four goal: Final preparations

Designer tasks

- Present character photos to producers (if not approved, producers must discuss with the director)
- Meet with hair and makeup departments to review fitting photos
- Meet with sound department to discuss sound-related concerns
- Get final logo clearances
- Write up wardrobe instructions for extras, if extras are to supply their own wardrobe; coordinate with extras casting
- Double-check backup options for characters
- Gather stock, as necessary

Supervisor tasks

- Supervise returns
- Departmental clean-up and final organization
- Bring in product placement goods
- Final purchase of supplies
- Supervise truck preparation
- Finalize set-book preparation

Designer and supervisor: shared tasks

- Final fittings
- Develop strategies for stunt problems, extras wardrobe, last-minute changes, and, in general, "CYA" (cover your ass)

Set costumer tasks

- Prepare wardrobe truck
- Purchase truck and set supplies
- Aid supervisor in finalizing set-book preparation

Set costumer and costume supervisor: shared tasks

- Conference on costume changes and stock for trailer
- Plan purchase of supplies, rental of equipment for truck, and arrangement of truck stock
- Determine cleaning and maintenance policies and setup for "crunch" days

Setting Costume Breakdown and Budget Research Priorities

In addition to sourcing and price research, costume breakdowns of many types must be done early in prep. As a result, the costume designer and the costume supervisor must sort out, as quickly as possible, how this work will be divided. Detailing costume changes, "guesstimating" multiples and supplies, developing estimates for the preliminary budget are among the tasks that get split among the designer, the supervisor, and the assistant designer (if the department is lucky enough to have one). The route to a preliminary budget must be as direct as possible; as a result, all members of this team need to be clear on the territories they're responsible for covering.

For both the costume designer and the costume supervisor, first priority goes to doing the script breakdown and the costume scene breakdown (the "long form"). From the costume scene breakdown, they can start putting together the design and cost guidelines for the production, researching what's needed to make an initial presentation of the design concept to the director and producing a preliminary budget for presentation to the UPM. This process should begin by targeting the most important design elements and budget items, including (1) clothing styles (e.g., period details, rules of dress, design options) needed to finalize initial character-design guidelines and (2) the availability and cost of the goods and services needed to produce the designs.

Specifically, first priority in matters of character and costume research goes to all character or clothing-style research that helps the designer develop major design guidelines and costume stock priorities. This includes researching the clothing preferences, design ideas, and body information for principal characters and actors, and finding images that support the designer's ideas in presentations to the director and other key members of the production's creative team. For the costume supervisor, costs for mass rentals, made-to-order work, purchased goods, multiples, wardrobe-related services, and other costume budget line-items will need to be researched before the preliminary budget is submitted.

How do you determine exactly how much time can (or should) be spent on design, budget, and source research? It's not possible to give exact guidelines for this. The amount of research needed for a production varies with the scope and style of the project, the breadth of knowledge of the designer and his or her crew, and the level of detail to which the designer and the supervisor want to commit in the preliminary budget. If a production has the budget and the time, the costume designer and the costume supervisor may enlist assistant designer(s) or research services to streamline this stage of the research process. However, a savvy, well-trained costume crew can cut short research time and still deliver a quality look. A short prep period will force any crew to cut to the bottom line—to establish tough priorities and forego extensive research service costs in favor of bringing in both the big-dollar items and the logistically difficult necessities.

Regardless of the nature of the production, your researchers will require a clear picture of the range of design options acceptable to the designer. For maximum efficiency, it is imperative that your researchers be presented either verbally or through design graphics with clear design guidelines for characters and atmosphere. Sketches, collage boards, and detailed research pages can clarify mushy design language and delineate the costume designer's style priorities for the characters (fig. 7.2). Distributing portable copies of these materials to your shoppers will streamline their hunt for goods.

The importance of clearly communicating the designer's desires becomes abundantly clear when you realize that checking the price and availability of a nineteen-forties gray suit can require answers to the following questions: Does the suit have to be a cool gray or a warm gray? Light, medium, or dark value? Single- or double-breasted? Peaked or standard notched lapel? Striped or plain? Chalk stripe or pinstripe? Wool or silk? Time spent with a costume designer who knows how to describe what she wants is time well spent by any member of the preproduction costume team.

While the costume designer is developing the design priorities for the production, the costume supervisor is forging ahead, setting up the office and establishing supply

FIG. 7.2   255

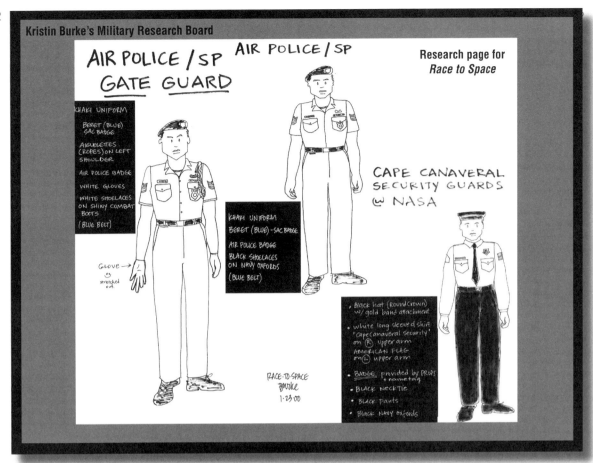

Kristin Burke's Military Research Board

AIR POLICE / SP GATE GUARD

AIR POLICE / SP

Research page for *Race to Space*

KHAKI UNIFORM

BERET (BLUE) SAC BADGE

AIGUELETTES (ROPES) ON LEFT SHOULDER

AIR POLICE BADGE

WHITE GLOVES

WHITE SHOELACES ON SHINY COMBAT BOOTS

(BLUE BELT)

Glove → stretched out.

KHAKI UNIFORM
BERET (BLUE) - SAC BADGE
AIR POLICE BADGE
BLACK SHOELACES ON NAVY OXFORDS
(BLUE BELT)

CAPE CANAVERAL SECURITY GUARDS (w NASA)

RACE-TO-SPACE BURKE 1-23-00

• Black hat (round crown) w/ gold band attachment
• white long sleeved shirt "Cape Canaveral Security" on (R) upper arm AMERICAN FLAG on (L) upper arm
• BADGE provided by PROPS + name tag
• BLACK NECKTIE
• BLACK PANTS
• BLACK NAVY oxfords

lines, equipment rentals, and wardrobe-related services like dyeing and dry cleaning. Once the preliminary design scheme is developed and the research for the preliminary budget finished, the designer-supervisor team can start to develop character worksheets, estimate multiples, and fill in preliminary budget details. As the design develops and research continues, other costs can be filled in.

The need for large numbers of multiples, or the availability of appropriate product placement pieces, can have a profound impact on the budget, so this kind of research gets done early in the budget research process. The careful scheduling, high costs, and long development periods required by some made-to-order work (very detailed period gowns, elaborate body padding, spacesuits or creature suits, for example) dictate early priorities for this kind of research.

Getting comparative bids from different workrooms or doing price-comparison shopping can help keep your budget at its trimmest, but bargain-hunting takes time. Costume designers and costume supervisors have to determine, at an early point in the prep process, how much time and labor they can afford to spend researching comparative costs or resources. To streamline the resource research and comparison shopping processes, consult the guidelines below.

GUIDELINES FOR STREAMLINING COMPARISION-SHOPPING AND RESOURCE RESEARCH

• Create shopping lists that divide the research load into source categories (e.g., "probable rental source," "probable MO," "probable buy," etc.), in order to take maximum advantage of any trip or call to vendors.

- Divide research problems into what can be done by phone and what must be done by on-site inspection. List the questions you need answered on style, sizing, color, availability, terms of usage, service fees and options, development process, scheduling, etc. Get all the information you need from a vendor the first time you call. "Giving good phone" is a highly prized skill in this industry.
- Target one-stop shopping sources—places where you can accomplish multiple research errands. At Western Costume Company in Los Angeles, for example, you can price its made-to-order work, do character research in its library, and scope its racks for rental alternatives to made-to-order work—all in one visit.
- Cut down travel time by shopping and running research errands at places close together. Prep personnel in New York and Los Angeles are especially savvy about the most efficient routes and modes of travel for costume-related trips: in L.A., the shortest, least-traveled, routes, the least-trafficked times of day; in New York, taxi, subway, car service, and delivery strategies. Prep personnel should know the general range of goods available in the primary shopping districts, malls, rental sources, and research libraries in their area, then cluster errands to these vendors and services for maximum efficiency. (Part 10, *Entering the Market,* lists key costume resource areas in New York and Los Angeles.)

Purchasing strategies and costume stock priorities

As research filters in, the team can start collaborating on the development of purchasing strategies and the establishing of costume stock priorities. To set purchasing priorities, the team must (1) identify unavoidable costs; (2) identify deals that might be cut; (3) determine costume coverage needs and costs for the principal players and day players; (4) determine costume coverage needs and costs for the specialty and general extras.

Identifying unavoidable costs and deals to be cut. Both the designer and the supervisor need to assess the script for unavoidable high-dollar and high-labor items—specialty craft costumes, multiples for big-ticket items, uniforms in large quantities, period costumes for atmosphere, formal wear for atmosphere, and character goods that require made-to-order work. Made-to-order services required for actor safety—fireproofing, for example—must be given top budget priority. Craft costumes for the principal actors are given a higher budget priority than their regular wardrobe, to insure the actors' comfort in these tricky costumes. Even craft costumes for the extras can take budget priority over principals' regular wardrobe.

Unique character touches required by the script—like pregnancy pads, catsuits, light-up leather jackets, or "icon" costumes (Marilyn Monroe's white, fan-pleated halter dress, for example)—can demand MO work when standard retail and rental sources can't provide them. And then, there's the piece of costume research that the director fell in love with (or is obsessed by) that can't be found for love nor money.

Casting research can reveal other unavoidable costs. If you need attractive suits for Arnold Schwarzenegger or Danny DeVito, you had better budget for made-to-order. Some actors' bodies are so difficult to fit that MO is your first—and sometimes only—choice.

The costume designer and the costume supervisor must also brainstorm on deals that might be cut, including rental package deals and the use of product placement (see Part 5, *Costume Budgets,* "Tight Budget Strategies," and below, "Product Placement").

Choosing sources wisely is a large percentage of the designer's work. (Hope Hanafin, costume designer)

Determining costume coverage and costs for principal players. Designs are divided into "principal player" and "atmosphere" categories. High-ticket items, designer goods, and made-to-order designs are usually acquired for only the principal players. Because fitting time is limited, the costume team should try to limit costume options for principal characters to three or four per look. This gives the director and the actors a comfortable number of choices while keeping the design concept in focus and fitting times under control. Too many options can overwhelm; too few can turn a designer into a shopper who serves only the actors' and director's demands.

As noted earlier, powerful stars may dictate the use of specific designers and brands. The costs of keeping a star happy can be astronomical. A request for a particular T-shirt and pair of jeans can seem reasonable until the star names the items' designer. Conversely, a star may insist on "absolute reality." If the part demands a chambray work shirt, he or she may be offended by the Calvin Klein version. Unless the members of the costume team are aware of a star's standard demands, they can only guess what a look will cost. And guesswork is never good. Getting the "skinny" on a star's eccentricities moves to the top of the list.

The pressures of prep are added to by the fact that principal casting is rarely fully set at the beginning (and often not by the end) of preproduction. Until casting is "locked," only limited costume purchasing and rental can be done. As a result, the costume team needs to leave room in the department budget for the costumes of not-yet-cast principal players. The designer and the supervisor will have to agree on how much "star treatment" they can afford to give these principals, then gamble that they have put aside enough money in the budget. If principals need more "budget room," carving cash out of the atmosphere budget may be the only solution—not a good one. And so with today's ever-shrinking prep periods, and later and later casting of principals, many costume teams are developing desperate, and wily, strategies for coping with last-minute fitting of actors, including second-guessing the casting, purchasing a range of sizes, and pre-fitting body doubles.

On one show, I got a call on a Tuesday night to revamp these two detective babes. Production said, "We're casting them tomorrow—Wednesday—and shooting Thursday." I said, "We'll fit on Wednesday, around five or six." I hired an assistant, and we started off at meetings at ten A.M. Then we "pulled" at Barney's, went over the hill, and "pulled" at Sherman Oaks Galleria. I pulled pieces in sizes 4 and 6, because you know your leading actress ain't going to be an 8. We just pulled the world, and we were able to get the looks we wanted. You know your ingenue is size 4 to 6, even a 2 or a 0, nowadays. I learned how to size people from working the set on *Miami Vice*, where we did twenty-six to thirty-six characters every week.

I did a film last year, in Canada. I didn't get to see the cast until the day before shooting. I had this one lead character playing a Mexican renegade, and he wears one costume. I took a chance and got his wardrobe at a discount place here [in L.A.]. I wanted these great twill pants that look so worn the way they come. I took a chance and bought four pairs of pants with a 33-inch waist, because that covers the range of good leading men in good shape. He's either going to be a 32 or a 34. I don't think he's going to be a 31—he's a big, strapping guy. He's going to be 5'10" to 6'. And I got extra-large flannel shirts, and large

Calvin Klein T-shirts. And it worked. From experience, you know your leading-man sizes. They're usually about 5'10", 165 pounds, a 42R, with a size 9½ to 10 shoe. Most leading men are small. Robert Redford, Robert De Niro, Harvey Keitel, and Mel Gibson are small and well-proportioned. Of course, there are also strapping leading men, 43 to 44 Long, which would be more like Liam Nieson—the taller end. *(Eduardo Castro, costume designer)*

Determining costume coverage and costs for extras. Because the film production process requires costume designers and their crew to design extras at a break-neck pace—often in fifteen minutes or less per extra, on the set or at a mass fitting call—the costume stock for extras must be chosen shrewdly, with an eye to a broad range of sizes and character types. The garments and accessories in your costume stock for extras will determine how broad a range of characters you can contribute to the atmosphere of the film. (See fig. 2.8, which shows the extras in a nineteen-fifties' Indiana train station scene, in the 1997 film *Going All the Way*. Each of these extras was styled in ten to fifteen minutes, on average.)

When approaching the problem of costume coverage for extras, you need to ask the following questions: What scenes need high-ticket goods? Where can we get the best design "bang" for the buck? Where can we cut corners? Keep in mind when you're acquiring atmosphere stock that you'll have to fit a broad range of sizes. If the script dictates a wide spectrum of ages, from children to the elderly, garment types and size range must reflect this. If the script dictates character and costume eccentricities—for example, the "double-D" tendency of the women in Federico Fellini's films—the costume department must adapt its stock rental and purchase lists accordingly. The range of sizes that must be stocked for extras will also vary with the shoot's location. For example, if you are working in L.A., on a scene with generic "attractive" extras, you can anticipate that the majority of women extras will be in the 6-to-8 size range, men in the 40-to-42 range, with a few in the 46-to-48 range. If you are working out of town, anticipate much larger sizes for the women.

The costume department will sometimes be able to exercise a degree of control over the sizes the of extras, particularly when it comes to extras hired to wear uniforms, or period garb; but, in general, the department needs to be able to adapt to the range of extras sent by extras' casting. Chatting up the person in charge of extras' casting can help you identify the body types being sought for different scenes. You can also anticipate problems by devoting a percentage of the costume stock to "cover-up" items—overcoats, aprons, big sweaters, and other garments used to hide the bad basic wardrobe often brought to the set by extras.

Atmosphere is often divided into "upscale," "nondescript," and "character" groupings. Additionally, atmosphere stock may be ranked "A," "B," and "C," according to its quality. In general, and whenever possible, look to mass-rental, thrift-store shopping, and the use of performer-provided clothing to solve atmosphere coverage problems. Palette and texture control can be achieved with performer-provided clothing if instructions to the extras are specific. (See below, "Coordination with the casting department," for advice on the art of giving wardrobe instructions, and fig.7.3, "Memo to Extras' Casting.")

Re: Background Wardrobe Info

---

casting department.

Hello there! I just wanted to give this to you before things get crazy. The following is a list detailing wardrobe requirements to be given to extras casting.

1)   **Rangers (SIX, including deputies with speaking parts)**
Must bring plain white crew neck t-shirt (NO LOGOS), black socks, & hiking boots (brown or black). Must be within the following size ranges: WAIST: 30" to 36"; INSEAM: up to 35"; NECK: 15" to 17 ½"; JACKET: 38 to 44. Due to the limited number of costumes we will be able to pull, *we will not be able to accommodate sizes in excess of these guidelines*. **Female Ranger: size 8 or 10 ONLY.**

2)   **Paramedics (2)**
Must bring plain white crew neck t-shirt (NO LOGOS), black socks, & black lace-up shoes. Size guidelines: WAIST: 32" to 36", INSEAM: up to 34", NECK: 15" to 17", JACKET: 40 to 42. Again, we will not be able to be flexible here. We can only pull two costumes. These are the sizes we are pulling.

3)   **Bear Handlers (6, including Trailer driver and Forklift operator)**
Must bring plain white crew neck t-shirt (NO LOGOS), black socks & black boots (combat style, thick high-top hiking boots are okay). These are coveralls, so size guidelines are as follows: HEIGHT: 5'8" to 6'1", **MEDIUM BUILD.** What this means, translated into sizes, is roughly JACKET: 38 to 42.

4)   **Conservatives (?)**
Must bring a minimum of three options, including the following: upscale casual, well-kept denim is okay, khakis, Dockers, sportcoats, dresses. This is SUMMER time – no fluffy jackets or big sweaters. Colors: Muted, not pure. Example – taupe, slate blue, deep/muted reds, greens, greys. NO OBVIOUS LOGOS.

Acquiring strong, eccentric pieces (jackets, sweaters, sport shirts, etc.) that can be combined with an extra's own clothing to create "character looks" is especially important. What percentage of the budget should you devote to purchases and rentals like this? It's impossible to give a specific percentage, since every project is different; it depends upon the nature of the project, and the costume designer's desire for a strong, specific "style" or "flavor" in given scenes. You can, however, use common sense. If you are doing Harlem, Cotton Club, nineteen-thirties, for example, you'll need a load of good, weird period accessories; so put aside a decent chunk of the budget for rentals and purchases in this category of goods. Are you working on a contemporary kid's movie? Then save your money. You won't need a ton of stuff for extras; the extras will bring their own choices.

In all events, a good percentage of the extras' budget needs to be devoted to accessories. A strong accessory stock can be a powerful design aid, giving life to bland outfits (fig. 2.9). This is especially true for period productions. Period hats, bags, gloves, scarves, bold ties, suspenders, spats, shawls, aprons, and jewelry all contribute greatly to creating a strong period look. Remember, it wasn't until the mid-nineteen-sixties that the fashion industry de-emphasized accessories for women and hats for men.

Regardless of whether a production is period or contemporary, a range of sizes is particularly important in items like footwear, since far too many extras show up with inappropriate shoes. Do not skimp on shoe stock!

Staffing and support negotiations

When costume stock needs have been established, the preliminary budget is finalized by the costume designer and costume supervisor and submitted to the unit production manager. In this category, items to be negotiated with the UPM or line producer include the size of the costume staff and the duration of staff contracts, requests for over-hire and freelance costume labor, and requests for facilities and wardrobe transportation support.

Costume department team members come on board at different times during prep. The designer and design assistant come on board first, the supervisor second, prep staff third, and lastly, set costumers, who, as a rule, come on board one to two weeks before shooting begins. To estimate your requests for staffing, transport, and facilities, you need to know the length of prep time, the conditions at shooting sites, the size of the wardrobe load, the number of extras, and the number of days when the numbers of combined principals and background players are high.

Hiring issues. After getting the UPM's approval of costume department staff-size and composition, the costume designer and the costume supervisor can approach prospective staff members to discuss the project and the terms of their employment, including kit rentals.

> The element that is going to save you is your crew. Nothing is more hideous than a weak crew. That can kill you. It just makes it so difficult. Your crew is everything. *(Eduardo Castro, costume designer)*

Putting the costume crew together is all about creating a family. Here, "chemistry" is important. Prep costumers who shop and pull need to have a sense of style and be able to work with the designer on a visual level. Set costumers need diplomatic skills, a strong sense of set etiquette, and an unwavering sense of loyalty. All need to support and protect one another. Personal virtues like flexibility, endurance, a positive attitude, courteous work habits, and a good sense of humor go a long way toward making the department "work."

> Through experience and time, you put together groups of people who work very well together, who understand each other. Some members of the group may be extraordinary in some situations and not comfortable in other situations. It's always about moving that piece of the puzzle around. A show that is predominantly about middle-aged women may take a slightly different crew than a show about a bunch of guys doing stunt sequences at night in the mountains. *(Catherine Adair, costume designer)*

Contract negotiations. Rates, overtime wages, kit rental fees, back-end deals, exclusivity, travel support, screen credit, and print advertising credit are all items to be negotiated by the costume designer and the line producer or UPM. Design assistants and costume supervisors also negotiate rate, overtime wages, kit rental fee, and other pertinent elements in final contract talks with the UPM or the line producer.

Non-union, non-exempt, non-supervisory staff are paid by the hour, and they get neither pension nor welfare benefits. Union prep and set costumers are also paid an hourly rate, but do get pension and welfare benefits. Prep-period paychecks are, as a rule, lower than shooting-period paychecks since, during prep, union prep and set costumers are generally not permitted to work more than ten hours per day. All union employees are guaranteed a certain number of work hours a week. Designers, design assistants, and non-union costume supervisors are paid a flat weekly rate.

While rates and work weeks differ only slightly for union personnel working in costume houses and in different production formats (television episodic, movies of the week, etc.), rates for costume crew on a production vary widely, according to the worker's expertise, the production format, artful negotiation on the part of an agent, and whether the work is in town or on location. The minimum union rate for a given job is known as "scale," but nobody works for scale if they can help it. Non-union rates may actually match or exceed union minimum rates because there are no benefits attached to the salary.

Costume designers also negotiate the following:
- *Overtime wages.* Days off, and overtime rates for additional days and hours.
- *Design kit rental fee.* This can include not just the design kit, but the cost of cleaning kit items, and equipment and supplies such as cell phones, computers, beepers, etc. Note: Kit rental fees are not treated as wages by the production company's accountant and, as a result, kit rental fees are not included in the figure on which pension and welfare contributions are based. The IRS, however, does treat kit rental fees as income.
- *Back-end deals.* "Back-end deals" come in many flavors. In general, they involve payment deferments and "point participation" in a project's profits. Deferred payments are usually made after the production company has sold a movie's distribution rights. (On some low-budget films, the whole crew may work for deferred payments.) "Point participation" grants an individual or company involved in the making of a movie a percentage of that movie's profits.
- *Exclusivity.* A contract provision that forbids an employee to accept work on additional projects until he or she has completed work on the project for which they're under contract.
- *Travel support.* Per-mile payments for in-town travel, plus per diems, car rentals, airfare, and hotel accommodations for location travel.
- *Screen credit.* A "single-card front" credit, the most desirable option, displays a credit alone (without any other credits appearing simultaneously on screen) during the main (opening) sequence of credits. A "single card back" credit displays a credit alone during the closing sequence of credits. (For most designers, a single-card end credit is considered a slap in the face.) If a credit appears in a "crawl," it will scroll up the screen accompanied by a list of other credits. (If, however, the credit appears alone for at least one frame of the crawl, it is considered a "single card" credit.) No billing is guaranteed unless it's written into your contract.
- *Print advertising credit.* This credit appears in newspapers and posters. Inclusion in these credits is a point of negotiation. So is the position and size of this credit.

The credits of costume supervisors, design assistants, and other costume staff are not included in a film's opening credit sequence or in print advertising. They don't have leverage for first-class travel or special hotel accommodations, but additional screen credits, payment deferments, kit rental fees, additional work pay, and other travel support can be a part of their negotiations. Most often, kit rental is a part of a set costumer's negotiations.

Contract negotiations are a fine art. If you are working as your own agent, heed the following instructions from a pro, Madeline Kozlowski, costume designer and head of the costume design program at the University of California, Irvine:

> You have to know the going rates—the costume house rates, the cable television rates, the feature rates—the going rates, not just the "scale" rates. Independent salaries are comparable to union rates. In fact, producers will pay a little extra because they aren't paying benefits. I teach my students that the secret to good negotiation is, "Never say anything. Let them do all the talking."
>
> Here's an example of a TV-movie negotiation with a production manager: He asks, "What do you cost?" You say, "What I'm really interested in is what kind of budget you have for the film. What I'm mostly interested in is if there's enough money to do this film well." (So, I haven't said anything.)
>
> Now it's the production manager's turn. He says, "What I've got here is about $75,000 for wardrobe purchases. I've got an assistant designer for you. Male and female supervisors. Set man. One costume crew. Extra help on six days that appear heavy."
>
> So far, they have lied about the budget. If they said "$75,000," you know they have $90,000. Their job is to get everything for as cheap as they can, and your job is to get as much out of them as you can. After breaking down the script, you will submit a budget estimate based on your expertise.
>
> So now, to your fee. The production manager asks again, "So, what do you cost?" You say, "Now, I know you have a budget. What are you offering?"
>
> The production manager pretends he's shuffling through the paperwork. He says, "Well, it looks like I've got about $2,500 a week for ten weeks." You say, "That's a bit lower than I usually make." (If you have worked for this company before, you now say, "You know me, you know how I work. You know you are going to get your money's worth and more.")
>
> The production manager says, "So, what do you want?" You say, "I'm making about $4,500 flat for five days." The production manager says, "How about $4,000?" You say, "Fine."
>
> Everybody's happy.

THE GOING RATES

Note: Rates vary according to the level of the production on which you are working—from lavish "A" productions to bare-bones "Z" productions. If you are working on a union production, rates will also vary according to contract. Rates also vary according to your level of experience.

Feature film rates
- For Costume Supervisors ("Key Costumers"), starting at $23.07 per hour*
- For First Set Costumers, starting at $21.13 per hour*
- For Costumers (including additional Costumers), starting at $18.81 per hour*
- For a stitcher, approximately $35 per hour (union rate)

*IATSE Single Production Signatory Low Budget Feature Length Motion Picture: "Low Budget Basic Agreement Wage Scales $1 – 3.6 Million Budget"

Made for Television minimum rates
- Costume Designers, $1601.95 per week (on call – flat rate)*
- Assistant Costume Designer, $1306.97 (on call – flat rate)*
- Key costumers (Costume Supervisors), $854.85 per week; $198.11 per day; $21.37 - $24.76 per hour*
- Costumers, $779.41 per week; $180.65 per day; $19.49 - $22.58 per hour*

*IATSE Made For Television Long-Form Agreement Rates, Effective through July 30, 2005. Weekly rates are for 40 hours of work (except for "on call" employees)

Comparative Made for Television salaries
- Art Director, $2028.04 per week (on call – flat rate)*
- Camera operator, $1294.78 per week*
- 1st Assistant cameraperson, $1182.03 per week*
- 2nd Assistant cameraperson, $1069.28 per week*
- Film loader, $924.14 per week*
- Still photographer, $1143.49 per week*

*IATSE Made For Television Long-Form Agreement Rates, Effective through July 30, 2005. Weekly rates are for 40 hours of work (except for "on call" employees)
- ß   Make-Up artist, $1091.83 per week*

After negotiations—deal memos and payroll paperwork. Once final contract negotiations are completed, all costume-crew deal memos and time cards go through the costume supervisor, who works with the UPM on hiring matters and kit rental arrangements. The supervisor also distributes paychecks and tracks fitting times for SAG wardrobe allowances (see below, "SAG Fitting Rules" and "SAG Fitting Compensation Guidelines").

Purchasing Power

Even before renting office and storage space, the costume supervisor must establish accounts with costume vendors, workrooms, and other wardrobe-related services, and arrange for a petty cash "draw" from production accounting. Script breakdown, research, and design work can proceed without an office, but stock gathering and office rental require cash flow, and proof that you and your production are legitimate. Setting up accounts can take time, so the earlier the costume supervisor can get petty cash and establish accounts, the better, since no rentals, loans, or purchases can be made until cash is available and accounts are actually open.

To keep petty cash demands to an acceptable level, costume supervisors will try to establish accounts with costume providers and services, including costume rental houses, cleaners, product placement sources, made-to-order workrooms, alterations services, and studio services departments at major retailers (principally, department stores). Be prepared: You can't just walk in and say, "I want to open an account." Some vendors are cash-and-carry only; some accept purchase orders or company credit cards; others bill only on an established line of credit.

When preparing to open an account with a vendor, make sure you get a detailed list of the information the vendor needs to set up the account. Also, identify the vendor's terms of payment and form of deposit. Each vendor will have its own rules and regulations for setting up accounts, although most will ask for proof from the production office of the legitimacy of the production company (credit references, credit history, bank information, tax identification numbers, and so on). They will also request proof of *your* legitimacy as purchasing agent for the production company, as well as a certificate of insurance, which proves the company is liable for loss and damage. (The production company accountant should be able to provide you with all this paperwork, including a billing/liability page that includes the company's tax status and billing procedures.) Vendors can take their time setting up accounts even after they get the paperwork they require. Some vendors attempt to make the wait less frustrating by accepting single-use purchase orders (arranged for by the costume supervisor) until the account is formally open.

Some companies limit lines of credit; some will require cash deposits for their goods. A costume vendor who allows a production company to establish an "open" account—a form of account that allows multiple transactions, up to a specified credit limit—requires purchase order, rental form, or credit card charge paperwork of one kind or another in order to process transactions. (Keep in mind that since "open" accounts have specific budget limits, the costume supervisor must track the status of each account as often as necessary, in order to be aware of when that limit is being approached.) A studio that provides supplies and services to a production allied with it does so through a kind of open account that requires requisition forms, for purposes of ordering and billing.

Some vendors will not work on an account arrangement and need to be paid up front, using petty cash, a production company check, or a credit card. All petty cash paperwork goes through the costume supervisor, who is responsible for accounting for all funds dispersed by the costume department. Petty cash limits vary widely from one production company to another, and the actual funds may take some time to arrive. To avoid the rapid depletion of department petty-cash funds, high-ticket items are best paid for with a production company check. These checks must be arranged for by the costume supervisor, and may take twenty-four hours or more to process.

Billing corroboration and returns tracking

To guard against unnecessary additional costs, a costume supervisor tracks not only the proper return of purchased garments, but goods taken out "on memo" (that is, documented, in a memo, before being taken off premises without charge, for approval by designer, actor, director, and, sometimes, producers; see below, *Studio services*). Invoices for shipped goods must be carefully checked for accuracy against the goods received, and the supervisor must arrange for corrections of any errors made. (For more on this, see part 9, *Final Wrap*.)

It is very important, this business of accurately tracking the bills for goods that are used or kept. It is also a constant headache, since the film costume business deals in high-volume rentals, high-volume purchases and returns, and goods taken out on memo. Many costume supervisors use a computer software program for tracking purchases, check requests, purchase orders, receipts, and so on, developed and copyrighted by costumer Betty Besio. Through ProSanity.com, Besio markets two programs, MoneyTrackPro, which tracks the spending of a costume department, and C/PlotPro, which breaks down a script into the information needed to prep, run, and budget a film or television series. There are also budget-tracking aids in the CostumePro and CMS Movie Breakdown programs.

Warning! Warning! Petty cash, credit card use, and production purchasing

Radically abbreviated prep periods can make setting up accounts and turning around petty cash an intensely frustrating waiting game. Some production companies provide the costume department with a company credit card, but still, this is only a single credit card and doesn't go very far when you have a "purchasing brigade" made up of designer, design assistant, one or more costumers, one or two shoppers, and a wardrobe PA. In any event, you don't want to turn over a credit card to any old shopper. Because of this, the costume supervisor must always fight to keep a workable stash of petty cash in the department.

The supervisor's ability to estimate the cost of purchases from vendors where no account can be set up will be the basis upon which your department determines a workable amount for a petty cash draw. All production companies impose restrictions on how much petty cash their costume department is allowed to draw at one time. Regardless of amount, production managers and production accountants can make it easy—or nearly impossible—to actually get petty cash.

The price for the privilege of using petty cash is impeccable accounting. Anyone handling petty cash must gather receipts, tally purchases, keep accurate accounts, write up petty cash reports, and return leftover currency. The really difficult part of handling petty cash—more psychological than logistical—is how dangerously easy it is for shoppers to borrow small amounts of dough from petty cash reserves (to be returned, of course), especially when they're so busy they don't have time to go to the bank. It is frightening how quickly the dollars borrowed can tally up to a tidy sum. Being scrupulous in the separation of your own cash from production cash is a basic survival skill for every member of the costume crew who shops a show.

When petty cash is short and time is tight, many designers and costumers are tempted into using their own credit cards to purchase stock using their own credit cards. This is a dangerous gambit. Using a personal credit card for production purchases can create chaos when tracking purchases and doing returns. Far too many designers and costume personnel have gotten burned doing this: Not only can production accountants be difficult about receipts, but productions can be slow—very slow—to reimburse. In many instances, a designer and design assistant have been "wrapped" on a production (taken off payroll) before purchases made on their credit cards are returned; often, their credit card are needed by the vendor to credit the account. To add to the headaches personal credit card use can induce, the IRS has been known to view reimbursements as income, and to tax them accordingly. Unfortunately, there are times in the business when using a personal credit card to make a wardrobe purchase is unavoidable. Some companies expect this—particularly in the world of commercials and print advertising—and getting reimbursed by them is often a struggle.

Choosing Costume Facilities and Services

Costume department workspace and storage space—and services like made-to-order work, crafts work, alterations, laundry and dry cleaning, dyers, distressers, and costume painters—have to be lined up early in preproduction. Many productions prefer to rent costume office and storage space in one facility, and sub-contract for made-to-order work and costume rentals from workrooms and rental houses, gaining the additional benefit of access to their fitting rooms and storage spaces.

When it comes to space and services, the best way for a costume department to go comes down to how much square footage it needs to house its costume stock, and the equipment and personnel it needs for costume construction, alterations, dyeing, distressing, and laundering. Productions with very short prep schedules (like television series) may also need instant access to costume rental stock. In all events, before a decision is made, the costume supervisor must ask these questions, among others:

- Will the volume of costume stock demand more than the usual storage space? ("Cage" spaces vary from facility to facility.)
- Does the department need costume construction done on-site?
- Will the workspace being considered support the costume construction and alterations operations the production requires?
- Is it more appropriate to contract workrooms to do made-to-order work or will doing made-to-order work at off-premises shops eat up too much travel time?
- Can the department avoid shop overhead costs by hiring a freelancer to do alterations?
- Does the department need to dye and distress costumes on-site or can dye shops or freelance dyers and distressers be used?
- Does the department need laundry facilities on premises?
- Can the department afford a week of rent to do star fittings at a posh studio fitting room? If not, what are the alternatives and are they suitable, given the level of "talent?"
- What about shipping services? Getting the goods to the right place at the right time can be costly. But the cost of mishandled and missing goods is dear.

Before designers and supervisors make critical decisions about facilities and services, they will have to compare the cost of renting all necessary space and contracting freelancers for every bit of work with the cost of subletting space and paying for in-house services at a costume house or professional workroom.

Varieties of costume department setups

Costume department setups can vary. Some production companies provide office facilities for the costume department and may even offer costume storage space. Productions originating at a film studio and shooting "in town" may run their costume department out of the studio's wardrobe facilities, which will offer a kind of package deal that generally includes office and storage space, workroom services, fitting rooms, and costume rentals. (Most studios require that their own productions use at least some of their own lot's wardrobe facilities and services.) Other productions—low-budget projects and studio films on location—opt to put together, from scratch, their own all-services costume department.

Whichever way you go, remember, the ideal costume department facility is convenient to the production office, shopping districts, and costume rental houses. It has ample costume storage space, a costume construction workroom, fitting rooms, laundry facilities, dyeing and distressing facilities, and an office space well outfitted with phones, fax, computer, and copy machine. It will also be relatively clean, climate-controlled, and secure.

Studio costume department or costume rental-house home base. Large film studios and costume rental houses in L.A. can provide all of the above—which is a saving grace for productions with extremely tight prep periods. However, the cost for this convenience can be steep. And, keep in mind that prep space at studio or rental houses are available only on a first-come, first-served basis.

In Los Angeles; studio and rental house "cages" rent for $100 to $350 a week; office space for $125 to $350 a week (fig. 7.4). Most studios and rental houses that offer cage rentals supply pipes for hanging the costumes, and may allow access to rolling racks while in the building. Office equipment may also be supplied, billed as a service charge to the costume department budget. Most of the rental house and studio facilities allow after-hours access to the office and the cage, but charge healthy overtime fees for access to the general rental stock. In addition to weekly cage-rental charges, costume houses and studio facilities bill the production for "facility charges"—fees for the use of fax, phone, Xerox, and staff services (e.g., rental-form processing, costume stock pulling, etc.). Some services, like re-filing pulled costumes, are, as a rule, included in the stock rental charge.

On a project with six weeks prep and one week wrap, you might expect the following basic charges from a studio or costume rental house:

FIG. 7.4

A typical wardrobe cage

FIG. 7.5

A typical wardrobe office

Office rental	$150 a week
Cage rental	$250 a week
$400 a week in base rate costs X 6 weeks of prep	= $2,400
One week of wrap using only the cage	+$ 250
	$2,650
Average phone bill	+$ 175
Average fax/copying charges	+$ 200
Total	$3,025

As noted above, many productions prefer to rent office and cage space in one facility and use multiple sources for MO and rental goods—sources that also provide places for fittings and costume storage. Most cage-rental facilities provide hanging pipes, but rolling racks and storage bins may be optional; some cages come with a mini-office—a desk with a telephone wedged between storage racks. (As noted above, prep supply and equipment charges can differ widely, depending on the facility you choose to rent.)

The do-it-yourself home base. Three different types of productions may find it more productive and economical to create an independent costume department, selecting the space, equipment, and staff to suit the needs of the production: (1) very large productions, where a lot of made-to-order work is required; (2) productions with lengthy prep periods, where costume stock is gathered over several months; and (3) low-budget productions that need to avoid expensive shop charges (fig. 7.5).

Any production that faces the need to assemble a very large costume stock, one that takes up hundreds of square feet of storage space, may find it more economical to rent a warehouse than to rent costume cages at costume rental houses or film studios. The big-budget *Batman* productions opted to create their own workrooms, as did *Mars Attacks*, another big-budget Tim Burton film, whose costume supervisor, Sue Moore, took over a warehouse, where she created a multitask office area; a mini costume workroom, complete with draping, stitching, finishing stations, and fitting areas; a huge costume storage area, with double-hung pipes, rolling racks, and box storage; laundry facilities; and, next to the laundry room, a mini dyeing/distressing area. Even moderately budgeted productions may find that investing in the installation of a rented washer and dryer (and the hiring of a freelance dyer/distress) can save thousands of dollars in dye studio charges.

> Big period or fantasy films often set up their own costume aging departments. You put someone
> on payroll so you can control them, and runaway costs . *(Dan Lester, costume designer)*

On low-budget productions, especially those shot on location, inventive solutions to solving the problem of department home base may provide benefits beyond budget savings. For example, on location in Great Falls, Montana, my costume supervisor and I (KB) were put up by production in a two-bedroom house, with an unfinished basement. In the basement, we built racks and tables, set up a fitting room with a mirror, a laundry room, a men's wardrobe room, and a women's wardrobe room. We had a lighting system installed and washers and dryers, to create a dyeing/aging room. It wasn't posh, but it was functional, and we didn't have to trudge out in the snow to get things done.

Determining equipment and supply needs

Once you have a home base for your department, you must determine your needs for equipment and supplies for the department office; for wardrobe storage and organization; for costume construction and alteration; for wardrobe maintenance; for wardrobe dyeing, teching, and distressing, and for the wardrobe trailer. In determining these needs, you must consider six variables: (1) the script; (2) the scale of the production; (3) the shooting conditions; (4) the size of the crew; (4) the availability of crew kits; and (6) the nature of your office, workroom, and storage setups.

Before you can place orders for equipment and supplies needed during prep and shoot, you need to do the budget research discussed in Part 6 (*Costume Budgets*). This includes reviewing the equipment and supplies that come with the space you are using for costume department offices, workrooms, and storage as well as the nature of the equipment available to the department via crew kit rentals. (Well-stocked kits are a godsend, often making available a broad range of equipment that can be rented to the production at a weekly rate, which, as noted earlier, usually comes out of the production's salary budget, not the costume department budget.)

If you are putting together your own department workspace, you'll have to arrange to rent and/or purchase all the equipment and supplies needed to get you through prep and shoot.

For the costume department office. If your choice of facility is the do-it-yourself home base, you'll need everything it takes to put together an adequate office: desks or tables, chairs, shelves; phone and fax access; computers; a bulletin board; and basic office supplies.

For home-base wardrobe storage and organization. The basics in this category include stationary and rolling racks and supplies to hang, box, size, tag, and bag wardrobe items. Standard items here include hangers of various styles and weights; safety pins; zip-lock baggies and accessories bags of various sizes; a cone of cotton string for hanging baggies; tags in manila and, if affordable, red; muslin-covered hangers; storage boxes; shelving; and some kind of hanging rack system (hanging pipes or racks, fixed and collapsible, and rack dividers). Heavy-duty clear-plastic zip-front garment bags are a major investment, but standard on most productions—and indispensable. (They can be purchased from motion-picture supply companies and display companies that also supply hangers, rolling racks, and steamers.) Polaroid cameras should come with designer and costume kit rentals, but film (Polaroid and 35mm, if necessary) must be ordered. These basic supplies should be acquired before you begin gathering stock or you will waste a lot of shuffling and re-hanging clothes. (For more on rack dividers and garment bags, see below, *Final Preparations*, "Camera-ready costume changes: tagging and bagging systems.")

For costume construction and alterations workspace. If the costume department is interested in setting up its own workroom for relatively elaborate costume construction, the determining factors for supplies and equipment are as follows:

- The historical period or place in which the story is set
- The size of the costume construction crew
- The size of the space that will serve as the workroom
- The quantity of costume pieces that must be built

Any costume construction setup needs to include the following equipment and supplies: cutting table workstations, for pattern-makers; sewing machines; ironing setups; steamers; sewing supplies (based on those listed below for the alterations stations). A workroom must also stock patterning supplies (muslin and mock-up fabrics, brown paper, French curves, rulers, pens); over-lock machines and supplies; structural supplies (interfacings, boning, and linings appropriate to the period). Most workrooms are also supplied with male and female dress forms.

Determining how many cutting and sewing stations are needed depends on the skill and speed of your made-to-order and alterations personnel, as well as the quantity of goods that must be produced. I (HC) visited one workroom that employed three individuals (a patternmaker, an assistant to the patternmaker, and a stitcher). The workroom was equipped with one cutting table, two sewing machines, and several dress dummies, a setup that served three television series. I've also heard stories about on-location workrooms that mainly consisted of folding tables, with sewing machines, folding chairs, minimal sewing supplies, and power cables.

However, unless the production is very small, the general rule of thumb says you need a minimum of two on-site costume maintenance/emergency alterations setups: one for the principals and one for the extras. If crew members have extensive personal kits, the costume department may have to provide only expendable supplies for emergency repairs and alterations. But if crew wardrobe kits are minimal, the costume department must be prepared to provide each station with the range of equipment and supplies listed in the Appendix ("Wardrobe Kits").

Fitting-room setups, even the most basic, require privacy curtains, chairs, table, full-length mirrors, and rolling racks.

For laundering, dyeing, and distressing. A washer and dryer dedicated to straight laundry (as opposed to dyeing and distressing projects) are standard. (All legitimate wardrobe trailers have washer/dryers, so you also need to plan for laundry supplies for the truck as well as the home base.) Large-scale dye/paint projects can dictate the purchase of an additional washer and dryer, the purchase or rental of stovetops (and the installation of 220-volt lines), airbrushes, compressors, and dedicated work tables and dress forms or mannequins.

Standard laundry supplies you'll need include liquid and powder detergents, for both "color safe" and "extra-whitening" effects (no perfumes, bleaches, or dyes in either liquid or powder detergents); Downey Ultra Fabric Softener and fabric softener sheets (non-scented); bleach (both Clorox and color-safe Clorox 2), laundry bags or baskets; clothesline and clothes pins; in-machine stain removers (Shout, Zout, Spray 'N Wash, Shout gel); spot removers Carbona, K2R, Picrin, Clear Choice, Everblum, Shout wipes, Stain Stick, club soda, Handi-wipes, Oxi Clean, Formula 409; TSP (trisodium phosphate, a heavy-duty fabric softening and/or costume aging/teching agent, available at any hardware or paint store (for more on dyeing and distressing techniques, see below, "Teching, distressing, and other garment treatments for character and camera"); and spotting brushes, including toothbrushes, to use for the purpose.

For fine washables, you may want a small rubber basin (for hand-washing) or mesh lingerie bags (for machine-washing) and liquid detergents designed for washing knits and delicate fabrics (e.g., Woolite or Hosiery Mate). For ironing or steaming you'll need spray starch (or liquid starch, for really heavy-duty starching), water spritz bottles, plain vinegar (mixed with water, and sprayed on silk fabrics, to keep them dye-fast), iron cleaner, and a lot of distilled water (for steamers). For extra protection, you may even want to supply "color-catcher sheets" (Woolite Dye Magnets or Shout Color-Catcher sheets), No Mildew (a de-humidifying anti-mildew cake), spray Scotch-Guard or Craft Guard Fabric Protectant (to help fabrics fight off dirt and stains), and EMU Leather Protector.

For un-washable garments you may want to use laundry-freshening supplies (e.g. Lysol disinfectant sprays, Endbac, Fresh Again, Fiebings Fresh Feet, or vinegar) and/or in-the-dryer dry cleaning products like Dryel.

For dyeing and distressing "in house" (that is, if you don't send out garments to be dyed and aged), you should have on hand Ivory liquid or Synthrapol, Cassalene, and fabric dyes that, at minimum, cover cool and warm teching colors, plus colors to help achieve "movement." You'll need extra fabric softener, sandpaper, razor blades or a file, and seam-rippers, to help prep goods for long-washing distressing. Also have on hand a stock of paper towels or newspaper, for "pocket stuffing" (to give the look of pockets stretched with wear). You may also need liquid leather dye, alcohol, shellac, and a sprayer. You need a spray bottle or plant mister, bleach, and Magix in a variety of colors, including Champagne, Avocado, Smoked Elk, Saddle, Gray, Olive, Brown, and Black, in case you are distressing dark goods. Deglazing fluid and Neatsfoot oil, for working with leather; Schmutz, in a full range of colors, and mineral oil and glycerine. For definitions

Fig. 7.6

The morning after a rough ride. Rolling racks need to be tied down for transport both at the top and the bottom or you're likely to face this the next morning.

of technical terms and product names and explanations of use, see below, "Preparing Costume Pieces for Shooting."

For wardrobe trailers. Wardrobe trailers may require additional box storage and other organizational supplies, including collapsible rolling racks. The physical room available for box and rolling-rack storage will dictate how much of this equipment, and how many supplies, you'll be able to carry on the truck (see below, *Truck Prep*, "Truck styles").

When it comes to organizing wardrobe on the truck, conventional wardrobe trailers have built-in metal rods for hanging costumes. In most trailers, these rods have built-in clamps that run the length of the rods, to keep hangers and garments from falling off the rack when the wardrobe trailer is in motion. "Improvised" wardrobe trailers—Ryder or U-Haul trucks converted for wardrobe transport—will need a host of supplies for rack storage and tie-down, including an ample supply of gaffer's tape and bungee cords, to secure hangers on rods for the move. This can be a healthy budget item in no time. However, the results of failing to lock down wardrobe can be devastating (fig. 7.6). Rack dividers are essential, to separate and mark sections devoted to individual characters and specialty and general stock categories (e.g., police uniforms; women's, men's, and children's "train station" stock), but because most lock-down systems do not accommodate convention plastic rack dividers, you may have to improvise. You'll also want a rubber washtub, a heavy-duty blow dryer, and a clothes-drying rack.

Wardrobe trailers built for the purpose have a built-in washer-dryer. What happens if you don't have a washer-dryer in the trailer? The laundry will have to be sent out, either with a costumer hired to do laundry, to a commercial service (which will be hard on the clothes), or, in the low-budget scenario, with a lowly member of the costume crew (the wardrobe PA, a department intern, anyone you can strong-arm into it; maybe you). We can speak from experience when we suggest that in a pinch you use the honeywagon restroom sink. Alternately, use your rubber tub, detergent, and distilled water and hang the garments on a clothing rack to dry. When washing by hand, make sure to rinse all garments thoroughly to avoid stiff, soap-laden clothing. (And remember that some people are allergic to dyes, perfumes, and detergents. Make sure you ask your actors about their allergies.)

Of course, a production needs bagging, tagging, and labeling supplies on the truck. A production that requires minimal costuming will be able to minimize its need for these supplies. However, dispensing with these supplies altogether puts a serious crimp in any department's ability to respond to the pressures of getting actors dressed and to the set on time. To rack items that have not been tagged or bagged is a dangerous business. Grabbing untagged, un-bagged garments from the rack can lead to irremediable disaster.

Beyond the basic supplies, trailer supply-lists are also shaped by the script and the conditions under which the crew will be shooting. Each production will dictate its own truck equipment supply list. If the script includes major shoot 'em ups, you'll need quantities of fake blood on the truck, for various stages of costume distress, and towels in the set costumer's kit bag, to clean up your actors. You'll also need quantities of costume-distressing supplies, including pounds of Fullers Earth (a fine powder used by distressers to make new clothing appear old and dirty), gallons of mineral oil, and Schmutz aging sticks galore, for extremely grubby extras. (For guidelines on aging techniques with these materials, see below, *Conversation Eleven: On Dyeing and Distressing Costumes for Film, with Edwina Pellikka*.)

"Suit shows" will need a stock of collar stays and spray starch on the truck. Period shows, with lots of vintage garments, can dictate lots of Endbac (an alcohol-based spray cleaner/disinfectant, with low-impact effect on vintage fabrics), padded hangers, sewing supplies, Stitch Witchery (an iron-on binding used principally for quick hems and other fabric repairs), dress shields, spray hat sizing (for stiffening hats, to withstand hard usage), hat stretchers, hat foam strips, corset lacing, and heavy hangers for heavy period wardrobe. Scripts with nude scenes can require a supply of G-strings, athletic supporters, bust pads, push-up bras, garter belts, mole skin (for pubic patches), "penis socks," and set robes (see Part 8, *Shoot*, "Nude Scenes").

Difficult shooting conditions demand additional wardrobe supplies be purchased for the truck. Cold-weather locations dictate stores of thermal underwear, hand-warmers, and shoe dryers. The cost of foul-weather gear for actors and crew and wardrobe gear for extreme shooting conditions (underwater, in snow, etc.) can place a real burden on a costume budget designed to cover only basic costs. The movie crew of *Titanic* needed 200 wetsuits, at $200 a pop. (Negotiate with the UPM for the cost of non-costume gear like this to come out of a separate budget.)

Even planned-for shooting conditions can require the costume department to supply a lot of non-costume clothing: thermals, wetsuits, gloves, knee pads, rain gear, towels, modesty robes, and other garments meant for actor comfort. Under duress, your department can also get hit for items like sun hats for the visiting producer or the camera guy who forgot his hat, and "sweats" or jackets for actors and members of the crew when the set turns unexpectedly chilly. The costume team should attempt to use general stock items and the inventory of rented crew kits to cover these non-costume needs. But while still in prep, it's best to consult with the members of your department to determine which of these non-costume items can be safely provided by kits and which must be budgeted for, and purchased, before shooting begins.

Long-distance or primitive locations also drive up the need for basics like laundry equipment and cleaning supplies, security and lock-up equipment and supplies, even basic office supplies. If access to favorite sources and goods is going to be limited, buy more than you think you'll need before leaving for a remote location.

MEMORANDUM

To:

From: Kristin Burke
        Wardrobe

Date: 2/8/99

Re: Ranger Uniforms

Just wanted to ask you about the specifics for the Rangers –

1) First set of Rangers is from Montana. I'll be researching those uniforms, and will pass along whatever I find. I assume we can use N/D nameplates, but we should coordinate on that.

2) The rest of the Rangers are from California. I am not sure whether or not we have clearance for Big Bear or anything else, but I can tell you what I found in the script for CUSTOM nameplates:

        BAUMAN
        BRADFORD (may need multiples)
        BROOKWELL
        JACOBS
        KNEPPER
        MARK
        PHILLIPS

    There is some discrepancy to the difference between "Deputy Mark" and "Deputy Brookwell", but I'll ask about that. I can get regular N/D badges included in our rental, but we should talk about the custom stuff.

3) I am going to try to outfit these Rangers with full dress uniform, including jackets and hats. When it's nighttime, these guys would be wearing their jackets. Just letting you know in advance where I'm headed.

Looking forward to chatting with you – please give me a call at ▮▮▮▮▮▮▮ when you get a chance.

Thanks,

KB

Production Meetings and Ongoing Collaborations

Production meetings can be four-hour-long affairs, with little time for real conferring. They are, however, necessary. They are key times to make contact with the UPM, the first AD, and representatives of the production's principal departments, a time to hear updated logistics of the shoot and to deliver progress reports. Because representatives of all the production's departments are present, these meetings are also key times for interdepartmental coordination. Costume issues that involve camera, special effects, stunt, location, art, and prop departments are best addressed at these meetings. The director, the cinematographer, and the casting department are present, as well. In episodic television, the production meeting can be the *only* real opportunity to talk with other departments. In all events, production-meeting etiquette dictates that you are well organized, clear and accurate in your information, never negative about other departments, and brief in your requests for information.

FIG. 7.8: LEGAL CLEARANCE CHECKS

Legal Clearance on telefeature: **Grizzly Lake**, Shooting Draft dated Jan. 10, 1999.

PLEASE NOTE:

A.   IT IS ADVISABLE THAT USE OF ACTUAL PRODUCTS, RECOGNIZABLE VOICES AND CHARACTERS, AND ITEMS PROTECTED BY COPYRIGHT BE AVOIDED.

B.   IN THE FOLLOWING REPORT, INCIDENTAL REFERENCES IN THE SCRIPT TO ACTUAL PERSONS, PLACES, OR THINGS ARE NOTED, BUT ONLY REQUIRE CONSIDERATION IF THE REFERENCE HAS POSSIBLE DEROGATORY CONNOTATIONS.

C.   THE SOURCES CONSULTED FOR THIS REPORT REPRESENT THE MOST CURRENT INFORMATION AVAILABLE AS OF THIS DATE, GIVEN THE DESCRIPTION OF THE CHARACTERS AND/OR ITEMS IN THE SCRIPT.

Setting: Fictional town of Grizzly Lake, CA in the vicinity of Big Bear, CA.

2.   The following items have been checked:

P/SC	REFERENCE
2/2	2 UNIFORMED RANGERS- Permission required if identifying any actual state or federal agency through usage of uniform, agency insignia, or name.
2/3	pulling a U-haul- Permission required to feature brand name rental equipment. Contact: U-Haul, ███████ ████████
3/4	wears a L.A. DODGER CAP AND TUNES blare from his Walkman- Permission required to feature protected any protected merchandising. Contact: L.A. Dodgers, ████ ████████████████ Also, permission required to feature brand name radio. Contact: ████████████
2/3	I appreciate your offer Ted- Single name use only.

Of course, as you know, collaborations among departments begin before the first official production meeting, and continue well beyond it. Once you are solidly into prep, interdepartmental meetings are supplemented by memos, and your mastery of the art of memo-writing will becomes critical to the success of any costume matter that involves more than the costume department. Because the property department is responsible for many character items, including handbags, briefcases, glasses, jewelry, weaponry, and some insignia, careful coordination with them is essential (fig. 7.7, "Memo to the Prop Department"). Logo and copyright issues can present problems and require clearance through the legal department (fig. 7.8, "Legal Clearance Checks"). As a result, pointed memos to these departments in particular can prevent future crises.

Coordinating with stunt and special effects

Coordinating costume work with the stunt department generally means establishing clear lines of communication with the stunt coordinator and the stunt casting agency. The stunt coordinator can give the costume department information on planned approaches to action sequences and the resulting requirements for stunt actors' clothing. The stunt casting agency can provide a stunt actor's contact information, and may have size information. The directing, camera, and stunt departments must all be consulted on the number of times a particular stunt may be shot. Although most stunt casting is done late in the production process, protective clothing and shoe requirements for the stunts are especially important to establish before arriving on set.

Special effects and camera departments can offer guidelines for working with blue-screen techniques, explosive and firework requirements, and design guidelines for working with animation, animatronics, aliens, and monsters. Special effects techniques can dictate color, fabric, and scale. Dressing dummy doubles is the costume department's responsibility (fig. 6.14).

Coordinating with the transportation department

Preproduction meetings with the transportation department will include negotiations for the number and style of the wardrobe trucks that the costume department will need. (The UPM must also be involved in these negotiation, which have an impact on the production budget.) Other major discussions with the transportation department will involve the fine points of *when* the wardrobe truck (or trucks) will be available to the department for prepping. To adequately prepare for the rigors of location shooting, the trucks must be carefully packed. As a result, the establishing of a deadline for the arrival of vans to transport wardrobe, equipment, and supplies from homebase to location is another critical negotiating point in discussions early in prep with the transportation captain.

Remember in your discussions with transportations that the particular type of truck that is used for wardrobe is paramount in determining how well the costume department functions, every day of the shoot. How easy is it to step on and off the truck, especially carrying armloads of wardrobe? How easy is it to move rolling racks on and off the truck? Does the truck have a ramp? A lift-gate? A rickety set of wooden steps? Does it have lock-down racks, adequate work areas, cabinets, shelves, bins, boxes? How durable are they? Distributing costumes to principal players involves moving costumes from the wardrobe truck to the actors' dressing cubicles. Distributing costumes to extras may mean handing them out off the truck. Dressing large crowd scenes often requires set costumers to pull racks and wardrobe bins off the truck, for easy access and quick distribution. The kind of truck you're working from makes all the difference (see below, "Truck styles").

When and *where* the wardrobe trailer (and/or trucks) will be delivered to each shooting location once principal photography begins is also a vital negotiating point for the costume supervisor. The exact timing of the wardrobe truck's arrival at the shooting site will determine how long the crew will have to set changes for the actors and distribute wardrobe to background players. *Where* the truck is located will have an impact on how fast the costume department can get emergency supplies to the set during a crisis. And *how far* the wardrobe truck is from the set (and from the dressing area) can be a critical factor in determining whether or not the costumes arrive on setting looking right. (Think actors walking for blocks in wiltingly hot, humid weather, or in the rain; think costumers dashing madly to the truck for a fresh shirt or an armload of jacket options. Not a pretty picture.)

Gathering Wardrobe

The order in which you begin to gather wardrobe is intimately connected not only to the shooting schedule but to the format of the production. Feature films and movies-of-the-week (MOWs) mandate that wardrobe for principals be gathered first, although a large percentage of atmosphere stock must also be gathered early on. The general rule of thumb is to collect wardrobe for those scenes that shoot first.

Some television is shot like a feature film, using one camera, film stock, set and location work; but if you are dealing with a television series, unlike film, you can't plan your costume stock in its entirety. In episodic television, you are dealing with many separate, and evolving, episode scripts—scripts that are being written while finished scripts are shot. As a result, the first episode's wardrobe and general stock are assembled in a overall prep period that lasts three to four weeks.

As in film, stock for principal players in an episodic is gathered first, the nature of the garments, and their quantity, based on the number of changes per principal times the number of episodes ordered. (A full season is twenty-two episodes; a trial order is generally ten to twelve episodes.) A portion of the startup stock is gathered with an eye to pulling from it for principal's changes—sometimes before the first episode's script is even locked. Even in episodic television, the assembling of contemporary stock for general atmosphere gets a relatively low priority. (Often, some basic wardrobe stock for principals—both running characters and recurring characters, in addition to atmosphere—has been acquired during production of the series' pilot.) "Safe" purchases—good basic garments, jewelry and accessories that will go with many changes—are also collected early in prep.

Since most episodics traditionally shoot on locations and soundstages in major production centers, a series' costume department may rely for general atmosphere stock on weekly fixed-price/open-stock deals cut with studio costume facilities or costume rental houses. If you are doing an episodic for a major studio, the studio may charge you a weekly fee of, for example, $1,700, for open access during shooting to its costume rental stock. If your series shoots in a location that lacks major costume rental facilities and the setting is contemporary, you may have to thrift-shop general atmosphere stock. (For details on budgeting and stock-gathering procedures for episodic series, see *Conversation Ten: On the Prep Process in Episodic Television, with Barbara Inglehart.*)

Regardless of medium and format, the goal of every costume department is to build its stock as quickly as possible, with principal players' wardrobes getting first priority. Late casting, however, seriously limits the amount of early work that a department can do on principals' wardrobe.

If you have no cast, you can still begin assembling wardrobe: You can proceed with assembling extras' stock. Big military sequences, formal party scenes, mass multiples, and period extras needs to be planned for and assembled well in advance, with size range, accessories, and specialty items well covered. Assembling the extras' wardrobe is good "fill" work and helps create sizing and tagging jobs for crew members who are waiting for principal casting to be locked. This is also a fine time for the supervisor to research sources like cleaners, fireproofers, MO workrooms, and other costume services.

Even without final casting information, some preliminary work on costumes can be started. A specialty craft studio can develop samples for surface treatments; a dye studio can prepare silkscreen artwork. Each MO workroom should be consulted, to see if any work can proceed without final casting. The designer can also concentrate on making product placement deals and researching principal wardrobe sources.

Whether film or television, once casting is finalized, the department goes to work, getting sizes and preference information from actors, purchasing and renting goods, arranging for promos, and ordering MO work. Items that need to be built—especially craftwork—need to be planned and shopped for as early as possible.

Stock will continue to be gathered throughout the prep and shooting period, as casting, actor availability, and shooting schedule information develops. Information from stunt and special effects sources frequently shows up during the later stages of the prep process, and this information must be integrated into the department's set of priorities.

> In film work, even for a long shoot, the ability to mix rental, made-to-order, and bought goods really allows designers more leverage when it comes to the range of goods they can use. Broadway has to have everything built for a show. You build for longevity on Broadway. But in film, it is really for the short term. A film is not going to go longer than seventy or eighty shooting days, and ninety-nine percent of the time, the actors are not going to be in the same costume. *(Pat Welch, costume designer)*

Purchases

Anyone who shops for a film or television show has to be brilliant at shopping. Armed with cell phone or beeper, you'll spend days on the road, hustling garments from one end of town to the other, all the time knowing that the road to purchases is also the road to returns.

Purchases on approval: studio services. "Studio services," available at flagship department stores in cities with film and commercial production presences, can be a godsend to a costume department. Studio services staff can pull garments for you (particularly if given the garment's SKU number, style, and brand information), they can track down multiples at branch stores, and they can provide quick billing.

Often, studio services will allow legitimate production costumers to take out goods for a five-day approval period, with no restock fees and no exchange of cash, credit, or receipts—a real boon to those swamped by returns and return paperwork. Of course, any items returned to a store must be in pristine condition—original tags in place, without pinning or alterations, the item's original packaging restored as closely as possible to its original state. Unfortunately, many designers and stylists have abused these privileges, returning garments in "used" or damaged condition. Costume people seem to fall into one of two camps about purchasing for productions: those who think they are doing the store a favor by using its goods in a movie and those who think the store is doing them a favor by lending its goods.

Purchasing with returns in mind. When you are not working with a store's studio services department, you must always clarify the store's return policy up front. Some stores grant only "store credit," not cash or credit card refunds. If this is the case, shop elsewhere.

If a store does full cash refunds, you need to make sure that the items you return (after a fitting or at final wrap) are properly credited. Occasionally, a sale on the item(s) you've purchased intervenes between the time of purchase and the time of return; if this is the case, make sure you're being credited the price you paid, not the discounted price. And in all events, make sure that sales tax, if any, is refunded in the proper amount. Always check the item's SKU number on the receipt against the SKU number on the tag, to make sure they match—something you should do *before* you return the goods. When you are returning dozens of bras to three different vendors, from two different purchasing trips, you will appreciate how helpful SKU numbers can be. While you're matching SKUs, it takes no time to sort the goods in billing order (especially if the pieces are folded or on hangers). This is an enormous time-saver when doing returns; and the clerk who gets stuck with this thankless—and, often, resented—task will appreciate your consideration.

Note: Some production companies require that a "return sheet"—a formal production company receipt for returned goods—be made out for each return—a painstaking process. (For more on returns, see Part 9, *Final Wrap.*)

Rentals

Most film productions draw on more than one rental house for wardrobe rentals. There are union and non-union costume rental facilities. A union label on costume rental stock does not mean that the goods are always better. Each stock house has its own strengths and weaknesses. Learning these strengths and weaknesses will add to your flexibility as a designer or supervisor. Knowing exactly where to pull the stock you need can make a tangible difference in the mileage you get out of your budget—and the limited time you have in prep.

In Los Angeles, costume rental house stock is generally organized for quick checkout by the same general stock-organization principles used by a production's costume department (see below, "Guidelines for Organizing Costume Stock"). Many stock houses make a point of hanging period or military garments in close proximity to their accessories, to help speed

FIG. 7.9

Costume sources can be fabulously organized or complete chaos.

FIG. 7.10

Costume rental collections may provide costume research libraries, costume workrooms, fitting rooms, and rent out production costume storage areas and wardrobe offices.

Costume workrooms may also be entirely independent of costume rental collections.

A costume research library

A costume workroom

FIG. 7.11

A typical well-organized Hollywood rental stock.

up the pulling process. And more and more rental houses bar-code their stock, for quick checkout. In New York, however, most costume rental houses are set up for use by theater companies, not film production companies, resulting in a stock-organization system that defies high-speed check-out (bar-coding and tagging are seldom used).

In addition to costume stock, studio costume departments and rental houses often provide small research libraries, as noted above (figs. 7.9, 7.10, 7.11). Rental houses in Los Angeles provide the additional service of holding stock, bagged and tagged, for a specified period after principal photography is completed, for possible use in re-shoots. Some rental companies automatically release the stock for re-filing at the end of this hold period (see Part 10, *Final Wrap*).

Made-to-order services

Your selection of sources for made-to-order work largely depends on four factors: (1) the quality and expertise you need; (2) the scale of the project; (3) the speed with which you need the work done and the workload limitations of the workroom; and (5) the history of the professional relationship between the made-to-order source and costume designer or supervisor.

• *Quality and expertise.* Knowing the quality of the work you need and the technical expertise required to accomplish it is primary in helping you decide on made-to-order sources. Couture-level work, beading and embroidery, custom-knit goods, tricky tailoring problems, accurate period construction, unusual materials (plastic or rubber, for example) demand highly skilled and specialized custom-made personnel. Does the shop have what you need to accomplish what you want?

• *The scale of the project.* Large-scale projects can swamp small workrooms. In competition with huge projects, small-scale projects can be assigned a low priority, regardless of the size of the workroom. Any project that needs to be subcontracted to several workrooms (a dress that requires separate services from a tailor, a dyer, an embroiderer, and a pleating company, for example) can easily run into coordination difficulties and deadline problems.

• *The speed of the project and the workload limitations of the workroom.* It is miraculous how much difficult, meticulous work can be accomplished overnight in a good workroom. However, every shop and every freelancer has a limit to what can be accomplished—and the quality of the work that can be delivered—when time is limited. The bottom line is this: How good does the work have to be? Just "nicely finished" or do you really need "couture finished?" A realistic assessment of the level of expertise a project demands will go a long way toward helping you determine the kind of speed and quality you need from a made-to-order source (see below, *Conversation Twelve: On Prep Collaborations with Craft Artisans, with Chris Gilman*).

• *The history of the professional relationship.* Costume designers and costumers often develop strong loyalties to individual workrooms, and vice versa. Doing repeat business with an MO source can mean clearer communication, quicker delivery of costumes, and richer, deeper collaborations between designer and workroom head.

FIG. 7.12

CRC's Mayreni Cam

Workrooms around L.A.

CRC's Gaudencio Jimenez

The Costume Collection's Donn Hook and Laurel Taylor

The MO development process in costume workrooms. In Hollywood costume workrooms (fig. 7.12), the usual garment-development process includes the following steps:

1. A detailed discussion between shop head and costume designer regarding the designs themselves, the actor's body, and the desired fabrics and trims.

2. Development, by workroom personnel, of a half (or full) mockup of the garment, on a dress form, in "patterning fabric" (a fabric that drapes like the real goods but is cheaper). The mock-up's key style-lines, and its cut and trim details, need to be approved by the designer before the garment is cut from the final fabrics. (The dress form will be padded and shaped to give the designer the clearest vision of the actor's proportions in the garment.) After mock-up approval, the cutter will then cut and assemble the garment in its real fabrics, in preparation for a fitting with the actor. (In Los Angeles these days, it is rare for a workroom to have more than one fitting with an actor, whereas in New York, there are most frequently two or more fittings, including one fitting of the garment in a mock-up fabric.)

3. The fitting with the actor, in the garment assembled in its final fabrics. During this fitting, the designer, with workroom personnel, will determine the final style-lines and seam adjustments, hems, closures, and trims.

With tricky garments, and to avoid problems late in the MO process, factor in the cost of additional fittings, to be safe. Extra fittings might include fitting the mock-up, so that the actor (and, sometimes, production) can see the garment on the body before the final version is produced. (The elaborate body padding required for Clown, the character in *Spawn*, for example, required a three-fitting process more typical of theater than film costuming. (See figs. 7.13, 7.14, 7.15.)

In general, the more time you can give a made-to-order shop to do the work, the better. As the piece is constructed, design changes alter the man hours required to finish it. Some changes are inherent in the MO process, especially when the piece is fit to the actor's body, and the costume workroom factors this into its original cost estimate. But exceptional changes will incur exceptional charges. Shops can be asked to formally give a written bid on a job, and then track workroom hours and expenses on the piece, but costume designers and costumers tend to develop strong ties to individual workrooms, and often bypass the MO bid-out process if the workload is small. (Aspects of the MO process that affect cost were discussed, in detail in *Costume Budgets*, in the section titled "Made-to-order cost guidelines and conditions.")

The MO development process in craft studios. Craft studios follow different processes, depending on the materials they are using. In general, you can bet that the more steps in the process, the more expensive the item is going to be. Some materials, like vacuform plastic, require positive molds (figs. 7.16, 7.17). Other materials, like foam latex, require the creation of both positive and negative molds (known as a "two-part" molding process) that are carefully interlocked in the casting process. Some designs require molds to be fragmented, to create joined, three-dimensional forms. There are materials that require a designer to commit to color when the material is being poured into the mold, while other materials can be colored and surfaced as a

FIG. 7.13

Mr. Leguizamo at the start of the fitting with his faithful dog.

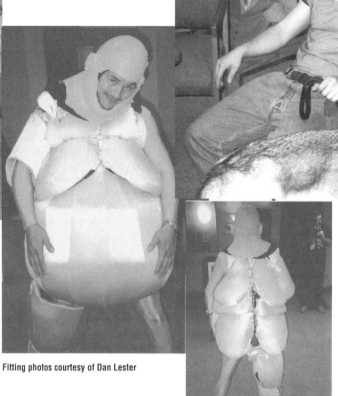

For *Spawn*, costume designer Dan Lester had to transform John Leguizamo from a svelt young man into a grotesque, fat clown.

Step number one was to create elaborate body padding that the actor could move in that was perfectly adjusted to the actor's proportions.

Fitting photos courtesy of Dan Lester

FIG. 7.14

Design by Dan Lester for The Clown in the film *Spawn* (1997)

Phase 2 of the fitting

Dan Lester's concern for John Leguizamo's comfort led to a more elaborate fitting process. Here you see the sketch, the adjusted padding, and the muslin mock-up being adjusted.

FIG. 7.15

The final fitting. Note that they used a mock-up of the final foam latex makeup prosthetic in order to judge costume proportions.

Fitting photos courtesy of Dan Lester

The final step of the character transformation John Leguizamo as The Clown in *Spawn*

Production photo courtesy of New Line Cinema

part of the finishing process. Dye and fabric paint processes are often complicated by multiple materials and multiple processes.

Before you finish your design, the head of the craft studio should describe the options and processes available to you that meet your cost and time constraints. You also need to understand the fitting process and the different stages of development through which your project will go. Often, the development process on craftwork requires further refinement of the design at key stages in the process. (For more craft process details, see Part 6, *Costume Budgets*, the section on "Craftwork cost guidelines and conditions," and *Conversation Eleven: On Dyeing and Distressing Costumes for Film, with Edwina Pellikka*, and *Conversation Twelve: On Prep Collaborations with Craft Artisans, with Chris Gilman*, at the end of this part.)

The MO-designer collaboration. The creation of custom costume pieces can be a fabulous experience for the designer and the workroom. But it can also be a nightmare. Trust, design clarity, a reasonable time frame and budget for the project, and respect for the artisans and their crafts all become part of the mix. Shops can be "burned" by designers who chronically change materials and design lines. Some designers don't know how to judge a mock-up, and, as a result, cannot approve a garment's proportions before it is made in final form—a tremendous waste of material and labor, if the garment is judged "not right." Some designers fail to heed workroom recommendations and demand the use of labor-intensive goods or methods when alternative solutions would be better for both design and durability.

FIG. 7.16

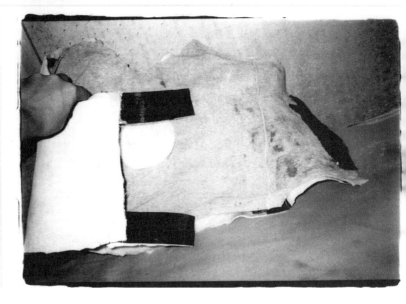

This foam latex pregnancy prosthesis by Sota Effects is intended to be worn with an open robe. Front and back views. Foam latex requires an elaborate preparation process. See the following example.

FIG. 7.17

1. Cast the actor's form and create a positive copy.
2. Sculpt the new shape in plastic clay and create a negative mold.
3. Clean the clay off the mold.
4. Mix and whip the foam perfectly.
5. Put the foam in the mold.

Josh Logan of Fast Cow Effects creates a prosthetic piece for the hand that will be pierced by a blade.

6. Lock the positive and negative molds together.
7. Cook them until the foam is set.
8. Peel the foam out, clean up the piece, and apply the piece to the actor.

Many designers fail to understand that clothing construction is, basically, a nine-teenth-century art. Since the invention of machines for sewing, embroidery, and knitting, only the invention of fusible interlinings and minor programming improvements for machine-embroidered and knit goods have had any impact on garment assembly speed. Tailoring and couture craftsmanship take time. Many film designers do not have a clear idea what the craftsman has to do to create beautiful goods. To be able to do beautiful work with only one fitting is enormously difficult.

Craft technologies can be very complicated. There are hundreds of different materials used in craftwork, among them: leather, steel, aluminum, open-cell foam, closed-cell foam, thermoplastics, resins, and coated fabrics. Each material has its own peculiarities. It takes a master crafter to be able to work equally beautifully in a wide range of goods. The time, care, and craftsmanship that go into craftwork can be more labor-intensive than the finest couture work. For designers and costumers unfamiliar with the materials, it is easy to underestimate, and misunderstand, the work that goes into a project that requires craftwork.

But designers are not alone in abusing the made-to-order collaboration. Craft and costume shops can take advantage of designers. Designers who are inexperienced in made-to-order work, or who lack knowledge about made-to-order resources, can spend money unnecessarily by selecting sophisticated workrooms for simple tasks. Some shops knowingly overcharge the naive. Work delivered to the shop "in a timely fashion" can get pushed back in favor of other projects, resulting in overtime charges down the line. Even the most scrupulously honest shop can over-book, committing to too many projects at the same time—a dilemma that damages all projects in the shop, and all persons involved.

Both designers and shops are regularly put in impossible situations by producers, yet many designer/shop teams manage to develop deep and abiding loyalties that carry them through hard times. Loyalty is a tangible force in the industry, and must be earned. One way to earn it is to be sensitive to a shop's needs: ask for changes at points in the process when they are best addressed, and inform the shop as quickly as possible about changes dictated by production that will have an impact on its work.

The on-the-road shopping kit

Whether you're shopping, pulling, or swatching, life on the road will be a lot easier if you carry a mobile version of a wardrobe kit, tailored to your needs on the road. The supplies you carry with you will help you stay organized not only while making purchases, pulling rentals, buying fabric and other costume-construction materials and supplies, but when you arrive, arms full, at the department office, the costume workroom, or the dyer/distressser.

The kind of "run" you are making determines the contents of your mobile kit. If you are making wardrobe purchases (even if you are first taking them out "on approval" from studio services), your kit should include the following:

Design aids

- Xeroxes of sketches and costume research (preferably in a small-scale format) that give style guidelines for the shopping errand
- Pantone color books or color-card rings made up of paint-chip cards; these are useful for color-matching but need to be edited, to keep kit weight down)

Purchasing aids

- A petty cash pouch, with separate sections for receipts from the purchase of goods and receipts related to travel expenses (gas, parking, and meal receipts, for example)
- All necessary purchasing paperwork (purchase orders, requisitions, return credit sheets, company account paperwork, petty cash-report envelopes, etc.), organized in a light, portable file that can be carried hands-free
- Petty cash and company credit cards, plus required identification

Shopping aids

- Measurement sheets for the actors (summary charts that list the actors' key sizes are useful here) and a measuring tape
- Shopping lists, organized by "like item," or source, or character, depending on your organizational preference. Add appropriate color chips to these lists, as necessary. If the price ranges within which you're working are very narrow, these ranges should be noted next to each item's entry.
- Tags, measuring tape, stapler, pins, and a pen for noting source information (price tags sometimes leave out the store name) and change-tagging goods. If you can tag the goods at check out, you can provide the information needed for returns and multiples purchasing. A stamp pad and custom stamps for the different tag styles illustrated below can speed the notation process (fig. 7.18).

If you're heading to a costume rental house to pull rental stock, your shopping kit should include the following:

Design aids

- Xeroxes of sketches and costume research (preferably in small-scale format) that give style guidelines for the shopping errand
- Pantone color books or color-card rings made up of paint-chip cards; these are useful for color-matching, but need to be edited, to keep shopping kit weight down)

Rental aids

- Measurement sheets or charts containing the actors' sizes and a measuring tape
- Rental lists organized by "like item" or source or character, depending on your organization preference (add appropriate color chips to these lists, as necessary)
- Tags, measuring tape, pins, and a pen, for noting sources, principal character changes, and sizes. If you can tag the goods when you are pulling and sizing, you can fill in key sizing information that may not be available on the rental company's size tag—and it helps you organize for stock filing. Tags of different colors (color-coded by rental company) are very useful for organizing returns. A rental tag stamp can also speed the garment identification process (fig. 7.19).

If you are shopping for fabric and other costume-construction materials, you should have the following items in your shopping kit:

Fabric purchasing and swatching aids

- Fabric shopping lists, with appropriate color chips, as needed
- Stapler, tags, pen
- Measuring tape
- Small scissors
- Swatch ring
- A fabric tag stamp (all fabric must be tagged for designer and draper—(fig. 7.20).

FIG. 7.18

Character:_____

Change #:_____

Garment:_____

Color:_____

Multiples:_____

Brand/Label:_____

Style#:_____

SKU #:_____

Fiber:_____

Price:_____

Source:_____

Quantity:_____

Shopping tag

FIG. 7.19

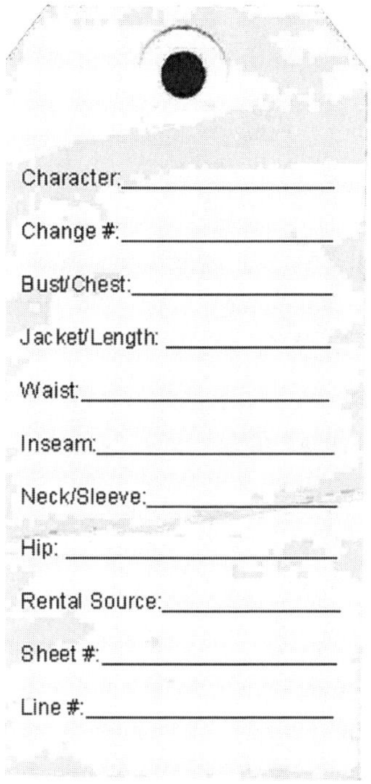

Character:_____

Change #:_____

Bust/Chest:_____

Jacket/Length:_____

Waist:_____

Inseam:_____

Neck/Sleeve:_____

Hip:_____

Rental Source:_____

Sheet #:_____

Line #:_____

**Rental tag color-code by
rental company**

FIG. 7.20

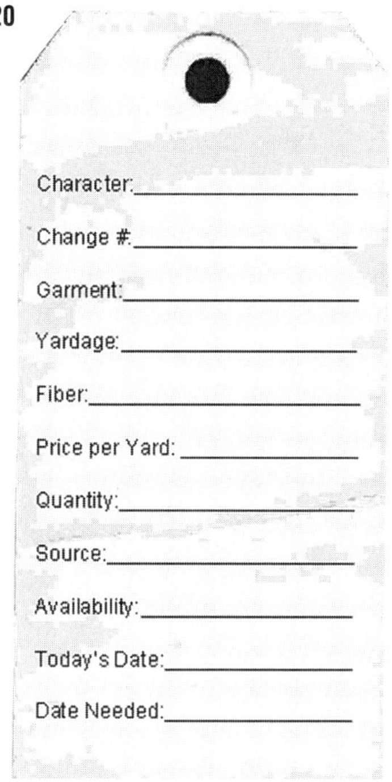

Character:_____

Change #:_____

Garment:_____

Yardage:_____

Fiber:_____

Price per Yard:_____

Quantity:_____

Source:_____

Availability:_____

Today's Date:_____

Date Needed:_____

Fabric/trim tag

Whatever the nature of your "run," you should carry the following with you, depending on the city you are in and your mode of transportation:

Travel aids

- In Los Angeles, you should have the *Thomas Guide* (a book of gridded street maps) and *Shopping LA: The Insiders' Sourcebook for Film & Fashion*. In New York, you should have a subway map and *The Entertainment Sourcebook*. Take Post-it notes with you, to mark these books for quick reference.

One more note: How light and portable your shopping kit should be depends on whether you are traveling by car or by foot. Shoppers can become pack mules in no time, so thought needs to go into how comfortably you can schlep all the gear you need.

Product Placement

Once you are ready to pursue clothing and accessories designers and companies for product placement deals, you can start by looking at the product placement agencies listed in *Shopping LA: The Insiders' Sourcebook for Film & Fashion*. Although costume designers can—and do—work directly with clothing and accessories designers and companies, it is also possible to use product placement contractors who procure free goods for production companies. Product placement contractors can save you time and trouble, but may not deal with the brands or labels you want. In addition, a product placement rep may not use the powers of persuasion a designer will use to procure particular styles or pieces they want or need. By approaching a company directly, a designer can make a compelling argument in favor of a making a deal. This will include describing the merits of the project and its design aesthetic. The designer who deals directly with a company can address questions immediately, and often negotiate from a position of authority.

Once a deal is made, be aware that most companies that provide wardrobe goods (mostly samples) to a production expect the goods to be returned to them without alterations. The rule of thumb for production placement deals is that the pieces in play are on loan, unless specific arrangements have been made to donate them. And remember, product placement deals are, as a rule, only available if you are working on a commercially marketed project, not a student film.

> It says in the [product placement] contract that the clothes have to be brought back in perfect condition. If they aren't, you pay for them. You can tape up a hem, but you can't stitch it. Or you can stitch it lightly, and not press it hard, and then send the garment to the cleaners before you send it back. But the clothes you borrow had better fit absolutely perfectly; if there is any damage, you pay for it. *(Madeline Kozlowski, costume designer)*

Stars, network connections, a major theatrical distributor all make the task of securing product placement easier for a production. In spite of these enticements, however, clothing and accessories companies remain concerned with their public image. They require information about both the project's plot and its cast before making a deal. Concerned about how their goods will be displayed on screen, they will want answers to questions like, Who will wear the pieces? How will they be featured? Will they be worn by the "good guys?" Many fashion designers place restrictions on the manner in which their goods are used. And although many production companies make deals with more than one product placement source, most fashion designers dislike the logos of rival designers appearing beside their own on screen.

Most importantly, fashion designers and manufacturers who have agreed to product placement deals must get the screen credit they were promised. Clothing companies have been badly taken advantage of by production companies: They lose hundreds of outfits and get little or no information on how their goods were used. They can even get rooked out of their screen credit. Daily television series often fail to run full credits at the end of each episode. As a result, some companies prefer to work with product placement contractors, whose reputations rest, in large part, on their ability to deliver on production company promises.

> Say I'm dressing the host on a show with "trade-outs." I take pictures of my host, every show. I blow up one to 8x10, and I have him sign it. I give this to [the product placement rep] for the store or the manufacturer. I also give them two to three tapes showing what the outfit looked like on screen, and what their credit is. *(Madeline Kozlowski, costume designer)*

Before you buy, rent, build, or borrow—"reading" the body and the garment

Whether buying, renting, building, or borrowing, finding the right size, style, and brand of clothing for an actor requires savvy. A designer and her shopping and pulling personnel can save hours of alteration and fitting time if they keep the following axioms in mind: Different brands cater to different kinds of bodies. Size tags can lie. Actors can lie.

- *Different brands cater to different kinds of bodies.* Different designers and clothing manufacturers cater to different body types. Subtle differences in cut can make an enormous difference in how the leading man or leading woman will look, and how many alterations will be needed for the garments to fit correctly.

> You need to know what's going to save you time. What is best for a person's body shape? Wesley Snipes looks best in Armani; but if you put that on Harvey Keitel, he looks short and schlumpy. He's better in Valentino, or certain cuts of Hugo Boss. They're all cut differently. Donna Karan looks good on certain people, but not on Bridget Fonda. She looks good in Escada. Sean Connery looks great in Armani, and good in Donna Karan. Prada is extra large on women—a size 1 is more like a size 4, in real life. Or take an Issey Miyaki, which can fit a lady, size 20, because it's like a tent. *(Eduardo Castro, costume designer)*

- *Size tags can lie.* In general, menswear is more reliably sized than womenswear, since it is less prone to trends in fit. For example, the nineteen-eighties saw the great women's "oversize" trend, in which fashionable women swam in garments that were deliberately oversized. A size-medium blouse in the nineteen-eighties could be a 2X now. Any size-14 woman who has wiggled into a size 10 knows that commercial sizing varies widely.

Commercial pattern makers, including Butterick and Vogue, give size charts for garment patterns. These charts are written up for each general size range, based on an "average ideal" figure that is proportionally balanced, top to bottom. In general, ready-to-wear men's suits are sold with the chest/waist proportions indicated in the commercial sizing guidelines in fig. 7.21, and in short, average, and long body proportions. Womenswear is often available in petite proportions, for the short and short-waisted, and only sporadically available in "long" (fig. 7.22).

For the big-bottomed, or otherwise disproportionate, you have to look at "mixed" sizing. Unusual body features, like body-builder thighs or biceps, triple E bra cups, or "bubble" butts, are not considered in standard size charts, and require you to up-size, or have garments specially made or altered.

> Designers and costumers need to develop an eye for reading the body and the garment to the point where they can virtually know the size without the measurements. They need to know when the size-8 actress can fit the size-6 dress. *(Eduardo Castro, costume designer)*

To really know if a garment is going to make it around an actor, you have to do some key measurements, of both the actor and the garment, because, as we all know…

FIG. 7.21: COMMERCIAL SIZING GUIDELINES

Men's commercial sizes

Range	X-Small	Small	Medium	Large	X-Large	XX-Large
Chest	30" to 32"	34" to 36"	38" to 40"	42" to 44"	46" to 48"	50" to 52"
Waist	24" to 26"	28" to 30"	32" to 34"	36" to 39"	40" to 44"	44" to 46"
Hips	31" to 33"	35" to 37"	39" to 41"	43" to 45"	47" to 49"	50" to 52"
Neck	13" to 13.5"	14" to 14.5"	15" to 15.5"	16" to 16.5"	17" to 17.5"	18" to 18.5"
Shirt sleeve	31"	32"	33"	34"	35"	36" +

Suit length	Short	Medium	Long	X-Long
Center back neck base to hem	27" to 28"	29" to 31"	32" to 33"	34"+

FIG. 7.22: COMMERCIAL SIZING GUIDELINES

Women's commercial sizes

Range	X-Small	Small	Medium	Large	X-Large	1X-Large
Dress sizes	6	8 to 10	12 to 14	16 to 18	20 to 22	24
Bust	30.5"	31.5" to 32.5"	34" to 36"	38" to 40"	42" to 44"	46" to 49.5"
Waist	23"	24" to 25"	26.5" to 28"	30" to 32"	34" to 37"	38" to 41.5"
Hip	32.5"	33.5" to 34.5"	36" to 38"	40" to 42"	44" to 46"	48" to 51.5"

Bra cup sizes	A	B	C	D	DD/E	DDD/F
The difference between the bust and underbust measurements.	1" to 1.5"	1.5" to 2"	2.5" to 3.5"	3.5" to 4.5"	4.5" to 5.5"	5.5" to 6.5"

- *Actors can lie.* Getting accurate measurements from actors can be murder. Even the most spectacular-looking person can be uncomfortable when asked to give his or her sizes. In a business that most often allows you only one fitting, you should protect yourself with down- and up-sized alternatives for important costumes. Of course, this can mean massive time spent in returns and major amounts of cash tied up in the "overage" you had to buy, but it is better to be prepared with alternate sizes for the fitting than to get caught short.

> Actors and actresses who feel that they can do a performance without a costume fitting are unprofessional and a waste of time to deal with. Let them dress themselves and see what wonderful reviews they'll get! *(Jean-Pierre Dorléac, costume designer,* The Blue Lagoon, Somewhere in Time, *and the television series* Quantum Leap, *among others)*

Buying every garment in a range of sizes isn't the only solution to the measurements dilemma. It's worth remembering that actors, extras, and stunt personnel often work through casting agencies, which keep contact information and measurements (accurate or not) on file. In a pinch, these agencies can give you preliminary size information. Stunt agencies may also have stunt actors who commonly double for specific stars. These doubles are generally very close in size to the star, and may be available for doing preliminary fittings of the star's wardrobe, if the star is unable, or unwilling, to be fit in advance.

Costume designer Madeline Kozlowski recalls how she responded to one particular "no measurements" crisis:

> I had a terrible problem with Eddie Murphy on a film. My God! He didn't show up for anything, for any reason—and I'm looking at shooting tomorrow! So I called Central Casting and asked, "Is there somebody you have who works regularly as Eddie's double?" They said, "Oh yeah; it's a bank teller in Van Nuys." I did all my fittings for Eddie on this same teller, who was his body double except for one inch in the waist. I went into the film never having had a fitting with the actor.

> "We should never have been called 'costume designers,' but 'costume magicians,' instead," Edith Head said. Oh, so true! I think the odds of winning the lottery are greater than having an actor or actress give you honest measurements. Yet, one would think they could perceive that only by doing so would they end up looking their best. But no; I get everything but the answers I need. So, I have devised my own way of guessing their true size. It came to me, over years, by recognizing the same vague answers to the same questions. When they hem and haw about how much they weigh, I generally know I have someone on my hands who will never cough up the truth.

> My advice to actors: "It is imperative for actors to know their sizes—all of them—every time they are cast, in anything. Buy a tape measure, and keep it next to the phone. For the most part, especially in television, the designer will have, at most, a day to find something for you. There is no time to have you in, find out that you are larger than anything that was pulled for you, and have you back again for a second fitting."

> Don't go according to commercial clothing sizes. No decent designer would ask you about them anyway, as every label uses different specifications to determine the size of their clothes. Women need to know their height, weight, bust, waist, hips (yes, your hips—no matter how much you dislike them), shoe size, hat size, glove size, and pantyhose. Men: height, weight, chest size, neck measurement, sleeve length, waist, inseam, shoe size, hat size, and glove size. (*Jean-Pierre Dorléac, costume designer*)

Organizing the Costume Stock

Research, purchasing, and made-to-order work may continue throughout the prep and shooting periods, but as soon as the wardrobe begins to be assembled, the stock needs to be organized. The costume supervisor determines stock organization strategies and notation systems. Naturally, setups vary with the nature of the design, the scale of the production, and the amount of storage space available.

Organizing in phases

As costumes are added over the course of a production, the way they are organized may have to change, so the organizing of costume stock is an organic, rather than a fixed, operation. There are, however, four major ways to organize costume stock, each of which is keyed to a different phase of prep and production. The first is what I call the *pre-fitting* phase; the second, the *post-fitting* phase; the third, the *shooting* phase; the fourth, the *wrap* phase.

The pre-fitting phase. During prep, before fittings have taken place, the costume stock is divided into two separate inventories: *character stock* (the costume options for the principal and supporting players) and *general stock* (the costume options for the extras). In the character stock, the principal-player options are grouped by character, and, within each character section, by change number, with, on average, three to four options for each change. The general stock is arranged, sized, and tagged to prepare for the speedy walk-in styling of extras. (The costume supervisor on the strongly styled Tim Burton film *Mars Attacks*, for example, divided general stock into "Las Vegas jazzy," "Washington drab," and "Military.")

The post-fitting phase. After the principal and supporting players have had their fittings, the fit goods—upon the director's approval—are given character change tags (fig. 7.23), organized for alterations, and, once alterations are complete, re-filed in each character's stock storage section. (This tagging process is detailed in the section below, on "Post-fitting notation and wrap procedures.") Any rejected items are restored to general costume stock or placed in a "return" section of the racks, for return to sources of origin.

If a film pre-fits any extras, a common practice in period films, the extra's fit changes are tagged and racked in their own section of the "character stock" area, grouped by scene or type of atmosphere. (For example, individual changes for "train station" extras will be hung

FIG. 7.23

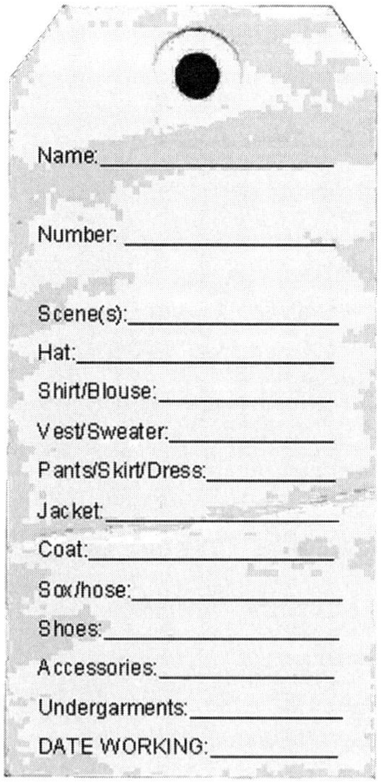

Name:_____

Number: _____

Scene(s):_____
Hat:_____
Shirt/Blouse:_____
Vest/Sweater:_____
Pants/Skirt/Dress:_____
Jacket:_____
Coat:_____
Sox/hose:_____
Shoes:_____
Accessories:_____
Undergarments:_____
DATE WORKING:_____

This tag can also be used on set to list items that the department supplies to an extra. It can be pinned to the extra's pay voucher to help track wardrobe items at final check in.

Background Change Tag

Actor:_____

Character:_____

Scene:_____ CH#:_____

Description:_____

_____
_____
_____
_____
_____

Attach picture from fitting here if available

Principal change tags can be filled in in pencil to allow last-minute on-set deletions and additions. These tags can help set costumers make out their continuity sheets during shooting.

Principal Change Tag

alphabetically, according to last name (or sequentially, according to assigned number), then grouped together on a "train station" rack of clothes.)

The shooting phase. When a production prepares to go on location, final preparations must be made to pull *location stock*, to be housed in the wardrobe truck or van. Location stock is made up of the character stock and general costume stock and supplies needed for at least a week of shooting on location (including stock for cover sets). The location stock is organized on the racks, and in the drawers and boxes, of the wardrobe truck, along the same guidelines as the character stock and the general costume stock is organized at home base. During the course of shooting, the character stock and general costume stock may be shifted back and forth many times between home base and the shooting site, depending on the amount of room available in the wardrobe truck or trailer.

The wrap phase. After each costume change (of principal players, day players, and "established" extras) is "shot out" (that is, finished being filmed), and the costume described in detail (for costume continuity purposes and general documentation), the change is tagged, bagged, and saved at home base, racked by character (for principal and supporting players) or by scene (for extras) in an area designated *wrapped stock* (see Part 9, *Final Wrap*, for more on this).

Organizing principles for costume stock

There is only one set of organizing principles when it comes to costume stock. It doesn't matter which phase of prep or shoot you're in, or whether the costume stock you're dealing with is character stock or general stock (fig. 7.24). These principles are as follows:

General principles
- Group pieces in logical, "like-item" divisions
- Hang items to the right of the rack marker
- Hang all items facing the same direction, with all hangers facing the same direction
- Hang all pants full-length, folded to maintain proper creases
- Arrange all hanging-storage divisions as follows:
- Inner to outer layer (e.g., underwear to overcoat)
- Head to toe (e.g., shirts to jackets to pants or skirt)
- Size-tag all like items in the same place on the garment, ideally the upper, outermost corner of the garment as it hangs, for single-level storage; or the lower, outermost corner, for second-tier storage (fig. 7.24)
- Hang pieces in like-item divisions in order of size, from small to large (size-sequencing takes precedence over color and texture groupings within a division)

Character stock
- Separate by sex, regardless of whether stock is boxed ("boxed stock") or on hangers ("hanging stock")
- Arrange in order of performer's importance (hanging stock only):
- Stars and lead players
- Secondary leads
- Featured day players

FIG. 7.24

shoes

STOCK STORAGE

blouses

gloves

hats
&
ties

- Pre-fitted extras, arranged by scene or type of atmosphere
- Principal-player changes (with options) hung sequentially, by scene (tagged and bagged after fittings; accessories, boxed or bagged, with changes)
- Rack "hanging stock" to the right of a divider, with all garments and hangers facing the same direction
- Tag, bag, and hang pre-fit extras' changes, including accessories

General costume stock
- Mark with easily visible size tags
- Organize in logical, "like-item" units, to enable costumers to access goods with maximum efficiency, for walk-in styling
- Separate by sex
- Separate adult stock from children's stock
- Separate uniforms and their accessories from the general stock
- Hang in size sequence within each group
- Hang to the right of a rack marker, with all garments and hangers facing the same direction

Accessory stock
- Hang accessories (color-sorted and pinned on muslin-covered hangers, if possible; see fig. 7.24), including the following:
- Ties, cravats
- Gloves
- Scarves, handkerchiefs
- Suspenders
- Cummerbunds, belts (sorted by color; tape size-tags behind the buckle on underside of belt)

Box the following accessories:

- Hats: separate felt, straw, and cloth; box by size range; stack or stuff crowns; tape sizes on inside of headbands (inside the hats) that need them; color-separate boxes, if space permits
- Shoes: box by size range; rubber-band pairs together; tape sizes inside the arch of the shoe; box by color, if space permits (fig. 7.24)
- Handbags: box by color

Principal player rack stock:

Men	A	B	C	D	Women A	B	C
change #1,2,3,4,5		1,2,3	1,2,3	1,2,3	change #1,2,3	1,2,3,4	1,2,3,4,5,6

Boxed accessories tuck under the different changes.

Menswear general rack stock:

shirts vests sweaters sport coats pants suits jackets overcoats belts suspenders

hats, felt	hats, straw	jewelry	underwear	sox, dark	sox, light	tennis shoes	dress shoes

Menswear boxed stock tucks under the rack.

Womenswear general rack stock:

blouses vests sweaters jackets skirts pants suits   dresses overcoats scarves belts

hats	jewelry	bras	panties	slips	sox, dark	sox, light	hose	flat shoes	heels	purses

Womenswear boxed stock tucks under the rack.

Children's rack storage	*Uniform rack storage*	*Stunt rack storage*
infants boys girls	cops baseball	stunt doubles
children accessories	uniform accessories	pads & Nomex

Accessory boxed stock tucks under the rack.

- Underwear, hose, and sox: separate by color, light from dark; separate by size into small, medium, large, and extra large; separate by style, depending on quantities
- Jewelry: put into small zip-lock baggies or jewelry-chest compartments. Group other items into color-sorted, like-item units. (Jewelry storage can easily become a tangled nightmare. Small zip-lock baggies and clear storage cases can keep the mess to a minimum. Pinning zip-lock baggies of jewelry to boards or muslin-covered hangers can allow good, quick access.)

COSTUME STOCK LAYOUT GUIDELINES

A NOTE ON SIZE TAGGING

While most rental stock comes with a size tag, a costume crew can spend a great deal of time and energy tagging purchased general stock with sizes. Because tagging a garment with its size speeds up the styling process, it is time well spent. But size-tagging itself is time-consuming, and so notation priority goes to the measurements most needed for fitting.

Regardless of whether the garment is new or used, its original size or altered, size-tag measurements should *not* reflect the *potential size* of the garment (the amount of hem that remains, or the amount of seam allowance left to let out at the waist, for example). Rather, for garments to be used in fittings (new or used), size tags should reflect the *current "ready-made" measurements* of the garment. If a garment is going to be used for general stock, the size tag should reflect the *current "camera ready" measurements* of the garment—measurements with hems shortened, sleeves shortened, waist let out, shrunk in the wash—whatever it actually is (see below, "Guidelines for Sizing Stock").

In all events, every piece that may be pulled to be used on an actor or extra on camera needs a size tag. Even garments sized and labeled by the manufacturer need manila size tags pinned to sleeves, for easy reading and pulling from the rack. And if manufactured garments are purchased used, prior use—laundering, cleaning, unrecognized alterations—may have changed their size and measurements. As a result, it is wise to have your crew measure and mark them again.

Each garment has its own points of measurement, by which size is determined. They are as follows:

GUIDELINES FOR SIZING COSTUME STOCK

Basic garments

- *Pants (men's and women's): waist and inseam.* Measure the waist and the inseam with the pants buttoned up. Note if pants are hip-huggers. Waists are low-rise or high-rise, according to historical period. Prior to the mid-nineteen-fifties, waists were high. If women's slacks are of a deliberately short style, like Capri pants or toreador pants, note only the waist measurement.
- *Shirts (men's): neck size and sleeve length.* Measure length from the neckband button to center of matching button hole. Measure long sleeves starting from the center back of the collar band, measuring across the top of the shoulder, down to the tip of the cuff.
- *Blouses: bust.* Button or zip the blouse, then measure the bust two inches below the armhole. You must allow for the two inches of ease that is built into every blouse by subtracting two inches from the raw measurement. You should also measure the waist on a tightly fitted style, and subtract up to two inches, for ease.
- *Dresses: bust and waist.* Button or zip the dress, then measure the bust two inches below the armhole. You must allow for the two inches of ease that is built into every dress by subtracting two inches from the raw measurement. Also, measure the waist. Measure the hips on slender styles.
- *Skirts: waist, or waist and hip.* Measure the waist buttoned up. For slender styles, lay the piece out flat and measure the hip at a nine-inch drop from the natural waist (one inch above the belly button's position, or, on a standard waist-banded skirt, the base of the waistband).
- *Bras: measure the under-bust,* with any elastic fully stretched.

Over-layer garments

- *Jackets: chest.* Lay the item flat, buttoned up, then do a chest measurement. Take two inches off the total chest measurement, for ease.
- *Sweaters and vests: chest.* Lay the piece out flat, buttoned up, then do a chest measurement, side to side, at armhole level. Take two inches off the total chest measurement, for ease.
- *Outer jackets: chest.* Lay the item flat, buttoned up, then do a chest measurement. Take four inches off the total chest measurement.
- *Overcoats: chest.* Lay the item flat, buttoned up, then do a chest measurement. Take six inches off the total chest measurement. For narrow styles, take off four inches.
- *Shoes: foot length and width.* Use a metal shoe sizer.
- *Hats: head circumference.* Measure the inner headband.

Paper tags with sizes are affixed to costume pieces for "quick read" purposes, but naturally, tags are removed when items are worn and cleaned. To avoid resizing garments that have had their paper tags removed, some costumers pin small cloth tags with laundry-marker size notations inside garments. (Cloth tags that are pinned with extra-small safety pins can make it through dry cleaning or laundry processes intact.) If these cloth tags are affixed with pins, you have the ability to move the tag if it shows on camera. This cloth-tag pinning and notation process take time, however, and tags must be removed for return to rental sources.

Fitting the Actor

For the costume designer and the costume supervisor, the fitting is at the heart of the work. In the fitting, all one's far-flung ideas about character and design boil down to what looks right on a particular actor. Hours of purchasing and preparation pay off as a design concept is distilled into final wardrobe choices.

Scheduling fittings with principals and day players

The more fittings that can be accomplished during the prep period, the more smoothly the shoot will go, and the more available the designer will be to handle matters that come up during shooting. Thus, fittings should begin as early as possible, to provide time for alterations or repurchasing.

> I have always lived by the rule of having *all* my fittings done before a film starts shooting, as [once shooting begins] there's always some change or another that requires the designer to be on the set. *(Jean-Pierre Dorléac, costume designer)*

The process of developing a fitting schedule for principals and day players begins with consulting the day-out-of-days (fig. 5.14) and one-liner (shooting schedule, fig. 5.13) to see when each actor works and what's shooting first. To schedule fittings with actors, you must contact the casting department or agency. Principal and supporting players can be contacted directly by the costume department only after casting has confirmed that the actor has been formally contracted for the production.

Once you are sure that you can bring in an actor for a fitting, you must face the difficulties presented by the actor's schedule, especially in view of the fact that, more often than not, a single fitting is all you will have. If a principal player's schedule makes availability difficult, you may be forced to wait to fit until a few days before the actor starts work. Often, even day players' fittings happen no more than two or three days in advance of filming them. Regardless of timing, however, you want to fit principal players in advance, off set when possible.

> More and more, the scenario is that you get a script, you get hired, you get Bridget Fonda. And Bridget Fonda is available tomorrow—before you've done research, or anything else—and then she's available the day before shooting, because she's in Paris doing another movie. Scheduling problems are constant. *(Eduardo Castro, costume designer)*

Once you know your "window of opportunity" with an actor, you can look at whether all the goods can be available for the fitting. Costume workrooms and product placement sources have their own working timeframes, and they need to be considered. If an actor has a wide window of opportunity, you can work backward from the "one-liner" shooting schedule to find the optimal time to schedule fittings—keeping in mind the time needed by the workroom if MO work must be fit.

The same principal of scheduling can be applied to the fittings of goods taken out on memo, on approval, or as product placement. (Goods taken out on memo must be fit and either purchased or returned within a day or two; rentals taken out "on approval" have their own rules for return—check with individual sources.) Fitting dates for made-to-order work that involves multiple sources (e.g., elements of one costume being produced by more than one craft source) should be carefully coordinated, to enable you to fit the costume change with all its appropriate pieces. Principal players who wear costumes that are complicated to alter (e.g., creature suits, armor, etc.) must also be fit early, to allow ample time for alterations.

On a union film crewed with Local 705 members, the costume supervisor has the task of calling the actors to schedule fittings and get actors' measurements. Technically, it is against the rules for a designer to do this. However, as we will see, designers do contact actors for discussions about style and character, one important way for a designer and an actor to build a trusting relationship.

> I always call the actors myself. I have to gain their trust. I want the actors to feel like they can approach me, personally. I give them my home phone number and let them know that they can call me at any time of the night or day with ideas about their wardrobe. I think it's cheesy to have everyone but the costume designer call the actor and/or his "people." I want the actor to know that I am there for him—not just key costumer number one or men's supervisor number four. It may be against the rules to pick up that phone and dial those numbers, but let's get real. *(Anonymous costume designer)*

A talk before the fitting

Costume designers must woo principal players. Among the most important means of achieving rapport with an actor, and assuring a successful fitting, is having a talk with the actor before he or she comes in. Whether you are lucky enough to confer in person with the actor or must accept the telephone as your instrument, having a talk with an actor before the fitting takes place will help you determine which garments to present and what kinds of conditions to create in what may be your sole opportunity to try on clothing.

In a conversation that precedes a fitting, the designer should ideally get the actor's thoughts on the character and a gloss of body-related insecurities and clothing preferences. Gaining an actor's trust before a fitting requires that a costume designer strike the right balance between promoting the actor's interest in the design and intuiting and assuaging the unexpressed insecurities all actors have about their appearance.

Ultimately, however, how successful you are in this important conversation rests entirely on the amount of time and energy an actor is willing—or able—to expend on planning the look of his or her character. In short, all of the methods for wooing actors listed earlier in this book require actors who are sufficiently intrigued with the process to collaborate with the designer. Unfortunately, many actors have neither the time nor the interest to collaborate with the designer in advance of their "start work" date. Instead, they abridge or eliminate fitting times, then expect things to be "right" when they get to set—which makes preparing for whatever fitting time you've got that much more important.

Preparing for an actor's fitting

The fitting process has two goals: to win the actor's confidence and to make on-the-spot design decisions and adjustments (editing and reconfiguring elements of the wardrobe, determining needed alterations, and so on). Aim to meet these goals in a single fitting with an actor; more often than not, this is all you will get. As a result, every costume change, every design option, every wardrobe item (including accessories, shoes, and correct undergarments—yes, sometimes even standard underwear), plus all appropriate personnel must be on hand whenever possible.

Character change-options should be well organized, ready to be fit on the actor, in the order in which they appear in the script. They should also be artfully displayed, to enable the actor to read at a glance the details of the character's costumes. For a made-to-order fitting, things that help the actor visualize the final look of the piece, like trims and accessories, are important to have on hand. The options you have available will help materialize your sense of the character, and demonstrate to the actor that you have taken seriously his or her requests.

An actor is fit individually, with as much privacy and comfort as possible. Costume designer Edith Head made a point of fitting stars in elegant, lavishly appointed fitting rooms, to set them at their ease and make them feel pampered. Simple elements can add comfort to the fitting: having beverages or simple munchies on hand, providing a comfy chair, flowers and music, lighting a candle, keeping the room at a comfortable temperature, preventing overcrowding (more on this below in "Who does the fitting?"). An attractive space in neutral tones and surfaces that set off the costumes and the actor is most desirable.

Edith Head also suggested that personnel doing fittings wear white, black, or beige. Everything should be background to the actor and his or her wardrobe. Costume personnel should make a point of looking appropriately stylish, as well as low-key. An actor's first real impression of the costume department—and its taste—may be based on the way its representatives look in the fitting. The designer's personal sense of style is an important means of gaining an actor's confidence.

The point of all this preparation is to create a space in which the actor can concentrate fully on the fitting. This should be the unspoken agenda in every fitting room, and it is worth finding ways to preserve it, even when fitting conditions are not quite so deluxe. In reality, actor fittings have been done in every conceivable venue. Actors have had fittings not only in the well-appointed fitting rooms of made-to-order shops and costume rental houses, but in their homes, in hotel rooms, in trailers, in rehearsal halls, in wardrobe vans and honeywagons, in tents, and in location bathrooms (fig. 1.9).

In all events, unless you are hopelessly stuck with primitive fitting conditions, every fitting room, regardless of how improvised, had better have adequate lighting, a place to hang costumes, a table to lay out accessories and supplies, one full-length mirror (or more, for three-quarter and back views), and adequate seating and standing room for the actor, the designer, and fitting personnel.

Who does the fitting?

In Los Angeles, Motion Picture Costumers Union Local 705 guidelines dictate that on union feature films, only key costumers, costume supervisors, or "custom-made" personnel are allowed to do the actual fitting—that is, pin the pins and so forth. Costume designers are not allowed to pin, sew, or push a rack, although designers "direct the fittings" of actors (and "direct the styling of the extras") by giving instructions to the 705 personnel on the job.

Whether the production is union or non-union, the costume designer or design assistant should be present at all fittings, to direct the selection and determine alterations of items. The costume supervisor (or his or her representative) should be present, to record the details of the costume changes and any fitting or alteration notes.

Made-to-order work should be fit by the cutter or crafts artisan who is creating the goods. If outfits that are the product of multiple workrooms are to be fitted, fitters from each of these sources may need to be present. On a union film, if rental or bought garments are to be fitted, the presence of an alteration-fitter may be required to do the actual pinning of the garments.

Child actors will most commonly want a parent at a fitting. But in non-child-actor fittings, it is a good idea to ban from the fitting room all non-costume attendees, including girlfriends, boyfriends, personal assistants, directors, and producers.

> Actors should come to fittings alone! This is the only time a costume designer has to create, in collaboration with the actors, the look that is required for the film. Actors who bring a friend along to offer opinions are usually neophytes, and have to be told that their friend can wait down at the corner soda shop until they are through. No one but the actor should be allowed into a fitting room. (*Jean-Pierre Dorléac, costume designer*)

The costume designer is expected to charm the actor being fit and create a comfortable, collaborative atmosphere. Costume support personnel (fitters, assistants, etc.) are expected to keep a low profile and create a quietly supportive atmosphere. Noise should be kept to a minimum. With few exceptions, the designer wants to hear only two voices in the fitting room: her own and the actor's.

Psychology of a fitting

For many actors, a fitting is an acutely uncomfortable occasion. They know they are being judged on their looks, their flaws are being analyzed in detail. It can make them feel especially vulnerable. As a result, it is important to put them at ease before plowing into the work. Give the actor a moment or two to adjust to the fitting space. Respect the actor's privacy. Every principal actor should be offered the opportunity to dress and undress unobserved.

You have to give actors a moment. You have to treat them like human beings, and not like mannequins. I learned from people who were bad about this. I remember once, we had a fitting with Bridget Fonda. She came in and she was an hour and a half late. I was the design assistant, and the designer came in with tons of clothes. Bridget was having a very hard time; it wasn't a bit fun for her, and she had a lot on her mind. The designer started out with, "Here, put this on, and I'm going to the bathroom." She left, and Bridget was in tears. I said, "Calm down. What's going on? I appreciate you coming here. I know it's very difficult for you. I'm sorry it's turned into this." And we got on with it. *(Eduardo Castro, costume designer)*

In order to prepare the actor for the business at hand, it can be helpful to review the costume arc of the character by doing a "walk through" of options for each character change. These changes should be hung sequentially on the fitting-room rolling rack. In addition, costume designers often present character design sketches and costume research boards to the actor, in order to emphasize how the costumes support the sequence of events in the script. Actors are sometimes curious to get a sense of the look of the whole production and may appreciate seeing atmospheric design research and sketches of other characters, to help them get a sense of how their character will appear in the context of the whole look.

Some actors, especially television actors, are unfamiliar with made-to-order fitting procedures and may need to be walked through them before the process begins. A *mock-up fitting* (a *mock-up* being a "test" garment made in a fabric not truly representative of the final costume's look) should be supported with a sketch and samples of the final fabrics and trims or paint-surface samples, in order to help the actor envision the final effect of a garment.

A designer can be an ambassador for the art and craft of film costumes and help make the job a little easier by initiating the actor in the little-known pleasures of the fitting process. Designers can promote collaboration by setting the actor at ease and beginning a dialog. Try to connect personally with the actor and establish a rapport, then move on to exploring the character the actor will play.

I learned how to handle a fitting with grace from costume designer Ann Roth. Ann Roth is great in the way she connects with the actor. It's establishing a rapport. It's really a matter of discussing what's important to the actor. I remember, I had a problem on my hands in Canada, with Goldie Hawn. Something from L.A. didn't work. I thought she was going to be very difficult, and she had every right to be. We kept talking about her son, because that was what was important to her, and everything fell into place, and we did the fitting. With Angelica Huston, I don't know what we talked about, but Angelica and I talked about a lot of things. It was so much fun, and we bonded. You have to be able to read actors. You have to have a quality about you. You have to discuss things that are interesting to the actor in terms of the character they are playing, in terms of what they like as a person.

When I was doing the movie *The Perez Family*, we had four core characters. They were all treated differently, and designed differently. With Angelica Huston, we did all of her clothes in two fittings, at the beginning of the movie, and we stuck to them. Angelica played a very refined character, so her fitting was about how good the clothes looked on her. Alfred Molina was "total trust," and everything worked on him. When I heard that Marisa Tomei was in it, my best friend and fellow designer said, "She's a holy terror. She's going to rip your heart out." But my assistant said, "That was his experience with her. It doesn't mean that that's going to be your experience with her." So, I go to New York and I meet with her. I talk to her, and things seem to go fine. We show her the designs, and then we meet in Miami. The way I approached her was that nothing was set in stone. You approach her more organically. You creep into the character. You go slowly, and you try things until they feel right. With her, everything was very, very slow and very, very organic. If she didn't feel right, we didn't do it. We went scene by scene through the whole film, with nothing set in advance. *(Eduardo Castro, costume designer)*

The fitting is a unique opportunity for designer and actor to explore character. If a fitting goes well, the designer's conception of the character and the actor's conception of the role will resolve in a tangible version of the character's look. The fitting can be particularly helpful to day players, who may not have been given the entire script, only the script pages in which they appear. Occasionally, if an actor has been considered for more than one role, even as late as the fitting, he may not know the part in which he's been cast. For an actor who is open to collaboration, the costume designer, with a deep and comprehensive understanding of the entire script, can be an important source.

If you exhibit confidence in a fitting, an actor will see that, and will feel much more at home in the costume. You gain their confidence. When you tell them, "This looks great," and it fits well, they feel that much better on the set. And they will go back and say, "Wow, I had the best fitting, I feel so great." And then the next actor comes in to his fitting thinking, "She had a great fitting; so should I." And he goes back and tells the director, and the director's going, "Yeah, I hired the right designer." It happens all the time—wonderful word-of-mouth. The more that the director can feel that their actors are happy, the better off you are.

You have to work with the actor. Sometimes, you'll have an actor coming in who doesn't really know what his character is. Because he doesn't have much rehearsal time, he is still trying to work it all out. And you have this wonderful time in the fitting where you work it out together, and they leave really excited that their vision and your vision are the same. *(Marcy Froehlich, costume designer)*

As noted above, gaining an actor's trust requires a costume designer to strike the right balance between controlling the design process and encouraging the actor to invest in the design idea. Many costume designers cater to the actor's design preferences, letting the actor dictate design choices, reject garments, select accessories. As I discussed in "Collaborating with actors," in Part 4, *Developing the Design*, the designer tries to maintain aesthetic control by presenting options an actor can live with. Of course, the actor's taste might be appalling, but a good designer just makes this another opportunity to exercise her superior diplomatic skills, her powers of persuasion, and her dazzling sense of design!

I was working with an actor who had a very obtuse sense of style and taste. Sometimes it worked and sometimes it was a little over the top, bordering on ugly. I'd say, "I understand you like it, but the camera is not going to be very kind to this." You can't say "no" to them right off the bat. By giving them a different perspective, you make them realize that maybe it's not the right choice. It's a lesson. "No" is not going to get you anywhere. It's just going to make the situation stagnate. And its going to hurt you more than benefit you. The best compliment you can get in this industry is when an actor says, after your first or second fitting, that he trusts you.

It's very rare that I don't agree with what ends up on camera. Of course. sometimes, you just have to "eat it" and say, "Okay, fine, she's being very, very difficult." You just have to weigh things and say, "Well, is it going to make that much difference?" I did a movie called *Shout*, and I had a problem with one of the actors, a singer. She had a problem wearing vintage clothes. She thought they were unclean. She brought this dress from home that was so wrong—very seventies—and this was the nineteen-fifties. So, we went to the producers and said, "Just shoot her in close-up." They did, and you never saw the dress. *(Eduardo Castro, costume designer)*

It is a truism in this business that the costume designer must work with an actor on the actor's terms. Even if stars refuse to do fittings, they *will be* accommodated—a most difficult position for the costume designer to be in. So it behooves a designer to be resourceful. If an actor prefers not to put on the clothes that you've pulled for a fitting, he or she may be willing to look at the goods. If this is the case, the costume designer should get "rack approval" from the actor—that is, the actor's okay on the garments the designer has on the rolling rack—garments that would have been tried on in a fitting. If even rack approval is out of the question, the designer may have to have a dress form made up to the star's exact measurements. Wardrobe options can be displayed on the form and photographs taken for the actor to review (fig. 4.12). Of course, in the most difficult circumstances, there are no advance approvals at all. The designer may not even get an actor's measurements.

> There are several actresses who won't be measured. What do you do then? You "eyeball" the measurements, and pray. *(Eduardo Castro, costume designer)*

Streamlining the fitting process for actors

To keep the actor comfortable, it is important to keep fittings as short as possible. But it is equally important that all costume details get checked. Streamlining the fitting process starts with the physical setup (see above) and moves on to efficient fitting strategies, among them, the following:

- Options should be hung sequentially, by change number, with all choices close at hand.
- When the actor arrives and gets oriented, but before fitting anything, check his or her key measurements. This will allow you to eliminate or adjust improperly sized garments.
- Start fitting the garments that make up a costume change from the bottom-most layer and end with the outermost layer. Getting the underclothes to fit correctly allows the garments worn over them to be fit with more accuracy.
- Always fit with the right side of the garment out. Alterations should be pinned in a manner that helps the actor and the designer visualize the final effect of the adjustments. (Remember that retail studio-service goods and product placement items cannot be altered if they are going to be returned.)
- All layers that are worn together should be tried on together, in order to check their proportions and their ability to function as a group (e.g., you'd love a fuller sleeve on the blouse, but it looks bulky when worn with the sweater you want to use).

Fitting standards for principals and supporting players

When fitting an actor with each change, the designer must take into consideration the actions the actor performs in that change. In a fitting, the actor should be asked to perform all physical movements done by the character, actions that might affect the fit of a garment or the selection of a shoe (e.g., she looks fabulous in the four-inch heels, but she can't do the tango in them).

The designer must also consider the overall conditions of the shoot. Accommodations must be made in the fitting for stunt padding or shoes that may need bracing and non-skid rubberizing, for example, as well as for silk thermal underwear that may need to be worn throughout a shoot done in cold weather conditions.

FIG. 7.25

Actor Kevin Kilner being
fit in a variety of suits for
Brainiacs

Dk Grey w/stripe
Alfani

DAVID

med grey
Alfani

Greenish Brown
Alfani

DAVID

Lt brown
Alfani

Designer Kristin Burke

FIG. 7.26

Shirt collar lies flat
around the neck with
room for one finger
between the collar
button and the neck.

The shirt body lies
smooth with the bottom
button three inches
below the waist.

The shirt cuff is 4½" from
the tip of the thumb.

Pants pleats lie dead flat.

The pants waistband is
perfectly horizontal to the
ground and worn slightly
above the navel. You should
be able to fit the flat of
your hand just inside the
wastband when standing.

The vest hem covers the waistband easily
with the two bottom pockets at waist height.
The lowest button remains unbuttoned.

Costume changes must be fit according to the "style" of the character and the "feel" of the production as a whole. Gritty realism suggests a particular character "fit"—drooping "butt-crack" waistlines for the plumber; soft, sagging shoulders and pockets on the jacket of the old man. Romantic comedies or thrillers can demand glamour styling—a custom-tailored, designer-label fit for the suits of middle-class businessmen and mid-level bureaucrats.

Fitting for the revealing eye of the camera demands painstaking attention to detail, particularly in the area around the face. This makes critical the fit of collars and the shoulders of a garment. To appear simply well-dressed, an actor's costumes must be fit meticulously; pulls, gaps, puckers, and other distortions—anything that takes away from a garment's drape and line—must be eliminated. Costume layers must be carefully adjusted. Panty lines should be eliminated, shirt tails cropped to keep the hips looking as slim as possible. A skirt made of translucent fabric may need the "turn-under" of its hem replaced with sheer fabric, to avoid the hem band of doubled fabric, which could show up on camera.

Because suits can be particularly subtle in their cut and fit, designers often try a variety of styles and brands on an actor during a fitting to find the ones that work best (fig. 7.25). Depending on the challenges to proper fit inherent in an actor's physique, and the degree of refinement required for the character, elaborate tailoring and alterations may be necessary in order to create a smooth, shapely appearance. (Glamorous womenswear is generally tapered, to keep bodylines as slim as possible. For standard and glamour fitting points for menswear, see below, and figs. 7.26, 7.27.)

FIG. 7.27

Jacket lapels roll lightly onto the body with no gaps or sags.

Sleeves are 2" larger than the bicep with no drag lines on the sleeve heads.

The jacket collar smoothly hugs the back of the neck.

Where you take a "military pinch."

The military pinch is taken to alleviate bunching (like the illustration above) at the center back of the neck where the collar meets the coat body. Shoulders should lie dead flat with no bunching.

The hem lies within the curl of the man's fingertips.

Cuffed hem option: cuffed hems lie perfectly horizontal to the floor with no more than 1¼"-1½" cuff depth.

The pants hems break lightly on the shoe in the front. Uncuffed hems are ½" to ¾" longer in the back.

MENSWEAR FITTING POINTS
FOR A CONTEMPORARY BUSINESSMAN'S LOOK

Dress shirt

- The collar should lay smoothly on the neck, with room for one finger between the collar button and the neck. Spread, height, and length vary in proportion to the actor's neck length and face shape, the jacket's lapel breadth, and the size of the knot of the tie. High collar, moderate collar points for a long face. Low collar, long points for a broad face and neck. Spread collars add width; straight collars add length. The knot of the tie should always fill the collar spread.
- The body of the shirt should lay smooth all around the body regardless of whether the actor is sitting or standing. The shirt should be comfortably loose, but not baggy. The bottom button should rest three (3) inches below the waist.
- Shoulder seams should be slightly outside the shoulder bone, but no more than one (1) inch.
- Sleeves end a fraction below the wrist bone, or four and one half inches (4½) above the tip of the thumb.

Pants

- The waistband lays perfectly horizontal to the ground, and should be worn slightly above the navel. You should just be able to fit the flat of the hand inside the waistband, and the fabric should lay perfectly flat under the belt.
- Any pleats should lay dead flat across the tummy. (Pleats are good for disguising pot bellies and give an elegant line when the hand is in the pocket.)
- Suspenders require inner waistband buttons and are never properly worn with a belt or belt loops.
- The seat should be comfortable for sitting, without sags or pulls across the butt or tummy. The crotch should not be too long (causing full-bottomed effects) or too short (causing snug discomfort and bun definition). Dancers need particularly high crotch-line placement and crotch gusseting or stretch in order to do high kicks.
- Hem: A cuffed hem goes horizontal to the floor, breaking lightly on the shoe. The cuffs themselves are one and one-quarter inches (1¼) to one and one-half inches (1½) in depth. Hems without cuffs should break slightly in front on the shoe, and go one-half inch to three-quarters (½ to ¾) of an inch longer in the back. Cuffs improve the line of light-weight trousers, but look bulky on heavy-weight goods. Cuffs also make short men look shorter.

Vest

- A vest should fit smoothly around the torso in the standing or sitting position, hugging but not constricting the torso. It may gather slightly into a belt in the back, but must be smooth across the shoulder blades. Armholes should never sag.
- Length: The hem of the vest must cover the trouser waistband easily, with the two bottom pockets at waist height.
- The highest button should be just visible above the jacket collar when the coat is buttoned.
- The lowest button may remain unfastened, in the English tradition.

Jacket

- The jacket should fit smoothly all the way around the body when the actor is both standing and sitting. It should lie dead flat on the shoulders, including the area where the center back of the collar meets the top of the coat (the area of the "military pinch," see fig. 7.27).
- The collar should rest beautifully against the center back of the neck, with no gapping.

- Lapels should hug the chest without gaps or sags, and lightly roll over onto the body, instead of being pressed flat.
- Back and side vents hang flat and perpendicular to the hem.
- The bottom hem of the jacket should lie within the curl of the fingertips when a man is standing with his arms straight down at his sides.
- Traditionally, two-button jackets button the top button, three-button jackets button the middle button, double breasted jackets button either the upper or lower button. (Double-breasted jackets, when buttoned, should always have the interior guard-button buttoned.)
- The sleeves should be two (2) inches larger than the bicep, and, if the shirt has a French cuff, may require more room at the wrist. The top of the sleeves should show neither pulls nor drag lines when the man is standing with his arms straight down at his side. Sleeve hems should show one-half ($\frac{1}{2}$) inch of shirt cuff.

Tie

- With a standard "four-in-hand" tie, the thickness of the tie should not crease or dent the collar. The knot should fill the area of the spread of the collar. When knotted, there should be a dimple, or crease, that falls in the middle of the tie below the knot. The width of the knot should be in proportion to the collar; the width of the tie should be in proportion to the lapels. When knotted, the tie should not extend past the belt buckle. Certain knotting styles may require longer ties.
- Bow ties must be in proper proportion to the face: The bow should be as wide as the distance between the outer corners of the eyes.

Hat

- Proper fit is a measure of how the hat looks on the head, but a hat normally sits just above the brow.

GLAMOUR FITTING POINTS
- Taper sleeves on shirts and jackets
- Take a military pinch at the back of the neck where the collar meets the body of the coat
- Re-hang sleeves to eliminate drag lines
- Taper the body of a coat and ease the excess out of a coat front, to mold the coat to the torso
- Adjust coat buttons and guard buttons, to eliminate pulls

Do I have a list of things I love to do to get the fit right for camera? Sleeve lengths. The military pinch, to get the back of the neck to lie flat on the jacket. Reset the buttons, because those buttons were stitched on flat, and they never sit right. If the jacket is single-breasted, the center button—the one that the actor is going to use—needs more room. If the jacket is double breasted, move both of those buttons, so it fits perfectly, so it doesn't pull. So many times, especially in double-breasted suits, you see a pull at the button, and it just looks terrible. Or the collar is sitting wide on the jacket, which is sort of like a halo effect. If you can just have enough time to pinch it up in the back, and take the collar in, then you get a nice rounded frame for the face.

Hopefully, if you've done a fitting, you've been able to determine what length the collar tab should be. Should it be spread, should it be close, should it be long, should it be a short point, according to the shape of the actor's face and neck. I always have my staff, or my crew, hand-press collars before they go in the actor's room in the morning. Even if they are just back from the laundry, get the iron out, press it flat, fold it, press it again. A little bit of starch. I always buy double shirts. At lunchtime, the crew can get the shirt that's not being used and touch it up. I always buy double shirts, absolutely. It's a cheap hedge. When you figure a shirt is $125, but if you hold up camera for an hour, it's like $7,000 to $10,000, $125 is pretty cheap insurance. For shirt-tail problems? I have, on occasion, used crotch straps. We would put a piece from front to back to hold the shirt tails down, to make sure the shirt stays neat. I don't put panties on blouses. I prefer to have the actress tuck it into her pantyhose, because you get a smoother line, especially if she's got wonderful tummy-control pantyhose that fit like an iron corset.

My least favorite phrase on the set is, "Don't worry, it'll never be seen on camera." That may be true, but I have producers, directors, and other actors looking at some poor guy whose pants are pinned up with safety pins. It just presents a bad image, and it could make the actor who's wearing the costume a little insecure—a risk I can't take. *(Pat Welch, costume designer)*

Fitting rules and regulations for actors

Although there are few formal rules that regulate fittings—no rules, for example, about where a fitting may take place, or the number of persons who may be present in a fitting—the rules that do exist are strict. Set up by the motion-picture costumers union locals on both coasts and by the Screen Actors Guild, fitting regulations are meant to protect their members, although in this day of shrinking crews and under-budgeted productions, they are particularly tough to enforce.

SAG FITTING COMPENSATION GUIDELINES
AND FITTING REGULATIONS

The following compensation guidelines are followed in SAG theatrical and television contracts for actors:

- Actors who earn more than $950 per day are not paid for fittings.
- Actors who earn less than $950 per day are paid according to the following guidelines:
- *Weekly players:* Producers are granted four hours of free fitting time with a performer for every week of employment (three hours for television personnel), when the fittings are held on days prior to employment. If fittings continued beyond the allotted "free fitting time," the player is paid in prorated fifteen-minute increments.
- *Day players:* Pay vouchers are provided at all wardrobe fittings. Log-in and log-out times are noted. For each fitting call held on a day prior to employment, the player receives one hour minimum pay. Additional time (beyond one hour) is paid in prorated fifteen-minute increments.
- *Three-day players (TV only):* Producers are granted two hours of free fitting time with a performer for every three days of employment, when the fittings are held on days prior to employment. After two hours, performers are compensated in prorated fifteen-minute increments.
- When fitting for actors who make more than $950 per day are held on official days of employment, fittings are only compensated if they occur *before* the actor's call time for rehearsal or shooting. If fittings are done during an official day of employment, but not before first rehearsal or first shot, fittings are considered "work time," and are counted as part of "the continuous work day." In general, no fittings can be scheduled during meal breaks.
- Fittings on work days must be arranged around the official call and break schedules that guarantee actors free time for particular intervals. Official break periods and

workday lengths vary with studio and location work. Studio and overnight locations guarantee a 12-hour (consecutive) rest period; nearby location shooting guarantees a 10-hour (consecutive) rest period once every fourth day of shooting.

- *Regardless of day rate, an actor who provides personal* wardrobe will get a weekly "cleaning allowance" of $17 per week for formal wear and $11.50 per week for all other goods. The actor must get two copies of a voucher that details the outfits they supplied.

Some principal players' agents may negotiate fat wardrobe-compensation deals for the use of their client's own garments, and occasionally, producers have been known to charge back those fat wardrobe compensation fees to the costume budget.

Fitting Extras

With extras, as with actors, the fitting is when your design ideas are materialized and tested. In the case of extras, however, the amount of fitting time you have with each player is a critical factor in the design process itself. If the production you are working on calls for period or other specialty costume extras (a bellhop, a nurse, a soldier, for example), you will have a budget to buy and rent stock that fits a design scheme, and time to pre-fit. In the case of contemporary dress, however, extras are fit with a combination of their own wardrobe and pieces from costume stock, on the day they shoot, sometimes right before their set call. In both cases, the "design time" per extra is very short.

Because of the fast pace required when designing extras (it's not called "speed styling" for nothing), you need to be able to take one look at the extra, analyze the personality inherent in his or her "look," evaluate body's strengths and weaknesses, then commit to an image. As a designer, you must create a process for yourself that allows you to respond to the moment, like an actor finds "the moment" or a cinematographer changes the shot based on a sudden inspiration. Given what you need in order to satisfy the overall design scheme, what kind of character can you turn an extra into? What inspiration can you take from an extra's face and body? How do you make the extra believable in the look? What key details will carry the correct message? And how do you do all this in a few minutes, with limited choices? You look at the raw materials and find inspiration. Then, you hit your well-organized general stock, and improvise a costume.

> It's hard to get everything to fit well when you are dealing with loads of extras. It's nice to think, well, they will be background guys, but, in fact, they aren't always. The camera can pick them out, and you can get horrible surprises. Or the director will fall in love with someone in the background, a wonderful character, and bring him right up to the camera. *(Pat Welch, costume designer)*

Scheduling fittings with extras

Extras who need to be pre-fit are generally only scheduled for a fitting one week in advance of shooting; but scenes with large numbers of pre-fit extras can create the need for large numbers of alterations, forcing fittings to be moved earlier in the prep schedule. If no pre-fittings are done, and extras are being asked to simply show up on location with appropriate wardrobe of their own, instructions are given to extras casting, in advance, via the second assistant director, who has already gotten clear written wardrobe instructions from the costume department (see below).

Fittings with extras—indeed all costume department arrangements and communications with extras prior to their arrival on set—are coordinated through the *extras casting* department or agency. If you are planning to ask extras to supply their own wardrobe, and are asking them to bring a selection of personal wardrobe items to a fitting or to the set, you must fax the extras casting department clear written instructions that tell the extras what to bring (fig. A.34, "Memo to Extras Casting").

Even with written notes and conscientious communication by extras casting and second ADs, extras are notorious for free-form interpretations of wardrobe instructions. All a costume department can do is send clear instructions, following the guidelines below, then keep its collective fingers crossed.

THE ART OF GIVING WARDROBE INSTRUCTIONS

1. Keep it simple.
2. Give day/night information.
3. Give interior/exterior information.
4. Give season and weather information.
5. Give a brief description of the status and tone of the goods you want. Keep specific language simple and universal.
6. Keep color palette and tone guidelines in simple terms; don't assume people understand technical color terms like "complementary" and "analogous," "low value," "high-intensity," even "cool" or "warm." Name specific colors that must be avoided.
7. Note any textures that should be avoided. Keep terminology simple.
8. Remember to request specific foundation-garment choices, if the line of the goods is affected by undergarments.
9. Detail briefly any accessories or garments that would be particularly helpful to bring. Try not to narrow the style choices too much.
10. Capitalize, bold-face, or underline the most important points. Assume that the reader will only skim the instructions.

Preparing to pre-fit extras

Pre-fittings for extras are generally handled en masse. This may require that well-tagged, well-organized general costume stock and wardrobe equipment and supplies be reconfigured in ways that more readily accommodate speed fitting and dressing by the costume department staff.

For any mass pre-fitting, the costume department sets up a holding area. In this area, costume department staff should set up a reception table manned by a costumer, a second AD, or a production assistant. Here, extras can line up to sign in and have their vouchers held. In this area, there will also be rolling racks, where extras can stash their garment bags and totes, and folding chairs, where they can sit until they are called by a costumer for preliminary measurements and the fitting itself. This holding area should be supplied with measuring tapes, pencils, and "priority measurement sheets" for women and men (see Appendix).

Extras are fit by scene, so the costume stock most desirable for the scene being fit must be arranged for quick pulling. A mass pre-fitting for a large formal scene may have costumers creating racks of men's and women's formalwear stock that can be rolled close to the reception area, for rapid disbursement.

When the department is seriously short-handed, or time is super-tight, extras can be instructed to select costume pieces themselves (most often, shoes, gloves, and uniforms), and costumers will organize or display stock to accommodate this process. Bins of same-size shoes and gloves, for example, can be arranged sequentially next to a seating area, so that extras can pull their own preferences, then sit and try them on. This can be successful, especially with hard-to-fit items, and, if you're lucky, a costumer's time can be saved.

It is a costume truism that when extras are left to their own devices, wardrobe chaos will rein: Garments will end up on the floor; sizes will get mixed; shoes of a pair will get separated; wardrobe will "walk away." You may get lucky and have an exceptionally responsible group of extras, but prepare yourself for the worst, if you must make this choice.

When large numbers of extras are being pre-fit, the costume department may need to construct additional fitting-room arrangements. At home base, as on location, dressing and fitting areas for extras will likely have to be improvised, with pipes and curtains, folding chairs, collapsible tables, rolling racks, and mirrors. It is not unusual for costumers to ask four extras of the same sex to change into wardrobe at the same time. Groups are cycled through at fifteen-minute intervals. As a result, fitting rooms, no matter how improvised, have to be spacious enough to accommodate a rolling rack and at least four sets of flailing limbs. It is a given that privacy and security are in short supply in extras' fitting or dressing rooms, and a note to this effect to your extras casting director in advance of a fitting or set call may save you—and your extras—the calamity of missing cash or jewelry.

Fitting standards for extras

The painstaking care taken in fittings with principal players is simply not practical when dealing with mass fitting calls. The goal is to make the extras look appropriately stylish in very little time, and this requires using goods that need minimal alterations, or none at all.

> When you're dressing extras—you know, two every fifteen minutes—you're just flying. You're just going on gut and instinct. You look at them and you try to figure out immediately what kind of characters they are. What clothes do we have in their size? How can I achieve a look quickly? That's tough, but it can also be exhilarating. It's fun, when you get it. But when you don't get it, when you're just trying one garment after the other and nothing works, it can be horrifying. Every once in a while, you get one of those.

A lot of it just comes from the experience of seeing it—of having done it so many times that you realize what works on camera. Dailies help a lot. You can go and see, "Did the choice that I made there really work? Is there something that I should do differently for the next outfit? I still have ten hours in between now and then that I can do it in!" I think it is a constant learning process. *(Marcy Froehlich, costume designer and co-author of Shopping LA: The Insiders' Sourcebook for Film & Fashion)*

As with principals, the fit of an extra's costume is determined by the style and feel of the overall design scheme and the "character" of the background players in a given scene. With extras' costumes, the goal is minimal alterations and repairs, although some alterations are unavoidable. As we discussed above, pre-fitted extras are sometimes sorted into "A," "B," and "C" groups that correspond to the grouping of the stock garments they've been assigned (group "A" stock being properly fitted and sharply detailed, group "B" stock being acceptable but not fabulous, group "C" being "please-don't-look-too-closely"). Making use of these rankings on the set requires a vigilant set costumer and a willing AD.

When pre-fitting extras, you must also address the comfort of the performer wearing the costume. Extras are often on their feet for most of a twelve-hour day, more often than not with only rudimentary shelter to protect them from inclement weather and other discomforts that invariably come with a location (fig. 7.28). Making them as comfortable as possible in costume, while supporting the overall look, should be a "given" when fitting extras. It is inhumane to give extras unnecessary layers of heavy garments on a hot summer day or shoes that are a misery. Such things should be avoided, if there's any way to do so.

FIG. 7.28

Extras on the set of the film *The Trial of Old Drum* (2000) designed by Kristin Burke. Twelve-hour shooting days often mean long periods of sitting around and waiting for camera setups.

Photos by Kristin Burke

Before I got my first wonderful break in costuming, I worked as an extra. I spent many evenings going home in tears. Why was I going home in tears? Insensitivity by certain costume departments. It may be a lack of time, maybe they were under pressure, but extras are really not treated very well. It's a lack of respect. And I remember what it felt like.

I think I owe an "atmosphere person" time. She's been given a work call, she's been told what to bring, if it's contemporary, and she's taken the time to go through her closet and pull things out and put them in a suitcase and bring them to work, I owe her the two or three minutes of time to look through what she's brought and say, "That's great" or "I love what you have on, but why don't you show me what you brought anyway, in case there is a second change?" It's so little to ask.

So whenever I design a show, I always do the extras. I love working with them. You need to pay them honor and respect, because if you take out the background, take out the back action, what have you got? A talking head. You may not notice what is going on in the background, but extras bring life to a project. *(Pat Welch, costume designer)*

Streamlining the pre-fitting of extras

The process of fitting extras during prep is choreographed for maximum speed and efficiency. As noted above, extras are lined up at the wardrobe reception desk, then seated in the wardrobe waiting area, where they await contact with the costume designer, the design assistant, or a costumer. Extras are then processed by the costume staff in the following manner:

- A member of the costume staff reviews all garment options brought by the extra.
- The costume staffer takes any measurements that are necessary, according to the "Priority Measurement Form [Women]" or the "Priority Measurement Form [Men]" (see Appendix).
- If the extra is being paid for a fitting, his or her pay voucher is collected by the costumer and the time noted.
- The costumer then proceeds to pull from the general costume stock any key wardrobe needed to supplement or supplant the extra's own wardrobe, then directs the extra to any wardrobe bin or rack from which the extra is allowed to pull. Once all the key items are pulled, the extra is sent to the dressing room. All extras need to be told *not* to remove tags from the stock garments.
- In order to be fit in wardrobe and assigned accessories, the extra must shuffle back and forth between the fitting room and the costumer, who remains at the fitting/stock distribution area. Extras are expected to dress themselves, freeing costumers to style other extras. Extras may be given several wardrobe options and encouraged to wear the outfit that fits them best.
- Once the costumer gives a preliminary okay to a change, accessories are pulled to complete the outfit.
- The designer or assistant designer, if available, makes final deletions and additions to the change, or approves the entire outfit, including accessories.
- The costumer does final fitting adjustments (pinning hems or marking needed repairs), if necessary, then Polaroids the dressed extra. A head-to-toe (full-length) Polaroid should be done of every pre-fit extra, in every change in which he or she will appear (fig. 7.29). Each photo gets labeled with the extra's name, scene number, and change number, if more than one. The extra is then ready for the post-fitting notation and wrap process detailed in the next section of this text.
- Before returning to the fitting area to disrobe, the extra is told that all unused or rejected items must be returned to the costumer properly hung up for restocking. Assigned pieces

FIG. 7.29

Bagged and tagged extra's costume.

Fitting photo of extra in costume.

must also be bagged or hung up in the proper manner by the extra. (This is detailed in the next section.) By holding the extra's pay voucher ransom for the proper return of all wardrobe items, costumers are spared a great deal of work.

• After the extra returns the wardrobe in the proper manner, the costumer records the assigned wardrobe items on the "extras costume chart" (fig. 7.30; for more on this, see below), gives the extra his or her wardrobe identification number, if one is assigned. The costumer then notes the check-out time on the pay voucher and hands it back to the extra, who is allowed to leave.

When it comes to recording the items assigned to pre-fit extras, an *extras costume chart* is used. You can make up your own (fig. 7.30) or buy the standard form, available from costume supply houses. The extras costume chart should include space for scene number and set (e.g., TRAIN STATION); an indication of the gender of the extra (M = Male; F = Female); a column for the names of the extras, and for standard items assigned from stock (hat, undergarments, shirt/blouse, jacket/dress, pants/skirt, socks/hose, shoes, accessories). Costume departments use these forms—one for female extras, one for male extras—to keep track of the garments assigned from general stock, and the garments provided by the extra from his or her personal wardrobe (marked with a "P").

To speed up the filing process, and to streamline the locating and handing out of pre-assigned wardrobe on the day of the shoot, a number may be assigned each extra at the time of the advance fitting. (Often, this is the pre-printed number that appears at the beginning of the line on which the extra's name appears on commercially available extras costume charts.) A prep costumer then records on a manila tag the extra's number (if one has been assigned) and the pieces that make up the approved/finished change. The tag is then pinned to the change.

FIG. 7.30: THE EXTRAS COSTUME CHART

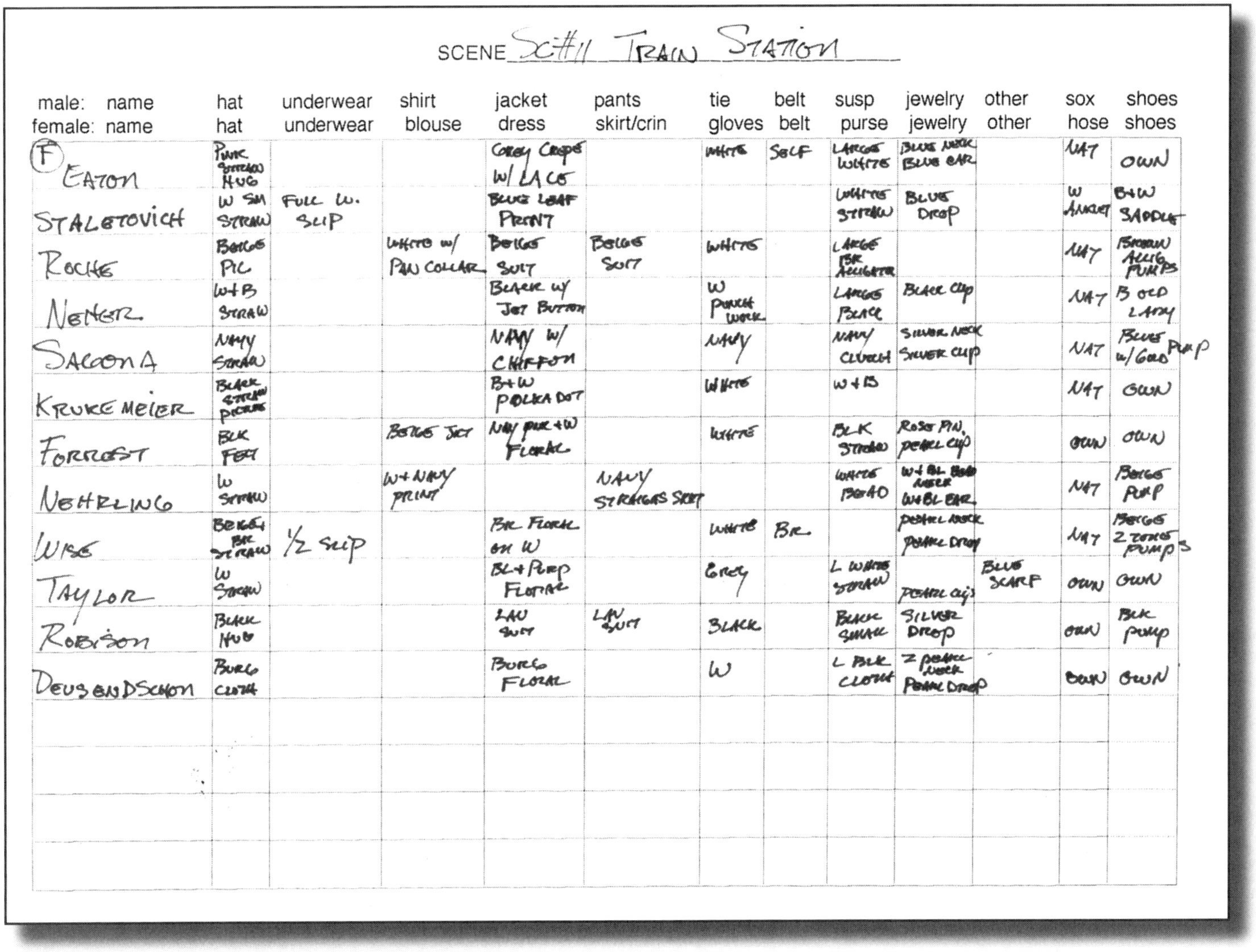

SCENE _Sc #11 Train Station_

male: name / female: name	hat / hat	underwear / underwear	shirt / blouse	jacket / dress	pants / skirt/crin	tie / gloves	belt / belt	susp / purse	jewelry / jewelry	other / other	sox / hose	shoes / shoes
(F) EATON	PINK STRAW HUG			GREY CREPE w/ LACE		WHITE	SELF	LARGE WHITE	BLUE NECK BLUE EAR		NAT	OWN
STALETOVICH	W SM STRAW	FULL W. SLIP		BLUE LEAF PRINT				WHITE STRAW	BLUE DROP		W ANKLE	B+W SADDLE
ROCHE	BEIGE PIC		WHITE w/ PAN COLLAR	BEIGE SUIT	BEIGE SUIT	WHITE		LARGE BR ALLIGATR			NAT	BROWN ALLIG PUMPS
NENGER	W+B STRAW			BLACK w/ JET BUTTON		W PUNCH WORK		LARGE BLACK	BLACK CLIP		NAT	B OLD LADY
SACCONA	NAVY STRAW			NAVY w/ CHIFFON		NAVY		NAVY CLUTCH	SILVER NECK SILVER CLIP		NAT	BLUE w/ GOLD P
KRUKEMEIER	BLACK STRAW PICTURE			B+W POLKA DOT		WHITE	W+B				NAT	OWN
FORREST	BLK FELT		BEIGE JKT	NAY PUR+W FLORAL		WHITE		BLK STRAW	ROSE PIN, PEARL CLIP		OWN	OWN
NEHRLING	W STRAW		W+NAVY PRINT		NAVY STRAIGHT SKIRT			WHITE BEAD	W+BL BEAD NECK W+BL EAR		NAT	BEIGE PUMP
WISE	BEIGE BR STRAW	1/2 SLIP		BR FLORAL ON W		WHITE	BR	PEARL NECK	PEARL DROP		NAT	BEIGE 2 TONE PUMPS
TAYLOR	W STRAW			BL+PURP FLORAL		GREY		L WHITE STRAW	PEARL CLIP	BLUE SCARF	OWN	OWN
ROBISON	BLACK HUG			LAV SUIT	LAV SUIT	BLACK		BLACK SMALL	SILVER DROP		OWN	BLK PUMP
DEUSENDSCHON	BURG CLOTH			BURG FLORAL		W		L BLK CLOTH	2 PEARL NECK PEARL DROP		BURN	OWN

After Fittings—Documentation, Adjustments, Sourcing

For principals, day players, and pre-fit extras, the careful documentation of each costume change is as important as the selection and fitting of the goods. This means documenting the actor or performer in the change(s), including taking photographs, making checklists of items in each change, and tagging the change with an "extras change tag" or a "principal change tag" (fig. 7.23).

This tag can also be used on the set to list items that the department supplies to an extra. It can be pinned to the extra's pay voucher to help track wardrobe items at final check-in. For more details on the post-fitting written documentation of changes, see below, "Notation system for post-fitting adjustments."

Photo documentation

Whether named characters or extras, when fittings are completed in advance of shooting, it is standard practice to photograph the performer full frame (head to toe) in each change and (for featured players) all possible options. Accessories and other details (the special way in which a garment is worn, for example) may require photo close-ups.

Each photograph (Polaroid or, for more detail and accuracy, 35mm stills) needs to be labeled with the following information:

- Scene number
- Name of the actor and character's name, or the extra's name and number, if assigned
- Change number, if applicable, and option numbers, if applicable

Often, these labeled photos are assembled on character-at-a-glance or scene-at-a-glance photo boards.

Notation system for post-fitting adjustments

After the first fitting, costume pieces may need alterations and other work, even additional fittings, to get them ready for shooting. Costumes may need to be distressed, dyed, painted, teched, and/or laundered, among other things. In *Pulp Fiction,* for example, four of the duplicate black suits for Jules and Vincent needed painting and distressing to look like they'd been spattered with brains and blood. Making note of what remains to be done to a costume piece, making sure the piece is sent to the proper source for that work, then restored to its proper place in the character change or costume stock: These tasks are critical and require a notation system that is both logical and precise.

Garments in need of additional attention before shooting must be pulled from a change and tagged for further attention.

Some designers and costume supervisors, especially on shows of modest size, find simple lists perfectly adequate (lists that include a description of the item, including character name and change number, a brief note of the work to be done, and the source or sources to which the item will be sent for additional work). On shows with large, costumed casts and many post-fitting adjustments, costume supervisors have contrived specific systems of notation that minimize the chances for error. One veteran costume supervisor accustomed to working on large studio pictures has her costumers write up two red tags for each item in need of additional work. (Standard tags come in red; when the budget is tight, try substituting fluorescent index cards.) One of the two red tags is written up with the following information:

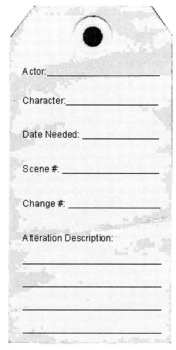

Actor: _____

Character: _____

Date Needed: _____

Scene #: _____

Change #: _____

Alteration Description:

_____

_____

_____

Alteration Tag

1. Actor's name and character name or pre-fitted extra's name and assigned number
2. Scene number and set
3. Change number, if applicable
4. Notes of work to be done (e.g., Alteration: "raise hem 1"; Dyeing/distressing: "tech sneakers and age for blood and mud")
5. The source to whom the piece is being sent (even if it's going to an in-house stitcher or ager)
6. The date it was sent out.

This red tag is pinned to the item in need of attention, which has been pulled from the complete change and hung on the appropriate rack or put in the appropriate box (the alterations and repairs rack, the laundry and dry cleaning rack, distressing and aging rack or box—good for shoes, hats, handbags, etc.). The second red tag, written up with the name of the item, the date, and the out-source (alterations, dyer, shoemaker, or dry cleaner, for example), is pinned to the manila change tag that is attached to the change bag or change unit (if the change is not bagged). This tag is meant to indicate that the item named has been removed from the change and is out to be altered, repaired, or otherwise attended to.

When the additional work on the item has been completed, the person doing the work crosses off the "work order" on the tag and returns the tagged item to a costumer, who restores it to the appropriate change, then destroys both red tags. This process may seem obsessive, but when dozens, even hundreds, of garments are flying between stitchers, agers, dyers, shoemakers, and dry cleaners, you need a way of knowing what's been taken care of, where in character or general stock the item belongs, and, if an item is missing, where it has gone, and when.

Sourcing post-fitting work

Alterations can be farmed out to made-to-order costume shops or freelance custom-made costumers, or, if the supervisor has created an in-house costume workroom, the work can be handled on site. A big-budget studio film or television show might use the studio's costume workroom for all of their alterations and made-to-order costume and craftwork. An independent film with a small budget might farm out only very difficult alterations to a made-to-order costume shop or a workroom at a costume rental house; it might have its own costume personnel handle all minor alterations, if they are sewing-savvy, or bring in an over-hire seamstress for a few days. If alterations work is light, a low-budget production might send its alterations to a dry cleaner who has a tailor or seamstress on the premises. If the alteration work on a costume is extensive, or if the made-to-order costume is very complicated, like the fat-suit costume for John Leguizamo in *Spawn* (figs. 2.8, 2.9), more than one fitting may be needed. Even on a modestly budgeted production, follow-up fittings are most efficiently, and most comfortably, handled in a well-equipped fitting room at a costume or craft workroom, where lighting, mirrors, tools, and equipment are at hand.

Because the norm is a single fitting with an actor in advance of the costume's shooting date, many supervisors hire a freelance tailor or seamstress to be available at the shooting site the first day the costume works, and will request an early call time for the actor so that the alterations can be accomplished in time. Of course, this means that the alterations required must be relatively minor, able to be accomplished in little time, with no glitches—and this assumes an on-site tailor or seamstress capable of working brilliantly, with great speed, under tremendous pressure. The risk you run? Holding up production. A better alternative is to bring a tailor or seamstress in on the first day an actor works, request an early call time, and sneak in a fitting of costumes that work later in the schedule.

Most tailors and alterations cutter-fitters know what they're doing, but you need to have some assurance of the level of their skill and the quality of their work before you bring them on. The trick is to get the right person pinning the garment for alteration. That's where the mistakes are made. Do not mess around with someone who is unskilled.

> If I have to fit on the set, I have an alterations cutter-fitter stand by, or a tailor—depending on whether the actor is a man or a woman. There is always some tweaking, always some alteration that I'll want to do. Tailors who work in the motion picture industry are a special breed. They know how to "quick-tailor." *(Pat Welch, costume designer)*

After any fitting alterations are made to the garments, dyeing, distressing, and other treatments may need to be applied, in order to make the garments work technically on camera. Costume supervisors and costumers must also carefully determine the number of garments that require "character" aging (fading, rumpling, tearing, staining, etc.) or spiffing up (starching, steaming, ironing, non-alteration repairs), in preparation for shooting. They must determine whether this work will be done by on-site personnel or farmed out to commercial dye studios, cleaners, or made-to-order workrooms.

Preparing Costume Pieces for Shooting

Checking garments for camera

Costumes may need to be checked to make sure that all elements will "work" technically on camera. (For more on this, review the section titled "Media Restrictions," in Part 3, *Composing Costume Images: The Art and the Craft.*) Is the intensity of any pure colors or whites in danger of causing over-burn or flare problems? Will the costumes clash with or disappear into the background? Will the film stock or film-processing impact the way the garment looks on camera? To avoid problems with color shift, color flare, or "black hole" effects designers are encouraged to consult with the director of photography, carefully research the colors being used on set, and ask for a palette test or camera test for any garments that may cause problems. Dipping bright colors down (that is, "teching" the goods in pale warm or cool dye baths) can solve a multitude of over-burn problems. Color shift or value/contrast problems may require deeper dye bath treatments. (See below, plus *Conversation Three: On Working with the Cinematographer and Collaborating with Actors in Film, with Catherine Adair* and *Conversation Eleven: On Dyeing and Distressing Costumes for Film, with Edwina Pellikka,* for a detailed discussion of factors effecting costume teching and dyeing.)

Costume textures may also need to be checked for how they read on camera (again, review, "Media Restrictions," in Part 3). Does the checked jacket moiré on screen? Does the metallic fabric over-burn on camera? Special effects and chroma key work can create color and texture palette restrictions, so it is wise to consult with the director of photography, in order to identify problems in advance. Some chroma-key blending or fabric-print moiré problems can be solved with over-dyeing or over-painting; but many texture problems can only be solved by replacing the offending piece.

Aging and distressing the garments for character

After you have fit and altered the costumes and checked them for camera, it is time to fine-tune the final look of the garments—the final stage of in designing the characters. Should the shirt be starched and crisply pressed, should it be lovingly wilted, or look slept in? Should the fabric be threadbare? Dirty? Bloody? Sweaty? Does the uniform look battle-scarred enough? Determining the final touches that are needed to have the garments embody the life of the character is a subtle art that can make all the difference in making the costume believable.

"Aging" is a costume term that refers to the subtle breakdown of a garment to reflect the life of a character. Unless the story dictates that a character is in absolutely brand-new garments, most garments need to look like they comfortably "belong" to the characters. The subtle softening of colors or textures can help garments lose their "too new" status. Subtle shaping of the garments to reflect the body or the habits of the character can make them feel "lived in" (stretching out the pockets on a character's comfortable old jacket, for example.) If a character lives a hard life, his or her garments must reflect appropriate wear.

The last step of the costume approval process is to thoroughly think through and how much aging (also called "distressing') and "teching" should be done to each costume. Talk with your director, and know these details before you finalize any costume. Make sure that your in-house and outside crew of dyers and distressers understand prior to doing the work exactly what you want, including the progression (or stages) of aging and teching a character's costume goes through. "Aging" or "distressing" is a costume term that refers to the more obvious break down or staining of garments to reflect damage from events or "hard living." For example, a script may dictate that a character gets mud-stained. A mechanic may be more believable if his work clothes look sweaty and grease-stained. A farmer may need dirt stains that reflect the color of the field that he is plowing.

To correctly distress a garment, you need to consider precisely the look of the garment in the context of the story, and specifically in the context of the scene or scenes in which it's worn. In addition to knowing how to use a wide variety of materials and techniques, you will need a carefully considered design for the aging of your costumes. For example, in the film I (KB) designed called *The Cooler*, starring William H. Macy, the costumes for Macy's character Bernie go through three distinct changes of age and tech. I called them stages A through C. Stage A was Bernie at his loser-y coolest: His suit was two sizes too big, not tailored, and aged to look ratty and pilled. Stage B was the transformation stage: The suit was one size too big, only slightly altered, and aged to a medium stage of wear. Stage C was the "hot," winning stage: The suit was pristine, perfectly tailored, the appropriate size; it fit him like a glove. We purchased two suits in each size, and everything needed to be aged to match. To amplify the look of each stage, we aged the other elements of the costume to heighten his progression. For stage A, we used rumpled dress shirts; for stage B, we steamed his dress shirt; for stage C, we did crisply ironed dress shirts. We also had two stages of shoe aging: very distressed and slightly worn.

Because this was a small show, our department worked together as a team, in the same workroom, creating the depth and intensity of the garments' aging. In this manner, we were able to understand the internal and external progression of the character as we created it in each stage of his costume. Before shooting began, I also walked the department through the stages of the costume, so that each member of the costume crew could understand the way they were meant to "play." There were three major stages of aging and tech but many sub-stages, reflected in subtle color shifts—a complex set of transitions. In the final film it all looks simple, and the aging and "teching" is largely imperceptible. The audience can feel it, but isn't hit over the head by it. This is subtle work, but it makes a world of difference in telling the story.

In order to design a plan for the aging of a character's costumes, you'll need to do the following:

1. Consider the nature of the character and his or her habits. Would the character be hard on his or her clothes? Is he or she naturally messy? Would the actor's body type naturally stretch out the clothing? Would the character's occupation be hard on the clothes? As discussed above, you can augment a character's qualities or eccentricities by the way you choose to distress a garment. (For tips on how to think about how people change the shape and surface of their garments, see the section below.)

2. Consider the impact of the setting on the garments. Look at the impact of season and weather on the characters. Look at how the time of day and the quality of the light will reveal the clothing. Look at how the colors of the set affect the way we perceive the colors of the clothing. (Costume designer Catherine Adair, in Conversation Three, is particularly revealing on this subject.) As you know, the colors that you use to age and distress clothing must always take into account the colors of the setting in which the clothing will work.

3. Consider the impact of the events of the script on the clothes. What damage or staining should be revealed on the clothing? How does the mood or the tone of the scene impact the state of the garments? For example, does the office atmosphere need very white, very starched shirts, or does it need sweaty, rumpled end-of-a-long-day shirts?

4. Consider the technical limits set by the fiber or construction technique of the garment you want to age. Aging and distressing techniques must vary according to what the garment is made out of, how many layers it has, how old or fragile it is. Bleaching, dyeing, and sanding techniques require natural fibers. Machine washing can ruin leather or wool garments and multi-layered garments like sport coats. (The conversation with Edwina Pellikka at the end of this part is particularly helpful in its suggestions for dyeing and distressing different kinds of materials.)

5. Consider whether you need to permanently or temporarily affect the look of the garments. Rental clothes, product placement clothes, and borrowed clothes can all demand the use of strictly temporary distressing techniques.

6. And, most importantly, consider the way the aged or distressed garment will look in close-up. Some materials (like spray paints, Nestle's hair sprays, and brushed-on acrylic paints) can sit on the surface of a garment and look phony on camera, unless they are very artfully applied. Softly layering colors, using materials that "work into" the fibers, and physically distressing the garments to soften them and wear down their surfaces can be most successful on camera.

As suggested above, aging (distressing) techniques fall into two primary categories, physical distressing and color manipulation.

Physical distressing. Physical distressing means changing the surface or shape of a garment by washing, starching, steaming, ironing, removing interfacings or padding, crumpling, stretching, sanding, filing, cutting, or tearing. Breaking down the fibers of a garment through multiple washings in a washing machine, or by sanding its surface, are examples of these techniques.

Clothing stretches and wears down according to how a body regularly fits and moves in it. Straining buttons, spreading bottoms, stuffing pockets all lead to shape distortion over the long haul. The repeated washing and drying of clothing frequently shrinks forms and fades colors. Fabric surfaces break down with repeated rubbing. To imitate these effects, costumers study how garments break down, stretch, and shrink with use or abuse; and they study how character qualities can seem to change as costume colors or shapes soften.

Color manipulation. Color manipulation includes processes like dyeing, painting, bleaching, staining, and adding dirt, when they are used to change the colors of garments in order to indicate age or distress. Some materials like dye, bleach, mineral oil, and wax are very "close-up friendly," because they work into the fiber and surface of a garment. Bleaching and dyeing garments artfully requires a thorough understanding of fibers, dye varieties, and construction techniques. For even the most experienced personnel, getting even, unblemished color change on a garment can still be a difficult task. Paint and dirt application techniques tend to work on all fibers, but can appear more obvious on camera unless they are artfully applied. (In Conversation Ten, Edwina Pellikka gives guidelines for a number of very valuable paint and dye techniques.)

Permanent versus impermanent techniques. In order to determine which techniques you may need to use on a garment, consider the following guidelines for permanent and impermanent techniques:

• For permanent aging/distressing: Fabric dyes (Rit, Tintex, Putnam, Pro-Chem, Aljo, to name only a few); fabric paints (Createx, Versatex, and Deka, among many); acrylic paints and most spray paints, which tend to have a permanent effect and will only partially disappear with repeated washing or dry cleaning. Leather dyes and colored wax products (shoe polish and Schmutz sticks) have a mixed reputation for leaving permanent effects, and often leave stains on high-contrast fabrics. Chlorine bleach and color remover permanently change garments and will, in fact, damage silks and antique goods irrevocably. Many physical distressing techniques—including fraying, sanding, cutting, ripping, shredding, stretching and the removal of padding or interfacing—change garments permanently.

- For impermanent aging and distressing: The least-permanent effects come with steaming, ironing, starching, rumpling or wrinkling, and appliquéing ripped-up pieces of fabric to make clothing look torn. Mineral oil, Reel Blood, Streaks & Tips, and dry Fullers Earth can generally be cleaned out of garments. Polyester fabrics and synthetics resist staining materials the best. When in doubt, pre-test the aging material on the inside of the garment, and have it cleaned, to be doubly sure that it won't permanently stain.

Laundering and pressing or steaming. Laundering and pressing or steaming are the most basic treatments used to prepare garments for shooting. Doing the laundry is often relegated to the lowliest crewmember, but in fact costumers need to be aware that many a glorious garment has been ruined by bad laundry practices. Ever had an "I-thought-it-was-acrylic-but-oops-it-was-wool" sweater go from large to extra small by mistakenly washing it in hot water? Garments made with wool, rayon, silk, or delicate interfacings may require delicate cleaning or specific laundry practices calculated to avoid shrinking, misshaping, or loss of dye. The "chemistry" of choosing the right products to clean the garments can be a tricky business. Bleach can cause a range of disasters: Dry bleaches can cause spotting if they are not liquefied before the garments go in the wash; chlorine bleach can cause silk garments to fall apart; liquid bleaches can spot garments if the bleach is poured on top of the wash load, rather than being added to the clothing in a mixed bath of bleach and water. Delicate embroidery, antique garments, sequined fabrics, and hand-painted or distressed garments can require careful dry cleaning or delicate hand washing with a broad range of cleaning supplies and techniques.

Even the simple ironing or steaming of garments can cause problems. For example, steaming cheap suits can cause fusible interfacings to warp (or "orange peel") into pebbly surfaces. Ironing some wool suits can cause them to shine on the surface. Pressing creases or hems in cotton or rayon shirt sleeves or pants can cause visible, semi-permanent, lines on the garments.

Aside from laundering the garments to keep them clean and comfortable for the actors, costumers may opt to "break down" garments to help them or appear "aged," by laundering them in strong laundry products that tend to leach the color or otherwise beat up the garment; for example, you can knock down the color of a brand-new shirt using the laundry product Biz. (For more information on the supplies and techniques used in dyeing or distressing garments, review the section above called "For laundering, dyeing, and distressing," in *Determining equipment and supply needs,* plus the material below, in "Preparing costumes for camera," and *Conversation Eleven: On Dyeing and Distressing Costumes for Film, with Edwina Pellikka,* at the end of this part.)

Preparing costumes for stuntwork. Some forms of stunt rigging (like flying harnesses) or padding can require garments to be specially rigged. Fire effects will require the garments to be treated by a licensed fireproofing company. Gunshot/squib effects require many garments to be sanded and prepared so that stage blood can easily come through the garments.

Production Tracking—"Bibles" and Set Books

Designers organize themselves according to their own manias. Most put together some form of a *design bible*—a master reference book—as a way of referencing key character and production information. Design bibles note sources, styles, and brands of important character pieces. The more well-organized and inclusive they are of design details, the more helpful they are. In very large productions, design bibles are key references for design assistants and supervisors when the designer is not handy. (See figs. 7.31 and 7.32 for the kind of detailed cost and source information filed in a design bible.)

The number of assistants a designer has, the scale of the production, the prep time scheduled for the production—all these factors are part of the information-organization equation. You may get away with one master design bible if your production is compact, with a manageable number of characters in a manageable number of changes, with few, if any, crowd scenes, and only rentals and purchase sources (no MO). If, on the other hand, your production has countless characters, takes place over a year or a decade, has vast crowd scenes, and uses made-to-order and craft sources to build these costumes, you may want to make up a separate bible for each MO and craft source, each containing all the information pertinent to the costumes being worked on by that source.

A *design bible* might be divided into the following sections:
- The script (that is, the *current version* of the script, with costume notations)
- Production office schedules and information, including:
- One-liner schedule
- Day-out-of-days schedule
- Daily shooting schedules and shooting-site information
- Crew and cast contact lists
- Production meeting notes
- Budget information including:
- Preliminary budget breakdown
- Revision memos
- Current master budget
- Purchase order and account source information needed for purchasing
- Costume breakdowns, including:
- Crossplot (optional)
- Scene costume breakdown
- Character summary breakdowns
- Extras summary breakdowns
- Individual character breakdowns (for principal and supporting players), divided into separate sections, and including:
- Actor's measurements
- Character breakdown
- Character bid sheets for different changes (see fig. 7.31)
- Copies of the sketches for MO work
- Made-to-order swatch sheets for MO work (see fig. 7.32)
- Character research and detail information

FIG. 7.31: CHARACTER BID SHEET FOR THE DESIGN BIBLE

CHARACTER _Sally_ ACTOR_____

CHANGE #_____

GARMENTS	SOURCE	BUY	MADE TO ORDER	RENT	ALTERATIONS	MULTIPLES	FINAL COST
						O	
Pink Dress w/ Applique	Stuntz Studio		$2400				$2400
UNDERGARMENTS							
White Bra w/ Pads	Palace Costumes			$10	1 @ $30		$40
Pale Pink Crinoline	Palace Costumes			$15	½ @ $30		$30
Seamed Natural Hose	e Costumes	$10				5	$50
Off White Fabric Pumps	Palace Costumes			$15			
OUTERWEAR							
ACCESSORIES							
White Gloves w/ Embroid	Palace Costumes			$5			$5
Pink Horsehair Hat	Costume Collection			$10			$10
Pink Pearls	Costume Collection			$15			$15
Pink Pearl Earrings	Costume Collection						
						TOTAL	$2550

A *supervisor's bible* might be divided into the following sections:

- The script (again, the *current version* of the script, with costume notations)
- Production office schedules and information, including:
- One-liner schedule
- Day-out-of-days schedule
- Call sheets and maps to locations (for section on call sheets, see Part 8, *Shoot,* "The call sheet")
- Crew and cast contact lists
- Production meeting notes
- Budget information, including:
- Preliminary budget breakdown
- Dated and revised budgets and revision memos
- Current master budget
- Purchase order and account source information needed for purchasing
- Made-to-order specs and bills
- Rental inventory lists and bills
- Petty cash reports and breakouts
- Cleaning account reports
- Purchase order and account tracking records
- Check requests
- Costume stock inventory list
- Crew payroll information

FIG. 7.32: MADE-TO-ORDER SWATCH SHEET FOR THE DESIGN BIBLE

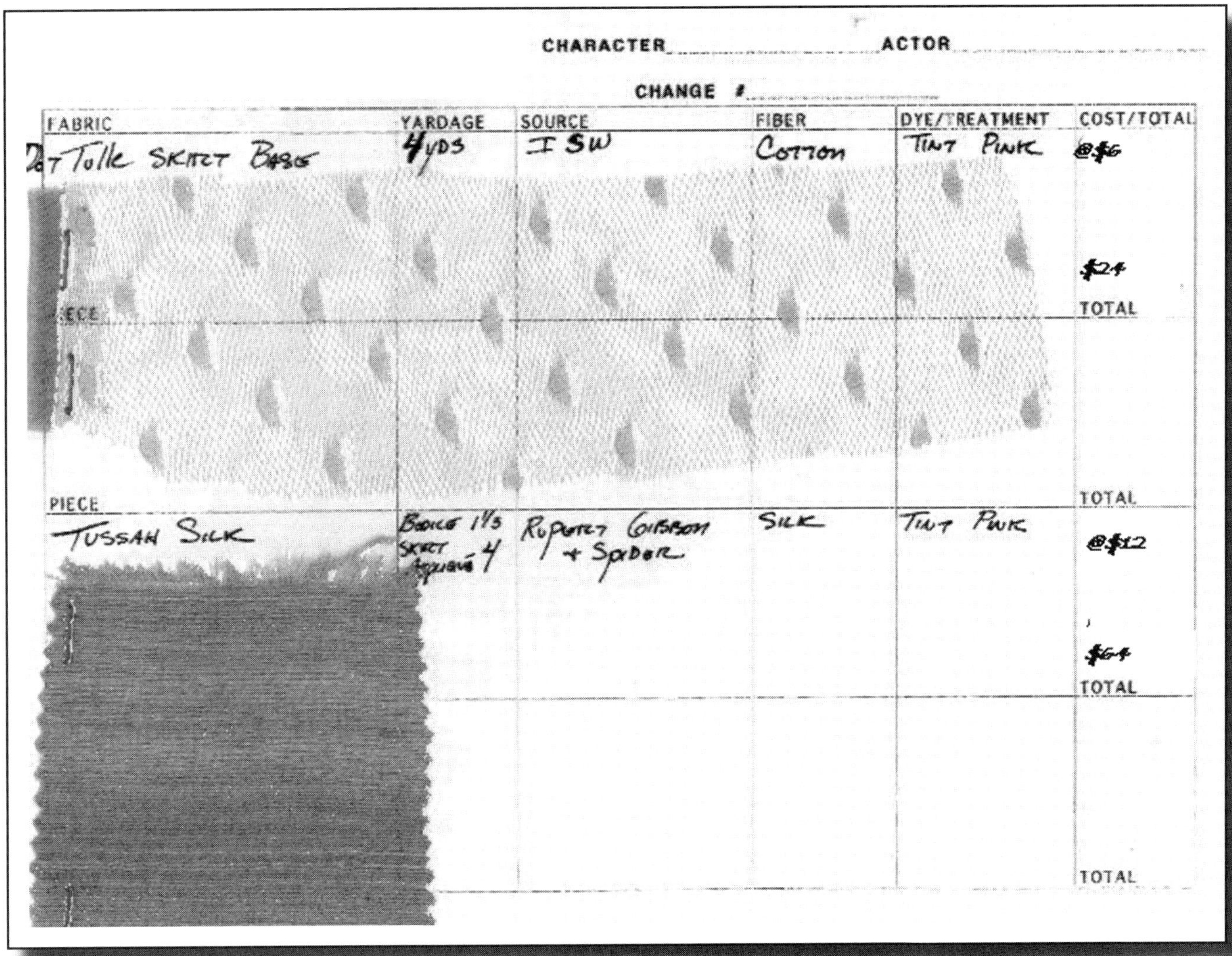

CHARACTER_____ ACTOR_____

CHANGE #_____

FABRIC	YARDAGE	SOURCE	FIBER	DYE/TREATMENT	COST/TOTAL
Dot Tulle Skirt Base	4 yds	I SW	Cotton	Tint Pink	@$6
					$24 TOTAL
PIECE					TOTAL
Tussah Silk	Bodice 1½ Skirt Approx 4	Rupert Gibson + Spider	Silk	Tint Pink	@$12
					$64 TOTAL
					TOTAL

- Costume breakdowns, including:
- Crossplot (optional)
- Scene costume breakdown
- Character summary breakdowns
- Extras summary breakdowns
- Individual character breakdowns
- Actors' measurements
- Character bid sheets

The set costumers' bible is called the *set book*. It gives a view of the whole show and becomes the storehouse for all continuity notations. (Large productions may require a separate extras set book, set up by scene sequence.)

The set book should contain the following:
- The current version of the script, and any and all revised pages
- Production office schedules, including:
- One-liner schedule
- Day-out-of-days schedule
- Daily call sheets
- Personnel contact information, including the crew and cast lists
- Costume crossplot (optional)

- Scene costume breakdown
- Character summaries/master charts
- Actors' measurements
- Character continuity sheets, with Polaroids of established costume changes
- Copies of any design guidelines for the scenes (sometimes, photocopies of approved fitting pictures will go in here)
- In a zippered pouch, supplies, including:
- White-out
- Sharpies
- Highlighters
- Scotch tape
- Adhesive tabs

All set books remain with the production company at the end of the shoot—motivation enough for making them look good (clearly organized, with neat, legible handwriting and neatly positioned photographs). This may be the last—and most lasting—impression you leave with producers, who may, or may not, hire you in the future. For more details on final set books, see Part 9, *Final Wrap*.

Final Preparations

As the first day of shooting approaches, final costume department preparations go into full swing. These preparations include:

1. Final contracting of the set costumers
2. Preparation of the set book and continuity pages
3. Final logo clearance checks, by production legal department and product placement offices, for costumes that have brand names on them
4. Final negotiations with the transportation department on wardrobe trucks and location logistics
5. Final gathering of stock from rental companies, purchasing and product placement sources, MO workrooms, craft studios, and alteration shops, dyers, distressers, and other custom-made work sources
6. Final tagging and bagging of changes
7. Final gathering of supplies and equipment for truck and on-set work
8. Walk-through of character changes and organization of general stock with costume designer, costume supervisor, home-base and set costumer(s), including notes on the ways in which garments are to be worn, and stages of distress.

Camera-ready costume changes: tagging and bagging systems

Once final work has been done and costumes are ready for camera, the contents of each change has to be recorded and organized. Lists, change tags, change-bagging systems, and costume and character breakdowns are the basic ways the costume staff keeps track of items assigned to principals, day players, and pre-fit extras. Ultimately, each changes should be tagged, and bagged, if possible, in the following manner:

- *Principal garments* should be grouped by change number and hung as a unit. Jewelry will be put in a zip-lock baggie; additional accessories, like ties, suspenders, handkerchiefs, etc., will also be bagged together, and hung with the rest of the outfit. Shoes and hats may be boxed or bagged, depending on the nature of your storage space. The clothing and bag(s) of accessories will then be enclosed in a clear plastic garment bag (available through display houses and catalogues).

A manila *character change tag*, which details the contents of the change and has a picture from the fitting stapled to it, gets attached to the garment bag. In addition to the master character change tag, a cloth label with the character's name and change number may need to be stitched on the inside of garments, for identification after cleaning, as noted above.

- *Extras' garments* are grouped together in the same fashion as principals' changes. Whether these changes are bagged or stored in boxes depends on the size of your costume budget. If proper garment bags are not affordable for anything but principals, accessories can be bagged together (as opposed to in separate zip-lock baggies for jewelry and other kinds of accessories) and hung on one of the hangers that makes up the actor's change. (Some costumers from the "old school," especially those trained at studio rental facilities, prefer to pin baggies of accessories and other non-hanger items on strings looped over the hanger hook; this allows the baggie to hang closer to the bottom of the gar-

The bagged and tagged change— the stuff that prep is made of.

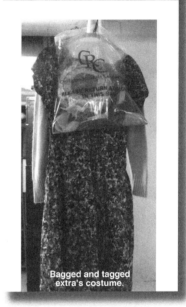

Bagged and tagged extra's costume.

ment bag, where items aren't getting squashed and taking up precious rack space). The change is then tagged, on the upper right shoulder of the change unit. Tags will list the extra's name, and, if assigned, a number.

Changes are then hung sequentially, in scene units.

> I was working on the first *Star Trek* movie. The Vulcan gal had a white wool crepe uniform blouse that was being made in multiple copies. We had a publicity photo shoot before filming started that needed this girl in that outfit. When I went to get it for the photo shoot, the shop, which was in the middle of assembling the multiples, had only one precious copy that was finished. The shoot was very close by, so I whisked the outfit out of the shop just as it was—no time for a garment bag. As I hand-carried the outfit across the muddy gutter at the site, the outfit slipped off the hanger and fell on the ground. No back-ups. No time. A real nightmare. It's a painful way to learn the value of a garment bag. *(Buffy Snyder, costume designer, costume supervisor, and former president of Motion Picture Costumers Union Local 705)*

Costume supervisor-set costumer collaboration

The costume supervisor and the set costumer collaborate on all on-set wardrobe planning. The purchase of supplies, the rental of equipment, and the arrangement of the truck stock are issues that these two should sort out together. Together they also determine cleaning and maintenance policies and the setup for "crunch" days. Shortly before the first day of principal photography, the costume supervisor and all set costume personnel, including the "truck" supervisor (if there is one), must reach an agreement about the department's "rules of the road," among them, how stock will be arranged at home base and on the truck, the style of wardrobe continuity notation, and the rules of comportment on the set. (Although these rules of comportment vary from supervisor to supervisor, it's a sure bet that they include the following: (1) never ever be late, (2) no gossip in the department, and (3) do whatever you can to help.)

The wardrobe truck supervisor (otherwise, the costume supervisor) is responsible for determining the way the truck will be organized and for acquainting the set crew, as well as the costume designer and the design assistant(s), with that system. In the press of principal photography, all department personnel may be called on to improvise costuming from the truck for just-cast day players, featured extras, and background players.

Orienting the set crew to the design

To make sure that the look of the costumes is "right" on screen, the costume designer must establish a close collaborative relationship with the costume supervisor, especially the supervisor who works the truck. The on-truck costume supervisor and the set costumers prep the wardrobe, "set" the dressing rooms, and make sure the actors are wearing their costumes according to the designer's wishes. As a result, it is vital that the designer and the truck supervisor understand one another. Before shooting begins, preferably before costumes leave home base, the costume designer should do a "walk-through" (an examination of each rack of featured players' changes, costume by costume) with the supervisor. In the walk-through, the designer needs to describe not only what makes up each change, but the way in which each change should be worn by the actor (for example, shirt's top three buttons undone, collar up, sleeves rolled up to just below the elbow, shirt tails out, neckchain outside the T-shirt) and stages of distress. The supervisor needs to make sure that the set costumers are clear on the designer's wishes, since ultimately it is the set costumer who must do what she or he can to make sure that the actors carry out the designer's wishes once cameras roll.

Making sure that the crew understands before shooting begins how the designer wants things to look goes a long way toward actually getting things to look this way on screen. Unless you can educate your crew in the correct design approach to a scene, the fast and furious demands of on-set styling for a large extras call can lead to design choices that the designer hates. This can lead to major "bad blood" between the designer and the on-set crew—especially when mistakes are discovered by the designer in dailies or at the screening, when it's too late to correct them.

Truck Prep

Rarely is there enough storage space in the wardrobe trailer to handle all of the stock needed for a shoot. As a result, throughout the shoot, stock will be traded out between home base and the wardrobe trailer. As character changes are no longer required on set, they will be tagged, bagged, and held at the home base, for possible re-shoots. A percentage of the general stock must be available on set, for walk-in styling; on shoots with no pre-fit extras, this will be a high percentage. Because storage space on the trailer is always at a premium, on-truck priority will go to principals' wardrobe (in case of last-minute shooting schedule changes). Extras stock can be traded out on a weekly basis.

Truck styles

Films with major budgets provide wardrobe trailers for both principals' and extras' wardrobe, if such an arrangement is necessary. (Take a look at the three diagrams of Star Waggons' top-of-the-line wardrobe trailers in figs. 7.33 and 7.34.) Unfortunately, many costumers do not work on such well-provisioned productions. Many productions provide a single wardrobe trailer, which must house wardrobe for principals, day players, pre-fit extras' wardrobe, and general wardrobe stock. (If you're lucky, a cube truck or a converted moving van may be provided if the show is heavy on pre-fit extras.) It is not uncommon on low-budget projects to be consigned to working in a cube truck outfitted with storage racks. In fact, there are companies that specialize in refitting rental trucks. (Truck Guts, in Los Angeles, is one such company.) On super-low-budget productions, costumers may be allotted nothing more than a dressing room in the "honeywagon" (a trailer truck with lavatories and multiple dressing rooms the size of a walk-in closet). I (HC) worked on a project for Showtime that gave the costume department one cubicle in the honeywagon. To complicate matters, it was only available when the actor assigned to it wasn't working. In the most miserable of circumstances, you may be working out of the back of your car.

Any wardrobe vehicle will test your abilities to adapt, organize, improvise; each truck requires its own solutions for storage and organization. However, most official wardrobe trucks do share a few things in common:

• A counter area for a mini-office/workroom arrangement, where the supervisor can set up a laptop computer and the crew can set up a sewing machine
• Lockable storage cabinets
• Overhead and under-counter storage areas and drawers, for supplies
• Rack storage, with lock-down features, to keep stock from swinging off the racks during transport (fig. 7.35)

Packing the wardrobe truck

Packing a wardrobe truck is a science that requires the costume supervisor and her staff to (1) anticipate the needs of the weekly shooting schedule, including costumes,

FIG. 7.33

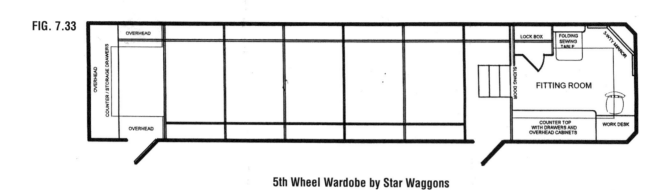

5th Wheel Wardobe by Star Waggons

FIG. 7.34

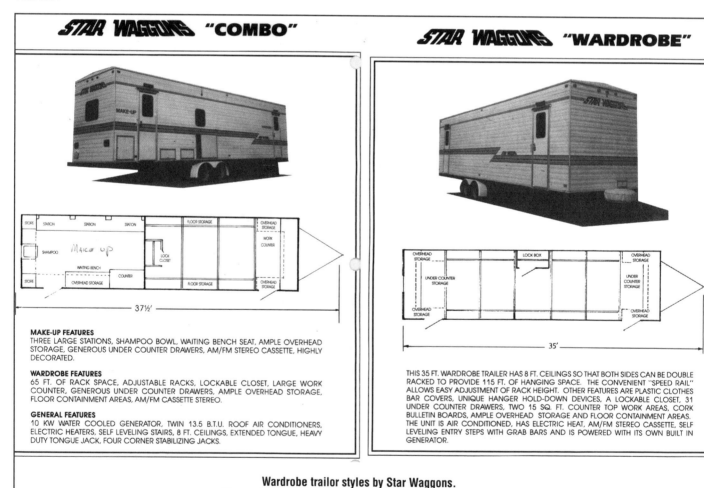

STAR WAGGONS "COMBO"

STAR WAGGONS "WARDROBE"

MAKE-UP FEATURES
THREE LARGE STATIONS, SHAMPOO BOWL, WAITING BENCH SEAT, AMPLE OVERHEAD STORAGE, GENEROUS UNDER COUNTER DRAWERS, AM/FM STEREO CASSETTE, HIGHLY DECORATED.

WARDROBE FEATURES
65 FT. OF RACK SPACE, ADJUSTABLE RACKS, LOCKABLE CLOSET, LARGE WORK COUNTER, GENEROUS UNDER COUNTER DRAWERS, AMPLE OVERHEAD STORAGE, FLOOR CONTAINMENT AREAS, AM/FM CASSETTE STEREO.

GENERAL FEATURES
10 KW WATER COOLED GENERATOR, TWIN 13.5 B.T.U. ROOF AIR CONDITIONERS, ELECTRIC HEATERS, SELF LEVELING STAIRS, 8 FT. CEILINGS, EXTENDED TONGUE, HEAVY DUTY TONGUE JACK, FOUR CORNER STABILIZING JACKS.

THIS 35 FT. WARDROBE TRAILER HAS 8 FT. CEILINGS SO THAT BOTH SIDES CAN BE DOUBLE RACKED TO PROVIDE 115 FT. OF HANGING SPACE. THE CONVENIENT "SPEED RAIL" ALLOWS EASY ADJUSTMENT OF RACK HEIGHT. OTHER FEATURES ARE PLASTIC CLOTHES BAR COVERS, UNIQUE HANGER HOLD-DOWN DEVICES, A LOCKABLE CLOSET, 31 UNDER COUNTER DRAWERS, TWO 15 SQ. FT. COUNTER TOP WORK AREAS, CORK BULLETIN BOARDS, AMPLE OVERHEAD STORAGE AND FLOOR CONTAINMENT AREAS. THE UNIT IS AIR CONDITIONED, HAS ELECTRIC HEAT, AM/FM STEREO CASSETTE, SELF LEVELING ENTRY STEPS WITH GRAB BARS AND IS POWERED WITH ITS OWN BUILT IN GENERATOR.

Wardrobe trailor styles by Star Waggons.
(Photographs, diagrams, and descriptions by permission of Lyle Waggoner)

FIG. 7.35

Lock-down pipes

TYPICAL WARDROBE COMBO-TRAILER

Lock-down drawers

equipment, and supplies; (2) discover the most efficient arrangement of costumes, equipment, and supplies for daily use and maintenance; and (3) arrange these elements to minimize loss and damage.

Needs for the weekly shooting schedule include:

- All character changes needed, including "cover set" changes for rainy days
- Emergency stock, for styling a broad size range of walk-in casting
- All supplies that are likely to be consumed in a week, and sufficient general emergency supplies
- All the equipment and emergency equipment that is likely to be needed during the week

The most efficient arrangement of costumes, equipment, and supplies for daily use and maintenance would provide the following:

- *Quick access to steamers, irons, and ironing boards, and all the costume stock that will be used at the start of each shooting day.* Have you ever camped? Your ability to get to the flashlight *before* you unpack the tent, the stove, and the ice chest makes a critical difference when you're standing in the pouring rain. Likewise, your ability to get the wardrobe distributed quickly while maintaining access to equipment needed for steaming and ironing is critical at the beginning of—indeed throughout—the shooting day.
- *Quick access to character changes and general stock.* Organize character changes and stock on the truck to mirror the organization at home base—a logical, familiar ordering of garments and accessories, for easy locating. Adaptation to the available truck space is, however, almost always necessary. Moving wardrobe from home base to truck can be like moving from a three-bedroom apartment to a studio: You get really good at solving storage problems. How the stock is "unpacked" for the day's work must be choreographed for efficiency. To speed setup each day, post copies of script pages, wardrobe breakdowns, and charts

for the principal characters, arranged by scene or by character. A setup rack of next-day changes, assembled before wrap the day before, can also hasten each morning's setup.

- *Designated rack space for garments to be cleaned and garments to be returned.* Lists of items out for laundry and dry cleaning, with dates, descriptions, and stock location are imperative for garment tracking.

- *Quick access to supplies.* Labeling drawers, cabinet doors, storage bins, and boxes can help immensely. It is very important that supplies used most often, and in emergency situations, be most easily accessible.

- *Designated work areas.* Plan carefully for daily work areas: a sewing area for minor alterations and quick repairs; an area for daily note-taking and other paperwork; an area for tag storage; an area for steaming and ironing. Of course, space is at a premium on the truck, and often, when weather permits, some of these activities end up outside the trailer. (Be sure you've stocked doormats, ground clothes, plastic tarps, and bungee cords.)

- *Assign storage areas for the normal accoutrements of each shoot day—places for the costume crew to stash personal gear, lock handbags, and leave kits.* This is an important means of organizing the trailer—and your crew.

Any arrangement of garments, equipment, and supplies that minimizes loss and damage will incorporate the following:

- *The ability to lock the wardrobe trailer.* When no official costume personnel are present on the truck, the truck should be locked. Only costume personnel and the transportation department should have keys. Star clothing and high-priced stock make security critical. In general, star wardrobe is placed where it can't be seen easily; lockable storage for jewelry, furs, and other expensive or one-of-a-kind items is mandatory. Uniforms can also require special security measures.

- *The means to keep the elements from damaging wardrobe.* Anticipate, among other things, mud and rain from open wardrobe trailer doorways and the effects of sun, which can fade unstable dye colors.

- *Enough space and ventilation.* Make sure that there is enough space on the racks and in cabinets, bins, and boxes to prevent clothing and hats from getting crushed. Make sure there's enough ventilation to keep to a minimum the sometimes toxic fumes from dry-cleaned garments and aged goods and supplies, and to keep shoes and other items damp from perspiration from molding.

Before the Shoot Begins: A Word on Setting the Tone

Because other departments on a production are often insensitive to the difficulties of costume work, the costume team must guard against feelings of martyrdom in their own ranks. In the depths of production craziness, you need to keep your eyes on the prize: a handsome design, a positive process. Good designer/supervisor teams counteract tension and mania by being protective of each member of the department, and by putting the most positive spin on the most difficult problems. Like many things in life, clear communication skills keep things moving efficiently. And simple acts of kindness—lavishing praise when even a mundane task is done well, working each day to keep things upbeat—go a long way toward making a team perform smoothly. A generous attitude, and humor, can energize a crew—and build lifelong professional relationships.

I (HC) learned the value of simple acts of kindness from costume supervisor Jennifer Barrett, while working together on a "production from hell." We worked in appalling conditions, with several insensitive types. Stupid planning, wasted time, stifling heat, and other conditions promoted real misery. But Jennifer got us through. She had the gift of genuine praise—not just the ability to say thank you, but a real eye for what people were going through. The knowledge that hard, thankless work was being noticed and appreciated was an incredible gift. It energized the crew. To get the best performance from a costume crew, a department's leadership must support, and inspire, the crew. In the midst of production purgatory, you must fan the spark of humanity.

> If you talk to ten designers and ten supervisors, each will have a slightly different take on how she makes the collaboration work. Because it is a marriage—a working marriage. (You are spending more hours with these people than you are with your own family.) They are seeing you at your most vulnerable, your most stressed, your most challenged, your most exhausted. They are seeing you at the most obscure hours of the day and night, and they are probably seeing you sleep-deprived. So you have to know that the team is solid, so that you can proceed.
>
> I say to my crews, "I need us to be a cohesive group so that we can deal with all the other challenges." If you've got challenges within your own "home," your own department, then dealing with all the other challenges that come your way is twice as hard. *(Catherine Adair, costume designer)*

Conversation Seven:

On the Role of Design Assistants, with Marcy Froehlich

Marcy Froehlich works as a costume designer on features, among them, *The Unknown Cyclist* (1997), *Unbowed* (1999), and television series (fig. 7.36). She also works as assistant designer on films, including *Road to Perdition* (2002) and *American Beauty* (1999). She co-authored *Shopping LA: The Insiders' Sourcebook for Film & Fashion*.

In general, is it difficult for a costume designer to hire a design assistant?

Yes, it can be, on films. I know of other design assistants who have had to be fought for by the designer. I think sometimes producers don't understand what it is a design assistant does that a costumer can't do. A lot of it has to do with educating producers and the general work force about why an assistant is so important. I think there is so much value in having another design eye on the show. The designer can't be everywhere. When the designer couldn't get to the fittings, I did fittings for her. I had to be the design eye. I'd bring pictures back, and maybe she'd make a few changes. The advantage was, there was someone at the fitting who was from the same kind of background—someone with the same knowledge of period costume, the same kind of research skills, and the eye of a designer. There are some designers who don't use assistants that much. A lot of the people who use assistants here [in L.A.] were New York designers who came from a theatre background.

Is your work exclusively prep-related, or are you working on the set as well?

I would say more of my work is done in prep. You can do "set tweaking," as I call it. You can dress extras. When they throw a new extra at you that you haven't pre-fit, you can do the fit-

FIG. 7.36

Unbowed produced by Filmanthropic. Designs by Marcy Froehlich.

Mark Abbott and Vincent McLean — Michelle Thomas

tings and you can pull together an outfit. I will often help the designer establish the particular costumes for a big scene, a scene for which we've been doing custom-made things. Once the costumes are all established, I'll go away, because the costumers know what the look is supposed to be. I'll go away and help the designer to prepare for the next big scene.

Often, I will be hired to stay until all the costumes are established, and then I will be let go (anywhere from a week to three or four weeks before the end of a production). But I'll be brought on right at the beginning, so that I can help prep. Once all the costumes are established and the costumers know what the look is supposed to be, producers usually like to dismiss the assistant.

Wasn't the concern of the producers on your last film that if they hired a design assistant, they wouldn't have the budget for a set person?

That's what they were concerned about. But the designer was concerned about getting the show done, and having someone able to prep the scenes that were coming up. I have bought fabric and pulled costumes and done that sort of thing, to keep us on time. In some cases, a costumer could do that, but a costumer is someone with a different approach.

I know you're very experienced with breakdowns and budgeting, and you're a whiz at resources. As an assistant designer, your background—working with made-to-order shops on Broadway—must also be very helpful. Not all designers understand costume construction.

I think it's essential. Some designers may not agree, but I think it's essential. I've had times when the person I'm working with doesn't know how to figure out a particular garment, so I've had to figure it out. And knowing how to fit a garment has given me a lot more confidence in fittings.

Whether it is film or theater, I have found that one thing that is challenging about being the assistant designer is that a shop will ask you questions about something that you don't always know the answer to—or that you can't answer decisively. It's tough, because they want the real and final answer, and you don't always have enough authority to give that answer. It's hard to be caught in the middle, sometimes. I think it's a bit of a dance, how you mesh with a designer. Especially if you are working with someone new and you don't know them that well, either personally or style-wise. You have to get to know what they might choose. After you know them for a while, then you have a better idea of whether they would choose this over that; but in the first few weeks, it might be a little bit of a challenge to figure out what they are doing.

A bit of your own taste comes into play, too. It always does if you are swatching. I will always swatch what I think they want, and then I'll swatch things that I think are cool. And often, those things that I think are cool will be chosen just because they've hired me for my design eye, and I might bring something totally fresh to the project. I've also had designers say, "What did you bring that back for?" You're trying to figure out what they want, but you can't possibly know all the time, so there is a bit of tentativeness involved in being an assistant designer. Sometimes I'm not as bold in my choices because I'm trying to think, "What is it that *they* want?" as opposed to, "What do *I* want?"

Conversation Eight:

On Working with Actors, with Pat Welch

Costume designer Pat Welch has designed for seven different television series, including *L.A. Law*. She garnered an Emmy nomination in 1988 for her work on the sitcom *Frank's Place*.

Even in television, you have to deal with major star power on a regular basis. How do you work with stars?

I've always made the assumption that when a star comes in for a fitting, he or she realizes that I'm not their personal shopper. I am here to do a character in a script, not the actor's personal-appearance clothes, or what the actor wears on the weekend. Together, we will create a "closet" for a character that will work for the actor. And "knock wood," I've never had a problem. Some actors don't want to wear certain colors, and I will honor that; that's not a problem, unless it's in the script. But I also skew the rack. First, I do a pre-show with the producer. If there is anything on the rack that he is not in favor of and wants to lose, it goes. I always put something on the rack for the producer to get rid of, and for the actor to get rid of—something for them to throw out so that they feel empowered. I really try to work very closely with them, because I can't afford to have an actor get on set and say, "I really hate what I have on."

Do you bring the director into the fittings with the star?

I prefer to deal with the actor, one on one, with the exception of the cutter-fitter and an assistant: "Many chefs spoil the soup." If you can control the number of "chefs" from the start, you are better off. I always try to lay out basic ground rules before we go into a fitting; otherwise, you can just have a runaway fitting, which lasts for hours. And I'm sure you've heard the horror stories of "angst for hours" over a quarter-inch cuff. I try to have a basic outline of where we can go, how far we can move laterally within the framework that's been given to me by the producer and director.

Are you shooting for one fitting, and one fitting only, because you have no other choice?

Most of the time, yes. Usually, I can get between six and eight changes out of an actor before he starts to fatigue. When an actor starts to get tired, it's best just to say, "I think we've got a great start. There are some things that I need to get that we talked about, so let's do a second fitting." But to actually do a second fitting is a rarity. It's usually one fitting, then on to the set.

Can you try something on an actor when you are actually on the set?

Once shooting starts, it's difficult. The set is the domain of the director and the AD. They are very careful in scheduling time, because if they do run into overtime, there are penalties to be paid. So an AD won't call the actors in too early, or keep them too late. A lot of elements enter the picture once you are on the set.

I've heard designers talk about the fact that occasionally an actor will not be willing to take a fitting, or may not be available for a fitting before shooting. Have you run into that?

I have on occasion, and at that point, I will go to the AD and say, "Listen, we didn't get a chance to do a fitting. I'll have a tailor on the set at six; would you please call the actor in early?" And we can usually pull it together.

You can only shoot one sequence at a time. You can only shoot one costume at a time. If I'm in trouble, you only get to shoot from the waist up. All the departments understand that. Sooner or later, every department is going to get into trouble. I can always slide over the DP and say, "Gee, that camera's sounding kind of funny, don't you think? Can you give me five minutes, and you have a look at the gate?" And he'll go, "Oh, sure."

It would be an incredibly pressured environment if every single actor had to walk straight into his clothes and have them be faultless and perfect every time.

It's not anything less than what the actor expects.

When fitting time is at such a premium, and speed and efficiency are necessities, how do you get accurate fitting information on an actor?

You can pick up a lot by the way an actor gives you sizes. If an actress gives me a junior size—"Oh, I'm a 5-7"—I'll know that she is not used to wearing expensive clothes. That's a real tip-off. Really expensive clothes run 4, 6, 8, and 10, and are cut a little more generously. If she's a 7-9, you are going to be able to get away with a six, or an eight, so you are going to bring those sizes to the fitting.

Often, when I am in a fitting, I can spot a chubby child within the actress, and it's very interesting. This woman who is 5'6", 108 pounds, is sort of squinting at herself in the mirror, not quite sure, very anxious; I will say, "Were you a chubby child?" I've had several actresses say, "Yes, how did you know?" And I say, "I could tell by the way you were looking at yourself." A lot of actors have no sense of self. I don't even attempt to get accurate measurements from them. Just give me vague numbers. "I'm a 6, 8; I'm a 7½, 8 shoe; pantyhose, I'm a B/C." This is a chubby child. Right away, I know this is a chubby child. She has no concept of what size she is. I usually get bra sizes, which is a big help. I would rather have somebody say, "I am a 36B," than, "My measurements are 36-24-36," because "36" is a range.

And on the guy side, all actors seem to think they've got the inseam of John Wayne. Inevitably, "I'm a 34 inseam." And I'll say, "Honey, get out a tape measure." Thirty-four inches, that's a lot of inches! That's the John Wayne syndrome.

You just bring in a range of sizes. But I try to control that range. I will not bring in an entire department store to a fitting. If I am doing three changes, I'll bring in five changes. And if somebody is really vague, I'll know that maybe there are some issues here. Maybe she is a little heavy around the hips, and I'll bring in some pleated pants. Let's not do little crop tops on her. Let's not do a bikini. Let's go for the one-piece, with maybe a wrap. So you hedge your bets; you kind of get used to it, talking to them on the phone. So much of our business, size-wise, is done on the telephone. It is rare that you will get accurate information for a fitting.

Can you get measurements from an actor's agent?

Oh, that's scary. Too much information that's out of date.

Do you see any body trends in the industry?

Television is going through a phase now with the "no female body shape on TV" phase.

Little skinny girls, remarkably little skinny girls. I have never seen more size twos, size threes, and size fours than I've seen in L.A. malls.

Did you overlook the size 0 racks? They're in all the stores now. Size 0 jeans.

Someone with a halfway normal body must be just cowed by all that.

I think an actor has to have a true center of strength. Unfortunately for actors, what makes them actors is that uncertainty, which brings the greatness to their talent. It can destroy an actress.

I had an actress who came to a fitting just recently, and she had had a costume designer tell her that she was fat and that she would never work in TV. Now, this is a woman who makes a very good living in TV. And she is a size 10. This is not an obese woman, but she was pretty shaky about the fitting until I reassured her. And it took a lot of reassuring. I think it can be very demoralizing.

Actors are in an incredibly vulnerable position, and their job is to be sensitive on camera, to *be* vulnerable.

Exactly. And that's what comes through on film. That's what the camera loves, that vulnerability, so it's a real yin-yang situation. Hopefully an actor is centered enough outside of her acting career to have that come through the acting part.

A costume designer has to be sensitive with the actors.

I try to make them believe that they are the ones who have the final say. If they really hate a garment, an item, a piece, I'll throw it out. I will not argue. Because I'd rather lose the battle in the dressing room than on the set.

Do you research an actor's tastes in clothing?

I try to have an in-depth telephone conversation with the actor. I have a long list of questions that I go through: What do you like? What won't you wear? When you open your closet door, what am I going to see—black and white, color? What colors to you prefer? What sort of necklines do you like? Do you like long sleeves, short sleeves? Can your upper arms pass the "wing test?" Usually, nobody over the age of twenty-two says "yes." I just try to sound them out, and then I always end up by saying, "Here is my phone number; if you have any questions, or if you think of anything, please call me."

And then, I have food at the fitting. Feed them.

In a comfortable space. I feel for actors in an improvised fitting room—a dark living room; a public restroom; a cubbyhole out of the way.

But that's the wonderful side of working with actors, that you can tap in to that child-like fantasy of, "Isn't this great? Isn't this wonderful? You are getting ready to play this part, and we are standing in this toilet stall in a honeywagon. You are standing on the toilet seat, and I am on my knees, doing the hem. And you just hope the toilet has a lid on it, so the actor can stand on the lid. Otherwise, it's real tight.

Have you seen actors' attitudes change in the last ten years?

No. I've worked with a lot of the great and the near-great, the on-the-way-down and the up-and-coming. I think this is really a magical industry that we work in. I think that we all go home at night and laugh and say, "Oh my god, look what we get to do."

Conversation Nine:

Prepping on Distant Locations, with Eduardo Castro

Eduardo Castro is the costume designer of the feature films *Nailed, City of Industry, Kama Sutra: A Tale of Love,* and *The Perez Family,* among others (figs. 1.11, 2.1, C.2). He has also designed for television, including the series *Miami Vice* and *Judging Amy.*

Eduardo, you've designed many commercials and features that have shot outside the United States. The feature film *Kama Sutra*, which prepped and shot in India, presented special problems. Will you describe your experiences? How did the project come to you?

I had gotten a call to do a commercial in Rome, with Sean Connery, for Italian Honda. Money was no issue there. Whatever we needed for Mr. Connery was fine. I selected the clothes in the States (mostly Armani and Donna Karen), then I went to London, to do the fittings and the alterations. We were two weeks in Rome. I fly back from Rome on a Tuesday. I get a call on Wednesday from this producer I worked with before who said,

"We're in trouble. Can you be in Bombay on Sunday?" That was for *Kama Sutra*. I ended up replacing a designer. I arrived in Bombay on Sunday—well, Monday morning, actually. We had two and a half weeks before shooting, and I had to come up with a total of two thousand costumes for the film.

My God, what did you do?

I just said, "What do we shoot first?" And the next seven days, I was on a plane. I was either in Delhi or Bombay or Jaipur or Khajuraho, or in Rajastan somewhere, gathering jewelry, fabrics, shoes in each place. We had a very healthy crew. I had inherited this crew from this other designer, and I was allowed to bring one person from the United States, so I brought my assistant. There was a network already built up for this other designer. She had been there for two and a half, almost three months and she just had designer's block. She just couldn't do it. A great visionary, she knew what she wanted; she just didn't know how to achieve it. I just had to walk in and do it. And so I came in, and the only reason I accepted the position was that I knew that everything in India was there. It had to be, because that's where everything is made. I said, "Just let India do it."

The production was based in Bombay, but the principal costumes were made in Delhi. Finding the fabrics was easy. The hardest part was fine-tuning our work ethics and work standards to some of the peasant crew. They don't believe in pinning and they don't believe in matching up things. They don't work the way we do.

My third day there, after my first fitting with the two principal girls, I was in a bit of a panic, and the production manager was on my back to present them with a budget. I said, "I have no idea of what things cost here. I don't know where we're going." I had never been to India before, so I said, "We will proceed responsibly. We will proceed with caution. I have to iron out all of these problems. Let's get the first week done, and after that we'll figure out where we're going."

***Kama Sutra* is a film entirely about ethnic dress. All those rules about how it's wrapped the right way.**

Exactly. There were many, many things we learned, and I learned very, very quickly. There were things I wished I had incorporated sooner in the film. We bastardized so much of it. But it was actually okay to do so—it ended up looking better. For example, my assistant, Loveleen, who's very talented, and very, very good—kept saying to me, "You can't use any paisleys because they weren't in the Mogul period of the sixteenth century." I said, "Who's going to know? This is also a very frothy adult fairy tale. I don't think it really matters. We really have to use these fabrics." I let it slide.

There must have been so many things to adjust to.

I had to send to London for steamers, because they don't have steamers there. There was a sequence where I wanted a very limp look. I had to have a steamer.

I remember we were preparing these two girl-principals. I'm not the world's greatest patternmaker, but I can solve certain problems on a mannequin. The Indian crew didn't work that way. I said, "Isn't there any place here with a mannequin?" "No." So I had a mannequin FedExed, from Los Angeles.

This gets better. In the first fitting I had with the two lead women, we had the problem that they were very, very full-busted, and they needed support. Well, try and find a bra in Bombay! It's not the easiest thing. The bras there are all heavily structured, and they show through the very delicate clothes we were making. They don't have the Donna Karan seamless under-wire bra. So I put a call into Neiman Marcus. I had called Neiman Marcus two weeks before, from Rome, to send me a Giorgio Armani suit for Sean Connery, because they didn't have a 46L in Rome. So I called, and they said, "Are you in Rome?" "No, I'm not, I'm in Bombay, and I need some bras." They arrived, and they were perfect, and we proceeded. You know, it ended up saving us money, and a headache. Time is money. People don't understand that time is money. If it costs you whatever it costs in terms of FedExing and customs, it was still better than the two days it would cost me trying to search for it in Jaipur or Bombay or wherever.

We ended up preparing that movie every single day. I had one day off the whole time. Every single day, we prepped, we prepped, we prepped. I think it was eight or nine weeks of shooting. It was very, very tough. At one point, I kept going to Delhi every five or six days and gathering up thousands of meters of fabric, because we kept running out of fabric. In the middle of production, we couldn't handle it—we needed another person. I got a second Los Angeles-based person, and I sent her to Delhi. I sent her and the production assistant to Delhi, to come back with seven thousand meters of fabric, which is like eleven thousand yards of fabric. I sent her to the "Old Delhi" flea market. It's miles and miles of little booths and bazaars. I said, "I need five hundred pairs of shoes." So they ordered five hundred pairs of shoes from this man. They went back a week later and they were all done. They came back with trunks of things. It was madness, but it continued throughout the whole show.

You have to realize, you're dealing with a third-world country, where things are so difficult. The easiest things are hard; the hardest things are easy. It's easy to *make* something, but try and find a safety pin or paper! We had three-ring binders brought in. People don't organize at all. No country has three-ring binders! I did a film in Argentina and we had the same problem: no three-ring binders. At least they had washing machines. We didn't have washing machines in India. We had the river and washer boys called *dobis*.

My best story from India: I have this whole group of courtesans to do, and they're supposed to be in beautiful fabrics. I'm at the end of my rope. It's Friday. I leave for Delhi. The Delhi flight is late by four hours. I miss the stores. My plane the next day is a one-o'clock-in-the-afternoon flight. The stores open at about 11:00. I get to the store at about 11:00, and I buy. I buy so much fabric that I had to take the fabric and leave an assistant there to count the money, because you have to count the money. I tore off for the airport with another five thousand meters of fabric. I got to the airport, got the flight, and had a fitting with all the courtesans that afternoon at five. They shot Monday morning. It was absolutely hellish. So, that was 1995, my most colorful year.

Conversation Ten:

On the Prep Process in Episodic Television, with Barbara Inglehart

Barbara Inglehart is a costume designer for feature films, television series, music videos (fig. 7.37), and commercials, in addition to being co-author of the book *Shopping LA: The Insiders' Sourcebook for Film & Fashion.* In the following conversation, she talks about the prep process on an episodic series, the most demanding work routine in the business.

You were the costume designer on an episodic series that presented the costume department with even more than the usual number of challenges. Can you tell us what they were and how you met them?

The basic premise of the series, a science-fiction TV show called *Sliders*, was that, in each episode, four lead characters "slide" to a different earth—a parallel earth, with a slightly different history than our Earth. Each parallel Earth, hence each episode, had a slightly different look. In each episode, there were three groups I had to design for: the four principal characters, the day-player characters, and the characters that populate the world of the episode. Each lead had a distinctive look, which was consistent from episode to episode.

One of my great challenges was designing for the wide range of skin tones among the principal actors. One actor was a very dark-skinned black man, one was a very fair-skinned black woman, one male had olive skin with dark hair, and one was a porcelain-skinned female, whose hair color changed from reddish to dark brown. The color palettes that I used not only had to look good on each of the actors individually, but had to work as a whole. The looks for the day-player characters were dictated by the demands of the script and the physique of the actor. I tried to give each world a unique look that complimented the storyline.

How does the prep period develop for a series? As I understand it, you actually took over *Sliders* when there was a major shift in the cast.

Two of our four principal characters were replaced at the beginning of the season, so new looks needed to be established specifically for these new characters. We had a three-week prep period at the beginning of the season, during which we set up our offices, had concept meetings about our new characters, and began to prepare for the upcoming season. During prep, I met with the line producer and executive producers on the design looks, and showed them tear sheets and garments that I had purchased for these characters. I shopped for all four lead Sliders, building a "closet" for each character that I would be able to pull from for the upcoming episodes. I had fittings with each actor and solidified their unique style. The director on an episodic series changes from week to week, so the producer sets up the look of the show, and the director on each episode accommodates to that look.

How did the budget work on the series?

Sliders had an average per-episode budget—a kind of budget "template." The per-episode budget figure for the new season was reached by adding the budget totals for each episode

FIG. 7.37

Barbara Inglehart's design for the music video "Beach of Gold" by Mike + the Mechanics

of the prior season, then dividing this sum by the number of episodes. This gave us a per-episode average budget for the season we were prepping. We also had an "amort" budget [amortization budget] for the season equal to an average budget for one episode. The amort budget was used for purchases to be used over the course of the entire season, such as wardrobe supplies or uniforms. For each episode, I turned in a budget based on the dictates of that specific script. The budget would include purchases, the cost of the rentals, dry-cleaning, and an approximation for the MO work and alterations.

Most TV series budgets range from $12,000 to $20,000 per episode. On *Sliders,* if the script for a particular episode required an historic period or specialty costume, the budget for that episode could be as high as $60,000. It depended on what was needed.

How about over-hire staffing?

That would be an additional line item in the budget—projecting how many extra days I would need a day-checker working on that episode. If the script entailed a historic period, I would ask to hire an assistant costume designer, in addition to the day-checker. This was a great help, because I needed their expertise during the prep period. The producer would approve the extra help when the budget was approved.

Were you based out of a studio?

Fortunately, we were based out of Universal Studios. Not all episodic series are tied to a studio. Other episodic shows may need to rent office and cage space at a costume house. Sometimes a production makes you work out of a warehouse space, where a good deal of your time is spent schlepping clothes back and forth between the rental house and the warehouse space.

Did the studio dictate that you had to do all your work within the Universal setup?

No, nothing was dictated, but we did have an arrangement with the Universal costume rental department that allowed us to rent directly from them, at a greatly reduced rate. Because *Sliders* was an in-house production, we could rent an unlimited number of garments for each episode for a flat rental fee. All of the clothes purchased for *Sliders* were inventoried as we purchased them and turned into the Universal costume department stock once the series wrapped. It was a great disappointment to many a day player who wanted to purchase the costume that had been altered for them, but couldn't, because it was destined to become part of Universal's stock. If an episode called for specialty items, such as a spacesuit or a military uniform, we would rent those from another costume house. If an episode called for a unique item that could not be found in stock, we manufactured it.

Episodic shooting schedules are, typically, tight. How do you get accounts set up at all the places you need in time to get the work done?

Every account was set up during the three-week prep period. The Universal costume accountant set up the accounts, using the vendor list we supplied. Typically, bills were paid with POs [purchase orders] or petty-cash reimbursements. The supervisor turned in the PO for each episode to the accountant, along with the vendor's receipt. The accountant then cut the check and mailed it in the specified time frame, usually thirty days. The turnaround time on petty cash was usually two or three days.

Were your budgets based on a breakdown of each costume into individual items?

No, I gave an estimate for each complete costume change, including doubles, stunts, et cetera. If there was any question as to the amount, I could give a more detailed estimate. As the script changed, I revised my budget.

How many people made up your costume department?

It was a four-person department: my supervisor, two set costumers, and myself. Then, on heavy-extra or stunt days, an additional day-checker would be added. We tried to use the same day checker, for consistency's sake.

How do you work with your supervisor?

A good supervisor is invaluable. I like to work very closely with the supervisor; we work together as a real team. My *Sliders'* supervisor, Riki Sabusawa, was terrific. She attended all meetings with me and was my second brain. It was always great when we had the time to go shopping together. But there were times when she had duties that she needed to attend to, separate from mine. More likely than not, I would go shopping on my own while she did other work. If there were special meetings throughout the week, such as an insert-shot meeting, she attended those meetings and coordinated the clothes required for those shots. Throughout the day, if there were going to be any big "scene switchovers" for extras (where extras are used in more than one scene, and the change of scene requires wardrobe to be changed, or "switched over"), she would plan ahead to go back to the set from our office, to help with those changes. Or, if we were on the studio lot and there were items that the set costumers needed at the trailer, she could zip back and forth in our golf cart.

Since we were prepping one episode and shooting another at the same time, we split our daily duties. My supervisor would always start the day with the crew at the trailer, and then swing over to work with me, in the office. Because we had very, very early calls for makeup—often 4:00 or 4:30 A.M. on Mondays—one costumer would start work with the earliest actor, and then my supervisor would come in with the next costumer. Their call time was typically twenty minutes in advance of the principals and extras' arrival.

The supervisor's job was to make sure that everything ran smoothly. The principal characters' costumes were set in their rooms. The extras had been instructed, in advance, to bring specific clothing looks, and, once they received their vouchers, they would line up and the costumers would look at their clothing and choose all of the outfits for their different characters for the day. They often played two or three different roles in one day. If they didn't have clothes that were appropriate, they would be given a costume from the trailer's selection of extras' clothing.

Our goal was to avoid all problems and foresee all needs, in advance. But of course, elements always arise as the shooting progresses.

If you were off set, how did things get handled?

Our production company furnished us with combination cell phone/walkie-talkies. I had one, my supervisor had one, and there was one with the second AD at the trailers. If my crew wanted to reach me, all they had to do was push the button, and there I was. These cell phone/walkie talkies are invaluable communication tools. I never want to work on another show without them. They gave me and my supervisor the advantage of constant communication. I could be in the middle of a hardware store and ask, "Didn't we need such and such?" And she could say, "Nope, I bought that already. We're fine."

Describe the shooting schedule on *Sliders*.

The shooting schedule for TV series vary, from a six-day shoot to an eight-day shoot. Our schedule was the six-day version, which has a very short prep-time. Generally, we would get the script on the Thursday or Friday before our first preproduction meeting, which would be held the following Monday afternoon. I'll describe a schedule as if our film week began on a Monday:

Day one: Monday morning, usually 6:00 A.M.. or so, I started the day at the costume trailer, with my crew. I liked to be in the trailer first thing in the morning, to set the tone for the day. I felt that that was really important—to be available to answer questions, to say good morning, to wander onto the stage to see how things were looking there. On average, my time at the trailer and on the set varied from one to three hours per day. I wasn't always present when new characters were "established" on film, but the costumes had been pre-approved, since, on a six-day turnaround to the next show, there was no time to waste. With a more typical eight-day format, there's a lot more time to see what's happening on the set. But with a six-day format, if I'm on the set, I am not prepping the next show.

The crew works on the present episode while I prep the next episode. I've read the script and already have a feeling for what my lead Sliders were going to wear, based on the dictates of the script and the stunt action anticipated. In the trailer, I've assembled a "closet" of clothes for each character. These clothes have already been fitted and altered.

This closet was started during the three-week prep period, and added to throughout the season, working fittings in on the set. Out of this closet, I pull the four lead Sliders' clothes for the next episode.

Returning to our office, the supervisor and I spend the rest of the morning doing additional research, breaking down the script, and putting together a potential budget for the next episode. We talk through my design ideas for the script and write down a list of questions to ask at the preproduction meeting. (I like to have a very strong idea of how I want to portray the characters, and what the costs will be, before the meeting.)

Of course, there were always things to attend to for the on-going shoot and the previous episode, so duties were split between the three episodes. After an episode was filmed, unused "memo" clothing was returned to the department store's studio services, and outside costume rentals were returned to their rental houses. POs needed to be filled out and turned in to accounting, petty cash needed to be reimbursed, and the budget needed to be wrapped up.

The producers, director, assistant director, department heads, and a Universal representative attended the preproduction meeting. As the meeting began, we were given a one-liner schedule, which told us when and in which order we would be filming each of the scenes. The script was read aloud, page by page, scene by scene. As groups of people or specific characters were introduced in the script, I presented my design ideas. If the director and producers agreed with me, I would go forward with my design process. If they had a slightly different take on it, then we discussed options and came to an agreement.

Anytime something came up in the preproduction meeting that specifically referred to the clothing or action, I asked the relevant questions. I inquired whether the actors would be photo-doubled or stunted, and if stuntmen were being used in specific scenes, whether it was for fights or specialty action. If the actor was going to be doing the stunt, would he or she be "squibbed" (equipped with built-in "blood"-emitting packets, to simulate being struck by a bullet)? If the actor was going to be squibbed, how many "hits" were needed?

Usually at this point the stunt coordinator does not know the answer to my questions, since the script is still being rewritten, and the schedule will continue to change. The stunt coordinator can't lock in the stuntpeople yet, because, once they are "locked in," they get paid for the day they're booked, whether they work or not. During location scouts, the director and the stunt coordinator discuss the blocking and the type of stunts that will be done. (The stunt and the blocking will often change from what was written in the script once the director and stunt coordinator visualize the stunt on location.)

In addition to stunts, the extras count is important: If extras are going to be dressed in uniforms or specialized costumes, our budget and prep time are going to be affected.

Once the main portion of the preproduction meeting is complete, I present the actual clothing I pulled from the trailer that morning to show the director and producers. At this point, I get either a go-ahead or directions for refining my choices. Based on the information learned during the meeting, my supervisor and I are ready to revamp the budget, which is usually due, in its final form, the next day, between ten and two o'clock.

To back up a minute, you said you got the script on Thursday or Friday, and by Monday you had already fit the actors?

Yes, but, prior to Monday, I had pre-fit them and sometimes pre-altered them, so that they were ready to be used. This was why assembling a closet was so important on this series. It was one of the many advantages of shooting many episodes over an eight-month period: If costumes did not work for one episode, they could work for another.

You're financially committed to these garments once you've gone through the alterations process. Was this a risky thing to do before you got approval at the meeting?

Not really. The clothing was within the color palette and design lines that I was using for each character, and they were clothes that the actors liked and had approved. I've found that it's very effective to have the actors approve the clothes first, before the producers see them. This way, the producer does not see a garment that the actor doesn't like. And I don't end up trying to talk the actor into wearing something that he isn't fond of, or back-peddling with the producers on my choice. I show the producers, director, and writer clothes that I like and the actor likes; then, I just have to make sure that *they* like them, as well. In TV, the writer often does have a say during this stage of the design process.

You've come to the meeting basically knowing that the actor was fond of the look. In the meeting, you'll see if that look works with what the director wants, and with the designs of the other departments?

Correct. It's especially important to make sure that the colors all work together.

After I show the clothing choices, I get an immediate response: either "Yes, we love them," or "No, we don't." If I get the "Yes, we love it" response, then my job on the four main Sliders is complete, except for tweaking, and I spend the next four days focusing on the rest of the characters within the episode. If I get a "no" response, which is very rare, then I have the rest of the week to find a solution to the problem. While I'm out shopping for the current episode, I keep an eye out for clothes the principal Sliders can wear in future episodes.

Tuesdays, you shop till you drop?

Days two and three, yes. On this show, Tuesday and Wednesday were typically shopping days. Lots of times, I would pre-shop for day players who had not yet been cast, so that, once I had their sizes, I could immediately call them in for fittings. On this show, the basic size range on the women was size 2 to size 6. Men's sizes varied a little more. On this series, pre-shopping day players turned out to be an incredibly failsafe method. I may have had to re-buy, for correct size, once the day player was cast, but I already had doubles. And we always needed doubles. Typically, there was either a photo double or a stuntperson, or just hard wear-and-tear over the course of the six-day shoot.

Of course, the budget was turned in. Theoretically, I should have waited for the budget to be approved before actually purchasing anything, but because of the time constraints in this format, I just charged forward. If there were any major purchases, I checked with the producer first.

We would also set time aside to go through the Universal stock and pull out any items that could be rented. Our extras typically fit into groups of looks. There might be a group who worked at the Chandler Hotel, a location that recurs in parallel worlds and is visited frequently by lead Sliders. Typically, there would be waiters, waitresses, a desk clerk, and a bellhop. The look of their uniforms would differ from world to world. If there were other extras who needed specific uniforms, we would rent from Universal or another rental house, or we would research which catalog had the look we needed and have the order sent overnight express.

Between Tuesday and Friday, depending on the demands of the script, the director and producers cast featured extras, often from head-shots, occasionally on the basis of a personal interview. Once the featured extras were set, I would decide if I needed to call them in for a fitting. It really depended on the type of body they had and the type of clothing they were going to wear. For a big-bruiser bodyguard type who had to wear a suit, we would definitely have him in for a fitting, because the suit would need to be altered. If it was going to be a regular guy in security-guard uniform pants and shirt, that could be done on the spot, at the trailer.

Somewhere in here, my supervisor would have received a one-liner, in script order, from the first AD. She would enter that information in our costume breakdown program. We used the CMSMovies computer program (costume breakdown program for movies and episodic TV scripts). Because the costumes for the four lead Sliders had already been approved, she could enter their changes into the computer. Then later, once the day players were fit, she could add their clothing descriptions to their pre-assigned costume change numbers.

Tuesday was also the day to catch up on finishing the previous episode's paperwork and returns. Monday through Wednesday, some casting could dribble in, but most casting was finalized on Thursday afternoon. As the week progressed, we would also get script and shooting schedule revisions. The first AD was the lifeline to this type of change.

Day four, Thursday afternoon, casting had their final callbacks. The actors who auditioned for the day-player roles read for the producers and the director. It was always our hope that the producers and director would lock in the actors during the next two to three hours, and then call us immediately with their contact information. Once they were cast, I would get their telephone numbers and phone the actors, to get their sizes. I usually talked to them about my concept of their character and asked them about their skin tone, hair color, eye color, and if they had any color preferences or dislikes. I would set up a fitting for the following morning. If I had guessed right about their sizes, I already had clothes from pre-shopping or pre-pulling from stock. If not, I'd have that night and early the next morning to go shopping.

Day five, Friday morning, we would finish preparing for the fittings and start to get ready for the producers' show-and-tell. Actors were usually fit between 10:00 A.M. and 1: 30 P.M. Usually, the fitting was the first time that I met the day player. More likely than not, I would have already purchased or pulled clothing for them, without ever having seen their picture and having only talked to them on the phone. I had an idea about their body type from their measurements, but had pretty much shopped "blind."

When I would first meet a day player, I would chat with them a little bit about how I saw the character and, more likely than not, show them the range of clothes that I had for them. I think the key is to be at ease during a fitting, since you're asking someone you've just met to take off his or her clothes. I never force an actor to wear something that he or she is uncomfortable with, because that discomfort shows up on camera. My goal is to make them look good and be happy with my character design.

On *Sliders,* my supervisor had tremendous responsibilities during fittings. Because I'm using my "eye" to look at the designs, she's listening to everything that I'm saying and taking down notes. She was there to record the changes. We used a tag system: Once a garment was fit, Riki would write down the alteration notes on an alteration tag and pin it to the garment. Then, she would write out a tag with the character name and description. This tag stayed with the garment when it was transported to the trailer, so that the set crew knew which character wore the garment and what number costume change it was.

The wonderful thing about working in a studio setting was that there was a tailor shop right there, for alterations, and we could just walk the garment down the hall and have the tailors get started. Often, one of the tailors would come in to fit the costume and mark alterations. Then, after our marathon fittings, it was time to head to the production meeting, which usually began at two o'clock. Along with the entire production staff, we would again read through the entire script, scene by scene. Anybody who had any concerns or problems, questions or comments, made them at that point. There were usually thirty-five to forty people who attended that meeting.

Immediately following the meeting, the producers, the director, the first AD, and, sometimes, the writer, all trooped over to the costume department, and we would have what's called a "show and tell." All of the clothes for the entire episode were organized on racks, scene by scene, including principals, day players, and extras' clothing. I had a file folder that had all the Polaroids from my fittings taped in it, with the character names and change numbers next to them, and I talked through the look of the entire show. It's at that point that all clothing was approved and locked in. After this meeting, Riki and I finished anything left unfinished.

Day six, Monday, was our catch-up day. We finished buying things like accessories, hose, jewelry—little details that hadn't been finished on day five. If we hadn't been able to complete our fittings, we scheduled the rest of them for this morning. Once all of the clothing was back from the tailors and organized, it was time to move them to the trailer. We called it a "roundy round," since it meant loading off the trailer onto the flatbed truck all the racks of clothing from the episode that was just finishing and taking them to the costume department, then loading up all of the racks for the new episode onto the same truck and off-loading them at the trailer. The set costumers would then organize the new show on the trailer.

Meanwhile, my supervisor was entering all the new day-player costume descriptions into the CMS breakdown computer program, and printing out the sheets for the continuity book. This was printed on cardstock, so that we could actually affix the Polaroids directly to it and have it hold up for the next week of constant use. I would head over to the trailer and go through each character and costume change with the set costume crew. I would show them the Polaroids of the day players, so that they could see how the costume looked on the actor, and talk through the flow of the show, explaining stunts, photo doubles, and any problems I foresaw. They would have read the script, and they often had specific questions that could be answered at this point.

After the set costumers meeting, I took the Polaroids to the hair and makeup departments. I wanted them to be aware of the characters I had created with the day players' clothing. This was also the first time they would see the day players' faces, and it helped them to start thinking about hair and makeup choices.

Day seven, Tuesday, the new episode started shooting. The cycle began again. And once it was up and running, I was pulling the four lead Sliders looks for the next episode, having read the script somewhere during the Thursday, Friday schedule.

Back at the department, we saved the costumes from the last episode for re-shoots, hanging them in our "cage." There was some lag time before the show was "locked" and the director's cut approved—usually two to four weeks. There were always re-shoots and insert shots on our episodes. There was an insert stage on the Universal lot, where re-shoots would take place. An example of an insert would be an actor reaching his hand into frame to pick up the telephone. Or, say, an actor is playing a character who plays the piano, but the actor cannot play correctly. A trained musician must be hired for insert shots. The musician must have the same skin tone and bone structure as the actor, and the jewelry and sleeves need to match what was shot during the rest of the scene.

In any event, once the show was locked, we could break down the clothes from that episode and return anything that we had rented.

Was *Sliders* a three-camera show? Did you use tape or film?

It was a one-camera show. Sometimes we had two cameras, when we were doing fights or specialized action: "A" camera, "B" camera. Also, the director sometimes had two film cameras set up simultaneously, side by side, with different lenses, to catch the same action in different ways. This helped save time filming, especially during stunts.

Usually, you find a three-camera setup in a sitcom or video shoot, since the cost of videotape is much less than film. Everything for *Sliders* was shot on 35mm film. We used traditional film techniques, with lighting setups specifically designed for each shot. *Sliders* tended to shoot faster than most productions. To save time, we would often shoot "green screen" or add "burn-ins" in post. There were a lot of special effects, and special effects was one of the topics we discussed in our preproduction meetings.

Except for the director and the first AD, the crew was the same from episode to episode. The first AD rotated on the odd and even episodes, so that while one episode was being shot, the next was being prepped by the alternate first AD.

Were you on location a lot in this series?

It varied. We were based on a soundstage, on the Universal lot, where the permanent sets were constructed. The costume office was located in the Universal costume building, right next to the costume rental department, at the other end of the lot. It was very convenient when we were working on the backlot or soundstage to just zip back and forth between our office and their shooting location. However, they did shoot quite a bit on off-lot locations, and then it was more difficult.

How big was your average costume load?

We had four principal characters and anywhere from three to ten day players in each episode. Then, there could be up to one hundred extras in a scene, depending on the episode. If there was a specialty-clothing look, that number was usually smaller. In "New Gods for Old," an episode where characters were in a cult, we dressed eighty people in clothes manufactured specifically for the scene.

How much lead-time did you have on that?

Four days. On that particular show, at the preproduction meeting, I proposed an idea that was different from what had been written in the script. I showed them a sketch of my costume design, as well as several garments that I had pulled from stock, to illustrate the look. They thought it was an interesting idea and asked how much it would cost. I estimated $4,000, and they approved the overage.

And the shop was ready to go? To get your MO in that short a time, was it just overtime like mad?

In this particular instance, I contracted with a manufacturer to build the clothing, but they didn't come through with it on time. In the end, I used the Universal shop to finish the project, and paid them for their overtime. It's one of those horror stories you hear about and hope never happens to you. On this particular episode, we began to film the scene in which these MO costumes were to be worn on a Wednesday morning, at 7:00 A.M. The shop had assured me the previous Wednesday that they would begin working on the project Thursday. On Monday morning, I called the shop to check in. I found that there might be a problem, but was assured that they would be able to handle the construction on their own. My supervisor and I called them every two to three hours, all day long, and, finally, at about nine o'clock that night, I was told that they were not going to be able to complete the job.

The next morning, Tuesday, I started to make phone calls to see who else could handle the construction, while I sent my supervisor to the vendor to pick up the cut garments. Once she arrived, she found they hadn't even patterned or cut out any garments. The entire day was spent trying to fix this problem, which never should have happened. Universal's shop was terrific, and a few of their tailors ended up working until 2:30 A.M. to finish the garments. We picked them up at 6:00 A.M., and had them on bodies by 7:00 A.M. The costumes ended up costing $5,500 with overtime included, which, in the end, wasn't a terrible overage. I had been able to save money in another part of the episode, so I didn't end up going over budget. That's one of the things about this business: You just have to be ready to handle anything.

Conversation Eleven:

On Dyeing and Distressing Costumes for Film, with Edwina Pellikka

Edwina Pellikka, owner of A Dyeing Art, an important dye studio in Los Angeles, has worked on many films, among them, *Dick Tracy, Return of the Jedi, The Flintstones,* and *Forrest Gump.*

People are sometimes confused by the terms used for aging a costume. Could you define them for us?

In Europe, there are two terms: "breaking down" and "distressing." People freak out about the term "breakdown," because they think "breakdown" means "distressing" and "aging." It doesn't. Breaking down a costume makes it look real for the camera. It gives it "reality," rather than letting it looking like a nice, brand-new costume. It just literally means taking the "newness" off. You do a little airbrushing, to knock the edges off.

"Distressing" *is* aging. You break the costume down more because you want to show that it has a history: The guy's worn it for ten years or he has lived on the street in it or he's a guy who works in a garage—that kind of stuff.

For a very subtle "breakdown," where do you begin?

If possible, you begin by putting the piece through a dye process, through a little "dirty tech." "Tech" is short for "technical." It started off meaning a "technical white" color, for camera. White was too bright for camera.

Something that would technically read as white, but not flare on film. You use the term to mean a mild dye bath, to change the tone of the costume slightly.

You would either do a warm tech, which is a creamy color, or a cool gray tech. If the piece is in red and warm tones, you have to use almost a greenish gray tech to "knock it down"—take the newness off, subdue the colors, as if the garment had been washed and worn for a time.

In our shop, there are three techs: a warm tech, a cool tech, and what we call a "half and half"—half cool and half warm. Starting from white, you'd go from number one, which is just off-white, to number four, and then darker, depending on the skin tone. Nowadays, I think you can get some pretty brilliant cameramen who are okay with white, but if you have a darker-skinned person on camera, you're definitely going to begin with a "four tech," and go darker if you need to. If a cameraman exposes for the face of a dark-skinned person, then the whites are going to be too light.

You can buy white fabrics that are a very cold white. If you look at them in the light, they've almost got a lavender look to them. Those are whites that have been treated with an optical brightener. If you tech them to indoor lights, they're great, they look fabulous. But if you go outside, into the sunlight, under the ultraviolet (UV) rays, they look bright white again, because the optical brightener is reacting with the UV light. If you then dye them for outdoor light, when you come indoors, they look much too yellow. Things that have been treated with optical brighteners glow under a black light—like in a Disney ride or a discotheque—so whenever we're going to dye something, I beg the designer to bring me natural white or off-white. You do not want that cold white, because it changes its color in every light.

Bernie Pollack, when he designed the film *Havana*, had all these linen suits made, but he wanted them teched. I knew the suits had been treated with optical brighteners, so I called Bernie and I said, "I've got to know, is it an indoor shoot or an outdoor shoot? A daytime shoot or a nighttime shoot?" This is something you have to ask. And I said, "If I dye this to your tech for outdoors, when you come indoors, they're going to look way too yellow and you are going to freak." He said, "That's all right, Edwina, I understand that. Dye it for outdoors, because it's all going to be shot outdoors." So I dyed them to outdoors and then sent them to Western [Costume Company]. The guy there freaked! He said, "How can you do this? These are so awful! We're going to have to bring them back because they are all yellow. We're going to have to call Bernie." I said, "You go ahead." They did, and it all calmed down. But that's how dramatic it is. So dyers have to remember to really beg designers not to use a white that says "super-white/optical white." If they do use that white, you have to be sure what light it's going to be photographed in.

Designer Hope Hanafin has said she doesn't want any white brighter than the actor's teeth or eyes.

That makes sense. In our shop, when we tech, we have one recipe made up for cotton tech and one recipe for nylon tech. As I said earlier, it goes from number one, which is just off-white, to number four, and then darker, depending on the skin. Rit Dye used to make a wonderful color called "Honey," which they no longer make. "Honey" made the best warm tech ever. Now they have "Ecru," which is way too pink. If you are going to use "Ecru," you know immediately that you are going to have to add yellow, and maybe a little blue.

How about the Rit color "Tan?"

"Tan" is too red, too dark. All of them have too much red in them for tech. On set, sometimes, people use other things. I know people who use tea. Tea tends to be a little pinker. Coffee, I think, tends to be a little greener. I never use tea or coffee. I have heard that some people have used Coca-Cola, but that sounds pretty gross to me.

I have found that, now, almost nobody except older cameramen know what "tech" is. The younger kids have no concept of it, nor do the younger directors, nor do the younger cameramen. I had one girl, a young thing, come in to me and say, "Oh god, I'm working with this old guy. Oh god, he wants this 'tech' something, whatever that is." She practically thought he was stupid. I told her that she should thank her lucky stars, and listen to everything that this guy said, because he knew what he was talking about. He could teach her a lot.

Speaking of working with lighting, do you have to compensate for lighting intensity? Does it have an impact on your dye colors and the degree of distressing that you shoot for?

Yes, the light cleans everything up, so you've got to be gutsier or it doesn't look like you've been there. When you're aging, distressing, you've got to know this and bear it in mind.

When you age, when you distress for designers, unless they really know their stuff, you do it in three stages. You do it like they want it to look on film—which is way not enough. Then, they go look at the dailies and they say, "Oh, yeah, right, I need a bit more." Then you do the bit more. They look at it on screen again, and it's still not enough. Then you do what you would have done in the first place, which looks like too much, but the screen cleans it up. If you don't have enough time, you just bang it on and they freak out, but then when they see it on the screen, they say, "Thank you very much." So, equally with certain colors, you should choose a stronger color than is needed, because on camera it will wash out to the color desired. Yellows, in particular, do this.

I've seen the elaborate dye facilities in your shop—the big vats where you can handle large quantities of fabric, washing machines that can cycle continuously for hours. It's a fabulous setup. Many people are stuck using a washing machine in a rental house. What's the biggest problem that they face with standard washing machine dyeing?

If you have to dye in a washing machine because that's all they've got, it's not ideal. It will not do big yardage or heavy fibers. In the water in a washing machine, the dye cannot successfully move through the fiber in an even manner. But the biggest thing is temperature. You cannot maintain the temperature. It doesn't do very deep colors well, because it doesn't get hot enough, and the cycle is too short. Fabric has to go through dye for about an hour. When I used to try to dye in a washing machine, I would have a hot plate on constantly, with two kettles. I would fill the machine with hot water and I would keep those kettles going. When the cycle would finish, I would stop the cycle, fill it with more hot water from the kettles, and reset the cycle again so it didn't rinse.

Spandex and similar fibers will dye happily in a washing machine. The more you leave the fabric in there agitating, the more the agitating will even out the color. But unless you want a distressed effect, you should never, ever dye wool in a washing machine: The very action of the washing machine shocks the fibers, and they'll "felt" (the wool fibers turn into felt).

There are so many factors that go into getting a fabric to take color: the fiber, the water temperature, the length of the soak, the brand of the dye. Each type of dye has its strengths and its weaknesses.

People use Rit Dye in washing machines. And Rit actually is a good "union dye," in the sense that it will dye nylon-synthetic blends. If you use Rit Dye in a washing machine, you should always try to use only the liquid Rit (in bottles). No matter what they tell you, with the packages (the powder dye), you will always get spots. When you look at Rit Dye in powder form, it's very granular, which is actually the salt in the mix. That salt develops the dye—it holds the dye in one place, with the dye powder trapped in and around it, until it is dissolved. But it doesn't always successfully dissolve. So it's way, way better to use the liquid dye.

I hate Rit because you have to use so much. It's a very, very expensive way of dying fabric. Four bottles of Rit Dye is like one teaspoon of regular dye. Rit brilliantly dyes nylon, and it dyes wool and silk very well. It does not dye cotton well, at all. Good cotton dyes have "aniline," a dangerous substance that gets through the pores of your skin and breaks down your hemoglobin. Obviously, they cannot sell that in the supermarket, so analine is not in Rit.

If all you have is the powdered dye, can you "paste" it to start with?

All dye in powdered form should be "pasted up," with warm water, to a roux. Try as much as possible to have it all wetted; then, pour boiling water on it slowly and keep dissolving it. Then, you can also put in Synthrapol, from the Dharma Trading Company, and Cassalene oil. Synthrapol breaks down the surface tension in the water, particularly hard water, so it helps the dye slide into the fiber. If you know you are in a hard water area, you should use Calgon as well. If you cannot get Synthrapol, then use a few drops of Ivory Liquid soap. A drop of that will also break down the surface tension.

Cassalene oil is a brilliant addition to dyeing. It helps the dye move evenly through the fiber, so that, over a longer period of dyeing, the goods won't be patchy. One of the central tenants of fabric dyeing is, *Keep it in the dye bath long enough.* Sometimes when you first put in the dye and the color "patches," you panic. If you just leave the fabric in the dye long enough, gently moving it through the color solution containing Cassalene oil, the color will even itself up.

If you are dyeing Spandex or Lycra or any of those dance fabrics, you must always pre-wash them in a washing machine with Synthrapol, because the action of the washing machine bashes the water and the Synthrapol through the fabric and completely wets it through. If you put it in dye without doing this (or if you think that you *have* pre-wetted the fabric, but, in fact, the water has not totally soaked through), you will get teeny white dry spots. It has to be bashed in a washing machine.

What colors are difficult to dye?

In cottons, red bleeds. Actually, red bleeds in almost every fiber, but especially in cotton. There is a product called Retayne, which you can rinse your reds in and the reds won't bleed. But the next time you wash the item, you wash out the Retayne, and then the red will bleed again. Even when people bring you fabric that's purchased red from the store, when you put it in the clean dye bath, red pours out. Only if you use cold-water fiber-reactive dyes on one-hundred-percent cotton will the red not bleed out.

In cotton, you absolutely cannot get a bright royal blue or an electric royal blue with any dye on the market. Every great blue dye has been banned by the Food and Drug Administration, because it's made from a benzedrine base proven to cause leukemia. You can get fabulous blue dyes in Indonesia and Bali and Thailand and China, because they don't care if their workers die. The average life expectancy of a dyer in Indonesia who does all that wonderful blue batik dyeing is forty-eight years old. Because of the Food and Drug Administration ruling, the chemical factories are sitting on everything. We can no longer get the bright oranges that we used to get, and the cadmium yellows. It is harder and harder to get good gutsy, vibrant colors.

How about blacks?

Black blacks? No black dye ever makes black. With the cotton dyes, the cotton black is green, and the silk and nylon blacks are more violet. So, with the green-y black, you would add maybe some wine, maybe some scarlet—more wine than scarlet—to counteract it. With the purple-y ones, you would add a turquoise or green. Linen will never be a one-hundred percent deep, deep, deep ebony black. With cottons, you can get a good black; but with cottons, you have to be careful that you don't put too much black in, or it goes what we call "rusty"—it gets that brown-y look, because you used too much dye.

When you're dyeing cotton, you must always use salt as the *mordant*, a chemical agent that helps fix the dye. With silks, the ideal thing to use is acetic acid, which helps fix the dye and develop the dye more strongly. (Sometimes, acetic acid also helps nylon dyes develop red.) I use eighty-seven to ninety percent acetic acid, which you can get from a chemical supply house or a photography supply source. You only use a little splash of it. You should never sniff acetic acid, because it will sear your sinuses. And you should wear gloves when you use it. If you splash it on yourself, you can just wash it away, it's not going to harm you. Vinegar is five percent acetic acid. You can use white distilled vinegar in place of acetic acid; you just need to use a lot more of it to achieve the same effect.

Are the problems with cotton dye in certain colors the same problems that occur with the acid dyes for silk, wool, or nylon in those colors?

Acid dyes get brilliant blues. For instance, if you are asked for chroma-key blue or chroma-key green, the blue will be duller if the fiber is cotton. But if you are using silk or nylon dyes, there would be no problem at all—absolutely, you'd get it. With nylon dyes, you would also use a dispersal agent like Synthropol or Ivory Liquid, to help the dye move into the fiber. I always like putting a little drop of Ivory Liquid in every dye that I mix up in powder form, because it breaks down the water tension and helps the dye dissolve better.

What about the current rage for neon tones? Are those hard to get?

The dyes for neon colors are getting better and better. It used to be such an awful process. It was ghastly, and fairly poisonous. But now, there are fabulous florescent yellows for all fibers. And then you can add red to make fabulous fluorescent oranges. There is an amazing fluorescent pink called Rhodamine. The only trouble with that is that it bleeds. It never stops washing out. But the color depth stays the same. The only fluorescent color that you can't really get is a true blue.

Let's get back to distressing. Why is it important, when aging a piece, to dye it as a first step?

The thing that everybody should remember when they distress is to use color. The reason that you want to dye it first is because then the color is in the fiber. When I break down anything, the first step is putting the fabric in the dye, if possible. If you are going to put any aging in, you have to also try to put in a little "movement." You very, very subtly "patch" the goods.

Like blotches of color, to break it up?

Yes, but very subtle, not hard-edged. You subtly pour pools of different colors, and then, hose them, so that they bleed into each other. After you've done that, you might put it through a wash, and soften it, to smooth that out even more. But you've still got movement in it.

After you've put in the patch dyeing or the tech colors, you will take the airbrush and put in shading. You have to get that subtle feeling underneath. You break down the edges, you put in shade. I airbrush belts and shoes and gloves and everything before I put in any other coloring.

You will subtly put in "breakdown," depending on the scenario and the kind of information you have been given. If the character is a mechanic, you know that he's got greasy fingers. He'll have wiped them on the top of his thighs; he might have wiped them on his bum. He'll have a pocket, where he sticks things. When you airbrush, you will put in shading, as though he's gone in to his pocket a lot of times; and you'll bend the pocket over a little bit and make a crease. You'll bend the crook of the arm and crease it up in pleats, so that, when you give it a quick over-spray with the air brush, it puts creases in there. You kind of crease up where he might have sat.

What kind of dye or paint do you use for the airbrushing?

Unless asked otherwise, my airbrushing medium is like an FEV [French enamel varnish], an alcohol-based dye with shellac (dye is added to a mixture with the proportions one-quarter shellac to three-quarters alcohol). Ideally, the dye should be aniline dye, but you can use leather dye, instead. The fabulous thing about that technique is that the alcohol immediately carries the dye into the fiber. It doesn't sit on top. The dye stays in the fiber, and the alcohol evaporates instantly, so you don't worry about wetness and drips, or the fact that it's going to bounce off the surface of a wool fabric or resistant fiber. The reason you use shellac is because the shellac sets the dye onto the costume for the run of the show, but will also dry-clean out at the end of the season, unless it's been applied very, very heavily. Originally, my training was from theater, where you had to think about stock. Everything you did had to be able to be reversible, for future productions.

In this business that uses so much rental stock, I know there are real advantages to impermanent aging techniques, but how do you get the aging to hold up to cleaning during the shoot?

If the costumer came to me and said that the character was going to be in a television series and that he was going to be looking this way throughout, then, definitely, all that kind of aging would start in the dye pot. For example, if the character is old and he's been walking through the streets, then you would dip the edge of his trousers and his cuffs and maybe his collar in the dye pot. And you would maybe put some tears in them and dip those tears in the dye, using an almost mini-*ombre* technique to give them a permanent *ombre*. [*Ombre* is a color effect in which a hue gradually goes from dark to light, like a sunset. It is achieved through the dye process.]

You make these permanent dye features before you put on the airbrushing, so when the designer gets the garments to the set, they've got the basic breakdown in the fiber; and then whatever is needed can be added on the set, by the day. Maybe the character is slogging through inclement weather and then, later on in the scene, he's fallen in a puddle of mud, or whatever. They can "Schmutz" that in.

"Schmutz" sticks are like big crayons—pigmented earth with a wax binder—that you can buy for aging things on set.

Schmutz is now made in all the colors you'd like: rottenstone, Van Dyke brown, raw umber, ochre, clear, charcoal, black. And they are so phenomenally fabulous. After you've done all you can with dye, you can do a little Shmutz here and there, to complete the effect. It will come out in the dry cleaning.

Today, we had two sweatshirts that we had to match to a sweatshirt this guy's had for two years. All the writing on the original sweatshirt has been washed and washed and broken down. Because these gals who brought the sweatshirts in didn't do enough research, they didn't know that you can actually print in a broken-down manner. They took the sweatshirts to any old printing place and had them print the letters with Plastisol. Number one: Never, ever, ever have anything that you want broken down printed with Plastisol, because Plastisol is shiny plastic stuff that will not dye. So, we washed them, sanded them, bleached them. Washed them, sanded them, washed them, sanded them, softened them, dried them, washed them, sanded them, softened them, dried them, et cetera. We over-teched them and the letters still went "hello!" We thought we had time to break it down, because the scene wasn't supposed to shoot till next week.

All of a sudden, they called us: "Today! It's shooting this afternoon!" Production brought the schedule forward. So, we took rottenstone Schmutz and just slightly, very carefully, rubbed it on top of the letters only. They immediately looked like they were worn out and broken down. Schmutz is a great finisher. You just have to pick your color, and you have to be careful that you don't go "over the top."

Schmutz strips out in cleaning?

Because it's a wax, the wax part comes out in the cleaning. But sometimes, on the darker Fullers Earth [pigments], there is a residue. On a rented piece of goods, if you are putting black on white, it can also leave a residue. But with the lighter colors, it's not really a problem—although it depends on how much you use.

If you want it to last longer or sink into the fiber more, do you set it with a hot iron?

No. Sometimes, it really is minutes before the camera gets rolling; there's not time to "set" something. If I had time and someone came to me and said it has to last for the run of the show and we are going to have to clean it, then I would use maybe a paint or a dye pigment, and paint that in. There are ways that aging can be made permanent (that's where the whole dyeing process comes in); but regardless of what I do, there is always going to be a change of mind on the set, where something else has to be done. So, you have to have your Schmutz.

I've also heard that costumers will take a rag that has mineral oil on it and roll it in Fullers Earth (a pigmented earth with no binder), and then "hit" the goods on the set.

That works. In a way, that's almost Schmutz. With the Fullers Earth, costumers will make these porous bags (called "pounce bags") and fluff the Fullers Earth dust all around. Actually, Fullers Earth is a carcinogenic lung irritant. It freaks me out when I see them pouncing these bag of Fullers Earth around little children. There is no need to do that. There are other ways to do that. You can do it in the spray booth. Or, at the last minute, if the designer says to you, "I want this pounced," take the piece off the actor. Don't stand right there and do it all around him. Or, at least, make the actor wear a mask.

Schmutz and Fullers Earth are for final touches and final visible dirt, like mud stains.

The biggest thing that people must remember when they do dirt aging is, for God's sake, know the country they're in! When I was doing *Return of the Jedi*, I remember saying to the designer, "We've got to put this muddy stuff on the Ewoks and soldiers. What type of soil is it?" And she replied, "Why do you need to know that? That's none of your business. It's private, for security reasons." I said, "I don't give a damn *where* it is, but I need to know the color of the soil."

If you are aging something by putting on your generic earthy gray-brown tone and they are in a sandy soil or red clay location, then you're totally out of whack. If the project is so top secret that they won't give you the script, you have to at least have them tell you the location and what the soil is. You need that information for continuity.

Here's a different problem: What about aging dark clothes, where dye techniques may not show up?

With a dark fiber, you might take some color out. A bleach spray is one thing you would do. Take a spritzer—probably the pint size—and pour in one to two caps of bleach. You just do one little cap first, to test. Some fabrics will go, "Hello, what was that? I'm not interested." The bleach just disappears. So, you try a little more. But on other stuff, it goes, "Bam-o!" So, you go subtly. You don't want the fabric immediately to show up as bleached, because then you've got too much. You want to spray it on and just let it appear slowly. It mustn't happen immediately, before your eyes, or you have no control.

Next, if you can, you want to be able to rinse out the bleach. If you don't, that bleach will continue to work, and eventually it will rot the garment. Some people say that adding vinegar to the bleach solution will stop the bleaching action. It doesn't, really. It might impede it, because the bleach is alkaline and the vinegar is acid, but in the long run, the bleach wins over the vinegar. And you *never* bleach silk.

The next stage in aging dark clothes is to airbrush in shape, shading, and character. (Really, the only time you *wouldn't* airbrush is if the garment is too dark for the airbrushing to show.) Next, what you use is Magix [spray colors]—Champagne, Smoked Elk, and colors like that. You'll dust with Avocado and maybe a red or brown. You do not use just a black or a brown. Green gives an effect of age and moss, you know. You just spray and dust with these colors. As you spray, you wave the spray over the garment, so it just gives layers of different colors. *Please* wear respirator masks, goggles, latex gloves, and use a spray booth!

Do you work the paint in?

No, absolutely not.

Airbrushing and Magix are all right for camera? They don't sit on the surface too much?

That's why you want the piece in the dyeing or the bleaching first. If you don't have some depth underneath, you don't have enough "3-D" [three-dimensional effect]. You have to put in a base color, a base breakdown in the fiber, with dye or bleach, if you can. The Magix that you are doing now is topical, it's surface. You're just dusting, you're not doing heavy stuff.

So, what you have done is put your base breakdown in the dyes, then you've air-brushed in shape, and then you've Schmutzed and Magixed areas, for final touches. What truly horrifies me is how much water and acrylic paint people use when they distress. It's a sin. First of all, it's a sin because it looks like shit. It sits on the surface and looks plastic. It doesn't look real, which is the biggest sin. I have to reiterate, with the Magix, you're doing just a subtle spray, you're doing a nuance—you are not spraying like you're spraying a pair of shoes. Spraying the Magix just breaks down the surface of the piece, gives it a dusty look. It's just a misting over, which will come out in the dry-cleaning. Afterward, when you put on the Schmutz and the Magix, you have to be careful: the Magix can be more permanent. There are instances, on lighter fabric, where you might get a little cream-colored or black residue.

I hate to see people use so much acrylic paint, when there are so many wonderful textile paints now which retain the hand of the fabric—unless they really want a muddy effect; then, that's something else. If that's the case, then I myself would use acrylic paint—maybe a raw umber or burnt umber base. I always put in a teeny bit of bronze or metallic, because these pigments really give that "shit" look much better; if you put metallic in, it doesn't look so much like paint, anymore. You put that on with bits of straw and stuff, to stick to the surface. Then, I would airbrush. There just never, ever is a moment when I won't airbrush shading and character into an item, even if it's a belt.

I was most intrigued by the washer in your studio, which can do extra long washing cycles. I also saw you prepare goods for the washing machine by very subtly sanding and grating the fabrics. This process yielded fabulous worn-edge results after the goods were washed. How might I make use of this technique without all the special equipment you have in your studio?

An example: Someone brings you a pair of jeans, and they are to be aged like they've been worn for five years. You don't have the facilities that I have in my shop that allow me to throw the jeans in a washing machine for extra long cycles, then put in a tech to achieve a yellowed, sandy look. So, what you'll do is put them in a washing machine and break them down, soften them. The washing is important, and maybe the first wash cycle will have a little bleach. But the biggest thing to remember is to put extra softener in the final rinse; the softener breaks down fibers, too. And then, you dry the garments thoroughly. And then, you do it again. You have to repeat the whole process. You can't just bleach, soften, and then bleach, soften again. You have to bleach, soften and *dry*, bleach, soften and *dry*, because every stage of this process breaks down the fiber. Sometimes, a very light over-tech is added in the final wash process, to give that old, laundered look. Then you will take your Schmutz, in the sandy color, and you will run it along the seam and just give it a "push" for the shoot. And it's all ready!

Do you have other favorite aging techniques?

I love mineral oil and glycerin, because they give that nice "sweat" look.

It darkens the fabric, right?

It does darken the fabric. I like to put the oil on, and then maybe hit it with Schmutz on top. You can also mix color in with the oil, sometimes. When I get hats, I tend to airbrush the hat first, and then put the tinted oil on. You might put in a dark tone, to help it "ring" along the edge. Cowboy hats and things like that, I will always airbrush in shading first. I might Magix them, as well.

I've heard the stories of taking a week to age John Wayne's hat.

Take a whole bloody week to do a hat? That's just storytelling. That's a lot of crap. It's people not knowing what they're doing—unless they did it and John Wayne said, "I want more." Then they added more for the next scene and the director wanted something different, and so on. *Then* they could spend a week, or more! I can tell you this because I have copied John Wayne stuff. It's just a question of knowing what you're doing.

On *Return of the Jedi*, costumes for the pig guards at Jabba the Hut's palace had been made out of brand-new natural pink cowhide. They were to be shipped to England the next day, for shooting. I had only that night to age them and make them look real. What you can do with airbrushing and topical mediums over night is amazing!

How do you age leathers?

There are all sorts of things you can do with leather. First of all, if you have a thick leather, like a cowhide, that needs to be broken down, you might first smash it with a mallet. There was a film called *Terminal Velocity*, with Charlie Sheen, where Sheen had these thick leather jackets. I decided that the leather had been well tanned for wear in all weathers, so I actually threw the jackets in a washing machine after covering them with conditioners. But that is a rarity, and not to be recommended!

Wow! Can't that harden and shrink the leather?

If leather has been properly tanned, the old-fashioned way, you can wet it and dry it. And these jackets—because they were all-weather jackets, like Harley jackets—are going to be worn in the rain, wind, sleet, get washed and come back and still be soft. Then, you can almost be sure they've been tanned the proper way—vegetable tanning. So you can sling them in the washing machine and put lots of softener in, and that breaks down the whole surface. And then you must tumble-dry them on "cold" for at least twelve to twenty-four hours, until they are completely dry. That cold air ensures that they remain soft and supple. If you just let them air dry, without being tumbled, they will go rock hard, and crack. The whole secret is in tumbling them until they are completely dry.

It's like, in the old days, the Indians would stretch the skin after they tanned it. They actually used calves' brains. They would wipe the calves' brains back and forth, back and forth, while the skin would stretch, so they were constantly kneading it, massaging it, until it was dry.

Do you ever add color using shoe polish?

Normally, to age leather, I will take all the surface stuff off with a leather conditioner, which will remove all that dye and stuff. I use a de-glazing fluid. And then, I sand it down in areas that it would be heavily worn down. Always sand along the seams, elbows, around the neck, pocket "thingies," anywhere that you imagine that gets heavy usage. Crease it up in pleats—

Like at the bend of the elbows.

Yes, and sand all that with fine sandpaper. You just keep working at it. And then, you can rub in mink oil or Neatsfoot oil. Particularly on leather of a regular pigskin color, Neatsfoot oil will instantly darken and age it like you want it. I will airbrush leather dye first, maybe a subtle greenish shade, for a little shading, and then rub the Neatsfoot oil on top. The Neatsfoot oil works the dye in, and puts an aged look to the leather.

That's a leather that has a slicker skin surface, as opposed to a suede?

For suede, I sometimes put in glycerin. I definitely airbrush suede—it takes it very well. You have to be subtle. You should always, always experiment first. Be light-handed, until you know what you are doing.

Do you use shellac with the leather goods, as well?

Yeah, but just not as much. If you have too much shellac with the leather dye, it sometimes coagulates. Very rarely, but sometimes. Leather dye on leather does not really need shellac.

How do you deal with aging regular cloth jackets? Jackets have interfacings and linings that can be tricky dye problems—not to mention their fiber contents.

Any jacket is easier if the interfacing is basted, as with the old, proper tailor's interfacing.

As opposed to the fusible interfacings?

Yes. The trouble with silk suits is that the interfacing is usually iron-on, and it will become what they call "orange peel." We used to say it goes "lumpy," "pebbly." The correct definition in the fashion industry, I was told, was "orange peel." The heat melts the glue and makes tiny little bumps. Sometimes you'll get this when you get a lady's suit back from the dry cleaners and they've pressed it too hot. When you go to dye it, the same thing can occur.

When you're trying to get suits to dye, you have to watch out for polyester blends. Polyester is everywhere. I always tell a designer, "You will never win an award with polyester." It doesn't drape right, it doesn't cut right, and it looks like shit. I hate dyeing it. With polyester, you have to put in a "pre-treat." You have to wear a respirator mask at all times, then you put the dye in and you boil it, to melt the molecules. When the molecules are in a melted state, you slam in the dye with a very lethal carrier. It all looks a murky gray, but as it cools, it cools to a color. But you have no control, because before it cools to a color, you can't see what's going on. Then sometimes, you have to put it through an "after-treat" [after-treatment]. Because it is so environmentally unfriendly and bad for Mother Earth, and because I cannot one-hundred-percent guarantee my color, it's just something I refuse to do. I will not dye polyester.

You can tech polyester if you use enough nylon brown (so it will stain the polyester), but you can't dye it a dark, dark color. It'll wash out. And if you try to dye it red, with synthetic dyes, it goes to a dirty brown-y red color. I hate polyester.

How about traditional wool suits? Can you do any dyeing, considering the way wool shrinks in hot water?

Sometimes wool suits will shrink up to an inch and half in length. Not in width, but in length, which is something to remember. With a wool jacket, if you dye it at a lower temperature and you block it, it should be all right. In the "olden days," everything that was made was pre-washed; they did not have dry cleaning, and the garment would shrink if it wasn't pre-washed, so you *could* dye it. Unfortunately, with more modern methods, they never pre-wash the fabric. Armani, actually, is the best, because his suits seem to have been made from pre-washed fabrics. We dyed every single suit for Elliot Ness, the character played by Kevin Costner in the most recent version of *The Untouchables*, and they were all Armani suits, and they all dyed fabulously.

You also have to watch out because, now, almost invariably, clothing manufacturers use polyester thread, which doesn't take the dye. But you don't have to worry about that as much as you used to. There is an amazingly wide range of designer-color markers now that are permanent and wash-fast, so you can get almost any color marker and go over the thread to match, as long as you have the time.

Sometimes when you're aging wool coats you will stuff the pockets and the sleeves with wet newspaper, which you'll leave in overnight; and you "peg" them—not only to stretch the wool out, but also to put in creases where they would be. You leave it damp overnight, so that in the morning, when it's dried, the wet wads of paper have stretched the pocket pieces. Then, the pockets have got a weighted look, like they've been used often. And then, you might airbrush.

I've heard some comments made about avoiding too much symmetry when you are aging a garment, for example, making sure your sweat stains from your pits are not exactly the same. Always have some "breakup," so it doesn't look too theatrical in its aging. Do you have any thoughts on symmetry when shading a garment?

You should always think like an artist. Truly, there is no symmetry: Different people and different storylines will dictate different sweat stains. The sweat stain might be more on one side; it should not look perfect. You should always imagine the figure and where they would sweat or have dirt or worn-places. It's good to know where the actor's knee cap is, what the elbow height is. Is the actor high-waisted or low-waisted? Of course, nowadays, we hardly ever, ever, ever know who the actor is. Often, two days before shooting, the costume department still doesn't know who their actor is.

It's even beyond that. It's knowing the script, knowing the characters. Who are they? What are they doing? What kind of life do they live? What's the scene? I would love it if every dyer could read the script so they would know who the character is when they make the colors. On instinct, you can subtly put a nuance in the color based on the character. If this is a good guy or a bad guy, you can make the color sort of warm and friendlier, or cooler and not so nice. There really is a good-guy gray and a bad-guy gray!

Also, with aging, with distressing, you must always, always, remember the inside. You must always break down inside the hem of the jacket, and up inside the side of the jacket, and maybe a little bit under the arms. With trousers, inside the trousers, inside the pockets. With shoes, the sole of the shoe. You never know when the director is going to say to the actor, "Take the jacket off and throw it over a chair." If the actor takes off that jacket and throws it over a chair and it's brand-new and clean inside, that's a problem.

One of the biggest faux pas with shoes I ever saw was in *Merry Christmas, Mr. Lawrence*. David Bowie has been in this Japanese prisoner-of-war camp, and his costume was wonderful and all broken up. He's exhausted and he cannot stand anymore, so he's lying against the wall with his feet up. And there, twenty feet high on the screen, are brand-new soles underneath his broken-down boots.

How do you handle rubber on shoes?

In *Forrest Gump*, we had to age Tom Hanks' sneakers. Aging sneakers is hard. We had a friend who has a grinding machine, and we ground down the soles so that they were worn down where you walk. And then you can actually put them in dye, and put them in the drying machine. The dye penetrates the rubber better than topical paints, which tend to rub off. But then in the scene where he wears these beautifully broken-down sneakers, he has brand-new shoe laces. They didn't break down the shoe laces!

How about knit goods?

Often, you will be asked to age socks and knitted fisherman hats and things like that. They *cannot* bring you acrylic. First of all, you won't get dye in it. No matter how much anybody says "Oh, I have this great recipe for acrylic dye," they don't; it washes out. The only way you can dye acrylics or polyesters or things like that is to boil the fiber. I have to tell you right now, you should never, ever boil acrylic, never! Because it destroys the fiber. It weakens the fiber and can put permanent creases in the fiber. If you want to distress something, you can boil it, but if you're dyeing it, you should never boil it. And in hot water, acrylic fiber loses its memory completely, which means that it forgets that it was a hat or a sweater and just comes out this horrible misshapen thing, and permanently creased.

To pull a dyeing and distressing kit together, you should have Ivory liquid or Synthrapol, Cassalene, and fabric dyes that, at minimum, cover cool and warm teching colors, plus colors to help achieve "movement." Fabric softener, sand paper, razor blades or a file, and seam rippers can help prep goods for long-washing distressing. Paper towels or newspaper for pocket stuffing. You also need liquid leather dye, alcohol, shellac and a sprayer for FEV techniques. You need a spray bottle or plant mister, bleach, and Magix in a variety of colors, including Champagne, Avocado, Smoked Elk, Saddle, Gray, Olive, Brown, and Black, in case you are distressing dark goods. Deglazing fluid and Neatsfoot oil, for working with leather. And you need Schmutz, in a full range of colors. Mineral oil and glycerine, for on-set distressing work.

The thing that I must stress, though, is that you should always, always, always, always use your best respirator mask. There is never a moment when you are using an airbrush that you should not use a mask, because you are breathing paint particles into your lungs. And wear goggles, to protect your eyes. And use latex gloves or surgical gloves.

Especially with the alcohol-based dyes and acetone and Magix and spray bleach. Because, depending on the chemical, if used in large quantities, it can go into the cellulose of your hair or the pores of your skin. It can effect your kidneys and your blood stream and, even, like acetone, kill your brain cells.

I just don't want to hear anybody saying, "I don't like to wear a mask." You get used to it, you do. The prop boys and the special effects boys are so macho, they laugh. They refuse to wear masks, and they laugh. And you know what? The saddest thing is, they're gone. By the time they are fifty-four, they have cancer, they are dying. By the time they have family and kids, boy, do they wish they wore their masks. But you cannot get the young boys to wear them.

If the respirator mask doesn't work for you, that's because it doesn't fit right. After you have it on, if you put both of your hands over the filters, try to breath, and if you get no air, then it fits right. If you get air, it's not fitting right. Everybody has to have, in their kit, a proper respirator mask that they've had fitted to their face, with the proper filters.

There are filters for organic vapors, and there are pre-filters, for any dust particles. You should wear a dust mask if you are mixing any kind of powder dye—even if you are mixing it with water until it's in a paste. Once it's in a paste, you don't have to wear a mask. You should always have neoprene-coated gloves—the "bluettes" in the supermarket—when you mix dye. You should use latex gloves, surgical gloves, whenever you spray or paint. Aniline dye goes through the pores of your skin and breaks down your hemoglobin. And it's worse in women than in men.

There is never any excuse not to use a mask and gloves. From the moment I started doing repertory theater and traveling, I had my own mask, my own gloves, my own things. Don't ever rely on anybody else for these necessities. In my shop, if you don't wear a mask and you don't wear gloves, you're fired. My big bugaboo is that people should not work in unhealthy conditions. And theater and the film industry, particularly, have the worst conditions in the world for aging and distressing. You work without enough ventilation, or out in the open, where the wind whips it all over the place, so you must at least protect yourself. You must never, never have food or drink anywhere near the dyes. Every year, you should have a physical, and you should have your liver and your kidneys checked, because dyes, particularly aniline dyes, can effect your liver and your kidneys.

What about these safety lectures that cover aging and dyeing that the producers are paying for?

There are huge laws that have come out now. All the big companies are doing these programs. It's the law. There are lectures that everybody has to go to about fitting the mask and about all the health and safety issues—which is very good. Now that they have to go to these lectures, it means that the company managers will insist that their crews wear masks or they will be fired. Hopefully, that will make a better and healthier environment for everybody.

If you don't work for one of the big companies, you can investigate it yourself. There are some wonderful books out, including a book by Michael McCann called *Artist Beware: The Hazards in Working With All Art and Craft Materials (and the Precautions Every Artist and Photographer Should Take)* and three books by Monona Rossol: *The Artist's Complete Health and Safety Guide, Health & Safety Guide for Film, TV & Theater,* and *Stage Fright: Health and Safety in the Theatre.*

Everybody should have copies of these books, so that they know what they are working with. A lot of doctors don't know what we work with, or the side effects. So if you're feeling a bit off and you're going to have a physical checkup and you've been working with something fairly nasty, you should take your book with you. Show it to the doctor, and say, "Look, I've been working with these. These are the side effects. Can you give me a blood test, to check this part of my body?" It really helps the doctors. Don't rely on the doctors to know, because they can miss stuff.

Any other thoughts you have for potential dyers and distressers in the field?

The definition of a really good dyer and distresser is this: If you do your job right, they'll never know you've been there. Because we make it look real. We are some of the unsung heroes.

Conversation Twelve:

On Prep Collaborations with Craft Artisans, with Chris Gilman

Chris Gilman is president of Global Effects Inc., a company that manufactures special costumes and props for film. Past projects have included the astronaut suits for *From the Earth to the Moon* (1998), the biohazard suits for *Outbreak* (1994), and Dracula's armor for *Bram Stoker's Dracula* (1992).

I'd like to continue our earlier chat, but focus on prep period and time constraints.

The biggest mistake that I see made in preproduction is trying to rush, rush, rush, rush, rush—not allowing enough time to build the costume or "spec" the costume or make the costume. In fabric work, you can whip together stuff pretty fast, but not with vacuform or cast plastic parts.

Because you have to deal with curing and drying times, baking times, blistering, mold-making.

Or if you have to do outside processes—processes that we can't accomplish here at the shop; if you have to have something plated, for example. We don't do plating here, because plating is half voodoo, half chemistry. It's a really tricky process, to get it to come out right.

Subcontracting brings with it problems: being able to meet your target delivery date, for example—especially if that date moves up.

Designers make a big mistake when they sit around and pontificate on the subject of what a great thing this is going to be. They have eight weeks of preproduction time, and they spend five weeks of it deciding what they are going to design! You burn up a bunch of time going on and on and getting everybody's opinion and being wishy-washy and not making a decision. Then, when it comes down to it, there's not enough time to build it correctly. Often, people would rather procrastinate; they would rather say, "Oh, well, the actor hasn't been cast."

Aren't you held up in a big way by an actor being cast at the last minute, since you like to sculpt on top of body casts of the actor?

There are a lot of things that can be done without the actor, like pre-design. If you have an idea of how big the guy is going to be, you can do a maquette. Of course, if they cast John Candy, and you thought it was going to be Rick Moranis, you kind of wasted a bunch of time. But, on the other hand, if you think it's going to be Rick Moranis, and you get Dustin Hoffman, then you're okay.

And I know that when some costume designs are done, samples are wanted. Well, you don't necessarily have to have the actor to do samples. Say, somebody wants to know what the material is going to look like cast in rubber. "Is this going to give us the look we want?" We'll grab one of our molds upstairs, grab a sample of their fabric, and cast the material. Of course, it's not the exact shape they want, but it gives you a feel for color and how it's going to react.

As an owner of the company, if you come in to me and say, "We have ten costumes that we're going to build in sixteen weeks, but we can't start for another eight weeks," that's good news for me—because that's work that I know I will have in eight weeks. If you give me a deposit, I can order materials, I can make sure that I can get the people who are very good in that specialty, who are going to be more efficient. I can also get samples started. If I have to get processes done that require subcontracting, I can alert the people who I'm going to need. You don't have to have the actor to get a sense of, Are we over budget here? Is this going to take too long? Is this a six-week job? A four-week job? A three-week job?

What we'll do is give the designer a timeline. We'll say, This is what's required, how many weeks, and we'll type it up in our quote. They can come to us and say, "Look, this particular producer is gonna drag his feet big-time. I know he is. I need some help here." So, for purposes of the quote, we'll say eight weeks, instead of six.

That's the other big problem in Hollywood: People don't like to make decisions. They don't like to say, "Okay, let's do this," because they are unsure of themselves, and they really don't know if it's going to be the right decision. There is a great Hollywood quote, from a famous television producer: "As to my opinion of the script, I don't know. I'm the only one who's read it."

But sometimes, good people get trapped. Even if they know the project is coming eight weeks down the line, it can take forever to get firm casting.

If they don't have cast members, they have to start leaning on production. This is really where it comes down to the costume department doing its job. If you do not have the people I need when I need them (watch my lips), *things will be late.*

I see this business going down the toilet because too many people out there are going, "Oh, yeah, sure, yeah, we can do that," and then walking out of the room going, "Oh, how are we going to do this?" instead of just, right up front, saying, "You don't have enough time." The problem is that people are too afraid of getting fired and having somebody else hired, so they will say yes. There needs to be a balance of pre-planning and gutsiness, the ability to put your foot down and say, "No, I need this."

I've heard so many nightmare stories about an impossible shortage of prep time. There are many materials in your business that require elaborate prep procedures and long prep times. Do you give first priority to materials that are right for the design and the action?

FIG. 7.38

Dracula's armor, designed by Eiko Ishioka, for Francis Ford Coppola's film *Bram Stoker's Dracula*. Armor by Global Effects.

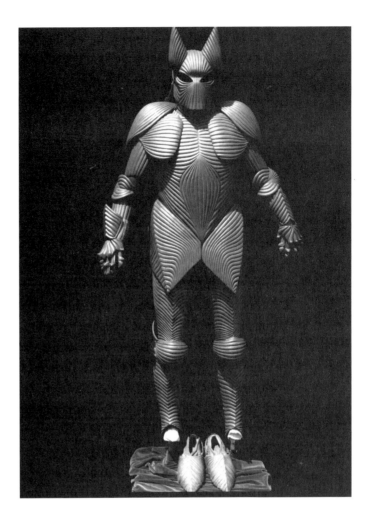

Photo courtesy of Global Effects

When we did *Bram Stoker's Dracula*, the costume designer, Eiko, designed a suit of armor that was, from a mechanical standpoint, totally impractical. Based upon the way she originally wanted it designed, it was almost impossible to put the person in it and have them do any movement. So, she said, "Well, we'll just make it all out of rubber." And we said, "Then it's really not going to be armor, it's going to look like a creature suit; so, wouldn't it be better to take the design and translate it into a mechanical shape that works, but still gets across your design?" I became the technical designer, taking her sketch and turning it into a mechanical shape that worked (fig. 7.38).

So, in your discussion with the designer, the exact degree of flexibility, of gloss, of surface detail, is of critical importance in choosing the materials and specing the labor?

Absolutely. Each project becomes a chain of events, a domino effect. And you have to know what materials are compatible. What materials shrink, what materials don't shrink.

How did you approach the *Dracula* suit?

The first thing that we did was sculpt a maquette of the actor Gary Oldman, using his measurements and his body cast. Because we were going to have to sculpt the armor to fit him exactly, we sculpted the rough sculpture in layers over the body cast and then made a mold. You have to take into account that some things shrink when you make molds, and then they shrink again when you make a casting out of that mold. We were going to make our sculptures of the layers, then make our molds of all those layers, and then make what we call "interpositives." Then, we sand out those interpositives, and make them perfect. Then, we would make a silicone mold, which requires a silicone "skin," and then a fiberglass jacket, to back up the skin, because the silicone is floppy and loose. If you don't have a rigid shape to hold the silicone skin in position, it won't ever be where you want it to be. We were going to do a final cast, in a urethane material, that was halfway between an elastomer (a rubber) and a rigid material.

In order to give some flexibility, for the action?

Yes. If you banged into something and flexed the armor, it would flex back, yet it would appear to be totally rigid.

The production didn't want to spend a lot of money making duplicate suits. The suit we were making would end up being the one suit that would be the most durable for all the action involved. And it would have the red of Dracula's armor cast right into it, so you could take a knife and gouge a big scratch in it and it would be the same color all the way down.

I understand that there were some serious changes on *Dracula*? With all these craft processes, how do you deal with production schedule changes?

First, we were delayed three weeks, because the designer didn't like the helmet. When the helmet was finally sculpted and the front view was translated into a three-dimensional thing, it looked like an aardvark. It did not look menacing, it did not look scary. So, it was re-design time. We re-designed the helmet and, after seventeen drawings and three weeks' worth of work, came up with a design that they were happy with. About six weeks before they were supposed to do the first shot, the costume department called us and said, "We would like to have the suit a few days early, so Gary can rehearse in it." And we said, "Well, we would like to have done that, too, but at this point we are going to be hard-pressed to make the fourteenth." And they said, "The fourteenth? The fourteenth of what?" "The fourteenth of December." They said, "What's on the fourteenth of December?" "Well, according to your shooting schedule, that's the first day up for Gary and the armor." "Oh no, no! Didn't you get the memo? That's all been changed. We're shooting this before Thanksgiving." And I just laughed.

When we got the call, we were in the middle of refinishing our interpositives and were still finishing up some of the sculptures. All of a sudden, instead of six weeks, we have three weeks. I just said, "There is no way that we can make this suit by then." The supervisor called me and said, "We are really trying to save some money. They're trying something with Gary's schedule. It would really be helpful." So, I said, "The only way we can do this"—and I kick myself for suggesting this—"is if we make the suit directly out of fiberglass, where we can sand and detail the parts as they come out of the mold."

It wouldn't move as well as the original material that you had intended use, but it might solve the time problem?

It would be more brittle, and the surface would have to be painted on, so it means that the paint could be scratched just as easily as taking a key to the paint of your car. It had a lot of downsides. I said, "The only advantage to this is that we can do it quicker. But it's going to break, it's going to scratch, it's going to crack, it's really going to be a high-maintenance thing. We should make that suit, and make a second suit right after it, and swap them out. When you are destroying one suit on set, we'll have the other suit in refurbishment." "Oh, we don't want to do that." So, we ended up making only one suit, in fiberglass.

The first day of shooting, we were on the set. They had sprayed the walls with the same material that you spray on the inside of a pool. It's very rough, it's like 36-grit sandpaper. In the first scene, Gary comes back and finds Winona Ryder dead on the steps, and he starts slamming himself into the walls and throwing over pots. We watched as this two-day, air-brushed, lacquered paint job got slammed into 36-grit sandpaper.

Another problem: The designer didn't want to see any visible closures in the suit. In the process of putting on all of these little hidden closures, two problems arise: (1) it makes it twice as hard to get into the suit, and (2) the closures don't hold well enough to hold the suit together during this highly athletic expenditure of energy, so pieces are popping open and flipping off.

Were you given no warning about how Oldman was going to move in the suit?

We didn't know that he had this *scene!* Francis Ford Coppola was very calm. He understood what pressure we were under, he understood what had gone on, as far as our time crunch. "Is there anything we can do?" he asked. I said, "Yeah, we can do this: We can drill a hole here, put a little screw in, you'll never see it." He goes, "Hey, fine, absolutely, go ahead and do that." So he gave us half an hour to go over and fix the stuff and put it back on Gary. It still cracked, and they still gouged the paint off of it, but none of the pieces popped free and came flying off. That night, we took the suit home, fixed it, re-fiberglassed it, re-sanded it, and re-painted it.

The whole moral of this story is, you should never, ever do that. And I will never do it again. I will turn the job down, or I will say, "Tough; can't do it." This, unfortunately, won't win you friends. Nine months later, as we were getting ready to do another big project, a designer came to us and said, "I was told not to use you guys." I said, "Why?" "Well, someone in the *Dracula* production office said that you guys had built some armor for them, and all it did was break."

A friend of mine once told me, "One dentist never criticizes another dentist's work." Because you don't know what the patient in the chair was like when that filling went in. So, no matter what we have done, you really don't know what the circumstances were surrounding it when it was getting made. Was it a twelve-week project that got cut down to eight? Was it a fifty-week project that got cut down to ten? Was it a one-hundred-thousand-dollar job that somebody tried to do for five thousand?

The difference between an expensive piece and an inexpensive piece is the fit and the finish. Take a look at a Yugo and take a look at a Mercedes-Benz. You don't have to know the mechanical difference, just look at the outside and you can see the paint quality is better, the fit is better. All the panels are straight, clean, every curve is perfect. That's where the money comes in.

Often, keeping the actors happy and coping with what they are willing to wear become elements in the mix. A lot of these suits are not very comfortable, even with

the meticulous fit you shoot for. Costume supervisors need to be able to plan for the actor's on-set comfort.

You have a guy in a big creature suit, and he's got to be on a hot stage all day. The human body generates a tremendous amount of heat. You put a guy in a suit, he starts sweating. There is no air circulating around him. You can't just pump air around the guy, because there is no way to get enough airflow.

We developed what we call a "cool suit," a vest system using liquid, for heat problems. This is an ultrasonically welded, urethane-coated nylon vest covered with one millimeter channels—one millimeter sealed areas filled with water. And we are able to make the cooling channels very, very close to one another. When these channels are filled with water, they inflate, becoming ellipses, and you get more surface contact. Our "vest" system works just like your blood stream: It circulates a fluid (close to the surface, in this case) that absorbs the heat from your body. It takes the liquid warmed by your body heat to a "heat exchanger," exchanges it for cold water, and circulates it back to your body. We use these suits to keep actors cool or warm.

And now, you can slip the cool suit in underneath the costume without having to take the costume on and off. This is extremely important in a costume that takes a while to get in and out of.

Can lack of coordination among a film company's various departments cause you headaches?

As a designer, you have to watch out because the area between costumes and props is sometimes seriously blurred. The prop guy wants to handle the helmets. Costumes wants to handle the costumes. Set dressing wants to handle costumes that have to get hung on the wall. Well, you don't really want to have three people doing that. You want to have one person doing that.

We worked on *Star Trek: First Contact*. They needed spacesuits. The costume designer knew that we were set up to do a wide range of things, but for some reason, they had another company do the helmets. They wanted us to do only the suits. So we did the suits. We went down to do fittings. The other company showed up with the helmets and the helmets weren't quite as far along as the costume department thought they were going to be. The suits were a little bit different than they thought they were going to be, so we settled on, "Move this up an inch; move that down an inch; move this over; change that; do this." We went away, they went away. They misunderstood what we were going to move. They moved theirs down an inch, and we moved ours up an inch. So, when they came back, it was worse. They had already made molds and this and that, so we had to rip apart our stuff again.

They were also trying to save time by modifying existing items. Sometimes it gets to the point where it's just cheaper to *make* it, but this was a battle that we lost. They wanted to modify stuff, and it just took forever. And when it was done, it didn't look as impressive as it could have. I don't know what the guys were up against, but the bottom line was, there were problems with the helmets. When they got on set, there was a three- or four-hour delay while they were trying to fix the problems with the helmets—which is a hot seat that I've been in, and I hate it. It's a horrible place to be.

PART EIGHT

Shoot

Introduction to a Shoot

Working on a film can be an exciting, unnerving, awe-inspiring, and mind-numbingly boring experience. The equipment, the manpower, the stunts, the stars, and the sheer mobility of it all can be very impressive. Even though every day of shooting carries "opening night" pressure, the full performance is a bit of a mystery: You never get to see the final product—the finished sequencing of shots and scenes—until well after your work is done. On set you're surrounded by waves of energy and neurosis; emergencies crop up on a regular basis. But unlike any other part of the business, being on set lets you feel the heartbeat of the film.

Set crews and actors can total a hundred or more individuals, and shooting days are long. For union shoots, calls depend on whether the crew is shooting in town or on location. In town, crews average a fifty-four-hour week, with a minimum nine-hour turnaround time between calls. On location, crews work fourteen-hour days, any five out of seven days, getting a minimum eight-hour turnaround days one through four and a forty-eight-hour turnaround after day five. This can mean that you start a week shooting from 5:00 A.M. to 7:00 P.M. and end the week shooting from 9:00 P.M. to 11:00 A.M., with a 5:00 A.M. start up two days later. A schedule can run the gamut, with all-day or all-night calls depending on the need for "daylight" or "night" exteriors.

Film crews aim for as much speed, and as little reliance on local resources, as possible. On location, it is the intent of production to be a self-sufficient unit. Generators, lights, costumes, and vast quantities of equipment are all part of the traveling production caravan. Film units even prefer to hire full-time caterers, rather than lose time while cast and crew search for local lunch sources.

Even though time is precious, filmmaking can feel like a very slow process, with a great deal of "hurry up and wait." The camera department sets the pace for the day. Most scenes will be shot from a variety of angles. Each angle requires its own camera and lighting setup. Moving the camera involves the complex workings of a crew made up of camera and lighting technicians who run cable, lay track, choreograph the movement of dollies and cranes, measure and mark focal lengths, and more. Sound recording may involve multiple takes if an airplane passes overhead, or a member of the crew talks too loudly, or an actor's shoes squeak repeatedly.

On set, everyone's priority is to get camera rolling. Rehearsals are short and sweet. Generally, the technicians only get one camera rehearsal, right before the cameras roll. Often, the action of a scene is worked out in the process of shooting it.

On-set personnel need to be on their toes at all times. The pressure is on to get it right every time the camera rolls. Fortunately, the time it takes camera and lighting to prep each shot buys the costume and makeup crews time to dress the actors, maintain their costumes on set, and make valuable notes on continuity. Off-set personnel have to have the goods ready to go. For the costume crew, the daily priorities revolve around prep, maintenance, and record-keeping. During the course of the shooting day, the costume department must respond to costume emergencies *and* prep the next scene's, and the next day's, work. No one wants to wait for wardrobe problems to be solved.

Filming is often a physically difficult process. Not only are the hours long, but the work can be dangerous, and the physical logistics are often awkward in the extreme. Filming in a jungle; on a busy street, in a suburb, in a museum, or in a tiny house all cause complications. Mud, rain, heat, noise, and access to electricity all have an impact on the shoot, and require great flexibility and problem-solving skills. The distance from the trailers to the dressing rooms, the distance from the trailers and dressing rooms to the set, the size of the set itself become critical concerns. The bigger the set, the more grueling it is to lug gear back and forth. The smaller the set, the hotter it is, and the more difficult it is to make costume adjustments.

I (HC) remember working on location in the small bedroom of a suburban house. The space was so small that the only members of the production team allowed in were those needed to make the scene happen on film—the first AD, the DP, two camera operators, and the sound boom operator. Wedged into an adjoining hallway were the director, a producer, the script supervisor, a makeup gal, and me, the set costumer—all vying for access to one video monitor. It was about 110 degrees, from the heat of the lights, and the actors were sweating like there was no tomorrow. The wardrobe van was about three blocks away, so I was perched on top of a precious pared-down batch of supplies.

At the end of each shot, I would whip out a blow dryer and towel, to cool the actors off. In between shots, the camera and lighting guys were hustling for all they were worth, and I had to choreograph my "runs" to take care of the actors with the camera's "dance" to re-set camera and lights. I could barely squeeze around the camera equipment to get to the actors. Everybody was uncomfortable. With each take, tempers rose. By three in the morning, the AD had virtually eliminated our time to "tweak" between shots. The pace was too fast, the set too damn tense to do the job. Wardrobe continuity became a low priority. Unfortunately, this happens. Working on set, you learn to recognize what must be done, and how to do it—with minimum distress and maximum finesse.

For all this, working the set can be stimulating, even, occasionally, thrilling. You can watch the lighting, sound, and camera crews do their thing. You can watch the actors work. Watching the video monitors that dot the set, you can see how scenes are shot, and learn to think like a camera. (If you can finagle your way into dailies, you will see the full-screen impact of what you saw being filmed. You will learn which "takes" the director thought most effective, and discover how costumes play on screen—which textures, colors, shapes work well, which subtleties of concept and construction "play" and which get lost; how designs that looked bad or boring on the hanger or on the actor can look remarkably right on film. All of this will help you design characters more effectively in the future.)

Seize every opportunity to work the set if you want a quick education in the film business. The savvier you are to the filmmaking process, the better collaborator you will be—and the better able you'll be to cover your boss's ass, and your own. Just as in the design and prep of a production, the shoot itself requires a costumer to be creative, flexible, diplomatic, have an eye for detail, strong organizational and administrative skills, superior endurance, and an unflaggingly great attitude.

The Wardrobe Trailer, Your Home on Location

Unless you are shooting your entire production on a soundstage, you will be shooting, more than likely, on location—at sites out in the real world. Because the production must carry with it everything and anything it might need, every department—including the camera department, electrical, grips, sound, costumes, makeup and hair, special effects, props, art department, catering, and the rest—has equipment and supplies standing by in trucks and trailers. These trucks and trailers are distributed around the site under the guidance of transportation coordinators and location managers. Film locations tend to sprawl, and departments end up jockeying for proximity to the set. "Near set" parking priorities go to the camera and electric department trucks, to allow them quickest access to heavy, cumbersome equipment. The craft services table, for all-day munching, is set up close to the set. The catering truck, on the other hand, is parked some distance from the set, near the area reserved for crew dining. The honeywagon (with dressing rooms and restroom facilities and continuously running electricity) is, predictably, a hike from most sets; the on-location production office is often crammed into one of these dressing-room cubicles, so the long-suffering second ADs and PAs get their exercise. Naturally, parking for personal vehicles can be hell.

The wardrobe trailer is also frequently a fair hike from the set, and is usually grouped with the hair and makeup trailer, the actors' motorhomes, dressing room trailers, and the honeywagon (fig. 8.1). A map showing where to park your personal vehicle, where the shooting sites are, and where the wardrobe trucks are parked is distributed along with the detailed daily schedule known as a "call sheet." (For more on call sheets, see below, "The call sheet.") The costume supervisor and set costumers need to take careful stock of where the wardrobe trailer will live, where it is in relation to actors' dressing rooms, extras' holding areas, and the set. The placement of the wardrobe trailer has everything to do with what the set costumers need to take with them to set. A quarter-mile run to the wardrobe trailer or dressing room for an actor's hat or a warming jacket or an emergency repair kit will not endear you to anyone on the set, or off, including the higher-ups in your own department. Imagine this run in the rain, in the snow, in sweltering heat, under the unhappy gaze of an entire crew. (If the costume supervisor needs to negotiate the wardrobe truck's placement on location, it must be done with the location manager and the head of the transportation department, well in advance of arrival—the day before, if possible.)

When it comes to the location of things inside the wardrobe trailer, the logic with which you organize trailer stock is critical to doing your job well, and to solving costume emergencies. In Part 6, *Prep*, I discussed the art of packing of a wardrobe trailer and gave some examples of trailer ground plans. As you know, wardrobe trailers can be elaborately designed, with air conditioning, windows, pipes that can be locked down and reconfigured for hanging stock, bins for storage, fold-down worktables and ironing boards, mechanical lifts for loading. In the low-budget land of independent film, you can get stuffed into the back of a U-Haul truck, crushed into one dressing room of a honeywagon, or, if you're really out of luck, stuck costuming out of the back of your

FIG. 8.1

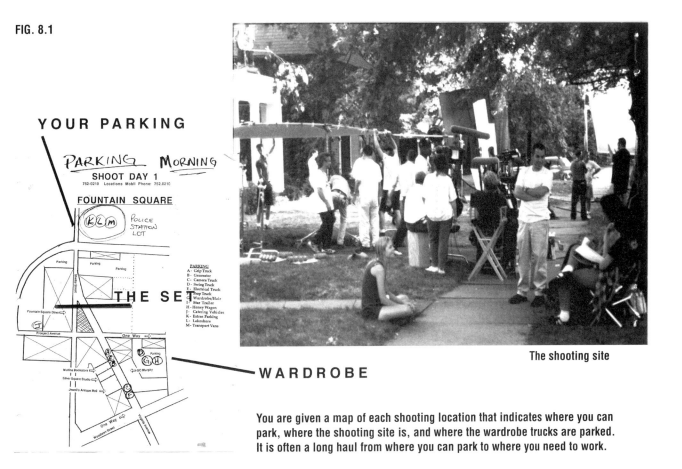

YOUR PARKING

PARKING MORNING
SHOOT DAY 1
752.0210 Locations Mobil Phone: 752.0210

FOUNTAIN SQUARE

POLICE
STATION
LOT

PARKING
A- Grip Truck
B- Generator
C- Camera Truck
D- Swing Truck
E- Electrical Truck
F- Prop Truck
G- Wardrobe/Hair
I- Star Trailer
H- Honey Wagon
J- Catering Vehicles
K- Extras Parking
L- Lakeshore
M- Transport Vans

THE SE

WARDROBE

The shooting site

You are given a map of each shooting location that indicates where you can
park, where the shooting site is, and where the wardrobe trucks are parked.
It is often a long haul from where you can park to where you need to work.

car. The lower the budget, the cheaper the trailer design, the fewer the trailers, and the
greater the need to organize well.

The design of the trailer or truck will dictate how and where supplies are stored
and set up for the shooting day. Hauling rolling racks in and out of the trailer, schlepping boxes of supplies from high cabinets and low drawers, setting up ironing boards
and sewing machines at the curb, hunting down power sources and water sources for
laundry hookups are all staples of the set costumer's job. Leaning on other departments
for supplies and aid is heartily discouraged, and all set costumers are expected to have a
personal *set kit* of supplies and equipment (see A.30-A.33). Nonetheless, the pressure that
comes with shooting does fuel the need for an attitude of cooperation among departments, which makes even more important a thorough understanding of department
jurisdictions—that is, which department is responsible for what, and who is responsible
for what in each department—starting with your own.

Costume Jurisdictions During the Shoot

Who does what during a shoot? Given basic, relatively fixed job jurisdictions, the duties of the key members of the costume department can be refined over the course of a production; from prep to shoot, they can shift, and often expand, depending on circumstances (especially on non-union productions).

Of course, the designer is responsible for establishing the look of the characters, but once shooting starts, it's the look of the characters *in the scene*. This means getting on-site approval (often *on-set* approval) of the clothes from the director, the cinematographer, and the producer. In all likelihood, actors will continue to be cast, and costume changes will have to be acquired and prepared while shooting goes on, even for already established characters. This, too, is primarily the designer's responsibility. (For more on the responsibilities of the costume designer during the shoot, see below, "The costume designer's daily routine.")

> The actual filming of a script is a very creative process—the only time a director has to show what he's all about. If you want your ideas to come through, you have to be there to represent them when the scenes are rehearsed. The only way to achieve this is to be on set as much as possible. *(Jean-Pierre Dorléac, costume designer)*

The costume supervisor is responsible for all costume-department work during the shoot—at home base, at the trailer, and on the set—from daily prep to final wrap. Set costumers have primary responsibility for what happens on the set itself. In preparing the actor to appear in wardrobe on set, the set costumers prepare the actors' dressing rooms, help dress the actors, clean and maintain the clothes, help style the extras, and work the set, attending to the actors, caring for the costumes, and tracking costume continuity. Importantly, they are the eyes and ears of the department on set, communicating the priorities and politics of the shoot to the designer and the supervisor.

The cheaper the production, the more costume personnel will be asked to double up on their duties. For example, on a low-budget film, the designer may double as the costume supervisor, a design assistant may double as set costumer. On a big-budget production, you'll have more lavish staffing, but it will come with the pecking order and job descriptions of guild and union. Work on small independent films can foster good survival skills, but, with some exceptions, it rarely teaches the job etiquette required on large-scale, moneyed union productions. (Detailed guild and union job definitions for designer, costume supervisor, and set costumers appear in fig.1.4 and will be elaborated on below, in the section called "Daily Routine.")

There are costume-related elements that are not solely the responsibility of the costume department. For example, while the costume department will supply stunt players with their costumes and help them with specific shoe and safety needs, stunt players generally provide their own special stunt padding. When it comes to hats, the costume department supplies them, and the hair department places them on the actors. Hair ornaments may be chosen by both the costume department and the hair department. (Generally, the hair department chooses them, although the costume department may find something that works, then seek the lead hairdresser's approval.) Again, the hair department places the ornament on the actor. When necessary, a makeup artist dirties the face and hands and any other part of the body; a member of the costume department dirties the clothing. The prop department distributes eyeglasses, weaponry, briefcases, umbrellas, nametags, and some personal jewelry. The costume department collects them at the end of the day, and returns them to props if the actor has forgotten. Who *chooses* these items can be a matter of acute sensitivity; as a result, a respectful and communicative relationship between the costume designer and the property master is critical, not only during prep, but throughout the shoot.

The costume department is frequently hit up for clothing items and accessories to be used by the prop and art departments for set dressing. The set dressing department may hit up costumes for a steamer, to unwrinkled drapes or tablecloths. The sound department may expect the costume department to supply *mike packs* (pocket and strap devices used to strap a microphone to an actor's body); *shoe booties* (slip-on shoe covers that encase the shoe) and other sound-muffling costume devices. Members of the camera and electric departments, in particular, may hit up the costume department for harsh-weather gear, in the event of excessive cold, sun, heat, rain, as can anyone on the crew, including actors, producers, ADs, and PAs. In general, any clothing or sewing needs that crop up during the day will get passed along to the costume department, on set or in the trailer, and it is up to the on-site crew to keep track of these unexpected demands.

Costume Tracking Procedures

Keeping track of costumes during the shoot is perhaps the preeminent responsibility of every member of the costume crew. This multifaceted task requires a fine eye for clothing detail, an excellent memory, a disciplined sense of organization, and a precise hand for record-keeping.

The principal reasons to track costume continuity:

• *Multiple takes and varied camera setups.* Scenes are shot from a variety of angles, in multiple takes, to provide editorial choices and help cover editing transitions. When different angles and takes of a scene are cut together in the editing room, the costumes—both what the actor wears and how he or she wears it in the scene—must match. An absent hat, an errant strap, the ever-shifting drape of a scarf can cause the visual gaffes that film hounds love to catch.

• *Out-of-sequence shooting.* Films are usually shot out of sequence. This means that an actor may film a scene on day one of the shooting schedule in which he boards an airplane in L.A. On day thirty of the shooting schedule, he films the scene in which he gets off that plane in New York. If the actor is wearing a pinstriped suit and a trench coat when he gets on the plane in L.A., he'd better be wearing the same suit and trench coat (even if he's carrying the coat on his arm) when he deplanes in New York. If you don't have a record of what he was wearing and how he was wearing it, and if you can't remember where it's racked, or if it's at the dry cleaner, you're in trouble.

- *Re-shoots.* When a problem is detected after a day of shooting, a scene or a portion of a scene may have to be re-shot (this is called a "pick up" shot). The wardrobe for all of the actors in that scene must then be reconstructed precisely, using the continuity notes and photos taken on set during the initial filming. This pickup shot may not be done until principal photography is completed; if the costume is a rental, it may have to be retrieved from one of many rental houses, so keeping track of the costume's whereabouts is also critical.

- *Actor doubling.* All stunt doubles, photo doubles, and body doubles need to have the details of the their outfit recorded exactly, so that the actor and his double look exactly alike.

Costumers have developed basic strategies for keeping track of costumes on the truck, in the performer's dressing room, and on the set. They include making sure that (1) the elements of a character's costume changes are clearly assembled, marked, and recorded; (2) the changes are bagged, tagged, and hung on the rack in an orderly fashion, for speedy access; (3) the costume change is laid out in a way that allows an actor to easily put on the correct costume pieces for a scene; and (4) accurate records are kept for the ways in which an actor wears a costume over the course of a scene.

To meet these requirements, film costumers have developed a costume tracking system that becomes part of the set costumer's routine. It is made up of four basic phases: (1) changes for principals and day players, which have been bagged, tagged, and organized, are pulled for the day; hanging stock for extras is chosen and organized for the day; (2) changes for principals and day players are laid out in dressing rooms, and change tags collected; extras are dressed with pre-fit changes or "speed-styled" using costume stock; (3) costume continuity notes and photographs are made on set; (4) written notes and photos are organized in the set book(s).

Phase one: Character changes and hanging stock pulled

Costume changes and extras stock for the day are pulled from their place on the trailer's racks. (They should already have been loaded onto the trailer.) This may be done the night before, in preparation for the next day's scenes—that is, if the costumes are not currently working on set. As noted in Part 6, *Prep*, "day racks" may be used on which all of the day's changes are hung, organized by scene, in shooting order, and within that scene, by character number (taken from day-out-of-days). To work at peak efficiency, the stock order and system of bagging, tagging, and re-stocking in the trailer must be maintained—or your cohorts will want to kill you. (See Part 6, *Prep*, for details on stock organization and change-tagging.)

Phase two: Changes laid out and change tags collected; extras' wardrobe assigned

For each day of shooting, the first outfits for all the day's key characters will be distributed to their various dressing rooms (in the parlance, a dressing room is "set," as a table is set). Garment bags and tags will be removed and saved, and the clothing the actors are to wear will be laid out in a logical and attractive fashion. (Principal actors should not be asked to re-tag their garments at the end of the day.) Additional changes for the day will either be placed on the day rack or kept bagged and tagged in dressing rooms, depending on the preference of the costume supervisor.

Extras may or may not have garments already assigned to them. The extras may be bringing options from their personal wardrobes that need to be approved and credited to their pay vouchers in order for them to receive proper payment for their goods. The costume department may also supply wardrobe on sight (fig. 6.17), so set costumers need to be prepared to keep a list of the goods that were given to, or supplied by, extras.

Costumers assigned to handle extras follow these steps:

1. At a predetermined site (this may be the door of the wardrobe trailer or an extras holding area), the costumer asks extras to form a line or respond to their name when called. When asked, the extra provides his or her pay voucher (or driver's license) and the personal wardrobe supplied according to the designer's guidelines (fig. 8.2).

FIG. 8.2

When the extras arrive, they are given a pay voucher by the casting department. They turn the voucher in to the wardrobe department for their new costume pieces. At the end of the day, when they have returned all of their costume pieces they get their voucher back.

2.   The costumer supplies a pre-fit change and/or new costume pieces, subject to the designer's approval. On an extras change tag or an extras costume chart, the set costumer notes the stock items that were supplied and the approved items supplied by the extra (see Part 6, *Prep*, for extras change-tag form, or fig. 7.30, for extras costume chart). The extra's change tag, any size tags that were on the pieces, and the pay voucher will be stored together and the vouchers filed in alphabetical order.

3.   At the end of the day, the extras return all of their wardrobe items, which are checked in on their tags or the master chart before their pay vouchers (or driver's licenses) are returned to them.

Phase three: Costume continuity notes and photographs made on set

Once shooting for the day has begun, the set costumer will take continuity photographs and make notes on both the photographs and on the accompanying continuity pages. The level of detail needed in both the photographs and the written descriptions is determined by two principal factors:

1.   *The amount of screen time the garment will get.* Costumes of featured players are noted and photographed in detail. Extras may be photographed in groups, with emphasis on those closest to camera; notes, if made at all, are only on the wardrobe of "character" extras and those in close proximity on camera to principals.

2.   *The similarity of pieces in the wardrobe.* A large number of like items, for example, a load of white dress shirts or a half-dozen gray suits worn by a team of businessman characters, makes it necessary for the set crew to keep detailed notes on garment label and brand information, in order to distinguish among principal characters' garments.

The set costumer is responsible for keeping wardrobe continuity notes on set for the characters he or she is covering. Formally, these notes are made on *wardrobe continuity pages*. (See figs. 1.6 and 1.7 for an example of a principal's wardrobe continuity page.) The set costumer keeps these pages in a three-ring binder, which goes with her wherever she goes. At the end of the day, these pages are transferred to the set book, for use by the truck crew and the set costumer in setting costumes for the next day's scenes.

If the costumes have not yet been "established" on film (i.e., filmed previously), the costume's master change tag (which lists every item in the change) might be kept on a ring on the set costumer's belt, allowing last-minute, on-set changes to be noted immediately. (For example, when the director takes the gray fedora off the actor before the camera rolls for the first time on this change, the costumer can cross off "gray fedora" on the character change tag; as soon as convenient.) This correction should also be made on the wardrobe continuity page for the character, so that neither the set costumer nor the truck supervisor sets the gray fedora with this change the next time the change is "up."

If possible, wardrobe continuity pages should be prepared in advance, by listing the different costume pieces in the change. The costumes are itemized in head-to-toe order, with key item brands or sources noted in the manner the supervisor desires. If the wardrobe continuity pages have not been prepared or completed by the time the actor works in a given change, a great time for the set costumer to finish making these notes is while the actors are rehearsing.

Once the camera is rolling, detailed usage/continuity notes are recorded on the wardrobe continuity pages for the characters who are working in the scene (see figs. 1.6, 1.7). Some costumers also take additional blocking and costume-business notes in the margins of the script, line by line, bit by bit. Final notes are recorded, and Polaroids taken, only *after* the camera has rolled. Notes should be made of wardrobe shifts within a scene, and of stains or other damage done in the course of the scene. These changes should be related to the scene's dialogue, to indicate when the changes occurred, for example, "He took the overcoat off when she said 'Take a load off,'" or "Quarter-size spaghetti-sauce stain between second and third shirt button on 'That's some spicy—'."

As soon as possible after "cut" is called, the set costumer must take a photograph of the actor in costume. The actor only needs to be photographed if the look is being established for the *first time*, or if the look shifts significantly during the course of the scene. Shoot with a neutral tone background when possible (high-contrast backgrounds can cause a loss of detail.) As a rule, the entire change must be photographed. Before taking the continuity photo, the set costumer should find out just what's in the frame. (Most film frames do not include quite as much as the camera lens sees; ask the script supervisor.) Significant and difficult-to-duplicate costume details should be photographed in close-up; if the detail is jewelry, the actor should be asked to hold up her arms to display jewelry more clearly (see fig. 8.3) If possible, the photo should be developed before the actor leaves the set, in order to check for clarity. The set costumer then punches a hole in the top corner of the photo and hangs it on a ring on her belt, until she can affix it to the official wardrobe continuity page.

As noted above, extras are frequently photographed in groups of three or more, to save film (see fig. 8.4). The date, the scene number, and the names of the extras should be written on each photograph. Supervisors will dictate the level of detail necessary in the notes for the extras. (Notes may be minimal, since, often, extras are "shot out" the day they work, and, as a result, "matching" is not required.)

Traditionally, wardrobe continuity photographs were done on Polariod film. However, most units now use digital cameras to record continuity. Both Polaroid and digital cameras create problems for costumers. Polaroid prints are famous for their inaccurate color and detail—especially when the figure is shot against a high-contrast background. Polaroid prints do not develop in cold-temperature conditions. Digital cameras can have similar problems with high-contrast backgrounds, and smoky or dark atmospheres can cause a loss of detail in the photos. But digital cameras often deliver better color and detail than Polaroid cameras, and digital images can be checked immediately for accuracy. Even though a digital camera allows you to store and check photos in its memory, you have to take the time to "come up to the trailer" and print. With a small table and some help from the electric department, you can set up a print station on-set; this is the ideal situation for set costumers. In this manner, you have the immediacy of a print, which you can affix almost immediately to the page in your continuity book. Some set costumers take both Polaroids and digital or non-digital 35mm stills, to ensure the accurate documentation of costume detail.

FIG. 8.3: CONTINUITY PAGE DETAIL

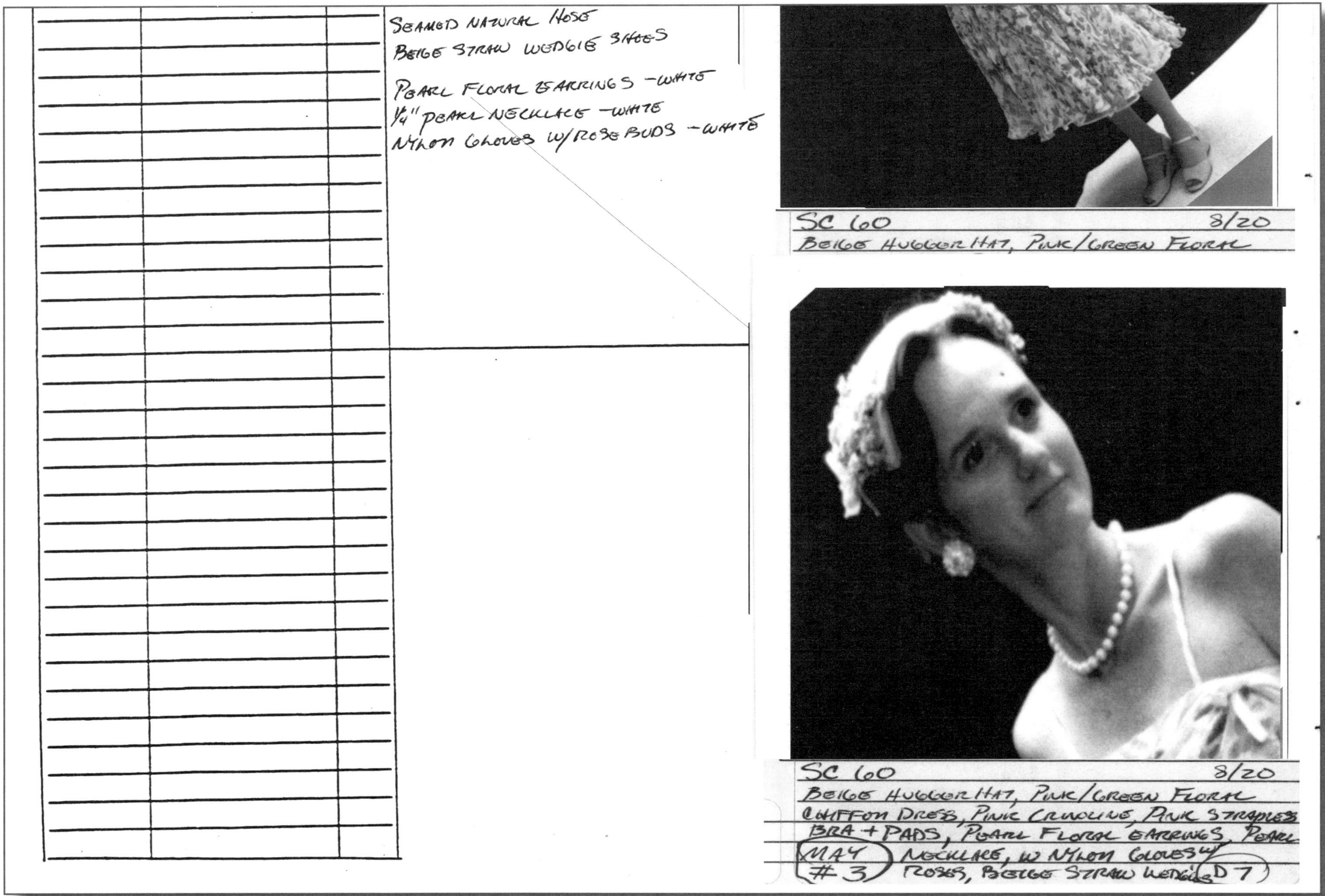

SC 60
BEIGE HUDGEN HAT, PINK/GREEN FLORAL
8/20

SC 60
BEIGE HUDGEN HAT, PINK/GREEN FLORAL
UNIFORM DRESS, PINK CANCANS, PINK STRAPPLESS
BRA + PADS, PEARL FLORAL EARRINGS, PEARL
MAY NECKLACE, W/ NYLON GLOVES,
3) ROSES, BEIGE STRAW HEELS,D 7
8/20

SEAMED NATURAL HOSE
BEIGE STRAW WEDGIE SHOES

PEARL FLORAL EARRINGS - WHITE
1/4" PEARL NECKLACE - WHITE
NYLON GLOVES W/ROSE BUDS - WHITE

FIG. 8.4: AN EXTRAS WARDROBE CONTINUITY SHEET

Character: Train Station Extras   **Production: Going All The Way**

Actor: As noted

Telephone: _____

Handwritten on photos: BARNES, SLAYMAKER, Ext Train Sc 11

Chg #	Sc #	I/E	Set/Action	D/N	Costume Notes - head to toe	Polaroids
1	11	E	TRAIN STATION	D2	Barnes – Porter uniform	
			Biff arrival			
					Slaymaker – Pale grey suit, white shirt,	
					red dot bow tie, own black shoes & sox	
					Russel – Brown fedora, yellow shirt,	
					brown tweed pants, grey/br stripe suspenders	
					brown & yellow zig tie, own black shoes	
					& sox	
					Gray – Pink dress w/ blk buttons, black belt	
					pink clutch, white gloves, pink hugger hat	
					own black shoes & hose	
					Simmerman – Summer sailor & cap	
					Heiple – White lace blouse, white full slip,	
					black A-line skirt, tan seamed hose, black	
					heels, black picture hat, black purse	
					Brennen – Black & yellow plaid dress, black	
					flats, tan seamed hose, black clutch	

If Polaroids are being shot, garment descriptions and dressing notes are usually written on labels, which are affixed to the back of the photos. Since the details in a Polaroid photo are often unclear, its colors distorted, it is wise to note the colors and brand names of pieces on your Polaroid labels. Notes should also indicate which items (if any) are from the actor's personal wardrobe. (Note: Taking Polaroids or flash photographs on set has its own etiquette. The flash of a camera, the time it takes to shoot a photograph, can turn into something intrusive, even dangerous, given the speed and precision needed to move heavy camera equipment and lighting gear, the concentration required by actors, and tense situations that may develop on set. Taking continuity photographs is a matter of delicate timing in a strained situation, but it must be done. While the camera and lights are being set up for the next shot, the savvy set costumer will pull aside the actor who needs to be photographed, out of the way of the director and the camera department. Before snapping the photo, call out "Flashing," so the electrical crew won't think a lamp or bulb has blown out.)

A word to the wise: Photos are often separated from their continuity pages—they travel back and forth from set to trailer for reference when pulling or restocking costumes—so it is vital to duplicate wardrobe notes on the continuity pages. (In this digital age, it is also useful to use a photo scanner to record the continuity photos and changes, or to shoot a set of digital continuity photos on set, as noted above, as is the routine of some set costumers. This makes it possible for a costume supervisor, using a laptop, to keep continuity photos on disk, for backup.)

In fact, prep costumers, costume supervisors, and designers all work from the set costumer's photographs and notes when doing the daily prep for shooting, as do over-hire staff and replacement personnel. As a result, the notes and photos must be accurate and clearly presented, and the procedures that follow from them precisely carried out (see below).

Phase four: Written notes and photos are organized in the set book(s)

At the end of the shoot day, all continuity pages, including photographs, should be filed in the set book(s). Most often, there are two set books: one for the principals and one for the day players and extras. (The contents of the set book(s) were discussed in Part 6, *Prep.*) As noted above, the set book is used daily at the trailer to help set up future scenes. It should never leave the truck overnight, with the following exception: On low-budget films with small crews, set costumers are taxed to the max taking care of the actors, recording continuity, clearing dressing rooms, inventorying wardrobe, making laundry lists, and reassembling changes. When no time is left at the end of the day to update the set book, the book may be taken home, if absolutely necessary, in order to finish mounting photographs and recording notes.

Even in the most trying circumstances, continuity must be recorded in detail for all principal characters, particularly those with the most screen time. After all, the set book is not only the key source of information for re-shoots, but the official record for all the costumes on the production.

The Daily Routine

Because change is the only constant in the filmmaking process, the routines of the day—the standard operating procedures of the production, and of the costume department—become sources of stability. To make sure that every member of the crew is "on the same page," a "call sheet" containing basic information on a single day's shoot is distributed to every member of the crew. This one-page or two-page guide is a kind of key map to the shooting day (see fig. 8.5).

The call sheet

Like every department during a shoot, the costume department's schedule and pace depend on the scenes to be shot, the action of the scenes, the way the scenes are to be shot, and the logistics of location and talent. How does the costume department learn this information? From the "call sheet." Once principal photography begins (and every day of the shoot until you hear the final, "That's a wrap!"), a call sheet is distributed to each member of the crew, usually by the second AD or key PA. Distributed at the end of each day, the call sheet contains information about the next day's shoot. More precisely, a call sheet is a detailed schedule, densely packed with information about the location, working crew and talent, and, most importantly, the scenes scheduled to be shot. The call sheet sets goals for the day and gives an advance schedule (usually, the scenes set for the next two shoot days of shooting, and the day's "cover set"—that is, a replacement for the scheduled set, should the scheduled set become un-filmable as a result of inclement weather or other site-related emergencies). Of course, what actually gets accomplished during the day is subject to the realities of the filming process, and scenes scheduled on the call sheet may not be completed, or shot at all, and may get bumped to later in the shoot. Not only weather, but stuntwork and special effects may cause shooting schedule changes.

If you study the day's call sheet, you will learn a number of things: the key scenes being shot and the cast members involved; key costume and prop pieces required for the scenes; call times for all the crew and cast. You can see whether any stunt of effects personnel are called; how many wardrobe vans, dressing trailers, and set costumers will be available; how many prop vehicles, animals, and wranglers will be involved; and who is in control of these departments. Since the members of each department are listed top to bottom (department head to department PA), you can see the pecking order of the entire on-site crew, a convenience that allows you to locate those in power—and avoid those with powerful opinions but no authority whatsoever.

The call sheet will also make it clear that the costume department has relatively little time to dress actors and extras, let alone accomplish final fitting adjustments. When you calculate the length of time between the scheduled pickup of an actor (p/up), the call time of the makeup department (m/u), and the set call (the time at which actors are expected on set, ready to shoot), you will see how much hustle is required of the costume department.

FIG. 8.5: THE DAILY CALL SHEET

Left panel

Hypothetical Pulp Fiction

Director's name here

Executive producers names here
Production Executive's name here
Producer's name here
Line Producer's name here

Crew Call	Day: Monday
	Date:
6am	Shoot Day: 1 out of 30
Shooting call	Production Office address
7:30am	Production Office telephone number
VANS LEAVE AT	Production Office fax number
5am	

Sunrise 6:01 am   Sunset 7:34 pm

24 hour set pager number:
Set phone number:

Breakfast will be served from 5:30am

Set A scene description	Scene	Cast	Pages	D/N	Notes
Ext.: Mason–Dixon Pawnshop * Day	80	4,7	2 1/2	D4	Address of shooting site
Marsellus hit by car/chase					
Ext.: Mason–Dixon Pawnshop * Day	87	4	1/6	D4	
Butch leaves on chopper					
Int.: Mason–Dixon Pawnshop * Day	81	4,7,13	1 2/3	D4	
Butch/Marsellus Fist Fight					
Int.: Mason–Dixon Pawnshop* Day	84	7	2/3	D4	
Butch gets sword					
		Total	5		

Cover set

	Scene	Cast	Pages		Set call
Int. Pawnshop Back Room	82	4,7,13,14,15	4 1/6	D4	7:30am
	85	7,15	1/6	D4	7:30am
Int. Russell's Old Room	86	4,7,13,14	2 1/2	D4	9am

Players

	Characters	P/Up	M/Up call
4 actor name	4 Marcellus	6am	6:30am
7 actor name	7 Butch	6am	6:30am
13 actor name	13 Maynard	7:30am	8am

Atmosphere

Gawker #1 & #2 @ 6am, 10 Pedestrians @6am
4 Stunt drivers @ 6am, Looky/Loo woman@6am
3 Butch stunt doubles @6am, 2 Marcellus stunt doubles @6am

Props
Donuts & coffee on tray(4)
Shogun [13], Samurai sword (7)

Vehicles
Butch car 6:30am

Costumes
Multiples for Butch and Marcellus

Makeup and Hair
Blood

Set Dressing
Pawn Shop dressing

Special Equipment
Tall pads

Vehicles
3 stunt cars @6:30am

Locations
Traffic control @ Int. Mason–Dixon
Street closure@ Ext. Mason–Dixon

Advanced Schedule

Date	Set		Scene	Cast	Pages	Location
Tomorrow's date	Int. Denny's - Day		1	1,2,5,6	5 1/6	Address of shooting location
The following day	Int. Denny's-Day		117-119	1,2,5,6	14 1/6	Address of shooting location

UPM signature ____   1st AD signature ____   2nd AD name & pager number ____

There will be a courtesy van provided to shuttle you to set and back.

Blocking rehearsal @6:30am

Right panel

Hypothetical Pulp Fiction   Day 1 out of 30   Today's date

	#	Position	Name	Call		#	Position	Call	Name
P	1	UPM	insert name here	O/C	W	1	Costume Design	5:45am	insert name here
R	1	Director	insert name here	6am	A	1	Assist. To Design	5:45am	insert name here
O	1	1st AD	insert name here	6am	R	1	Costume supervisor	5:45am	insert name here
D	1	2nd AD	insert name here	5:15am	D	1	On Set Costumer	5:45am	insert name here
U	1	2nd 2nd AD	insert name here	5:15am	M	1	Wardrobe intern	5:45am	insert name here
C	1	Key Set P.A.	insert name here	5:15am	/	1	Key Make-up Artist	5:45am	insert name here
T	1	Set P.A.	insert name here	5:15am	U	1	Key Hair Stylist	5:45am	insert name here
I	1	Set PA	insert name here	5:15am	P	1	Asst. Hair Stylist	5:45am	insert name here
O					H	1	Asst. Make-up Artist	5:45am	insert name here
N	1	Script Supervisor	insert name here	6am					
					L	1	Locations Mgr	O/C	insert name here
C	1	Extra Casting	insert name here	6am	O	1	Location Assist	O/C	insert name here
A					C	1	Location Assist	O/C	insert name here
M	1	Dir. Of Photo.	insert name here	6am	A	3	Police	O/C	insert name here
E	1	1st A.C.	insert name here	6am	T	1	Fire Marshall	O/C	insert name here
R	2	Loader	insert name here	6am	I	1	Medic	O/C	insert name here
A					O				
	1	Steadicam operator	insert name here	6am	N	1	Prod. Designer	O/C	insert name here
	1	Still Photo	insert name here	O/C	A	1	Art Director	as per	insert name here
					R	1	Art Dept. Coord.	AA	insert name here
G	1	Key Grip	insert name here	6am	T	1	Set Decorator	AA	insert name here
R	1	Best Boy Grip	insert name here	6am					
I	1	Grip	insert name here	6am		1	Leadman	AA	insert name here
P	2	Grip	insert name here	6am		1	Set Dresser	AA	insert name here
	2	Preng crew	insert name here	TBO		1	Set Dresser	AA	insert name here
						1	On-Set Dresser	AA	insert name here
						1	Asst. set decorator	AA	insert name here
						1	Art Dept. PA	AA	insert name here
E	1	Gaffer	insert name here	6am	O	1	Prod. Coordinator	O/C	insert name here
L	1	Best Boy Electrics	insert name here	6am	F	1	Asst. Prod. Coord.	O/C	insert name here
E	1	Electrician	insert name here	6am	F	1	Office P.A.	O/C	insert name here
C	1	Electrician	insert name here	6am	I	1	Assist to Dir.	O/C	insert name here
T	1	Electrician	insert name here	6am	C	1	Assist to Prod.	O/C	insert name here
R	2	Preng crew	insert name here	TBO	E	1	Assist to Prod.	O/C	insert name here
C						1	Accountant	O/C	insert name here
S						1	Assist Accountant	O/C	insert name here
S	1	Sound Mixer	insert name here	6:30am	C	60	Caterer	5:30am	insert name here
O	1	Boom Operator	insert name here	6:30am	A		Breakfast	12N	
U	1	Cable Wrangler	insert name here	6:30am	T	1	Lunch		
N					E				
D	26	Walkies	insert name here	C/O	R	1	Craft Service	6am	insert name here
					T	1	Transportation Coord	O/C	insert name here
	1	F/X Coordinator	insert name here	N/C	R	1	Driver	as per	insert name here
F	1	Rain F/X Coordinator	insert name here	N/C	A	1	Driver	B.B.	insert name here
/	1	F/X Assist.	insert name here	N/C	N	1	Honeywagon Driver	B.B.	insert name here
X	1	Visual Effects	insert name here	N/C	S	1	Make-up/Wardrobe	B.B.	insert name here
	1	Make-up FX	insert name here	6am	P	2	15 Pass van		
	1	M/U FX Assist	insert name here		O				
					R			Vehicles	
P	1	Prop Master	insert name here	6:30am	T	1	Props		
R	1	Prop Asst.	insert name here	6:30am	A	1	Fueler		
O	1	Prop Asst.	insert name here	6:30am	T	1	M/U & Wardrobe		
P	1	Prop Intern	insert name here	6:30am	I	1	Camera		
S					O	2	Grip/Electric		
					N	1	Honeywagon/8 Hole		
	1	Stunt Coord	insert name here	6am		2	Motorhomes		
	1	Stunt Driver	insert name here	6am		2	Shuttle Vans		
	1	Stunt woman	insert name here	6am		1	Production Car		
	1	Stuntman	insert name here	6am		4	Picture Cars		
		Writer							
		Writer							
		Studio Teacher							
		Publicist							
		Animal Wrangler							

The call sheet prepares you for what is scheduled. But to cover what isn't planned, the costume department must improvise. Filmmaking is an organic process. Although at times it may feel mechanical, the artistry of the process keeps it growing and changing. A shot evolves as the actors, the director, the camera department explore the text—and so will the costume department's tactics.

One of the things that I learned early in my career was the "option" thing. You just can't go into the fitting room or onto that trailer with just one choice. It is always nice to have a backup—always, always. I've been there so many times. For example, I did a film with Harvey Keitel called *City of Industry*, and we had prepared this one huge stunt scene. We had prepared five lightweight parkas, five shirts, five pairs of khaki pants, five pairs of shoes. Harvey was going to go into a river, and all these other stunts, in this change. We prepared it, and all the multiples, in May, and shipped out the scene somewhere in July. But things changed.

It was the hottest day of the year, and we were about to shoot this sequence, and Harvey, ten minutes before we shoot, calls me to the trailer and says, "Eddie, Why?" I go, "What?" He says, "You know, I don't know about this. This seems awful hot." Meanwhile, my wardrobe supervisor is having a cow. I said, "Okay, let's get every possible thing that we have from the other changes over here."

The scene's about this: Harvey is in a trailer and he's about to leave and suddenly he gets shot at. This all happens very, very fast. He has to be caught off guard. We brought in this Hawaiian shirt that was meant for another scene, and I said, "You know, if you wear this Hawaiian shirt, you'll really be caught off guard. You won't be like you're traveling to the bus station, like you were before; you'll be really caught off guard, and you'll be, like, almost naked." So, he loved that idea, and we went with it. We didn't have five of them, but they didn't all have to work that day.

But they would work within the next three days. What we did for a second shirt was really funny. The Hawaiian shirt was a bamboo print, but we had this great costumer on the show who could make things. We took a beige silk shirt. We cut off the sleeves and, with bleach, we did a bamboo print, for the second shirt. And it worked, it worked great—really, really great. Meanwhile, the costume supervisor is calling around, and we finally got hold of four more shirts, from Macy's, San Francisco.

If I hadn't done that, I think we would have caused more tension on the set. I think Harvey would have been unhappy throughout the rest of the film. He wouldn't have trusted me. It's one of those things I've just learned to deal with. The last-minute things are what moviemaking is about. And it isn't so much about creating something. It is, and it isn't. Every character is different. Every actor is different. So, the way you prepare is different for each character, each actor, each director. Certain directors want to see everything. Other directors put their trust in you. *(Eduardo Castro, costume designer)*

Fundamentals of the filming process: what to expect

Before developing the detailed daily routines of each principal member of the costume department during shooting, it might be useful to summarize the predictable activities and rhythms of the costume department, and of the entire crew *on set*, the destination of all costumes during this phase of filmmaking. If you've never worked on a film, you'll be lost unless you understand these fundamentals of the filming process.

For the costume department, each day of shooting begins by reviewing the day's call sheet, setting up the trailer for the day's work, including firing up the ironing board, the steamer, rolling racks, costume supplies, and so forth. This is followed rapidly by studying the "sides" (the script pages for the scene being prepped) and the costume breakdown forms and continuity pages for the characters to be dressed. Character changes are pulled, along with stock for atmosphere and any other items required for the first setup of the day (warming jackets, for example, if the weather is cold). Tags are removed and saved; changes are prepared. This may entail pressing or steaming out the folds in garments which have be crushed for days in hanging garment bags. Conversely, it may entail intentionally wrinkling, sweat-staining, or dirtying up pieces.

Character changes are carried to actors' dressing rooms (temporarily back in their garment bags—for protection). There, they are attractively laid out and de-tagged, the tags saved along with the empty garment bags. (Some supervisors allow garment bags to be left in dressing room closets, along with garment tags for that change; others prefer empty bags and tags to be returned to the wardrobe trailer until that change is wrapped.)

Once the principal actors are in wardrobe, they are sent to the set. The usual routine for setting up a shot gives the actors a chance to work out their blocking with the director and the DP, and then gives each technical department a crack at perfection before the cameras roll: "last looks," as called by the first AD.

Without much variation, except in scale and duration, the following procedure is repeated every time the camera changes position.

STANDARD SHOOTING PROCEDURES

1. *Camera and lighting setup.* Conventionally, each scene is covered from many angles, or camera positions. Each time the camera takes up a new position, lighting must be changed. As a consequence, camera and lighting equipment—sometimes, set pieces— must be moved. Most often, camera and lighting setups are worked out using a *stand-in,* a man or woman who literally "stands in" for an actor, allowing camera and lighting departments to have a human reference point for technical decisions, without requiring highly paid actors to stand patiently—or impatiently—on set. Stand-ins wear wardrobe that approximates the color and shape of the wardrobe worn by the principles in the scene. (This stand-in wardrobe is called "color cover" and must be provided by the costume department, unless the stand-in provides his or her own, in consultation with the department.)

When a scene is being shot for the first time, the principal actors dress and get made up while camera and lights are set up. Meanwhile, the first and second ADs work with extras who will be in the shot, choreographing their movements and rehearsing them. Once the principal actors come to the set and are wired for sound or special effects, the following steps take place:

2. *Camera blocking rehearsal.* The actors go through a "blocking rehearsal"—a rehearsal in which camera blocking (or movement), lighting, and sound are checked. The camera and the actors must hit a series of specific marks in order for the shot to work technically, as planned.

3. *Adjustments.* Lighting, camera movements, and marks (for both actors and cameras) are adjusted as a result of the rehearsal. The shot's action may be rehearsed again.

4. *Last looks.* Before shooting, the first AD gives wardrobe, makeup, and hair a last chance for adjustments. Since the director wants to get rolling while the rehearsal is fresh, the time given to "last looks" is very brief and very pressured.

5. *Rolling.* Once the camera is rolling, costume and action continuity are tracked, and off-camera silence is enforced.

6. *Multiple takes.* The director will shoot the scene over and over, until satisfied with that setup. (The camera only holds roughly eleven minutes of film; reloading the camera can take two to three minutes.) Not every take will be printed. The director will announce that a shot should be printed; however, for safety's sake, continuity is tracked and makeup, hair, and costumes adjusted to match the previous take *every time the camera rolls.* Between takes, the pressure is on to keep things moving, to get the camera rolling again and get on to the next setup.

7. *New camera and lighting setups.* Over the course of a day, there will be many camera setups. More often than not, more than one scene will be shot. While set costumers are working on set—maintaining the appropriate "looks," carefully documenting the process with written notes and continuity photographs, providing actors with warming jackets, handheld fans, a cup of coffee or a cold soda from craft services—the costume supervisor who works the truck is studying the call sheet, confirming the next scene number with the second AD, pulling, prepping, and setting costumes and stock for the next scene's changes.

Most scenes will be shot from a variety of camera angles and setups. Each new camera setup requires a new lighting setup and a new camera blocking rehearsal. These setup times give set costumers a chance to record continuity and solve costume emergencies.

When the cameras are rolling and sound is being recorded, quiet is enforced—on set and in the immediate area. Just before camera and sound roll, the first AD and several production assistants devote their efforts to announcing, loudly and firmly, "All quiet!" Once camera and sound are rolling, "Rolling!" is announced. Why? Because noise is a chronic problem: The microphones (booms and radio mikes) used by the sound department can pick up not just the sound of errant footsteps, but the sound of a stapler or the flipping of a script page. As a result, when sound is rolling, entry to the set is barred, usually by a determined PA. The location and transportation departments make sure that the area around the set is clear of extraneous vehicles (for sound and camera purposes). Additional production assistants control pedestrian traffic. Even off-set generators and production trailer air conditioners may be shut down in the interest of getting the best possible sound recordings. (When you're trying to get tomorrow's ironing done, you will see the advantage of having the wardrobe trailer parked well away from the set.)

When you've got a "tight set"—that is, when the space is limited and working crew are packed in—you may have to go through the *second* second AD or his or her production assistant to gain access to the set: They know when and where the camera is shooting, and it is their job to make sure that no one inappropriate is caught on camera.

Indeed, developing a sense of exactly *where* the camera is and *which way* it is facing can help you figure out how to sneak emergency supplies onto the set.

A tight set, and camera and sound rolling, are not the only reasons an AD may limit access to the set. A blocking rehearsal or the filming of a particularly sensitive scene may be reason enough to restrict access to the set, out of respect for the actors. (For a case in point, see below, "Sensitive set etiquette: shooting nude scenes.")

The costume designer's daily routine

Generally, designers are on and off set during the day, planning future scenes. Costume designers come to the set when character changes are being *established* (when the change gets final approval from the director on set and is recorded by camera for the first time). The more the designer can be on site, the better—not only to approve the clothing of the added-at-the-last-minute extras, but also to answer the day-to-day questions of the principal players. Harvey Keitel, Robert De Niro, and a number of other important actors are concerned with the "design" of their characters, and expect the costume designer to be available to answer their questions. To keep the actors happy and to be in tune with the heartbeat of the production, the designer should be available on the set a part of each shooting day.

> I spend as much time on the set as possible. Actors always seem happier when they can ask the designer—inevitably, at the last moment–if they can tie their tie a certain way, or switch a pin to the other side. I have always dressed all my extras, no matter how large a call or how early a call time. I feel that this is the costume designer's job. If you don't do this, you should be calling yourself a stylist, not a costume designer. Having ideas may be one thing, but actuality and application separate the wheat from the chaff. *(Jean-Pierre Dorléac, costume designer)*

The costume supervisor's daily routine

Once shooting begins, the supervisor's focus shifts to running the set operations. Most supervisors make the location their base of operations, directing the daily routine of the crew, monitoring the off-site preparations, supervising the budget, and preparing the wardrobe for the upcoming scenes from the wardrobe trailer. (When a department is structured in a way that assigns costumers exclusively to the set, the "truck" costume supervisor will take care of many of the duties that would otherwise belong to the set costumer assigned to the truck; see below, "The set costumer's daily routine.") Depending on the size of the crew, the complexity of the shoot, and the need for off-site preparation, a supervisor may also go on and off location during the day. However, many costumers feel that it is the supervisor's duty to stay on location.

The set costumer's daily routine

If the costume department is well staffed, with two or more set costumers, duties may be divided. One set costumer may work exclusively on the truck, prepping and maintaining wardrobe, while other set costumers track continuity on the set itself. On some stream-lined productions, once shooting begins, the costume supervisor may take up residence in the truck, as noted above.

Off the set, set costumers focus attention on the most mundane tasks—hanging and tagging the clothes; making laundry and dry-cleaning piles and inventory lists (doing laundry, if you have a washer and dryer on the truck); re-filing cleaned garments; recording notes on costume changes; laying out the costume changes; pulling stock for extras; prepping changes for scenes coming up. Keeping the trailer tidy and well organized is a big part of the job. How the dressing rooms are prepped can be vital to getting the actor dressed correctly and to the set on time. Any time costume pieces are returned to the general stock after cleaning, they must be retagged or size-tagged again. This, too, is the set costumer's job.

The costumer who works the set must be present whenever the camera rolls, and before the camera rolls, in order to track costume continuity and maintain the "look" of the characters. As you already know, continuity notation and costume retrieval are a big part of the set costumer's job. All items that the costume department gets hit up for—the foul-weather gear for the camera crew, the last-minute accessories for the extras, the "set dressing" clothing for the art department—must also be tracked down by the set costumer at the end of the day. Improvised dressing areas for the extras can be the starting point for trails of costume pieces that set costumers must faithfully follow. The educating of extras in the subjects of where to dress and how, where to store valu-ables, and how to return costumes is a constant challenge. Since an extra may only be making $35 a day, for what can be fourteen hours of endless boredom, many an extra has been known to depart leaving a scattering of costume pieces, or worse, taking them along. Checking items in and out and itemizing loss and damage are a part of the set costumer's job.

The job of maintaining the look of the characters means not only making sure that a jacket sits correctly on the actor's shoulders and the shirt is buttoned as pre-scribed, but that wardrobe emergencies can be handled on the spot. This means that the set costumers must have personal set kits. These kits include a smattering of every portable tool and supply available on the truck. (For a solid basic list of sug-gested set kit contents, see A.30.) Costume supervisor Jaci Rohr has this to say about the set costumer's kit:

> I certainly recommend that set costumers purchase a real cheap Polaroid camera. The production will buy the film for you. If you have your own camera, you're familiar with it, you're not fumbling around to see how it works. And a little sewing kit that you can get at the 99-Cent Store, one where all the needles are threaded in different color thread, they're fabulous! And I like an assortment of different-sized safety pins— particularly the eensy-teensy 00 blacks and golds—because you can fix a hem better than you can with tape.

I also like to wear a big old vest with lots of pockets; I add a bunch of loops with jump rings on them, so I can hang my pictures on me. I put my scissors on an elastic strap, so I'm never losing them, and that way I can keep mostly what I need on me. I try to keep everything on my body in small amounts, so that I'm not lugging a big giant kit over to an actor twenty yards away. Keep enough small things with you. If there's something you don't have, it's in your kit bag.

The best set bag I've discovered is a "bucket buddy" from Home Depot (fig. 8.6). It's a five-gallon plastic paint pail with a lid that can also function as a seat. It's has a "bucketeer," which is usually a plastic vinyl-y thing with a zillion pockets, that sticks over the bucket. It's a seat and a set bag all in one. And it's waterproof, which is really important in dusty, dirty conditions. I had a canvas set bag that rotted from being wet. When I'm feeling really ambitious, I have two bucket buddies, which I stack together and put on a little luggage carrier that I can drag around.

As if keeping wardrobe continuity, maintaining the look of the costumes, keeping track of non-costume wardrobe, and responding to wardrobe emergencies on set is not complicated enough, the set costumer must be a diplomat. A set costumer must be well-versed in the rules of "set etiquette," including when to take Polaroids, when to record continuity notes, when to "tweak" costumes that are in disarray and when not to. (For a more detailed discussion, see below, section titled *Set Etiquette.*) Because the hours are long, the pressures intense, and the action occasionally difficult or dangerous, diplomacy, efficiency, preparedness, and just plain savvy are required set costumer skills.

Because some productions will not pay set costumers to start work much before the first day of shooting, set costumers are often stranded, with little time to learn the script or become familiar with on-site personnel. As a result, it becomes especially important for set costumers to bring with them not only a set of good work habits, but a clear understanding of daily shooting routines and a knowledge of the responsibilities of the job.

THE SET COSTUMER'S RESPONSIBILITIES

Personal prep

- Assemble your personal set kit.
- Dress in practical clothing—clothing that is easy to move in and won't impede your work.
- Don't wear noisy jewelry or squeaky shoes.
- Be tidy and low-key.
- Study the daily call sheet. Note crew call times, actor call times, the shooting order, scene numbers, and any extras descriptions. Note "cover set," stunt or special effects personnel info, and any special costume notes. Study the pecking order of personnel, particularly in the costume and AD departments.
- If available, review the script and costume paperwork—crossplots, scene breakdown, and character breakdowns for special action, doubling, and potential maintenance problems.
- Study potential emergency resources (supermarkets, laundromats, malls) on your way to work on location. You never know what can crop up during the day, and scoping out local sources has prevented panic in many a costume emergency.
- Study the location parking and department location arrangements for the day.

Costume department prep

- Report to the costume supervisor and to the person who hired you.
- Unlock the trailer and help set up the trailer, changes, and stock for the day.

FIG. 8.6

395

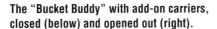

The "Bucket Buddy" with add-on carriers, closed (below) and opened out (right).

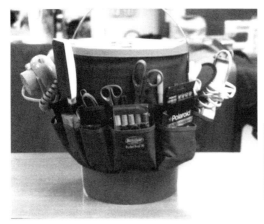

THE ESSENTIAL ON-SET KIT

The set bag

- Get a copy of the call sheet and mini scene-pages (called "sides").
- Confirm with an AD and your boss that the day's scenes are to be shot "per call sheet," and where and when the actors should be dressed.
- Assess the dressing requirements for the day: the costumes required; any special design or styling instructions; the dressing facilities; special dressing room prep instructions; and the location of the wardrobe trailer, actors' motorhomes, honeywagon, and extras holding areas in relation to sets. (This may be done the night before.)
- Help finish any ironing, steaming, or alterations for the first changes of the day.
- Prep and lay out principal and day-player changes in the dressing rooms.
- Prep any pre-fit or "special" extras racks for the day.

Actors to wardrobe

- Principal and day players dress in their own trailers and dressing rooms, and may be asked to do final fittings, for last-minute design approval. Any items supplied by the actors from their personal wardrobes are noted on garment tags.
- Extras report to the wardrobe trailer or designated holding/dressing area, exchange their pay voucher or driver's license for any costume pieces they receive (fig. 8.2).
- Period and special-costume films will pre-fit extras and bag and tag their changes like those of principal players. Racks of pre-fit extras' changes are arranged by scene (within the scene, alphabetically, by background player's name). Contemporary films will style extras on site, and extras will be instructed by casting to bring options from their own wardrobe (fig. 6.16).
- Whether the film uses contemporary or period costumes, set costumers style the extras from any available goods, noting any garments supplied by the department and any garments supplied by the actor, for pay and wrap purposes. Notation systems may vary from supervisor to supervisor.
- Extras are advised how to re-hang and retag their costumes, and where to store their personal garments for the day.

Actors and extras to makeup and hair

This period can buy you time for emergency alterations, pressing and steaming, and accessorizing. Instruct actors to come to you for "last looks" and final accessorizing before going to the set. Often, however, the assistant directors will pull actors and extras directly out of makeup and/or the extras dressing area, to speed the production along.

Costumers to set

After the actors are dressed (but several minutes before set call time), the on-set costumers head to set with kit, and rolling racks containing extra stock, warming jackets, color cover, modesty cover, and whatever other pieces and supplies seem necessary. Once on set and "camp" is established, final checks of costumes on actors and background players are done before shooting begins.

Set costumers tracking principals must be on the set whenever cameras are rolling. Because extras are often still dressing for a scene at set call, key set costumers must cover for the extras set costumer, solving problems and taking continuity photos and notes on background until all extras are dressed and the extras costumer arrives on set.

DURING SHOOTING

Off-set costumers

- Prep all of the day's changes for the actors on call.
- Dress all actors that are called after shooting has started.
- Make sure that the next change of costumes for each actor is laid out.
- Make sure the next day's changes are on the trailer and ready to be used.
- Check in the cleaning, and make sure that all the cleaning is present and ready to be used. Re-stock, re-tag, and re-size the wardrobe, as needed.
- Send out the dry cleaning and laundry.
- Help with fittings, as necessary.
- Prep future scenes, per the costume supervisor's priorities.
- Keep in close contact with the on-set costumers, to help handle emergencies and act as a source of supplies.
- Keep the costume supervisor fully advised of any changes to the wardrobe stock and supply shortages.

FIG. 8.7

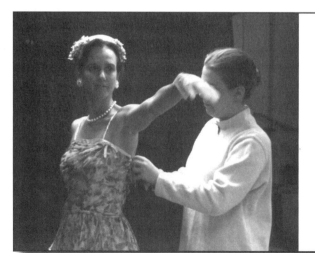

Knowing when to tweak, and when not to, is the art of dressing on set.

On-set costumers

- Adjust the costumes, as needed, to maintain the look of the characters at the start of each shot (fig. 8.7). Set costumers should try to check out in one of the video monitors on the set how the characters they are covering look (fig. 8.8).
- Track and record costume continuity, and match all costume aging and distressing for each shot. Set costumers take Polaroids, and attach them in the set book, to support their notes. However, they do not rely only on Polaroids for documentation.
- Cooperate with fellow on-set costumers to help maintain continuity on *all* actors, including principal players, bit players, stunt players, and extras.
- Stay on set. The set costumer may not leave the set without notifying a fellow on-set costumer, or the first AD or second AD. If you must leave for any reason, you must find another costume department member to take your place.
- Handle any on-set costume changes.
- Care for the actors between takes (warming coats on, off; hand fan, if necessary; something to drink, etc.).
- Keep in close contact with the script supervisor, and inform him or her of important wardrobe-matching details.
- Keep the costume supervisor fully advised as to what is happening on the set, and let him or her know of any potential or actual changes to the wardrobe.
- Stay in touch with the wardrobe trailer. At least one costumer on set should have a walkie-talkie, for quick contact with costume personnel at the trailer.

DAILY WRAP PROCEDURES

- Check the set for costume items mistakenly left behind before leaving the set for the day.
- Tag and collect extras changes, and check them for missing costume pieces. When all the pieces are together or accounted for, return the extra's pay voucher or driver's license.

FIG. 8.8

Set etiquette dictates: Don't hog the monitors and don't sit in someone else's chair.

- Keep a record detailing the extras' personal wardrobe items that were used, and those costume department pieces that were lost.
- Check extras' dressing areas and holding area for additional costume pieces.
- Reassemble all principal players' changes used that day, and remove them from dressing rooms. At the trailer, tags are replaced, and any pieces that are missing are noted.
- Double check with the AD at the end of the day for any changes that may not be on the next day's call sheet, and the names of any extras who may be called back for tomorrow's shoot.
- Check garments for prop items; return prop items to prop department.
- Separate laundry and dry cleaning, and prioritized according to the needs of the next day's shooting.
- Organize on the prep rack(s) the changes needed for the next day of the shoot, and check to make sure they are ready.
- Record properly and legibly continuity notes on the character continuity pages, and file in the set book. Store set book in a prearranged place in the trailer.
- Clean and sweep out the trailer(s). Lock down, for transport.

Second unit: "the other white meat"

Inevitably, every show has some degree of additional photography, concurrent with principal photography. A single parallel unit filming additional footage is called "second unit," and is made up minimally of a director of photography, two camera assistants, an assistant director, a script supervisor, a PA, and occasionally a sound mixer and boom operator. (If more than a "second unit" is shooting concurrent with "first unit," it will be called "third unit," and so on.)

Additional units are generally used to shoot stunt coverage, "drive-bys," establishing shots, "B-roll" (addition "illustrational" footage, including moving and static point-of-view shots and time-change shots—including weather change, light change, sunrises, sunsets, full moons), and any number of other transition shots. Second unit (and all additional units) that require characters shoot with stunt doubles, drivers, photo doubles, and occasionally, the actors themselves, when they are on call but not being used in the main action. When second unit photography is being done with actors, a representative of the costume department should always be on set with the actor. Always. Although if second unit is scheduled for additional hours (after the balance of the crew is wrapped, or on a day in addition to the scheduled shooting days—a Sunday, for example), producers will put up a fight, because of the high cost of overtime rates. (If you are on a union shoot, check your contract.)

Second unit work is usually discussed in preproduction, and the dates of shooting are usually settled before shooting begins. If possible, the costume supervisor will book additional costumers for those days. Shows that find themselves shooting third unit will have to book *additional* additional costumers. Clear all bookings of additional costumers with production first. Make sure they know that the second and third units will mean more costume crew. In the event that the schedule changes (and it always will), costumers are booked on the fly to come in for the additional photography.

Sometimes on low-budget shows, including, surprisingly, television pilots, production will not be able to pay for additional costume department crew to work additional units.

This is a highly undesirable situation. You may be forced to pull a member of your crew from the set or the truck to go out in the follow-van; you may even have to send an actor out to be shot alone with the skeleton crew and cross your fingers that the costume looks right. Try to impress upon the producer that this is a big risk. Sometimes a producer will suggest that the set book be given to a production department PA or the script supervisor accompanying the second unit. This may be your only recourse. Sometimes, you have to just trust the universe.

Occasionally, additional units will shoot on a day that was never scheduled. For example, production may decide (on the day) to use second unit to shoot drive-bys on a wide lens. What this means is that photo doubles will be dressed in the top-half of a principal character's wardrobe, placed in a picture vehicle, and shot as they drive past camera. In this case, make sure that you have checked the photo doubles before the vehicle being shot takes off. It is not unusual with drive-bys for there to be no follow-van for production personnel; as a result, you will not be able to be as vigilant as you can be on first unit. If at all possible, make sure that you are present when second unit returns to base camp, to take the wardrobe back from the photo doubles. When the decision to use second unit is spur-of-the-moment, try to be a good sport, and go with the flow. Crying over having no warning does not solve the immediate problem. Send the photo doubles to set, then sit down with the line producer to discuss future second-unit activity.

Usually, second-unit scheduling is listed on the call sheet. This information is located close to the bottom of the call sheet, next to the advance notes. Often, there is an entirely separate call sheet for second unit. Pay careful attention to all details of the call sheet: "Forewarned is forearmed."

And lest we forget: meal breaks

Production companies provide breakfast at the beginning of each call, and a "craft service" table of snacks is provided all day long. By union rules, a meal must be provided every six hours during the production day. (If meals are not provided, "meal penalties" are levied, according to contract.) Even cheap production companies provide meals, in the interest of keeping the crew happy and efficient. For costume folk, getting breakfast can be a killer as you hustle to get things ready for the day, so the craft service table can be a godsend when prepping, and when emergencies interfere with meal times.

Set Etiquette

Once shooting starts, set costumers are the most visible members of the costume department team. As such, they present to the entire crew an image of the costume department's efficiency. Good work habits, a good attitude, a cooperative manner, clear communication skills, and the ability to accurately handle information are important assets for a set costumer. On all union shoots, set costumers need to fully understand jurisdictional job etiquette.

Whether union or non-union, most costumers have strong feelings about members of other departments touching the wardrobe. Rules of thumb in this matter include "PAs should not handle wardrobe," and "Wardrobe puts blood on wardrobe; makeup puts blood on skin; art department puts blood on the set." Someone sitting on a set costumer's kit box or camp stool is often felt to be in more serious violation of jurisdiction than a member of the art department who clears the set of costume department wardrobe. A makeup artist removing lint from the lapel of a costume jacket might or might not be in line for a gentle reproof, but a grip spraying dulling spray or Streaks 'N Tips near an actor—that's clobbering time. Within the costume department, some are more sensitive (and more militant) about jurisdiction than others.

In all events, when someone from another department, even the producer or director, asks a set costumer to change the costume in any way, take a deep breath—this is touchy political territory. Call the designer. If the designer is not on location, try the cell phone. Remember, a set costumer is the designer's liaison on set, as well as an employee of the production company.

A GUIDE TO SET ETIQUETTE

1. Always be early.
- Arrive on location and begin work ten to fifteen minutes before call time. However, understand that, if you are on a union shoot, the call time that appears on the call sheet will be the time from which you will be paid (unless contract or negotiations with the line producer establish otherwise, and changes are duly made on the call sheet).

2. Don't delay an actor's call time.
- If an actor is late to the set, don't let it be because of a costume problem.

3. Respect the production's power structure.
- Study the call sheet to know the names of your bosses.
- Get information on hidden power sources (e.g., the producer's relatives, friends, allies on the crew). For information on set, deal mostly with the first AD, who knows the right time to bug the director.
- Understand from whom you do and don't have to take orders. (For example, a DGA (Director's Guild of America) trainee may not have official authority, but you may want this person on your side.)
- Fully cooperate with your boss's work priorities—even when they shift moment to moment.
- Respect union job jurisdictions.

4. Be self-contained on the set.
- Bring with you everything you will need.
- Be neat and organized with your kit, and with set costume stock and changes.

5. Keep a low profile and respect others' turf.
- Don't sit in someone else's set chair.
- Don't hang out at craft services.
- Don't hog the video monitor.
- Don't flirt with others at the cost of job efficiency.
- Don't pester the actors.

- Don't get in the way of the first AD, camera, lighting, stunt or special effects crew members.
- Always be conscious of the direction in which the camera is shooting.
- Practice smoking etiquette on set and at the trailers.
- Let others do their job. Do yours, and only yours, and do it well.

6. Cooperate with other departments.

- Do what you can to help other departments when it does not put your department at risk.
- Cooperate with the prop department in all matters of mutual interest, including the return and exchange of prop items left with costumes.
- Respect all noise restrictions set up by the sound department.
- Cooperate with the lighting department as much as possible. Never plug into a lighting department power cable without first checking with an electrician.
- With your boss's approval, give emergency sewing aid to other departments.
- Help solve costuming problems and casting-related costume emergencies, with your boss's approval.
- Respect the shot priorities established by the first AD.
- If there is a major continuity problem, alert your department boss.

7. Follow continuity-photo protocols.

- Before taking a continuity photo, call out "Flashing!"
- Shoot continuity photos only after the scene has been shot.
- Shoot continuity photos during breaks for lighting or camera adjustments.
- Be careful about shooting continuity photos just off set during rehearsals, when the flash might break an actor's concentration.
- Make proper and legible notes on both Polaroid labels and character continuity sheets.

8. Care for, and respect, the actors.

- Respect actors' privacy: always knock on dressing room door, and ask permission before entering.
- Anticipate actors' special needs for nude scenes with set robes, penis socks, G-strings, and privacy patches (see below, "Sensitive set etiquette: shooting nude scenes").
- Anticipate problems with inclement weather and excessive heat or cold. Keep warming jackets or handheld fans standing by, as necessary. Stand ready to remove warming coats and other comfort items before cameras roll.
- Respond to the needs and requests of actors, within the limits of the design. Defer to the designer or costume supervisor in matters of garment choice.
- Be sensitive to an actor's prep for a scene. Keep a low profile while maintaining the costume continuity. Don't "bug" the actor. As much as possible, make necessary costume adjustments only immediately before shooting.
- Stay out of the actor's eye line during shooting, especially during tense or intimate scenes.

9. Make your boss look good.

- Be cooperative, pleasant, efficient, calm, supportive, low-key, and highly visible.
- Be loyal: don't volunteer sensitive information to anyone outside the costume department.
- Look out for wardrobe needs and problems, and help to protect the design.
- Inform your boss of on-set tensions and priorities that may effect the costume department.
- Stay flexible, positive, and calm in a crisis.
- Be cooperative and flexible with type-A personalities who can't see beyond their own needs.
- Cultivate a low-key ego and a good sense of humor.
- Give accurate estimates on dressing time. (Be conservative in your estimates.)
- Make yourself indispensable to the department.

10. Anticipate problems, when possible, and find ways to solve them with awareness, diplomacy, and grace.

- Double check the problem in the monitor and/or ask about the frame size (close-up, full shot, etc.).
- Always defer to your boss for a final decision, but try to help to solve the problem.
- If you don't know the answer to a question raised by an authority figure, say, "I'm not sure, but I'll find out."
- If you catch a continuity problem on set, inquire discreetly whether the camera has rolled. Discreetly inform the costume designer or your boss (using the walkie-talkie on a channel not used by production), so that you or the designer can immediately talk with the script supervisor. See if the first AD can buy you some time, via rehearsal or camera prep, to address the problem.
- Don't whine. Nobody wants to hear it.

11. Follow trailer and stock protocols.

- Respect and maintain the costume tracking and continuity documentation systems set up by the costume supervisor (including keeping inventories, tagging, bagging, hanging systems, photo and written documentation).
- Maintain order in the trailer; respect it. Be precise in your attention to the most mundane details.
- Always hang hangers facing right, with garments facing the front, tags pinned to the top-left shoulder or corner of the garment. Sensitive or delicate garments may need special tagging.
- Neatly hang all parts of a change ganged together and tagged, with accompanying accessories hanging or in attached bags and zip-locks. If possible, put changes in individual garment bags, and tag them on the outside of the bag.
- Use the hanger type appropriate for a given garment (dress hanger, skirt hanger, suit hanger, padded hanger, heavy-gauge hanger, etc.) to prevent hanger collapse and keep garments from wrinkling, snagging, slipping, and stretching.
- Hang changes sequentially, according to the order established by the supervisor.
- Make sure that the set book is always accessible to the entire costume crew. Always store it in the same location.
- Keep your personal kit supplies in the trailer as neat and self-contained as possible.
- Always tag the changes for which you are responsible. Make your motto, "If I die, my clothes are tagged" (fig. 8.9).

FIG. 8.9

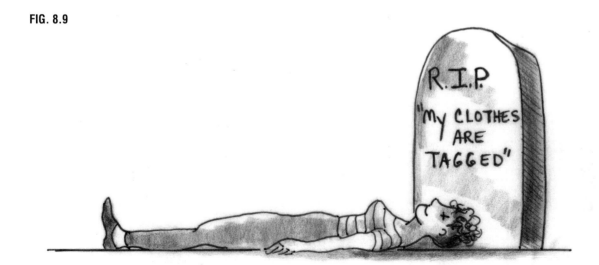

Sensitive set etiquette: shooting nude scenes

There are two types of nudity in film: (1) *non-sexualized nudity,* which includes, among other things, streaking, physical comedy, showering, changing clothes, giving birth, and the revealing of an unclothed corpse; and (2) *sexualized nudity,* which includes acts of seduction, lovemaking, and post-coital snuggling.

There is an enormous psychological difference between these two types of nudity. Non-sexualized nudity is generally much more hassle-free than sexualized nudity. The only occasions when non-sexualized nudity is always a problem is when stunts are to be performed. (It is very difficult to put stunt pads on a stunt man and have him appear naked, even a hundred yards away.) When sexualized nudity is the subject, approach the actors with care. Not every actor is comfortable, or experienced, in this realm. Even the most acclaimed actor may never have done a nude scene. And in most cases the poor actor must do this nude scene in front of a small crowd, including the director, the first AD, the DP, the script supervisor, the camera crew (camera operator, focus puller/loader, dolly grip), and one set costumer. The crowd may grow to include a lighting technician, a makeup person, a hair person, a prop person, and any number of producers who feel that they have a right to be present.

To support the actors in this difficult work, you need to do the following:

1. Establish a solid rapport with the actors before getting to the set. Many times, the first discussion that the actors have regarding nudity is with the costume designer, so it is essential that the designer be clear about how the director wishes to handle it. (Information on how much nudity will be visible on-camera, what will happen in the action of the scene, and so forth should come from the director in early design meetings.) The designer must then be able to convey this information to the actor adeptly and diplomatically.

2. Discuss nudity with the actors in a comfortable and professional manner. When you talk to the actors about nudity, speak professionally and clinically. If it seems appropriate to the actor, you might even make it light-hearted and funny. The more comfortable you are discussing nudity, the more comfortable the actor will feel. One can never tell how sensitive to nudity or specific body images the actor will be. Be sensitive and respectful of these issues, whether or not you sense them. Offer support and whatever garments they request to make them comfortable (robes, pubic patches, G-strings, etc.).

If during prep you sense that an actor is on edge and uncomfortable with any part of the action that involves nudity, talk it out thoroughly with the actor before you seek outside help. If, just before shooting a nude scene, an actor creates a problem—refuses to come out of the trailer or throws a screaming fit, for example—stay out of it. At this point, it is incumbent upon the director and/or producers to assuage the actor. Only if you have a close personal relationship with the actor, or if the actor requests your presence, should you step in, and then, with extreme caution.

3. Provide pubic area coverings for actors in a lovemaking scene and modesty clothing (or pieces) for private parts that will not be revealed on camera. There are a variety of garments commonly used to provide psychological and physical "protection" to actors required to do nude scenes, among them *pasties, penis socks,* and *privacy patches.* Pasties are disks that cover the nipples, usually cut from flesh-toned adhesive fabric like moleskin or surgical bandages. A penis sock (also known as a "marble bag") is a flesh-toned, stretchy Lycra bag with an elasticized opening, designed to completely cover and hold the penis and testicles. A privacy patch is a teardrop-shaped piece of flesh-toned Lycra that's taped, with double-faced Topstick (toupee tape), to the top of the pubic area, then brought through to the buttocks, where it is taped between the "cheeks." For water work, this patch is made with moleskin, carefully cut so that the adhesive is only on the edges. *Dance briefs* are available at dance stores. *G-strings*, for men and women, can be fabricated (as can *tube bras*, for over-the-shoulder nudity coverage) from flesh-toned Lycra.

 4.   Provide robes and towels for the actors when they are off-camera. Just because the actors are not wearing much doesn't mean that the set costumer has nothing to do on set. During camera setups or lighting changes, it is a good idea to supply actors with robes, or anything comfortable and familiar, to provide a sense of security.

Also note that while modesty clothing is important for the actors, it is also important for the crew. Buck-naked bodies on the set, particularly in a sexual context, can hinder a crew's efficiency. It is also easier psychologically on the crew to have happy, comfortable actors, who are secure in what they are doing.

 5.   Respect the actors' privacy. On set, during filming, the designer, and all costumers, should respect an actor's privacy by staying out of his or her eye line (direct point of view) and, if possible, facing away from the action.

> There is a lot of nudity in film. As a new costume designer, I thought, "Okay, intellectually, I know how to deal with this, and I know, from other costume designers, how to deal with nudity and how to make this work." But there I was, on maybe my second film, and I had to deal with fifteen, twenty nude extras.
>
> And then, of course, I wondered, "When it comes to the nude scenes, who's going to 'patch' the actors? Does it have to be me?" So, I'm cutting the patches out: "Okay, next person in the trailer; okay, next person…" Some of the stuff that I saw on that film I will never forget. I'm glad I come from a family with a medical background: I can look at this objectively, and realize that everybody has a body, and nudity is not the enemy.
>
> Many years ago, I worked with an actress who did not feel that she could go out to set and perform comfortably nude from the waist up, wearing only pasties. She was mortified. We talked about it at length in her trailer, and I proposed a compromise: If it would make her feel better, I, too, would come to set naked from the waist up, wearing nothing but pasties, and sit on a chair by the camera. When she realized I was serious, she understood that as professionals we support and watch out for each other. She understood that I would be there for her, no matter what. While she did not take me up on my offer, she did ask that I closely watch the monitor, and stand by on set. It made her feel more comfortable. Providing that level of comfort for an actor is what we, as costume designers, are charged to do. *(Anonymous costume designer)*

Dealing with Conflict

In an ideal world, we would get along with everyone. There would be no conflict, and life and work would flow freely. Unfortunately, the real world operates differently, and moments of such sublime harmony are the exception, rather than the rule. There will be occasions in your work in the film industry when your "people skills" will be put to the test. How you handle yourself in difficult situations will reflect not only on your work, but also on your character.

The ability to manage conflict is not always innate, as some assume. We can not always predict how we will react to a new situation, particularly one for which we are unprepared. We hope that by sharing with you lessons that no one will ever teach you in the classroom—lessons we've learned coming up in the film industry as costumer and costume designer—we can shed light on how to handle the conflicts that inevitably, in one form or another, arise during production. Our philosophy is, the more you know about what *could* happen, the more prepared you will be to deal with what *does* happen. If the tone in this section is frank, our intention is not to demean, but to forewarn.

Conflict can arise from many things, including ideas, experiences, beliefs, personality, work methodology. It is important to remember that work is *work*: The people you work with are not members of your family; you should not take things personally. Remember, too, that all work situations in this business are temporary, although bad behavior and ungracious conduct will be remembered for a long time. You must be professional and treat others in a manner that befits professionals—even when you doubt the professionalism of others.

Your comportment: keep it cool

The most important piece of advice we can give you is to "play it cool." In the face of bad behavior by another member of the crew or cast, it is important not to be reactive, no matter how egregious the infraction. Passions run high on the set, and "mixing it up" action/counter-action style is a sure way to get into trouble. I (KB) have observed fist fights on the set—unscripted; I have observed abusive language and aberrant behavior; I have observed sexual harassment of the most blatant kind. Rather than bludgeoning the offenders with a nine-iron, which may be your impulse, the more professional thing to do is to talk with someone who can make a difference, usually a producer or an AD. Stifling the urge to assault may be difficult, but, in the long run, addressing the problem with frank dialogue will polish, not tarnish, your reputation.

Recognizing signs of impending doom

Costume design is primarily about creating characters. A character is based upon a psychological profile. Rather than bore you with a dissertation on the works of Freud and Jung, we encourage you to study psychology and sociology, to better understand not only the origins of conflict among characters in a script, but among people on a production.

Many signs, if you learn to read them, can alert you to the possibilities of conflict on a set. Personality clashes, behavioral problems, outbursts of anger, drug or alcohol abuse, and sleep deprivation significantly affect the ability of a crew to work together harmoniously. When you see signs of any of the above, tread carefully. Recognize the early signs of conflict, and steer clear—or mediate in a manner that serves everyone involved.

Cutting them off at the pass

When you find yourself personally involved in a conflict, it is wise to resolve it before it gets ugly. If you can, speak to the person with whom you have the conflict, and try to diffuse it directly. If such dialog is impossible, speak to your superior (if you are a member of the costume crew) or a trusted producer (if you are a costume designer). If the conflict is intradepartmental (that is, with someone in the costume department), always speak with the costume supervisor or the designer. Taking your concerns directly to a producer will serve only to alienate you from the ones who run your department, and could exacerbate the situation. If you are a member of the costume crew, and the conflict is with another department, discuss the situation with the designer, so that she or he can discuss the conflict with the other department head.

The longer a conflict drags on, the worse it will become. The sooner you voice your concerns about a situation, the sooner it can be resolved. Deal directly with people; be straightforward and forthright. Everyone will appreciate it, in the end. Nonetheless, sometimes conflict cannot be avoided entirely, nor can it be cut off at the pass, so you'll need to buckle up and get ready for a bumpy ride.

Sources of conflict during the shoot

Different kinds of work relationships produce different kinds of conflict. Working in the costume department, you will find that most conflicts on a production during the shoot arise from difficulties with actors, with the director, with producers, with the members of your own department, and with members of other departments whose work directly affects yours.

Conflicts with actors. Actors often draw their characters from personal experience. Sometimes what makes an actor an artist is his or her experience of pain, and the ability to draw on that pain in the work. Occasionally, the deeply personal emotions an actor uses in a performance leak out into an actor's dealings with other people. These emotions can produce anxiety attacks, explosions of anger, or other violent outbursts. If you are the object of an attack like this, try not to take it personally. It is not about you. Let it go in one ear and out the other. By recognizing what is going on beneath the actor's surface, and arming yourself emotionally, you can save your own sanity.

If you are a costume designer working with an actor whose behavior is impeding your work, it may be wise to assign the actor a "personal dresser." A personal dresser should be a costumer who has a friendly rapport with the actor, and who can serve as liaison between the actor and the designer. Many actors' contracts call for personal dressers. If this is the case, the designer will work in tandem with the personal dresser to achieve a particular character look.

On projects with lower budgets, where a personal dresser is out of the question, the designer—and the set costumers—may simply have to live through the experience. As lamentable as this may prove to be, it is well worth the effort it takes to find a place in your heart where your own professionalism can coexist with the suffering—and insufferable—actor.

Another common problem is the actor who chooses, consciously or not, to embody the character he or she portrays both on-screen and off. Be particularly alert to the actor who takes this approach, and who is playing an angry character. Recognize that the anger the actor is experiencing is not related to you or your work. While this acting method may seem extreme, remember that creating a character from deep within is a challenging, often unsettling, experience. Some actors can snap in and out of character effortlessly; others prefer—or are compelled to—live the experience.

Then, of course, there are the "divas." These are the actors who think of themselves as beyond human. They are the "all-about-me" types. It is not always the bona fide A-list movie star who fits this description, it may be a lesser-known actor. Divas are the ubiquitous complainers, the attention-grabbers, and, often, the most insecure people on the set. Recognize this, and try your hardest to treat them with love. While they may crack the whip and boss you around, listen to what they are saying: There may be valid reasons for their demands. Try to determine which of their requests have merit and which are fluff. A costume designer's job is to create characters, but it is also a costume designer's job to enable actors to become those characters. In all events, the bottom line is, more often than not, you've gotta suck it up.

A more unfortunate condition is known clinically as *body dysmorphic disorder* (BDD). This is a condition characterized by the often-warped body perceptions that go hand and hand with having one's image projected on a vast screen and viewed by countless members of the public, who are quick to judge. While an actor may have an impressive physique, she or he may not be able to accurately recognize her or his own shape. An actress may complain of looking fat, when, in fact, she is 5'6" and weighs 90 pounds. Seen more frequently among women than among men, it is related to, although separate from, eating disorders, and is frequently the source of conflict between an actor and a costume designer.

No matter how troubling the constant cry, "I look fat," and no matter how often the actor takes out his or her frustrations on the costume department, try to treat the actor with compassion. Learn about the condition, listen, and help in any way you can.

Conflict with directors and producers. Although you have been hired in part because of your ability to work with the director and the producers, there are occasions when conflict may arise. The costume designer can be particularly vulnerable under certain conditions, among them the following: when the designer is hired as a "safety valve," or as the result of a deal cut between director and producer; when design matters are in dispute; when budget overages and the wishes of the director are at odds; and when the legitimate logistical needs of the costume department exceed the limits of the budget.

Everyone in the production office has his or her favorite candidate for any given job. The job of costume designer is no exception. Sometimes, the bargains struck in the production office are unspoken. ("I'll let you have your editor if you let me have my costume designer.") Other times, hiring like this, done overtly, is what I like to call the "safety-valve" hire.

Being hired as the "safety-valve" on a production puts the costume designer in a precarious position. It means that the producer is your closest ally, and often you have been hired specifically to execute the producer's vision, not the director's. The director may have a visual style that the producer does not want reflected in the film. You, the designer, are hired to override the wishes and inclinations of the director, with the producer's blessing and support. This makes for an awkward and complicated work environment. If you feel that you have been hired as a "safety valve," talk it over with the producer. Make sure that all parties are aware of the situation, and above all, make sure that you do indeed have the full and unconditional support of the producer who brought you on to the project.

Even when the designer is hired by unanimous approval of producers and director, conflict can arise around matters of design. Everybody who gets dressed in the morning has an opinion about clothing. As a costume designer, your job is to find the most appropriate look for the character, given the input from the director, right? Not always. An actor has a say in what is, and is not, appropriate for the character he or she plays. Producers and executive producers will want a say. (It's their money—or they're responsible for it.) Where do you draw the line, and how do you make it work?

As the costume designer, you must make the situation work, balancing the requests—and demands—of the parties involved. This can be a tall order. Group meetings are a great idea, but scheduling them may be impossible. The best advice I can give you is to make sure that all parties know about the design choices in the works. If you find yourself in the middle of a design conflict, describe your design ideas visually and distribute copies of sketches, tear sheets, and swatches (when available) to everyone concerned. After a fitting, distribute copies of Polaroids to all parties involved. Keep everyone in the loop. The key to resolving a situation like this is to keep the lines of communication open. Beyond that, grace, finesse, and diplomacy will be your greatest assets.

Speaking of assets, money is always a source of potential conflict, especially when the needs of the costume department or the wishes of the director are at odds with the facts of the budget. Producers are primarily money and logistics experts. Their major concern is the budget. Of course they care about the look of the project, but no one cares as much about the budget as they do. How, then, do you avoid conflicts over budget matters?

Production has given you a budget. In your estimation, it is too low. Tell them immediately. If you suspect for a second that you will go over budget, put this in writing, and be specific. Distribute copies of your budget memo to the producers, line producer, UPM, and production accountant. The sooner you let production know about your concerns, the sooner you can remedy the situation.

Your trailer is too small, you need an additional costumer for two weeks, an actor's availability has changed, you need to contract for laundry services in the middle of nowhere. Put your request in writing and send it to the producer. To avoid unnecessary conflict with production, write those memos, and make sure you are very clear about what you need. Production is there to help; use them when you need them.

Intradepartmental conflict. Tight quarters, long hours, day after day with the same people: familiarity breeding contempt? It doesn't have to be that way. Here are some common interdepartmental conflicts, and ways to deal with them.

You're stepping on my toes! Within the costume department, everyone has his or her assigned duties. Everyone likes to do a good job, and everyone likes to feel productive in what they do. Occasionally, there is overlap in job duties. Occasionally, someone may step on someone else's toes. What do you do?

If you're a costume designer, try to ensure, from the beginning, that this never happens. Once you've have hired your crew, gather everyone together socially, to break the ice. This helps build relationships that transcend work. Try to pick a crew with a sense of humor, whose personalities will mesh well. When everyone begins work, tactfully delegate responsibility to each member of the costume crew, and not only according to union rules (when union rules apply), but according to disposition and aptitude. Finding the right fit between a person's strengths and the job that needs to be done is easy when you are familiar with your crew, and when your crew is familiar with one another. When you have encouraged your crew to bond outside of work, there less of a propensity to step on toes. Crew members become friends before they become coworkers. When each member of the costume crew knows his or her responsibilities, and knows them in the context of the entire department, within the greater dynamic, your crew will develop its own rhythm and work together with confidence.

But still sometimes, conflict happens. If you find yourself on a show where the members of your crew are stepping on one another, and where animosity rears its ugly head, you, as costume designer, must break it up. You must hear each party's complaints and decide how to solve the problem. If it means coming up with a written list of job tasks, there you have it. It may seem childish and trivial to have a list hanging in the trailer, but if such a list prevents coworkers from scratching each other's eyes out, it will not be a waste of time. Above all, encourage dialogue. A friendly work environment is a healthy and efficient work environment.

If someone in the department displays blatant disregard for coworkers, and this happens consistently, the costume designer must make a tough decision. If the person's presence is disturbing the efficiency of the department, it is sometimes best to cut the person loose. Firing a subordinate is one of the hardest things you'll ever have to do on a production, but these decisions have to be made, for the benefit of the bigger picture.

If you do decide to fire someone, be firm but gentle. Don't make a scene, and don't make an example of the person. Remember, the way you give someone the boot says something about your professionalism.

Sleep deprivation. The longest day I (KB) ever worked on a film was twenty hours. We had just finished our "third" meal, and the crew was "zombified." How do you keep your crew going under these circumstances? If you can, encourage naps at lunch time. Break crew members one by one, staggering the work hours. Let your crew take naps on the "QT," staggering nap-times. Sleep deprivation is a real, and serious, threat to productivity. Moreover, it is unsafe to drive when sleep-deprived. There are many documented cases of film crew members falling asleep at the wheel on the way home from a long day's work.

It is the responsibility of the designer and the costume supervisor to ensure that the costume department crew is operating with enough sleep. If the hours are ridiculously long, speak with the producer and the AD staff. Encourage change. Sleep deprivation makes everybody crabby.

Having fun. The costume designer and the costume supervisor are the leaders of the costume department team. On a stressful show, they must put on a brave front and encourage the best work from their crew. They must not allow the stress of their jobs to trickle down to the crew, who depend on them to set the tone. The best way to relieve stress on a tense show is to simply go a little bit nuts. It doesn't matter what you do, just as long as the fun doesn't affect your job performance. Never underestimate the power of laughter and the galvanizing effect it has on a working team.

Conflicts with other members of the crew. A filmmaking crew is a kind of organism, like the human body: If one part fails, the entire body suffers. So what happens when someone on the crew fails to function properly? "It's not my job." "It's not my department." You may hear these statements from time to time. What they really mean is, "I screwed up," or "I don't have it," or "It's not in my budget," or "I don't care." Whatever the meaning behind such statements, the implications are clear: You have a problem to solve.

"It's-not-my-department" problems are most easily solved in the production meetings that take place before principal photography begins. To avert conflicts with the prop department, for example, make time to have a long, sit-down chat with the prop master. Bring to the meeting a written list of the items that the costume department believes fall to props to provide, and go through the list point by point. Sunglasses, jewelry, watches, handbags, name tags, badges, briefcases—in theory, these are all props. However, in practice, the costume designer knows more about the look of the film's characters than the prop person. The designer has had fittings with the actors, knows what they look like, may even have had conversations about the prop elements of their costumes. Based on this knowledge, the designer may want to make some of the prop purchases. Whether or not a sit-down meeting with props is possible, the designer and the prop master must agree on who is responsible for what, and must approve of one another's choices for crossover items. This is essential so that efforts and objects are not duplicated, nothing is left undone, and the "look" remains coherent.

Set dressing is another area of overlap and potential conflict. On a big-budget show, the art department provides its own wardrobe items to use as set dressing (hanging in closets, hung on hooks, strewn on the floor, and so on). The art department's choice of set-dressing wardrobe is, of course, based on information about character clothing provided by the designer. On shows with smaller budgets, the set dresser may approach the costume department to borrow a character's actual wardrobe. Be very careful. Make sure that a running list of wardrobe items borrowed from the costume department (including notes on who borrowed it, and when) is kept in the wardrobe trailer, with a copy to the set costumer, who will have to keep an eye on these items (and may end up collecting them when the set is wrapped).

Trust among departments is always important, especially on a small film. The loss of a single piece of wardrobe may prove to be a costly mistake—a cost determined by more than its replacement value. Make sure that you have discussions with art department about who is responsible for these garments *before* you get to the set, so that problems like this can be avoided.

Another category of "crossover" can create conflict between departments—the crossover that comes when someone outside your department tries to do your job. We all like to do our job well, but what happens when someone does your job for you, without being asked? Straightening a collar is the job of a member of the costume department, not the job of the DP, or the AD, or a PA, or the makeup department. How do you gracefully handle a situation like this?

Begin by making it clear to the individual that, while you appreciate the help, this is really a job for a member of the costume crew. Usually, this is all it takes. If the problem persists, remind the person that this is costume's job. If the behavior doesn't change, take it up with your boss (the costume designer), who can then take it up with the boss of the "problem person."

Of course, this works the other way around—to wit, no member of the costume department crew should fix or tweak anything that is not within the province of the costume department. It is not recommended, for example, that you fix an actor's hair (even if it's messy). It may be messy on purpose; by fixing it, you will have unwittingly compromised the continuity of the scene. In general, if you have concerns about continuity (whether it's art department, props, makeup, or hair), take up those concerns with the department in question.

Cooperation: borrowing, lending, helping

We all get into a jam at one time or another. We may need a "stinger" (an extension cord) to run a hair dryer, in order to dry an unwanted wet spot on a garment. We may need someone in the locations department to find us a changing room. We may need gaffer's tape. It is production protocol to help fellow members of the crew. With this in mind, if the art department needs to borrow the costume department's steamer, if a dolly grip falls in the mud and ruins his pants, you can, and should, help. There are, however, limits. You can say no. You are not required to sew patches on twelve pairs of jeans brought from home to the costume department by a grip. This is not part of production work.

If the costume department finds itself repeatedly helping a particular member of the crew, or a particular department on the production, *say something*—particularly if this extra work keeps costumers from doing their jobs. Doing a good deed is one thing; being hoodwinked into doing someone else's job is another.

Unfortunate behavior

Once in a blue moon, you may come across a person who, it would seem, was born in the Dark Ages. You may hear language stream from lips that could wilt flowers. You may see behavior that is illegal and unprofessional. If such behavior infringes upon your ability to do your job, you must *immediately* talk to your boss (if you're a costumer), or to a trusted producer (if you're the costume designer).

Sexual harassment, racism, misogyny, anti-Semitism, homophobia, lewd behavior, verbal and/or physical abuse must never be tolerated in the workplace. You have a right to protest uncivil work conditions, and producers have a responsibility to ensure that the work environment is a productive one, free from the scourge of violence and hatred.

Cleaning up the mess

If all sticky problems could be avoided by taking this advice, we'd be living in a world more predictable than this one. Sooner or later, something—or someone—on a production will get out of hand. When this happens, you must take measures to remedy the situation. Making amends is never easy, but it is a necessary part of being a professional. You can write a letter, send an email, whatever you choose, but it is important to at least attempt to resolve an unhappy situation. If you are at fault, be the bigger person. Admit it, say you're sorry, and move on. You'll feel a lot better about it in the end.

Whatever you do, do not slander others after a bad experience on the set. People in the film industry have big ears. Vent to family and trusted friends, but when it comes to coworkers and professional acquaintances, keep your lips buttoned.

Learning from mistakes

You will make mistakes in your career, I guarantee it, but look to them for growth. Don't beat yourself up over a mistake you made. Learn your lesson and move on. Listen to others when they tell you about their mistakes. Learn from their experience. Study psychology and sociology. Develop compassion for others. Learn to understand what motivates people. In the end, this will make you a better conflict manager, and a consummate professional.

A Field Perspective: Working on *Going All the Way*

The realities of costuming during the shooting period are best comprehended by taking a look at a relatively low-budget film production, on which the challenges expected by every costume department are amplified and added to by a relatively small budget. We are on the shoot of the independent feature *Going All the Way*, written by Dan Wakefield, directed by Mark Pellington, with a costume budget of $35,000. *Going All the Way* is the story of two young men who come back from the Korean War to their homes in Indianapolis, Indiana, and spend the summer trying to pick up the pieces of their lives and sort out what they want to do next. Our stars are Jeremy Davies and Ben Affleck, as the boys, and Jill Clayburgh and Lesley Ann Warren, as their respective moms.

Today, the first day of shooting, we are at Fountain Square in Indianapolis, to shoot three and one-half pages of the script—three different scenes altogether. There's a big public street scene and two different scenes in a diner on the street. The art department has spent the last day or so dressing the set to look like 1954. The police are rerouting traffic, and production assistants are rerouting pedestrians—which makes us fairly unpopular with both the pedestrians and the local shopkeepers. "Picture" vehicles—a collection of nineteen-fifties cars and trucks—are cruising up and down the street as camera, lighting, and sound crews furiously set up for the first shot. (Light diffusers and reflectors will be manipulated all day long, in an effort to get the light to look the same throughout the entire sequence.) Camera dolly track is being laid, and the director and DP are going through their shot plans with the first assistant director. We have this street and the diner for only one day, so the pressure is on.

The costume call is at 5:45 A.M., and we'll go until 9:00 P.M. tonight. On location, the costume department lives in a parking lot two blocks from the main camera setup on Main Street. Home base is made up of two-thirds of an official wardrobe trailer (one-third going to makeup and hair); one Ryder rental truck, into which we've built hanging racks; and a large honeywagon, with fairly large dressing cubicles and a small toilet stall. When Jill Clayburgh and Leslie Ann Warren are working, Winnebago trailers will be brought in for them. Off site, at the administrative offices on the other side of town, there is a mini costume department, a fifteen-by-fifteen-foot room packed with additional costume stock, a washing machine and dryer, a table or two for sewing, an office area for the designer and costume supervisor, and a fitting room.

We are a small costume crew. The only paid members of the department are the designer, Arianne Phillips, her assistant designer, Jennifer Barrett, the costume supervisor, Julie Glick, and the set costumer, Danielle Valenciano. Costume department interns are unpaid, and their number will vary over the course of the shoot, subject to availability. This week we have four. After a hurried three-week prep in Indianapolis, during which we received costume stock, sized, tagged, and conducted fittings on a few principal characters and the first week's worth of extras, we are as ready as we can be for this first week of shooting.

We have been blessed on this production in several ways. Our director, Mark Pellington, is a dream to work with: He gives clear notes and is generous in the creative freedom he gives our designer. The director of photography, Bobby Bukowski, has also been easy to work with, and good about collaborating in advance. Our stars have been particularly pleasant and cooperative. Costume neurosis is at an absolute minimum: no major divas, no "hissy fits" about "inappropriate" costume choices. Since *Going All the Way* is a period film, the costume department has been able, as a rule, to fit extras and alter their costumes before shooting begins—a decided advantage on a low-budget, minimally staffed film. Our producer, Tom Gorai, is a charming young man who, before this outing into feature film, has produced only music videos. He is pleasant and supportive, but the problems inherent in costuming a period film are new to him. Although the tenor of the production during prep has been generally friendly and efficient, the budget is exceptionally tight.

The problems that arise on this shoot will be many, varied, and often chronic. The trucks are too small; staff members, too few. We can't afford enough racks or shop supplies. We don't have enough costume stock, and can't get a quick turnaround on most of the laundry or dry cleaning. We will shuffle stock onto and off our few rolling racks, and generally dig into our private kit supplies. We will rely on our pick-up seamstresses to supply their own machines, ironing and steaming supplies, and sewing supplies, including buttons and fasteners. We will buy supplies on an as-needed basis only. Every walk-in volunteer will be welcomed. Unpaid production assistants, who will be given camera time as extras, work in every department.

Over the course of the shoot, the costume team will be divided between the production-office and the shooting site. The costume stock is also split between the two sites, so that the designer, the assistant designer, and the costume supervisor can do advance fittings at the home base, and the set costumer and interns can style walk-in extras at the location. On every shooting day that requires extras, there will be a few walk-ins—special friends, substitutes for extras who don't show up, additional bodies needed to pad a scene. Since we will fit and accessorize at two sites, and the stock is fairly small, there will be times when a costume intern must shuttle stock across town.

At the shooting site, precious goods are stored in the wardrobe trailer: all of the principal and day-player costume stock; the set books; most of the general maintenance and office supplies; wardrobe equipment; personal wardrobe kits; and some extras costume stock, on racks and in boxes. Each change for a principal character, including accessories, is tagged and hung behind the character's name card/rack divider. At one time or another, each of us in the department will have to claw through stock, so proper tagging is a must.

The converted Ryder truck is largely devoted to the extras. In it, we store the general hanging costume stock, and rolling racks of pre-fitted extras' costumes, which are tagged with scene number, set, and extra's name, sorted by scene, and hung on the racks in alphabetical order. Cases of jewelry and boxes of hats, purses, stockings, socks, and shoes are sorted by color and given size tags, where appropriate. Underwear, scarves, ties, handkerchiefs, belts, suspenders, and gloves are all sorted by color and size, size-tagged where appropriate, and grouped, for easy display, on muslin-covered hangers. The general costume stock is separated into uniforms, menswear, womenswear, and childrens' stock, and arranged, head to toe and inner to outer layer, on pipes.

At the start of each shooting day, the set costumer "unlocks" the wardrobe trailer's hanging pipes and drawers. She pulls out the principals' changes for the day and puts them on a prep rack. The clothes are fairly packed onto the pipes, so garments get crushed, and daily ironing and steaming is required. The principals' changes are then delivered to the dressing cubicles, the garments laid out for the actors, and the garment tags collected and saved on a bulletin board in the wardrobe trailer. On moneyed productions, changes may be stored in garment bags, and carried in them to dressing rooms; but on this production, we can't afford garment bags.

On the Ryder truck, there is no air conditioning, no power, and no easy lock-down system. The rolling racks are tied up and taped down each evening. Crawling underneath the racks, and on top of them, to tie them off is a less-than-pleasant task. If you do not tie and tape them down, you are greeted with chaos—a costume dump on the floor of the truck—a sight that will greet us on the second day of the shoot. Driving to a location, garments can swing so violently on the racks that either the garments end up on the floor or the entire rolling rack tips over (fig. 7.6).

So, on the Ryder truck, each day starts with untying and untaping racks, rolling them out, and pulling out any boxed storage to which we may need easy access for on-site styling and accessorizing. Irons, ironing boards, steamers, and electrical hookups are quickly hustled curbside, to get ready for the onslaught of extras. The first extras arrive within the first half hour of call, while we are frantically doing touch-up ironing.

"Hurry up and wait" is the name of the game at the beginning of each day. Technically, the actors have one-half hour scheduled to get into their costumes. In reality, however, it may take hours before an actor gets before camera. As the principal players go to their dressing cubicles, the extras, with their pay vouchers, come to the wardrobe trailer, where they exchange the vouchers for a costume. We note the pieces that we must collect at the end of the day, but since most of these are pre-fit outfits, we already have notations on check sheets.

There is no way of knowing which extras will be used first, so we simply hustle, dressing as many of them as possible as quickly as possible. With few exceptions, we have between fifteen minutes and one-half hour to style walk-in extras, and have only three "windows of opportunity" to do emergency repairs, final accessorizing, and ironing of their wardrobe: when we first give the extra his or her outfit; after the extra is dressed and has reported back to us; and right after he or she has been through makeup and hair. Most shoot days, extras have to scrounge for dressing room space. Today, we get lucky: The diner we are using for the second scene has a large set of bathroom stalls, so extras have a place to dress. Miraculously, by set call, we have a fabulous set of fifties' families, college kids, teenagers, business folk, farmers, shoppers, and diner staff (fig. 8.10).

Before camera rolls on the first shot, the set costumer, Danielle Valenciano, arrives on set. The designer, Arianne Phillips, and her assistant designer, Jennifer Barret, arrive, to establish new looks on the principals, help us style walk-ins, and check all of the extras. Mark, the director, and Bobby, the DP, look over the characters, and Arianne directs final costume adjustments. When filmmaking begins, interns are still finishing extras at the wardrobe truck, so Danielle is stuck covering continuity and tweaking costumes for *everybody*. Once Arianne approves the costumes and they are established on film, she and Jennifer head back to the production office, along with costume supervisor, Julie Glick, to fit next week's extras. At the truck, the interns finish dressing extras who are not in the first shot. They clean up the truck a bit, then the ones who can be spared head to set, to spend the rest of the day there.

All day on set, our set costumer attends to the principals' wardrobe—tweaking details, recording continuity, and generally making sure they look right. Interns take

FIG. 8.10

Extras on set

turns doing the same for the extras. We Polaroid the principals in individual shots (with additional shots for costume details), the extras, in groups. With only two interns to handle dozens, sometimes hundreds, of extras, careful continuity notation on extras' costumes will be impossible. Taking wardrobe continuity notes on so many feels like drowning in minutia: How far were his sleeves rolled up? How many buttons were undone? Where did his pants break on the shoe? In what order did she wear her bangle bracelets? As a result, only leads will get comprehensive wardrobe notes—a shortcut we'll pay for two weeks into shooting, when film stock problems are discovered in dailies. We will need to re-shoot a scene in a bar, assembling the clothing for extras overnight, with only poor Polaroids to work from. Ideally, the clothes would have been tagged, bagged, and held for re-shoots. But this was not possible (even if we could have afforded garment bags): Our stock was inadequate for the demands of the show and, as a result, it was constantly being recycled. In order to find the pieces that had "played" in the bar scene, we would have to pick through the entire costume stock. A real nightmare.

Traditionally, once the shooting begins, the pace of the day is up to the first AD, the DP, the grips and electrical personnel. In general, there is sufficient time at the wardrobe trailer to prep, restock, and reorganize. However, with our tiny budget and skeleton staff, we are stretched thin covering the set, keeping wardrobe continuity notes, prepping principals and extras, and cleaning up. The second day of shooting will bring us piles of cleaning and laundry to refile and resize. Since we are recycling stock, we must constantly retag stock garments, to get them ready for new extras.

Our long shooting days take a heavy toll on the clothes we have, as actors and extras sit around waiting to be filmed. Because the budget has forced us to work with the absolute minimum number of costume doubles, there are no back-up shirts or pants that can be used, halfway through the day, to help the leads look fresh. On several occasions, the set costumer will have to work magic, cleaning costumes without doubles, for the next shot. The extras simply wilt in the course of the long summer day. Meanwhile, the interns are buried in racks of ironing for the next several days of shooting. Moneyed productions have the staff to maintain the look of the costumes. We do not have this luxury.

Minor emergencies keep us hopping all day. An instant "invented" food stain is needed for the apron of the diner's cook. The car drivers need hats and shirts, to make them look more "period." An elderly lady extra needs a change of shoes if she is to continue walking up and down the block for two more hours. A hair dryer is needed to dry the water stain on the lead's cotton shirt. An emergency supply line from the wardrobe trailer to the set needs to be maintained all day, and the interns quickly learn which supplies they had better carry with them, and which they can safely leave at the truck.

Our first day of shooting brings us a potential political crisis. Late in the day, word comes back to the interns at the truck that featured extras must be re-costumed. They've clocked a lot of on-camera time in the outfit in which we sent them to the set, and the second AD wants them recycled as different characters—*right now*. Because the designer is back at the office, the interns will have to work without the designer's approval. Interns designing on their own? Eeek! But holding up production is even more taboo. So, via walkie-talkie, the interns get approval from the set costumer, Danielle, then re-style the extras and send them back to set.

The meagerness of our department's supplies and equipment lead us to tease out the "secret" lines of supplies and information on location. Finding distilled water for the steamer at 6 A.M. is impossible—unless you have a friend among the caterers. The transportation guys are a godsend when we need electrical hookups. They will also save us, more than once, in the course of loading, unloading, and tying down the racks. The second second assistant director finds us walkie-talkies; the caterer lends us chairs.

Of course, there is some nonsense, and, occasionally, poor communication on set. The second AD demands costume changes that the costume supervisor has already negotiated against. A PA who is friendly with the second AD tries to make us redesign an extra to his liking. The extras casting director makes a number of costuming suggestions. But somehow, we get through the day.

At the end of the day, we collect the costumes from the principal players' dressing rooms, and collect the costumes from the extras, checking in all of the pieces and giving back their pay vouchers, noting missing items for which they will be charged. We search the set and dressing areas for stray costume pieces. (Of course, extras have left piles of clothes in three different locations.) We hunt down all of the costume items loaned to crew—the hat for the cameraman who needed a sunshade, vintage hats and shirts for the "picture car" drivers; the shoes for the little old lady.

We organize the laundry and cleaning to go out according to penny-pinching principles. Because we need to recycle as much of the extras stock as quickly as we can, we collect only the sweatiest and dirtiest of the garments for laundry and dry cleaning. We spray Endbac in any shoes and pants we can, allowing us to recycle the garments more quickly, and cut down on cleaning costs. We retag pieces that don't need laundering or dry cleaning, reinstate them in the proper change, or in the proper order on the stock rack. We hang tomorrow's changes for the featured players on the daily prep rack in the wardrobe trailer, prep the extras' rack for tomorrow, and double-check everything for readiness.

Then, we start "lock-down"—locking or tying down racks and drawers, moving the rack of extras' stock and boxes of accessories and supplies for tomorrow to the front of the truck (so it's the first thing off in the morning), and generally getting the trailers swept up and ready for transport. For the supervisor who faces a crew of walking wounded at the end of a grueling day, getting the paperwork done at wrap can feel like an uphill battle. But, come rain or come shine, updated continuity pages need to be filed daily so that the show can go on, regardless of staff emergencies. Call times, wrap times, and meal breaks must be accurately recorded for every member of the crew, or time-cards at the end of the week will be wrong and paycheck problems will ensue. When all of this is done, we crawl home and get ready for the next onslaught.

Funnily enough, at the end of this long, hard day—a day in which moments of real mania are interspersed with long periods of relative tedium—we still feel energized. This is fortunate, since we are heading into a marathon week of shooting that will take us all over the script, and Indianapolis, covering a mix of big public scenes and little private scenes. Monday sees us costuming roughly thirty to forty extras and three principal players, as we do the street and diner scenes. Tuesday is an all-day shoot at a swimming pool, again using thirty to forty extras—a mix of adults and children. Wednesday, we're in the suburbs, in two different backyards, shooting little scenes with our leading man and a handful of featured day players and extras. Thursday, we shoot the biggest scene of the picture—a dinner-and-dancing date at the courtyard restaurant in the historic Athenaeum building. We'll have the four leads, one hundred-plus extras, and a band. We'll shoot from 3:30 P.M. Thursday until 9:00 A.M. Friday. After ten hours off, to sleep, we'll shoot all night Friday inside an art museum, with roughly thirty extras and three principals. Saturday, we'll be back in the suburbs, shooting all night, with the principals doing love scenes from various points in the script. Sunday is our day off.

When working on location, independent films most often work six-day weeks. But "day" in filmmaking lingo does not mean sunup to sundown; it actually refers to any single shooting period, regardless of whether the period starts at 6:00 A.M. and ends at 6:00 P.M. or begins at midnight and ends at noon. Producers sequence the scenes in the shooting schedule according to requirements for daylight or night sky, and all-day and all-night shoots are permitted as long as the crew gets a ten-hour "turn-around" between wrap and the next call. In week one of *Going All the Way*, the producers had scheduled a "night for night" shoot for Thursday night—the night-time dinner-and-dancing date in the open-courtyard restaurant. As a result, the first three "days" of the week will be nights, spent shooting interiors. This split day/night schedule is grueling over the long haul, and by the end of the first week of filming, it will feel as if we've been shooting for a month.

At the end of each day, and on that blessed Sunday off, we will simply have to breathe deep, regroup, and regain our sense of humor. By nature, filmmaking is a marathon. It can run roughshod over your personal life by demanding all your attention and every bit of energy you possess. You have to build your own personal strategies to stave off the crabbiness and sloppiness that are too easy to give in to. Working with close friends, indulging your sense of humor, treating yourself to an expensive "toy" afforded you by your paycheck—any number of survival techniques can be honed to help you maintain a good attitude. And let's face it, while filmmaking may often be unnerving, it is rarely dull for very long. The adrenalin "high" that you get just surviving a shoot can keep you going for a very long time.

PART NINE

Final Wrap

The Art of Final Wrap: An Introduction

At the end of principal photography, the costume crew faces the monumental task of returning or liquidating all the goods, equipment and supplies that have accumulated during the shoot. This phase is called "final wrap." "Wrap." Everybody loves this word. All of your hard work is finished. Or is it? The tasks entailed in "final wrap" are some of the most important of a production. This is the time when all of the loose ends are tied up, the set books are completed, the thank-you letters go out, and the wardrobe is inventoried and set aside for possible re-shoots. This is the last chance to make a favorable impression on production.

On a film, the two key objectives of final wrap are to prepare for re-shoots, inserts, pickups, and other new footage that may be needed after principal photography has ended, and to return or liquidate stock, supplies, and equipment not needed for future shooting. Readying thousands of costume pieces to be stored, returned, or sold off is a labor-intensive, time-consuming process. To complicate matters, once principal photography ends, the pressure is on to downsize staff and wrap the costumes as quickly as possible.

Who gets downsized first?

Depending on the shooting schedule, it could be the costume designer. Once the look has been established for the characters, a producer may feel that the costume designer is superfluous. (This has been known to happen on many TV series, where the costume supervisor takes over and runs a design established by a costume designer.) Why would a producer even contemplate letting a designer go before the end of production? Often, late in the shooting schedule, scenes require fewer and fewer actors; the scenes remaining on the schedule may require work solely by principal players. If no new character costumes or major costume changes for extras are required, the priority becomes the maintenance (rather than the creation) of character looks—the job of the set costumers and the costume supervisor. So unless the producer is willing to continue to pay the costume designer or design assistant to begin preparations for the final wrap, they could be the first staff downsized. Costume personnel who work predominantly on prep—shoppers, fitters, alterations personnel, dyers and distressers, and other custom-made personnel—are often let go as soon as their work is completed—well before final wrap.

Indeed, wardrobe wrap is generally completed by the costume supervisor and costumers. On a bigger show, the costume designer usually has only a few days of wrap—enough time to complete thank-you cards to vendors and get his or her kit packed up and shipped home. If time is of the essence, the supervisor may hire additional hands for wrap. But usually it is a process undertaken by just the supervisor and the two key set costumers. Most costumers who have been through the entire show have one day of wrap in their deals. That one day of wrap is usually spent downloading the trailer and getting their kits refurbished and packed to go home.

Wrapping before shooting ends

Wrap doesn't have to wait until the last minute. The wrap process can be undertaken along the way, to avoid a log jam at the end of the show. As the number of costume crew dwindles toward the end of principal photography, production exerts more and more pressure on the costume supervisor and set costumers to wrap the production. If this is the case, a basic tactic for costumers is to start wrapping wardrobe before the shoot is over, a move that will save the department time and headaches later.

> When you have enough time, I, personally, like the return portion, because it's like a puzzle. Say, you have a thousand pieces of wardrobe, and they have to get back to five different places, and they're all marked in some way: Some have labels and some don't, some are bar-coded (occasionally, more than once). The goal is to make sure everything gets back to the right place, but it's tricky. In doing the little puzzle thing, we try to find the most error-free process we can. *(Jaci Rohr, costume supervisor)*

While the costume designer is still "on board," the designer and supervisor should spend some time deciding on "wrap" priorities. To wrap or not to wrap, that is the question The answer is to wrap whatever you can, whenever you can, in a way that allows you access to the garments if you suddenly need them. For example: You have finished shooting the big flashback scene in this period film, the high-brow, black-tie cocktail party. You have moved on to a new location and are never coming back to the mansion where the flashback was shot. Safe bet to wrap the wardrobe? Ask production. Make sure that your decisions are informed. The important thing is not to get caught in a situation in which you've prematurely returned wardrobe that you unexpectedly need. Rule of thumb: Plan carefully. Pull accordingly.

The safest bet in this case is to dry-clean, bag, and tag the wardrobe. Hang it up in a far corner of the trailer, organized according to the return rental sheets, then rope it off and forget about it. (Note: This is assuming that you pulled the garments as part of a twelve-week production rental. If, for some reason, you have pulled these garments on a short-term rental, make sure that everyone knows that the garments are going back to the rental source. Send a memo to the production office, with copies to the ADs and the director, so that it is clear to all that the garments will need to be pulled from the rental house if inserts or re-shoots are necessary. If possible, put the garments on "hold" at the rental house they came from.) (For more on rental sheets and rental holds, see below, "Returning rental goods.")

Of course, finding time to do this can be a problem. While principal photography is still under way, the set costumers will be focusing primarily on the task at hand—the ongoing shoot. As a part of this work, however, they can pave the way to final wrap by keeping the set book current and wrapping character changes when they've been "shot out"—bagging them, tagging them, and moving them to the back of the trailer. The costume supervisor, too, will have her hands full during the final weeks of shooting, overseeing the on-going set operations and wrapping up the accounting paperwork (for more on this, see below, "Final accounting"). The costume designer—if he or she is still on the show—can help support the supervisor by working closely with the production office: getting the most up-to-date information on re-shoots, for example, and procuring production stills of actors wearing product-placement stock or other borrowed garments. The costume designer can also oversee the sorting and storage of the re-shoot stock (see below, "Holding goods for re-shoots"), and send out the thank-you notes and appropriate production photos to the sources that lent garments to the production.

Preparing returns: basic protocols

As shooting starts to wind down, any members of the costume staff who are not needed to record continuity or prep costumes for future scenes can be "liberated" to prepare stock and supplies for returns. The work of doing this can be assigned according to which crew members can be mobile and which are tied to a location (set or home base).

Regardless of who is doing the work of preparing returns, certain protocols are required, in order for final wrap to happen with minimal hitches.

1.   All items must be returned in accordance with the rental or receipt paperwork used to obtain the goods, to make sure the production is properly credited. The general policy for returns is that the goods need to be returned in (or restored to) their original condition. All rental houses require that garments are professionally cleaned in advance of their return. Since each source's return policy may have rules and regulations beyond standard practice, crew heads need to keep track of return policies, and prepare goods for return accordingly. (For more details on proper return protocols, see below, "Returning rental goods").

2.   The order in which "wrapped" goods are returned is determined by deadlines imposed by the vendors, and the labor required to prepare the goods for return (for details, see below). Returning unused goods to department stores generally occurs throughout the shoot, with the costume designer or wardrobe supervisor's approval. For product placement or loaned goods, carefully confirm the return date in the agreement to see if goods can be held until final wrap. (Note: Goods taken out on memo through studio services departments must be returned within five days or they are considered purchased and will be charged to the production's account.) You may simply have to let go of some of your "safety net" garments if your sources won't allow you to keep their goods through final wrap.

3.   All goods to be returned need to be sorted by source, and all production character and size tags removed.

Re-shoots and other additional photography

Hold all principal and day player changes and specialty wardrobe, including bought goods, made-to-order, and rentals, for re-shoots and any other additional photography. In addition, hold established extras stock that is easily recognizable—the outfit with the big feathered hat worn by the lady at the bar, for example.

The costume changes for featured players (principals, day players, featured extras, stunt players, stunt doubles, and photo doubles) can get bagged and tagged after their final use and held in storage, for safekeeping. Rental garments are usually held at the rental source, grouped together and tagged for re-shoots, for six weeks after the end of principal photography. (For more, see below, "Returning rental goods.") Supplies and equipment needed to support re-shoots are kept to an absolute minimum on most productions, especially when storage space is at a premium.

The "wrap" system used for re-shoot wardrobe must be logical and the documentation and organization of re-shoot stock meticulous. Garments should be bagged and tagged by change. All elements of each costume change should be grouped together and listed on the change tag (e.g., "Paul Smith: multi-stripe short sleeve shirt, Guess brown leather belt, Fawn Timberland boots, size 10") and a note made as to the location in the total series of a character's changes of any garment used more than once (e.g., "Charlie, Change #3, scenes 24-36: Teched white Hanes underwear, teched white tube socks, Diesel 5-pocket blue jeans, with frayed hem (*located with Change #1*).")

In the event that a garment in a change is a rental, it must be marked as such on the change tag, and the tag annotated with (1) the manufacturer's name, (2) the costume house from which it was pulled, (3) the sheet and line number of the rental (on the original rental paperwork), and (4) the end-hold date. Additionally, this information should be written in the set book, on the continuity page for the costume change in question.

Notes on all bagged and tagged wardrobe, whether rented or purchased, should include the manufacturer's name (in case many garments in the character's wardrobe look similar). In the case of shoes, mark the tag and continuity sheets with not only the manufacturer's name but the size (so shoes assigned to the actor are not mistaken for shoes assigned to a stunt double). All of this information should be written up in lists or entered on a computer spreadsheet, and handed in to production, with copies retained by the costume designer and the costume supervisor. (As you can see, wrap is all about the details. It involves a good deal of paperwork, so make sure that someone on the crew has a laptop.) Once this is done, the hanging stock is stored on racks, or in wardrobe boxes. Non-hanging stock is boxed or stored in bins clearly labeled with their contents (e.g., "Charlie, Changes #1, #2, #3).

You will never regret this level of detail and organization—and production will thank you in the end (whether or not they say so). So will the wardrobe person who gets stuck doing re-shoots, pickups, and inserts. With an organized wrap system, including an accurate, clearly presented set book, any wardrobe person off the street will find everything she or he needs. (For more on set books, see below, "Wrapping and storing set books.")

While principal photography continues, "wrapped" changes get stored in the wardrobe trailer or truck (as noted above), or at home base, depending on the amount of storage space available (see below, "Storage"). If push comes to shove, rental goods can be sent back to the rental houses from which they came, as long as they are placed on hold, as can product placement goods that must be sent back to their sources, again, as long as they are put on hold. (For more, see below, "Returning rental goods" and "Product placement returns.")

Before the shoot wraps: the wardrobe sale

As noted above, all wardrobe that has been prominently featured in the film, either on principal players or on featured background characters, should not be sold; it should be kept for re-shoots and other additional photography. (In order to determine what must be held and what can be sold, or otherwise liquated, see below, "Liquidating purchased stock.") However, unnecessary stock is an asset to the production, and may be sold or auctioned at considerable profit. Some costume departments, in fact, arrange to hold a sale of leftover wardrobe before the cast and crew disperse—usually during the final days of principal photography.

Let's say you're over budget and the show has four days of shooting left. You have a trailer full of cool wardrobe purchased for extras—assets to the production, but not principal wardrobe (which might require storage for re-shoots). How can you help solve your budget problems? A wardrobe sale to the crew! Make sure that the sale is approved by the production office and the producers, then advertise your sale with a note stapled to the call sheet. Direct sales to the crew (or members of the cast) are handled in cash, or checks made payable to the production. You can make back hundreds, sometimes thousands of dollars in this manner, and the crew gets souvenirs for cheap. The standard policy for selling to the cast or crew is to value the goods at half-price.

A sale like this is conducted more or less formally, and is run by the costume department. Once principal photography is over, costume departments should not be involved in the auction-for-profit of these garments. At this point, the responsibility belongs to production.

When shooting ends: wrap procedures (continued)

When wrap time comes, download the truck first, basically sorting the wardrobe as you do it. Production will want to get rid of the wardrobe truck and driver as soon as possible—well-equipped wardrobe trucks are too expensive to keep. When wrapping the truck, you would be well to leave it in the condition in which you received in. Sweep the floors, wipe down the counters, take the stuff off the corkboards. The "transpo" guys will love you for it.

Where do you finish wrapping? Wrap can be done just about anywhere where there is racks and space. Many wardrobe facilities will rent out cages and/or offices for wrap. But, rental costume cages are costly. If you are on a low-budget show, you may find yourself wrapping out of the producer's garage, or a production office. If wrap home base is a room in the production office, you are good to go: Production will be in residence longer that the costume department.

Once the stock is out of the truck and you are set up to finish wrap, the job of sorting changes and stock for laundry, repairs, and restoration takes priority. Once changes, general stock, and supplies have been pulled and prepped for additional photography, all unneeded costume stock needs to be sorted for return, resale, or donation (for more details, see below). Used goods need to be tagged for repairs or restoration, including cleaning, according to rental agreements. Rental or product placement stock should be restored to "original condition," unless the production has received express permission to age, alter, or change the goods (or substitute items for damaged goods). Items in need of repair or restoration must be farmed out to the appropriate sources (see below, "Returns to rental houses"). After sorting for repair and restoration, the general stock is then sorted according to where it will be returned. Rental and product placement stocks are separated by source. Purchased stock is grouped according to how it will be liquidated. Guidelines for the dispersal of costume stock follow.

Returns to rental houses. The biggest headache for both production companies and costume rental companies is the proper return of rented goods, especially when it involves a mass return at the end of a shoot. Rental companies charge for the time and trouble it takes to check in their stock and organize it for re-filing. If stock is returned in a condition not permitted by the rental agreement, they also charge for the repair or replacement of damaged goods, and for cleaning. Each rental source has its own rules for acceptable return conditions. However, when in doubt, restore garments to their original rental condition (unless otherwise specified in the rental agreement).

The following are some of the most frequent problems experienced in the return of rented good, and some of the most common solutions:

1. Unorganized returns.

Problem: Productions have been known to return rack after rack of garments in utter disorder. Checking hundreds of items against checkout sheets can be a long, tedious process for rental company staff, and the rental company charges accordingly.

Solution: Wardrobe must be returned to rental houses on hangers, in "sheet order." "Sheet order" is a major buzzword for returns to both rental houses and studio service departments. Staff at both venues check in garments as they were checked out—in the order in which they were written up on the rental sheet forms, and it is imperative that the wardrobe crew is "with it" in this regard. Note: Rental pieces do not need to be size-tagged for return; costume houses will do this as part of check-in, without added charge.

2. Returns in unacceptable condition.

Problem: Occasionally, a production company returns rental garments in a condition not allowed by the rental agreement. Garments have been damaged (in the course of filmed action, or by accident); garments have been altered and not restored to their original condition (either because they are altered beyond the ability to restore them, or because time was not allowed or available to do so); garments are soiled (everything from mud to sweat to simply having been on a body and not laundered or cleaned).

Solution: It behooves the costume department to return rentals in their original condition, if this is what the rental agreement calls for—unless, that is, the department has the budget to pay the stiff fees charged by rental houses to have their garments restored to original condition (cleaned and/or alterations removed). After all, the rental house is the middle man; they charge more than a laundry or cleaner would because it takes the rental house's time and personnel to sort the goods, employ in-workroom tailors, and arrange for outside cleaners to pick up and deliver. In addition, while the garment is being restored, it isn't available for the next production rental.

426 COSTUMING FOR FILM

When your department does send rentals out to be cleaned, make sure the cleaner has a reputation in the industry for working with vintage and other potentially delicate garments. You don't want the garments damaged in the cleaning process. When it comes to the damage repair and "de-alteration" of rental garments, your on-staff stitcher, if you had one, is no longer on payroll by the time final wrap is this far along. An alternative? There are a few cleaners in L.A. that will actually repair garments in the cleaning process (Milt and Edie's Drycleaners, in Burbank, California, is one of them), and this can save you time if you have minor damage to the garments. If the repairs are major, take the garment to a trusted tailor first, then clean the garment.

3.   Inadequate description on rental sheets.

Problem: There is nothing more frustrating to a costumer than trying to wrap a show using rental sheets that don't adequately describe the costume pieces and thus make rentals difficult to identify.

Solution: If this is the case, try adding clarifying notes to the one-line descriptions on the rental sheets when you check in the garments during prep. If this is not practical, check the SKU numbers on the rental company bar-code tags against the SKU numbers on the rental sheets—a tedious, but unavoidable, process.

4.   Bar-code duplication.

Problem: Occasionally, rental companies bar-code garments twice, by mistake. This creates two tags, two check-out numbers, and endless confusion when the goods are checked in.

Solution: Not much of one. Most of the time, just bite the bullet. Either the costume rental house will cut you some slack, or, if resistance is too great, handle it as you would a lost garment problem (see below, "Damage and loss").

5.   Returns to the wrong rental source.

Problem: Production companies can return garments to the wrong company by mistake. These things happen all the time. Often, when you look inside a pair of pants at, say Western Costume, you will see labels from Palace and Warner Bros. as well. Sometimes, the costume house doesn't catch it; sometimes, it is too late. Sorting this out can be a nightmare, for the costumers who are wrapping and for the rental house staff.

Solution: What happens if, by accident, you return garments to the wrong location? Track them down and try to swap them out. Sometimes, tracking down missing garments is an impossible task, and substituting stock is your only option (see below, "Damage and loss").

> Every costume house in town has pieces with another rental company's name in them. Let's say there's a black turtleneck missing. Maybe it wasn't marked well. It should have gone back to Western Costumes, but it got accidentally returned to Eastern Costumes. Then, two days later, when all we have to finish are returns to Western Costumes, we find a turtleneck labeled Eastern Costumes. We return it to Western because we don't have time to go back to Eastern, and we know the other turtleneck has already been restocked at Eastern, anyway. (*Jaci Rohr, costume supervisor*)

6.   Damage and loss.

Problem: Costume rental houses have chronic problems with loss and damage to costume stock by productions. Some rental sources allow productions to supply substitutes, some prefer to get damage fees.

Solution: If you find yourself in a situation where garments are missing, talk with the rental house about a "swap out" or replacement-garment deal *before* you make the return. See if you can give them three new ties for the one you lost. Sweeten the deal by being generous. Loss and damage charges can be pretty high, and most costume rental houses are reasonable and willing to exchange in this manner. Be up front about the damage and loss that you have incurred, and offer liberal amounts of substitute garments, if you can.

As noted above, in the process of preparing rental goods to be returned, make separate rack sections for each rental source to which costumes are being returned. Within each rental house section, a separate section should be devoted to "holds." When character changes are to be held at the rental house, make sure that each is tagged, including a list of items in the change, the name of the production, and a contact name and telephone number. Traditionally, a rental house will hold changes, intact, for six weeks, if prior arrangements are made.

An alternative to sending rentals back for "hold": If a production company has enough storage space, and production wants to keep rental stock on premises for re-shoots, it can pay for an extension on the rental time. This is a good insurance policy. Rental wardrobe is held by production until "picture lock," and you always know where it is. When the picture has been locked, the wardrobe is returned to the rental house.

Returning product-placement goods. All production tags must be removed from product-placement goods, and other goods on loan. They must be sorted according to source, and grouped together to tally exactly with loan paperwork. Used and/or principal wardrobe that came from a product placement or other loan source should be held for re-shoots, unless your agreement with the vendor says otherwise. Product-placement garments that were never worn, with tags still attached, always go back to the vendor that supplied them. (Product-placement vendors don't sell used merchandise, but unused garments with the tags still attached can be re-stocked and sold.)

Returns to department stores. Unused purchased stock from department stores will be returned for refunds. To make sure that each item is properly credited, SKU numbers on store tags should be checked against the SKU numbers listed on the receipts.

Returns made on the designer's credit cards are, occasionally, complicated. Sometimes, the designer will give his or her credit card to a trusted costumer, along with a photocopy of his or her driver's license and a signed note giving the costumer permission to use the card for returns only. (This is usually not a problem, since the account is being credited, and no charges are being incurred.) What if the designer is unwilling to sign over the card to whomever production is paying to do returns (usually, someone who costs less than the designer)? Then, the designer does the returns—on her own time.

In most cases, cash returns are simpler than credit card returns. If a vendor doesn't have enough cash in the register to cover a very large return, a refund check will be cut and sent, usually from corporate headquarters. If this is the case, the check should be made out to the production company, and sent to the production office. Ask for the vendor to give you a receipt indicating the items returned and the amount to be refunded. This receipt should be given to the production accountant, with a note to expect the refund check in the mail.

Liquidating purchased stock. Each production has its own policy when it comes to what's to be done with leftover costume stock and supplies. On a major studio production, purchased goods may get absorbed into the studio's rental stock and supply store. On an independent production, the producer may prefer that unused goods be returned for cash, sold off, or donated for a tax write-off (see above, "Before the shoot wraps: the wardrobe sale"). On television series, the principal character stock bought or made for the production may be held intact, awaiting next season's shoot, in a cage at the costume rental facility allied with the studio that's producing the series. "Mini-majors," like Miramax or DreamWorks SKG, that don't own studio lots with costume rental facilities, have their own approaches to wrap. After a shooting is completed on a DreamWorks production, for example, all principal-player wardrobe is either integrated into the stock they've warehoused from other productions, or inventoried and set aside for donation or auction. DreamWorks usually makes its clothing donations to the MPTF—the Motion Picture and Television Fund—which sets up on-line or on-site auctions, with proceeds going to the fund itself. The purchased stock that's not donated is considered "leftover goods." Because DreamWorks does not run a costume rental service, warehoused costume stock is periodically sold off, in bulk, to a consignment dealer, wardrobe house, school, or theater company. Sometimes DreamWorks even has production sales, which are open to the public, held, customarily, ninety days or more after a film's release. (For more on wardrobe donations, see below.)

In all events, it is incumbent upon the costume supervisor and designer to familiarize themselves with the policies and procedures for wrap held by the production on which they're working. Once an overall plan is in place for stock and supply liquidation, they can set about determining what can be wrapped or returned while shooting continues.

Before unassigned purchased items (stock or supplies) can be liquidated, the costume supervisor and the costume designer must agree on which goods are truly available. Several factors affect this decision:

1. *The need for re-shoot stock.* Purchased stock not assigned to principals, day players, and featured extras during the course of principal photography should be combed for pieces that might work for these established characters—in the event that additional scenes must be shot. In the case of television, this makes sense since additional episodes or seasons may be ordered, and these pieces can become part of a character's "closet." In addition to stock that is suitable for named characters, pull and hold general stock that conforms to the designer's palette for background players in major scenes.

2. *Actors' agreements.* Occasionally, actors will have clauses built into their contracts that guarantee that they be given some of the wardrobe purchased or made for them on a show when production ends. If no such contractual agreement exists, an actor may

want to buy his or her costumes, and expect them to be available for purchase. If this is the case, the costume designer and the costume supervisor must get clear information from the production office, and guidelines on any wardrobe deals that are to be made with actors. When wardrobe is given to actors as a gift, or sold to them, items listed in the set book must be annotated with their eventual location (e.g., Charlie, Change #1, Diesel 5-pocket blue jeans, 1 pr. actor purchase). This list (complete with the location of absent garments) should be duplicated and distributed to the UPM, the production accountant, the costume designer, and costume supervisor.

3. *Rental and wardrobe-loan agreements.* If the costume designer or costume supervisor has struck deals with rental and wardrobe-loan sources that commit the production to giving purchased costume stock back to these sources in exchange for low rental rates or screen credit, production must approve these deals. If rental items have been lost, or cannot be restored to original condition, substitutions may be made from the general stock, by mutual agreement. These problems should be solved before "leftover stock" is still available for substitution.

4. *Wardrobe kit restoration.* Before supplies or stock can be sold or given away, crew kit stock and supplies that have been used up during production must be replenished, and crew kit stock that has disappeared, been abused, or co-opted by principals and featured players must be replaced (or substitutions made). Since many members of the costume crew are let go shortly before or after principal photography is finished, those who have provided wardrobe kits (at no cost, or for a rental fee) need to collect and restore their kit stock, supplies, and equipment before they are dismissed.

> Typically kit rental is provided to either the designer or the supervisor—not the set person, in my experience. However, if you come with four boxes of Topstick in your kit, you want to leave with four boxes. The stuff is expensive. At the end of the show, everybody replenishes their kits. *(Jaci Rohr, costume supervisor)*

If after filling all other potential needs, unassigned purchased stock remains, it can be sold or donated, with the approval of the producer. Independent production companies may opt to sell off their stocks to rental houses, actors, crew, or staff and will require the costume staff to document the goods and where they're going (as described above), then deliver them to these sources. On a studio production, any leftover purchased costume stock is added to the studio's rental stock; leftover supplies are added to the studio's supply store. As a result, studio productions may require costume department staff to inventory and "cost out" leftover stock and supplies with values exceeding $25—in order to credit the production unit for the cost of the goods. Once this is accomplished, the goods can be delivered, for restocking, to the studio's rental and supply storage facilities.

If purchased stock is to be donated, whether to a costume rental company (without the production's account being credited) or to a non-profit entity (Goodwill or Salvation Army, for example, or the Motion Picture and Television Fund), the costume supervisor will be required to prepare detailed inventories of the goods, including costs, for tax purposes. Studios and charitable sources may have varying policies on the valuation of donated articles, and specific forms to be filled out. The supervisor must learn these policies and practices before submitting the goods. As with rentals and other returns, purchased stock and supplies to be donated or sold after production should be sorted and grouped by source.

When the goods are finally dropped off for donation, a receipt for the goods should be issued. It should describe the general content of the donation (wardrobe and wardrobe supplies, for example) with its assigned value. Checks should be made payable to the production company.

Storage. Once the "wrap crew" has decided which supplies and equipment to keep, which costume pieces can be returned, and which must be liquidated (sold or donated for tax or cost credit), postproduction storage becomes a question. If wardrobe is to be stored, production will have arranged a place to store it. First storage priority goes to the set books, usually held by a producer, and the featured character costume stock mentioned above. After that, the size and availability of storage space will dictate how much additional stock and how many supplies and hard-to-find pieces of equipment will be kept. It is really up to the producer where the stock gets held. Some producers store assets in their garage; some producers store assets at a studio costume rental facility, a warehouse, or commercial storage site.

Wrapping and storing set books. The set book, which details principal player and extras changes scene by scene, is vital to the re-shoot process, and important to the final wrap of the production. Wrap is the time to finalize and clarify the details of every costume change. Any costumer should be able to come in, look at the set books, and be able to figure out what needs to be pulled for re-shoots. Every change for each principal, day player, and featured extra must be listed completely and accurately, including notes on how the garment is worn (e.g., "Yankees baseball cap, worn backwards") and documentary Polaroids.

As noted above, if any pieces of the costume are rentals, they need to be marked in the book with the following additional details: (1) manufacturer's name; (2) the name of the costume house from which it was pulled; (3) rental sheet number and line number on which the item is described; and (4) the end-hold date. Highlight this information on the page with a fluorescent highlighter. If a garment in a costume change is actor-owned, mark it and highlight it, as well. The set book should also include a master inventory of general stock and supplies and an indication of where items are stored (rack, box, or bin number). Additionally, the names and phone numbers of the designer, costume supervisor, and key costumers should be put in the book, so that they can be contacted if questions arise. Once the books are completed, they should be turned over to production, for future reference.

Remember, the completed set books should be works of art. They should be in binders that look good and are easy to use, the contents logically organized, the pages simple, clean, legible. These books will be your representatives once you have left the show. Those who depend upon them—not only the costumer hired for re-shoots, but the producers who may hire you in the future—will be left with a lasting impression of you, and your work.

Final accounting. Final accounting for the department is completed by the costume supervisor, after all the returns and loss and damage settlements have been completed, petty cash and charitable-donation receipts turned in, and, if possible, refund checks accounted for. This final settling of accounts can be an arduous process. Everyone needs to settle their petty cash with the supervisor before they are off the books. All studio service and rental accounts need to be settled before the supervisor is off the books.

Looking to the Future

"Parting is such sweet sorrow." "Wrap" means leaving the friends you have made over the course of a shoot. "Wrap" also means leaving behind those folks who really bugged you. How do you wrap relationships? My personal experience has led me to send out a flurry of thank-you cards and copies of snapshots taken over the course of filming. I think it's important to acknowledge these relationships, to celebrate them, and a supply a sense of closure. Of course, you will find your own way to take your new friends with you—or leave them behind. This business is based on personal contacts, so tread carefully if you've had an unsavory relationship with a fellow crew member or actor. The toes you step on today could be attached to the ass you must kiss tomorrow.

PART TEN

Entering the Market

Preparing to Work in the Film Industry: Further Training for the Field

Now that you have an understanding of film costume processes and costume job descriptions in the film industry, you can examine how to get started in the profession. Before you head to Los Angeles or New York, I advise you to prepare yourself carefully. Over are the glory days of the studio system, during which vast costume departments were maintained and hundreds of films a year produced. To get work now in film or television, in Hollywood or New York, you have to be very good, very well-connected, or willing to work cheap.

With a little training, a lot of charm, and more luck, you may still be able to work in film or in television. But to build a career in the film industry in the United States, you need solid skills, a thorough comprehension of the film costuming process, and the willingness and ability to meet standards set in the cradle of the motion picture industry. Just as Broadway sets the professional craft standards for theater in this country, Los Angeles sets the craft standards for film and television.

Film costumers have grown accustomed to training people on the job. Why? Because there is very little formal training available for aspiring film costumers, especially training that addresses the nitty-gritty of costuming a film. Most basic training for the film industry combines formal training at film, theater, or fashion schools with on-the-job training in the professional theater market, costume rental houses, independent film or television productions, and made-to-order workrooms. However, by acquiring a range of skills in costume research, character design, costume construction, dyeing and distressing, costume stock organization, and production wardrobe support (dressing actors and maintaining costumes), you can become more employable when you start out.

> For someone starting out in the film costuming business, the more background you have, the better served you will be. I think you should know costume construction. You should know how to work with a draper. You should know modern fashion. You should know period research and be able to recognize a period garment, not just when you're looking at it in a book, but when it's hanging on a form—even when it's hanging on a really bad hanger, squashed in some dark corner. You should know all of it before you come out to L.A., because you don't know what you are going to be doing. *(Marcy Froehlich, costume designer, and co-author of* Shopping LA: The Insiders' Sourcebook for Film & Fashion)

Academic training opportunities

Academic programs in film costume design. Formal academic programs in film costuming are available at very few universities. Ohio University offers a costume design and technology master of fine arts (MFA) program that allows a specialization in film costuming. California State University, Long Beach, Extension Services, offers a professional designation program (a vocational certificate) for costuming for film and television. Los Angeles City College Theatre Academy offers a two-year professional certificate (a vocational certificate) for theater costuming that includes film and television costume studies. The Fashion Institute of Design and Merchandising, in Los Angeles, offers an advanced degree in film costume studies for students who have gotten their undergraduate degrees at that institution.

There are also several classes in film and/or television costume design at University of California, Los Angeles (UCLA); University of California, Irvine; New York University (NYU); and Otis Parsons Art Institute, in Los Angeles. Several universities with strong film departments offer formal training in theatrical costume design; occasionally, these include film project work.

Film schools. Film schools do not generally make costume classes an important part of their program. Instead, they emphasize writing, directing, cinematography, editing, and film history. Occasionally, you will find classes in art direction, but for the most part, set and costume training is relegated to adjunct classes in theater departments.

There is great value to training in film and television production. Developing a basic understanding of the whole filmmaking process—from the points of view of the producer, the director, the cinematographer, the sound designer, the production designer, and the editor—will help you analyze a production situation, assess a production's needs, and understand your role in satisfying them. This type of training teaches you to think and talk like a filmmaker. If taking classes is not possible, at least read Sidney Lumet's book *Making Movies*, this director's perspective on the shooting process.

Theater schools. Theater schools traditionally provide technical training in costume construction and costume crafts, dyeing and distressing, costume stock organization, production wardrobe support (the skills needed to "run wardrobe" during a theater performance), and costume maintenance (cleaning and repair). However, although there are exceptions, the technical training you get in a traditional theater program may not meet craft standards and protocols of the film industry.

Theater-school costume-design programs do provide training in script analysis, character development, costume research (historical, symbolic, and "tonal"), fashion history, sketching and collage work, and the process of collaborating with costume workrooms, set designers, lighting designers, sound designers, choreographers, and directors. However, with few exceptions, theater costume design training de-emphasizes modern dress (rarely using film scripts or the type of costume breakdowns seen in film) and rarely gives costumers the opportunity to work on a film shoot. (Courses in set design, lighting design, script analysis, acting, directing, and film history can help fill this gap, and can be very useful in preparing a student for the collaborations encountered in the field.)

Theater school training does provide a wealth of experience—in low-budget production, improvisational styling, stock-garment adaptation, and sleep deprivation.

Fashion schools. Fashion schools provide technical training in costume construction, fashion marketing, fabric construction and textile analysis, mass-production practices, and production wardrobe support for live fashion shows and print work (catalogues, print advertising, etc.). The garment-construction training offered by fashion schools often matches film industry standards, but, depending on the program, may not be oriented to film's high-speed construction practices.

Fashion schools can also provide training in sketching, thematic and event-centered research and design (formalwear, swimwear, uniforms, etc.), fashion history, current-market design practices, and the process of collaborating with fashion workrooms and clients. While fashion schools can develop in their students a sophisticated understanding of the current fashion market and the work of important fashion designers, they tend to de-emphasize historical research, and do not train students in detailed script analysis or the skills needed to work with other designers.

Independent research

Any formal training program can help you gain some professional skills. But to be well-grounded in film practices and standards, to stay current with film market resources, and to help you identify potential employment sources, you must be prepared to study the film and fashion markets on your own. The following are some ways to go.

Polish your sense of film and television history. Study production values throughout the history of film and television. You need to know the work of the giants of the film industry, and of film costuming, past and present, and understand what is characteristic of their work. Studying the illustrious careers of costume designers past will show you what shaped the "studio standard" and the "Hollywood image," and will provide you with rich resources for costume history research.

Curl up in front of the television and watch the vintage movie channels available on cable. Watching films of the past, you can study the work of the industry-honored costume designers whose work established the gold standards for film costume design in the twentieth century, including, for the nineteen-thirties and nineteen-forties, Adrian, who designed for Greta Garbo, Katherine Hepburn, and Norma Shearer in films that include *Anna Christie, The Philadelphia Story,* and *The Women;* Travis Banton, who designed for Marlene Dietrich and Carole Lombard in films that include *Shanghai Express* and *My Man Godfrey;* and Bernard Newman, who designed for Ginger Rogers in *Top Hat* and *Swing Time.*

Extending from the nineteen-thirties and forties into the nineteen-fifties, you'll find Howard Greer, who designed for Katharine Hepburn, Ingrid Bergman, and Jane Russell in films that include *Bringing Up Baby, Spellbound,* and *The French Line;* Orry-Kelly, who designed for Ingrid Bergman, Bette Davis, and Marilyn Monroe in films that include *Casablanca, Now, Voyager,* and *Some Like It Hot;* Walter Plunkett, whose films include *Gone With the Wind* and *Singin' in the Rain;* and Travilla, who designed for Marilyn Monroe in *How to Marry a Millionaire, The Seven Year Itch,* and *Bus Stop.*

The nineteen-fifties and nineteen-sixties saw the rise of Helen Rose, with films including *High Society, Silk Stockings,* and *Butterfield 8),* and witnessed the continuing mastery of Cecil Beaton *(Gigi, My Fair Lady);* Jean Louis *(Gilda, The Misfits, Ship of Fools);* Irene Sharaff *(The Best Years of Our Lives, The King and I, Who's Afraid of Virginia Woolf?,* and *Hello, Dolly!),* and Edith Head, whose astonishing career began in the late nineteen-twenties and included such classics as *All About Eve, Sunset Boulevard,* and *Butch Cassidy and the Sundance Kid.*

Extending into the nineteen-seventies, you'll find stalwarts like Theoni V. Aldredge (*The Great Gatsby, Network, Moonstruck, The First Wives Club*); Dorothy Jeakins (*Little Big Man, The Way We Were, Young Frankenstein*), whose career includes epics like *The Ten Commandments* and musicals like *The Sound of Music*; Bob Mackie (*Lady Sings the Blues, Funny Lady*, and countless hours of television, including *The Sonny and Cher Show* and *The Carol Burnett Show*); and Theadora Van Runkle (*Bonnie and Clyde; The Godfather, Part II; Leap of Faith*).

From the nineteen-seventies to the present, look to the work of the prolific Ann Roth (*Midnight Cowboy, Silkwood, The English Patient, The Talented Mr. Ripley, Signs*), and Albert Wolsky (*All That Jazz, You've Got Mail, Road to Perdition*). Having made their marks in the early nineteen-sixties, these designers continue to produce work worth studying.

The books *Those Glorious Glamour Years: Classic Hollywood Costume Design of the 1930s*, by Margaret J. Bailey; *Edith Head–The Life and Times of Hollywood's Celebrated Costume Designer*, by David Chierichetti; and *Gowns by Adrian: The MGM Years 1928-1941* by Howard Gutner explore the work of the key costume designers of Hollywood's glamour era. The book *Costume Design in the Movies: An Illustrated Guide to the Work of 157 Great Designers*, by Elizabeth Leese, gives the filmographies of some of the most important costume designers in the business, up to 1976.

Current designers with Academy Awards and A-list careers define today's standards. The up-and-coming designers with hot careers trigger tomorrow's industry trends. Since 1980, Academy Awards for best costume design have gone to the following designers: 1980—Albert Wolsky, for *All That Jazz;* 1981—Anthony Powell, for *Tess;* 1982—Milena Canonero, for *Chariots of Fire*; 1983—Bhanu Athaiya, John Mollo, for *Gandhi;* 1984—Marik Vos-Lundh, for *Fanny and Alexander*; 1985—Theodor Pistek, for *Amadeus;* 1986—Emi Wada, for *Ran;* 1987—Jenny Beavan, John Bright, for *A Room with a View;* 1988—James Acheson, for *The Last Emperor*; 1989—James Acheson, for *Dangerous Liaisons*; 1990—Phyllis Dalton, for *Henry V*; 1991—Franca Squarciapino, for *Cyrano de Bergerac;* 1992—Albert Wolsky, for *Bugsy;* 1993—Eiko Ishioka, for *Bram Stoker's Dracula*; 1994—Gabriella Pescucci, for *The Age of Inno- cence*; 1995—Lizzy Gardiner, Tim Chappel, for *The Adventures of Priscilla, Queen of the Desert;* 1996—James Acheson, for *Restoration;* 1997—Ann Roth, for *The English Patient;* 1998— Deborah Lynn Scott, for *Titanic;* 1999—Sandy Powell, for *Shakespeare in Love;* 2000—Lindy Hemming, for *Topsy-Turvy*; 2001—Janty Yates, for *Gladiator;* 2002—Catherine Martin, Angus Straithie, for *Moulin Rouge!*; 2003—Colleen Atwood, for *Chicago;* 2004—Sandy Powell, for *The Aviator*. (For more information on current major designers, see page 558.)

Study current trends in the film and television markets. Watch a broad range of contempo- rary films and television programs to gain a working knowledge of current trends in production and costume design. Focus on who is doing the most acclaimed and innova- tive work in the industry, and where it is being done. Develop a strong awareness of the business side of filmmaking—the box office successes and failures, the power brokers, the rising and falling stars. Read the trade papers, and magazines like *The Hollywood Reporter, Premiere*, and *Daily Variety*, to keep up with news in the industry.

Identify the production companies, artistic staff, and costume supervisors for the work you admire. To pursue employment with directors, costume designers, or costume supervisors, you need to have a sense of the range and quality of their work. (For a list of contemporary costume designers who have done notable work in period and high-concept films, science fiction films, whose work includes strong and eccentric character designs, stylish modern dress, and trend-setting designs, see Appendix pages 557–558.) For the filmographies of key film personnel, try the website www.IMDb.com. Also useful are the many creative directories and sourcebooks available in hard copy and online.

Study fashion market trends and sources. You need to keep abreast of current trends in the full range of fashion markets for young and old, from haute couture to mid-market ready-to-wear. And you need to know where to shop these looks. The greater your shopping and styling skills, the more marketable you become. Study a broad range of fashion and news magazines, websites, clothing stores. Hone your people-watching skills in a range of districts and neighborhoods.

Training in professional theater and film markets

Working as a shopper, costume technician, costume crew member, costume designer, or design assistant in the professional theater can help you develop a number of skills that will be useful to you in film. Working in any costume workroom will refine your understanding of fabric, fitting techniques, and made-to-order pattern-development processes. Any theatrical wardrobe position will train you in a variety of costume cleaning and maintenance techniques. Any theatrical costume design job will help you develop skills in script analysis, costume graphics, character design, and shopping. The salt mines of summer stock, Off Broadway, and regional theater are rich grounds for training in the costume crafts, and in the survival skills required on film and television productions. Film employers will always prefer to employ people with film experience, but high-quality theater credits on a résumé sometimes enable you to enter the film market above entry level.

Two kinds of theater experience are particularly useful. The first is to work as an IATSE wardrobe member in New York or in the regional theater market. IATSE has chapters across the country that represent theater and film wardrobe personnel on union productions in their areas. The theater branch of local chapters deals exclusively with costume wardrobe personnel—the workers who "run wardrobe" for productions, dressing the actors nightly and dealing with garment maintenance and repairs. Working freelance as a theater wardrobe technician can train you in costume maintenance and organization, develop your attention to the fine points of dressing the actors, hone your ability to work with difficult personalities, and help develop your networking skills. An IATSE wardrobe card can also put you in the loop for word-of-mouth information on film or television shoots in the area. Union films that shoot in your local's region will often tap local IATSE personnel. IATSE wardrobe members must acquire separate membership cards in film and theater categories if they wish to work in both, but, as a rule, the union is more open to crossover memberships than it is to new applicants.

Becoming a member of an IATSE theater wardrobe union local can be difficult. Pay rates for union wardrobe staff are some of the best in the theater business and, as a result, the union is inundated with requests from people who want to join. One of the best ways to get into this union is to find work in a costume workroom attached to a union theater. (In New York, Radio City Music Hall and The Metropolitan Opera, among others, have IATSE costume workrooms on their premises.) Schedule an interview with the shop head, who can hire non-union members with the expectation that the new employee is earning hours toward union membership.

In New York, once you have worked in a union workroom for a period of time and have decided to apply for union membership, you can ask union members in the shop to write you recommendations, which are a required part of the application process. While this approach does not guarantee acceptance into the union, if union members in the shop appreciate you and your work, and if there is an opening on the "run crew" of a show at the theater to which the shop is attached, you may be lucky enough to find sponsorship for union membership. Additionally, if you have solid costume construction skills, you can apply to union wardrobe crew heads for work as a "day-check" technician—doing repairs or maintenance when regular wardrobe members are unavailable or uninterested. Most other routes to union membership involve nepotism—a father, a mother, a sister, a brother who are union members in good standing, and can pave your way.

Working on Broadway in a costume design studio, a costume rental house, or a costume workroom can also be an entrée to the film and television industry. Working as a design assistant or shopper for a Broadway theater workroom can help you develop a detailed knowledge of New York research and costume resources—all of which can be directly applied to film and television industry work. The budget for a Broadway show is the closest theater gets to the scale of the average film budget. (Of course, some Broadway theater budgets are bigger than small film or television project budgets.) Made-to-order costs in Broadway costume workrooms are on par with MO costs in the film industry, and the quality of clothing purchased for Broadway from retail sources matches the standards for film costume purchases, so Broadway training can also develop film-costume budget savvy. Many New York workrooms and rental houses serve not only theater but the film and television industries. Some Broadway designers work on film and television projects, affording the design assistants in their studios opportunities to make connections in the worlds of film and television.

The film world's respect for Broadway's standards is based on the quality of prevailing Broadway costume-construction methods and Broadway's demand for large-scale made-to-order work. In addition, the intensely collaborative nature of theater work, particularly among designers, stars, and artistic staff, matched with the demand for garments that hold up under the high-stakes performance requirements of a Broadway show, become sources of instruction and experience for practitioners of the costume arts who wish to make the transition from theater to film.

Entry-level positions in New York include working as a costume or craft technician (if you are sufficiently skilled), as a shopper for a workroom, or as an intern in a design studio. Pay rates are low and vary with your qualifications. For young graduates of theater or fashion programs, the easiest route to employment with a New York workroom is as a "first hand" (assistant to a tailor or a cutter). This work requires you to join the International Ladies' Garment Workers Union (the ILGWU), an easier feat than joining IATSE. With sufficient skill, you may gain entry to a craft studio as a craft artisan (dyer, painter, milliner, etc.). Both high-caliber college training in craftwork and high-quality professional regional theater credits will help you get work as a craft artisan. To intern in a Broadway design studio, you need connections to a good theater training program or strong design talent, a pleasant manner, and a willingness to work for free.

Hollywood is full of New York theater professionals who abandoned Broadway to migrate to the more lucrative film market in Los Angeles. Bill Hargate and John David Ridge, who design and run costume workrooms in Los Angeles, came from Broadway. Costume designers Ann Roth, Jeff Kurland, and Richard Hornung are also examples of Broadway émigrés. (For an additional perspective on breaking into the film market with a Broadway background, see below, *Conversation Fourteen: On the Difference Between New York and L.A., with Marcy Froehlich.*)

Film and television internships

To develop film contacts and fill in gaps in their training, many people start by working for free—interning—on films, television shows, and commercials produced by independent production companies. Interning is a fundamental test of your basic job skills and professional qualities. Among basic job skills are a mastery of costume crafts useful in film, a command of production etiquette, and an ability to work collaboratively. Professional qualities that will be tested include promptness, endurance, and how much fun you are to work with—even under adverse conditions. Many interns spend days sorting, sizing, and tagging costume stock, running shopping and laundry errands, returning garments, ironing, doing alterations, loading and organizing wardrobe trailers, packing and shipping goods, and if they're very lucky, dressing extras. Costume work is often prosaic—long hours filled with thankless, dirty little tasks—whether you are an intern or not.

Costume interns run the gamut from trained costume specialists to people with absolutely no costume or film training. People are often chosen as interns because they are pleasant, have a car, and consistently show up to work. Occasionally, interns feel like Rodney Dangerfield: They "don't get no respect." In fact, many of the tasks an intern performs require relatively little skill. It doesn't take an MFA to iron a shirt.

The cons—and pros—of internships. The disadvantages of interning? Aside from poverty and long hours, an intern must depend on the kindness of strangers. Crew members can sometimes be mean-spirited about sharing information. Even though you're working for free, there's no guarantee that the people you're working with are going to be generous or fair with you. There are no guarantees that you will be exposed to the whole film costuming process, let alone work on set. Interns are generally not allowed to see dailies, where you really get a chance to see what shows up on the screen and study how the camera is used. You can be stuck off site or in a corner for long periods of time. And interns naive about the business can be taken advantage of, even abused. You might be asked to drive for miles on errands and never be reimbursed for gas. The production can make off with your equipment and supplies and never reimburse you for them. You can hear a lot of promises, but receive few results. Filmmaking is not kind to the naive.

So why intern? As thankless as it sounds, it's worth it. By learning from the ground up, you will gain an understanding of the whole film costuming process, an understanding that will help you throughout your career. You can study the process and feel some of the pressures without being expected to shoulder major responsibilities.

For beginners, the principal advantages to internship are as follows:

1. An internship will give you access to people who can help you professionally, and provide you with film résumé credits. With luck, during an internship, you may find an "angel" who will take you under his or her wing and help you get started in the business.

2. During an internship, you will learn how to work at the pace of film production. Production priorities will be clarified, and you will be able to study others' solutions to production crises, and develop a few of your own.

3. An internship can teach you vital prep and set skills. Working on a production during prep can teach how to set up a costume office, organize costume stock, delegate costume labor, compensate for late casting or low budgets or small staffs, and allow you to sharpen your sense of an area's costume resources for goods and personnel. You can learn survival strategies and meet the people who may help you make it through the next project.

4. An internship will allow you to witness what actors and crews go through in the course of shooting. Working on set will allow you to feel the pulse of the production. You will learn set etiquette and job jurisdictions. You'll learn how and why you need to collaborate with other departments. Watching the shooting process (and the video monitor at the shooting site) will train you to think like a camera. You'll learn the attention to detail demanded for continuity tracking, and the kinds of garments needed to withstand the rigors of shooting. You'll learn how careful stock organization pays off in on-set "speed styling." You'll learn the cost of delaying camera.

How do you choose an internship? It depends on your background and the gaps in your understanding of film or costume processes. Unless you have a solid understanding of the craft standards of the business, low-quality productions incline you to bad work habits (e.g., poor standards of costume fit, garment maintenance, continuity notation, and a poor understanding of job jurisdictions). While it is ideal to intern on a big-budget production that uses crew working at the top of their form, internships on productions like this are difficult to secure. Competition for jobs is fierce—and film unions battle to protect their own.

Furthermore, interns who work without pay present two problems to the industry:

1. Interns are not covered by production company insurance policies. This presents serious liability problems and can put a production company at great risk.

2. Interns can take work away from union personnel. It is forbidden by union guidelines for non-union workers to work on union production units. Occasionally, unpaid internships can be had on a big-budget productions when they are shot away from major filmmaking centers, and when productions are desperate for help. Low-budget productions (which are much more interested in interns) can strive for high production values when they are managed by good people, and these productions

can be fertile training grounds. Try to get background information on the production company, costume designer, or costume supervisor and watch any of their films that are out on video or in theaters.

In exploring possibilities for internships, make sure you get answers to the following questions:

- Will you work at the shooting site? (Working at the shooting site—whether a studio or on location, at the trailer or on the set—will mean that the production will provide you with meals: important to an unpaid intern!)
- Will you get a chance to observe any made-to-order processes?
- Will you get to observe fittings?
- Will you get to work closely with the costume designer or the costume supervisor?
- Will you be compensated for the use of your wardrobe kit, including equipment and supplies used by the production? In what amount?
- Will you get mileage? At what rate? Will you be reimbursed for gas receipts and other travel-related expenses incurred for production purposes? Will you be reimbursed for production-related cell phone calls?

Formal internship sources. In Los Angeles, the American Film Institute (AFI) and the Academy for Television Arts and Sciences host internships for newcomers. These internships are available on a competitive basis. The Academy for Television Arts and Sciences internships are open to qualified full-time students pursuing degrees at universities in the United States. Interns participate in the production of episodic television, mini-series, soap operas, or movies-of-the-week, from prep through taping; they assist the designer or costumer in purchasing, rentals, and made-to-order work. Applicants must submit photographs of their portfolio work and have a theater or fashion design background. The Saks studio service department also takes interns, and non-union workrooms and rental collections around L.A. can be approached about internships. Other film industry internships are listed on the web at sites including www.reeldirt.com and www.showbizjobs.com.

The Costume Designers Guild is developing a Trainee Program to guide young people toward design careers in motion pictures, television, commercials, and music video production. Trainees will follow a curriculum that couples technical training with real-life experience and be financially compensated for their work. Eligibility requirements have not been established yet. The goal is to start accepting applications in the fall of 2006.

In New York, you can intern with a variety of costume designers who work in film and on Broadway. You can also approach costume workrooms or rental collections in New York for internships, although work at these facilities will be oriented to the theater.

> Nobody seems to apprentice anymore. Nobody believes they need to—especially graduates from college who want to come out to L.A. and earn the big bucks right away. They don't realize that after receiving their diplomas they have to pay their dues; they may have to work for up to ten years before qualifying for the big bucks, because you have to learn your craft. People don't seem to realize anymore that this is a craft that requires special training. *(Edwina Pellikka)*

Work in the regional film market

To prepare yourself to enter the film industry in New York or L.A.—to polish the skills and develop the contacts you'll need to enter the market there—get some regional film work under your belt, at local television stations and film production companies, at studios around New York, or on L.A.-based feature films that are shooting on location. In addition to New York and Los Angeles, the United States has three other particularly strong regional centers for feature filmmaking. They are Wilmington, North Carolina; Chicago, Illinois; and Orlando, Florida.

In addition, there are hundreds of regional production companies scattered across the country that produce features, documentaries, music videos, commercials, TV series, business films, educational films, animated shorts, print ads, and now, CD-ROM (compact disc) and Internet-targeted productions. If your goal is to head to New York or L.A., you'll want to develop a network of contacts that will help you when you get there, so try to connect with the feature film units based in New York or L.A. that are planning to shoot in your region.

Many production companies don't need much in the way of costume support, especially companies that specialize in documentaries, animation, and training films. In order to get costume work, you need to look for work with production companies that shoot commercials, music videos, features, or television shows. Most feature film productions that shoot on location hire key costume department staff (the costume designer, costume supervisor, and key costumers for prep and set work) out of L.A. or New York. As a result, most entry-level positions on these films are as costume department interns or made-to-order and alteration costumers. Occasionally, these films rely on "local hires" for dyers and distressers, prep costumers (for shopping and costume stock organization), on-set extras costumers, and, occasionally, assistant designers. To get work as a costume designer, a design assistant, or a wardrobe stylist, you will, most often, need to approach regionally-based production companies.

Most aspiring film designers and costumers enter the regional film market by being in the right place at the right time—lucking into a connection with a film unit in their area. Local regional theaters, colleges, or independent costume shops can get tapped by regional films for the use of their costume stocks, or for job referrals for costume construction or other costume-related work. IATSE film work and commercial work can come to you through connections made doing day-check work for a regional theater that employs an IATSE wardrobe crew. If you do not live in a region that has easy access to film production companies, you are going to have to work very hard (and be willing to travel) to make film connections in your region.

To root out information on what is shooting in your region and who is hiring costume personnel, you must be dogged in your search. One way to connect with regional productions is through state film commissions, which can tell you what is being shot in a given state, and if a production is union or non-union. State film commissions and established regional production companies are listed in several publications, among them the *Film & Television Directory*, available through Peter Glenn Publications (www.pgdirect.com) and your city and state film commission production guides. You can also use the search terms "film commissions," "film organizations," and "regional film commissions" to research the Internet.

Many states have a "hotline" you can call for information on what is currently shooting. You can get listings for specific regional films that are in production in the Tuesday edition of *The Hollywood Reporter* (www.hollywoodreporter.com), a daily film trade publication available by subscription and at selected newsstands and bookstores, principally in New York and LA. Every Tuesday's edition of *The Reporter* lists the feature film projects that are "in production" (currently being shot), "in preproduction" (shooting this month), "in preparation" (films with a definite shooting start date), and "in development" (don't hold your breath). These listings identify the production company, the costume designer (when available), and the unit production manager through whom you can apply for work. *The Reporter* lists shooting locations, dates, and key artistic personnel for each production. The films that advertise in these sources are generally "highly visible" productions that originate in the U.S., and are shooting in Southern California, New York, and other places around the country and the globe. On the Internet, Reel Dirt (www.reeldirt.com) provides a free job listing service that posts Hollywood and regional jobs.

Micro-budget productions preparing to shoot outside New York or L.A. may be eager to take on novices. You can track down these productions through your local film commission, or on the web at Reel Dirt, Shoots.com (www.shoots.com), and any number of other entertainment industry job-search sites. If you own a costume rental collection, or have worked as a stylist, a costume technician, or wardrobe personnel, you can advertise in directories, among them, the *Film & Television Directory*, noted above (Peter Glenn Publications, www.pgdirect.com). Or, if your local film commission publishes a production guide, you can buy a listing.

While ads in *The Hollywood Reporter* and listings on the Internet and in directories can be useful in your job hunt, many production companies do not advertise when they have jobs. Instead, they rely on word of mouth for résumés, on recommendations that come from mutual friends, and from crew members with whom the company has already worked. Even if you advertise in print, until you are part of the filmmakers' grapevine—thus privy to the buzz on film productions looking for costume staff—you will need to be aggressive in your hunt for a costume job.

Entering the film market

Before you apply for a job, you need to assess your strengths as a film costumer. What do you really have to offer an employer? Are you more skilled at prep or set work? Do you have the technical training you'll need to work to industry standards? What experience do you have shopping or renting clothing in the area or doing costume research locally? Can you organize, size, and label costume stock by film standards? Have you run wardrobe for any film or theater productions? What do you really want to do, and how can you prove that you will be good at it?

An ability to take measurements and fit, a knowledge of local costume and clothing resources, an ability to navigate the city where a production is shooting, and a willingness to help with anything are all valuable skills to offer film productions in your region. If you have wardrobe equipment or costume stock a production needs, you are even more marketable. If you have a car that's big enough to haul costume stock or equipment, that's another plus.

Beyond assessing your skills, you must examine your attitude toward the work. How much are you willing to sacrifice to get into the field? What are you willing to settle for (in salary, work hours, working conditions) and still maintain a cheerful disposition? What are your shortcomings?

> Film is a great leveler: You either get it, or you don't. In spite of good skills or good training, work habits are all. Your energy level, the ability to make yourself useful and anticipate problems are the most important skills. *(Catherine Adair, costume designer)*

If you are applying for work on a production that is passing through your region, you should expect to apply for *entry-level work*, unless you have already racked up some professional film or television credits. Be prepared to intern or do alterations, unless you have advanced technical costume skills or professional wardrobe experience. Low- to micro-budget productions may look for design assistants and set costumers locally, but they may try to fill these jobs with interns. If you are applying for work with a local non-union production company, you can approach them for design work, but until you have some professional film, commercial, or TV credits, you may be asked to do the work for little or no pay.

Introducing yourself: cover letters, résumés, and sampling pages

When you apply for work as an entry-level intern, production companies do not always expect you to submit an elaborate résumé or prepare a professional portfolio. Frequently, these jobs are given on a first-come, first-taken basis to people who show up at the production company door asking to be interviewed for any available non-paid work. But if you are applying to work for free beyond the entry-level, or for paid work, you must prepare cover letters and résumés that will appeal to the personnel who control the jobs you want (directors, costume designers, costume supervisors, and production managers).

Cover letters and résumés should be customized, not boilerplate or form letters designed for a mass mailing. Content and tone should complement the character of the production and the position for which you are applying. List first the credits most closely related to the job you are seeking—credits that reflect your expertise in the job and show the kind of work you prefer to do. If you are switching job positions and have only a few credits, or none, in the position for which you are applying, the cover letter you write will need to be especially strong in order to offset your lack of direct experience.

The tricky part about contacting a production unit for work via the mail is getting your letter to the person who can hire you. More often than not, production companies ignore blanket mailings of résumés and cover letters. Telephone calls to companies can be frustrating, and sometimes futile, attempts to connect with the right person. Résumés often don't get passed along to the right people. While it is standard procedure to mail a résumé and a cover letter before any interview, you may find it difficult to get a résumé to the appropriate person without hand-delivering it. Your best bet is to call the production office and get the names of the wardrobe crew. Persistence may be required, but at least you'll know who you're sending your résumé to.

In order to get hired on a feature film that is coming through your region, you need to set up an interview with the production unit's costume supervisor or costume designer. Call your local film commission or check its website for information on who is shooting in your area and where their local production office is set up. Go to the production's local office and ask for the costume department office. Show up on the costume supervisor's doorstep with a résumé and ask to set up an interview. Bring a portfolio of technical work or film styling work, just in case the costume supervisor is interested.

To approach local production companies for work as a stylist, costume designer, design assistant, or design intern, you will need to send a cover letter and résumé. If you are applying as a stylist or costume designer, request an interview with the director, the producer, or the staff production manager. If you are applying as a costume design assistant or design intern, request an interview with the costume designer. For work as a prep or set costumer, you can apply to the costume designer or the costume supervisor.

COVER LETTERS. Many of the film personnel you need to contact get dozens of letters monthly from costume designers and costumers. To even begin to get noticed, you need to approach your prospective employer with a personal touch. You must try to give the employer a sense of who you are—your tastes, your background, your awareness of their work. Gushing and "brown-nosing" are not appropriate forms of address. Instead, show the employer how smart you are.

Whether you are going to write a cover letter or go to an interview, prepare by researching the past projects of the person or production company with whom you are making contact. Study the production company's advertising and ask for any literature that details their past productions. Filmographies and contact information for directors are listed in *Hollywood Creative Directory Film Directors*. Costume designers are listed in *Hollywood Creative Directory Below-the-Line Talent* (which also lists cinematographers, production designers, and film editors). Both of these books, along with *Hollywood Creative Directory Producers* (which is a great source for current production company addresses) are published by IFILM Publishing. IFILM's website, www.IFILMpro.com, may also direct you to the *Hollywood Creative Directory*'s website (www.hcdonline.com), which includes a job board.

Another way to research the credits of potential employers is via the *Costume Designers Guild Directory*, which you can obtain through the guild's office in Sherman Oaks, California, or their website (www.costumedesignersguild.com). The directory lists contact information and key credits for costume designers, stylists, design assistants, and sketch artists. Information on costume supervisors is much more difficult to find. The Motion Picture Costumers union directory is not available to the general public; the union has no website and will not give out contact information on the telephone. You need to know a union member, or work in a union studio or workroom, to have access to this directory.

Of course, many consider the best source for production research to be IMDb, the Internet Movie Database (www.IMDb.com), which has pretty comprehensive credit listings and a place for agent's listings, too.

When you have a list of your prospective employer's past film work, rent any available videos of the work and study it. If you're applying to a production company for work as a designer or stylist, you need to note those aspects of your work that best suit the project at hand. If you are applying to assist a costume designer, your cover letter should reflect your appreciation of the designer's work and the skills you have that will be useful on this production. If you are applying to work with a costume supervisor, note the skills you will bring to this position and describe why the current project (or projects the supervisor has worked on in the past) fit particularly well with your abilities and interests. For letters to a workroom or rental company, go to the shop, look at their goods, examine their publicity flyers. In your cover letter to the workroom, comment on what attracts you to this particular workroom's specialties.

The tone of your cover letter is important. Your prose should sparkle, and you should seem like you'd be fun to work with. Your writing needs to embody your positive attitude. If you are looking for work as a costumer, you can show you're hip to costume lingo by asking about "day check" positions, and expressing your pleasure in doing "returns" or detailed research work. If you are not targeting a specific position, you might say you "will do anything to be of assistance in costuming." You can also show you're costume-savvy by reflecting on how what you do best fits the job at hand. For example, stress your love of costume detail, your shopping skills, your organizational skills, your character styling sense, your clothing distressing abilities and your skill as a dyer, your computer literacy, your actor-wrangling skills, or your wardrobe-maintenance skills.

A sense of humor may get you noticed, but don't push it. Charm is great, obnoxiousness is not. Read your letter carefully before you send it, to see that it reflects a calm, patient, charming personality and a good sense of humor. You never want to come off as needy or egocentric. Keep the letter as brief and to the point as possible.

Designer Eduardo Castro gets stacks of résumés and cover letters each year from people who are anxious to work with him. If the cover letter catches his interest, and the applicant is persistent, Castro may set up an interview—he interviews many who write him letters. Known for his generosity to people new to the field, Castro has this to say about the art of the cover letter:

> You should have a couple of different letters. If you're directing a letter to a costume designer, it should be written one way. If you want to be a PA on a film, and you got the production-office phone number or fax number through *The Hollywood Reporter*, do a general letter to the department head: "I just graduated from such and such. I've come to town. I am very much interested in a wardrobe production-assistant job, if you have one." Address it to the head of the wardrobe department, and include, "I'm willing to work on any level."

> The best advice I can give you for cover letters is to make them personal. Do some research on the person you're writing to, if possible. The thing about it is, it does make a difference to be able to say, "I really admired your work on such and such." I get the letters that are full of flourishes, that call me a genius and this and that. That's awfully desperate and pushy. Just say how much you admire something, and how you respect the person's place in this industry. Say, "I would really love a chance for you to look at my work," and, "Any conversation that we may have, and any advice you can give would be appreciated." You will get a response, at least from certain people. I can't get to everybody, but I do try.

> I'll give the person more of a shot if they give their letter a personal edge—a personal edge, and savvy. I see as many people as I can, and I keep many of their names right

here in my book, where I have costumer-type PAs. I keep them in order of who I would like to use next; and I recommend those who are most persistent.

What I don't like are desperate letters, often from people who are already in the industry. "I'm a good worker. I'm really good at what I do. I can shop, and I can do this." I prefer letters that say, "I really would love to get a chance to meet with someone like you. I like the projects that you do, and the range of them." Sure, tell me where you're coming from and what you've done and what you want to be, but don't be desperate.

You'll hear from a lot of people, "Don't say that you're a designer." I don't think that's right. It's a lot of jealousy. But what you might want to do in your cover letter is, if you're a new designer, say, "I want to connect with someone I can learn from. I want, in my long-range plans, to be a costume designer. I know I'm not there yet, but I would really love to learn from the best. And I'm in no hurry." Because if you say you're a designer, and you want to be that right off the bat, there's a certain language, a certain way you need to phrase it.

RÉSUMÉS. Your résumé needs to be simple, to the point, and professional. It should be easy to read and should reflect film industry terminology for job classifications (wardrobe intern, set costumer, key costumer, etc.) and production formats (feature films, episodic series, MOWs, etc.). Names and references should be accurate.

Résumé formats vary a great deal—some costume personnel shoot for single-page formats, some do postcard-like "résumé highlights" cards, and some do elaborate foldout résumés. It is important to stress the range of production formats in which you have worked, and the scale of the productions on which you've worked (e.g., epic series, music videos). Give a place of importance to the "quality" productions and production companies for whom you've worked. Don't list high school credits. Eliminate college credits once you have a respectable number of professional credits.

Résumés must prominently feature:

• *Date.* Put the date on your résumé at the top of the page. Regularly update the résumé for new credits.

• *Your contact information.* Include your address, phone, fax, email, and cell phone/pager information.

• *The type of work in which you are expert.* List your credits by job categories (e.g., your supervisor/key costumer credits would be listed separately from your set costumer work, etc.). At the top of the first page of the résumé, list the credits for the type of work you are targeting in the job application. Reconfigure the résumé according to the different kinds of work you apply for (see A.35, Jean Rosone's résumés for costume design work and for costumer work).

• *The title of the production, the type of production, the production company, and your job on the production.* This information should be formatted to be easily read. For example, Jean Rosone's résumés (cited above) separate the production information into different columns and list the work under different job-title headings. The more famous the projects that you have worked on, or the personnel that you have worked for, the better. If possible, group your credits by production format (e.g., make separate listings for episodic TV work, MOWs, and feature films).

If you are coming straight out of school, list professional jobs (including internships and summer work) under "Professional Experience" and student film project work under "Academic Experience." If you don't have a lot of film experience, you need to set up your résumé to feature the work that most closely relates to the film industry jobs you are looking for. For example, for a design position, list print-ad stylist work or theater costume design work; for a workroom job, list fashion or theater costume technology work; for a prep job, list shopper or studio services work, styling and design work, or costume technology; for on-set work, list theatrical wardrobe experience; for dyeing and distressing work, list costume technology experience.

- *The designer, director, and stars involved in the film.* Note that in both Jean Rosone's and Robert Joyce's résumés, key artistic staff members are noted (see A.35, A.36). Famous names on résumés are extremely helpful. For television work, add producer names.

- *Additional key information.* Some résumés, like Jean Rosone's in A.35, also feature very brief *descriptions of the project*, in order to give potential employers a taste of the nature of the design challenges in films that are not well known. If you include project descriptions on your résumé, you must do so consistently, even on well-known projects.

Some résumés feature a section on *special skills*, listing the specific kinds of work and materials in which you are expert. For example, a design assistant might list additional competencies in sketch artistry, military or period research, styling, fabric shopping, computer breakdowns, and budgeting. A costume technician might list additional expertise in leather work, tailoring, period garment construction, foam constructions, padding, and lingerie. A set costumer might list expertise in menswear, distressing, computer skills, military detailing, and creative storage solutions.

Some résumés feature *education/training* credits. You may benefit by listing college degrees in theater, fashion or film, and special training courses or professional internships.

- *References.* At the bottom (or on the flip side) of any résumé, you should list your references: costume designers, costume supervisors, workroom heads, directors, and producers who would be willing to vouch for your work habits and expertise.

Contact your references to make sure they are comfortable recommending you *before* you list them. Include telephone numbers, email address, and street address information for these sources. Be advised that anyone listed in any way on your résumé may be contacted by a potential employer. It is a very small business in many ways, and employers examine résumés closely, looking for the name of someone they know who can give them the inside story on you.

Résumés need a personal touch as well—something that gives a prospective employer a taste of who your are and what you are like. The paper stock and the type font you use convey an impression. While loud colors, difficult-to-read fonts and cutesy graphics detract from the professional impression you want to make, stylish papers and graphics can help. A small photo of your face included in your résumé can plant an image of you in the mind of your potential employer.

SAMPLING PAGES. When a potential employer sorts through a stack of résumés, the inclusion of supporting visual materials will help your résumé stand out from the rest. Costume designers and technicians should also attach a *sampling page*—a sheet with several photographic examples of their work. The sampling page should make clear the range of design and technical accomplishments in the work. (See A.36, the sampling page of Robert Joyce's craftwork, and A.37, the sampling page of Robert Turturice's design work. These examples display some of the range and expertise of both of these artists.) The owners of the Muto-Little costume workroom, in L.A., suggested that sampling pages be good quality non-laminated color Xeroxes (they dislike laminated pages). They also pointed out that sampling pages don't always prove that the individual actually did the work.

If you have already sent résumés and sampling pages to potential employers, refresh their memory by sending a *sampling card* that has a photograph or design on one side and new résumé highlights and contact information on the flip side (see Laurel Taylor's card in A.38). Even small photos of your work—as long as they are well-lit and sufficiently detailed—can reveal beautifully designed or constructed work, although they can equally reveal poorly designed or badly made goods. Any sampling page must be printed well and reflect top-quality work: It represents your standards.

PORTFOLIOS. Portfolios are important for costume design and costume technical job interviews. (Costume supervisors are not interested in looking at the portfolios of applicants for prep or set costumer work.) For many directors, it is more important in their first meeting with a costume designer to establish a rapport and discuss the current project than it is to look at old design work. No portfolio can verify whether or not you met your deadlines, came in on budget, or handled the costuming process with grace. For this reason, your résumé and your references are your first line of attack in the job-hunt process.

But, a portfolio can show the quality and range of your work like nothing else. Even your current on-the-job performance speaks only to your current job skills—it does nothing to show the range of work of which you are capable. When you are ready to break into the business at the next level, you will find it necessary to show more of what you can do. Photo portfolios, sketch work, set books, and breakdown paperwork can help "prove" the range of your skills.

The following words of advice will help you put together a compelling portfolio presentation:

• *Keep it short and sweet.* Portfolios vary in format and content, according to the job you are targeting. In preparing your portfolio for an interview, assume the interviewer has a short attention span. Stress your range and special skills in as few pages as possible. (Costume Designers Guild guidelines suggest a maximum of twenty pages.) Start with a high-quality project, to establish your standards. End with a "conversation provoker," to extend your rapport with the interviewer. Avoid extended written comments on the pages. (Further union guidelines for design portfolios are discussed in Part 11, "Joining Costume Designer's Guild Local 892.")

• *Put the work that is appropriate to the interview toward the front of the portfolio.* Interviewers will always want to see something on the order of the project for which you are interviewing—even if it is only project work (that is, not tied to a film production). Choose a setup for your portfolio that allows you to rearrange the photographs and sketches according to the needs of each interview. You never want to spend time in a presentation flipping through the book looking for particular images. Support materials like supervisor "bibles," continuity pages, and script breakdown forms that show organizational skills are only appropriate in interviews with costume designers and costume supervisors.

• *Keep the overall size of the portfolio fairly small.* Fourteen by eighteen inches maximum. It should be able to be displayed comfortably on top of a desk or a restaurant table. Pages should be neat, easy to read, and clear on the nature of the job that you did. Be careful and spare with collage presentations: Dense presentations can be difficult to "read." Employers complain chronically of cluttered portfolios and portfolios that contain too much work. Less is more when what's there is exactly right.

• *The portfolio should stress the way the work looked on camera.* High-quality photo work and detail shots are of primary importance for design and technical presentations. Shots that show the context of the work in the film's art direction can also be good. For designers, dramatic shots are very important. Polaroids of extras can be used, but it is better if the Polaroids can be enlarged.

A "reel" of your work can also be part of a presentation. Most reels are dubbed on VHS, for ease of viewing. Recently, however, costume personnel have been posting a selection of their work on websites or burning film clips of their work on CD-ROM or DVD. But a reel is rarely asked for—usually only for advertising design projects—and the interviewer may not have the appropriate equipment to show a reel in his or her office. If you do put a reel together, shoot for a five-minute presentation that shows a range of looks and production challenges.

DESIGNER PORTFOLIO GUIDELINES. Film portfolios tend to represent individual projects in concentrated fashion, using only a representative image or two. A theater portfolio tries to show, through costume images, the world of a known play, in an effort to promote dialog with a director on interpretations of the text. A film portfolio, on the other hand, rarely presents images from well-known texts; rather, it presents "new" work from productions a director may or may not have seen. As a result, dialogue with a film director is sparked solely by the quality of the designs and range of styles represented in the portfolio. It is the *variety* of character types, clothing styles, and atmospheres that prove important in a film portfolio.

Design portfolios are generally "photo heavy" and "sketch light." Designers who draw well tend to have more sketches in their portfolios, but, for the most part, photos are the preferred presentation medium, since they demonstrate the camera-worthiness of a design more literally than sketches. It is useful to include a sketch or two with photos of the realized costumes, to show the relationship of the finished product to the sketch on which it was based. (This is particularly appropriate for projects like science fiction films, which rely heavily on made-to-order work.) Portfolio photos should show the costumes in the context of the set, to prove how the costumes blended with the art direction. Close-ups of detail work and strongly dramatic photos are highly desirable. Page layout should be kept simple, and explanatory text kept to a minimum (figs. 10.1, 10.2).

The first project in your portfolio must establish your design standards. You must include work in a style appropriate to the job. The work should display the range of

FIG. 10.1

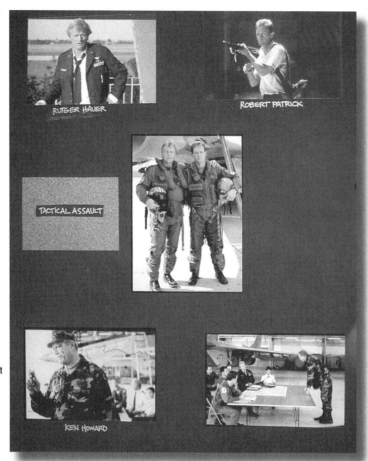

Design portfolios frequently feature hyper-realistic work and military projects, like this *Tactical Assault* (1999) designed by Kristin Burke.

Photos published by permission of Tactical Assault LLC and Hess Kallberg Associates, Inc.

FIG. 10.2

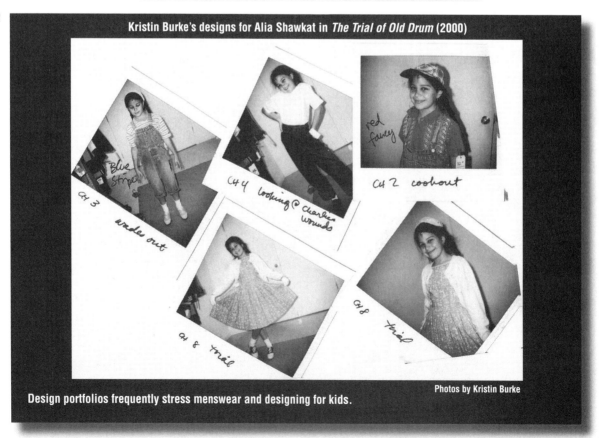

Kristin Burke's designs for Alia Shawkat in *The Trial of Old Drum* (2000)

Photos by Kristin Burke

Design portfolios frequently stress menswear and designing for kids.

your design abilities, in a maximum of twenty portfolio pages. Each project is generally represented in one to two portfolio pages. (When a portfolio is not customized for a specific interview, it can look like a "design smorgasbord"—something for everyone.) If you present theater work in your portfolio, the designs should be appropriate for film. Purely theatrical work (e.g., Shakespeare done for the stage, an opera, a dance piece) can be a turnoff in a film portfolio.

Particularly good projects to feature in a film portfolio include projects with famous actors; visually compelling, high-style images; and menswear, childrenswear, and/or uniforms. Designs that show character arcs (Denzel Washington in *Malcolm X*, for example) and figure and "image" transformations (one actor transformed into different characters (Meg Ryan in *Joe vs. the Volcano*, for example) also work well in a portfolio. Designs that show high-quality work on a low budget and high-quality work done with little prep time are, of course, hugely popular in portfolio interviews with producers.

Design portfolios tend to be heavy on modern dress, featuring work in keeping with the styles most commonly represented on contemporary commercial screens, among them:

- *The gritty or highly realistic looks* of films that trade on naturalistic sets, and costumes with truthful detailing—films like *Taxi Driver* (1976) and *Heart and Souls* (1993), *Tactical Assault* (1998), and *The Trial of Old Drum* (2000). (See portfolio pages for these film in figs. 10.1, C.13, 10.2.) These designs are characterized by low-key, "anti-glamour" styling that avoids notably trendy fashions and features "average-Joe" fit (slightly oversized or undersized). Characteristically, these designs do not have overly controlled color palettes, and the clothing is lovingly aged to produce the look of well-washed, well-worn goods. Crime, war, and hospital dramas demand uniforms with accurate patches, name tags, insignia, and other costume details. The bottom line for this type of design is "real clothing worn the real way by real people." This often translates into shirts hanging out, sleeves rolled up, jackets carried, coats unbuttoned—in short, all costumes "humanized."

- *Youth culture looks* featured in films that target the under-25 crowd, including comedies like *There's Something About Mary* (1998). These films—among them school-wise flicks like *Clueless* (1995), *Legally Blonde* (2001), and *The Lizzie McGuire Movie* (2003)—tend to give free rein to design caricatures that trade on trends in fashions. Also included in this category are more naturalistic, "street-wise" films—like *Trainspotting* (1996) and *Jesus' Son* (1999)—that that explore anti-establishment chic. An audacious sense of design and youth-fashion savvy are needed for this work.

- *Fantasy looks* featured in films like *The Matrix* (1999) or *Spawn* (1997), sci-fi films, and films like *The Terminator* (1984) that combine contemporary dress with fantasy elements (figs. 10.3, 10.4, 10.5). This category also includes films for the children's market like *How the Grinch Stole Christmas* (2000), *Kazaam* (1996), and the 2000 TV movie *Geppetto* (figs. 10.6, 10.7, 10.8, 10.9).

- *Romanticized looks* that feature current fashions in a life-as-it-should-be context, where gorgeous people perpetually look beautiful—films like *Pretty Woman* (1990) and *The Thomas Crown Affair* (the original 1968 version, with Steve McQueen and Faye Dunaway, and the 1999 version, with Pierce Brosnan and Rene Russo). Stylish crime capers, romances, and

FIG. 10.3

Design portfolios include contrasting designs for scenes and character progressions.

Dan Lester's designs for *Spawn* (1997): scenes and the costume progression for the character of Spawn. Photos courtesy of New Line Cinema.

FIG. 10.4

Design portfolio pages can show both the original graphics and the way the final work photographed.

Designs by Dan Lester for *Spawn* (1997). Illustrations courtesy of Dan Lester, photos courtesy of New Line Cinema.

FIG. 10.5

Films inspired by comic books have been a theme in the '90s. This design by Shawna Leavell is for a film that did not finally get produced called *Rogue Trooper*.

some screwball comedies trade on this mode of design, which is characterized by casual elegance—well-groomed, well-tailored looks featuring faultless fit.

- *"High-concept" looks* that, in design terms, create "alternate" versions of known worlds. Examples of this kind of design include the 1995 *Richard III*, starring Ian McKellan; the Jim Carrey vehicle *The Truman Show* (1998); most of the Coen brothers' feature film output, including *Oh Brother, Where Art Thou?* (2000) and *The Man Who Wasn't There* (2001); and Baz Luhrmann's work, including *Moulin Rouge!* (2001). This work is highly stylized and demands a designer with strong interpretive skills.

- *Period looks* for films that tend to fall into two camps: lavish costume dramas and low-key first-half-of-the-twentieth-century nostalgia. The designs for 1973 version of *The Three Musketeers*, designed by Yvonne Blake (figs. 10.10, 10.11), and *Kama Sutra: A Tale of Love*, designed by Eduardo Castro (figs. 10.12, 10.13), are excellent examples of the lavishly designed end of the spectrum, while designs by Jenny Beavan and John Bright for *Remains of the Day* and Jenny Beavan's designs for *Gosford Park* exemplify the low-key end of the spectrum.

> Unless you have it in your portfolio, people do not think you can do it. If you have your *Three Penny Opera* or your *Twelfth Night*, it doesn't mean that you should get rid of them, because that's what got one of our biggest designers of the nineteen-eighties, Richard Hornung, started. But, in a world where many people don't know anything about theater, and producers are twenty years old (all they know is Dolce and Gabanna and Prada), it's a little difficult to get them to realize what a portfolio is. *(Eduardo Castro, costume designer)*

FIG. 10.6

Shaquille O'Neal in *Kazaam* (1996) by
Touchstone Pictures.

© Disney Enterprises, Inc.

FIG. 10.7

Hope Hanafin's designs for
Shaquille O'Neal in *Kazaam*
(1996) by Touchstone Pictures.

© Disney Enterprises, Inc.

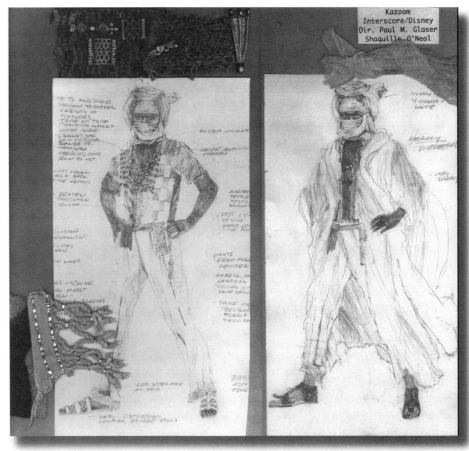

FIG. 10.8

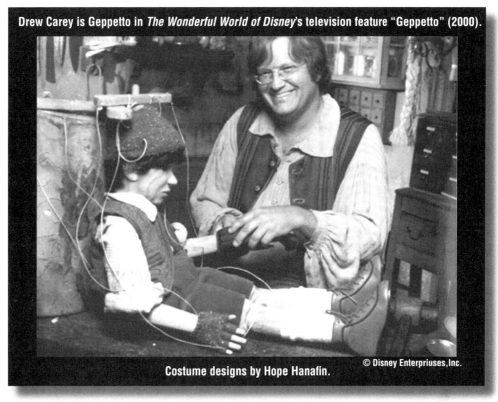

Drew Carey is Geppetto in *The Wonderful World of Disney*'s television feature "Geppetto" (2000).

Costume designs by Hope Hanafin.

© Disney Enterpriuses, Inc.

FIG. 10.9

Photos of well-known actors enhance every portfolio. Brent Spiner is seen here in "Geppetto" (2000, designed by Hope Hanafin for *The Wonderful World of Disney*'s television feature.

© Disney Enterprises, Inc.

FIG. 10.10

Yvonne Blake's designs for Oliver Reed and Richard Chamberlain in *The Three Musketeers* (1974).

FIG. 10.11

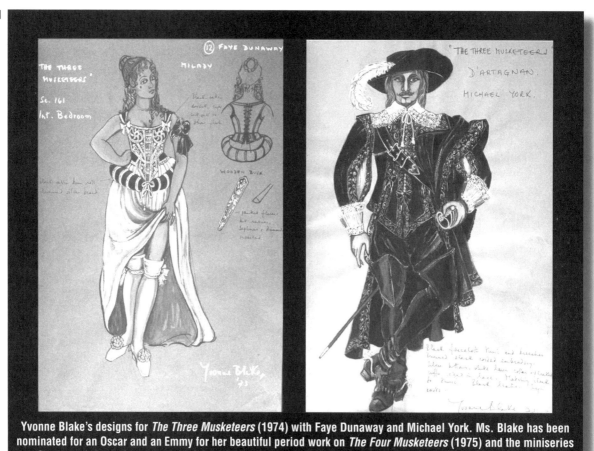

Yvonne Blake's designs for *The Three Musketeers* (1974) with Faye Dunaway and Michael York. Ms. Blake has been nominated for an Oscar and an Emmy for her beautiful period work on *The Four Musketeers* (1975) and the miniseries *Casanova* (1987). Co-designing with Antonio Castilla on *Nicholas and Alexandra* earned her an Oscar in 1972.

FIG. 10.12

Design portfolios most importantly feature photos.

Designs by Eduardo Castro for the film *Kama Sutra* (1996).

Photos published by permission of RASA Film, Inc.

FIG. 10.13

Eduardo Castro's designs for Maya in *Kama Sutra* (1996).

Photos published by permission of RASA Film, Inc.

PORTFOLIO GUIDELINES FOR DESIGN ASSISTANTS. If you are looking for work as a design assistant, augment the contents of the design portfolio suggested above with materials that display your research and organizational skills. These materials might include: (1) design-bible work that shows off your script and character breakdown skills and your budgeting abilities and (2) detailed costume research work, including research on historical, military, and quirky character costumes.

You can also add to your portfolio evidence of your design support skills (sketching, shopping, swatching, fitting, and character-styling) by including:

- A broad range of costume graphics and sketch artistry;
- Swatched sketches that display a range of fabric-swatching skills;
- Styling shots of actor transformations or clever stunt-double or rental solutions;
- Character conversion work (by "character conversion," I mean the transforming by way of costume changes of one performer into several entirely different characters; see fig. 10.14).

INTERVIEW SUPPORT MATERIALS FOR PREP COSTUMERS. In introductory interviews with costume supervisors, describe your knowledge of shopping and research resources, discuss a range of prep experiences that exemplify your responses to preproduction problems, and, of course, show what a great attitude you have. Many productions hire personnel with back-up skills in construction, dyeing, and distressing, so you may want to discuss your work in those areas, too. Portfolios tend to be unwelcome; in fact, several costume supervisors have told me that they have never seen a prep costumer portfolio.

Once you have established a rapport with a costume supervisor, you may be able to promote a second interview, especially if you would like them to consider you for a

FIG. 10.14

Extras are frequently restyled into other characters during the course of a shoot. Character conversion pages, such as the one above, can prove our skills with this.

range of work beyond the relatively narrow job jurisdiction of prep costumer. In this second meeting, you might consider presenting supporting materials that reveal the range of your technical and organizational abilities. These could include the following:

- Script and budget breakdowns that display your computer savvy;
- Photos of a range of costume construction and craftwork, including dyeing, distressing, and alterations work;
- Fabric swatches, with copies of sketches, for made-to-order projects that display your shopping skills;
- Photos of costumes on actors that focus on styling and fitting solutions.

INTERVIEW SUPPORT MATERIALS FOR SET COSTUMERS. Like prep costumers, set costumers must prepare to describe their skills and demonstrate a great attitude; portfolios are never seen. Skills in alterations work, distressing, improvisational styling, and crisis-cleaning solutions can be stressed in interviews. Your familiarity with period work, and military and formalwear, can be a plus, and you should be prepared to present evidence to this effect. You should also be prepared to discuss the rate of speed at which you can style extras. After the supervisor has seen how you hold up under pressure, she or he may give you an opportunity to present evidence of your other skills, so prepare to present script, character, and budget breakdowns; evidence of computer literacy and other technical competencies; documentation of on-set styling, fitting and alterations abilities; and competency in distressing and other craftwork.

COSTUME CONSTRUCTION PORTFOLIOS. In general, portfolios should stress modern clothing construction techniques (figs. 10.15 and 1.10). Fantasy, futuristic, and

FIG. 10.15

Technical portfolios stress modern dress projects. Shop: The Costume Collection. Draper: Donn Hook.

craft constructions are also a plus (figs. 3.21 and 6.1). When you assemble a costume construction portfolio, follow the guidelines below:

- Stress the range of your work, grouping projects together according to the nature of your responsibilities. Draping and tailoring projects should be grouped together; stitching and alteration projects should be grouped separately. Group examples by construction techniques or type of materials used, e.g., leather work, bias dresses, period garments, tailored garments, foam constructions, dancewear, etc.
- Document your ability to handle radical alterations by using before and after photos.
- Stress craftsmanship. Display photos of the inside and the outside of some of your beautifully finished garments and close-ups of tricky garment details. It can also be helpful to present a few well-chosen photos of each stage in the construction of an intricate garment, as can photo documentation of actors wearing beautifully fitted garments made by you. Bring a sample of one of your beautifully finished pieces to the interview.
- Show your interpretive skills by presenting examples of the sketches from which you worked, and photos of the final products derived from those sketches.
- Label the photos with the names of the production, the designer, and the techniques and key materials used. Note unusually tight deadlines that you nevertheless met.

CRAFT PORTFOLIOS feature photos of work in a range of materials—metals, leather, foams, fiberglass, rubber, and plastics, for example. When assembling a portfolio of craftwork, follow these guidelines:

- Group examples according to the materials used.
- Feature photos of work using a range of techniques, including vacuform work, moldmaking, sculpture, flat patterning, draping, and mechanical solutions to costume movement problems (figs. 3.21, 6.1, 10.16 and 10.17). Group your examples according to the techniques they display. Photo-document some of the processes. If your specialty is dye/paint work, show a range of techniques, including dyeing, distressing, stenciling, and silk-screening (figs. 10.18, 10.19).
- Feature your decorative and finishing techniques in close-up photos.
- Get photo documentation of actors wearing your work, when appropriate.
- Show your interpretive skills. Show examples of the sketches you were given to work from and photos of your final creations.
- Label the photos of the work with the names of the production, the designer, and the techniques and key materials used. Note unusually tight deadlines that you nevertheless met.

The interview

An interview tests your powers of observation and character analysis, gives you the opportunity to shine as an engaging personality and show that you can listen well. Your interview goal: to click with the interviewer. In most interviews, you'll have twenty to thirty minutes maximum to win over your interviewer.

THE APPROACH. Film professionals can be surprisingly generous with information, if you approach them the right way. If you're interviewing for a job, the interviewer wants to know as quickly as possible why you are the right choice. Organize your support materials (résumé, portfolio, etc.) to display as quickly as possible the type of work for which you are interviewing. If you are being interviewed "on spec" (that is, on speculation, without the immediate prospect of a specific job), you have been granted the opportunity to show your work—and yourself—to someone who may hire you or recommend you in the future. This is an act of generosity on the part of the interviewer,

FIG. 10.16

Craft work by Robert Joyce

FIG. 10.17

**Masks by
Robert Joyce**

FIG. 10.18

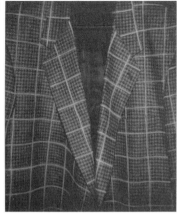

Painted plaid lines.

Heavily distressed boots.

Painted 2-tone shoes.

Painted fur pants for Steven Segal.

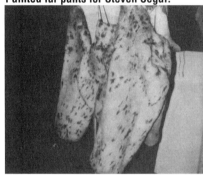

German stencil technique
for imitation fur.

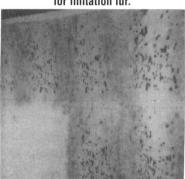

**Paint and
distressing
techniques by
Robert Joyce**

FIG. 10.19

**Distressed jeans for
*Grace Under Fire***

**Distressing techniques
by Robert Joyce**

whose time and knowledge are valuable. Asking directly for a job, or asking for comments on naïve or mediocre work, can put an interviewer in a most uncomfortable spot. Avoid creating this discomfort by asking the interviewer for advice, rather than a job. Whether you are seeking advice or a job, you must charm the interviewer.

Trying to set up an interview with someone famous in the field will be an uphill battle. Many famous costume designers and directors field inquiries through their agents, in order to avoid wannabes and other riff-raff. To be given an appointment with someone of significant stature in the business, you must have a particularly interesting project, a cover letter that commands attention, a personal connection that will help you rise above the crowd—more than likely, all of the above. If you can intrigue the person you approach, he or she may be fabulously generous with information. If you are good at what you do, having them see you work can be the key to eventual employment. Consider working in places where you will be seen by designers, producers, directors. Costume rental-house jobs and on-set work are good for this. Of course, working with friends of the famous is the best "in" of all.

For "cold" interviews (no previous contact with the interviewer, and no connections that can help you), you must be very well prepared. For film design work, it is not uncommon for production to provide you with a script, in preparation for the interview. As noted above, rent videos of your interviewer's work and study them; for interviews with a workroom or a rental company, go to the shop and study their goods in advance of the interview. It is also good to know something about the interviewer's training. If you are interviewing with a director or costume designer, learn if he or she comes from a theater background. (This may have exposed them to formal costume design training.) Many directors who come purely from film, and some costume designers who come from a stylist background, can be repelled by an interviewee's display of period and theatrical work. Presentations of science-fiction projects, period pieces, fantasy projects, and construction work may confuse them. That's probably not what they do, and probably not what they need for the job. Customize your interview support materials (résumé, sampling pages, portfolios) to feature the type of work that will appeal to them, and suit their current project.

> Ninety-five percent of what I do is modern design and construction. Please don't show me another beautiful period corset! *(Bill Hargate, costume designer and owner of the union costume workroom Hargate Costumes)*

TIMING. If you are responding to an advertised job, rush to make interview arrangements: The world is chock full of people who want to do this work. If you are interviewing "on spec," give your interviewers a generous timeframe in which to grant the interview: You will need to accommodate their inevitably busy, ever-changing schedule. Between projects is a good time to schedule interviews with people in demand. Even though the interviewer you approach may not be able to hire you immediately, he or she may be more relaxed and open during "down time." The Christmas holiday season and June and July are slow times in the television industry, and are good times to schedule interviews with television personnel. In film, busy and slow periods are less predictable. Check *The Hollywood Reporter* to see when a film wraps; this is a good indication that a director or a costume designer may soon be available to interview you.

Similarly, when you learn that a director or designer is about to start a new project (again, the "trades"—*The Hollywood Reporter* and *Variety*—are your best sources of information), contact the interviewer again, by phone. As the quality of your work improves, as your credits grow more impressive, call for an "update" interview.

STYLE AND MANNER. You might as well present yourself in an honest fashion, because if you do get the job, the people you work with are going to get to know "the real you," in detail. Edith Head may have gotten into the industry by presenting a portfolio of sketches stolen from her classmates, but to stay in the industry, she must have eventually demonstrated her ability to be indispensable—especially when it was discovered that she couldn't draw. Even if you think you're the next Edith Head, I don't recommend flamboyant lying as a means to entering the market.

Learning to interview well is important. Be aware of the personal style you project in an interview, and what it reveals about your taste, your manner, your sense of humor, your attitude. The things that make an interview click can be ephemeral. It's like going on a blind date: You may know in the first two minutes, or it may take the whole session. You can connect with an interviewer in dozens of areas, among them, attitude, background, taste, world view or sense of humor, your attitude toward your kids, your sense of confidence or vulnerability, a shared sense of personal style.

In fact, "clicking" at an interview has a lot to do with personal style—especially if design and styling choices are at issue in the job. The personal style appropriate for an interview—the way you put yourself together and the way you behave—varies tremendously from interview to interview. However, it is fair to say that the first two hurdles in *any* interview—especially for a costume designer—are appearance and manner. The way you present yourself, visually and behaviorally, will be scrutinized closely. Remember, not only your work, but your person, will be a reflection on your boss.

With this in mind, do your best to look good. The film business values appearance in a lot of different ways. If you can't be beautiful, be well groomed. For costume designers, seemingly effortless grace and casual hipness are the general targets to shoot for. But hipness in an interview is relative. Dressing too formally or too casually can be a turnoff. For costumers, casual grace must be balanced with practicality: Don't wear clothes that you can't schlep around in, even to an interview.

If you are interviewing as a costume designer, try to get the lowdown on your prospective employer's personal sense of style, and the style of the personnel with whom he or she works. A producer or director may be looking to a designer for better style solutions than he or she can provide. In all cases, a wise interviewee comes armed with an understanding of her prospective employer's tastes.

> Sometimes, the prettier you are, the more you're going to get work. *(Eduardo Castro, costume designer)*

There is room for personal eccentricity on the job, but only if you have a wildly engaging personality. Newcomers who push the envelope of personality run the risk of being deemed too much trouble to train. Even fabulously experienced personnel may fail to get the job if their personality is deemed "difficult" by the interviewer.

> The industry is made up of people on a short list, and you want to be on that short list. You can't afford to be flaky, and you can't afford to be whiney. You can't afford to be anything negative when you're starting out. When you're young, you can't afford to be meek, you can't afford to be too quiet. You really have to be a communicator. You just have to sparkle one hundred percent of the time—because that's what we need. *(Eduardo Castro, costume designer)*

Common turnoffs are obviously needy individuals, slobs, starfuckers, "princesses" and "princes," "bitter Betties," airheads, backstabbers, crybabies. And, of course, workers with major commitment restrictions and schedule conflicts. This is not a business for the hobbyist. Commitment, plain and simple, is the name of the game.

PACING THE INTERVIEW. Enter all interviews with a calm and friendly demeanor, even if the interviewers are frazzled or preoccupied. Don't rush. Let the interviewer set the pace of the interview. Take coffee, if it is offered. Let the interviewer establish the range of the discussion. The getting-to-know-you phase is very important. Stating briefly why you are here and what you want should help draw out the interviewer, and promote dialogue. Unless you've come to interview as a costume technician, don't assume the interviewer wants to see your portfolio on a first interview. Because of the extraordinary pressures of the business, the priority of preliminary interviews is to establish a personal rapport.

> I leave the portfolio at the door, and pull it out only if they ask for it. It's more important to establish a rapport. *(Richard Hornung, costume designer,* Raising Arizona, Barton Fink, Nixon*)*

Costume supervisors do not want to see design portfolios. What they want to see is professional savvy and people skills. Costume supervisors want to know, Do you love to clean and organize? Do you love to do returns? Do you have a great background in military minutiae? How many extras can you style in fifteen minutes? Do you have a background in dyeing or distressing? Can you stitch in a pinch? How well do you know the local resources? Ever been around the block with a diva? How about kid-wrangling? How well do you cope with all the paperwork? If you should die, will your changes be bagged and tagged?

Costume designers, too, are looking for staff with professional savvy and people skills. Since a costume designer's endurance and creativity are tested thoroughly over the course of most projects, support staff must be truly that—capable of supporting the designer. This is something you will need to demonstrate in the course of your interview. A costume designer will also want to know if you have worked with made-to-order goods, if you have "the skinny" on the shops or rental collections in town. Got a horror story for shortest prep? How about your research skills when it comes to the nitty-gritty details of period or uniform goods? Do you have any special background with unusual design problems, such as arctic wear, robots, circus goods, uniforms?

Interviews with directors or costume designers for design-related work (assistant designer or shopper, for example) also cover matters of taste and interpretation. Often, you will be asked about work that you love. Prepare yourself to answer this question in a way that reveals the range and subtlety of your tastes. If you are a candidate for a design-related position, you must also be prepared to paint a verbal picture of your ideas for the film's design—to do the "tap dance" about the script, the characters, the atmosphere, as you see them. If your interview is with a costume designer, you can also talk about fashion designers, sources, labels, and your tactile responses to goods.

If you are interviewing with a director for the position of costume designer, he or she will want to hear about your instincts for the particular project; this will be the focus of the first interview. There is always a bit of you-show-me-yours-and-I'll-show-you-mine in a design concept meeting; so you may have to take the plunge and lay out your thoughts on the script—even before you learn the director's views. This is a way for the director to test a new designer's instincts. Discussing the script and its themes gives a director a sense of whether your tastes mesh, and whether or not you bring an original vision to the mix.

Whether you are interviewing as a designer or a costumer, stories that exhibit humor, grace, and the ability to improvise in impossible conditions are good stories to tell. Such tales should feature, in a modest way, your willingness to roll up your sleeves and deal with the realities of the business. Everybody loves stories of endurance. Stories like these address subtleties and depths of knowledge and experience that don't show up on a résumé. Just remember that these stories can also be an index to both your understanding of the job you are seeking and your cynicism about the business. Shape stories to show your personal flexibility, your ability to adapt spontaneously to work challenges, your willingness to work long hours and mold your life to a production's needs.

> When I go into an interview, I try to establish a dialogue by telling a few horror stories—of those impossible jobs where you have to work miracles. *(Hope Hanafin, costume designer)*

Paint a verbal picture of your sense of detail and your understanding of the realities of the film business. Many interviewers ask you to assess your strengths and talk about what you love to do. The way in which you describe these traits and the kinds of stories you tell reveal a lot about your ability to understand an employer's needs and the sophistication of your understanding of the industry's processes and protocols. Tailor your strengths to the interviewer's needs.

> Have self-confidence. Be assured of who you are, and of your ability as a designer. Everything else will follow suit. I don't tend to dwell on negative things that have happened to me in the past, or catastrophic problems that I've solved. I do tend to be very positive because I feel that I am a very positive person in life, and that's how I like to present myself. I don't want to come in as the savior; I want to be the person who prevents problems from ever occurring.

> This is a business entirely about being flexible. Every interview situation is different. If you are being interviewed by somebody who is totally unknown to you, you have to size them up pretty fast, and then go with the flow. There can be from one to seven people in an interview, so you have to figure out who to focus on.

> I like to talk about my strengths as a designer, and as a person. In this business, you're not being hired because you're clever and creative, you're being hired because of who you are and how you deal with people. I find that it's always helpful in an interview if you can be seen as a problem-solver. I like to ask about their design concept for the

new production—any specific design ideas they've had before they're ready to hire a designer—then talk about how my design concepts might fit in with these ideas.

It's really great if you can turn the interview into a miniature design concept meeting, because then you can really see how you'll work with them. Then, you just have to be clever: You have to come up with it right there on the spot—answers you can live with later. *(Barbara Inglehart, costume designer, and co-author of the book* Shopping LA: The Insiders' Sourcebook for Film & Fashion*)*

Your interview may move toward a look at your portfolio, but your portfolio is a "conversation piece," not the heart of the interview. It is the dessert to the verbal main course. When you show the portfolio, avoid extended commentary. Try to reduce the verbal part of your presentation to sound bites. Keep the presentation on a positive note. Don't wear out your welcome. Keep carefully attuned to the interviewer's body language, and know when to quit.

When do I show a portfolio? It's interesting. Portfolios are viewed differently every time. One of my first experiences, when I was starting out as a young designer, was with a director who looked at two pages of the portfolio, then said "Thank you." I was very naive, I actually had a few of the drawings that I'd done in school. He wasn't interested at all. That was it.

When I did *Sugar Hill*, I didn't show a portfolio. I had it with me, but they never saw it. Instead, I talked about the film. I said I wasn't interested in doing this film if it was about "baseball caps turned backwards" and hip-hop clothes. I said, "I'm viewing this film as grand opera. Here you have a story about a bad brother and a good brother—one in the drug world and one trying to get out. Why couldn't you do it elegantly, as an opera in modern dress?" Of course, I took a risk by saying that. Turns out, that's what they were looking for. I said the right thing at the right time. They never looked at the portfolio. *(Eduardo Castro, costume designer)*

Danger signals

Designers are sometimes asked to design "on spec"—on speculation—for a project. Depending on how hungry you are for the job, you may or may not be willing to work up designs for the interview. Some designers do this with regularity, some have been burned. Unscrupulous producers and directors may ask that you not only design on spec, but present a budget for the work. They may ask you to drop off your portfolio *and* "spec" designs, for review by key production players. Later, you may find out that your designs have been shown to others who underbid you and are then given the work. It is up to you whether or not you are willing to take the risk.

You might also be asked to do a job for which you have no background. How dangerous is it to attempt the work? It's your call. In reality, the business is always asking you to stretch and grow, so risk is a normal part of the job. It simply depends on the stakes. Your research skills could pull you through, or you may want to delegate some of the work to experts. You need to gamble, but you also need to know how to cover your butt.

Never let them know you don't know how to do what they are asking you to do. Just figure out how to do it, or find a way to do it. [In the film business,] you are always being faced with new challenges. *(Barbara Inglehart, costume designer and co-author of the book* Shopping LA: The Insiders' Sourcebook for Film & Fashion*)*

PART ELEVEN

Working in New York and L.A.

Orienting to the Market

In the United States, most people who seek work in the film industry migrate relatively early in their careers to New York or Los Angeles. There is one simple reason for this: The range of film and television work available in these two cities is greater than in any regional market. To work in these cities, however, you need to know the costume job jurisdictions and industry power structures, the employment sources and costume resources characteristic of these major production centers.

Getting your bearings: moving to New York or L.A.

If you feel that the time has come in your career to make the move to New York or Los Angeles, you need to look closely at your finances. Don't come to either city without a hefty savings account: You may be unemployed for quite some time. In fact, expect to be unemployed from one to six months when you are starting out—and this is a conservative estimate, unless you come to town with fresh contacts. Costume designer Madeline Kozlowski suggests that if you decide to move to Los Angeles, you should come with one year's worth of income in the bank:

> You have to have some kind of support to start out in Los Angeles. You just can't come here with enough money in your pocket for one month, and say, "If I don't make it in a month, I'm leaving." You're not going to find anything in a month.

In addition to bringing with you a financial "cushion," you should also equip yourself with one or more of the many guidebooks to breaking into the film business that are available at bookstores and online sources. While none of these books is written specifically with the costumer in mind—and, of course, no book is a substitute for having your own private "angel" to guide you and sponsor you in the business—many of them do provide insights into the work of producers and other members of the production team with whom you'll be collaborating.

The following books can help you gain some perspective on the business of film production and the art of the job hunt, and provide you with an overview of production priorities and standards:

The Hollywood Job-Hunter's Survival Guide: An Insider's Winning Strategies for Getting That (All-Important) First Job…and Keeping It, by Hugh Taylor (Lone Eagle Publishing Company), gives a good overview of the business side of the industry, including a guide to major studio and network power structures. It gives tips on the art of the deal and detailed information about how producers put productions together. It is particularly good on production-office job descriptions.

How to Make It in Hollywood: All the Right Moves, by Linda Buzzell (HarperCollins), gives an overview of the various jobs in production, development, and postproduction work, and a lot of artful "schmoozing" advice. Practical tips on interview techniques and the Hollywood status game are liberally doled out.

Getting Into Film, by Mel London (Ballantine Books), gives an overview of production company divisions, kinds of production companies, and information on training sources and job hunting.

What a Producer Does: The Art of Moviemaking (Not the Business), by Buck Houghton (Silman-James Press), is an illuminating guide to the art of producing. It details how producers put productions together and gives detailed information about factors that affect collaborations between the producer and each of the major design and production departments on a film.

What an Art Director Does: An Introduction to Motion Picture Production Design, by Ward Preston (Silman-James Press), is a detailed guide to the ways in which a film's art department works.

From Script to Screen: The Collaborative Art of Filmmaking, by Linda Seger and Edward Jay Whetmore (Henry Holt and Company), looks at the collaborative process of writers, producers, directors, actors, designers, editors, and composers in a series of interviews with professionals in the film business.

Getting Started in Film: The Official AFI Guide to Exciting Film Careers (Prentice Hall) has forty-nine interviews with professionals from all aspects of the film business.

Job Descriptions for Film, Video and CGI: Responsibilities and Duties for the Cinematic Craft Categories and Classifications, by William E. Hines and Thomas C. Short (Ed-Venture Films/Books), gives detailed descriptions of non-costume area craft jobs.

Costume resources in New York and L.A.

Before you can work in New York City or Los Angeles, you need to learn about local costume resources. The sooner you know the full range of costume resources and the sooner you learn how to get around town quickly, the more marketable you will be. In Los Angeles, buy a *Thomas Guide* (a spiral-bound book of street maps) and *Shopping LA: The Insiders' Sourcebook for Film & Fashion*. If you land in New York, treat yourself to a subway map and the current edition of *The Entertainment Sourcebook*: *An Insider's Guide on Where to Find Everything*. Visit workrooms, shops, rental collections, and other costume research sources; more often than not, the owners and staff of these industry-oriented businesses are happy to let a newcomer look around.

Jeffrey Kurland, an Oscar-nominated film costume designer noted for his design work on *Erin Brockovich* and many of Woody Allen's movies, offered some useful insights on the differences in the two cities' costume resources. Shopping contemporary clothing is easier in New York, he feels: The seasons are represented more fully in New York than in Los Angeles, there are better multi-ethnic sources in the city, and many of the department stores, like Saks and Barneys, are larger in New York than they are in Los Angeles. On the other hand, in L.A., there are many more costume rental houses, and garment services and made-to-order sources are more attuned to the industry's eccentricities. The little-to-no-fitting-time realities of costume work, the need for multiples, and the costume requirements of stuntwork are, as a rule, better understood in Los Angeles than in New York.

> You've got to know the right people who do the best job in town for what you need. What you do depends on who you work with. *(Eduardo Castro, costume designer)*

For costume construction and craftwork. In Los Angeles, for costume construction work, look at Elizabeth Courtney Costumes, Bill Hargate Costumes, John David Ridge, Muto-Little, and the studio workrooms at Universal, Warner Bros., and Disney. For crafts, look at A Dyeing Art, Prop Masters, Global Effects Inc., and Stan Winston Studio.

In New York, for costume construction work that epitomizes the industry standard for made-to-order, look at Barbara Matera's costume studio (Barbara Matera Ltd.), Parsons-Meares Ltd., Carelli Costumes, and Eric Winterling Costumes. For hats, look at Rodney Gordon. For fabric painters and dyers, look at Martin Izquierdo Studio and Gene Mignola, Inc.; for costume craft and specialty costume work, look at Henson Associates.

Costume rental collections. In Los Angeles, look at the Costume Rentals Corporation (CRC) (figs. 11.1 and 11.2) and Eastern Costume for uniforms and uniform accessories; E.C. 2 Costumes for Bob Mackie-style glamour and theatrical clothes; American Costume Company, Palace Costume and Prop Company, Warner Bros. Studios Costumes, and Western Costume Company for period clothes; and Universal Studios Costume and Warner Bros. Studios Costumes for contemporary clothes. These sources are really only the tip of the iceberg in Los Angeles.

In New York, for twentieth-century clothing, look at Odds Costume Rental and Dodger Costumes; for earlier periods, look at Broadway Costumes.

Costume research. In New York, go to the New York Public Library Picture Collection and the Lincoln Center Performing Arts Library. In Los Angeles, go to the Margaret Herrick Library of the Academy of Motion Picture Arts and Sciences, the Burbank Public Library, and the Warner Bros. Research Collection, as well as the libraries at the Costume Rental Corporation (CRC) and Western Costume Company. Walk-in customers are welcome at these sources. *Shopping LA: The Insiders' Sourcebook for Film & Fashion* and *The Entertainment Sourcebook* list a wide array of other costume research collections.

Shopping the fabric districts. For shopping fabric and notions, no other place in America is like the New York "garment district." In midtown Manhattan, between Sixth Avenue and Ninth Avenue, and 36th and 40th streets, lies the heart of the trim and fabric districts. Visit M&J Trim, Art-Max Fabrics, and B&J Fabrics. Decorator goods, fur, and low-price-fabric districts spread out all over town, from the Upper East Side to the Lower East Side. If you've got to pinch pennies, the low-price-fabric and trim shops on lower Broadway and Orchard Street (between Houston and Canal) shouldn't be missed.

In Los Angeles, you should visit International Silks & Woolens, Michael Levine, and F&S Fabrics, for fabric and notions. Unlike New York, Los Angeles has far fewer fabric stores clustered geographically. Instead of just setting out to "explore," you're better off studying the sourcebook *Shopping LA,* then mapping your travels in advance, using your *Thomas Guide.*

FIG. 11.1

The Patch Room
at CRC

Patches, insignia, and uniform decoration galore.

FIG. 11.2

CRC has one of the most extensive uniform
collections in the United States. In addition to
their uniforms, they also have a broad range of
other costumes and accessories.

HazMat suits

The Indian collection

Shopping clothing. In New York, for fabulous designer goods, crawl through the upscale East Side neighborhood around Bloomingdale's. Greenwich Village (especially along Eighth Street from Eighth Avenue down to First Avenue, and down lower Broadway to Canal) and the neighborhood known as Chelsea are both loaded with funky and trendy goods, as is the Upper West Side. Classic midtown and East Side department stores and designer boutiques go from Central Park and Fifth Avenue (Bergdorf Goodman, Henri Bendel, Saks Fifth Avenue, and others) across to Madison (Barneys and an abundance of designer boutiques) and Third (Bloomingdale's), down to Herald Square (Macy's). Be sure not to miss Daffy's (great bargains on high-quality merchandise), Canal Jean Co. (trendy casual wear), and Peter Fox Shoes.

In Los Angeles, the choicest area for designer clothing is around Rodeo Drive in Beverly Hills. For the funky and chic, try the boutiques on Melrose Avenue, Montana Avenue (in Santa Monica), and Main Street (in Santa Monica). Malls also abound. Particularly lavish malls are the Century City Shopping Center and the Beverly Center. For the low-price spread, go to the garment district called "the alley," in downtown Los Angeles, by the California Mart.

Beginning a Job Hunt in New York or L.A.

Once you've gotten your bearings, you're ready to start job-hunting in earnest. Whether in New York or Los Angeles, start your search by looking up the contacts you've acquired at school or in the regional market. These contacts are the vital starting point, enabling you to broaden your professional network and arrange for interviews. Even one "angel" can lead you to your first paying job.

> You've got to have an angel in this business when you're getting started. *(Pat Welch, costume designer)*

Now, prepare yourself. Many who make a respectable living in the film industry began their careers by interning—working for free on productions. Film costume personnel work without pay for a variety of reasons: to sharpen their skills; to gain résumé credits in a new job classification; to acquire photos for a design portfolio; to broaden their network of professional contacts. The formal internships (described in Part 10, "Film and television internships") are one source of non-paying work. Taking costume design and supervising jobs on student film is another non-paying way to build experience and résumé credits. For work like this, post your resume on film department bulletin boards at the many colleges and universities in Southern California and the New York metropolitan area.

What kind of work is available?

If you can't afford to work for free, you will need to find someone who will pay you to learn on the job, a place where you can learn the local resources and make the contacts that will help you reach your "make-movies-or-bust" goal. Film costume personnel stay alive by working in a wide variety of venues, including workrooms, rental collections, independent production companies, film and television studios, and commercial production companies.

Costume rental houses employ rental stock clerks; a few even provide design assistants. Many provide costume construction and alteration services. Of course, costume and crafts workrooms employ construction personnel, but they may also employ shoppers and project managers. The major studios—MGM-UA, Paramount, Sony, 20th Century Fox, Universal, The Walt Disney Studios, and Warner Bros.—produce a variety of films and television programs; their facilities provide rental collections and workrooms, as well. These studios employ a full gamut of costume personnel for prep and set work, construction and rental work.

Many production companies opt to hire as crew the costume designer, supervisor, and prep and set costumers, but leave the costume construction work to freelance costume artisans, and the staff of independent costume rental houses, workrooms, and dye shops. Among the hundreds of independent production companies that work like this are Morgan Creek Productions, Imagine Films Entertainment, New Line Cinema, and Miramax Film Corporation, the major broadcast television networks (ABC, CBS, NBC, and Fox) and cable stations (HBO, Showtime, TNT, USA, Disney, and Lifetime, among them). These independent companies, networks, and cable companies produce a vast array of television programming, including episodics, sitcoms, movies of-the-week and miniseries, soap operas, live shows, and television commercials.

Whether you are starting a career or broadening or sharpening your skills, the following is a breakdown of the kinds of work you should consider.

Independent film work. Independent productions provide much of the work for non-union costumers and costume designers in the business. Even when you are working for free on the lowest of low-budget projects, these films can teach you a great deal about the hustle and politics of the film business in L.A. and New York.

Independent productions can in the prep phase help you learn your way around local resources, through shopping and contact with workrooms and rental collections. You can learn purchasing procedures; how to quickly pull and shop a film; how to organize costume stock; and how to fit, bag, and tag changes. You may even be able to design or supervise on one of these productions and, as a result, polish your script breakdown, budgeting, and stock-acquisition strategies.

By working on set, you can polish your extras styling skills; learn what the camera picks up; polish your stock organization skills; learn emergency solutions for cleaning problems and stock shortages; work on your set etiquette; and develop an understanding of set politics.

Independent television production work. Television work provides many of the same training opportunities as film work, but demands greater speed in the process. The work is extremely varied, including movies-of-the-week, miniseries, episodic drama or comedy series, talk shows, game shows, and commercials.

Compared to film, television series with half-hour and one-hour story formats tend to have fewer events, smaller casts, and demand fewer location setups. Some programs present high-volume, multi-situational costume demands that must be satisfied in three to four days. Script breakdown, shopping, and rental skills are tested to the max by the speed required by television production. Many shows demand interaction with product placement sources, studio service departments, and made-to-order sources. Depending on the production, you may need experience in working on location. If you spend some time working in television, the short prep that film designers complain about may feel like a luxury to you.

There are many TV shows produced every year, but only a small percentage of them are non-union. The competition is very stiff for these jobs. While interns are hired in television, beginners are seldom hired in paid positions: Too many qualified costumers are available for hire in these markets. (The formal internship with the Academy for Television Arts and Sciences is one entry route into television productions for costumers and costume designers.)

Unless you have acquired some film or television credits regionally, you will have a hard time getting television work upon entering the L.A. or New York market. You may, however, be able to parlay your film work in the regional market into television work in New York or L.A. once you've thoroughly learned local resources and have some professional contacts—especially if your regional credits are convincing (L.A. or New York-based productions with major designers and a cast with "name recognition"). And, it does pay to look for opportunities on pilot projects, and in the non-primetime part of the market (morning and afternoon programming, including soap operas, children's shows, and quiz shows).

In all events, to work in the television medium, you must learn the differences in the processes and the aesthetics of film and television. As discussed in "Designing for the Camera," in Part 2 of this book, some television productions are shot on film, some on videotape. Some productions are shot using a single camera and multiple lighting setups; others—particularly sitcoms and soap operas—are three-camera productions (studio setups that use three video cameras and a full-stage lighting approach that covers all the shots). Episodic TV series shoot one episode per six-day week, seven to eight pages per day. Movies-of-the-week shoot six pages per day, for twenty to thirty days.

Half-hour episodic formats demand costumes that work as easy-to-read character statements, although character complexities can be explored through the range of costume details revealed in characters' wardrobes over weeks of shooting. The small screen also demands designs that make a strong visual impact (heightened character details, strong color statements, clear costume images), in order to pull the audience's focus to a small screen in a room filled with distractions. Television screens shrink and shorten visual elements; even in close-up, detail is lost. To compensate for the flat lighting effects seen in many TV productions, costume designers use strong textures or use color break-up to add more depth visually.

TV designers frequently complain that they rank lower than film designers in the business. In fact, in union television work, the pay rate is significantly higher for work on film than work on tape. Nevertheless, television series work is considered by some to be the most desirable work in the business. If you live in Southern California or the New York metropolitan area, series work permits you to stay close to home. This is because series tends to shoot predominantly on soundstages. If you are on the payroll of a series, you are guaranteed twenty-two weeks of employment, which, when the series is long-running, may expand to years of work. On a series, you have a *hiatus*—a break—of one week every three to four weeks of shooting, which can be a blessed relief.

Music videos and commercials. Music videos and commercials can be among the best-paid work in the business. Made by many different kinds of production companies, they run the gamut from super-low-budget to extravagant. A lot of this work is non-union, and can provide training for work in feature film and television.

Music videos demand compelling, trendy presentations. Music-video costume designers must be well versed in both video and music markets for the performers. Dealing with the star image of the group or the solo performer becomes all-important. Often these productions involve short prep periods, location shooting, styling extras, made-to-order work, and "memo'd-out" goods.

Often, commercials have prep periods of three days or less. As a result, they demand strong organizational skills and strong knowledge of local resources. Commercials may involve styling extras and stars, and are often shot on location. Rarely do you get sizes much in advance of shooting, since most of the casting is done in the few days immediately before the shoot. Ultra-rush made-to-order work and quick-fire shopping practices, including the use of memo'd-out goods from studio service departments and rental sources, are standard in the world of commercials.

> There may be around two hundred films shot each year, but there are roughly ten thousand commercials shot in the same period. *(Pamela Shaw, costume designer, co-author of* Shopping LA: The Insiders' Sourcebook for Film & Fashion*)*

If you succeed in landing work as a stylist on a commercial, you need to know how the process works. Since there is not a script, per se, on a commercial, the stylist (the title given the designer in the world of commercials) will most often be given a scenario or a storyboard, which includes dialogue and a simple line drawing of a key frame in each sequence in the "spot." This scenario or storyboard becomes the basis of the stylist's costume breakdown.

With very few exceptions, commercials require that both product and performer look perfect. This means that the product being sold (the "hero" product), the actor who holds or wears the product (the "hero actor"), and the principal objects that "reflect" the effect or power of the product (the "hero objects") must be styled meticulously for camera. The exact number of sesame seeds on the "hero" bun; the lacing pattern, length, color, and tips of the shoelaces on the "hero" sneakers; the color, style, and brightness of the "hero" towel that was washed by the "hero" soap can, and will, be the subject of lengthy debates among producers, director, client, and ad agency personnel. The stylist will be nothing but a bystander. Logos other than the hero logo are not allowed on camera. Pleasing the client, the agency, the production company, and dealing with demands of product "branding" require flawless presentation and exquisite diplomacy.

When it comes to working with wardrobe, commercial production companies run the gamut from highly experienced to "not a clue." Many production companies shoot more product-oriented "spots" than people-oriented spots, others may have done a host of testimonials (using "real people" wearing their own clothes). These companies may have little understanding of what a stylist does, and how he or she does it. If you work for a commercial company new to wardrobe styling, you may need to educate the producer and production accountant in the subtleties of how to set up accounts with costume workrooms or rental companies, including the standard conditions for the use of memo'd-out goods (items must be returned in pristine condition; charges incurred for on-camera use). On the other hand, you may be privileged to intern or assist on a sophisticated commercial production where a costume budget can run as high as $100,000, a top stylist can make more than $1,000 a day, and the whole thing is over in a matter of weeks. Obviously, this work can be seductive. Pamela Shaw, an experienced commercial stylist, has shot major ad campaigns in Paris, Saint-Tropez, and Edinburgh.

Entry-level work as an intern or assistant stylist can be had, especially when many major commercial production units are using one or more assistant stylists. Pay rates for assistants can start as low as $80 a day, but can go up radically, depending on experience and budget. While some commercial production companies do offer internships, it is generally more effective to apply directly to the costume designers and stylists who do commercials. Many of these are listed in the *Costume Designers Guild Directory of Members* and *The Image Makers Source of the Madison Avenue Handbook*.

Job connections in New York and L.A.

Start with friends in the industry, then pursue interviews with (1) costume departments on advertised non-union productions; (2) non-union costume rental companies and workrooms; (3) costume designers; and (4) costume supervisors.

There are many sources you can tap into to learn about upcoming and ongoing productions, and to get contact information for job sources and industry personnel, including the following, some of which have been described above.

For current production job postings:
- *The Hollywood Reporter*'s Tuesday edition, at selected newsstands in Southern California and New York City (or online at www.hollywoodreporter.com). The first and third Tuesdays of every month, *The Reporter* lists the television productions that are shooting;
- *The Hollywood Creative Directory* website job board (www.hcdonline.com);
- *Dramalogue* magazine, which caters to the independent market, and *Backstage*, *Screen*, and *Playbill* (available at selected newsstands in Southern California and New York City);
- The L.A. *Daily Variety* Friday edition (at selected newsstands in Southern California). Issues sent out by subscription may not list the jobs listed in the Friday daily edition;
- Entertainment careers (www.entertainmentcareers.net), an excellent free site that lists wardrobe jobs separately;
- Reel Dirt (www.reeldirt.com), which lists Hollywood and regional jobs;
- Shoots.com (www.shoots.com), a free job-listing source that lists many lower-budget production jobs around the country;
- Showbizjobs.com (www.showbizjobs.com), a free job-listing source that is a great place to look for internships with studios.

Note: Many of these sources duplicate job listings. Neither *Daily Variety* nor *Dramalogue* lists costume crew jobs. Some entertainment job-listing sites on the Internet are free (like those listed above), others like Crew Net (www.crewnet.com), In Hollywood (www.inhollywood.com), and EntertainmentJobs.com (www.eej.com) charge a membership fee and/or a monthly subscription fee (with or without minimums).

For film production company and producer contact information:
- *Film & Television*, which is updated yearly and lists twenty-seven regional companies, plus film and video production companies in New York and L.A. (Peter Glenn Publications, New York, www.pgdirect.com, 203-227-4949);
- *The New York Production Guide*, which lists production companies in New York (www.nypg.com);
- The *LA 411 guide*, which concentrates on L.A. production resources. Production company listings are updated yearly and separated into specific categories, among them, film, television, music video (LA 411 Publishing Company, Los Angeles, 800-545-2411, www.LA 411publishing.com);
- *NY 411*, which is the New York equivalent of *LA 411* (updated yearly; www.ny411.com);
- *Hollywood Creative Directory's Producers Directory*, updated yearly, is a great source for production company addresses and credits (IFILM Publishing, www.ifilmpro.com and www.hcdonline.com, 800-815-0503).

Determining which production companies produce feature films, movies-of-the-week, TV shows, music videos, and commercials and which are union-only companies can be a challenge when using these references.

For film, television, and commercial directors:
- *Hollywood Creative Directory's Film Directors*, which gives filmographies and contact information (IFILM Publishing, with websites at www.ifilmpro.com and www.hcdonline.com, 800-815-0503; updated yearly).

For costume designers and stylists:
- *The L.A. Costume Designers Guild Directory of Members*, which gives filmographies and contact information for union members, including costume and television designers, commercial stylists, sketch artists, and costume design assistants (available by writing the Guild's office at 4730 Woodman, Suite 430, Sherman Oaks, CA 91423, 818-905-1557, www. costumedesignersguild.com; updated yearly);
- *LA 411*, which lists phone/fax numbers for a selection of union and non-union costume designers and stylists in Los Angeles (LA 411 Publishing Company, Los Angeles, 800-545-2411, www.LA411publishing.com; updated yearly);
- *NY 411*, which is the New York equivalent to *LA 411* (www.ny411.com; updated yearly);
- *Hollywood Creative Directory's Below-the-Line Talent*, which lists contact information and filmographies for feature film costume designers, as well as for cinematographers, production designers, and film editors (IFILM Publishing, www.ifilmpro.com and www.hcdonline.com, 800-815-0503; updated yearly);
- *Film & Television*, which lists contact information for New York, California, Florida, and Illinois stylists (Peter Glenn Publications, New York, www.pgdirect.com, 203-227-4949; updated yearly);
- *The New York Production Guide*, which lists film costume designers in New York (www.nypg.com);
- Local 829, IATSE, United Scenic Artists, in New York, will give contact information on individual New York members, including theater and film costume designers, by request (212-581-0300, www.usa829.org);

- *Shopping LA: The Insiders' Sourcebook for Film & Fashion* (ShoppingLA@aol.com) lists phone numbers for Costume Designers Guild members or their agents;
- New York and L.A. telephone directories can list designers by name, but the multiple boroughs that make up New York City and the numerous cities, towns, and unincorporated areas that make up Southern California require multiple directories (and area codes). This makes tracking down film personnel by name a complex, tedious, and often impossible, process.

As you can see, finding a designer's address and telephone number is not always easy. Many designers choose to remain unlisted in public directories, principally in an effort to avoid receiving unsolicited calls and mail from vendors and job-seekers. If you want to get in touch with a designer, contact the designer's agent and ask to have your correspondence forwarded to his or her client.

For costume supervisors:

- Motion Picture Costumers Union Local 705, IATSE (Los Angeles), directories are unavailable to the general public. You can call their office at 818-487-5655 and leave a message for an individual member to contact you.
- Wardrobe Local 764, IATSE (New York), covers film, television, and theatrical union wardrobe crews (545 W. 45th St., Second Floor, New York, NY 10036, 212-957-3500); it can provide you with a list of film costume supervisors and member contact information, upon request.
- Motion Picture Studio Mechanics Local 52, IATSE (326 West 48th St., New York, NY 10036, 212-399-0980), covers the states of New York, New Jersey, Pennsylvania (with the exception of the 50-mile radius around Pittsburgh), Delaware, and Connecticut.

You can get referrals to costume supervisors through costume designers and workroom heads, or you can meet them at costume rental houses and workrooms in the cities.

For costume rental companies, costume and craft workrooms:

- *Shopping LA: The Insiders' Sourcebook for Film & Fashion,* which lists detailed contact information on costume rental sources, costume and craft workrooms in Los Angeles, and some references to national sources: The best source for L.A. costume resources (ShoppingLA@aol.com);
- *The Entertainment Sourcebook: An Insider's Guide on Where to Find Everything* (updated yearly), which provides detailed contact information on costume rental sources, costume and craft workrooms in New York (plus some references to national costume sources) is the best compendium of New York costume resources (Applause Theatre Books, New York, 212-765-7880, www.applausepub.com).

In large part, what makes a neophyte's job hunt difficult is the task of sifting the "non-union-need-not-apply" production companies and personnel from the production companies and personnel friendly to beginners. Many of the industry guides listed above provide minimal information on a staggering number of production companies, costume designers, costume design assistants, sketch artists, commercial stylists, producers, and directors. Nonetheless, getting your letter to a person who can actually hire you can be very difficult. Some production companies hire only union personnel. It is not unusual for a unit production manager to lose your application in stacks of résumés. Mailings to the agents of famous designers and directors can be fruitless: Agents frequently fail to pass on interview requests. Many film personnel commented that it is utterly ineffective to do blanket mailings of résumés.

To repeat: Many film costume professionals worked their way into the industry by interning, or working in costume workrooms and rental collections, where meeting costume designers and costume supervisors is possible. (Read the Conversations One, with Eduardo Castro, Six, with Marcy Froehlich, and Twelve, with Jaci Rohr, to get a taste of the wide variety of ways in which people begin working in this field.) And of course any interviewer, any college pal working in the industry, any contact who remembers you from the salt mine of some regional shoot can be a connection to work. For all the agony of finding and making job contacts—the first hurdle—you *can* reap rewards. This book began with three key contacts in Hollywood that, in six months time, grew to over two hundred. Each interview you set up can potentially net you referrals. [This was my experience.—HC]

Least we forget, when it comes to building a career network, working the party circuit is an age-old method for both New Yorkers and Hollywood folk. Break into the film-world party circuit by attending film markets and festivals, premiers and parties thrown by film organizations that you join simply by paying a membership fee. Once you begin to get work, you can schmooze with costumers, prop and set dressing personnel, assistant directors, actors and other production personnel, a time-honored path to more work, if done diplomatically.

More formally, a few organizations exist primarily to foster such networks, among them, nonprofit organizations like Women in Film (www.wif.org), which specializes in helping minority personnel, handicapped workers, people over forty, and women find work in the industry. Also helpful are alumni groups whose members are heavily represented in the film industry in both Los Angeles and New York (Brown University, Emerson College, Northwestern University, Harvard University, Carnegie-Mellon University, Columbia University, and NYU, among them). Special-interest organizations for British filmmakers, independent filmmakers, and a number of other special-interest groups provide additional means of extending your contacts.

Paths to career development: non-production work

You know that building a career in film costuming, particularly in Los Angeles or New York, depends on your training, your performance, and the opportunity to be recognized for the work you do. As a result, you must build your skills through progressive challenges; develop job contacts with professionals who work steadily; and seek work in high-profile places, and with high-profile personnel. In the beginning, you cannot always accomplish these goals immediately (see below, "The union hurdle" and "Joining the union"), so you will have to be determined and resourceful. If you cannot immediately find work in production, there are alternatives.

For costumers and designers. Because it can be a challenge to get a contact system going, some aspiring costumers and designers who cannot get film production work immediately turn to work in studio service departments, production offices, product placement bureaus, and film research services. These are circuitous routes to working in film costuming. Employers may find themselves confused about your career goals, and may "type" you incorrectly, so make sure that the work you seek makes sense for the costume career that you would like to appear on your résumé.

Working with obscure companies, or on productions with low production values, can foster bad work habits and get you pegged as a "schlock" worker, even if you do learn survival skills and earn some much-needed cash. To develop a solid reputation in the business, it helps to seek work at costume service sources known for high-quality work or goods. Regardless of the position to which you aspire, or the position in which you begin, it is wise to work on independent productions run by well established film professionals, or up-and-comers who will work at the center of the business in the future.

For costume technology work. In Los Angeles, you are advised to apply first to non-studio workrooms that can help you establish made-to-order network connections. This includes independent film industry workrooms—among them, The Costume Shoppe, J&M Costumers, and Jeran Design, and the smaller union workrooms like Bill Hargate Costumes, John David Ridge, Inc., Muto-Little; and costume workrooms for the following theaters: the Los Angeles Opera, Pasadena Playhouse, and Center Theatre Group.

In New York, some of the best made-to-order network connections can be made by applying to the following: for costume construction work, Barbara Matera Ltd., Parsons-Meares Ltd., Carelli Costumes, Dodger Costumes, Grace Costumes, Euro Co Costumes, Eric Winterling Costumes, and Donna Langman Costumes/Couture; for costume craftwork, Martin Izquierdo Studio, Henson Associates, Parsons-Meares Ltd., Rodney Gordon, and Lynne Mackey Studio.

To attract clients in Los Angeles, you may want to advertise your skills in *Shopping LA: The Insiders' Sourcebook for Film & Fashion*, in New York, *The Entertainment Sourcebook; An Insider's Guide on Where to Find Everything*.

Employment in costume workrooms and craft studios. Costume workrooms use a wide variety of techniques and materials. Many workrooms develop specialties, and they look for artisans with particular expertise in the work for which these shops have become known (fine dressmaking, for example, or speed tailoring). Couture-quality dressmaking and tailoring are common in many costume workrooms, but particularly prized are the range of techniques used to create dancewear, foam body padding, period garments, and leatherwork. Also coveted in workrooms are skills in fabric embellishment, speed sewing, garment assembly, and special effects and stunt rigging. Los Angeles costume workrooms look for personnel with a range of skills in twentieth-century and contemporary clothing construction, including mass-production techniques and speed-alterations skills. Muto-Little, a union workroom in Los Angeles, gives a sewing test to applicants that includes work on stretch fabrics, welt pockets, zippers, and topstitched collars.

New York workrooms serve both theater and film industry clientele, so they look for personnel with a broad spectrum of modern and period dressmaking techniques, dancewear expertise, and soft-sculpture skills for the creation of theme-park style costumes and fantasy work. Among the entry-level positions available in many workrooms are assistant to a patternmaker, and machine or handstitcher. To begin work in a shop as a tailor or draper or patternmaker is exceptionally rare, and requires strong, specialized skills. The volume of custom-made work in New York tends to make workroom entry a bit easier than in L.A.

Craft workrooms offer a range of craft construction techniques (manufacturing puppetry and theme park-style walk-around characters, spacesuits, creatures and armor, and other costume-related products); or costume specialties like millinery, glove-making, embroidery and beading, shoemaking, costume painting and dyeing, and leatherwork. Shops like these may be looking for staffers who have draping and patterning skills, dye and paint expertise, sculptural skills with foam, fiberglass, plastics, and metal, or expertise with mask-making or mold-making materials, according to the specialty of the workroom.

In New York, there are three primary categories into which most craft workrooms can be divided: those that serve dance productions (costume painting and dyeing specialists), those that serve theme parks and fantasy projects (soft sculptural and mold-making specialists), and those that serve the fashion and dressmaking industries (fabric embellishment and accessory specialists). In Los Angeles, craft workrooms tend to fall into the following three categories: those that do sci-fi and fantasy film work; those that produce specialized clothing or accessories (custom knitwear, millinery, beading, and embroidery); and those that do costume dyeing and distressing. Many craft studios are small operations. In New York, some costume workrooms cover costume craftwork. In L.A., craftwork is rarely covered in costume workrooms; in fact, much of the craftwork produced in L.A. is done by special effects studios. Applicants for costume or craft workrooms should apply to workroom owners or division heads.

In New York and Los Angeles, union workrooms welcome non-union applications during busy times of the year. In New York, the busiest period of the year tends to be September through May. In Los Angeles, the busiest period of the year tends to be August through November, and January through May.

Working in costume rental. For work in costume rental, or for help developing connections with costume designers and costume supervisors, you are advised to apply to non-union costume rental collections. In L.A., look into Glendale Costumes, Palace Costume and Prop, and The Wardrobe Wing. The most popular rental collections in Los Angeles (Costume Rentals Corporation, Eastern Costume Company, Universal and Warner Bros. Studios, Western Costume Company) are all union costume houses. In New York, look into Odds Costumes, Dodger Costumes, and Early Halloween. Costume rental houses are listed in *Shopping LA: The Insiders' Sourcebook for Film & Fashion* and *The Entertainment Sourcebook*.

The traditional route by which to enter the film industry is to work as a "rag picker" in a union rental house for thirty days, then join the union. Nowadays, costume rental houses have few positions open, and it can be a matter of remarkable timing to get one. If you succeed, you can learn how to organize and file stock, check billing and inventories, recognize period garments "on the hanger," get the patches and accessories right, deal with boxing and shipping, pull garments with an eye to different design solutions, and pull them under pressure. Most importantly, you can learn just how long it takes to pull a show. Working in a rental house often gives you a chance to watch workroom processes and interact with a variety of different designers and prep costumers. (See

Conversation One, with Eduardo Castro, and Conversation Thirteen, with Jaci Rohr, for personal experiences with this traditional route to entering the business.)

You apply to a rental house by filling out an application and interviewing with a department head. Theater or fashion training in costume history or costume stock organization is desirable. Some rental houses also look for special experiences and skills that result in knowledge of special costumes. Were you in the armed services or medical work? Do you know uniforms? Have you worked for a formalwear company? In Los Angeles, if you can work in a union rental house for at least thirty continuous days, you may get the opportunity to join Local 705—but be aware that many union rental houses in Los Angeles have long waiting lists for non-union hires. In New York, there are far fewer rental sources, so a very limited number of positions are available.

If you do find production work

Unless you have a background in regional film work, or a knowledge of area resources, entry-level costume work on a production is frequently as an intern or wardrobe PA on low-budget commercials, television pilots, and independent films. For paying work on a production, follow these suggestions:

For work as a costumer. Apply directly to the costume supervisor for "day-check" or "pick-up" work, or an entry-level staff position on projects that are posted in *The Hollywood Reporter* and other publications and websites, and described as "in production" or "in preparation." As noted earlier, many prep and set costumers enter the business by interning, working at rental companies, "massaging" their theatrical wardrobe contacts or their personal connections in the business.

Stamina and a flexible attitude are the most valued attributes in a costumer, prep or set. Basic skills for prep costumers include stock organization and/or shopping (especially local sources). Experience with dressing actors, laundry and costume maintenance, and costume emergency skills are basic requirements for set costumers.

For work as an assistant designer. Design assisting is generally something you work up to. There are two common routes to becoming a design assistant: the recommendation of a working costume designer and a presence and reputation in the design community earned by working at venues frequented by the designers who might give you a chance. In Los Angeles, many costume design assistants enter the market with professional backgrounds in theater or fashion design. They seek work as interns, shoppers, or sketch artists with costume designers on independent film and television productions, or as assistant stylists (on-set design assistants) on commercials. In New York, many costume design assistants start as shoppers (or in-house assistants) in workrooms, as rag-pickers at rental houses, or as interns in Broadway design studios. They get into film by working with theatrical costume designers who also design costumes for film.

Design assistants aim to assist well-known costume designers. Not only do well-known, well-respected designers get more than their share of productions (the work for a design assistant will be plentiful), but the quality of the designer's work and level of his or her connections will become critical to the assistant designer's professional future. But while working on high-profile productions does build a great résumé, it is no guarantee of a fabulous costume-design career. If the designer for whom you work is unavailable for a job, few producers will settle for the assistant designer, although it is not unheard of for a prominent designer to take on an independent project if the elements are compelling, especially if they trust the assistant designer. In an instance like this, the assistant designer will work (and sometimes be credited) as "associate designer"—an important step up. Working on a high-profile project also allows a assistant designer to make connections that can lead to job opportunities and creative collaborations in the future.

To approach a well-known costume designer for work, you should:

- Work with the designer's colleagues and friends, then get a personal referral;
- Work in a good rental house or made-to-order shop, or as a costumer on one of their productions, where you can demonstrate your knowledge, your sense of style, and your professional manner;
- Charm a costume designer at a social or professional event (of course, charm only goes so far—you must have the skills and gifts they need);
- Have the gods smile on you (and your cover letter); luck into an interview where you can work your magic.

Endurance and the patience of a saint, among other talents, will help in your job search, but solid skills in sketch artistry and/or shopping, script breakdown, budgeting, rental, and styling are basic requirements for the assistant designer.

For working as a costume designer. One way you can enter the market as a costume designer is to work up from the design-assistant position. Another, more common (and more likely) route, is to hitch your wagon to a rising-star director or producer by taking work as a costume designer on their no-to-low-budget production. Like beginners to film costume work, many burgeoning directors and producers start out in low-budget film. With luck, you can connect with these talented beginners, who may then take you with them as they work their way up the ladder. If you can design a series of well-made low-budget productions, you can build a reputation as a talented designer. A steadily employed costume designer gets more design opportunities than those who work only intermittently.

In Los Angeles, several production companies welcome beginners, among them Concorde New Horizons, Chanticleer Films (PM Entertainment), and CineTel. Look at the conversation with Kristin Burke at the end of this part for more tips on working your way up in the industry as a costume designer in the world of low-budget film.

> I don't recommend that aspiring designers in Los Angeles begin by working as stitchers, I recommend they work as assistants or shoppers. I don't believe you know who you are and what your goal is unless you're focused on design. *(Madeline Kozlowski, costume designer)*

Remember, to survive as a young designer in independent film or television, you need (1) a gift for, and knowledge of, design; (2) solid research skills; (3) a detailed knowledge of local resources; (4) an ability to do script and budget breakdowns at lightning speed; (5) an unending ability to improvise; (6) and a real love of making design decisions quickly. Add grand diplomacy and schmoozing skills, and you start to cover what it takes to endure the kind of schedule outlined in Part 7, *Prep* ("A Typical Independent Production's Four-Week Prep Schedule").

The Union Hurdle

As a newcomer to New York or Los Angeles who is not yet a member of a guild or union local, you will need to address the question of where you are allowed to work. Even though there are a great number of independent productions, it is not easy to break into film and television work in either of these major production centers. Largely, this is because of the power of the labor unions.

The major networks, film studios, and production companies are all IATSE (International Alliance of Theatrical Stage Employees) *signatories*—entities that have signed binding agreements with IATSE to employ only union members in all but a very few positions. Personnel in a broad spectrum of industry crafts, from grips to art directors, belong to IATSE. As a result, its influence in the entertainment industry is pervasive. Non-union workers in these fields are prohibited from working on union films, except in all but a handful of positions, including "production assistant." And although it is against union bylaws for its members to work on non-union productions, many union members do moonlight, especially when television series are on hiatus and union feature work is thin. So while you may not be able to qualify for work on a union shoot, you may still be competing with experienced union personnel for independent production work.

If you are non-union, you can still apply legally to costume designers and costumers who work on independent projects, regardless of whether they are union or not. Simply make it clear that you are applying to them for future work on non-union productions on which they may work. By traditional union-entry guidelines, you may apply for an *entry-level position* at a union signatory rental company or costume workroom. Many of the interviews in this book refer to situations where non-union beginners found jobs with union personnel on major projects (or for union-signatory companies) when work was fast and furious, and timing, good fortune, and talent were on their side.

IATSE's influence is particularly strong in Los Angeles because, unlike New York, which has a strong theater and fashion-industry presence, Los Angeles is a one-industry town, and IATSE alone covers the full range of costume personnel, including those who design, build, and handle wardrobe: In New York, the Broadway theater market and the fashion industry serve to dilute IATSE's control of local costume services.

IATSE in Los Angeles

In Los Angeles, two branches of IATSE serve the film costume market: one for costume designers (Costume Designers Guild Local 892) and one for costumers (Motion Picture Costumers Union Local 705), which includes separate divisions for costume construction personnel and "finished costume" personnel. The costume service industry in Los Angeles almost exclusively serves film and television markets, and most union job-jurisdiction guidelines restrict crossover work among designers, costume construction workers, and finished costumers.

When approaching IATSE work sources, be realistic about your prospects. These union shops have every right to say that they cannot hire non-union help. In Los Angeles,

IATSE workrooms and rental companies may be willing to grant you an interview—after all, the traditional route into the union is to work in a union shop for thirty consecutive days. However, most union shops are awash in résumés. Unless you have fabulous luck, exceptional connections, or rarefied skills, prepare yourself to be denied entrée.

Many job-contact information guides do not list the union affiliations of personnel or workrooms. Major union employment sources are listed below. To find non-union employers in Los Angeles, eliminate the venues listed below from the comprehensive list of costume workrooms and rental sources published in *Shopping LA: The Insiders' Sourcebook for Film & Fashion*. Those that remain on the list may or may not be union shops, but at least you will have narrowed the list and can begin making query calls. For the union situation in New York, see below, "New York employment sources."

Los Angeles union employment sources

Private workrooms and rental collections: American Costume Company; Bill Hargate Costumes Inc.; C&J Custom Tailoring; Costume Detail West; Costume Rentals Corporation (CRC); Custom Tailoring Inc.; Eastern Costume Company; Elizabeth Courtney Costumes & ECII; Dominic Gherardi Costumes; ICSS; Marilyn Madsen Brands; Motion Picture Costume Co.; Private Collection Costumes; John David Ridge Costumes; Wardrobe Wing Costumes; Western Costume Company.

Studios with workrooms, rental collections, and production units: Among them, Beachwood Services Inc.; CBS/MTM; NBC; Paramount Pictures; Sony Studios; 20th Century Fox; Universal Studios; The Walt Disney Studios; and Warner Bros. Studios.

Union-only production companies: Among them, DreamWorks SKG, Morgan Creek Productions, and Tig Productions.

New York employment sources

Broadway and the fashion industry have had an impact on the way costume unions claim turf in New York City. New York film, television, and Broadway theater wardrobe staffs belong to IATSE Local 764. Many film costume designers are part of the Costume Designers Guild, but some are solely members of United Scenic Artists Local 829 (the IATSE-affiliated theater designers' union).

The costume workrooms that serve the fashion and theater industries are generally run independently or are signatories to the contract with International Ladies Garment Workers Union (ILGWU). Theatrical costume workrooms and rental collections are kept busy with work for film, television, Broadway (including national tours of Broadway productions), commercials, the Ringling Brothers circus, ice shows, theme parks, and regional theater work. Only a handful of workrooms that are attached to theaters are run on IATSE wardrobe contracts, among them, Radio City Music Hall and The Metropolitan Opera.

Because the theater and film industries share costume personnel and shops in New York, and because IATSE does not hold exclusive sway in this market, union costume personnel with the appropriate range of skills can job-hop from workroom to rental collection to design studio with some degree of ease. However, because IATSE union pay scales for film and television work are substantially higher for costume designers and wardrobe personnel than most equivalent theater jobs, union film or television work can be as difficult to break into in New York as it is in Los Angeles.

Joining the unions

Not only is IATSE the key film union for costume designers, costumers, costume illustrators, commercial designers, and costume construction personnel (see below, "Los Angeles IATSE costume classification guidelines"), it is also the union of art directors, story analysts, cartoonists, set designers and set decorators, scenic artists, craftspersons, graphic artists, set painters, grips, electricians, property persons, set teachers, make-up artists, hair-stylists, motion picture and still camera-persons, sound technicians, editors, script supervisors, laboratory technicians, projectionists, utility workers, first-aid employees, and inspection, shipping, booking, and other distribution employees. A host of video engineers and sound personnel unique to television also work under the IATSE insignia. CBS, NBC, and the Fox network are IATSE signatory operations.

As advocates for their members, IATSE has negotiated a wide variety of contracts with signatories—twelve different categories of contract, to be exact, each of which has its own job definitions and benefits package. Here are some examples of these contract categories: the "Videotape Contract," for sitcoms or talk shows; the "Episodic Contract," for first-year, one-hour TV shows or pilots; "The Basic Contract" or "Studio Contract," for feature films and filmed TV shows after their first season; the "Long-Form TV" contract for movies-of-the-week and miniseries; the "Commercial" contract; "Individually Organized" contracts, which follow the "Basic Contract" guidelines, but allow room for modifications.

Benefits for union members include pension plans, health plans, dental plans, and credit-union membership. The broadcast networks have negotiated specific benefit-package deals in their contracts, which may not include health benefits or provide "flex-plan" health coverage.

Because unions do provide health plans, and pension and welfare services (albeit with qualifications), freelancers find membership in a union most attractive. To get into any of the unions, however, you must have a track record of work in film or television. And a union is not an employment service (contrary to popular belief)—even after you become a union member, it is up to you to make job contacts and hustle the work.

> For would-be designers in Los Angeles, I suggest that if you get a chance to get into Local 705 [the Motion Picture Costumers Union] before you join the Costume Designers Guild, you'll work more. There are more jobs. I can hire you as a costumer with a design sense easier than I can hire you as a design assistant. And you'll make more money. (*Eduardo Castro, costume designer*)

In L.A., in particular, to move with grace in the industry, you must understand the union job classification and ranking systems detailed below, and the individual costume job jurisdictions set out in appendix A.

Los Angeles IATSE costume classification guidelines

For members of the film and television costume community in Los Angeles, there are only two IATSE locals to which they can belong: the Costume Designers Guild Local 892 and Motion Picture Costumers Union Local 705.

Costume Designers Guild Local 892

You can enter the Costume Designers Guild Local 892 in one of the following four categories: costume designer; assistant costume designer; costume illustrator; commercial designer. Each category has its own fees and requirements, in addition to the standard application fee and procedures (see below, "Joining Costume Designers Guild Local 892").

Costume designer—Costume designers must show a design portfolio; three letters of recommendation (which should include letters from producers); pay an entrance fee of $4,040, processing and stamp fee of $125, and quarterly dues of $205.41. To qualify for membership, designers must have at least one design credit for a commercially released film or television production.

Assistant costume designer—Assistant costume designers must show a design portfolio; three letters of recommendation (which can include letters from designers and producers); pay an entrance fee of $2,020, processing and stamp fee of $125, and quarterly dues of $168.29. Assistant designers can upgrade to a higher category if offered a project, or if they have two years in service in this category.

Costume illustrator—Costume illustrator applicants must show a sketch portfolio; three letters of recommendation (which should include letters from designers); pay an entrance fee of $2,020, processing and stamp fee of $125, and quarterly dues of $128.24. Costume illustrators can upgrade to a different category if offered a project, or if they have two years in service in this category.

Commercial designer—Commercial designers must show a design portfolio; three letters of recommendation (which should include letters from producers); pay an entrance fee of $3,030, processing and stamp fee of $125, and quarterly dues of $205.41. Commercial designers must have one to three commercial credits.

JOINING COSTUME DESIGNERS GUILD LOCAL 892. There are three routes by which you can become a member of Costume Designers Guild Local 892: (1) by the standard application process, (2) by working on an "organized" production, and (3) by the "force entry" method.

1. *The standard application process.* The standard application process requires paying a $50 application fee, and submission and application forms for the category you wish to enter; a one-page résumé; three letters of reference and/or recommendations from professionals in the field (detailed by category; see below); and a portfolio of no more than twenty pieces. (A *costume design portfolio* covers male and female characters, period,

modern, and "character"—eccentric—clothing.) Sketches should include swatches, if possible. Photos of produced work are necessary. The designer is not required to do his or her own sketching, but submitted sketches should indicate the illustrator who did them. A reel of filmed work can also be included, but a reel cannot be submitted in lieu of a portfolio. A *costume illustrator portfolio* must include original sketches.

All applicants must appear before a review committee to answer a broad spectrum of questions on their work, including questions on budget, atmosphere coverage, doubling and stunt strategies, and your conceptual approaches to the work. This review tests your ability to communicate ideas and examines the aesthetic and technical choices made in your work.

2. *The "organized production" entry method.* You can enter the guild if you are working as a costume designer on a non-union project that is "organized" during the course of production—that is, brought into the union by a labor union (IATSE) organizer. You must pay the union entry fee if this happens.

3. *The "force entry" option.* If a producer of a union film reviews the Guild "designer availability list" and prefers to use a non-union designer on the film, he or she can choose to "force" entry into the union for that designer. The designer must pay the union entry fees, but will not be a full Guild member until he or she has gone through the standard interview process.

Motion Picture Costumers Union Local 705

MEMBERSHIP GROUPS AND RANKING SYSTEM. Motion Picture Costumers Union Local 705 has six different membership groups: (1) Men's Finished Costumers; (2) Women's Finished Costumers; (3) Men's Custom-Made Costumers; (4) Women's Custom-Made Costumers; (5) Live TV Costumers; and (6) Costume House Costumers. For decades, costumers specialized in either men's or women's wardrobes, because the quantity of productions serviced by the studio wardrobe departments warranted having personnel work exclusively in a single area of expertise. During the Golden Age of Hollywood, the nineteen-thirties and nineteen-forties, Southern California studios and major costume companies cranked out great quantities of custom-made work, and supported massive wardrobe departments. Vast workrooms housed multitudes of construction and craft personnel (fig. 11.3).

As the television industry took off in the nineteen-fifties, and the studios got on the bandwagon of producing television, new job definitions came into the unions, including a broadening of job jurisdictions for costumers working under union "Live TV" contracts.

Today, many workrooms consist of no more than a few cutters and tailors, with their assistants, working under a head of the department. Some shops specialize in tailoring, dressmaking, or craft ("specialty costume") work, and rental companies may or may not be attached to workrooms. However, the range of skills and their pecking order established in the complex world of studio and costume-company workrooms during Hollywood's "golden age" led to the current union categories of costumer jobs (see fig. 1.5).

FIG. 11.3: MOTION PICTURE COSTUMERS UNION LOCAL 705 MEMBERSHIP RANKING SYSTEM

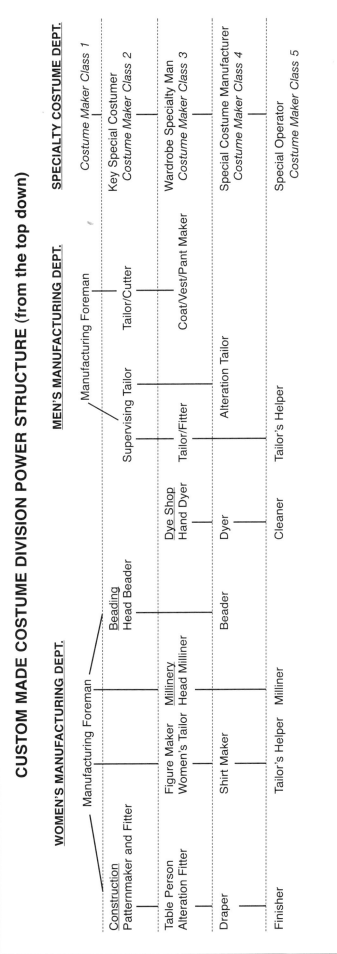

FINISHED COSTUME DIVISION POWER STRUCTURE (from the top down)

FILM

Costume Designer
Design Assistant and Sketch Artist
Costume Supervisor
Costume Dept. Foreman (M&W)
Key Costumers and Set Costumers
Costumers (Journeymen)
Costumers (Entry-Level)

LIVE TV

Costume Designer
Design Assistant and Sketch Artist
Costume Supervisor
Wardrobe Master (M&W)
Wardrobe (M&W)
Junior-Grade Wardrobe (M&W)
Seamstress

COSTUME HOUSE

Head of Stock Dept.
Costumer
Costumer Stocking Clerk
Stock Sizing Clerk

CUSTOM MADE COSTUME DIVISION POWER STRUCTURE (from the top down)

WOMEN'S MANUFACTURING DEPT.

Manufacturing Foreman

Construction
Patternmaker and Fitter

Beading
Head Beader

Beader

Table Person
Alteration Fitter

Figure Maker
Women's Tailor

Millinery
Head Milliner

Shirt Maker

Draper

Finisher

Tailor's Helper   Milliner

MEN'S MANUFACTURING DEPT.

Manufacturing Foreman

Supervising Tailor   Tailor/Cutter

Tailor/Fitter   Coat/Vest/Pant Maker

Dye Shop
Hand Dyer

Dyer

Alteration Tailor

Cleaner   Tailor's Helper

SPECIALTY COSTUME DEPT.

Costume Maker Class 1

Key Special Costumer
Costume Maker Class 2

Wardrobe Specialty Man
Costume Maker Class 3

Special Costume Manufacturer
Costume Maker Class 4

Special Operator
Costume Maker Class 5

DUTIES AND RESPONSIBILITIES. Each of the six categories and rank of membership has a specific, defined range of duties and responsibilities (see fig. 1.5).

Categories 1 & 2 (Men's and Women's Finished Costumers). Men's and women's finished costumers work with built costumes in a production setup. These two groups include traditional "dressers" as well as prep costumers and shoppers. According to union guidelines, finished costumers are allowed to "coordinate the manufacturing, refurbishing, and alteration aspects of any costume apparel items."

Within groups one and two, there are three different classes of finished costumers, ranked high to low, in the following order: Key Costumer; Journeyperson; Entry-Level.

Categories 3 & 4 (Men's and Women's Custom-Made Costumers). Custom-made costumers build, refurbish, and alter new and used costumes. There are five different classes of custom-made costumers, ranked according to the level of supervision and expertise required in their work.

Category 5 (Costume-House Costumers). Costume-house costumers are the personnel who do finished or custom-made work in a rental house. Rental-house workroom members follow the ranking system established in the "Custom-Made" category. Rental-stock personnel follow Motion Picture Costumers Union rankings, namely, men's and women's finished costumers, and men's and women's custom-made costumers.

Category 6 (Live TV Costumers). These are the personnel who work in television production facilities in the finished *and* custom-made areas of TV production. In television, costume job definitions allow individuals to do both finished and custom-made work, and, as a result, the job titles are a bit different. Ranking guidelines are indicated in fig. 11.3.

In each of the six membership categories, job class—that is, supervisory authority and seniority—are based upon degree of job responsibility and work experience. The higher the classification number, the higher the degree of responsibility and seniority; conversely, the lower the classification number, the lower the degree of responsibility and seniority (e.g., "entry level" for the Finished Costumer group is Costume Maker Class 4 or 5).

Live TV costumers and costume-house costumers are permitted to do both finished and custom-made work. As a result, a member who belongs to either category can count work days in either finished or custom-made work toward the work days required to ascend in rank in either the Finished or Custom-Made groups.

> I was a costume supervisor on a show that got organized. This got me into the union, but only at entry level. Members of the other creative department on the show—the art department people—all tested right to their level. They all entered their unions at higher-than-entry level. As far as I'm aware, the Costumer's Union is the only local that doesn't allow you to test to your skill level. *(Jaci Rohr, costume supervisor, member of Motion Picture Costumers Union Local 705)*

JOINING MOTION PICTURE COSTUMERS UNION LOCAL 705. For finished costumers, entry-level applicants can enter in the following three ways:

1. *By working for union production companies.* A costumer can apply for Local 705 membership after thirty days of employment by union production companies (thirty days of employment within the year immediately prior to the application). All thirty days of

work need not be from the same union production source. Entry fee: $1,000. This is the most difficult way to gain entry to this union local.

2. *By working on a non-union production that gets "organized" by the union.* If the non-union production on which you are working is "organized"—becomes a union-signatory company—you are credited with the required thirty days of entry-level work required to join the union. Entry fee: $1,000. If you enter this way, you come in to the union at "entry level," even if you were the supervisor on the non-union production. However, if you work for the same production company again, the union permits you to work in the more-highly ranked classification, even while your union ranking is lower.

3. *By working for a union costume house for thirty days.* Working at a union costume house for thirty days will get you in to the union under the Costume-House Costumer classification, for an entry fee of $500. But if you wish to reclassify as a "Finished Costumer" in order to go into production work, you must pay an additional reclassification fee of $500.

Application to Motion Picture Costumers Union Local 705 requires the following steps:

• *For finished costumers.* In writing or by telephone, request the application information be sent to you. You will get a letter giving information about the union and the application process. (Alternatively, you can make an appointment at the union office to receive an application packet in person.) Submit the following documents and fees: (1) the application form; (2) a cover letter with an overview of your relevant background and experience; (3) a current résumé; (4) three letters of recommendation and a list of references with contact information (recommendations should be from costume supervisors, directors, producers, and unit production managers); (5) a "Qualifying-Jobs-Worked Details Form," with required documentation attached, including paycheck stubs, call sheets, crew lists, and deal memos from your different jobs; (6) an "employer-verification" letter from each of the sources listed, verifying your "qualifying days worked"; (7) a nonrefundable application fee of $50; (8) half the total initiation fee for your category. You are also required to appear before a review committee for a formal interview, in which your application for membership will be considered.

• *For custom-made costumers.* For custom-made costumers, the application process is similar to that required of finished costumers, with the exception of a requirement that you provide proof of work on Class 4 or Class 5 "costume-maker" projects for the film or television industry. In union terminology, you are providing proof of "having performed the duties of the level applied for" for no less than three hundred workdays within the four calendar years immediately prior to the date of application. The only projects that count toward these days are costume construction projects done for "recorded or filmed productions" for employers involved in the motion picture industry.

• *For live TV costumers.* For live TV costumers, the application process is similar to those for the applicants in the categories above; however, applicants for membership in the Live TV category must have completed thirty workdays under a Live Television contract. Workdays in this group can count toward the requirements for membership in either "Finished" or "Custom-Made" categories.

- *For costume-house costumers.* For costume-house costumers, the application process is similar to those above, but applicants in this category must have completed thirty workdays within the prior year for a union costume house. According to the tasks they have been doing at the costume house, they can qualify to count these workdays toward the requirements for membership in either the "finished" or "custom-made" categories.

Dues vary according to category and ranking, and the amounts change yearly, based on salary upgrades. Entry-level costume-house employees pay $48 quarterly; live TV beginners pay $75 quarterly; Class 5 and Class 4 costume makers pay $95. Local 705 can provide you with the figure for quarterly dues in your classification and "grade." Generally speaking, your quarterly dues will be the same amount as four hours' pay. All dues are tax deductible.

To upgrade from an entry-level position to a higher-ranking position within your classification, you must meet the following "time-in-grade" minimum requirements:

- *For finished costumers.* To upgrade from entry level to journeyman, you must have a minimum of 200 entry-level workdays for union companies. You cannot apply for an upgrade in less than one year from the time you entered the union, and if you take more than one year to earn the upgrade, you must have accrued 250 workdays within the four-year period prior to your application date. You must have worked under the direct supervision of a key costumer, handling finished costumes in all phases of costuming, and provide documentation that you have worked both the thirty days required to join the union and the 200 or 250 days of entry-level work required to quality for the upgrade to journeyman. The fee for an upgrade is $1,000, and, upon upgrading, quarterly dues rise to $135, or four hours' pay.

To upgrade from journeyman to key costumer, you must have a minimum of 200 workdays doing journeyman-grade work for union companies. You cannot apply for an upgrade in less than three years from the time you entered the Journeyman category. You must also pass a test administered by the Contract Services Administration. If you take over three years to earn an upgrade, you must have accrued 250 workdays over the six-year period immediately prior to your application date. You must provide documentation of your employment for the thirty days required to achieve entry level, the 200 or 250 days of entry-level work to achieve journeyman grade, and the 200 or 250 days of journeyman-level work. The fee for the upgrade to key costumer is $1,000. After upgrading, the quarterly dues rise to $147, or four hours' pay.

No finished costumer can "fast-track" from entry level to key costumer in less than four years and 400 workdays.

- Custom-made costumers who wish to qualify for an upgrade from Costume Maker Class 4 or Class 5 to Costume Maker Class 1, 2, or 3 must provide proof of having worked no less than 300 days at the Class 4 or 5 levels, and no less than 200 days "at the level applied for." All work must have been accomplished within the six years immediately prior to the application. The upgrade fee is $1,000. Upon upgrading, quarterly dues rise to $105 or $111, depending up the rank to which you upgrade, also based on four hours' pay.

Once you are a union costumer, Motion Picture Costumers Union Local 705 members are required to attend four mandatory membership meetings a year. Benefits do not kick in until after you've worked 600 hours. While dues are paid quarterly, a member who works less than six days in a quarter can opt to pay half their full quarterly dues rate if that figure is equal to or greater than the minimum dues requirement of $48 quarterly. The union provides potential employers with an "availability list" of its membership, but the real job hunt boils down to members contacting designers, supervisors, and studio department heads. Getting on the IASTE "roster" can be a function of the contract under which you work. Network contracts with CBS, NBC, and Fox do not give roster status to their workers.

Union job-jurisdiction issues

The strict guidelines for job jurisdictions set forth for costume personnel by IATSE establish the costume-department pecking order. In a union costume department, for example, a costume designer belonging to Costume Designers Guild Local 892 is not allowed to pin an alteration, move clothes on racks, or unload or deliver costumes from a shopping trip. He or she needs a Local 705 costumer to do these things.

The highly specialized nature of union job jurisdictions is a legacy of the Hollywood studio system of the nineteen-thirties and forties, when the scale and style of studio productions—indeed, the workings of the studio system itself—demanded a degree of specialization among costume personnel that is only occasionally demanded today. Now, costume designers must design entire productions, not just costumes for female stars, and most costumers need to have a breadth of knowledge, including an ability to work with both men's and women's wardrobes. IATSE guidelines do recognize that several costume jobs, particularly those of the costume designer and the costume supervisor, have overlapping duties, among them script breakdown, budgeting, and research. This, too, is a holdover from the grand old studio days, when designers principally designed costumes for the female stars while costumers put the rest of the production together, a division of labor that necessitated overlapping duties.

In this day and age, finding adequately schooled costume staff is a perpetual problem. As a result, following union guidelines to the letter is often impossible. Non-union films can seldom afford to follow the union's strict jurisdictional guidelines, and, more often than not, require costume-department personnel to cover many more tasks than union rules allow.

> I worked on a non-union film in San Diego, early in my career. I was treated very badly by the designer and the supervisor, and was left to my own devices. So the prop guy and I kind of went to bat for each other. We were considered the fluff-and-fold team. He would not only "break" me so I could go to the honeywagon, he would step in and do all the wardrobe stuff. And when he needed to leave to go to the prop truck, I would step in and do all of his prop stuff. That's easy to do on a non-union film, but in the union, it's unheard of. You're really stepping on toes and boundaries if you do that. You're encroaching on someone's territory, even if it's just to help a guy move the big table out of the way. *(Jaci Rohr, costume supervisor, Motion Picture Costumers Union Local 705)*

When non-union personnel with independent film experience are admitted to the union, they must adjust many of their work habits to conform to union jurisdiction guidelines. The independent film movement has given newcomers entrée to the unions through productions that get organized; however, there is still a stringent pecking order, as well as "time-in-grade" requirements for new members, particularly for Local 705 members. The fact that you have advanced skills does not help you enter Local 705 at a higher-than-entry level, since the local requires that you qualify for reclassification by proving time-in-grade at the levels that precede the level to which you wish to advance. The Costume Designers Guild, in contrast, allows you to enter as a full designer if you meet their work requirements.

New York and beyond

United Scene Artists (USA) members design for theater (in the Broadway and regional theater markets) and some film and television productions in New York, Chicago, and Florida. USA has branches in New York, Chicago, Los Angeles, and Orlando, Florida. Each branch office has different entry requirements and procedures, which are detailed on the organization's website (www.usa829.org).

IATSE film, television, and theater costumers in New York City belong to Local 764. Applicants for membership as custom-made or finished wardrobe crew members must request application information by writing the local at 545 W. 45th St., Second Floor, New York, NY 10036, or calling them at 212-957-3500. IATSE costumers, among others who do production and theater work fifty miles outside the jurisdiction of the New York City local, belong to Motion Picture Studio Mechanics, Local 52. For membership information and applications, write to Motion Picture Studio Mechanics, Local 52, 326 W. 48th St., New York, NY 10036, or call 212-399-0980.

Current conditions for entering the unions

The unions are anxious to keep their memberships busy and in the forefront of the business. Both unions are actively pursuing hot independent productions, hoping to get them to "go union." Most new members of both unions are coming in through productions that get organized.

The unions want their members (indeed, *need* them) to be the cream of the crop. Since recent waves of relatively inexperienced union recruits have, in most cases, entered the union via non-union productions that have been organized, costumers' locals have been forced to reexamine their standards and find ways of making certain that their members meet those standards. Motion Picture Costumers Union Local 705, in Los Angeles, is particularly proactive in this regard, organizing workshops and training sessions for union members who are interested in upgrading their skills. This local is also examining the possibility of instituting new internship and training programs for their members, a plan that may lead to formal training-session requirements and examinations for upgrades.

Career-Building Strategies

In an industry under the gravest financial pressure in its history, the unions are fighting back, encouraging political involvement by rank and file, closing ranks where they can, lobbying the Congress for production tax breaks and subsidies, and pressuring production companies that shoot outside the U.S. to attach as many U.S. union crew members as possible to their production roster. If you are a newcomer to the business, prepare to run into the "union wall."

If, in the beginning, you do get stopped at the "union wall," remember, there are strategies to get up, over, and around that wall, strategies that will help you build—and survive—a durable costume career in the film industry.

DEVELOP A NETWORK

Non-union crews are often made up of "diamonds in the rough"—good, hardworking personnel, who learn fast and can work up to speed. Making connections with these gems can foster lifelong loyalties and lead to more work. Some of the designers and supervisors for whom you work on a non-union production may precede you into the union—and write you those letters of recommendation.

If you haven't gotten your "big break" yet, and aren't working on a production, find another industry niche for yourself, in an area related to what you really want to do, in a job that allows you to learn more about the business. Many costume designers and costumers with whom I've chatted have talked about connecting with a workroom or rental collection that was their safe haven. Bill Hargate's studio, J&M Costumers, The Costume Collection, and Eastern Costume Company have all taken talented newcomers under their wings. And, because the industry is filled with freelancers, many employers are flexible about allowing you to come and go for freelance gigs.

As you learn the business, you must recognize the "angels" who will save you. Workroom heads as well as crew members can save your butt. Designers can protect and promote you. Producers, directors, art directors, and stunt crews can help you at key times. To create a network of job contacts, you must cultivate a sense of loyalty to the people with whom you work. The world of independent films trades on favors—not only from fellow crew members, but from vendors and service personnel. They deserve your loyalty, too.

STUDY FILM-MARKET TECHNICAL DEVELOPMENTS

Study the technical advances made on the craft side of the industry. Digital technologies coming into film are revolutionizing filmmaking, creating the need for sweeping changes in film training. The costume design rules for adjusting color and texture to work with different film stocks, videotape, and special effects will shift as the technology develops. But these digital technologies are also changing *who* can make movies, the stories they can tell, and how they tell them. This may mean more work for you.

DEVELOP A THICK SKIN

Freelancing is not for the faint of heart. Said one costume designer, "They don't hold talent against you in this business, but it doesn't always help." There are many stories of weak personnel chosen over more talented workers because they were "known"—previously employed—by the company. Your charm, your looks, your status in the industry, your loyalties, the favors you do and for whom all play a part in the politics of getting hired. Connections to a director can get you work, or backfire on you.

> Most often, you just don't know where your next job is coming from. You never know what's going to get you a movie. There are times when you think, "I have this job," and all of a sudden, you don't. So, the hardest thing for any newcomer to learn is to take it all in stride and to roll with the punches. You never know when you're trying too hard, or not hard enough. How to sparkle. How not to sparkle. How nervous you are. Sometimes the nervous thing works, and other times, it doesn't. There are many talented people who don't get the work. It's unpredictable. *(Eduardo Castro, costume designer)*

LEARN TO SAVE YOUR MONEY

Everybody goes through periods of unemployment in this business. To survive in this business, you can't make your sense of self-worth dependent on getting hired for every job, or you'll drive yourself crazy.

> The producer on a project [for which I interviewed] was very, very, very fond of my work, and very, very interested. And I didn't get the job. For one reason. This was the director's first time, and he felt I didn't have a blockbuster under my belt. He wanted someone who had done a blockbuster. That happens an awful lot. *(Eduardo Castro, costume designer)*

VARY YOUR WORK

Some film personnel luck into long-term careers with only a few key connections; but most of us try to develop a broad network of connections by varying our job sources. Early in your career, make a point of working in as many places and with as many different people as possible. The greater the range of work that you are willing to do, the broader and deeper your network of contacts—and the more steadily you'll be employed.

> For me, the saddest thing I see now is that so many wonderful people at the apex of their careers, when they should be in high demand for their years of experience and wisdom, are being treated so shabbily. It's very heartbreaking. It seems that if you are over a certain age, you become disposable. You see some unbelievably talented people, who haven't worked in over a year, actually losing their homes! *(Edwina Pellikka)*

Whether your long-range career goal is to work on a soap opera or win an Academy Award, you need to be able to work in a variety of media and production formats. Look at the film and television costume designers with long careers. You can see a list of their credits in the Costume Designers Guild *Directory of Members, Hollywood Creative Directory*'s Below-the-Line Talent (www.hconline.com), or the Internet Movie Database website (www.IMDb.com). Many have done film *and* television design; feature and episodic formats. Costume designers must be capable of designing for a range of styles, including period and modern work, ultra-realistic and strongly imaginative work.

> Sometimes it seems like as soon as you know what you're doing, you're out of style. *(Dan Lester, costume designer)*

Every year, hundreds of new style trends take off; if you want a long-term career, you have to stay in touch with fashion and be adaptable. Even James Acheson, the brilliant three-time Academy Award-winning costume designer of historical epics (*Dangerous Liaisons, The Last Emperor*), started by designing for television, worked on science fiction and fantasy films (*Brazil, Time Bandits*), and worked as an art director (*Little Buddha*).

IF AT FIRST YOU DON'T SUCCEED, TRY, TRY AGAIN

Persistence pays off. If you want to forge a career for yourself, you must dig in and not become discouraged.

> The thing I tell people is, you have to be persistent, you have to hound people. I met a gal from Carnegie-Mellon University, and I can't remember her portfolio at all. It was typical theatrical, and needed to be worked on. But what I got from her was her personality. I knew that I would like working with her. She met Ann Roth, and Ann said, "Go over to Western and stand in front of Jane Greenwood's desk. She's doing this thing and she's going to need help." She stood in front of Jane Greenwood's door, and Western hired her. *(Eduardo Castro, costume designer)*

A Little Inspiration

While interviewing Academy Award-winning designer James Acheson, he shared with me a quotation, by Scottish mountaineer and writer W. H. Murray, that has been an inspiration in his own career:

This may sound too simple, but is great in consequence. Until one is committed, there is hesitancy, the chance to draw back, always ineffectiveness. Concerning all acts of initiative (and creation), there is one elemental truth, the ignorance of which kills countless ideas and splendid plans: that the moment one definitely commits oneself, then providence moves too. A whole stream of events issues from the decision, raising in one's favor all manner of unforeseen incidents, meetings and material assistance, which no man could have dreamt would have come his way. I learned a deep respect for one of Goethe's couplets:

> Whatever you can do or dream you can, begin it.
> Boldness has genius, power, and magic in it!

Conversation Thirteen:

On Getting into the Business as a Costumer, with Jaci Rohr

A member of Motion Picture Costumers Union Local 705, Jaci Rohr has worked in costume rental and on productions as a set costumer, costume supervisor, and designer.

What advice would you give someone coming to Los Angeles for the first time, looking for work in film costuming?

If you're coming to town and you're not familiar with Los Angeles, I recommend that you go out immediately and buy a *Thomas Guide,* the detailed map book of Los Angeles, and learn how to use it. It can be hard to find a starting point when you begin looking for work in the business. I found my job through an ad in *Daily Variety.* Of course, it's always good to have an "in"—to know someone. But you can always go in "cold" to the costume houses. When times are good, they may hire you off the street. You should be able to say what your skills are, and what you can do. You don't necessarily have to have your portfolio with you, certainly not for a stocking job at a costume house. But you have to be willing to get your hands dirty. And it is back-breaking labor. People have no idea how physical the job is.

Any other advice on getting the lay of the land?

I think it's really important to go into every costume house and say, "Hi, I'm new to the business. I want to learn about it. Can I just wander around your stalls and see what you have, see what's in your aisles?" They're very accommodating about that, they really are. And if you need help, sometimes they will have someone escort you around so that they can tell you what they specialize in. For instance, Western Costume has all this wacky Renaissance stuff, from the fifteen-hundreds. They specialize in period things, and they go all the way up through the nineteen-sixties. They do have some contemporary items, but that's not what they're known for. They also have a fabulous workroom.

Eastern Costume and the Costume Rental Corporation (CRC) have fabulous work-rooms and collections, as well. CRC is known for its uniforms. Eastern is also known for its uniforms, and for being very accommodating to those with small budgets. They're both very nice to work with. Since everyone's feeling the crunch these days, everybody in town is becoming accommodating.

One of the places to start is a really friendly place like Eastern Costume. It's a little bit smaller shop; it's not as forbidding as going into Western or CRC and seeing I don't know how many thousands of square feet of rack space! You say to yourself, "Oh my god, I'll never be able to figure out what all this is."

Do you really think that some places are more friendly than others to newcomers looking for work, or is it the luck of the draw? Is it just a matter of showing up on the right doorstep at the right time? When you're applying for work, is there a difference between a union and non-union house?

When the business is slow, you may get laughed out the door if you go to a union house, because everybody will want their (required union) hours. During slow times, finding a job even in a non-union house may be difficult. But be persistent, and go in with a good attitude, and say, "I'll mop the floors until you have something for me to do." You have to be willing to put yourself out—even for something that you don't necessarily want to do—just to get the job.

My niece comes to the set and works with me. I always tell her that her job is to smell the socks. And she always tells me, "I'm never going to be a costumer, Aunt Jaci, 'cause I'm never going to smell the socks." You just have to be willing to deal with the icky stuff, too. If you go in and say, up front, that you're willing, I think you'll make many good friends, because people will realize you're not in it for the glamour. And, believe me, there's very little glamour.

Of course, a lot of getting your first job is being in the right place at the right time. TV shows, I think, are harder to get on to. I think it's easier to get on to an independent feature that has nothing to do with the union or the studio, only because the budgets are low and the productions are willing to exploit you. If you're willing to be exploited, there are a lot of little independents out there. They're proliferating.

Where do you hear about them?

When I first came into the business, I picked up *Daily Variety* and *The Hollywood Reporter*, and I used to diligently read those. I would send out fifty to a hundred résumés. I didn't have any theater or movie experience, but I was willing to do whatever. And I never got a single job from any one of those "résumé calls."

What was your background?

My background was a degree in art from San Jose State University. I started dressing my dogs when I was five, and I've been interested in costumes ever since—particularly vintage costumes. So, I studied on my own. I already had a pretty massive collection of costume and art history books. I was interested in theater, so I did a lot of that on my own. I had taken several millinery classes, and I really liked them. I applied for a job as a milliner at CRC. I just went in and accidentally got the job. This was 1990. I had just been in L.A. for a month, and I wasn't even unpacked, really.

What luck! A union house, to start with.

CRC was not a union signatory at the time. I worked there for ten months that year. It's funny, I never made a hat the whole time I was there. They put me in the tailor shop. I'm not a tailor. And Gilbert, the head of the tailor shop, wanted to boot me out, because, he said, "She can't sew!" I can sew, but I did not have tailoring skills. So they put me in women's stock. Liz Petrithelis took me under her wing. She taught me all about how to do the women's stock, and I started pulling orders. I didn't get bored with women's stock, but I wanted to learn everything I possibly could, so I lobbied to get into the men's department. Then, I lobbied to get into police-uniform stock. Although I am not a military person, I love that little fussy detail. Johnny Napolitano was there, and Johnny was so sweet. I used to go show him what I was doing, and he would make sure I was correct.

It was really "learn by doing." You learn how to measure the garments, add the two inches for the butt, and allow for this and that. Much of it was on-the-job learning— and just being practical and using common sense. Enough cannot be said for common sense. Don't hang that pant on the hanger with the crease in the wrong place! Fix the crease, *then* hang it up. Just organizational things. Things about being neat, doing things in a consistent way.

Eventually, I moved into the research department, working as a research librarian in their collection, putting together research packages for people and referring them to different sources. The research part is an ongoing education. And it's so important in the business. It's funny, the only time I worked on hats at CRC was when I was working in the library. I would go to the stock, find the hats most in need of refurbishment, take them in my office, and when I wasn't looking up stuff, I'd fix them. I needed that "hands on" thing.

While you were working at CRC, did you make contacts that eventually got you on set?

I met costume designer Evelyn Thompson at CRC, and pulled orders for her. She was a key contact for me, eventually. But the first job I got on a set was by word of mouth, after I had quit the costume house. Somebody said that a little production company was looking for a set costumer. I went to the designer and said, "I have no set experience, but I would be willing to do whatever it takes to get the experience and learn." She had interviewed several other people, but we really clicked. I did have the costume house experience, which I think was very helpful, so she knew that I kind of knew the ins and outs of that part of it. And in rental, you learn a little bit about the behind-the-scenes prepping part, which is a really big part of making movies.

Compared to working at a cutting table, where you might get a nice sensitivity to shape and the made-to-order process, the rental process's tagging and sizing and organization has such an on-set connection.

Absolutely. The sheer number of costumes is mind-boggling, even for a very small show with just a few principals. When you're working at a costume house, you begin to *handle* all the stuff. You realize the physicality of it. And then you start pulling orders. Someone will call you up and say, "I need a bag lady and I need a grocery clerk; I want the grocery clerk to look not too 7-Eleven, but I want him to have some kind of funky polyester top and a little soda-jerk paper hat." You get a feel for interpreting what that person has said to you. You also get a feel for going and getting those physical clothes and bringing them in. You work the sizes, so you figured out how to do the sizing: I don't have a medium, but I can give this person a large, because it's an oversize thing. All those common-sense details aren't really that obvious when you first start.

Did any of your friends start out in similar ways?

One friend went to film school because she wants to direct. She's done a little bit of everything—set work and prepping, designing and directing. Many of my friends come from theater backgrounds. As much work as that is, it still doesn't quite prepare you for the chaos that is film. Some have come from fashion design, which I think is a good base to start with—understanding clothing. But I think that the people who come from fashion design really are in a different world. The whole emphasis in fashion is different than in film—just the physicality of what happens on a movie set—and it doesn't neces-sarily serve them well.

I've also worked with people who have said, "Well, anybody can buy clothes." I've heard that from plenty of producers. "Well, I wear clothes, I can certainly pick them out." Sure, *you* go ahead and break down the script and figure out who needs to be in blue or red and all of that stuff! People told me this when I got into the business: "It's just not like you think it's going to be. You won't have a life when you're on a movie." I didn't believe that I wouldn't have a life. I imagined this romantic notion of Edith Head and design swatches. Oh boy, was that a crock.

The reality is that there is a lot less respect for the costume department than there is for any other department on a movie. Costumers make less money than any other craft crew on a movie. The grips can pick up a twenty-pound sandbag, but they never have to crack the script, or do a breakdown, or figure out a characterization; and yet, gosh, they're paid more. What's wrong with this picture? The people who are starting out, I don't try to discourage them. I say, "You're going to learn very quickly that you're not going to have, right off the bat, the level of respect that you might aspire to. And you may never achieve the respect you think you're owed, because in this business, you're low man on the totem poll."

Why do it? Does anything still dazzle you?

I don't know if it's a dazzle, but there really is this perverse little part of me that loves the clothes—especially on a period piece. I just love the old clothes, the history, the way that the tailoring is different. I go to work in sneakers and leggings and a big old shirt, but what I really love are Lilly Dashe suits. Even when you're on a contemporary film, you just get to feel the pieces. Sometimes I'll be working in the trailer and, oh, I want to touch these things—because it's corporeal design. So you didn't design it, someone else bought it off the rack, but that little piece of wardrobe is kind of like a little piece of art. Then it gets painted, and then this actor puts it on, and then it's put together with other actors in costume in the whole big scene, and you see how it all fits together. That's really cool.

Let's get back to your first set job.

I didn't have anything when I went to my first job. The designer said, "Don't worry about it. I will provide everything." That was very kind of her, because a lot of times now, people expect you to come with your Polaroid and your pins and your tags and your Sharpie markers and clippers, a seam ripper, and a little sewing kit—all of those things you should have. But I didn't know that at the time.

I think a lot of people have a pretty good tolerance for real raw recruits.

In some ways, I think that's true. One of the things that's not so prevalent now as it was when I first started is the use of a lot of unpaid interns. For insurance reasons now, that's really slacked off. I, for one, am glad, because I know that they were really abused. My theory about interns is this: They're on a production to learn, not to be slaves, not just to make copies all day, or iron shirts all day.

I hired a theater person in Virginia, the sweetest kid. He was so excited to be given his first movie job. I said, "I'm going to run you ragged, but I will show you everything that you want to know, and more. I'll show you my job, which you don't have to do, but that way you'll get a feeling for it." So I showed him the "book," and how it's broken down, and why we do this and that. He was the kind of kid who came in and said, "I'll do anything. I'll shine shoes, I'll spit-polish the shoes." And he really did do anything. In five weeks, he started spit-shining shoes, and then he was setting rooms and helping on the set. I just brought him along, in a major crash course.

That's very generous. Not all folks are that way.

I've run into those people. They used to really bother me, but I've developed a much thicker skin. Every time you walk on the set, the dynamic of the crew is different. On one set, you might have somebody who is kind to you, and on the next set, you might have someone who's just really mean. You have to learn to adapt, especially when you are going to work on a set where you haven't met anybody.

I have jitters when I go onto a new set and I haven't met anybody. I'm really eager, and I want to please them, but every supervisor has quirks. You must learn to adapt to those quirks, and roll with the punches. You should not take things personally. You should be able to say, Okay, she wants these socks folded, and the other guy wanted them rolled up in a ball; just do it, and adapt to the powers that be.

When I'm with a new crew, I probably drive them absolutely insane asking questions. I'll say, "I've worked this way before; please tell me if *you* want it done in a certain way." Or, "If you need me, call me from the trailer to the set whenever you want." If it's a real bad day on the set, often just walking off the set for fifteen minutes can rejuvenate a set costumer, get her to the point where she can get back in there. When I have the opportunity, I'll say, "You go back to the trailer for fifteen minutes; I'll just stay on the set. I can watch what's going on." There are also times on set when you just sit there for hours and watch the paint dry. *You* need a break, then.

What should newcomers to the business be cautious about?

It depends on how star-struck you are. I am not a star-struck person. Actors are people. I've had young people work for me who thought that, just because they were on the set, they could go up and talk to the actors and ask for an autograph. They're few and far between, the people who are this clueless or naive, but they do exist.

One of the first things a newcomer should learn is that a film shoot is a working environment. Even though there are egos and there are actors, there is a structure. If you stick to yourself and you observe for the first couple of days while you're doing your work, you'll really learn what that structure is. It will become obvious. You'll be able to tell where you can go with impunity if you have to ask a question.

Is it important for newcomers to learn about job jurisdictions?

Yes. There is a real power structure. If you come in as an extras' set costumer, you're not allowed to deal with the principals. That's because there are people who deal specifically with the principals—that's their job. There can be a little bit of overlap, but you also have to learn to respect the boundaries between your job and everybody else's. The line is fuzzy sometimes between the set costumer and the extras costumer. I've worked with a set costumer who didn't want you to have anything to do with the actors; they wouldn't even let you come to the set. Then again, you sometimes have to "swing," to do a little bit of everything. A lot of set costumers who do the principals don't want to be bothered with extras. And you know what? That's bullshit. Your department should back you up.

The whole thing really boils down to teamwork, and getting the job done, and having fun while you do it. If you're not having fun, what is the point? The best of all possible worlds is when you get on a crew, and you click with the people in your department, and you run interference for each other. You cover each other's butt, and you don't let your ego, or your job description, get in the way of getting the job done. The whole point of making the movie together—the ultimate result—is to make a good piece of film with very few mistakes.

I like to tell people who are new to costuming that if someone asks them a question, no matter who it is—whether it's the director or the actors or the prop people—if they don't know the answer to the question, say, "I don't know, but I'll find out." Then, go find out, follow up, and report back. Don't just blow it off and think it will get taken care of, because nine times out of ten, everybody has twenty things they're doing at the same time—and it won't get taken care of. And then it will fall back on your department.

If you follow up, you will become known as someone who can get things done. And then people will come to rely on what you have to say. The bottom line is this: If your costume department functions well as a team, with lots of energy and a minimum of conflict, then the project will be fun, and well done, and an integral part of a successful film experience.

Conversation Fourteen:

On the Difference Between Working in New York and L.A., with Marcy Froehlich

Marcy Froehlich has worked as a costume designer on features, among them, *Unbowed* (1999), *Contact* (1992), and television series (fig. 7.36). She has also worked as assistant designer on films, including *Road to Perdition* (2002) and *American Beauty* (1999). She co-authored *Shopping LA: The Insiders' Sourcebook for Film & Fashion*.

You came to Los Angeles and the film business after being a very successful Broadway assistant costume designer. Can you talk a little bit about why you chose to come Los Angeles?

Well, I came to L.A. because I felt like I wasn't really progressing in my career. I was assisting and I was designing in regional theater, but I didn't feel like I'd ever make it to design on Broadway. It was not that easy to make a living, and I felt that I needed to explore something else, especially film. And film was happening in L.A. My family lived out here, and my apartment lease was coming up, so I decided to put everything in storage and see what L.A. was all about. It was kind of a wild thing to do.

It was harder for me to get started out here, but I think that may be partly because I really was into design-assisting, and I was looking for work at that level. Still, I think that there may be more openness in the market here in L.A. than in New York. In New York, I wouldn't call it snobbery, but getting someone to give me the big design opportunity wasn't happening; it didn't come my way. When I left New York, the same designers were designing as when I had come to town ten years earlier. It does seem to be a smaller market in New York.

I also think that it is easier to live out here in L.A. The creature comforts are easier: You can get an apartment for less money; you can go to pretty places cheaper; and you can have a normal life in Los Angeles much easier than you can in New York. Overall, I was unemployed longer in New York than I was here, except for the first chunk of two or three years when I was just getting started in L.A.

Did you have any film or television background when you came out here?

Yes. In New York, I had been working at Costume Arts, followed by a job at Barbara Matera's costume shop, as a shopper. After nine months at Matera's, I was starting to search around for something else. At Costume Arts, they suggested to film designer Kristi Zea that she try me as an assistant. She gave me a chance; and that was my first film in New York.

I had a few other film experiences in New York. In fact, I had already designed a TV series and a film when I came out to Los Angeles, so I was not a novice, I'd had some experience both as a designer and as an assistant on films. In fact, I was out here for a year, and then I went back to New York for a few months to do a film before I came back here for good.

I thought I would get work faster here than I actually did. It took me several years to get established. Most of my contacts out here, film-wise, have been people who have come from New York. I find that my communication is best with those people who have a theater background. Not only designers, but also directors. That is my particular niche.

I think it is hard to get started in L.A., as a new kid. The business in New York is very much about contacts, but I think perhaps a little more so in L.A. There is much more of a union hurdle here, too.

In those first tough two or three years, how long were the on-and-off periods of unemployment? What was the longest stretch of unemployment that you ever had?

I seem to remember a month or six weeks, but I've never been unemployed for months and months at a stretch. There are some people who are definite that they will only take design jobs, but I haven't been as strict with that. Therefore, perhaps, I've worked more. And there have been times when I've been an assistant and have been offered something as a designer that I've not been able to take because I didn't feel that it was fair to leave in the middle of a job. To be offered something that seems yummy and yet feel bound ethically to another project is difficult.

Did you find that your manner had to change for L.A.?

I think that I have become better at schmoozing, networking. My ability to just talk to people has improved out here, and I think that was something that I needed to improve. I couldn't rest on who I knew because I didn't know that many people, so I had to join organizations where I could meet new people.

What kind of organizations did you join?

Women in Film—which men can join, too. Also, Independent Feature Project West—IFP West. I've purposefully gone to more screenings and more parties than I might personally have wanted to, because I felt that this was a way to meet people.

In such an image-conscious business, did your personal style have to change from New York to L.A.? Have matters of personal style affected your job hunt?

I think it is important to look stylish, to present yourself well, to be in shape. I became much more body-conscious out here, whereas in New York, I was more culture-conscious, I guess. In New York, there is much more concern with what you know, and how many operas you've been to. In Los Angeles, I would say that there is more emphasis on presentation. As to whether a sexy hot-shot gets the job over you, I think that this can happen in any business. That's just part of it. Perhaps it happens more often in the film business. I would say it happens more to actors and actresses than to designers and costumers. And it certainly depends on who's interviewing you.

I think it is important to be up to date in what you are wearing. But after a while, once you have a career established, that isn't as important as the kind of work that you do. It may be important at first, when you're hoping to get the job out of a field of people; but I really think that your rapport with the person who's interviewing you is more important. And how that rapport is established is sometimes enigmatic. You can't put your finger on it. You just keep going for interviews until you find those people who are your kind of people.

Maybe once a week, or once every two weeks, I talk to some young person coming into town who asks me how to get started. I tell them that every person gets started in a different way, and I give them a list of things to look into, like going to AFI—American Film Institute—and designing some movies for free.

How did you end up breaking into the business in L.A.?

The very first day I arrived, I got a phone call to do an AIDS benefit. It's a freebie. I thought, "Sure, I'm not doing anything else." One of the guys on that benefit, a director, was an actor in my last show. The lighting designer on that benefit and I got to know each other pretty well. He brought me on as a costume designer when he was a production designer on a small film. That was my first film in L.A.

Did you have any theater contacts—directors or designers—who were already out in L.A.?

I had a friend who taught at Occidental College, so I designed a show out there. I had another friend who was a costume designer, but she was working in crafts. She got me two little jobs. I knew Cynthia Hamilton, who was doing a lot of assisting out here, especially with the costume designer Ellen Mirojnick. Cynthia and I had assisted on *Phantom of the Opera* together in New York. She happened to be in Bill Hargate's shop when Bill said he needed an assistant. Cynthia said, "Why don't you hire Marcy?" That was the beginning of working a lot more. I've worked for Bill on and off now for five, maybe six years.

A sort of a home base for you?

In a way. He's had two, sometimes three, shows a year—mostly theater—that I've worked on with him. I've done a little bit of TV with him. But more importantly, I've met a lot of people through that shop. I've gotten to know the people in the shop very well, as well as a lot of the designers who come through there.

I assist him. It's being an assistant/shopper. Sometimes it's shopping for his shows; sometimes it's shopping for the shop. He pulled me in because of my theater background.

Did that also give you entrée into the Costume Designers Guild?

In New York, I was in the Broadway design union, United Scenic Artists (USA). When I came to L.A., I thought, "Oh, I should join the Guild," which I did. I joined it shortly after coming to L.A. I got in on an interview with my portfolio. I didn't have to do the test project they required because I was a USA designer. There was sort of a gentlemen's agreement then—it's become a little more "in writing" now—that if you were a member of USA and if you had the credits, then you could get in the Costume Designers Guild on interview.

I became an assistant first, instead of a designer. I was spending thousands of dollars to move my furniture, buy a car, and put money down on an apartment. With joining the Guild, I just thought I couldn't afford the extra thousands of dollars to go for full designer status. I've now upgraded to designer.

Please talk more about ways to pursue work in Los Angeles.

In Los Angeles, as in New York, if you want to become a costume designer, try to go for jobs that are closest to designer, such as a shopper. There are a few shopper positions at some of the "shops" (workrooms). If you want to be a draper, then start as a seamstress. But if you want to be a designer or a design assistant, the shop is maybe not the best place for you—unless you just need a job.

Or be a costumer, where you will be on the set. If you are on the set, you will meet production assistants, for instance. You want to meet the PAs and the assistant directors—the young people in film who may be directors ten years from now. You also want to meet the other folks on the set—folks you'll develop a rapport with, who will take you with them for their first film.

Being on the set is the best way to get to know those people?

And to get to know how a film is really made. Work begets work. Someone may be better at the job than you, but the person that you have met on a film doesn't know *that* person, they know you. So they'll take you—someone they know—over the better-qualified person they don't know. If you're a newcomer to L.A., or you're going to New York, you do anything. Because you want to get *to* people, and you want people to get to know that you have integrity and creativity and endurance, and that you're a good person for the future.

What I've said is very unique to my own experience. What I see as "usual practice" may be very different for someone else—especially for someone who comes from the MTV styling world. That's a very different kind of approach from the kind of approach that I have taken. An MTV stylist looking to work in feature films would have a very different take on how to get jobs, and what shops to use and that sort of thing.

Did you ever have luck getting work through *The Hollywood Reporter?*

A lot of people send out résumés every week to the shows in *The Hollywood Reporter,* hoping to get a chance as an assistant or a designer. I've interviewed for a couple of films this way, but I haven't gotten work this way. I know people who have: Young designers coming into town have gotten work that way.

I think it is important to pick and choose the projects you work on. At first, you are eager and you want to do anything, but you need to make sure that the producers and the companies that you work for have integrity. Especially at the beginning of your career, your reputation—the way you're sized up in the business—has a lot to do with the companies you are willing to work for. If the company that you work for doesn't have a sense of integrity, or if you try to pull a fast one on a costume shop, the costume shops will get to know this about you. They will be less and less willing to do you favors.

You need to use your intuition to size up the company. Demand that they follow certain ethical practices; if they won't, don't work with them. For instance, there are some companies that want you to use clothes on the actors and then return them to the store. I have refused to do that. Maybe I haven't worked with those companies again, but my relationship with the store, and the costume shop, is going to last for my entire career.

In an interview, you can "feel" what a company is. Sometimes, though, you'll still get mashed. But if you do, and can make the costume shop understand that you had no idea that this was going to happen, if you try to make amends—those two things go a long way. If you have a reputation for being someone who cares about the clothes and cares about your reputation, you'll have favors done for you. A costume shop or rental house will be much more willing to do something for someone who has been good to them than for someone who is constantly taking advantage of them.

As a designer, have you noticed any difference between the interviews in New York and the interviews in L.A.?

I have to package myself for film work differently in L.A.—something I learned by making a big mistake in an interview with a director. I took my entire portfolio with me—film, TV, and theatre work, all sort of mixed up. When the director came to the pages on *Madame Butterfly,* I could see his eyes glaze over. When we came to a half-hour "short" in which I had two soldier uniforms, he goes, "Oh, yeah, this is more like what I do." I thought, "Here I've shown him *Madame Butterfly,* where I have painted these costumes and created this whole show, and he doesn't relate to it. He relates to modern blood-and-guts stuff."

I had seen the ad for this film in *The Hollywood Reporter,* and it had caught my eye because it was being shot in Pittsburgh. I sent in my résumé, saying I was born in Pittsburgh. The director gave me the interview, I think, because he was born in Pittsburgh, too. Unfortunately, that was the only link we had. If I really wanted that job, I should have done more research on who he was and what kind of films he did, and tailored what I showed him to that.

You didn't have the script before you went in to the interview?

Sometimes you have the script, sometimes, not. It is nice if you have a script, because then, you can go in with some ideas about how you want to see it.

A friend of mine had an experience with a director who was interviewing several people. This director wanted everyone he interviewed to go home and do some sketches and come back for another interview. She said she didn't do that. Someone else must have, because they got the job. That, I felt, was taking advantage of people wanting a job.

A lot of times, you get the job because you have a rapport with the director. Whether it's a personal rapport or just a good vibe, or you see the project the way they see the project, somehow you click. Even if you are a designer of huge stature, you might not get a job if you don't click with a particular director. There are a lot of first-time directors out there who are just looking for somebody they can connect with. If someone of great stature comes in, they're a little afraid. They'd rather go to someone who is a little less experienced, who is a little more along their own lines.

Every interview is different. It's hard to put your finger on how to do it, but I think that the most important thing is to do your homework: know who this director is, and know a little bit about his or her work. See if you jibe. I think, eventually, you will find a group of people with whom you share an ethos. This group will become the group who takes you along.

On every film, every project, you develop a little family. Then, when that project is over, the family dissolves. It's nice when you are going in to be comfortable with that family, because it is such a tough few weeks that you spend together. To go in having a little security or peace with each other is very important. When I come out of an interview and realize that there wasn't that sense of connection, I think, That project's not going to be for me.

Is there a different pace in L.A. than there is in New York?

I have found the pace in California equal to or greater than the pace in New York. One of the things that contributes to this is Southern California's car culture. In New York, you take buses and taxis and subways. In L.A., the shopping is much more dispersed. In a day, you will drive ninety miles, going from shop to store to fabric store to cobbler to some other place. Trying to get the same amount of work done in the same amount of time, you feel that you are working at a little madder pace. Another difference is that in L.A., work can start as early as 5:00 A.M., and go on until it's dark. In theater, in New York, you start a little later, maybe 9:00 A.M., but you go until midnight. Getting up really early in the morning to go out to some field where it is deathly cold and still dark is very different.

I think working on films can be harder on the body, harder physically, than working in theater. Not that I didn't get tired in New York. I remember when I first started shopping in New York, I came home at 7:30 and went to bed. But here, in L.A., it's more demanding to be outside in the hot sun, running back and forth to the set, aging things on set. In New York, I was running back and forth to the shops, and buying fabric, and hauling it into a taxi in the rain or the snow. That would tire me out, but there wasn't the same kind of driving pace. Also, when you are doing film, there is more last-minute casting. Often, you'll get principals way up front and you'll have time to deal with them. But last-minute casting seems to be getting worse and worse, happening more and more frequently, with the actors trying to cut the best deal and agents postponing and postponing, until the last minute.

I have done more last-minute, gotta-have-it-tomorrow-morning kind of stuff in L.A. than I have in New York. And the shops in L.A. have always come through. You'll always find someone who can work overnight. For example, on a film about the nine-teen-twenties, the actor was cast, and they got sizes from the agent. The actor didn't come in for the fitting until, I think, after five o'clock the evening before he was going to be filmed. But all the clothes that the costume department had pulled for the fitting were useless because the actor was not the size that the agent said he was. By the time they realized this, the rental houses were closed. They took new measurements and, that night, the tailor did a three-piece suit. A three-piece suit overnight! I was rather impressed. It's hard trying to convince a producer that we can't always custom-make something in twenty minutes.

What do you miss about New York?

I miss the fabric stores the most. In L.A., there is nothing like the range of fabric stores that you have in New York City. That's because New York is the center of the garment trade. The wide variety, and the quality, of fabric and trim—there is nothing else like it in the U.S. When doing a period show, a lot of L.A. designers will go back to New York to swatch and shop. In L.A., I've become very adept at finding new sources.

How about rental collections around town?

There are more rental clothes out here than in New York, and the rental houses in L.A. have a broader range of clothes than the rental houses in New York. In L.A., you have four or five big studio collections; then, you have Western, CRC, Eastern, and Motion Picture Costumes. And then the smaller ones, like Palace or Helen Larson Collections, that have, mostly, real period stuff. And the costume rental houses here in L.A. are better organized than the rental houses in New York. Bar-coding is becoming a big thing out here. Now, even Western and Disney are jumping on the bandwagon. It does seem to be easier. Rental houses are even starting to use photographs of costumes: They can take a digital picture of a costume so they'll know that they are getting that garment back in original condition.

How about research resources?

I do miss the New York Public Library picture collection, because it is great. But you have wonderful research collections in Los Angeles, at Western Costume, Warner Bros., the Academy of Television Arts and Sciences, the Margaret Herrick Library of the Academy of Motion Picture Arts and Sciences, and at the Burbank Public Library. The Costume Designers Guild and Motion Picture Costumers Local 705 have established costume research libraries of their own, and if you are a member of the unions, you can use these libraries for free.

There are other research collections for film that are quite extensive, but you pay for them: usually $50 an hour and up, to have a librarian work with you. Most of these research collections have a $25 minimum charge for a librarian to pull things for you, but then you can sit there for free, for hours, doing the research yourself. Whenever you have a librarian working with you, it costs money; but sometimes, when something's thrown at you, you can call one of these research collections and have a librarian do the research. You send them a purchase order and they send the research to you. So, that's a wonderful service.

Research collections in Los Angeles are specifically geared to the industry. CRC, for instance, is known for uniforms, and they have an extensive research library on uniforms. You can get all the patches and details for police groups all over the United States, and the world.

There are also independent folk, in New York and in L.A., who do research. There are people out here who are experts in uniforms. If you have a uniform show, you hire them, because they know the details.

I know New York has studio-services departments in a few department stores.

But there are more studio services in L.A. I think there are more businesses out here that try to cater to the industry, because the industry is just bigger out here—and it's so visible. New York is known more for Broadway.

One thing that I've noticed in Los Angeles is that when you need crafts on a movie, you usually create your own shop, whereas in New York, for crafts or millinery, you often go to a shop that's already established. Some of the major shops in L.A. do occasional millinery, but when it's creature crafts, they put together a shop, or go to special effects groups. There is nothing like New York's Martin Izquierdo Studio, or Parsons-Meares Ltd., which has several full-time people doing dyeing, painting, and crafts. There is a full-time cobbler at Western Costume, and a full-time milliner, but I'd say that Western is the only shop that I know of in L.A. that has full-time craftspeople of any type. If a production needs something special, a shop will bring it in. A costume studio will have full-time drapers and seamstresses and such, but not a full-time creature sculptor. Maybe at a props house or a special effects place; but not at your basic costume studio.

There is a company in Los Angeles that does dyeing, exclusively. But as I said before, a lot of times when you have a movie that needs a lot of dyeing, the production's costume department will set up its own dyeing and distressing shop. A lot of designers like to do that.

Do they "build" more costumes in New York?

There is more custom-made work done in New York than there is in L.A. because they're set up to make an entire show. Broadway shows have to make everything, whereas in L.A., there is a lot of rental. In L.A., extras' costumes are usually rented. If it's a modern piece, extras will often bring their own clothes. In L.A., you usually custom-make the principals, and maybe important day players, but, overall, you don't do as much custom-building in L.A. as you do in New York—unless you have major film stunts, or a *Batman*, where you have a certain look, or in a production like *Geppetto*, where you have to have clothes that are made specifically for dance movement. In a regular period film, you often don't have the money or the time to custom make an entire ballroom scene.

Does the bid process for made-to-order feel different in L.A. than it does in New York?

I think that there is less "bidding-out" of shows in L.A. than in New York. Usually, you establish a relationship with a shop. Or you get to know that this shop is better for this and that shop is better for that. But usually, who gets the work has a lot to do with relationships and where you have had work done before, where they have a certain language you understand.

For purposes of getting bids on custom-made work, a designer and a costume supervisor will work out what the budget is for the film. They will guesstimate how much these custom-made things should cost, and then go to the shop and say, "Here's what we need; what do you think it's going to cost?" The shop will tell you, and you'll go ahead.

In film, not as much time is spent going around finding out what each piece is going to cost. Part of the reason for this probably has to do with how little time you have. You don't always have the luxury of having a week or two to wait and find out what it's all going to cost. You are designing all the way through the movie. It takes a lot of time to do bids. In theater, it's easier to come to a decision early in the process about what the particular custom-made item is going to be. In film, there seems to be a lot more fingers in the pie: the actor, the producer, the producer's wife. All these people seem to have a say about what gets made. As you're getting toward the shooting moment, you find out, Oh no, it's going to be a special effect; or, Oh no, it's going to need to be flown in a harness. The decision-making is not all up front, like it seems to be in the theater. In film, it's more of an ongoing process: deciding what, exactly, this costume is, up front, and having it really remain the same, is a little more shaky in film.

Conversation Fifteen:

On How I Got Started in Independent Film, with Kristin Burke

Costume designer Kristin Burke has done dozens of independent features and television series, including *The Big Empty* (2003), starring Jon Favreau; *The Cooler* (2003), starring William H. Macy and Alec Baldwin; and *Star Maps* (1997). She is co-author of this book.

You got into designing features very quickly. Give us a little background on how you got into "the biz."

I studied theater costume design at Northwestern University. It was not my major; I was a film major and a French major, but I found myself drawn back to my roots in sewing, which I learned in the 4-H Club.

When I was in school, I did an internship with Columbia Tri-Star. I had written the production company a letter saying, "Hi, I'm at Northwestern University, and I'd like an internship with your company. Can you help me?" They called me and they said, "Can you come out for an interview?" So I went out to L.A. over spring break of my junior year in college. I interviewed with a woman named Adrienne Levin, and she was lovely. She had a lot of toys in her office, and we played for hours, like little kids. Then she called me a couple weeks later, and she said, "You know, you'd be perfect for this movie *Hudson Hawk*. I'd love it if you could be the assistant production coordinator. Are you interested?" I was like, "Sure!"

The production coordinator does not work in the costume department, right?

Not at all. The production coordinator works for "production." Production is a completely different department. Production is like reception: It's the door through which everybody comes. I was working as an assistant production coordinator, and the costume department was calling me for little things: "We need travel things," or "We need petty cash," or "We need—." So I got to know them. I thought, I've been sewing all my life and I think I'd like to meet these people, because they are very cool. So the costume designer, Marilyn Vance, got on the phone with me and she said, "You know, it's been really crazy here and we could really use an extra hand. I know you are interested in wardrobe; would you like to help us?" I said, "Yes!"

I kind of blew off the assistant production-coordinator job, which really made the production coordinator upset, but, as it turned out, the wardrobe department was very cool. I worked with them, and I got a sense of what they were doing, and their procedure. This was a fifty-million-dollar movie, which was a big-budget movie in 1991. Working with the costume department, I got to see how a big-budget show worked. They were shooting in five different countries, so I learned how you could ship things here and there, and do things more efficiently.

For example, they had cast an actress for the lead role, but three days away from shooting, they recast it, with Andie MacDowell. The costume department had to take all of the design concepts they had developed for the first actress and transfer it to Andie—another person, another body, another look. I saw that happen, and I thought, "You know what? This is cool. This is a challenging job. It would put all my creative skills and all my intellectual skills to use. I think this is perfect for me."

I got back to school and it was my senior year. I produced music videos and TV shows, and that was really fun, but it wasn't as creative for me as the hands-on nature of wardrobe work, so I petitioned the school of theater to get into the design program. I wrote costume-design teacher Virgil Johnson a letter and said, "I've done this work on this film, and I want to do it for a career. I hope that you can understand my motivation and my desire to do this, not to mention my devotion to the craft." And he let me into his design classes.

When I got out of school, I went to Europe for a while. When I came back, I said, "I'm going to move to L.A., but I need a reason, to placate my parents. So, I looked in *The Hollywood Reporter* and I sent off about one hundred-thirty letters saying, "I'm here, I can work as your assistant, or as your intern, or whatever. Hire me, hire me, hire me." And I got one letter back, from costume designer Patricia Zipprodt, in New York, saying, "I'm sorry, I'm retired." That was the only reply I got back from one hundred-thirty letters I sent out.

Do you feel you had a dud cover letter?

No. I knew what I wanted to do; it was just kind of a sign to try something else. I contacted MPCA [Motion Picture Corporation of America], which was, at the time, a low-budget movie entity. They were doing a film. I spoke with the costume designer. I said, "I'll intern, whatever." And she said "Okay, here's my start date." I stayed with my family in Long Beach.

Did you have major debts when you came out here?

No. I'm really lucky that my parents covered my education, and I didn't come out here with debt. With that sort of security, I could pursue what I needed to pursue. To come out to L.A. with twelve-, fourteen-, thirty-thousand dollars worth of college debt—which I know a lot of people have—would have made it hard, really daunting, for me to do what I did.

On the MPCA show, I was treated poorly. I was driving the costume designer everywhere, and not being compensated for my gas or my mileage. She was griping at me constantly, and didn't seem to think that this was not a nice thing to do. It was one of her first design gigs and, clearly, she was in over her head. There were big-name actors, and it was just a disaster. It made me so mad. I went home crying every day. Anybody who knows me well knows that's really bad. After that movie, I said, "Fuck you. If you can do a low-budget film like this, I can do it ten times better *and* be a nice person in the process." So, I went off and interned on *Bram Stoker's Dracula*, which Francis Ford Coppola directed.

A big union film. Boy, did you get a break.

Richard Schissler was the associate designer on the film. I called him, and I said, "I know this is a huge movie, I know that you're understaffed, and I know that you need help. I'm here to help you, what can we do?" And he said, "You can start by coming in and talking with somebody." I said, "Okay, who do I talk to?" And he said, "Sue Moore," who was the women's costume supervisor. So, I met with Sue, and she took my hand and she looked at my fingernails. They were ratty as hell. And she said, "Well, I can see that you are accustomed to hard work." And I said, "That's absolutely right."

Sue Moore really gave me quite a perspective on the film world. By taking my hand and looking at my fingernails, I thought, "Right on, sister, I get you." So I worked on *Dracula* for a while. I took the costume stock that had been shipped over from [the costume house] Angels, in London, sized it, and organized it for their fittings. *Dracula* had a thousand extras. One city scene required five hundred extras, in period costume. They were doing it "to the nines"—toe to top of the head. Every extra had a corset, every extra had a bustle, everything. They had these women's costumes, and a lot of them were original—which is astounding, when you think about it.

Richard had gone to England to pull the wardrobe, and then he shipped it all back. None of it from Angels was sized. None, zero percent, none was sized. So my job—measuring tape around my neck—was to size the wardrobe and hang it, in order. I had those fitting rooms so organized! Evening wear, day wear, sloppy wear, by sizes. By bust size, by waist size—everything was organized. They were like, "Oh, Kristin, it's so great," until the day that somebody from a neighboring office called and said, "Who is this person you have working with you who you've been talking about? Is she union?" And they said to me, "You know what? You probably shouldn't come in to work today."

It was a union shoot, and you were a non-union kid.

I understand that, but at the same time, it was kind of like, "Oh, rats." This was my big break. I really enjoyed working with them. I thought it was totally excellent. I was thrilled because I was using everything that I had learned in school as far as period detailing goes right away, right out of school. I was so happy. But when that job fell through, I thought, "Okay, what am I going to do now?" Having had been treated so poorly before, and having this experience on *Dracula,* where they really respected me, I said, "That's it, this shit is mine. It's all about me. Get out of my way." I went to AFI [American Film Institute] and put my résumé in.

I did a couple of first-year student films, just to meet people and see what they were doing. Then I was hired on a couple of second-year AFI projects. Young student directors work there—I think the average age is about 27. The projects prep for a month and shoot for three weeks. Both of the "shorts" that I did for AFI were period pieces: one was set in the nineteen-seventies and one was set in 1893. For the one set in 1893, AFI had an agreement with Warner Bros., whereby I would get office space and all of my rentals free.

At the time, Warner Bros. had three wardrobe facilities. The "period" facility was on Flower, and the people there were old-school wardrobe types. They did *Shazam!* and *Isis* and *Little House on the Prairie* and all of those seventies' TV series that I grew up on. When I got there and told them what I was doing, they were like, "This is great. We will help you in whatever way we can." I thought, "I have arrived!" They gave me mannequins. I would dress them with the half-cage bustle and the petticoats and the outfit, and shoot pictures to show the director what I was looking for, because he wasn't really familiar with the period. They took me aside later and said, "You know, you're one of a few costumers we've ever seen who's actually done the undergarments the right way." And I said, "Oh, God bless you! This is a good thing, thank you." It was really cool.

This film that I was working on was set in 1893, and was a relatively big student film. It was called *Lucky Peach,* and it was a musical set in rural Wisconsin. We had a whole town of people, and a marching band, and lots of extras. For me, it was a great experience. It was very empowering, in that regard. I thought, "I don't have much money in the budget, I'm not getting paid anything to do this, but I know that I *can* do this. I've made the contacts, so I know where things are as far as wardrobe goes."

That was really a good start. After that, I thought, "Now, I'm ready to sort of do my own thing." One of my friends, who was a makeup artist on one of the AFI films, said, "There's this company called Concorde, and this guy named Roger Corman, who does all of these low-budget films. They are doing this skateboard movie. You'd probably be perfect for it because you know what's going on in that world." So I called the producer of this film at least ten times over the course of two weeks. "Hello, it's Kristin Burke, I'm calling about *The Skateboard Kid.*"

As luck would have it, I lived two blocks away from the production office. After two weeks of not having my calls returned, I thought, "All right, I'm going to go down there." I got on my business suit—because this is how much I know about interviewing for stuff! I got on my business suit and I took my portfolio, with all my pictures from all the things that I've done from theater and these AFI films, and I walked two blocks, down to the office. I went in to the reception area and I said, "Hi, I'm here to see Mike Elliot." And they said, "Do you have an appointment?" I said, "No." They looked at me kind of funny. I said, "I don't have an appointment, but I'll wait." So, I sat down and

I waited for about fifteen minutes. This guy came out and said, "Hi, I'm Mike Elliot." And I said, "Hi, I'm Kristin Burke. I've called you ten times about this movie *The Skateboard Kid*, and you haven't returned my calls. I wanted to show you my book, so you can see what I'm capable of doing." And he said, "Okay." We sat in the lobby of this office and I showed him my book. He said, "That's great, thanks for coming in. It's nice to meet you." And I said "Okay, thanks, bye-bye." I shook his hand and l went home.

A week went by and I hadn't heard from him. I thought, "This is no good." So I put on a different suit, took my portfolio, and marched down to his office again. I said, "Hi, I'm Kristin Burke. I'm here to see Mike Elliot." "Do you have an appointment?" "No, I don't." And I waited for ten minutes, and then he came out and said, "Oh, it's you again." And I said, "Yes, I'm here about *The Skateboard Kid*. I know that you're doing this thing. Do you want to see my book again?" "Okay, thank you for coming in." "Okay, bye-bye."

I went home and another week passed and I'm like, "That's it, I'm over it. He's going to hire me on this movie!" I was not in a business suit this time, I was in my funky early-nineties grunge gear. I went down there with my book. You know the routine, "I'm here to see Mike Elliot." "Do you have an appointment?" "No." "Hold on." Five minutes later—the time was shortening—he came out and said, "Oh, it's you again. Come back to my office." So I followed him back to his office. Mike Elliot's maybe five years older than me. "Sit down." So I sat down. He picked up the phone and called somebody. And he said, "Yeah, yeah, yeah. There's this girl here, she's been here three times unannounced to see me. She's really annoying me, could you please just see her and get her off my back?" It turns out that he was on the phone with the head of their studio in Venice. He gave me the address of the studio. I drove down there that day and presented my book.

You're still in your grunge gear, right?

Yes, I was still in my grunge gear. These guys at the studio were thinking, "Okay, well, she's been recommended by Mike." They said, "Let's set you up with a meeting with Larry, who is the director." They set me up for a meeting with Larry, and Larry thought that I had been hired. They had given me a script to read, and I had sort of, in a preliminary sense, broken down the script. I understood who the characters were. When I went to meet with him, I had ideas for their wardrobe. He sort of thought that I was hired on the film, and then when I went back to the two people at the studio, they thought that Larry had said okay. It just turned out to be this default thing, so I was hired on this movie.

Persistence pays off—although I don't recommend it: It is humiliating, sometimes. From that point, I did nine movies for Roger Corman, because I was able to bring the wardrobe in for the budget, I was an enthusiastic worker, I had a sense of humor, I was good at it. I was hard working, and had a positive attitude.

Did you get flack in the business because Roger Corman is sort of a renowned horror-film guy?

Most people, whether they admit it or not, have worked for Roger at one point or another. And that's just the God's honest truth. A lot of people won't admit it, because there's some stigma to it. Concorde is a place where people learn, and Roger Corman is often a person's first break. Jack Nicholson, Jonathan Demme. I could go on for hours about who got their first break at Concorde. It's a great place to be, especially if you're young and you can endure it. At age 22, I could do it. I was straight out of college. It was perfect. The whole crowd there was like that.

If you can survive at Concorde, you can survive the business. It's not a glamorous job. Let's just be straightforward about that. Even for people who work in theater, I've got to tell you that film is a whole lot less glamorous than theater.

Once you'd lost the comfort of being able to work out of the AFI/ Warner Bros. base, you had to be able to hustle shows quickly, and learn the resources in the city very fast.

Back to back to back. I have never owned a *Thomas Guide*. I needed to get to know the city by myself. So, when somebody said to me, "It's in this part of town," I'd go, "I'm just gonna drive and find it. At that time, in the early nineties, there was no such resource as *Shopping LA [The Insiders' Sourcebook for Film & Fashion]*. You just had to learn your way around.

With the rental houses, it all depends on what you need. I know if I go into a lower-budget contemporary corporate drama where I need men's Armani suits on everybody, I go to Warner Bros. Warner Bros. has the best contemporary stock of anybody in town. I can rent Armani suits for about $80 a suit, instead of spending $1,800 per suit to own them.

Who else do you use consistently?

CRC for uniforms. They are underrated for the rest of their stuff: They have great period men's and women's clothing. For *Beach Movie*, which was all late-sixties/early-seventies, they had beachwear, bikinis, bathing suits, beach cover-ups, everything. CRC has a lot of stuff for women, so I pulled a lot there. I pulled a lot at Disney. I did a lot at Palace Costumes. Palace has a lot of interesting garments. As you work in different periods, you find where the bones are buried, who has what. It's a matter of experience, knowing where things are. If you don't have that experience, you gain it very quickly.

A lot of costume designers for Roger Corman, or designers in that genre, shop in "the alley," in downtown L.A. "The alley" is a series of little shops around the garment district, open storefronts where people sell knockoffs or overstock. I would also go to places like The Citadel factory outlet center. In those days, our budgets were so small that there was no way to make things look perfect. They didn't look bad, but we just had very little money.

On the movie *Carnosaur*, we didn't even have $5,000 for a wardrobe budget, and everybody died in the movie! We needed to get doubles, triples, quadruples of things, because, in the film, the dinosaurs come and kill people. You can't pull from people's own wardrobes; you have to buy the garments, because you need five of them. We also had police, and people in Hazmat suits, and this was sucking the life out of the budget, because those things are so expensive to rent. We started shooting the day after Thanksgiving, and I had only a week of prep—well, really, five days of prep. So, on that show, I got really creative. I went to every thrift store I knew that had doubles—and in L.A. there *are* thrift stores that have doubles. I went to Target and the sale rack at Kmart, and all of these places where I knew I could get really cheap clothes.

That's when I learned about product placement, and made my own contacts with these people to get it going. I really think that low-budget production work is a valuable training ground. I went into film work as a designer, not as an assistant. When I think about it, I say, "Oh my gosh, what was I thinking?" The first film that I did for Concorde, in 1992, I was paid $400 a week to design, but they knew that I needed that experience.

Did you have any kind of kit?

When I started designing costumes, I really didn't have much of a kit. But I'm one of those notorious pack rats who saves everything. I have all of my clothes from the late seventies and early eighties, the late eighties and the early nineties: Every piece of clothing that was ever in my closet. I added to my kit on those shows where I could buy extra stock from the show. When I went to Footlocker Outlet and I saw that kids' Converses were a dollar a pair, I bought fifteen pairs.

I am a tightwad—but not in an unstylish way. I can save money, but make it look good. When I go to a place and I see stuff on sale, I realize the value of it for me as a costume designer. I think, "Buy it!" I can recognize the beauty of buying a pair of shoes for $100 that were originally $500: They fit beautifully, and they look perfect. It's that kind of sensibility that sets you up to create a good kit, because it shows you have a good eye. If you have a good eye, and if you have a good sense of what is going to last and what is not going to last, what makes an enduring style and what makes a fleeting style, you can choose your purchases with that in mind. You'll have a great kit, and it'll be timeless. You'll be able to use it for ten years, or more.

How do you package yourself to appeal to different directors?

My major strength is that I'm a young person. There aren't that many people my age who are doing costume design, proportionally speaking. However, that is changing. There are an awful lot of young producers and directors out there. I speak their language, they get it, and we understand each other.

But at the same time, my weakness is that I'm a young person. When I was starting, I would go in to job interviews with my résumé and people would say, "Uh huh. You made up your résumé." They wouldn't believe me. That was extremely frustrating. It was very difficult for me in the early times, and that's why I worked for the same company for such a long time. They knew me and they knew what I was capable of.

If you are a good person and you have integrity, if you are sincere and industrious— an enthusiastic worker for the company—people will recognize that. No matter what you do, even if it's scrubbing the floors, do it to the best of your ability. You never know who's watching.

There's a lot of independent work that's extremely well-respected, but there's also a substantial amount of mediocre work out there. Do you find it very important, when you are on low-budget stuff, to prove that you are working beyond the level of the production?

I think that is the goal for most people.

Do you ever get frustrated by the scripts?

I've read a lot of scripts. I've read a lot of scripts set in a lot of different periods, in a lot of different genres. The thing that intrigues me most about a script is not its period or its genre, but the story it has to offer. When I get a script and it really "sings," I think about it for days after I've read it. It doesn't leave me. That's a good script. That's a script that I want to work on.

For me, a film has to have some import, some filmmaking in it. I want to create things that give meaning to what people see. My job is to move people. If I can do that by creating characters visually, then I have done my job.

Appendices

Blank Forms

For Script Breakdown

A.1: COSTUME CROSSPLOT FORM

Sc#	I/E Set/Action	D/N	Characters																									

A.2: SCENE COSTUME BREAKDOWN

Sc#	d/n	Set/Action	I/E	Character	Change	Costume	Notes

s - indicates stunt/stunt double   d - indicates a destructive action that indicates costume multiples
a red dot indicates blood   a brown dot indicates dirt   a blue dot indicates water
x's indicate phases of distress   + indicates an added piece or layer   - indicates a stripped piece

A.3: SCENE WORKSHEET

Scene # _____   Set Location _____

	Char	Char	Char	Char	Char	Char
Totals						
	Char	Char	Char	Char	Char	Char
Totals						
	Char	Char	Char	Char	Char	Char
Totals						

A.4: CHARACTER WORKSHEET

Char	Chg#													
Totals														

Char	Chg#													
Totals														

Char	Chg#													
Totals														

A.5: CHARACTER BREAKDOWN

Production: _____

Character: _____

Actor: _____

Telephone: _____

528

Ch#	Sc#	D/N	I/E	Set/Action	Costume	Notes

A.6: CHARACTER BREAKDOWN FOR SHOPPING

Character: _____   Production: _____   Agent: _____

Ht. _____ Wt. _____ Suit _____ Shirt n_____ Telephone: _____

Pants: _____ _____ slv _____ Shoe _____ Actor: _____

Allergies: _____

Chg#	Sc#	D/N	I/E	Set/Action	Costume	Notes	Source

A.7: EXTRAS SCENE BREAKDOWN

Chg#	Sc#	D/N	I/E											Set/Action										Costume				Notes			Source			

A.8: CHARACTER SUMMARY FORM

Ch#	Sc#	D/N	I/E	Set/Action	Costume	Notes

A.9: EXTRAS SUMMARY BREAKDOWN

Sc#	D/N	I/E	Set/Action	Costume types	Quantity	Character Notes

For Design Bibles

A.10: CHARACTER BID SHEET

Character: _____
Change # _____

Actor: _____
Telephone: _____

Items	Source	Buy	Made to Order	Rent	Alterations	Multiples	Final Cost
Garments							
Undergarments							
Outerwear							
Accessories							

A.11: MADE-TO-ORDER SWATCH SHEET

Character: _____

Actor: _____

Change # _____

Fabric	Yardage	Source	Fiber	Dye/treatment	Cost/Total
					Total
					Total
					Total
					Total

For On-Set Notation

A.12: WARDROBE CONTINUITY SHEET

Character: _____

Production: _____

Telephone: _____

Actor: _____

Chg#	Sc#	I/E	Set/Action	D/N	Costume Notes - head to toe	Polaroids

For Budget

A.13: BUDGET SUMMARY COVER SHEET

Production: _____

COSTUME BUDGET SUMMARY
Prepared by: _____

From the script dated:

Principal Actors _____ Sub total

Supporting Cast _____ Sub total

Specialty Atmosphere & Extras _____ Sub total

Alterations _____ Sub total

Dyeing and Fabric Treatment _____ Sub total

Cleaning _____ Sub total

Supplies and Equipment _____ Sub total
(including wardrobe and office supplies)

Loss and Damage _____ Sub total

Miscellaneous _____ Sub total
(including facility fringe charges, Xeroxing, research, shipping,
sketch artists, and overhire set costumers)

Tax _____ Sub total

Total:

Budget conditions:

A.14: MASTER BUDGET BREAKDOWN: PRINCIPALS

Production: _____

Production # _____

Character/notes	Ch#	Sc#	Costume Pieces	MO	Rnt	Buy	Mult.	Sub total	Total

*Indicates possible promo goods

A.15: MASTER BUDGET BREAKDOWN: SUPPORTING ACTORS

Production: _____

Production # _____

Character/notes	Ch#	Sc#	Costume Pieces	MO	Rnt	Buy	Mult.	Sub total	Total

*Indicates possible promo goods

A.16: MASTER BUDGET BREAKDOWN: SPECIALTY ATMOSPHERE/GENERAL EXTRAS

Production # _____

Production: _____

Character/notes	Ch#	Sc#	Costume Pieces	MO	Rnt	Buy	Mult.	Sub total	Total

*Indicates possible promo goods

A.17: MASTER BUDGET BREAKDOWN: ADDITIONAL COSTS

Production: _____

Production # _____

Category	Overhire Services	Subtotal	Total
Supplies & Equipment			
Cleaning/Laundry			
Alterations			
Miscellaneous			
Tax			
Loss and Damage			

Hypothetical *Pulp Fiction* Project Budget Breakdown

A.18: BUDGET SUMMARY COVER SHEET

Production: Hypothetical *Pulp Fiction* Project

COSTUME BUDGET SUMMARY
Prepared by: _____ Holly Cole _____

From the script dated: _____ April 28 2000 _____

Principal Actors	Sub total	$81,853.00
Supporting Cast	Sub total	$5,437.00
Specialty Atmosphere & Extras	Sub total	$19,575.25
Alterations	Sub total	$6,852.00
Dyeing and Fabric Treatment	Sub total	$3,600.00
Cleaning	Sub total	$13,000.00
Supplies and Equipment	Sub total	$7,480.55
(including wardrobe and office supplies)		
Loss and Damage	Sub total	$10,686.00
Miscellaneous	Sub total	$3,951.45
(including facility fringe charges, Xeroxing, research, shipping, sketch artist costs, and overhire set costumers)		
Tax	Sub total	$11,694.29
	Total:	**$164,129.54**

Budget conditions: This preliminary budget was prepared without access to the director to help determine the exact number of required extras and stunt multiples. Star costumes were estimated before consultation with the actors.
    This budget assumes a feature film shooting period of 50 shooting days and a prep period of four weeks.

A.19: MASTER BUDGET BREAKDOWN: PRINCIPALS   Title: Hypothetical *Pulp Fiction* Project   Production #___

Character/notes	Ch#	Sc#	Costume Pieces	MO	Rnt	Buy	Mult.	Sub/total	Total
Vince	1	1,11-13	USanta Cruz tee shirt		$20.00			$20.00	$75.00
		112-119	Red shorts			$40.00		$40.00	
			thongs			$15.00		$15.00	
	2	2-8	black suit w/ thin lapel	$1,000.00			7	$7,000.00	$12,656.00
blood splash from Marvin	2D	93-99	white shirt			$50.00	7	$350.00	
phase1 bloody,stunt driver	2xs	105-111	thin black tie	$50.00			7	$350.00	
phase 2 bloody, wet	2xx		black belt			$20.00	2	$40.00	
			black sox			$10.00	2	$20.00	
			black shoes **			$138.00	2	$276.00	
			jewelry			$100.00	2	$100.00	
lose for scs 105-111			duster	$1,500.00			3	$4,500.00	
	3	14-15	jazzy black suit			$800.00	4	$3,200.00	$10,538.00
sweat potential for dance	3D	33-41	jazzy tie	$50.00			4	$200.00	
phase 1 distress from Mia	3x	16-35	white shirt			$50.00	4	$200.00	
driving double	3xs		black belt			rpt			
			black sox			rpt			
			slip on shoes **			$138.00		$138.00	
			overcoat			$800.00	4	$3,200.00	
	4	45-51	hit man black suit	$1,000.00			6	$6,000.00	$6,600.00
stunt double blown away	4s	60 &76	white shirt			$50.00	6	$300.00	
			thin black tie	$50.00			6	$300.00	
			jewelry			rpt			
			black shoes **	rpt					
			sox			rpt			
lose duster for shooting			duster	rpt					
Jules	1	1	I'm With Stupid tee shirt	$50.00				$50.00	$105.00
		11-13	White shorts			$40.00		$40.00	
		111-119	thongs			$15.00		$15.00	
	2	2-8	black suit w/ thin lapel	$1,000.00			7	$7,000.00	$12,636.00

*Indicates possible promo goods

A.20: MASTER BUDGET BREAKDOWN: PRINCIPALS

Title: Hypothetical *Pulp Fiction* Project   Production #_____

Character/notes	Ch#	Sc#	Costume Pieces	MO	Rnt	Buy	Mult.	Sub/total	Total
blood splash from Marvin	2d	93-96	white shirt			$50.00	7	$350.00	
phase1 bloody,stunt driver	2xs	97-107	thin black tie	$50.00			7	$350.00	
phase 2 bloody, wet	2xx	109-111	black belt			$20.00	2	$40.00	
			black sox			$10.00	2	$20.00	
			black shoes **			$138.00	2	$276.00	
			jewelry			$100.00		$100.00	
			duster	$1,500.00			3	$4,500.00	
Mia	1	18-24	designer blouse	$400.00			9	$3,600.00	$7,650.00
sweat potential, shoeless	1d	26-32	slacks			$250.00	5	$1,250.00	
		33-34	shoes **			$290.00	2	$580.00	
food stain,sweat potential		39	fancy bra/bustier	$200.00			5	$1,000.00	
lose jkt, nose bleed, vomit	1d	29-37	jacket			$1,200.00		$1,200.00	
phase 1 distress,stunt driver	1xs	41-49							
blouse rip, EFX chest stab	1xxs								
phase2 distress,driving double	1xxs	50-51	over shirt			$20.00		$20.00	
	2	60	dress **			$1,050.00		$1,050.00	
			jacket **			$2,000.00		$2,000.00	
			jewelry **			$400.00		$400.00	
			hose			$15.00		$15.00	
			pumps **			$100.00		$100.00	**$3,565.00**
	3	100	negligee **	$500.00				$500.00	
			slippers			$50.00		$50.00	$550.00
Marsellus	1	10-13	jazzy suit **			$1,500.00		$1,500.00	
			jazzy shirt **			$135.00		$135.00	
			sox			$10.00		$10.00	
			shoes **			$65.00		$65.00	
			jewelry **			$200.00		$200.00	$1,910.00
	2	60	jazzy suit **			$1,500.00		$1,500.00	
			jazzy shirt **			$170.00		$170.00	$1,715.00

*Indicates possible promo goods

A.21: MASTER BUDGET BREAKDOWN: PRINCIPALS   Title: Hypothetical *Pulp Fiction* Project   Production #___

Character/notes	Ch#	Sc#	Costume Pieces	MO	Rnt	Buy	Mult.	Sub/total	Total
	2	54	boxing trunks **			$75.00	3	$225.00	$2,565.00
stunt double, bloodied phase	2xs	56-61	boxing shoes **			$75.00	3	$225.00	
			boxing gloves **			$100.00		$100.00	
			sox			$5.00	3	$15.00	
			robe w/ "Battling Butch"	$1000.00			2	$2000.00	
	3	61	slip on pants			$35.00	2	$70.00	$120.00
gets rained on	3d	62-64	tee shirt			$25.00	2	$50.00	
			school jacket			rpt			
	4	66	boxer shorts			$10.00		$10.00	$10.00
	5	66-80	jeans			$35.00	11	$385.00	$4,739.00
stunt driver	5s		tee shirt			$12.00	12	$144.00	
distress phase 1	5x	80	sox			$5.00	3	$15.00	
stunt runner, distress doubles	5xs	80	tennis shoes **			$65.00	3	$195.00	
distress phase 2, stunt fighter	5xxs	81	high school jacket			$400.00	rpt +10	$4,000.00	
bloody phase 3, no jacket	5xxx	82-90							
Fabienne	1	64	dress			$200.00		$200.00	$350.00
lose layers for lovemaking			underwear			$150.00		$150.00	
	2	65	terry robe **			$70.00		$70.00	$70.00
	3	66	sleep shirt			$30.00		$30.00	$40.00
			underwear			$10.00		$10.00	
	4	88-90	Frankie says relax tee sh	$50				$50.00	$595.00
			pants			$70.00		$70.00	
			shoes **			$65.00		$65.00	
			sox			$20.00		$20.00	
			jewelry		$30			$30.00	
			jacket			$260.00		$260.00	
			purse			$100.00		$100.00	
Lance	1	15	red flannel shirt		$20.00			$20.00	$195.00
			speed racer tee shirt	$50				$50.00	

**indicates possible excess spends

A.22: MASTER BUDGET BREAKDOWN: PRINCIPALS   Title: Hypothetical *Pulp Fiction* Project   Production #____

Character/notes	Ch#	Sc#	Costume Pieces	MO	Rnt	Buy	Mult.	Sub/total	Total
			drawstring pants			$35.00		$35.00	
			sandals			$90.00		$90.00	
	2	44-49	tee shirt			rpt		$15.00	$35.00
			jams			$15.00		$20.00	
			bathrobe		$20.00				
Jody	1	14	tee shirt			$25.00		$25.00	$400.00
			overshirt			$50.00		$50.00	
			black jeans			$40.00		$40.00	
			jewelry		$30.00	$50.00		$80.00	
			sox			$5.00		$5.00	
			boots **			$200.00		$200.00	
	2	47-49	XL tee shirt w/Flintstone	$500.00				$50.00	$570.00
			robe			$70.00		$70.00	
Capt. Koons	1	53	Airforce captain's uniform		$200.00			$200.00	$200.00
Wolf	1	102-116	tux **		$125.00		2	$250.00	$390.00
			tux shirt **		$15.00		2	$30.00	
			tux accesories **		$30.00		2	$60.00	
stunt driver double			black sox			$10.00	2	$20.00	
wet potential			black shoes **		$15.00		2	$30.00	
Jimmie	1	99	bathrobe			$70.00	2	$140.00	$330.00
wet potential		105-114	tee shirt			$25.00	2	$50.00	
			pajama bottoms			$40.00	2	$80.00	
			slippers			$30.00	2	$60.00	
								Principals	
								Final	
								Total:	$81,853

* Indicates possible promo goods

A.23: MASTER BUDGET BREAKDOWN: SUPPORTING ACTORS   Title: Hypothetical _Pulp Fiction_ Project   Production #___

Character/notes	Ch#	Sc#	Costume Pieces	MO	Rnt	Buy	Mult.	Sub/total	Total
Brett	1	8	tee shirt			$6.00	8	$48.00	$676.00
2 phase shooting-shoulder&kill	1x		blue shirt			$25.00	8	$200.00	
stunt double	1xxs	93-94	khakis			$35.00	8	$280.00	
			sox			$2.00	2	$4.00	
			topsiders **			$72.00	2	$144.00	
Marvin (stunt man)	1	8	La coste shirt			$50.00	7	$350.00	$648.00
2 phase shooting	1x	93-95	jeans			$32.00	7	$224.00	
dummy double	1xxs	96-106	sox			$2.00	2	$4.00	
			sneakers **			$35.00	2	$70.00	
Roger (stunt man)	1 s	8	jams			$30.00	4	$120.00	$289.00
		93-94	tee shirt			$15.00	4	$60.00	
			sox			$2.00	2	$4.00	
			tennis shoes **			$35.00	3	$105.00	
Fourth College kid (stunt)	1 s	8	college sweatshirt			$45.00	4	$120.00	$271.00
bloody murder		92-94	jeans			$34.00	4	$136.00	
English Dave	1	12-13	jazzy shirt		$15.00			$15.00	$84.00
			slacks		$20.00			$20.00	
			sox			$4.00		$4.00	
			shoes **		$15.00			$15.00	
			jewelry		$30.00			$30.00	
	2	60	jazzy shirt		$15.00			$15.00	$124.00
			jacket		$45.00			$45.00	
			dress slacks		$20.00			$20.00	
			dress shoes **		$15.00			$15.00	
			sox			$4.00		$4.00	
			jewelry		$30.00			$30.00	
Esmarelda	1	56-63	floral shirt			$20.00	2	$40.00	$82.00
			jeans		$15.00			$15.00	
Esmarelda driver double	1 s		boots **		$15.00			$15.00	

*Indicates possible promo goods

A.24: MASTER BUDGET BREAKDOWN: SUPPORTING ACTORS   Title: Hypothetical *Pulp Fiction* Project   Production

Character/notes	Ch#	Sc#	Costume Pieces	MO	Rnt	Buy	Mult.	Sub/total	Total
rain splash potential			sox			$2.00			
			jewelry		$10.00				
Maynard	1	81-86	tee shirt			$6.00	6	$36.00	$760.00
dirt potential from Marsellus			jeans			$35.00	6	$210.00	
gets chest slit, stunt double 1s			western belt			$25.00	2	$50.00	
			flannel shirt			$30.00	6	$180.00	
			trucker cap			$15.00	2	$30.00	
			western boots **			$125.00	2	$250.00	
			sox			$2.00	2	$4.00	
Zed	1	82-86	cop shirt			$40.00	6	$240.00	$632.00
shot in groin, stunt double 1s			cop slacks			$49.00	6	$294.00	
			belt			$15.00	2	$30.00	
			motorcycle boots**		$20.00		2	$40.00	
			sox			$2.00	2	$4.00	
			patches			$6.00	4	$24.00	
The Gimp	1	82-85	mask			$300.00	2	$300.00	$1,240.00
gets beaten			leather jock strap			$400.00		$400.00	
			leather leggings			$200.00		$200.00	
			leather chest straps			$200.00		$200.00	
			gloves			$40.00		$40.00	
			boots **			$100.00		$100.00	
Monster Joe	1 *	115	dirty tee shirt			$6.00	6	$6.00	$35.00
			work shirt		$7.50			$7.50	
			jeans		$12.00			$12.00	
			sox			$2.00		$2.00	
			shoes		$7.50			$7.50	
Raquel	1 *	116	flannel shirt		$15.00			$15.00	$55.00
			knit top		$8.00			$8.00	
			jeans		$15.00				

*Indicates possible promo goods

A.25: MASTER BUDGET BREAKDOWN: SUPPORTING ACTORS   Title: Hypothetical *Pulp Fiction* Project   Production #___

Character/notes	Ch#	Sc#	Costume Pieces	MO	Rnt	Buy	Mult.Sub/total	Total
			sox			$2.00		
Trudi	1 *	14	shoes **		$15.00			$65.00
			shirt layers		$15.00			
			shirt		$15.00			
			sandals**		$15.00			
		44-49	jeans		$20.00			
Buddy Holly (prefit)	1	31-34	dinner jacket&tux pants		$125.00			$158.00
			formal accesories		$15.00			
			dress shoes **		$15.00			
			sox			$3.00		
Ed Sullivan (prefit)	1	31-34	grey suit		$100.00			$138.00
			thin tie		$5.00			
			white shirt		$15.00			
			dress shoes **		$15.00			
			sox			$3.00		
Young Butch (prefit)	1	53	tee shirt		$10.00			$38.00
			shorts		$15.00			
			sox			$3.00		
			sneakers **		$10.00			
Butch's Mom (prefit)	1	53	dress		$40.00			$67.00
			hose			$12.00		
			pumps **		$15.00			
Klondike	1 *	54	casual shirt		$7.50			$75.00
			slacks		$12.00			
			zip jacket		$45.00			
			shoes **		$7.50			
			sox			$3.00		
							Supporting Player	
							Grand Total	$5,437.00

*Indicates possible name goods

A.26: MASTER BUDGET BREAKDOWN: SPECIALTY ATMOSPHERE/GENERAL EXTRAS

Title: Hypothetical _Pulp Fiction_ Project
Production # _____

Character/notes	Ch#	Sc#	Costumes	MO	Rnt	Buy	Mult.	Sub/total	Total
Denny's waitresses (2x1.5)	1	1,117-119	uniform		$55.50		3**	$166.50	$166.50
Denny's manager(1x1.5)	1	1,117-119	Suit+ access		$131.00		1.5***	$196.50	$196.50
Denny's cooks(3x1.5)	1	1,117-119	uniform		$88.00		4.5***	$396.00	$396.00
Denny's busboys(2x1.5)	1	1,117-119	uniform		$62.00		3**	$186.00	$186.00
Denny's patrons (35x.5)	1	1,117-119							
casual men(12x.5)			casual day*		$50.00		6*	$300.00	$300.00
casual women(10x.5)			casual day*		$50.00		5*	$250.00	$250.00
businessmen(5x.5)			biz day*		$108.00		2.5*	$270.00	$270.00
character men(3x.5)			casual day*		$60.00		1.5*	$90.00	$90.00
children(5x.5)	1		casual day*		$50.00		2.5*	$125.00	$125.00
College apt. dwellers(5x.5)	1	4	college casual*						
frat boys(2x.5)					$50.00		1*	$50.00	$50.00
sorority girls(2x.5)					$50.00		1*	$50.00	$50.00
punk guy(1x.5)					$50.00		0.5*	$25.00	$25.00
Ricky Nelson (prefit)	1	31-34	50's idol		$108.00	$4.50		$112.50	$112.50
Marilyn Monroe prefit	1	31-34	7 year itch idol	$1000.00	$30.00	$4.50		$1,034.50	$1,034.50
Zorro (prefit)	1	31-34	50's idol		$115.00	$4.50		$119.50	$119.50
James Dean (prefit)	1	31-34	50's idol		$37.50	$69.50		$107.00	$107.00
Donna Reed (prefit)	1	31-34	50's idol		$100.00	$4.50		$104.50	$104.50
Dean Martin (prefit)	1	31-34	50's idol		$170.00	$4.50		$174.50	$174.50
Jerry Lewis (prefit)	1	31-34	50's idol		$170.00	$4.50		$174.50	$174.50
Phillip Morris midget(prefit)	1	31-34	bell hop uniform		$150.00	$4.50		$154.50	$154.50
Mamie Van Doren (prefit)	1	31-34	50's idol		$70.00	$4.50		$74.50	$74.50
Slim's uniformed staff	1	30-34							
carhops(1x1.5)	1		50's uniform		$125.00		1.5**	$187.50	$187.50
busboys(2x1.5)			50's uniform		$100.00		3**	$300.00	$300.00
bartenders(2x1.5)			50's uniform		$125.00		3**	$375.00	$375.00

*Indicates possible pull from the actor's own wardrobe. The extras that are supplying their own clothing will need an additional 50% of outfits for color coverage
**An additional 50% of outfits will be needed for coverage for late casting.

A.27: MASTER BUDGET BREAKDOWN: SPECIALTY ATMOSPHERE/GENERAL EXTRAS   Title: Hypothetical _Pulp Fiction_ Project
Production # ___

Character/notes	Ch#	Sc#	Costumes	MO	Rnt	Buy	Mult.	Sub/total	Total
Elvis(prefit)			50's icon		$128.00	$4.50		$132.50	$132.50
Brenda Lee(prefit)			50's icon		$106.00	$4.50		$110.50	$110.50
Jerry Lee Lewis(prefit)			50's icon		$128.00	$4.50		$132.50	$132.50
back up musicians(4x1.5)			50's rock		$128.00	$4.50	6**	$795.00	$795.00
Slim's patrons (120x.5)	1	31-34							
Melrose upscale casual men(30x.5)			upscale sporty*		$118.00		15*	$1,770.00	$1,770.00
rose upscale casual women(30x.5)			upscale sporty*		$111.00		15*	$1,665.00	$1,665.00
Dressy casual men(20x.5)			dressy casual*		$195.00		10*	$1,950.00	$1,950.00
Dressy casual women(20x.5)			dressy casual*		$171.00		10*	$1,710.00	$1,710.00
Twist men(10x.5)			dressy casual*		$118.00		5*	$590.00	$590.00
Twist women(10x.5)			dressy casual*		$111.00		5*	$555.00	$555.00
Dead Willis bloody (prefit)	1	60	boxing outfit			$150.00		$150.00	$150.00
Willis's trainer(1x1.5)	1	60	casual sport		$50.00		1.5**	$75.00	$75.00
Fight crowd(85x.5)	4	60							
tough hoods(10x.5)			casual daywear*		$108.00		5*	$540.00	$540.00
upscale casual men(20x.5)			dressy daywear*		$118.00		10*	$1,180.00	$1,180.00
upscale casual women(10x.5)			dressy daywear*		$111.00		5*	$555.00	$555.00
character men(15x.5)			casual daywear*		$108.00		7.5*	$810.00	$810.00
ordinary men(30x.5)			casual daywear*		$50.00		15*	$750.00	$750.00
Looky loo (stuntwoman)	1d	80	casual daywear			$85.00	3	$255.00	$255.00
Accident bystanders(6x.5)	1	80	casual daywear*		$50.00		3*	$150.00	$150.00
Camaro driver (stunt man)	1	80	casual daywear		$50.00			$50.00	$50.00
Gamblers(5x.5)	1	102	tuxes*		$125.50		2.5*	$313.75	$313.75
Lucky Ladies (2x.5)	1		dressy cocktail*		$125.00		1*	$125.00	$125.00
Croupier(1x1.5)	1	102	spencer tux		$125.00		1.5**	$187.50	$187.50
								Extras total	$19,575.25

*Indicates possible pull from the actor's own wardrobe. The extras that are supplying their own clothing will need an additional 50% of outfits for color coverage
**An additional 50% of outfits will be needed for coverage for late casting.

A.28: MASTER BUDGET BREAKDOWN: ADDITIONAL COSTS

Title: Hypothetical *Pulp Fiction* Project
Production #____

Category	Overhire Services	Subtotal	Total
Principal players $81,853+Supporting Cast $5,437 + Extras $19,575= the materials budget $106,865		$106,865	
Supplies & Equipment	7% of the materials budget($106,865)	$7,480.55	$7,480.55
Cleaning/Laundry	$200 a day for 50 shooting days for a generally low key design	$10,000.00	$13,000.00
	+ a full cleaning at wrap	$3,000.00	
Dying and Fabric Treatment	three 40 hour weeks of dying and distressing @ $30 an hour	$3,600.00	$3,600.00
Alterations			
@ $28 an hour	29 principal chnges x 6 hrs of alterations	$4,872.00	$6,852.00
@ $18 an hour	28 changes for featured specialty characters x 3 hours each	$1,746.00	
@ $18 an hour	13 major multiples @ 1 hour per	$234.00	
Miscellaneous			
Overhire set costumers @$216 a day	for Jackrabbit Slim's- 5 set costumers for 1 day,2 for 3 days	$2,376.00	$3,951.45
	for the fights- 2 set costumers for 1 day	$432.00	
Xeroxing, shipping	.1% of the combined materials and supplies budget($114,345.55)	$1,143.45	
Tax	8.25% of the combined materials, supplies, and services budget.	$11,694.29	$11,694.29
	($106865 +$7,480.55+ $13,000+$3,600+$6852+$3,951.45=$141,749 combined budget)		
Loss and Damage	10% of the materials budget	$10,686.00	$10,686.00
Loss and damage costs are sometimes			
hidden in the rest of the budget			
in order to create a contingency that			
won't get cut. You may want			
to let your producers know that			
you're giving your department			
a contingency, but keep the			
amount quiet.			

The question of how many supplies you need in your kit gets varied responses from film professionals. High-budg[et] productions will provide many general supplies; low-budget productions will provide as few as they can get away with. If y[ou] wish to make yourself indispensable, have the large kit detailed in the following three lists and keep track of the expendab[le] supplies you use on the job. If you want to pinch pennies, go with the essential on-set kit to handle minor emergencies.

A.29: THE ESSENTIAL ON-SET KIT

In your waistpouch or on your person:

*Topstick	$3.50
*2" safety pins	
*small safety pins	$5.25
small scissors	
*garment tags	$2.00
pre-threaded multi needle & thread kit	$6.25
lint brush	
*call sheet	$0.57
*mini scene pages	$8.00
3" ring for Polaroids	$1.00
single hole punch	$18.00
fine-line Sharpie	$1.75
small Snakelight	$2.98
tailor's chalk	
Stain Stick	
*Polaroid lables	$35.00
set chair	
Plus any emergency on-site changes the actors may need in order to speed the filming.	

In your set bag:

a mini office: Polaroid camera & *film	$45.00
pencils & mini sharpener	$50.00
Sharpie fine-points	$2.29
*tape dispenser(s)	$2.00
*White-out	
highlighter	$1.15
mini stapler and staples	$3.00
Post-it pads or notepad	$1.15
*garment tags	
*binder with character continuity forms	
*dividers, Polaroid lables, character tabs	
*blank continuity forms	
*Polaroids of characters	
first aid kit: aspirin	$1.00
Tampax/panty liners	$3.00
Band-Aids	$1.50
sunblock	$4.00
insect repellant	$4.00
Binaca	$2.00
tube of Barge	$3.00
water spritzer	$2.75
small jewelry repair kit	$2.00
epoxy	$5.00
Super Glue	$7.50
optional aging kit: Schmutz stick set	$2.75
*glycerine and Fullers Earth	$7.75
pounce bag and oil rags	$2.00
sandpaper	$0.69

sewing kit: small varied thread kit

*safety pins	$2.50
seam ripper	$1.20
elastic	$2.50
*small bag of buttons	
small bag of fasteners	$4.50
Buttoneer & refills	$22.00
cleaning kit:	
hairspray	$1.25
small container of Picrin	$1.29
Picrin rag in Ziplock	
small Zout	$6.00
mini Lexol with rag	$5.00
colored tailor's chalks	$2.15
hand steamer	$35.00
hairdryer & extension cord	$23.00
*Wet Ones towelettes	
dressing kit:	
*Static Guard	
*moleskin	
*insole sets	
*heel grips	
shoe horn	$0.50
clear nail polish	$1.00
Zipper-ease wax	$1.20
crochet hook	$1.85
leather punch	$18.00
*Topstick	
emergency accessories:	
*sound buffer supplies	
*shoe laces	
*modesty supplies	

A.30: THE PERSONAL AT-THE-TRAILER KIT

Item	$	Item	$	Item	$
Office Supplies: 3-hole punch	$5.00	assorted Schmutz sticks	$45.00	Fraycheck	$3.15
stapler & staples	$6.00	assorted Fullers Earth pounce bags	$17.00	Stitch-Witch	$1.75
staple remover	$1.29	oil rags in Ziplocks	$6.00	assorted bias tape, hem tape	$10.00
calculator	$4.00	Old English polish	$4.50	assorted fasteners	$16.00
12" ruler	$1.00	candles & matches	$1.60	assorted threads	$13.25
Glue Stick	$2.19	wire brush, rasp, sandpaper	$40.00	assorted buttons	$10.00
paper scissors	$5.00	sponge, plastic scrubber	$4.00	thimble	$1.35
duct tape	$3.00	glycerine	$6.00	poly batting	$2.50
rubber stamp for tagging	$13.50	mineral oil	$4.00	**Cleaning supplies:**	$13.00
stamp pad	$3.50	bucket	$6.00	silver-cleaning cloth	$3.00
Equipment: rolling racks (2)	$260.00	matt knife & blades	$4.50	suede brush	$2.00
3-way grounded plug	$1.69	dulling spray	$3.50	Carbona spotting bottle	$1.30
10' grounded extension cord & adaptor	$9.25	**for millinery-** hat stretcher ring	$70.00	dish soap	$1.30
clip lamp & extension cord	$11.50	spray hat sizing	$7.00	Clear Choice or Picrin	$25.50
golf umbrella	$14.00	horsehair braid	$4.00	iron cleaner	$3.50
rain poncho	$2.50	millinery wire	$10.00	assorted shoe polishes	$15.00
steamer	$165.00	wire cutter	$3.00	shoe brush & cloths	$4.25
iron & ironing board	$41.00	hat sizing foam	$5.00	Military shine	$5.00
sleeve board	$40.00	**adhesives-** E6000	$6.00	Stain Stick	$3.00
velvet board	$19.00	spray adhesive	$7.50	trash bags	$4.00
spritz bottle	$2.00	Sobo	$2.00	EndBac	$7.00
carry-alls for supplies	$7.00	Duco cement	$3.00	**Dressing supplies:** ring	$10.00
Craft supplies: Hudson sprayer	$32.00	hot glue gun & pellets	$23.00	shoe sizer	$35.00
clothes line & pins	$6.30	Fabri-tac glue	$5.00	no skid pads for shoes	$1.50
for distressing- respirator	$35.00	Barge	$2.75	heel grips	$1.50
Bluettes gloves	$5.00	**Sewing Supplies:** sewing machine	$400.00	assorted shoe insole sets	$20.00
apron	$5.00	sewing machine oil	$2.75	assorted shoe laces	$10.00
particle masks	$0.50	8" shears, pinking shears	$18.00	Shoe Stretch & stretchers	$16.00
Preval sprayers (3)	$16.50	hem marker	$3.00	bra back repair kit	$3.75
spritz bottle	$2.00	tracing wheel & paper	$6.30	collar stays	$1.35
bleach	$1.30	measuring tape	$1.25	collar extenders	$2.35
assorted Magix (4)	$32.00	seam ripper	$1.90	shirt studs	$10.00
assorted fabric paints and brushes	$30.00	18" ruler	$4.15	bust & shoulder pads	$7.50
leather dyes	$15.00	magnet box of straight pins	$2.45	knee pads	$8.00
shellac	$5.50	needles: hand, machine, leather	$8.00	elbow pads	$8.00
alcohol	$10.00	beeswax	$2.00	Ace bandage(s)	$4.00

A.31: THE EXTENDED PERSONAL KIT

Office Supplies:	airbrush gun & compressor	paper towels
portable computer	buckets	Lysol
portable printer	box of examination gloves	towels
computer paper	dye – assorted colors	more of any general cleaning supplies
power strip & adaptor	dye measuring spoons	**Dressing supplies:**
computer carry all	Ivory Liquid or Synthrapol	sweater comb eyeglass repair kit
zip-up binder/carry all	Cassalene	dress shields
rubber stamps & pad	fabric softener	**underwear-** assorted sizes & styles
rubber bands	Neatsfoot Oil	v-neck & crew-neck tees
paper clips	stage blood	men's briefs & jock supports
Stock Equipment:	more of any of the paint and distressing supplies	bras & panties
hangers: padded, muslin-covered rolling racks	listed in the previous lists	assorted slips
jewelry compartment storage	dance rubber	**general supplies-** athletic sox assorted
garment bags	**Craft supplies for shoe work:**	men's dress sox assorted
clothes dividers	grommet set & 00 grommets	nylons & knee sox
styrofoam heads or hat blocks	eyelets & eyelet punch	handkerchiefs & scarves
tagging gun	more of any of the shoe and leatherwork	cuff links & stud sets
General tools & equipment:	supplies listed previously	jewelry of all varieties
fire extinguisher water cooler	**Sewing Supplies:** overlock machine	belts & suspenders
clip lamps & cords	overlock tweezers	boot jacks & hooks
flashlights	overlock thread	**modesty wear:** jocks
bungies	dress forms	body stockings & G-strings
bulletin board	loop turner	penis sox
stools	10" shears, 5" tailor snips	set robes
staple gun & staples	boning	**foul weather gear:**
hammer	bobbins	rain suits sun hats
pliers	interfacings	umbrellas
swiss army knife	iron-on patches	rain ponchos
X-Acto knife & blades	marking pencils	galoshes
awl	muslin	thermals
screwdrivers, assorted	push pins & t pins	**stunt support:** elbow, shin & knee pads
hand drill	zippers	**sound support:** baby bottle nipples
sabre saw	more of any sewing notions	sound booties
WD40 detergent	**Cleaning supplies:**	foot foam
nail and fastener assortment	Woolite	
Craft supplies:	lingerie bags	
paint & dye kit		
hot plates & dye tubs	broom, whisk broom & dust pan	

General supplies

- Fabric steamer
- Steam iron
- Plastic bins
- Clothes line
- Clothes pins
- Spritz bottle for water
- Spritz bottle for bleach water
- Extra spritz bottles
- Hudson sprayer
- Towels
- Buckets

Safety supplies

- Custom-fit Respirator with organic vapor cartridges and paint pre-filters
- Dust masks
- Safety goggles
- Rubber gloves
- Lab coat or paint smock

Dye supplies & equipment

- Synthrapol or Ivory Liquid
- Color remover
- Bleach
- Assorted fabric dyes (Rit, Tintex, Putnam, Pro-Chem, Aljo, etc.) in a variety of colors* and types (including union dyes, silk (acid) dyes cotton/rayon dyes, acetate/nylon dyes, fiber reactive dyes)
- Dye additives including:
- Cassalene
- Vinegar

- Salt
- Soda Ash
- Baking Soda
- Assorted colors of leather dyes
- Denatured Alcohol
- Garbage bags
- Multi-burner hot plates
- X-large steel canning pots
- Small steel pots
- Dowel or x-long spoon
- Hot pads
- Pint canning jars
- Quart canning jars
- * minimally have a variety of union dye colors to cover cool and warm teching

Paint supplies & equipment

- Magix (or NU Life Spray in a variety of colors including: Champagne, Brown, Black Avocado, Smoked Elk, Saddle, Grey, Olive)
- Airbrush fabric paints in assorted colors (Createx, Versatex brands)
- Reel blood
- Air brush & hoses
- Portable air compressor
- Airbrush bottles & custom lids
- Extension chords
- Fine-mesh screening
- Pipe cleaners
- Mineral spirits
- Assorted paint brushes
- Tooth brushes

Distressing supplies & equipment

- Fabric softener
- Laundry detergent
- Bleach
- Sand paper
- Paper towels
- Deglazing fluid
- Neatsfoot Oil
- Schmutz sticks in assorted colors
- Fullers Earth in assorted colors
- Mineral Oil
- Glycerine
- Cloth baby diapers
- Cheese cloth
- Gallon Ziplock bags
- Old English furniture polish in assorted colors
- Twill tape
- Safety pins
- Shellac
- Wax shoe polish in assorted colors
- Surform files (different sizes)
- Electric sander
- Seam ripper
- Scissors

A.33: PRIORITY MEASUREMENT FORM [WOMEN]

FITTING: _____

ACTRESS _____ PHONE _____ SCENE/CHARACTER _____

HEIGHT _____ WEIGHT _____ HAIR COLOR _____ SKIN TONE _____

SHOE _____ FOOT ISSUES* _____ HOSE _____

BUST _____ BRA _____ HIP _____ WAIST _____ INSEAM _____

DRESS SIZE _____ SWEATER _____ HAT/HEAD _____ GLOVES _____

CORRECTIVE LENSES _____ PIERCED EARS _____ ALLERGIES _____

RING SIZE _____ WRIST SIZE _____

PRIORITY MEASUREMENT FORM [MEN]

FITTING: _____

ACTOR _____ PHONE _____ SCENE/CHARACTER _____

HEIGHT _____ WEIGHT _____ HAIR COLOR _____ SKIN TONE _____

SHOE _____ FOOT ISSUES* _____ TEE _____ JOCK _____

CHEST _____ WAIST _____ INSEAM _____

SHIRT: neck _____ sleeve length _____

SUIT SIZE _____ SWEATER _____ HAT/HEAD _____ GLOVES _____

CORRECTIVE LENSES _____ PIERCED EARS _____ ALLERGIES _____

RING SIZE _____ WRIST SIZE _____

* "Foot issues" refers to actor problems or preferences that have an impact on the fit of shoes. For example, arch supports, bunions, or different foot injuries can affect the style of shoe that is acceptable to the actor.

List of Current Designers with Major Careers

PERIOD WORK

James Acheson. *Time Bandits* (1981), *Brazil* (1985), *The Last Emperor* (1987), *Dangerous Liaisons* (1988), *Restoration* (1994), *Spider-Man* (2002), *Daredevil* (2003), *Spider-Man II* (2004)

Milena Canonero. *Barry Lyndon* (1975), *Chariots of Fire* (1981), *Out of Africa* (1985), *Dick Tracy* (1990), *Titus* (1999), *Bulworth* (1998), *In the Boom-Boom Room* (2000), *Affair of the Necklace* (2001), *Solaris* (2004)

Yvonne Blake. *Nicholas and Alexandra* (1972), *The Three Musketeers* (1973), *What Dreams May Come* (1998), *Carmen* (2003), *The Bridge of San Luis Rey* (2004), *Joan of Arc, The Virgin Warrior* (2004)

Gabriella Pescucci. *Age of Innocence* (1993), *Les Misérables* (1997), *Dangerous Beauty* (1998), *Van Helsing* (2004)

Jenny Beavan and John Bright. *Room with a View* (1986), *Howard's End* (1992), *Sense and Sensibility* (1995), *Anna and the King* (1999), *Tea with Mussolini* (1999)

And Ms. Beavan has additionally designed: *Gosford Park* (2001), *Possession* (2002), *Timeline* (2004)

Deborah Scott. *Titanic* (1998), *Legends of the Fall* (1998), *Wild, Wild West* (1999), *The Patriot* (2000), *Minority Report* (2002), *Bad Boys II* (2004)

HIGH CONCEPT & PERIOD WORK

Anthony Powell. *Nicholas and Alexandra* (1972), *Death on the Nile* (1978), *Tess* (1980), *Evil Under the Sun* (1982), *Indiana Jones and the Temple of Doom* (1984), *Hook* (1991), *101 Dalmations* (1996), *The Avengers* (1998), *102 Dalmations* (2000)

Colleen Atwood. *Edward Scissorhands* (1993), *Philadelphia* (1993), *Little Women* (1994), *Ed Wood* (1995), *Wyatt Earp* (1995), *Mars Attacks* (1996), *Gattaca* (1996), *Planet of the Apes* (2001), *Chicago* (2002), *Big Fish* (2003)

Julie Weiss. *Twelve Monkeys* (1995), *A Simple Plan* (1998), *American Beauty* (1999), *Frida* (2002), *The Ring* (2002), *The Missing* (2004)

Rita Ryack. *Apollo 13* (1995), *Ed* (1999), *How the Grinch Stole Christmas* (2000), *The Human Stain* (2003), *The Cat in the Hat* (2003)

SCIENCE FICTION

John Bloomfield. *Conan the Barbarian* (1982), *Waterworld* (1995), *The Postman* (1997), *The Mummy* (1999), *The Scorpion King* (2002), *Being Julia* (2003), *The Chronicles of Riddick* (2004)

Bob Blackman. *Star Trek* (the series, 1992-1994), *Star Trek: Generations* (1994), *Enterprise* (series 2001), *Enterprise: Broken Bow* (2001, TV)

Bob Ringwood. *Dune* (1984), *Batman* (1989), *Alien III* (1992), *Artificial Intelligence: AI* (2001), *Star Trek: Nemesis* (2002)

Jean-Paul Gaultier. *The Cook, the Wife, the Thief, and the Lover* (1989), *The City of Lost Children* (1996), *The Fifth Element* (1997)

Deborah Everton. *The Abyss* (1989), *Earth 2* (TV series 1994), *Virus* (1999), *Spy Kids* (2001), *Clockstoppers* (2002), *The In-Laws* (2003)

Joseph Porro. *Tombstone* (1993), *Stargate* (1994), *Independence Day* (1996), *Stuart Little* (1999), *Shanghai Noon* (2000), *Equilibrium* (2002)

STRONG AND ECCENTRIC CHARACTER DESIGNS

Ruth Carter. *Malcolm X* (1993), *Amistad* (1997), *Dr. Doolittle II* (2001), *I Spy* (2002), *Daddy Day Care* (2003), *Against the Ropes* (2003)

Deborah Nadoolman. *The Blues Brothers* (1980), *Raiders of the Lost Ark* (1981), *Coming to America* (1988), *The Stupids* (1996), *Mad City* (1997), *Susan's Plan* (1998), *Blues Brothers 2000* (1998)

Jeff Kurland. *Radio Days* (1987), *Bullets Over Broadway* (1994), *Man on the Moon* (1999), *Erin Brockovich* (2000), *What's the Worst That Could Happen?* (2001), *America's Sweethearts* (2001) (for Julia Roberts), *Ocean's Eleven* (2001), *Hidalgo* (2003)

Judianna Makovsky. *Big* (1988), *Reversal of Fortune* (1990), *Pleasantville* (1997), *Legend of Bagger Vance* (2000), *Harry Potter and the Sorcerer's Stone* (2001), *Seabiscuit* (2003)

Joanna Johnston. *Forrest Gump* (1995), *Saving Private Ryan* (1998), *Sixth Sense* (1999), *Unbreakable* (2000), *Castaway* (2000), *About a Boy* (2002), *Love Actually* (2003)

Aggie Guerard Rogers. *American Graffiti* (1973), *The Return of the Jedi* (1983), *The Color Purple* (1985), *Beetlejuice* (1988), *The Fugitive* (1993), *Mr. Holland's Opus* (1995), *The Hurricane* (1999), *Rockstar* (2001), *Holes* (2003), *The Assassination of Richard Nixon* (2004)

STYLISH MODERN DRESS

Ellen Mirojnick. *Wall Street* (1987), *Basic Instinct* (1992), *Chaplin* (1993), *Face/Off* (1997), *What Women Want* (2000), *Don't Say a Word* (2001), *Unfaithful* (2002), *It Runs in the Family* (2003), *The Blackout Murders* (2004)

Bernie Pollack. *The Natural* (1984), *Rain Man* (1988), *A River Runs Through It* (1992), *Clear and Present Danger* (1994), *The Horse Whisperer* (1998), *Message in a Bottle* (1999), *What Lies Beneath* (2000), *Hollywood Homicide* (2003)

Robert Turturice. Television series *Arliss, Cybill, Moonlighting; Batman and Robin* (1997), *The Flintstones in Viva Rock Vegas* (2000)

Marlene Stewart. *JFK* (1991), *Terminator II* (1991), *The Doors* (1991), *True Lies* (1994), *The X Files* (1998), *Gone in 60 Seconds* (2000), *Adventures of Rocky & Bullwinkle* (2000), *Coyote Ugly* (2000), *Ali* (2001), *Tears of the Sun* (2003), *21 Trams* (2003)

Gloria Gresham. *When Harry Met Sally* (1989), *Avalon* (1990), *6 Days 7 Nights* (1998), *The Kid* (2000), *The Hunted* (2003), *Envy* (2003), *Providence* (2004)

Nolan Miller. Television series, including *Dynasty, Charlie's Angels, Life of the Party: The Pamela Harriman Story* (1998)

UP-AND-COMING DESIGNERS

Sandy Powell. *Shakespeare in Love* (1998), *Velvet Goldmine* (1998), *Gangs of New York* (2002), *Far From Heaven* (2002), *Sylvia* (2003), *The Aviator* (2004)

Deena Appel. *Austin Powers* (1997), *Bedazzled* (2000), *Austin Powers in Goldmember* (2002), *Stuck on You* (2003)

Wendy Chuck. *Varsity Blues* (1999), *Election* (1999), *About Schmidt* (2001), *Bad Santa* (2003), *Saved* (2003)

Denise Wingate. *Melrose Place* (TV series 1992-1996), *Cruel Intentions* (1999), *She's All That* (1999), *Soul Survivors* (2000), *Novocaine* (2001), *The Sweetest Thing* (2002), *Radio* (2003), *The Cinderella Story* (2004)

Mona May. *Clueless* (1995), *The Wedding Singer* (1998), *Never Been Kissed* (1999), *Loser* (2000), *Stuart Little II* (2002), *Master of Disguise* (2002), *The Haunted Mansion* (2003)

Louise Mingenbach. *The Usual Suspects* (1995), *X-Men* (2000), *K-Pax* (2001), *X-2* (2003), *The Rundown* (2003), *Starsky & Hutch* (2003)

Mark Bridges. *Boogie Nights* (1997), *Magnolia* (1999), *Blow* (2001), *Punch-Drunk Love* (2002), *8 Mile* (2002), *The Italian Job* (2003)

Molly Maginnis. *As Good As It Gets* (1997), *Mighty Joe Young* (1998), *Town and Country* (2001), *Life as a House* (2001), *Dreamcatcher* (2003)

Isis Mussenden. *The Astronaut's Wife* (1999), *American Psycho* (2000), *Thirteen Days* (2000), *Shrek* (2001), *Jay and Silent Bob Strike Back* (2001), *The Breakup Handbook* (2004), *Havana Nights: Dirty Dancing II* (2004)

Kym Barrett. *Romeo & Juliet* (1997), *Matrix* (1998), *Red Planet* (2000), *From Hell* (2001), *The Matrix Reloaded* (2003), *Gothika* (2003)

Ruth Myers. *The Addams Family* (1991), *LA Confidential* (1997), *Emma* (1997), *Proof of Life* (2000), *Iris* (2001), *The Four Feathers* (2002), *Nicholas Nickleby* (2002), *Carnivale* (TV series–HBO 2003)

Resumes are reconfigured by the type of job that you are going for. Note the way Jean mentions the production format, stars, and key job contact sources. These are two different resumes that Jean submits depending on the available job.

Jean Rosone
Home address
home phone number, pager number
work phone number

COSTUME DESIGNER:

HIJACKED: FLIGHT 285 MOW HILL FIELD ENT.
Ally Sheedy, Perry King, James Brolin, Michael Gross
1995 contemporary drama
Charlie Correl, director

THE CHRISTMAS BOX* MOW THE POLSON CO.
BONNEVILLE PROD.
Richard Thomas, Maureen O'Hara, Annette O'Toole
1995 contemporary drama
Marcus Cole, director
1996 Emmy Award

RETURN TO PARADISE MOW TOPEKA PROD.
Shelley Long, Mel Harris, Delane Matthews
1994 contemporary, 3 ladies go on spring break
Bill Norton, director

A PLACE TO BE LOVED MOW THE POLSON CO.
Richard Crenna, Linda Kelsey, Rhea Perlman
1992 contemporary, the authorized story of Gregory K.
Sandy Smolen, director

A MESSAGE FROM HOLLY MOW THE POLSON CO.
Shelley Long, Lindsay Wagner
1992 contemporary Southwest
Rod Holcomb, director

SINS OF THE MOTHER MOW THE POLSON CO.
Elizabeth Montgomery, Dale Midkiff
1990 contemporary Northwest, upper class
John Patterson, director

GUESS WHO'S COMING FOR CHRISTMAS MOW THE POLSON CO.
Richard Mulligan, Beau Bridges, Barbara Barrie
1990 contemporary midwest small town
Paul Schneider, director

TURNER AND HOOCH* FEATURE TOUCHSTONE
Tom Hanks, Mare Winningham, Craig T. Nelson
1989 contemporary police story
Roger Spottiswoode, director

Jean Rosone
Home address
home phone number, pager number
work phone number

KEY COSTUMER / SUPERVISOR:

GET REAL SERIES 20TH CENT. FOX
Jon Tenney, Debrah Farrentino, 3 teenagers
1999 - 2000 contemporary family
Sharon Day, Kathleen Detoro, Costume Designers

SHANGHAI NOON FEATURE EAST WEST PICTURES
Jackie Chan, Owen Wilson, Lucy Liu
1870's western
Joseph Porro, designer

THE ARMY SHOW SERIES WARNER BROS.
Dave Higgins, John Sencio, Harold Sylvester
1998 contemporary "Sgt Bilko" - type show
Sharon Day, designer

THE 13TH FLOOR FEATURE CENTROPOLIS
Craig Bierko, Gretchen Mol, Vincent D'Onofrio, Armin Mueller-Stahl
1937, 1998, & future sci-fi
Josef Rusnak, director / Joseph Porro, designer

GODZILLA FEATURE BIG FIN PRODS.
Matthew Broderick, Jean Reno, Hank Azaria, Maria Pitillo
1997 contemporary sci-fi
Roland Emmerich, director / Joseph Porro, designer

HARD RAIN (aka THE FLOOD) FEATURE THE FLOOD PROD.
Morgan Freeman, Christian Slater, Randy Quaid, Minnie Driver
1996 contemporary drama
Mikael Salomon, director / Kathleen Detoro, designer

OVERNIGHT DELIVERY FEATURE SPECIAL DELIVERY PROD.
Paul Rudd, Reese Witherspoon, Larry Drake
1996 contemporary comedy
Jason Bloom, director / Kathleen Detoro, designer

A DANGEROUS HEART CABLE CITADEL ENT.
Peter Onorati, Alice Krige, Richard Portnow
1995 contemporary
John Harrison, director / Kathleen Detoro, designer

THE GREAT MOM SWAP MOW GETTING OUT PROD.
Shelley Fabares, Valerie Harper, Sid Caesar
1995 contemporary , Jr. Hi School kids and their families
Jonathan Prince, director / Kathleen Detoro, designer

EXTREME SERIES EXTREME PROD.
James Brolin, Cameron Bancroft
1994-95 contemporary extreme mountain rescue unit
Tony Hickox, Michael Keusch,directors / Sharon Nye, designer

A.35: ROBERT JOYCE'S RÉSUMÉ AND SAMPLING PAGE

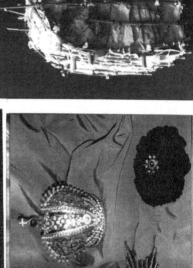

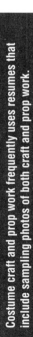

ROBERT JOYCE
Specialty Costume and Prop Design

Selected Features

Hook   (Rufio & Lost Boys' Jewelry, Tinkerbell's Jewelry)   Costume Designer Anthony Powell

The Addams Family   (Granny's Props)   Prop Master Robin Miller; Prod. Dsgnr Richard MacDonald

The Mambo Kings   (Paper Mache Palm Trees for Night Club Sequence)   Prod. Designer Stuart Wurtzel

The Invisible Man   (Chevy's Costume)   Costume Designer Joe Tompkins

Edward Scissorhands   (Edward's Costume-Painting & Aging)   Costume Designer Colleen Atwood

Hudson Hawk   (Wraparound Book & Illuminated Manuscript a la Da Vinci)   Prod. Designer Jack DeGovia

Life Stinks   (Mel Brooks & Leslie Ann Warren Cstm. Painting & Aging)   Costume Dsgnr. Mary Malin

Pacific Heights   (Key Album & Old Pictures)   Production Designer Neil Spisak

Back To The Future II   (21st Century Jewelry)   Costume Designer Deborah Scott

Postcards From The Edge   (Shirley MacLaine Portrait, Clinic Sign)   Prod. Dsgnr. Patricia von Brandestein

Joe Vs. The Volcano   (Wapone's Costumes/Accessories/Painting)   Costume Designer Colleen Atwood

Backaroo Banzai   (Mud & Weird Masks, Dr. Lizardo Props)   Prop Master Erik Nelson

Smooth Talk   (Art Director)   Production Designer David Wasco

A Trip To Bountiful   (Prop Decors & Dressing Whole Picture)   Production Designer Neil Spisak

Space Hunter   (Prop Decors & Prop, Dressing Whole Picture)   Production Designer Jack Degovia

All That Jazz   (Laser Mask Lites, Mirror Mask, Flashback Props)   Production Designer Tony Walton

The Wiz   (The Winkkies, Principal Costume Accessories, Props)   Production Designer Tony Walton

The Island   (All Costumes & Props)   Costume Designer Ann Roth

The Goodbye Girl   (Inventive Costumes Richard III Sequence)   Costume Designer Ann Roth

Broadway Stage
The Best Little Whorehouse In Texas; Liza Minnelli Show; Camelot (Burton Revival); Tartuffe; Tiny Alice; Joel Grey Show; Tommy Tune Shows; Hair; Jesus Christ Superstar

Television
The Passion of Dracula (HBO); Mr. Belvedere; Tales From the Crypt; The Muppet Show, Dirt Devil, Maricela KCET (1987 Emmy Award Winner)

Costume craft and prop work frequently uses resumes that include sampling photos of both craft and prop work.

A.36: DESIGN SAMPLING PAGE BY ROBERT TURTURICE

COSTUMES DESIGNED & DRAWN BY
ROBERT TURTURICE

Sampling page formats show range and career highlights at a glance. When they accompany a résumé, they immediately display the applicant's standards.

A.37: LAUREL TAYLOR'S DESIGN SAMPLE CARD

LAUREL M. TAYLOR
WARDROBE ASST./ SKETCH ARTIST
Street address
Phone number
Pager
email

As a follow-up to an employer who has one of your standard resumes on file, sampling card postcards can be good for quick reminders on your availability.

Guidelines for Estimating Costume Multiples

FOR STUNT DOUBLES

- Stuntmen and stuntwomen who substitute for principal players must be dressed to exactly match the actors for whom they double. In general, the star's clothing must match the state of the stunt double's clothing at the beginning and the end of the stunt sequence. Insert reaction shots can require them to match at some of the points in between.
- One duplicate of the principal costume is needed for each "low impact" stunt performed (where the level of clothing destruction is low, e.g., driving doubles, horseback riding doubles, water work, and flying stunts). For some low-impact stunts, padding may be required. If the actor does not do the stunt, a stunt double may be used, and, as a result, a duplicate of the costume may be required.
- For each major stunt specialty (e.g., driving, water work, falls, fire), you should be prepared to costume a new stunt artist, with the costume fitted over appropriate padding and stunt rigs.

FOR DISTRESS DOUBLES

- For each destructive action (e.g., squib work, fire work, actions that tear, actions that stain), have a minimum of two duplicates available, for retakes for stuntmen and principal players.
- For possible re-shoots, maintain a copy of each major phase of distress of a principal's or stunt double's costume.
- For each deliberately destructive sequence that uses a stunt double, the stunt double's costumes need to be duplicated, for distress, just like the principal player's.

FOR NON-DELIBERATE DIRT AND STAINS DUPLICATES

- Have a minimum of one duplicate change available for each principal involved in a scene with a high risk of dirt or staining problems. Light-colored garments are of greatest priority.

FOR USAGE DOUBLES

- New women's hose should be supplied for each day used.
- Intimate articles that are needed two days running should be duplicated.
- For each consecutive day of shooting, men with starched dress shirts should get a fresh shirt every half day; for two consecutive days of shooting, up to four matching shirts.
- High-maintenance garments that shoot for four consecutive days should be duplicated.

Estimating Staffing Requirements for Different Kinds of Films

ON A BIG BUDGET ($150 MILLION+) PERIOD MOVIE

Number of extras: 1500

"Big Days": 20 *

Additional hires: 1 costumer for every 10 to 15 period extras

Special facility needs: 20 days of a dressing tent.

ON A LOW-BUDGET ($5 MILLION) CONTEMPORARY KIDS' MOVIE

Number of extras: 450

"Big Days": 5, all school children

Additional hires: 1 costumer for every 15 to 20 extras

Special facility needs: none, they should come to work dressed.

ON A SUPER-LOW-BUDGET ($1.5MILLION) "SUNDANCE"-STYLE CONTEMPORARY MOVIE

Number of extras: 300

"Big Days": 4, all adults

Additional hires: 1 costumer for every 30 extras

Special facility needs: None, they should provide their own wardrobe.

*"Big days" are days in which you are dressing more than 20 extras with "repeat" dressing needed to recycle extras in additional outfits. On this scale of film some days could require 150 extras.

See the section on "Estimating over-hire" in Part 4 for more details on formulating labor estimates.

Selected Bibliography

For a general orientation to filmmaking and industry practices:

BOOKS

American Film Institute. "The Costume Designer," *Getting Started in Film*. New York: Prentice Hall, 1992.

Burke, Kristin M. *Going Hollywood: How To Get Started, Keep Going And Not Turn Into A Sleaze.* Lincoln, NE: iUniverse, 2004.

Buzzell, Linda. How to Make It in Hollywood. New York: Harper Perennial, 1992.

Charlotte, Susan. *Creativity in Film: Conversations with 14 Who Excel.* Troy, MI: Momentum Books, 1993.

Chase, Donald. "The Costume Designer," *Filmmaking: The Collaborative Art.* Boston: Little, Brown and Company, 1975.

Helton, J.R. *Below the Line.* Los Angeles: Samuel French Trade, 1996.

Houghton, Buck. *What a Producer Does: The Art of Moviemaking (Not the Business).* Los Angeles: Silman-James Press, 1991.

LoBrutto, Vincent. "Costume Designers," *By Design: Interviews with Film Production Designers.* Westport, CT: Praeger Publishers, 1992.

London, Mel. "Costume, Styling and Wardrobe," *Getting into Film,* New York: Ballantine Books, 1980.

Lumet, Sidney. *Making Movies.* New York: Alfred A. Knopf, Inc., 1995. Reprint, New York: Vintage Books, 1996.

Preston, Ward. *What an Art Director Does: An Introduction to Motion Picture Production Design.* Los Angeles: Silman-James Press, 1994.

SAG, *Screen Actors Guild 1998 Contract Summary: Theatrical Motion Pictures and Television.* Los Angeles: Screen Actors Guild Publication, 1998.

Seger, Linda, and Edward Jay Whetmore. *From Script to Screen: The Collaborative Art of Filmmaking.* New York: Henry Holt & Company/Owlet, 1994.

Steel, Dawn. *They Can Kill You but They Can't Eat You: A Lesson From the Front.* New York: Pocket Books, 1993.

Taylor, Hugh. *The Hollywood Job-Hunter's Survival Guide.* Los Angeles: Lone Eagle Publishing,1993.

Taylor, Theodore. "Art Direction, Set Decoration, and Costumes," *People Who Make Movies.* Garden City, NY: Doubleday, 1967.

Webb, Michael. "Costume Design," *Hollywood Legend and Reality.* Boston: Little, Brown and Company, 1986.

ARTICLES

Farren, Mick. "The 1,000 Dollar Static Cling Job," *The Village Voice,* Vol. XXVII, No. 51, p. 41, 21 Dec. 1982.

Hale, Alice, Steve Pollock, Susan Lieberman, and Jeff Wachtel. "Living and Working in Los Angeles," *Theater Crafts,* Vol. 19, No. 1, p. 32, Aug./Sept. 1985.

Hollander, Anne. "Costume and Convention," *American Scholar,* Vol. 42 (1972-1973), pp. 671-675.

———. "Movie Clothes: More Real Than Life," *New York Times Magazine,* Vol. CXXIV, No. 42,680, Section 6, pp. 68-71, 1 Dec. 1974.

———. "The Gatsby Look and Other Movie Blunders," *New York Times,* 27 May 1974.

Wasserman, Lisa, and Denise Tilles. "What Do They Wear? Designing Television," *Theater Crafts* Vol. 26, No. 2, p. 5, Feb. 1992.

Wernick, Ilana. "Have Costume, Will Work: Some Pointers for Extras," *Back Stage,* 10 Feb. 1995.

On the history of Hollywood costume design and costume designers:

BOOKS

Academy of Motion Picture Arts & Sciences. *50 Designers, 50 Costumes: Concept to Character.* Los Angeles: AMPAS, 2004.

Bailey, Margaret J. *Those Glorious Glamour Years: Classic Hollywood Costume Design of the 1930's.* Secaucus, NJ: Carol Publishing Group/Citadel, 1982.

Chierichetti, David. *Hollywood Costume Design.* New York: Harmony Books, 1976.

Crump, Irving. "Wardrobe and Make-Up," *Our Movie Makers.* New York: Dodd, Meade & Co., 1940.

DelGaudio, Sybil. *Dressing the Part: Sternberg, Dietrich, and Costume.* Madison, NJ: Fairleigh Dickinson University Press, 1993.

Engelmeier, Regine and Peter W. Engelmeier, eds. *Fashion in Film.* New York: Prestel, 1997.

Head, Edith. *Edith Head's Hollywood.* New York: Dutton Books, 1983.

La Vine, W. Robert. *In a Glamorous Fashion: The Fabulous Years of Hollywood Costume Design.* New York: Charles Scribner's Sons, 1980.

Leese, Elizabeth. *Costume Design in the Movies: An Illustrated Guide to the Work of 157 Great Designers,* rep. ed. New York: Dover Publications, 1991.

McConathy, Dale, with Diana Vreeland. *Hollywood Costume: Glamour! Glitter! Romance!* New York: Harry N. Abrams, Inc., 1976.

Nadoolman Landis, Deborah. *Screencraft: Costume Design.* Burlington, MA: Focal Press, 2003.

Sharaff, Irene. *Broadway and Hollywood: Costumes Designed by Irene Sharaff.* New York: Van Nostrand Rheinhold Company, 1976.

ARTICLES

Calhoun, John. "Transforming Tracey: Jane Ruhm's character costumes for *The Tracey Ullman Show,*" *Theater Crafts* Vol. 22, No. 9, pp. 54-57, Nov. 1988.

———, "Costuming the Westerners: *Lonesome Dove.*" *Theater Crafts* Vol. 23, No. 2, p. 40, Feb. 1989.

———, "Heightening Realities," *Theater Crafts,* Vol. 23, No. 4, pp. 58-67, April 1989.

———, "The Wonder Years," *Theater Crafts International,* Vol. 24, No. 2, p. 50, Feb. 1990.

———, "A New Spike Lee Joint," *Theater Crafts,* Vol. 24, No. 7, p. 26, Aug./Sept. 1990.

———, "Mystery: Keeping Agatha Christie's Characters Dressed to Kill," *Theater Crafts,* Vol. 25, No. 2, p. 40, Feb. 1991.

———, "Robin Hood, Prince of Thieves," *Theater Crafts,* Vol. 25, No. 7, pp. 48-53, 86-87, Aug./Sept. 1991.

———, "*Batman Returns*: A New Design Team Reinvents Gotham City," *Theater Crafts International,* Vol. 26, No. 7, pp. 34-39, Aug./Sept. 1992.

———, "*1492*: Charles Knode Costumes the Discovery of America," *Theater Crafts International,* Vol. 26, No. 8, pp. 30-33, Oct. 1992.

———, "*Used People,*" *Theater Crafts International,* Vol. 27, No. 2, pp. 40-41, Feb. 1993.

———, "*Malcolm X,*" *Theater Crafts International,* Vol. 27, No. 2, pp. 38-39, Feb. 1993.

———, "Costuming *Chaplin,*" *Theater Crafts International,* Vol. 27, No. 3, pp. 22-23, March 1993.

———, "They'll Never Be Hungry Again," *Theater Crafts International,* Vol. 27, No. 4, p. 6, April 1993.

———, "*Erin Quigley,*" *Theater Crafts International,* Vol. 27, No. 5, p. 48, May 1993.

———, "*Rising Sun,*" *Theater Crafts International,* Vol. 27, No. 7, p. 10, Aug./Sept. 1993.

———, "Dean Tavoularis," *Theater Crafts International,* Vol. 28, No. 8, pp. 42-49, Oct. 1994.

———, "The Journey Inside," *Theater Crafts International,* Vol. 28, No. 8, p. 78, Oct. 1994.

———, "Colleen Atwood," *Theater Crafts International,* Vol. 28, No. 9, pp. 38-41, Nov. 1994.

———, "Anthony Powell," *Theater Crafts International,* Vol. 29, No. 2, pp. 38-42, Feb. 1995.

———, "*Tom and Viv*: Phoebe De Gaye Recreates the Eccentric Couture of the Bloomsbury Group," *Theater Crafts International,* Vol. 29, No. 3, pp. 38-39, March 1995.

Cashill, Robert. "Western Costume," *Theater Crafts International*, Vol. 29, No. 4, pp. 52-53, April 1995.

AFI. "Dialogue on Film; Edith Head," *American Film*, Vol. 3, No. 7, pp. 33-48, May 1978.

Harris, Julie. "Costume Designing," *Films and Filming*, Vol. 4, No. 2, p. 17, Nov. 1957.

Hutera, Donald. "*Little Dorritt*," *Theater Crafts*, Vol. 23, No. 1, p. 34, Jan. 1989.

Lampert-Greaux, Ellen. "*Middlemarch*: Anushia Nieradzik Costumes a 19th-Century Village for a BBC Series," *Theater Crafts International*, Vol. 28, No. 3, pp. 36-39, March 1994 .

On Hollywood and New York costume resources and personnel directories:

BOOKS

The Association of Theatrical Artists and Craftspeople. *The Entertainment 2001 Sourcebook: An Insider's Guide on Where to Find Everything.* New York, NY: Applause Books, 2001.

Costume Designers Guild. *Directory of Members.* Los Angeles, CA: Costume Designers Guild Publication, 2001.

Debbies Book: The Sourcebook for Professionals in Entertainment Industries. Pasadena, CA: Debbies Book Publishing, 2002.

Froehlich, Marcy, Barbara Inglehart, and Pamela Shaw. *Shopping LA: The Insiders' Sourcebook for Film and Fashion.* Burbank, CA: Shopping LA Publishing, 2000.

Hollywood Creative Directory – Below the Line Talent. Hollywood, CA: IFILM Publishing, 2001.

Hollywood Creative Directory – Film Directors. Hollywood, CA: IFILM Publishing, 2001.

Hollywood Creative Directory – Film Producers. Hollywood, CA: IFILM Publishing, 2001.

LA 411: The Professional Reference Guide for Commercial Film & Videotape Production. Los Angeles, CA: LA 411 Publications, 1991.

Motion Picture Costumers. *Directory of Costumers: Motion Picture-Television.* Hollywood, CA: IATSE Local 705 Publication, 1994.

MPE. *Motion Picture, TV and Theatre Directory.* Tarrytown, NY: Motion Picture Enterprises Publications, 1999.

PG Direct. *Film & Television 2001.* Westport, CT: Peter Glenn Publications, 2001.

General costume references:

BOOKS

Aoki, Shoichi. *Fruits.* London, England: Phaidon Press, 2001.

Arnold, Janet, *Patterns of Fashion: English Women's Dresses and Their Construction c.1660-1860.* New York, Macmillan/Drama Books, 1972.

————, *Patterns of Fashion: English women's dresses and their construction c.1860-1940.* New York, Macmillan/Drama Books, 1977.

————, *Patterns of Fashion: The Cut and Construction of Clothes for Men and Women c. 1560-1620.* New York, Macmillan/Drama Books, 1985.

Cabrera, Roberto and Patricia Flaherty Meyers. *Classic Tailoring Techniques: A Construction Guide for Men's Wear.* New York, NY: Fairchild Publications, 1983.

Chenoune, Farid. *History of Men's Fashion,* trans. Deke Dusinberre. (Paris, New York: Flammarion, 1993.

Gioello, Debbie Ann. *Profiling Fabrics: Properties, Performance & Construction Techniques.* New York, NY: Fairchild Publications, 1981.

Held, Shirley. *Weaving: A Handbook of the Fiber Arts.* New York, NY: Holt, Rinehart and Winston, 1978.

Hunnisett, Jean. *Period Costume for Stage and Screen.* Studio City, CA: Players Press, 1996.

Jean Hunnisett. *Period Costume for Stage & Screen: Patterns for Women's Dress, 1500-1800.* Studio City,

CA: Players Press, 1991.

Jean Hunnisett. *Period Costume for Stage & Screen: Patterns for Women's Dress, 1800-1909.* Studio City, CA: Players Press, 1991.

Kirke, Betty. *Madeleine Vionnet.* San Francisco, CA: Chronicle Books, 1998.

Laubner, Ellie. *Fashions of the Roaring 1920s.* Atglen, PA: Schiffer Publishing, Ltd., 1996.

McGregor, Malcom, Andrew Mollo, and Michael Chappel. *World Army Uniforms Since 1939,* New York, NY: Sterling Publishing, 1983.

Molloy, John T. *Dress For Success.* New York, NY: Warner Books, 1975.

Moss, Sylvia. *Costumes and Chemistry: A Comprehensive Guide to Materials and Applications.* Hollywood, CA: Costume & Fashion Press, 2001

Pizzuto, Joseph. *Fabric Science.* New York, NY: Fairchild Publications, 1987.

Polhemus, Ted. *Street Style: From Sidewalk to Catwalk.* New York, NY: Thames and Hudson, 1994.

Prichard, Susan Perez. *Film Costume: An Annotated Bibliography.* Metuchen, NJ: Scarecrow Press, 1981.

Shaeffer, Claire B. *Couture Sewing Techniques.* Newtown, CT: Taunton Press, 1993.

Tortora, Phyllis and Keith Eubank. *A Survey of Historic Costume: A History of Western Dress.* New York, NY: Fairchild Publishers, 1989.

Villarosa, Riccardo and Giulano Angeli. *The Elegant Man: How to Construct the Ideal Wardrobe.* New York, NY: Random House, 1990.

Vogue Patterns. *The Vogue Sewing Book.* New York, NY: Vogue Patterns Publishing, 1973.

Waugh, Nora. *The Cut of Men's Clothes: 1600-1900.* New York, NY: Theatre Arts Books, 1964.

Waugh, Nora. *The Cut of Women's Clothes: 1600-1930.* New York, NY: Theatre Arts Books, 1968.

Wilson, William. *Man at His Best: The Esquire Guide to Style.* Reading, MA: Addison-Wesley Publishing Company, Inc., 1985.

Wolff, Colette. *The Art of Manipulating Fabric.* Iola, WI: Krause Publications, 1996.

Other general references:

Cuthbert, Neil and Vince McKewin, Andrew Scheinman, Adam Scheinman. *Pluto Nash.* Hollywood, CA: Castlerock Entertainment, 1999.

Craddock, Jim. *VideoHound's Golden Movie Retriever 2001.* Farmington Hills, MI: Visible Ink Press, 2001.

Parramon, Jose. *The Book of Color.* New York, NY: Watson-Guptill Publications, 1993.

Quiller, Stephen. *Color Choices: Making Color Sense Out of Color Theory.* New York, NY: Watson-Guptill Publications, 1989.

Tarantino, Quentin. *Pulp Fiction.* New York, NY: Miramax Books, Hyperion Press, 1994.

Cumming, Valerie and Elaine Feldman, editors. *Fashions of a Decade* series, including:

Carnegy, Vicki. *Fashions of a Decade: 1980's.* New York, NY: Facts on File, 1992.

Herald, Jacqueline. *Fashions of a Decade: 1970's.* New York, NY: Facts on File, 1990.

Blum, Stella, editor. *Everyday Fashions As Pictured in Sears Catalogs* series including:

————. *Everyday Fashions of the Forties as Pictured in Sears Catalogs.* New York, NY: Dover Publications, 1992.

————. *Everyday Fashions of the Thirties as Pictured in Sears Catalogs.* New York, NY: Dover Publications, 1986.

————. *Everyday Fashions of the Twenties as Pictured in Sears and other Catalogs.* New York, NY: Dover Publications, 1981.

Videotaped Lectures by Film Professionals:

(Note: These tapes are not available for purchase by non-union members.)

Costume Designers Guild. Specialty Crafts Seminar, Costume Designers Guild Special Collections

Library, 1992

Costume Designers Guild. Special Effects Seminar, Costume Designers Guild Special Collections Library, 1992.

Costume Designers Guild. Jurisdiction and Contract Seminar Costume Designers Guild Special Collections Library, 1992.

Costume Designers Guild. Script Breakdown, Costume Designers Guild Special Collections Library, 1992.

Costume Designers Guild. Agents Seminar/Portfolio Presentation, Costume Designers Guild Special Collections Library, 1992.

Costume Designers Guild. Budgeting, Costume Designers Guild Special Collections Library, 1992.

IATSE Wardrobe Union. Teams of Designers and Costume Supervisors, Wardrobe Office Library, 1991.

IATSE Wardrobe Union. Key Costumers, Wardrobe Office Library, 1991.

IATSE Wardrobe Union. Three-Camera Tape and Film, Wardrobe Office Library, 1991.

IATSE Wardrobe Union. Set Procedures, Wardrobe Office Library, 1991.

IATSE Wardrobe Union. Aging Costumes, Wardrobe Office Library, 1991.

IATSE Wardrobe Union. Script Breakdown, Wardrobe Office Library, 1991.

IATSE Wardrobe Union. Budgeting, Wardrobe Office Library, 1991.

INDEX